FILMMAKERS SERIES
edited by
ANTHONY SLIDE

1. *James Whale*, by James Curtis. 1982
2. *Cinema Stylists*, by John Belton. 1983
3. *Harry Langdon*, by William Schelly. 1982
4. *William A. Wellman*, by Frank Thompson. 1983
5. *Stanley Donen*, by Joseph Casper. 1983
6. *Brian De Palma*, by Michael Bliss. 1983
7. *J. Stuart Blackton*, by Marian Blackton Trimble. 1985
8. *Martin Scorsese and Michael Cimino*, by Michael Bliss. 1985
9. *Franklin J. Schaffner*, by Erwin Kim. 1985
10. *D. W. Griffith and the Biograph Company*, by Cooper C. Graham et al. 1985
11. *Some Day We'll Laugh: An Autobiography*, by Esther Ralston. 1985
12. *The Memoirs of Alice Guy Blaché*, 2nd ed., translated by Roberta and Simone Blaché. 1996
13. *Leni Riefenstahl and Olympia*, by Cooper C. Graham. 1986
14. *Robert Florey*, by Brian Taves. 1987
15. *Henry King's America*, by Walter Coppedge. 1986
16. *Aldous Huxley and Film*, by Virginia M. Clark. 1987
17. *Five American Cinematographers*, by Scott Eyman. 1987
18. *Cinematographers on the Art and Craft of Cinematography*, by Anna Kate Sterling. 1987
19. *Stars of the Silents*, by Edward Wagenknecht. 1987
20. *Twentieth Century-Fox*, by Aubrey Solomon. 1988
21. *Highlights and Shadows: The Memoirs of a Hollywood Cameraman*, by Charles G. Clarke. 1989
22. *I Went That-a-Way: The Memoirs of a Western Film Director*, by Harry L. Fraser; edited by Wheeler Winston Dixon and Audrey Brown Fraser. 1990
23. *Order in the Universe: The Films of John Carpenter*, by Robert C. Cumbow. 1990 *(out of print; see No. 70)*
24. *The Films of Freddie Francis*, by Wheeler Winston Dixon. 1991
25. *Hollywood Be Thy Name*, by William Bakewell. 1991
26. *The Charm of Evil: The Life and Films of Terence Fisher*, by Wheeler Winston Dixon. 1991

27. *Lionheart in Hollywood: The Autobiography of Henry Wilcoxon,* with Katherine Orrison. 1991
28. *William Desmond Taylor: A Dossier,* by Bruce Long. 1991
29. *The Films of Leni Riefenstahl,* 2nd ed., by David B. Hinton. 1991
30. *Hollywood Holyland: The Filming and Scoring of "The Greatest Story Ever Told,"* by Ken Darby. 1992
31. *The Films of Reginald LeBorg: Interviews, Essays, and Filmography,* by Wheeler Winston Dixon. 1992
32. *Memoirs of a Professional Cad,* by George Sanders, with Tony Thomas. 1992
33. *The Holocaust in French Film,* by André Pierre Colombat. 1993
34. *Robert Goldstein and "The Spirit of '76,"* edited and compiled by Anthony Slide. 1993
35. *Those Were the Days, My Friend: My Life in Hollywood with David O. Selznick and Others,* by Paul Macnamara. 1993
36. *The Creative Producer,* by David Lewis; edited by James Curtis. 1993
37. *Reinventing Reality: The Art and Life of Rouben Mamoulian,* by Mark Spergel. 1993
38. *Malcolm St. Clair: His Films, 1915-1948,* by Ruth Anne Dwyer. 1997
39. *Beyond Hollywood's Grasp: American Filmmakers Abroad, 1914-1945,* by Harry Waldman. 1994
40. *A Steady Digression to a Fixed Point,* by Rose Hobart. 1994
41. *Radical Juxtaposition: The Films of Yvonne Rainer,* by Shelley Green. 1994
42. *Company of Heroes: My Life as an Actor in the John Ford Stock Company,* by Harry Carey, Jr. 1994
43. *Strangers in Hollywood: A History of Scandinavian Actors in American Films from 1910 to World War II,* by Hans J. Wollstein. 1994
44. *Charlie Chaplin: Intimate Close-Ups,* by Georgia Hale, edited with an introduction and notes by Heather Kiernan. 1995
45. *The Word Made Flesh: Catholicism and Conflict in the Films of Martin Scorsese,* by Michael Bliss. 1995
46. *W. S. Van Dyke's Journal: White Shadows in the South Seas (1927-1928) and other Van Dyke on Van Dyke,* edited and annotated by Rudy Behlmer. 1996
47. *Music from the House of Hammer: Music in the Hammer Horror Films, 1950-1980,* by Randall D. Larson. 1996

48. *Directing: Learn from the Masters,* by Tay Garnett. 1996
49. *Featured Player: An Oral Autobiography of Mae Clarke*, edited with an introduction by James Curtis. 1996
50. *A Great Lady: A Life of the Screenwriter Sonya Levien,* by Larry Ceplair. 1996
51. *A History of Horrors: The Rise and Fall of the House of Hammer,* by Denis Meikle. 1996
52. *The Films of Michael Powell and the Archers*, by Scott Salwolke. 1997
53. *From Oz to E. T.: Wally Worsley's Half-Century in Hollywood—A Memoir in Collaboration with Sue Dwiggins Worsley*, edited by Charles Ziarko. 1997
54. *Thorold Dickinson and the British Cinema*, by Jeffrey Richards. 1997
55. *The Films of Oliver Stone,* edited by Don Kunz. 1997
56. *Before, In and After Hollywood: The Autobiography of Joseph E. Henabery*, edited by Anthony Slide. 1997
57. *Ravished Armenia and the Story of Aurora Mardiganian*, compiled by Anthony Slide. 1997
58. *Smile When the Raindrops Fall,* by Brian Anthony and Andy Edmonds. 1998
59. *Joseph H. Lewis: Overview, Interview, and Filmography*, by Francis M. Nevins. 1998
60. *September Song: An Intimate Biography of Walter Huston,* by John Weld. 1998
61. *Wife of the Life of the Party*, by Lita Grey Chaplin and Jeffrey Vance. 1998
62. *Down But Not Quite Out in Hollow-weird: A Documentary in Letters of Eric Knight*, by Geoff Gehman. 1998
63. *On Actors and Acting: Essays by Alexander Knox,* edited by Anthony Slide. 1998
64. *Back Lot: Growing Up with the Movies*, by Maurice Rapf. 1999
65. *Mr. Bernds Goes to Hollywood: My Early Life and Career in Sound Recording at Columbia with Frank Capra and Others*, by Edward Bernds. 1999
66. *Hugo Friedhofer: The Best Years of His Life: A Hollywood Master of Music for the Movies*, edited by Linda Danly. 1999
67. *Actors on Red Alert: Career Interviews with Five Actors and Actresses Affected by the Blacklist*, by Anthony Slide. 1999
68. *My Only Great Passion: The Life and Films of Carl Th. Dreyer*, by Jean and Dale Drum. 1999

69. *Ready When You Are, Mr. Coppola, Mr. Spielberg, Mr. Crowe*, by Jerry Ziesmer. 1999
70. *Order in the Universe: The Films of John Carpenter,* 2nd ed., by Robert Cumbow. 2000
71. *Making Music with Charlie Chaplin,* by Eric James. 2000
72. *An Open Window: The Cinema of Víctor Erice,* edited by Linda C. Ehrlich. 2000
73. *Satyajit Ray: In Search of the Modern*, by Suranjan Ganguly. 2000
74. *Voices from the Set: The* Film Heritage *Interviews,* edited by Tony Macklin and Nick Pici. 2000
75. *Paul Landres: A Director's Stories*, by Francis M. Nevins. 2000
76. *No Film in My Camera*, by Bill Gibson. 2000
77. *Saved from Oblivion: An Autobiography*, by Bernard Vorhaus. 2000
78. *Wolf Man's Maker: Memoir of a Hollywood Writer*, by Curt Siodmak. 2001
79. *An Actor, and a Rare One: Peter Cushing as Sherlock Holmes,* by Tony Earnshaw. 2000
80. *Picture Perfect,* by Herbert L. Strock. 2000

Wolf Man's Maker

Wolf Man's Maker

Memoir of a Hollywood Writer
Revised Edition

Curt Siodmak

Filmmakers Series, No. 78

The Scarecrow Press, Inc.
Lanham, Maryland, London
2001

SCARECROW PRESS, INC.

Published in the United States of America
by Scarecrow Press, Inc.
4720 Boston Way, Lanham, Maryland 20706
http://www.scarecrowpress.com

4 Pleydell Gardens, Folkestone
Kent CT20 2DN, England

First edition © 1997 by Curt Siodmak: *Even a Man Who Is Pure in Heart. . . . The Life of a Writer, Not Always to His Liking.* Three Rivers, CA.: Three Rivers Press. First Scarecrow Press edition 2001

All rights reserved. No part of this publication may be reproduced, stored in a retrieval system, or transmitted in any form or by any means, electronic, mechanical, photocopying, recording, or otherwise, without the prior permission of the publisher.

British Library Cataloguing in Publication Information Available

Library of Congress Cataloging-in-Publication Data

Siodmak, Curt, 1902–2000
    Wolf man's maker : memoir of a Hollywood writer/ Curt Siodmak.
      p. cm. — (Filmmakers ; no. 78)
    Originally published: Even a man who is pure in heart. Three Rivers, Calif. : Three Rivers Press, 1997.
    Includes index.
    ISBN 0-8108-3870-2 (alk. paper)
    1. Siodmak, Curt, 1902–2000 2. Screenwriters—United States—Biography. I. Title. II. Series.

PN1998.3.S538 A3 2000
812'.52—dc21
[B]

00-041284

∞™ The paper used in this publication meets the minimum requirements of American National Standard for Information Sciences—Permanence of Paper for Printed Library Materials, ANSI/NISO Z39.48-1992.
Manufactured in the United States of America.

*Dedicated to America, the country that was good to me, a stranger—
the only country that told me "Come in" and not "Get out."*

Even a man who's pure in heart
And says his prayers at night
May become a wolf
When the wolfbane blooms
And the autumn moon is bright

> (from the motion picture screenplay *The Wolf Man* by Curt Siodmak)

Contents

List of Illustrations	xv
Foreword: Hans-Helmet Prinzler	xvii
Author's Prologue	xxi
1. Europe	1
2. Loss of Innocence	71
3. The Golden Years	89
4. The Cat's Prediction	143
5. America	175
6. The War and Hollywood	299
7. Did I Really Write That Much?	341
Epilogue	435
Filmography	445
Index	449
About the Author	457

List of Illustrations

1. Curt and Robert, 1905
2. *People on Sunday*, 1929
3. Schuss in Tonfilmatelier, 1931
4. Dolly Haas, 1931
5. *F.P. 1 Does Not Reply*, 1932
6. *Der Mann der Seinen Moerder Sucht*, 1932
7. *La Crise Est finie*, 1934
8. *The Tunnel*, 1936
9. Letter from German Publisher, 1937
10. *The Wolf Man*, 1941
11. *The Wolf Man*, 1941
12. *Tarzan's Magic Fountain*, 1941
13. *The Lady and the Monster*, 1941
14. *The Invisible Agent*, 1942
15. *Son of Dracula*, 1943
16. *The Climax*, 1944
17. *The House of Frankenstein*, 1944
18. *Four Days Leave*, 1948

19. *The Invisible Woman*, 1949
20. *The Return of the Invisible Man*, 1949
21. *I Walked with a Zombie*, 1949
22. *Donovan's Brain*, 1953
23. *Earth Against Flying Saucers*, 1954
24. *The Beast with Five Fingers*, 1954
25. *The Creature with the Atom Brain*, 1955
26. *Curucu, Beast of the Amazon*, 1956
27. Henrietta
28. Robert and Curt, 1962
29. *The Lightship*, 1963
30. Order of Merit First Class, 1992
31. Postage Stamp and Postmark, 1997
32. Siodmak Brothers Poster, 1998

Foreword

The author's capital are his ideas. The stories he tells awake the reader's curiosity and fantasy. His most important tool is his language. What terrifying and devastating misfortune when a young author—together with his gifted colleagues—is forced to flee his country and change his language, just after his first literary success. Kurt—later Curt—was thirty when he and his wife Henrietta escaped the Nazis. Switzerland, France, England, and finally faraway America became stations on his exile. He decided never again to write in his native language and composed his stories, novels, and screenplays in English. When he, thirty years later, returned to Europe, he visited Germany as an observer, distrustful, and with guarded emotions. Destructions of a livelihood are difficult to heal and are never forgiven.

Curt Siodmak, trained engineer and mathematician, created highly original and fantastic stories, especially in science fiction and Gothic "horror" tales. But he also supplied the story idea of the classic avant-garde film *People on Sunday*, a technique called, thirty years later, "*la nouvelle vague*" in France, "the new wave" in the United States, and "neorealism" in Italy.

People on Sunday, that simple story of four young people who flee the crowded city with a million others only to take the city with its noise and haste along, spawned its collaborators, Robert Siodmak, Billy Wilder, and Fred Zinnemann, who after their forced exile became some of the most important motion picture directors of that period. The originator's name was not mentioned, a fact that still irks Curt today.

Directors are well advertised, but never film authors, and Curt stood in Hollywood under the shadow of his highly successful film director-brother Robert. Still today, Curt considers the importance of directors and actors as highly inflated. Their contributions to motion pictures can be replaced by dozens of other directors and actors. The technical conception, the screenplay, can be written by hundreds of film writers. Directors and actors might shine brightly, not like stars but rather like comets that cross the sky and disappear. But the author's original contribution to the film is irreplaceable. As the head of a film museum I cannot agree with Curt's evaluation of his craft, but I am inclined to respect his contention. When I sent him a book with the inscription "Reading is important, not only writing," he replied with a fax: "If it's not written, it can't be read."

What personal and great fortune that Curt for more than seventy years has Henrietta, a strong and beautiful woman at his side, who assists him with her strength and optimistic outlook on life. He likes to describe himself as a lonely scribbler who withdraws every morning to his study, composes his stories, only to reappear in the evening, refusing to be interrupted but otherwise appreciative, despite his doubts and depressions, of the good fortune of a long life and of destiny having led him to Three Rivers, that bucolic paradise at the foothills of the High Sierra mountains, where raccoons, foxes, bears, and people live together in harmony.

Curt's friends know many of his personal stories, which he also tells in his autobiography, but I find them in a new context, floating through a large stream of life of political and human experiences. How fortunate that an author in his late years still has the energy to register his experiences. The strain and also the torture to remember shine through his stories when his memory, not as "after this followed that, then after that followed this . . . ," wanders into deep contemplations, a quarry of broken stones that reveal hidden, suppressed, and undigested painful observations. This book is not the work of a historian but an assembly of remembered history of a time that only seemingly is anchored in a past.

Actually two different times are registered in Curt Siodmak's remembrances: the years at the turn of the twentieth century until the middle of the 1930s in Europe and the present time in America. It is, of course, the same person that lived through those momentous changes. But he has sharply defined his experiences in two different worlds: the forced exile to escape the world of the Nazis; the loss of his tool, the German language; and his country of birth, twice growing up in different cultures, to learn anew his profession, to create a new identity and adjustment to a different society. He never lost his curiosity, sometimes with skepticism or sarcasm, but with sharp evaluation of human frailties.

People whom Curt Siodmak encountered in his life stand in clear focus of his recollections: good friends, colleagues, and some less good "friends." If all were mentioned in the index, it would take even more pages to cite names of prominent people and also unknowns who drifted through his life. These people are no shadows. They have, when Curt told about them, character, fate, and reality. In his reports the author is blending back and forth. He creates a mosaic, which also leaves empty spaces that we, the readers, must fill ourselves. The people whom he describes are weaving two large panoramic views of the cultural history of the twentieth century: the image of a tradition that perished in hatred and persecution mania, and a freedom in America based on talent, wealth, and success. Both worlds have branded their stamp on Curt Siodmak, but his sympathies belong to the New World that accepted him and became his steady home.

What rare gift that he has the ability to spin fictitious, often mysterious and magic tales based on his experiences and visions. It is our fortune that he also wrote a very realistic story: that of his life.

Hans-Helmut Prinzler
Director of the Stiftung Deutsche Kinemathek

Author's Prologue

"A young man who wants to be a writer is looking for an older writer to talk him out of it."

I qualify for that request, though I would never interfere with a budding Shakespeare to forego his talent.

I believe that I am the only professional writer who has lived through the entire twentieth century and was able to write down its history as I saw it, since history is what we experience and not necessarily as historians interpret it.

I was born in Germany in 1902, the year the first plane, the *Kitty Hawk*, was airborne for 120 feet. Now ten thousand airplanes are in the air every day.

I witnessed the most astonishing inventions of the world's history but also its most bloody century, in which 160 million were slaughtered, as many lives as the combined populations of England, France, and Spain.

But I also witnessed the emergence of a new art, motion pictures, and was part of that industry, from story cards to the latest state-of-the-art computerized techniques.

After my few years of great success as an author and film writer, the moon came back over the hill, carrying the Swastika on its back. I was thirty years old when this occurred, changing me into an outcast because I was born Jewish. My relatives were murdered, and I escaped into a world I did not know.

I became an expert on horror pictures, which became the trademark of Universal Studios. The production staff assigned me to create a third character to add to their main moneymakers, the Frankenstein monster and Count Dracula. I was well suited for this assignment since I was brought up with Germany's Gothic tales. It was the turning point in my life as a film author. I became the first writer whose imaginary character would appear on a U.S. postal stamp. I had added a new character, one that would outlive me, to American folklore.

"Even a man who is pure at heart and says his prayers at night may become a Wolf when the wolfbane blooms and the autumn moon is bright." The Wolf Man knows that his fate might change when certain circumstances come together and that he is powerless to fight fate.

It dawned on me that all of us are "Wolf Men," that fate rules our destiny. This very simple revelation made me write my autobiography, a ten-year effort that still covers only part of my life. I had four hundred copies printed for my family and friends and then accepted an offer from Scarecrow Press to make it accessible to others who might see some value in it.

For the young writer: Write, if you have something to say. But don't ever talk about it to anybody until it is finished to your satisfaction, and your pencil will become an instrument of power.

Curt Siodmak

1

Europe

The United States had 146 million Americans when I arrived in 1937, a stranger in a new land. Now, more than sixty years later, it has almost double this number.

The male ejaculation, as my neurologist informed me, has 250 million sperm. One intercourse could produce all the inhabitants of the United States of America if properly raised in vitro. The sperm that was the basis of my existence was one of the 250 million that grew into a human being with two legs, two arms, a body, a brain, and no hair on my head because I inherited that shortcoming from my father. That penchant for baldness was built into each of the 250 million sperm. When I look in the mirror I see the result of the sperm that started me. I must have been the fastest swimmer among 250 million competitors since I reached my mother's egg ahead of all the others. One sperm out of 250 million, and it became me! That is a smaller chance than winning the Irish sweepstakes. This thought should instill awe in people about their personal uniqueness.

Being born has its shortcomings: you are given no choice of time, country in which to be born, or, of course, the family background that goes with it. I was born in 1902, a time so far back that I now have lived through almost a century. Dresden, the capital of Saxony, a kingdom in pre–World War I Germany, was the city where I first saw the light of day. Saxony was still ruled by a king, August III, of the House of Wettin. The Wettins had reigned over Saxony for eight hundred years. When, after the war, August III finally had to abdicate, he quit with the historical remark, "Let' em shovel their own shit."

It is a fact that the tempo of history accelerated the last hundred years with astronomical speed. It took the Essenes, the Jewish tribe in which Jesus was born and who wrote the Dead Sea scrolls, two hundred years to change one single sentence of the Bible. It took them that long to make up their mind what words to change, while in our time a new religion is created almost every day. Time does not move in a simple mathematical progression as it did for billions of years. It now accelerates in the square. That's why I have seen in my short life more history than all my ancestors combined. Even a stroll with Moses through the desert took his disciples forty years. A jet plane crosses it in a few minutes. We now are confronted daily with more scientific discoveries since the day when the man who invented the bow and arrow believed that his invention would be the beginning of eternal peace. Being able to kill from a distance would be the inevitable end of wars. When you can kill a man from far away, what chance does he have to survive? That man was sadly mistaken.

Second, I wasn't asked in which country I would prefer to appear on Earth. I was born in Germany, August 10, 1902. If I had had the choice I'd love to have been born during the Greek time of Aristotle, Plato, and other great Greek thinkers. That was the time of immense mental intercourse. It also was a very human time. The god of the Greeks, Jupiter, to cheat on his wife, Juno, transform himself into a swan to have an affair with Leda, a juicy girl. Jupiter also was aware that the swan's penis is formed like that of a human. If he felt very horny, he transformed himself into a bull. That was the time I'd have preferred to live in, where the gods were human and not a god of suffering like that broken image with a crown of thorns that is nailed to a cross. The Greek sense of sin was human. Maybe they didn't even know what sin was.

I also would have been extremely happy to have had as teachers the great Greek brains of that time, who were not prevented by religious taboos from thinking, the way the Judeo-Christian church stopped human intelligence from developing thoughts that would have made the world a utopian paradise. But being born in 1902, without my consent, I wasn't offered any choice. I was also born in a Jewish home, to Jewish parents. Would I have chosen to be a member of a minority that has been persecuted for two thousand years, taught to believe in a stern, macho God of revenge, and to be born in sin?

I don't believe in heaven or hell, since it was the human mind that made up these frightening conceptions, which finally debilitated the function of the Greek brain and impeded its world-changing intelligence for thousands of years.

The Christians believe in the gospel. If I had been born 1,500 miles west of Rome, I would have been told to die for the Koran; a couple of thousand miles to the northeast, I would have been a Buddhist and believed that Buddha was born in a lotus flower, which makes sense since the petal of that flower is formed like a vulva. I could have been a Japanese and been brought up in Shintoism, and a couple of thousand miles to the south I would have been a tribal member at the New Guinea Peninsula. To find favor with my paramour I would have had to offer her a freshly cut human head. Born in Italy I might have been a Catholic, a religion that knows the absolute truth and in the name of that truth spilled so much blood that the Niagara Falls could tumble down for a week with the blood of slaughtered heathens.

But I was born a Jew, wearing the invisible Star of David all my life. I would have liked to have been a Greek, and not a member of a minority which, though its number consists of only one-third of 1 percent of the world population, is the most persecuted tribe in history. God, by divine neglect, hasn't found time to replace his chosen people with another race whose destiny is to suffer.

I once had the idea that would be the solution to the Jewish question: ship all of them to Israel, but also Jesus Christ, and let the Christian religion find another Messiah who this time would not be Jewish. Maybe a Korean, and make the Koreans the Jews of the future.

Gifted with a good memory, I remember the King of Saxony, August III, taking his morning constitutional by walking from the Schloss, the lovely baroque castle on the Elbe River, down the Seestrasse, crossing the Altmarkt, which was the town square of Dresden. Thirty years later seventy-five thousand human corpses were piled up in the Altmarkt and were incinerated after that lovely baroque city was senselessly bombed to ruins in World War II by the Allies.

In my early childhood, nobody thought of war. Every morning, the king walked down the Seestrasse, crossed the Altmarkt, then strolled to the railway station at the end of the Pragerstrasse. He was followed by his coach, in case he got tired. He is still in my memory: a tall man, with a kind face, dressed in a German officer's coat that reached down to the pavement. He had a Great Dane with him and called her, "Diana, you beast, come over here!" The huge dog ran into me. The king picked me up, brushed me off, apologized, and asked, "To whom does the little boy belong?" None of the pedestrians turned around, used to the king's early-morning constitutional.

The years between 1902 and 1914 were the only time of peace I can remember. Then only unrest followed. World War I broke out in 1914, followed by an epidemic of the "Grippe," a deadly virus that killed more people than died in the war. Germany had its inflation where the German mark was finally stabilized with 4.5 billion mark for one dollar, a scheme of the German government that wiped out the war debt, for the price of a postage stamp with money left over.

Then came a few years of success in my life, until the Nazi hordes took over Germany with almost every German citizen's patriotic consent. This was followed by my emigration, adjustments to foreign countries, and learning new languages to be able to stay alive. Again a long war followed that killed fifty million people, among them generations of future scientists and artists, and maybe a new Messiah, who might have saved humankind.

After years of life's struggle my wife, Henrietta, and I finally settled down in a peaceful place called Three Rivers in the High Sierras of California. What would we have given for a glimpse into the future when life seemed to be without hope?

The human race is a storytelling breed. Every tribe from the North to the South Pole produced local bards, who invented fantastic tales to explain the creation of the world as they visualized it. Their imagination sometimes became the gospel of the tribe, and many races went to war to proliferate their unalterable truth, forcing other tribes to accept their special myths.

"Truth" is what people believe in. It cannot be verified, since truth is and always will be subjective. The ancient Greeks were especially adept in inventing gruesome tales of how the world was created. The imagination of our bards sounds tame in comparison. Hesiod, a Greek poet of the eighth century B.C., explained the creation of the universe thus: It started with Chaos, "vast and dark." Then appeared Gaea, the "deep-breasted Earth," and finally Eros, "the love which softens hearts." The early Greeks must have been a very human race to have included love as a part of the Earth creation. No other religion ever devised a god personifying sensual love.

But Hesiod also conceived horror stories, which mythologists like Joseph Campbell are able to analyze: Gaea, united with her son Uranus, produced the first race, the Titans. Uranus and Gaea—a mating between mother and son, the earliest incestuous relation ever mentioned in mythology and history—gave birth to the Cyclops, who had only one eye in the middle of the forehead. While Uranus slept, Cronos, his and Gaea's son, armed with a sickle, mutilated his father atrociously and threw his genitals into the sea. From Uranus's terrible wound black blood dropped into the ocean and gave birth to the Furies, a very unpleasant breed of females, who grow poisonous snakes instead of hair on their skulls. The debris that floated on the surface of the waves created a white foam from which was born a young goddess, Aphrodite, whose beauty inspired painters and poets for thousands of years.

Despite reveling in the poetic beauty of women, the human mind did not become less warped than the fairy tales of the Greek past. Many families, even in our time, have their own horror tales to tell, which often are much more original than writers of soap operas could invent.

The grandfather on my mother's side, David Blum, fell off the roof of the building on Paradeplatz 6 in Leipzig, a thriving city in Saxony. The Jews lived in Germany for a thousand years. They had arrived with the Roman legions. The proof is that a synagogue existed in Ulm, in southern Germany, built in the ninth century. The Nazis razed it in 1942. Though he was despised, tortured, and imprisoned in ghettos during the Middle Ages, the German Jew tried to be more patriotic than his German hosts. That's why it was fitting that my grandfather should fall to his death while hoisting the black, white, and red flag of the German Empire. The year was 1898. His haberdashery on Paradeplatz was on the verge of bankruptcy. To escape the shame of having failed in business, he camouflaged his death by slipping off the roof of the five-story building while hoisting the flag on the emperor's birthday. He died a true patriot, wrapped in the black-white-red German national colors.

To save the haberdashery for her beloved son Hugo, my grandmother Anna turned the only family asset left to her into cash. She sold her seventeen-year-old daughter, Rosa Phillipine, to a man who, highly recommended by the local matchmaker, contributed money to keep grandfather's store afloat. That's how my father, Ignatz (Ike) Siodmak, got married to my mother, Rosa Phillipine Blum. It was an ill-matched marriage that deeply clouded my life and that of my three brothers. In my early youth I felt the alienation of my parents. It was a vague, nebulous notion, which had not clearly taken shape in my mind. I was lonely, since I don't remember my father or my mother ever hugging me.

Since nobody talked to me about my insecurities, I confided my fears on paper, withdrawing into a world of make-believe, a surrogate for a life that was more true to me than reality. I created a world of my own, in which I felt protected and which I did not share with anybody. Searching for an elusive quality of life, which is love, I was looking for the unknown, the ephemeral.

Real princes and princesses, the children of kings and queens, still existed in my early youth. They lived the way I did, I supposed, a similarly detached existence. Their parents were busy ruling and giving big parties while their children were left in the care of servants.

I wrote a story that expressed my search for the nebulous, the unattainable, and called it "The Key."

"Once upon a time [most fairy tales I knew started that way], there was a castle with a thousand rooms where a young Prince lived. He had innumerable toys but no companion to share them with, like friends, a dog or cat, even a bird. The Prince rarely saw his parents, and then only at official receptions. The servants were mute and the windows so high that the Prince could only see a few clouds floating by. He sometimes heard dogs bark and birds sing, but he didn't meet any dogs, cats, or birds, because the King was afraid his son might be contaminated by strange diseases. The young Prince was fading away, suffering from loneliness. He became so thin that he had to walk twice through the same door to be seen [a sentence that indicates that I might become a writer]. The King, afraid for his son's life, invited wise men, astronomers, astrologers, doctors, and magicians to find a cure for his ailing son. Whoever could restore his health could take as much gold from the treasury as he could carry.

"The wise men had different ideas about how the Prince could be cured. One suggested mixing a concoction of hearts of lizards with the powder of butterfly wings. Then one old man produced a key. He predicted that this key would open one of the thousand doors of the castle, and behind that door the Prince would find his cure and salvation. But nobody should be allowed to watch the Prince while he was looking for the right door that the magic key would open.

"The young Prince walked from door to door, testing the locks. But the key did not fit any of them. When, discouraged, he gave up the search, he discovered a small door he had overlooked. The key fit, and the Prince found himself outside the castle."

It was my mother's story. She wanted to escape but could not find the door.

I wrote that story with a quill (a sharpened goose feather quill on parchment), decorated it with sequins, and I bound it with a colored ribbon, which I fastened with sealing wax to the paper. I gave that little book to my mother.

One of her friends was the editor of a children's magazine, *Kinderwelt* (World of Children). He published that story. Thus I became a published author at the age of nine.

From that moment on I got only "A"s in school for my compositions. But, though the teacher read stories of other children to the class, he never mentioned mine. They must have been so intimate that he did not want to expose me to my classmates. I don't remember any of the stories I wrote for the teacher. But from the day on which I saw my story in the magazine *Kinderwelt,* I composed stories as a catharsis and a cure for a loneliness that has never left me during my life.

Uncle Hugo, Grandmother Anna's son and my mother's brother, took over the haberdashery with my father's financial help, and through years of toil and thrift he made a comfortable living. He and Grandmother Anna were respectable citizens of Leipzig's Jewish population until the day Hitler became Reichskanzler and wiped out that ancient Jewish community, which dated back to the exodus of the Sephardic Jews from Spain in 1492.

Uncle Hugo's bookkeeper, Helga, who had worked for him for twenty-eight years and whom he had treated like a family member, denounced her boss and benefactor to the Gestapo, concocting a story that her employer had cracked a joke about the Fuehrer. Uncle Hugo was arrested and sent to a concentration camp near the town of Osnabrueck. There, on a cold winter night, some bored Nazi guards turned a water hose on the Jew and froze him into a block of ice. His haberdashery—Grandmother Anna had died mercifully a decade before—was given by the Nazis to the bookkeeper, as a reward for her patriotic deed.

In 1944 British bombers set Leipzig aflame, creating a firestorm in which ten thousand citizens died. The Paradeplatz and Uncle Hugo's haberdashery went up in flames. As far as I could make out, Helga the bookkeeper was burned to death. There is no great difference in dying by ice or by fire.

Like a tree just before it dies, throwing all of its strength into its last fruit, producing them abundantly, my hometown Dresden reached the peak of its culture just before World War I. At its opera house, Caruso was a regular performer, and when he died was and even today is a legendary name. The composer Richard Strauss tried out his works, such as *Electra* and *The Rosenkavalier*, on its stage. Hugo von Hoffmannsthal was Strauss's lyricist. When Hoffmannsthal died in 1929, Strauss chose his close friend, Stefan Zweig, to write the librettos.

When in 1935 the Strauss opera *Die Schweigsame Frau* (The Taciturn Woman) was performed, the opera was forced to close after three days, since the Gestapo, on Goebbels's orders, threw rotten eggs on the stage because a Jew had written the libretto. Zweig had to flee Europe and committed suicide. Strauss became, I assume against his wish, a high government official during the Nazi time. But he did not fight the Nazi intrusion of the arts. After the rise of Hitler, he did not compose anymore, except an elegy bemoaning the demise of his fatherland. Dresden, the most beautiful baroque city in the world, first mentioned in the thirteenth century, went up in flames in 1945, a barbaric, senseless act of Allied bombers.

Fifty years later while in Germany, I was invited by the mayor of that unhappy city to visit. Germany miraculously had been built up again. Nowhere in Germany did I find a trace that a war had ravaged that country.

The affable young mayor of my hometown asked me to sign the "Golden Book" of the city. I wrote, "Peace, Pace, Pax, Friede, Shalom. Will it ever happen?" I couldn't think of more words for peace in other languages. My question was half a century too late to influence the history of that city.

Except for impressive government baroque buildings along the Elbe River, the king's castle and its adjoining sixteenth-century church, the Saxonian capital had been rebuilt hastily. Houses and streets lacked character or variety, just giving shelter to people who had lost their homes in the rain of British phosphor bombs and blockbusters. But I found the house on Mozartstrasse 5 where I grew up in my teens, undamaged.

All homes in the Mozartstrasse, except that massive brick building, had been burned to cinders. That rubble had been removed. Not one was left standing except the house of my youth. It was deserted, the garden overgrown with weeds. It looked soulless, numb, and shell-shocked to me, still exuding a smell of brimstone and fire. Except for the house number, I would not have recognized it. Its picture had disappeared from my memory.

I could not feel any pity for the city's demise, since my emotions had dried up remembering the boundless cruelties of its population against the Jews. My hosts and I were strangers to each other, though I was treated with an intimate friendliness, as though I had left only days before. A pleasant young woman was the city's official historian. Since she was born decades after the war's end, I will never learn how she was able to cope with her historical research, or whether she was able to analyze and judge the times of her parents. Meeting me, a relic from the past, must have defied her comprehension. Though city governments record in publication the excesses of the time of the Nazis with German thoroughness, those books dryly record facts but never voice a judgment about the limitless cruelties and insensitive proclivity of their parents. It does not seem to be in the genes of the Germans I met to be able to say, "We are sorry."

I could not see the real faces behind the friendly masks of this new generation, since I too suffered from an amnesia that the flow of time had imposed on me.

My memory of my early youth, when a king ruled Saxony, is like a stage play whose curtain rises and then falls, a show that has a beginning but a sudden last curtain.

I was brought up in an atmosphere of culture and beauty, the kind I could not offer my son or my grandchildren.

Richard Strauss was my father's skat partner. Skat, similar to bridge, is an auction card game played by three. Strauss and my father Ike met almost daily in the back room of Mr. Hub's delicatessen in the Seestrasse. Sometimes my father took me along. I liked Mr. Hub's delicatessen since I got two small hot sausages, as delicious as only Mr. Hub could make them.

Strauss's love for the card game skat has been mentioned in many of the famous composer's biographies. I remember my father, who had a short temper, scolding his card partner, "Strauss, you idiot, why didn't you play the ace!"

The skat-afflicted players (Strauss, Ike, and Mr. Hub) also met in our apartment at the Seidnitzer Platz. I could walk to the school, which was only a few hundred feet away. Our large apartment, where I was born, contained a music room with white silk-covered chairs, depicting French Fragonard scenes with shepherds and shepherdesses, a Bluetner piano, though none of our family played any instrument, and a gilded round coffee table where Ike played skat with his partners. Strauss was a tall, heavyset man of about forty with a moustache and always sporting a bow tie. During the hiatus in their games, when my mother served tea in paper-thin china cups, Strauss repeated a melody endlessly on the Bluetner. He was composing his opera *Electra,* which was performed in 1909.

At that time Ike was affluent. Rosa, our mother, a dark-haired lively beauty, created a "salon," inviting painters, actors, and famous personalities. She surrounded herself with artists. A young painter and writer, Oskar Kokoschka, who became famous by illustrating his poem "Dreaming Boys" and later was the director of the Dresden Academy of Art, brought his friends, the creators of dadaism, that nonsense art that telegraphed the times of upheaval to come. Emil Nolde, who already was a recognized painter, was in that group. Strauss came with his collaborator Hugo von Hoffmannsthal.

We children were not allowed to sit at the long refectory table, which was laid out with Dresden porcelain and crystal glasses and decorated with flowers. Young actors playing at the Albert Theater, and always very hungry, were steady guests. One of them drank champagne out of the shoe of a dark-haired young woman. I did not find this very sanitary. Ike, enjoying the cultural atmosphere that his beautiful wife had created, sunned himself in the attention also given to him.

My mother offered a toast before each meal and threw a glass of wine over the table, a graceful gesture to make her guests feel comfortable should they spill food on the damask tablecloth. Of course she had help: a cook, Frau Schrubber, a young French nanny for her children, a maid, and a washerwoman who appeared every Thursday to wash in the cellar all the used linen in a steaming cauldron of soapy water. No paper towels or plastic cups at that time.

Robert and I, being older than our brothers, knew that the marriage of our parents did not go well. But what did we children know about our parents' relationship? Communications with parents were unknown in the late Victorian age. I remember on one Sunday morning musicians appeared. Father had hired a quartet, including a young woman who played the Bluetner and a violinist wearing a Tyrolean hat, which he didn't take off. There was a cello and a flute. Those four performed in the music room, all by themselves since Rosa had locked herself in the bedroom and cried. Ike, knocking at the door, begged her to come out. There must have existed a romance, my father constantly wooing his wife, though my mother, a spoiled Jewish princess, never accepted that marriage to a man chosen for her by a matchmaker and forced on her by our grandmother.

That mismatch deprived us as children of a parental love that nothing in my or my brothers' lives could replace. In my case even a marriage, despite its closeness for seventy years, could never completely fill that void of my childhood. Robert was searching all of his life for love, which he never found. Werner became an unfulfilled and bitter man, and Rolf (Roland) chose death as a way out of his loneliness when he was nineteen.

There was only one time of peace for Germany, an empire created by Otto von Bismarck, chancellor of Kaiser Wilhelm I, the years between the Prussian-French war of 1870 and the outbreak of World War I in September 1914. After World War I came the second one, followed by the Cold War. There was never again a period of innocence like that between 1870 and 1914.

In my early youth, Dresden was a city made of sugar and spice, with lovely baroque buildings, small colorful streets, majestic bridges spanning the Elbe River. It was the center of art, musicians, painters, the hub of theater culture. It also had the air of a small town. Every month a country fair was held at the Altmarkt, the town square. Farmers came in horse-drawn carts to sell pigs and live chickens; there were gypsy fortune-tellers; and Uncle Hugo and his brother-in-law and partner, Arthur Wildau, came from Leipzig, a two-hour train ride away, to sell cheap cloth ("three meters for one mark") from a rented booth. It was great fun for us children. I saw my first motion picture in a "Kinomatograph" on the second floor of a building in the Seestrasse. A narrow escalator carried the audience up to it, where a huge black man in a uniform helped the people to step off the moving stairs. He was the first black man I ever saw in my life. One of the moving pictures was the head of a beautiful woman who could contort her features into ugly, frightening shapes. The main event was a boxing match between Jeffries and Johnson, a white and a black. I believe the black won. It was a cruel, gruesome fight. I still don't like boxing matches. I have never been to one, nor do I watch that macho sadism on TV.

The problems of the time before World War I seem fairy-tale-like and inconceivably primitive.

Saxony was ruled by the House of Wettin, a family from which several royal houses in Europe have sprung. It was an ancient family, dating back to the Nordic king Wittekind, who died about 807. The English House of Battenberg, the Mountbattens, the present British ruling family, also had its roots in the Wettins, an obviously fertile family. On June 7, 1902, a month before I was born, King Albert of

Saxony died and was succeeded by his brother George. The most conspicuous event of his reign was the affair of Crown Princess Louise with a M. Girot, who was the French tutor of her children. This resulted in a grave scandal, broadcast throughout Europe and ending with a papal dispensation of divorce.

The Catholic religion does not allow a divorce since marriage is registered in heaven's files. The Wettins were members of that religion, but adultery in a royal family has a different connotation. The child the crown princess bears might not be that of the future king, and a bastard might inherit the throne of Saxony! Though George must have loved the beautiful princess, he was forced to divorce her.

But Louise didn't stick to her paramour, either, and married the Italian composer Enrico Toselli, who had composed a great deal of music, among them two symphonies and the widely known "Serenade." That relationship also didn't last. She supposedly married again and died, anonymous and poor, a midwife in Brussels. A scandal like that was so important to European society that the Crown Princess Louise's tryst with M. Girot is mentioned in the eleventh edition of the *Encyclopaedia Britannica* of 1911, page 272. Who slept with whom made world-shaking history at that time. There was a rumor that Queen Victoria, after Prince Albert, her husband, died, had skin contact with her coachman, Mr. John Brown, a part of history about which Hector Bolitho, an English playwright, wrote a play. During 1936, when I worked in England, I wrote a screenplay about that scandalous incident for the London film company Gaumont British. But an unknown government power stopped its production.[1] That screenplay had been my last European job in England. I sailed, on my clairvoyant wife Henrietta's insistence, to America. She must have felt the coming European upheaval. In our marriage her intuition is never wrong.

When I arrived in New York, Charles MacArthur, the writing partner of Ben Hecht (authors of the successful play *Front Page*), threw a party for a young German actress. She wore a deeply cut dress, exposing lots of luminous skin on which, surprisingly, sprouted five long black hairs. Some men might find that exposure sexy; I did not.

Charles MacArthur, an alcoholic, loved giving parties, since only then did he have access to unlimited quantities of liquor that his young wife, the young actress Helen Hayes, otherwise strictly ra-

---

[1] Eventually this story did become a movie, *Mrs. Brown*, 1997.

tioned to him, but not during his parties. I remember sitting at the great actress's feet, and being an expert on Queen Victoria on account of my research into the life of that English queen, we discussed the reign of Queen Victoria. Miss Hayes at that time was playing *Young Queen Victoria* on the stage. It was the one time in my life that I had the opportunity to talk with that gifted lady, who died in 1994. I remember our conversation vividly, she having the image of a twenty-year-old innocent girl in her mind, and I that of a lonely woman in her fifties.

The scandal of Crown Princess Louise, who would rather sleep with a man she loved than be queen, shook the European royalty to its foundation. There is a parallel in the Battenberg family with the abdication of Edward VIII, who would rather marry the woman he loved than be king, and also with the divorce of Charles, Prince of Wales, from his wife, Diana Spencer. The marital fickleness of the royal family of the Battenbergs and Windsors seems to be endemic and was an essential story source for tabloids the world over. But when at the French prime minister François Mitterand's funeral not only his wife but also his mistress and the child he had fostered took part, the media only chuckled. But Queen Victoria's private life was treated with reverence by the British nobility. In the nineteenth century there was more resentment about the influence that Prime Minister Benjamin Disraeli had on Queen Victoria than her stepping out with a servant. Lord Clarendon, a contemporary member of the House of Lords and ingrained anti-Semite, wrote about Disraeli, "The Jew, the most subtle beast in the field, has, like Eve's tempter, ingratiated himself with the Missus!"

Lord Clarendon's "Missus" was the queen; the beast, Disraeli, who, despite having embraced the faith of the Church of England, always remained a Jew to the British nobility.

Now values have changed. Who cares if the president of France has a mistress whom he displays openly? Or if Mitterand's wife, mistress, and illegitimate child are present at his funeral? Or if an English prince takes girls of questionable repute to Balmoral Castle? But the sexual exploits of the Victorian age were of major concern to the empire, despite that an extensive pornographic literature flourished, especially in puritan London, where every sixtieth house was a brothel, where underwear was called "the unmentionables," and when offered a chicken, the customer was asked if he preferred dark or white meat, since it was not in good taste to utter the word *thigh* or *breast*. That Victorianism hasn't changed in the present-day British royal house. The future queen of England has to be virginal before her marriage. Her child might be that of a M. Girot and thus would spoil the purity of the clan. The future queen of England had to go through the medical embarrassment to prove that she never had a sexual affair before she married the Prince of Wales. That's why King Solomon kept a harem, guarded by eunuchs, to make sure that every one of his two hundred children was the result of his own sperm.

To ensure the continuation of the family, virginity was an essential part in marriages. The Greeks parade the bloodied bedsheet of a wedding night through the village to prove the virginity of the bride and that the firstborn child undoubtedly was that of the bridegroom and not of a previous lover. That's why the husband of my cousin Else never believed that her absent virginity came from her training as a dancer. That's why the Jews step on a glass, breaking it, at their marriage ceremony. It used to be a pomegranate, and the symbolism is obvious.

The blonde daughter of cantor Hofstein in Dresden got pregnant out of wedlock. She tried desperately to seduce a young Hasidic Jew before they married. But she did not succeed, since her future husband was not allowed intercourse before the rabbi gave his blessings. She had to be shipped out of town to give birth to a child of shame! Times have changed, and women demand the same sexual freedom as men. In my father's time, monogamy, which didn't pertain to women, was the connubial law.

My parents liked to be seen among the Dresden society that frequented the operas. The Dresden opera house was as famous as the Teatro alla Scala in Milan. It was run by a theatrical genius, Count Seebach.

There was no radio to be listened to, no television to look at. Books and theater ruled the entertainment world. Honoré de Balzac's novels (thirty-six volumes) of family stories were the equivalent to today's soap operas. I sometimes had to go with my parents to the opera. I must have seen Wagner's *Ring* a dozen times. His opera *Parsifal* took six hours to perform. I still remember the clock above the stage, which I watched hoping the show would be over soon. In the opera *Lohengrin,* a swan made of wood appeared on the stage, pulling a small boat to give Lohengrin a free ride. One day the swan didn't arrive in time, and I, sitting in the first row, heard the tenor sing three times, "If he returns, though I may ne'er receive him, this horn, this sword, this token I leave him." I never found out who "he" was. Finally, the swan was pulled on the stage. Lohengrin was great fun, because of the wooden swan. I also liked Wagner's *Walkyrie,* since buxom ladies on horseback rode on the stage and the horses sometimes misbehaved.

But, even today, I would never voluntarily go to see an opera, not even on television. I had seen too many operas in my youth by parental decree.

The film industry was organized by Jews, who developed it into a world power. When I arrived in the United States in 1937, there was still a *"numerus clausus,"* a quantity fixed as the maximal percentage admissible to an academic institution. Only 4 percent admitted at certain universities could be Jews. Why did anti-Semitism extend even to the teaching professions? What were the Gentiles afraid of? Because a Jewish dropout is a guy who didn't get his Ph.D.? The Chrysler Corporation didn't accept Jews, not even as a car salesman. Henry Ford was a rabid anti-Semite. He even financed an anti-Semitic newspaper. The Jewish-controlled film industry in Hollywood never showed a Ford car in their motion pictures, except wrecked ones, which made Henry Ford officially abandon his policy, though not his prejudice.

To educate oneself is a strong Jewish belief, so teaches the Talmud, that Jewish guidebook of the laws of life. Education is the highest accomplishment in the Jewish existence. If a Jew has the wish to bring a child into the world, but if that added burden would prevent him from educating himself further, it is his duty to forego his progeny so as to continue his learning. Since the Jews in any European country were not permitted to own land, only the professions of craftsmen, medicine, and dealing in money were open to them. The Christians, also Mohammed, forbade collecting interest, which exempted the Jews. That strict religious law has been drastically changed by the believers since money is more powerful than any creed.

At the turn of the twentieth century, a loophole in the prohibitive numerous clauses opened up for the Jews: the invention of moving pictures. That new discovery had no restriction imposed on the Jews, since producing films was a commercial industry without congressional interference. Jews, mostly emigrants from Eastern European countries, flocked into that new medium, sensing its potential. Samuel Goldfish Americanized his name to Goldwyn, and with Louis B. Mayer formed the MGM studios. William Fox, whose name was Friedmann, opened up Twentieth Century–Fox studios.

Carl Laemmle from Laupheim in Germany started Universal Studios. Harry Cohn was master of Columbia Pictures. The Warner brothers, four of them (sons of a Russian emigrant), built the Warner Brothers Studios. Every big studio was ruled by Jews, except Fox Film, which changed hands and was headed by Darryl Zanuck, an Episcopalian, and therefore it was known as "the Goy Studio"— *goy* being a non-Jew as *"giour"* is a non-Muslim. The root of those two expressions seems to be related.

The actors were, with very few exceptions, non-Jewish, but many writers, producers, and directors were. The Jewish heads of the studios, despite their primitive education, became tycoons, and it is astonishing that a sense of story values seemed inborn in them. Their products disseminated American culture and its way of life to every country of the globe. The spread of the American world power is partly based on the influence of the moving pictures that came from Hollywood.

Even members of my family saw the potential of pictures in motion. In 1906, the four sons of my father's brother Usher (Hermann, Martin, Leo, and Julius) acquired a newfangled American invention, the Mutoscope—wooden boxes in which printed cards turned rapidly, creating the illusion of a moving object. There was a man on a galloping horse, dancing couples, even a woman who started to undress. But the picture stopped when she had removed her stocking, which was a daring feat at that late Victorian time.

Since the czar of all Russians forbade Jews to enter Siberia, my enterprising cousins changed their religion to that of the Russian Orthodox Church and went with their Mutoscope boxes to Siberia. At night the newly baptized Gentiles congregated and, facing the east, prayed in the direction of Jerusalem. For one kopek the startled peasants in Siberian villages could observe this twentieth-century miracle.

With enough rubles in their satchel, my cousins returned to Germany, the city of Dresden, renounced their Gentile religion, and now with enough cash started a wholesale distribution of butter. Their enterprise prospered.

If the American industry had been aware of the power of the photographed moving image, it would have tried to curtail the Jewish participation in that industry. But Jews were already too deeply entrenched in that still unexplored culture. They monopolized it.

My father missed his chance of becoming a Hollywood tycoon. We found out that he was proud of my brother Robert and me, when we worked in the German film business. He would never admit it, though he often secretly carried one of my novels with him. I remember that when we were well known in the German film industry, we invited our father to the gigantic UFA film studios in Babelsberg at the outskirts of Berlin. Babelsberg was the German Hollywood.

The year was 1932, and the German film industry with its world-renowned films like *The Blue Angel* was at its peak. We took the "old man," as we called him behind his back (he died when he was sixty-three), to the UFA studio. There Robert was directing the motion picture *Stuerme der Leidenschaft,* with the world-renowned star Emil Jannings. *F.P. 1 Does Not Answer* (Flying Platform One Does Not Reply), a gigantic science fiction film based on one of my novels and screenplays, was filmed in three languages in Babelsberg. My conception of a floating platform in the ocean was the prototype of the present airplane carrier. But since I forgot to patent that idea, I could not sue the governments for patent infringement.

At Babelsberg, Father shook hands with the actors Charles Boyer and Conrad Veidt, who played in the picture based on my book. He met Erich Pommer, the most gifted producer I ever worked for in my life. Ike was very pleased with his sons when he left and pronounced, "I've lent you a part of my brain, and I'm very happy to see how well you use it." That was his way of identifying himself with our success. "When I went to America as a very young man, a friend of mine worked with me in Oshkosh, rolling cigars. His name was Zukor, a Hungarian. He had the idea of producing little flickers, moving pictures, but not as big as they do them now. Zukor formed a corporation. He wanted me to become his partner. I declined since I had an idea how to make money in Germany. I wonder what has happened to him?"

His friend was Adolf Zukor, the creator of Paramount Pictures in Hollywood. If my father had accepted Zukor's offer, he would have become a producer at Paramount, would not have returned to Germany to follow up his idea of how to make money in a special way. He would not have met my mother through a matchmaker in Leipzig, and his four sons would never have been born. And the one hundred thirty motion pictures that Robert and I created in our lifetime would never have been made. The question is still open as to whether my father had made the right decision for himself. But not for my mother. She might have found a man with whom she could have been happy.

What memories stay with all of us during our lifetime? Memories are like photographs, often stopped in motion, unmovable, precise pictures. Others are events, like the wars we lived through, which did not affect us personally. We live on the outskirts of disasters and remember them like the Vietnam War, the dust bowl, World War II, or, if we are old, World War I, from tales of our parents or grandparents.

But there are other incidents that engrave themselves like motion pictures with all their details in our memories. Occurrences that seem trivial can have a deep impact on our lives, our future, and often even in forming or engraving our character with opinions that we are unable to shed. One of them is as vivid in my mind as if it were a motion picture that I had seen only the night before.

It was the ball at the opera house in Dresden before World War I, in 1913. Once a year, sponsored by the royal court, a fancy dress ball for the Dresden society was held at the opera, by special invitation of the House of Wettin. The seats in the auditorium were removed and replaced with tables. Guests were carefully chosen according to their prominence and wealth. They tried to outdo each other with imaginary costumes.

My father and mother were invited, though they certainly did not belong to the Dresden society. Richard Strauss had provided tickets for his skat partner. Elated by the honor bestowed on him, my father had a clown's costume tailored for him. He was a small man but powerfully built. He could hold out his right arm, and my mother and we four children could hang on it. He wore for the occasion a clown's hat and a peacock feather on his nose.

Father came to our bedroom to perform for us as a clown. I was eight, my brother Robert, ten; the youngest one, Werner, then three, started to cry, since he did not recognize father.

His performance, possibly encouraged by a few glasses of slivovitz, the hardy Polish plum schnapps he often frequented, was monstrously obscene to us. In the adjoining bedroom was our mother, dressed as Carmen in a low-cut gypsy outfit. She wore a rose in her hair, and for the first time we saw her long, well-formed legs in black silk stockings.

Just then the doorbell rang, and since the maid was busy dressing Mother, the clown opened the door. A plainclothesman stood outside with one of Ike's employees. The man had stolen half a crate of eggs, and Father had reported him to the police. The man pleaded tearfully with the clown to drop the charge. Should he be sent to prison, his family would starve. But the clown lifted his arm in a biblical gesture and exclaimed, "Whoever steals my possessions, steals my luck! To prison!"

It was like a scene from an Erich von Stroheim picture. A peacock made of brass stood in our living room, with wings made of real feathers. And the clown wore a peacock feather on his nose. I did not like that bird's image and connected it with bad luck. Even today I cannot stand peacock feathers in my home and resent them as carriers of bad luck.

A thousand guests were invited to the opera ball by the king's fiat. His Highness, the Crown Prince, appeared in the royal box. All female members of the king's family had to stay home from carefree festivities like the opera ball, to keep the strain of the Wettins pure. King August III grounded the unmarried princesses to prevent them from meeting another M. Girot.

For thousands of years virginity in unmarried women was demanded. It was the only guarantee that the firstborn was the husband's child. The French cut that Gordian knot by adhering to the Napoleonic Code, which states that if a woman declares a man to be the father of her child, it is indisputable evidence.

During the opera ball, officers of the guard, dressed in white, mixed with the masked crowd. Champagne flowed from magnum bottles. Curtains closed at private boxes on the first balcony, which was reserved for the king's court. The orchestra played waltzes under the direction of my father's skat partner. At midnight, when the spirits were high, an adjutant of the Crown Prince approached my father's table to invite the beautiful Carmen with the flowing black hair and the shimmering velvet shoulders to a dance.

The merchant of eggs, son of the Rabbi of Podgorze, was overwhelmed by the honor. My mother was eager to have real fun, since my father was hardly a good dancer.

But Carmen did not return for two hours. Prodded by the cynical remarks of some of the guests at his table, the clown left to find his wife. He went upstairs to the royal balcony. Possessed by an unbridled temper, of which we children suffered often at home, he burst into the royal box, pushing the guard aside. There among the resplendent uniforms of gold and white, the naked shoulders of the ladies of the court, the silk dresses and shining jewels, was his Carmen on the lap of a young, high-ranking officer, who was kissing my mother! The red rose, which Carmen had been carrying in her hair, was gone, her dress was in disarray, and her black hair needed combing. The officer in the gold and white uniform was the Crown Prince, who prudently had left his wife at home.

Ridi Pagliacci. The clown was thrown out. He went home alone.

The next day the Jewish community tittered with amusement about the Crown Prince's affair with a Jewish princess. My mother was not permitted to return home and stayed with the blonde Rosa, who enjoyed that scandal with great relish, since she got her sexual pleasures from other women's adventures. My father, who was easily moved to tears, stayed home for days, crying that his wife had humiliated him and made him a laughingstock among the Dresden Jewry. Though he and mother had frequent fights about her flirtatious ways, this time my father was determined to divorce his wife.

Grandmother rushed from Leipzig by express train. Dressed in black, she fell on her knees in plain view of us children and cried, imploring Ike to take his repentant wife back, not to make orphans of his children and bring shame to the good name of Leipzig Blums.

Later Mother appeared, dressed in a tight-fitting black costume that accentuated her small waist and full breasts. She wore a huge black hat, and her face was hidden by a black veil that was the fashion of the time, which she finally lifted. Her large eyes were red from crying. As had happened before, she brought presents for us children and coached us on what to say should Father ask us if he should take her back. I believe that every child assures him- or herself that his or her mother was very handsome, but on that day in my memory she looked devastatingly beautiful in her remorse and grief, her skin translucent from lack of sleep and worry. What chance did a divorced woman have in the year 1913? She had never done a day's work in her life. She would, a Jezebel, have to return to her mother, with whom she never got along.

Despite his wife's seduction by the Crown Prince of Saxony, which after all contained a certain glamour, my father was still in love with her. He forgave her. We children were not unduly upset by our parents' quarrel. It had happened before, though not as dramatically.

Nine months later my mother gave birth to a boy. Frieda, the midwife who had delivered all of us, assisted her. My mother turned her head against the wall and did not want to see the baby boy. The wet nurse arrived from the Spreewald, since Mother never had nursed any of us, in order not to spoil her well-shaped breasts. Rabbi Winter came with his surgical instruments to perform the Brith, the circumcision. Grandmother Anna and Uncle Hugo came from Leipzig. The child cried, not wanting his penis shortened.

My father gave him a very Teutonic name, Roland, which we shortened to Rolf. Though we older boys had a strong family likeness, he did not look like any of us. He grew up tall, handsome, and aristocratic and did not possess the family drive that helped us stay alive during the exodus.

During his short lifetime, he tried several times to kill himself and finally shot himself, a refugee of Hitler's victims at the age of nineteen, in 1933 in the park of Versailles.

Do the impressions, the joys and hurts of our childhood and of our later life, stay with us forever? Do we ever recover from the loss of people close or dear to us? Their ghosts might appear in later years and cause "depressions," a word that seems to explain everything, though it does not clarify anything. In our present time, families are spread out over this vast continent. The older generation doesn't move anymore into a small house in back of the ranch. The main house used to be taken over by the children who would cultivate the land and raise food and cattle, as a cycle of life that had been the rule for centuries. The mobility of communication has changed all that, smashing up the continuity of life forever.

Now too much emphasis is given to the age of people. Since the next generation does not stay with the older one, their relation is kept alive more by a sense of duty to each other than of love. The family structure has collapsed. I have asked numerous people how much they know about their parents' intimate lives. No one really knew much about them.

Staying young as long as possible has become a profession, though a very precarious one, though this too is just make-believe. Aging can be camouflaged only for a very short time. Every added year brands its often minute stamp into faces.

Youth has become a commodity. A gifted screenwriter in his fifties takes his twenty-two-year-old son with him to studio conferences as his "collaborator," since only the young ones, for the producer, possess the wisdom of the contemporary trait and know what the audience wants. Youth is "being with it." The people who frequent motion pictures are mostly under thirty. That's where the tickets are sold. To cater to youth is guaranteed money in the bank. There is a condescending tolerance by the young for the old, though that borderline of years is not clearly defined. For the twelve-year-old girl a man of eighteen is ancient; those over sixty had a dinosaur on a chain instead of a Weimaraner. My friend the director Fred Zinnemann, who was the director of *High Noon, A Man for All Seasons,* and *From Here to Eternity* and has a handful of Academy Awards decorating the mantelpiece of his fireplace, was invited by the film company of Warner Brothers for an "interview" with a young producer.

"Please, Mr. Zinnemann," the twenty-five-year-old producer said, "tell me something about yourself."

"You first," Fred replied.

An old friend of mine, Charles Bennett, the author of many Hitchcock films, among them *The 39 Steps,* wrote a play and the film *Blackmail* sixty years ago. Since he is a "plot constructionist," he knows how to tell a story. Discovering the picture, which can be found on cassettes, a studio decides to buy its rights, which fortunately had reverted back to Charles. The studio bought Charles's play to produce it again in a "modern way."

They assigned two film writers who, not having reached thirty, obviously were gifted with the knowledge of present-day tastes. Then the company, to be courteous, asked Charles for his opinion. Charles created a forty-page "commentary" of the young writer's screenplay, pointing out its weaknesses. The company, impressed, asked Charles to write his own version. That decision created a national stir in the motion picture sections of newspapers. A man of ninety-two was assigned to write a contemporary screenplay! The prestigious "Calendar," which is part of the Sunday edition of the *Los Angeles Times,* printed a three-page enthusiastic commentary about that unusual assignment. The *New York Times* reported about that author who, despite having reached a biblical age, had been entrusted with writing an important film. Charles's name appeared even in British newspapers, as though his job were an item worthy to report, since it seemed a miracle that a man of that advanced age still possessed a working brain and could express himself more precisely than young writers whose brainstorms have watered down the present film industry to a commercial wasteland.

To attract the public, stories have to show more brutality and depravity, and their success is measured by the amount of blood spilled on the screen. Themes in books and motion pictures do not shrink from showing cannibalism or necrophilia. The "arts" are mirrors of our maniacal times, which, though moving scientifically forward with lightning speed, glide inhumanly back into the darkest ages of our creation.

It seems that the human brain consists of three parts: that of the caveman, a "social" part, and a "mystical" one. The social brain enables us to deal with each other without murdering each other. The mystical one, which religions have taught for thousands of years, humankind has not yet reached.

What is the driving force in modern American society that caters to the inexperienced young and judges an older man's well-seasoned conceptions of his work as dated?

Youth tries to discard the old, to eliminate them in their short span of youth. I know that my granddaughters, when they were in their early teens, resented violently if I conversed too "intimately," as they thought, with their female peers. Even the possibility of a mental contact between the young and the old was repugnant to them, because their subliminal emotions were basically concentrated on sex, which might be explained by the height of their testosterone or estrogen level. Youth, in their opinion, belongs to youth, forgetting that a huge army of younger people pushes the presently young into the categories of the middle-aged. The criterion is the number of years that relentlessly accumulate, creating schisms between the generations.

At my busiest time in my forties, I was advised by the studios to "write down" to the level of the twelve-year-old. If I would do that today, those films would be X-rated.

Since the time that I was a teenager, the age of puberty has dropped at least five years. When I was sixteen, I was still virginal. Nor were my peers well informed about sex. Books about that subject were not available in my youth. Though physical maturity now comes earlier to the young, the development of their brain power has not kept pace at the same rate. Of course, the bridgeless cleavage between old and young always existed. Didn't Aristotle complain that youth has no respect for the old?

In my youth I also experienced the same stage of alienation with older people. I still suffer from the lack of communication I had with my parents and cannot even remember that my mother ever hugged me or that my father kissed me, except for one incident. My bedroom adjoined that of my parents. I was five at that time and staying alone in the dark room was scary for me; I saw ghosts in every dark corner. Suddenly a rooster crowed. But there were no roosters in the huge apartment building where we lived. I listened, panic-stricken. Then the rooster crowed again. I called my mother. She was at my bed immediately and took me in her arms. There must have been concern and love of my parents for their children, the memory of which I have suppressed, since my brother Robert, until his death, assured me that he was our mother's favorite child. Though we might find much love in our lifetime, the void of not being loved in our early youth can never be filled, since our brain, which is most impressionable in the first years of our existence, remembers that omission forever.

The social structure of a Jewish family at the turn of the century deliberately isolated the young from the old. The parents of the generation my father belonged to did not know any better. They repeated the treatment they themselves had suffered from their parents. Looking at the picture of my grandfather Abraham Siodmak, rabbi of Podgorze in Galicia, Austria, a hand-colored photograph taken a century ago, showing a man wearing a skullcap, long curly sideburns and a beard, I can hardly imagine that he ever hugged any of his thirteen children. How can we blame our parents for something they did not know? I am aware that their inability to give vent to their feelings misshaped the life of us four brothers, their children.

My father, to overcome his insecurities, tried to create a macho image for his patriarchal status. When I was five, I had to kiss his hand when he came home from work. The breadwinner, up to the beginning of the twentieth century, was the undisputed master of the house. He was above the law. He could beat his children or wife brutally and with impunity. My brother Robert was often cruelly chastised by my father, while my mother and we children huddled in the adjoining room in terror. He could not make the ten-year-old Robert cry, which made Father unreasonably furious. His power went so far that since he believed we masturbated at that age, he had leather corsets fashioned for us with a metal container for the penis and testicles, which we had to wear day and night. Those corsets had locks to which only Ike had the keys. I can't even visualize the embarrassment if other children had discovered that medieval virginity belt. I was terrified to go to the toilet in school, afraid of exposing myself.

I talked to Dr. Friedrich Hacker, the well-known Viennese psychiatrist who died in 1989, about that medieval torture my brother Robert and I had to endure. He tried to appease my memory that it "was the fashion of that time," where masturbation was considered a deadly sickness. Didn't the God of the Bible kill Onan, son of Judah, as described in Genesis 38:9, because, instead of making the childless widow of his brother pregnant, as Jehovah demands, he let his seed fall between her legs, preventing her pregnancy? That's where the expression *onanism* derives from. A sexual act without the intent to create a child was a biblical sin. A psychiatrist whom I consulted, and whom I told that story, asked me, "Didn't you ever fight your father when he forced that chastity belt on you?" A revolt of a child against his father was almost inconceivable in those days.

Right through human history, and even a hundred years previous, a father was not even held accountable for killing his son or daughter. Women and children were considered chattel.

That's how we children, born at the turn of the century, were brought up. All those incidents of my youth still created deep and unexplored depressions in me and my brothers. Since I never knew my parents intimately, I am still searching for information on why my father, at sixteen, went to America in 1886. He did not tell me, and what I know I heard from my cousins who were of my father's age. On a Sabbath he went to the marketplace in Podgorze in his chasidic clothes, threw his skullcap away, cut off the hemp of his caftan, snipped off his sideburns, and ate ham! On the holy Sabbath! In plain view of the Podgorze Jews! I marvel at his rebellious spirit. He must have suffered under his father's domination as we four brothers suffered under his.

He had somehow acquired the equivalent of twenty-two dollars, which paid for his ship's fare to America. Steerage. The emigrants took along a sack of beans or some other nonperishable food that they were permitted to cook on board. I cannot even conceive the deprivation those travelers had to endure. The journey must have resembled that of a slave ship. How many hundreds were packed into those hulls? What prompted Ike to shame his religious father and leave the small village for a continent of which he had only heard?

Jews ran away from the Austrian army or from the czar's, afraid to be pressed into military services. They hated, by tradition, military organizations since they are trained to kill. Their religion, unlike the Christian and Mohammedan, was a gentle one.

My grandfather Abraham must have forgiven his rebellious son. He gave him an Austrian stamp on the way, asking him to write home when he arrived in that faraway country.

In New York my rebellious father met on a horse-drawn bus a woman who once had worked in his father's house. Since he spoke only Yiddish and Polish, she got him a job with a tailor she knew. At night he slept on the bundles of old clothes in the tailor's cellar. He knew of a relative in Cuba, and after three years of menial work, he had enough money saved to make the long trip to that strange island. There he met his Uncle Itzrak Baum and learned to roll by hand "Baum's Little Havanas" cigars. Then he went to Oshkosh in Wisconsin. There he also rolled cigars. Cigars were a commodity very much appreciated at that time. Henry Clay, the United States statesman and orator, remarked, "What this country needs is a good five cent cigar." That was as important a problem as killing Indians.

Then Ike went to New York. I remember that he talked about the gigantic Hotel MacAlpine, its splendor and luxury, which the Mellons, the Rockefellers, and the Vanderbilts frequented.

When I arrived in America in 1937, I also went through Ellis Island, but since I had made the boat trip first class, I didn't have to go through the emigration routine of being checked for TB, lice, or mental illness. But I walked on the same stony floor my father had.

The MacAlpine was still standing, a shabby, rundown hotel frequented by commercial travelers. I walked through the lobby, relishing that I touched the same floor that my father had crossed a half century before. Here I was, Ike's son, in an unknown country, trying to start a new life, plagued by the same insecurities and fears my father had experienced, a repeat of family history.

What Ike did in New York I don't know, but he stayed a few years. The pay was a dollar a day for ten hours' work. But, one could go to a brewery, buy a glass of beer for five cents, and eat at the buffet for free.

Cousin Hermann also was in New York. Broke and starving, he asked Ike for the loan of one dollar. Ike, with his fierce, unbridled temper, threw the dollar on the pavement for Hermann to pick it up. Hermann told me about that incident thirty years later in Dresden, where he had become affluent with his wholesale butter distribution.

There are insults in life that we never forget. How much damage do we do to people without being conscious of it?

I cannot visualize my father as a teenager or as a young man. There is no picture of him, except for a photo in a smart sporting outfit, holding a bicycle. When he took it out for the first time, a horse kicked it. He had the bicycle repaired, had a picture taken with it and himself, but he never mounted that bike again. But, what made the then thirty-year-old leave America, though he became an American citizen in 1892 in Memphis, Tennessee, I don't know. What was he doing in Tennessee? He kept that document of naturalization, which was adorned with a large red seal, proudly in his safe. That's why we children were American citizens by birth.

In 1898 Ike returned to Germany, to Dresden. He must have had a very fertile and inventive brain. He had figured out that in the cold winter in Germany the hens did not lay eggs. That of course was not a scientific discovery. Renting a huge storehouse in Dresden, he installed large concrete pools that he filled with water, saturating it with sodium silicate. He traveled to Serbia, Poland, and Russia, and bought eggs. Since the only international language in the world is Yiddish, I am sure one could find a Jew, even among the aborigines of Australia, who speaks Yiddish.

My father never had difficulties in foreign countries, since he always contacted a Jew who spoke Yiddish, and who could negotiate for him. The eggs, packed in thin wooden crates, arrived in Dresden by railway, each crate containing 24 times 120 eggs. Some were broken and rotten. By dumping them into the concrete pools, the bad ones floated to the top and were removed; the rest sank to the bottom, preserved until Christmas. My father was the only merchant in Dresden who had eggs at Christmastime when the bakeries produced their famous Dresden Christmas stollen, a fruitcake that they could not have baked without Ike's eggs. It made Father wealthy until World War I broke out. Russia and the Balkan countries became communist. My father's access to eggs dried up. He could never create another business for himself and became frustrated and cruel. The result of his unhappiness, created by the change of the world's economy, destroyed his marriage and our family.

When I was still in my mother's belly, she often visited the "Zwinger," which was part of the king's castle in Dresden. To "zwing" somebody is to enforce a situation. The Zwinger originally had been the Royal Zoo, since in the eighteenth century wild animals were kept there in cages. That's how that building got its name. The Zwinger building, one of the most beautiful baroque buildings in the world, had been rebuilt into a palace by the Wettins. Nothing was standing after the destruction of Dresden. After the war it was restored to its original condition. It now contains as before the treasures that the kings of Saxony had stolen or bought during the centuries of their reign. Among them is Rafael's painting of the Madonna, depicting the Holy Virgin looking rather worldly and seductive, holding the Jesus child. Small, fat little cherubs, reposed and contemplative, are watching Madonna and child. My mother did not visit the Holy Virgin. She visited the little angels to persuade herself that the child she was carrying should have their looks.

Curiously, she succeeded. I was born an angelic-looking blonde child like one of those winged rotund cherubs in Rafael's masterpiece. But, alas, that heavenly beauty did not last. I lost that alluring innocence when I reached maturity. My curly hair also thinned out and then completely took leave of me, despite the many advertised wonder medicines I used externally and internally. None did its job. Part of that hair just slipped to my chest.

Robert and I were brought up like dolls. My parents bought clothes identical to those of the Crown Prince's children. And when "Mademoiselle," whom we called "mad maeusels" (little mad mouse), our seventeen-year-old French governess, took us to the Schloss park, the gardens surrounding the king's castle, we were often mistaken for the royal princes. But that chimera also evaporated early in our lives. Robert always believed himself to be ugly, which he was not, since his tremendous energy favorably enhanced his exterior. He always considered me, the younger brother, as the better looking, just because I was taller, blonde, and rather aloof. Though we had all the physical comforts of children of the affluent middle class, my father tried to keep my mother's love all to himself. I believe that he was jealous of his children, who demanded part of my mother's love. To tie her to himself, he kept her for years constantly pregnant. I'm convinced that she had many abortions. Robert, many years later, told me that, as a child peering through the keyhole of the paternal bedroom, he had watched mother doing something to herself that might have been an attempt to abort an unwanted child. It made her very ill, and Dr. Korn, our house physician, completed the abortion as he might have done before.

Dr. Korn spoke eighteen languages fluently. He practiced them as a hobby every night for three hours. He also invented a machine of revolving red, blue, and yellow disks that changed black and white motion picture film into color projection. He suffered from the thyroid illness known as Grave's disease, which made his eyes bulge, and had to swallow every day a whole raw, bloody ox gall, uncooked, to keep his hypertrophic gland under control. Now people just take a pill.

An inventive physician, he saved Robert's life. When I was twelve, a fiacre approached the house. In it lay my brother, his face greenish blue. Dr. Korn was summoned and pronounced that my brother had an intestinal occlusion. Filling a container with warm soapy water, he attached a ten-foot-long rubber hose to it, then climbed on the top of a cupboard in our bedroom. The water pressure in the syringe straightened out my brother's twisted bowels. That horse cure might also have burst his intestines. Robert always was a sexually promiscuous child. I believe that he had his first affair when he was twelve, while I had to wait six more years.

He discovered that our mother kept an erotic library in her bedroom hidden behind stacks of bed linen. He read *Lady Chatterley's Lover,* which mentioned the penis that the gamekeeper in that story lovingly called "Thomas." He read the classic *Fanny Hill,* the English story of a whore and madam, literally well written a century ago. He found that Felix Salten, author of *Bambi,* the innocent fawn, also had indulged in writing a pornographic novel, *The Mutzenbacher,* the story of a Viennese girl who, raped by her father when she was four, liked that act of incest so much that she developed a penchant for the oldest profession.

Hidden in folders of velvet were exquisite watercolors by Honoré Daumier depicting old men wearing nightcaps, satisfying country maidens with their tongue, an exercise that we youngsters didn't quite understand.

Gustave Doré, who also illustrated the Bible, produced a series of sexual watercolor drawings, as did Felicien Rops, whose lithographs baffled me, but not my older brother Robert, proficient even at that age in sexual kinks.

What do we know about the sex life of our parents? We cannot follow them behind their bedroom doors, and it might be that my mother needed sexual stimulation. To mention that stimulation was of course taboo during the Victorian times, despite that a titled Englishman had written a twelve-volume encyclopedia, *My Secret Life,* that described his carnal exploits minutely and graphically. He seduced only kitchen help, parlor maids, and poor country girls who hardly could defend themselves. He must also have had numerous affairs with women of his social stratum. Those women, obviously promiscuous, were not written up in that voluminous biography, since never mentioning the depravity of the English was an unwritten law of the hypocritically prudish Victorian age.

The approach to sex has changed considerably since Freud tried to explain our inner erogenous drives. When I worked in Sweden in 1960 directing a TV series with Lon Chaney Jr., a woman was accused in court of advertising sex films in Stockholm's biggest newspaper. Her defense was that, if certain people could achieve orgasm only by watching pornographic scenes on the screen, is the government empowered to interfere with this deviation by law? The Swedish judge did not forbid her selling those films, but she was not permitted to advertise them in newspapers, lest children might buy them. That did not make sense either, since sex education in Sweden is taught in schools from a very early age. That prudent teaching method did not increase the sexual activities of teenagers in Sweden. The results are fewer teenage abortions and the complete absence of prostitution. No promiscuity exists, either.

My contention is that the world is accepting politically and socially, though not fast enough, the Swedish way of life. As Sweden socially moves, so moves the Western world, but only after a twenty-year hiatus. The Swedish church is government controlled and Lutheran, and the *pfarrer*, the minister, is an employee of the state. The Swedish state religion has no influence on the laws of the land, the way the Catholic Church tries to dominate the sex life of its sheep. There is an absence of sexual "guilt" in the Nordic countries, the power that the Christian and Jewish religions thrive on. The Nazis' first decree was to control the sex life of Jews, who were forbidden to contact Christian girls. The world seems to be split by religious beliefs, rabid nationalism, and the color of people's skin. In America, citizens pride themselves in having had an Indian great-grandfather. I never heard a white American boast that he had a black one in his ancestry.

World War I raged for four years. Germany was allied with Austria, which still was ruled by the senile Emperor Franz Joseph of Habsburg, and Turkey. Those three states, named "The Axis," fought the French, the British, the Italians, and the Russians. At the end the Americans joined the slaughter. We in Germany were sitting in a besieged fortress. During that war no foreign soldier ever set foot on German soil, except as a prisoner of war, while part of northern France and Russia, also Minor Asia, went up in flames. All we knew about the war was the censored daily news, the constant "victories" of the German army, and the disappearance of anything edible. We watched endless railroad wagons with the Red Cross painted on, then packed with wounded soldiers, passing through Hauptbahnhof, the Dresden main railroad station.

Otherwise life continued for us children as though there was no carnage going on in the world. None of our family was in the army. They tried to draft Arthur Wildau, Uncle Hugo's partner in his haberdashery business in Leipzig. Arthur, terrified of any killings, an antisoldier if there ever was one, went to a hospital with "chest pains." His wife smuggled the sputum of his tubercular sister into his room. By examining that sputum the doctors sent the "dying" man home.

Father still possessed his renewed American passport, and we had no trouble from the German government since that country still was not yet actively involved in the slaughter.

The year 1918 was the coldest winter of the century. Even birds fell off the trees, frozen. The same harsh winter plagued Europe during World War II and decided the battle of Stalingrad, where Hitler's divisions, led by General von Paulus, succumbed and turned the German "victories" into a defeat that decided the outcome of that insanity. Napoleon's armies also were defeated by an extremely harsh Russian winter. It was as if nature deliberately was taking sides in the fighting, to bring humankind to its senses.

Money was quickly losing its buying power, and people invented a barter system. Our barter was Father's broken eggs in glass jars. Mother exchanged them for meat, whose animal origin we did not question, or flour, sugar, salt, anything edible. Father brought home a brick of real butter. It was a treasure too good to be consumed. To keep it fresh, Mother kept it outside on the ice-cold windowsill of our apartment, which was located on the fourth floor of our apartment building in the Blochmannstrasse.

Suddenly a huge black bird appeared, coming seemingly from nowhere. It had a long neck and a sharp pointed beak. I had never before, or after, seen a bird like this. It flew straight to the kitchen window, stabbed the lump of butter, and flew away with it.

I and my close friend, Johannes Schweisinger, collected tin soldiers. There was a toy shop in the Seestrasse that specialized in minute lead soldiers of any army, German, French, Russian—friends and foes. One also could buy whole villages, houses partly destroyed by fire, cannons, graves and even "dead" tin soldiers. We two boys created a gruesomely realistic battlefield, done with the precision that only the warped mind of the patriotic German could conceive. I don't believe that British or French children had corpses of tin soldiers for sale.

There is a macabre streak in the German soul that appears as far back as in songs of the troubadours, the traveling minstrels. Those bards of the Middle Ages wandered through Germany, singing songs of fighting and slaughter, of the Nibelungen, of Lancelot, Siegfried, and the dragon. Or of a war that the king fought in some part of Germany, winning or losing. Those instant poets were the newspapers of that time, since no other communication existed.

Death and the German spirit are brothers. My friend, the author Erich Kaestner, who went to the same school in Dresden with me, wrote a satirical poem, "Kennst du das Land wo die Kanonen bluehn?" (Do you know the country where the cannons blossom?), a version of the famous song "Do You Know the Land Where the Oranges Bloom?"

To get the money to buy those soldier toys, my crooked friend, Johannes Schweisinger, and I stole money without any moral compunction. We, like other schoolchildren, volunteered to take tin collection boxes from house to house, asking for contributions for some charitable causes, such as paralyzed soldiers, the Red Cross, or starving children. At home with the help of tweezers, we relieved the boxes of most of the paper money and bought the toy armies at the toy shop in the Seestrasse for our private war.

On the wall of my bedroom hung a large map of Europe, the battle lines marked with colored pins. One day as we moved the colored pins backward to the German border, Johannes remarked clairvoyantly, "We are losing the war." It meant little to us, since except for the scarcity of food we had never been close to it. Besides, never having had a good meal in years, our taste buds had shriveled.

Daily life, though having become shabby like worn cloth, continued. We went to school, the vacations started, and Father sent us to the Baltic Sea to a boys' camp. There were traveling minstrels as in medieval times singing "Marmalade, Marmalade, ist Parole jetzt im deutschen Staate" (Jam, jam, is the order now in Germany). Jam, made of sugar beets, was still plentiful, though the bread we ate was partly made of wood shavings, which filled the stomach.

At school the teachers had to give patriotic speeches to keep the morale alive. They talked as though by rote: "The superior morale of the German troops makes up for the greater number of the decadent French, the 'perfide Albion' [as the English were called], the stupid Russian peasants, and the moronic American soldiers, mostly nigger slaves, who did not know how to fight." The German youth was "weapon-ready," ready to die for the right cause, and would triumph over the soulless mercenary spirit of the enemies. The war is a necessary lightning rod that would clean the atmosphere from which a new Germany will arise, creating a nation of supermen in spirit who would extinguish the degenerate world and lead it to new idealistic heights. War cleanses poisonous ideas. The future belongs to Siegfried, not the treacherous Hagen of the Nibelungen, who slew Siegfried from the back. The weak will die because there is no place on Earth for them. "Viel Feind, viel Ehr" (Many enemies, much honor).

Our teachers delivered those speeches in monotonous voices since they no longer believed their own words. Adolf Hitler and Joseph Goebbels performed the same soliloquies, twenty years later. They only replaced the French, English, Americans, and Russians with the Jews. The official Nazi government order was that whenever the word *Jew* was mentioned or printed, it had to be accompanied by an odious adjective, like "the deceitful Jew," "the treacherous Jew," or the "conniving Jew," to hammer the image into the German mind that the real enemy that made them lose the war was not Hitler's inferior war strategy but the personification of all evil, the crafty Jew. As one German guard in a concentration camp remarked to his comrade as they watched emaciated men, women, and children tottering to the gas chamber, "You don't know how powerful those people are."

During World War I, I was not aware that I was a Jew, since Jewish bodies were rotting in mass graves together with their gentile peers.

After four years of senseless slaughter, the German front lines disintegrated in 1918. There was no final, devastating last battle that vanquished the German army. The German soldiers became tired of the butchery and went home. Walter Rathenau, an industrialist, tried to rally the Germans militarily, but his efforts and ideas were turned down by the German high command, who knew that the enthusiasm of their army for further killings was exhausted. Philip Scheidemann, a social democrat, formed a new government and Rathenau became the secretary of state in the newly created Weimar Republic. He was assassinated in 1922 by right-wing fanatics, nascent Nazis, for being Jewish.

The gruesome face of the war was experienced only on the fronts. The Russian army had collapsed. The Bolsheviks had signed a separate peace treaty with Germany at the town of Brest Litovsk and became communist for seventy-two years until this system disintegrated due to its inefficiency, corruption, and the inability to feed its own people.

The Germans at home were starving, but not one single bomb fell on their cities during the war, certainly not on Dresden, which was out of the reach of Allied bombers. Dresden had to wait twenty-five years for another war and its complete destruction.

The kaiser fled to Holland and spent the rest of his days in a castle near the town of the Hague, where he cut wood for recreation. The Wettins left Saxony, visiting their relatives, royals in other countries, of which they had many, since the European royalty was hemophiliac and interrelated.

In the Altmarkt, the town square of Dresden, a revolution broke out, led by front soldiers. Germany in its history never had a bloody revolution like the French, English, and Americans. In Germany, by tradition, a few people gather in a beer hall and throw dice to determine who should run the country. In 1918 on the Altmarkt, burghers shouted excitedly at each other, but no shot was fired during that confused riot. Hot-headed youngsters wanted to storm the armory where guns were stored, but just then the bells of the Frauenkirche, the Church of Our Lady, chimed the midday hour and the revolutionaries went home—it was lunchtime.

Those bells didn't ring at the end of World War II, since the Frauenkirche with its round dome, a miracle of architectural construction, was flattened in 1945 by British bombers. Its ruins are still there as a reminder of the deadly futility and stupidity of war.

There was shooting at the Zwinger near the king's palace, and I ran there to find out what the commotion was about. A crowd of curious people surrounded the lovely baroque building. The air smelled of cordite. For the first time in my life I saw soldiers in action. They looked like lansquenets of the sixteenth century in their iron helmets and baggy trousers, carrying their rifles so proficiently as if that weapon were an appendage to their body. Shots were fired. I didn't know at whom. A woman was standing beside me, watching, as I did, with curiosity the display of warfare. Suddenly she was gone. As I looked down, I saw her lying at my feet. Her head was missing, and blood was spattered all over the pavement. I ran away and did not stop until I reached our house in the Ludwig Richter Strasse.

It was the first time in my life that I had been confronted by death, in the shape of a headless body. For years I vainly tried to dispel that gruesome picture from my mind. Now, more than half a century later, it still is vividly etched into my iris like an indelible photograph. If the bullet had veered a few inches to the left, the gray matter of my brain would have spattered the cobblestone. On that day I clearly understood what war was like: the smell of cordite, headless bodies, the sudden disintegration of human flesh, which a second before had moved about, directed by that mysterious two pounds and three ounces of brain tissue, nerves, and serotonin.

A few days later I got hold of a tin can with pork and beans, the iron ration of British soldiers. It might be that the Allies supplied the starving German population with leftover soldier rations. But it certainly was the best meal I ever tasted in my life, including that of the Auberge in Avignon, France, which I visited seventeen years later and which at that time was a three-star Michelin eating place. I was convinced that Germany could never have won the war, when the enemy soldiers were fed so royally, while the bread rationed to us was mixed with sawdust, and the sausages stuffed with crushed horse bones.

An American, John Harvey Kellogg, through the "Kellogg plan," almost single-handedly fed the starving people of Europe. Kellogg, the inventor of breakfast cereals, had trained his country to ingest puffed rice and dry grains. Packed in fancy cardboard boxes, it proved how much money could be made by selling raw wheat and corn by the ounce, calling it health food. The farmer made two cents a box, the seller a hundred. Kellogg became a multimillionaire.

Upheaval followed the Armistice. The German national pride was deeply humiliated. It was "*der Dolchstoss von hinten*" (the stab in the back), as the German jingoists called it, who could not imagine that Germany could ever be defeated except by treachery.

There was the Peace Treaty of Versailles, signed in a railroad car. To chastise the French, the same wagon was used twenty-two years later by Hitler when he imposed his peace treaty on the defeated French nation.

Governments often act like children, creating hate and an urge for revenge, which years later erupts into another conflagration. All the seeds of coming misery are contained in the ephemeral conception of "national honor," a nebulous notion for which millions of people have perished during the ages.

After the demise of the communist conception, Europe looked forward to a time of democracy that would bring prosperity and peace to its tortured history. Instead, it was falling apart into nationalistic states and racism, which, rallied around a piece of colored cloth, again led people to slaughter each other, defending their ethnic pride. The choice to create a peaceful world was within their grasp. But the dormant nationalism, stirred up by its own brand of dictators, has found new fertile grounds for age-old xenophobic hatred.

How many children ever have a chance to talk intimately to their parents, not only about their own lives but of that of their father and mother, their fears, hopes, wishes, frustrations, and the secrets that are hidden behind their bedroom doors? I now wish that my father or my mother would have been intimate with us children. But that was a traditional impossibility in our Jewish family. Sex, of course, was never mentioned. Children in Germany were delivered by the stork, a bird, big enough to carry a bundle that he dropped through the chimney stack. That was in the time of my early youth. Now a twelve-year-old could enlighten the neuropsychiatrist Krafft-Ebing.

I, at sixteen, had only a vague notion of the secret parts of girls' bodies, whose construction was a mystery to me, but not for my sexually enlightened brother, Robert, who had acquired that mysterious information at a very early age. He did not share his carnal knowledge with me. He was sexually active until he died at the age of seventy-three, still had a girlfriend and a strong compulsion to work.

I believe that sex drive and creativity are closely related. Lose one and you lose the other. When Michelangelo fell in love with a young patrician, he was in his eighties. That late love affair gave him the power and imagination to paint the ceiling of the Sistine Chapel at the Vatican in Rome. Today the rampantly revived American Calvinistic morality would prohibit an old homosexual painter from despoiling the cupola of a church, depicting a naked male with his penis in full view, even touching the finger of God.

Since Michelangelo was inspired by love so late in his life, he would today be called a "dirty old man." I always wondered at what age a male would be called "dirty." When he has his first erection, which babies display when they are born? That would prove that any male born heterosexual or gay is born "dirty." Curiously that distinction does not apply to the opposite sex, which is driven by the same impulses.

With the outbreak of World War I, our father's egg business collapsed since it depended on the connection with Eastern European countries. He could not feed his family so in his frustration made money dishonestly.

Postwar Germany was swarming with police to squash any possible revolution. They were everywhere, stopping people in the street, watching the trains and their passengers, rummaging through their luggage, looking for "contraband." Only years later did I find out what the contraband was.

The German military had forced the citizens of the occupied countries, including Denmark, Belgium, part of France, and the occupied part of Russia, to accept currency issued by the occupation force. The thousand-mark notes, which were printed for that purpose, carried a red serial number, to distinguish them from money circulating in Germany.

The government-induced inflation had already started. The German monetary system was rapidly losing its value. A thousand-mark note, once worth two hundred fifty gold dollars, had sunk to the low exchange of sixteen dollars, and it continued its freefall until it lost all of its buying power. The government scheme was transparent to anybody with some knowledge of money. The "devaluation" has been practiced by every country since gold pieces were replaced by cheap metal. The rich ones did not need cash, since they owned the production machinery of their country. The workingman was "indexed," and his remuneration rose with the fictional value of paper money. The middle-class citizens' savings were completely wiped out. The mark was finally stabilized when it reached the astronomical sum of 4.2 billion paper mark for one dollar. To print a banknote was more expensive than its value. To send an ordinary letter, the postage stamp was marked 500 million. A German industrialist, Hugo Stinnes, tried to buy the whole German railway system. It would have cost him the equivalent of ten American dollars, paid in inflated paper money. Since money finally had to be transported in pushcarts, the government finally eliminated seven zeros and started the German currency with 4.20 mark for one dollar. The middle class was financially wiped out, having paid for all the government's war debts.

The victorious Allies forced the Weimar Republic to honor the occupation money at face value with hard currency. Since the inflation had not yet reached its peak, a thousand-mark banknote with a red number was worth eight times as much as those with black numbers that circulated in Germany.

An underground Mafia bought up those red-numbered notes in the former German-occupied countries and cashed them in at the German treasury, which was forced to exchange them for "hard" currency. Father entered that shady business. He sent me to Berlin with a suitcase filled with red-stamped occupation money where it was to be sold on the black market. He took the chance that the police wouldn't suspect a teenager, traveling railway third class, with smuggling contraband banknotes. The police passed me by on the train. I didn't know anything about that kind of traffic or the danger I was in. I didn't even know what the small battered suitcase contained.

I delivered that piece of luggage to Mr. Himmelfarb, a nice name, meaning the "color of the sky," who was father's contact man in Berlin. Then I stayed a few days at Ahlbeck, a resort at the Baltic Sea, waiting for Mr. Himmelfarb's call to pick up a suitcase with laundered money. I lived at a small hotel, sunbathing at the beach, swimming in the blue clean water, which now reckless pollution has changed into a sewer.

My carnal knowledge was only that which I had discussed with friends of my age and by smooching with my teenaged cousins. The virginity of those Jewish princesses was jealously sheltered by their parents, to be deflowered only on their wedding night, an often gruesome process since the young women did not know how to cope with that act. That painful and sudden connubial rape often made the young women frigid and afraid of sex for the rest of their lives.

It was not so many years ago that girls of the Victorian age were not permitted to be nude in their own bathtub. They had to wear a shirt to hide their own bodies from their own view, to prevent carnal thoughts from enticing their minds.

That night in Ahlbeck a young waitress kept me company as I sat at the hotel's dining room having a beer. Nothing was further from my mind and experience than a sexual overture.

But when I was in bed, she suddenly appeared in a long flannel nightgown and pulled my bedcovers off. I only knew in theory what she was up to and what a girl's anatomy was missing, though Lotte, one of my older cousins, had opened my fly when I was thirteen and had treated me to a well-executed act of fellatio, while not permitting me to touch any part of her body I wanted to explore. I don't think I had much fun at that encounter.

That night in Ahlbeck I behaved as stupidly as I did with Lotte. When the girl climbed on top of me, this time without the flannel armor, I said, "Help me, please." I was through in a few seconds, in what the Germans call a *"Perueckenniesser"* (a sneeze in a wig). She must have thought that at my tender age I was already sexually worn out. She did not know that she had seduced a male virgin. That knowledge might have made her more tolerant in her instructions.

The situation in Berlin seemed to have heated up, and Mr. Himmelfarb found it safer to send his two teenage daughters with the exchanged money to Ahlbeck. He wanted me to leave the seaside resort without having to go through the heavily controlled Berlin railway station.

Ella and Fina stayed in the small hotel with me in an adjoining room. I, having gained a carnal knowledge that was 48 hours old, met two virgins, who, though curious, knew even less about sex than I did.

That night I sneaked into the room of the Himmelfarb girls. They were wheat-blonde Polish Jewish princesses, always having lived as well protected as a pearl in its oyster shell. They were receptive, though slightly jealous of each other. Fina was seventeen, Ella fifteen. I was permitted to lie between them, and the warmth of their bodies was pain-inducing, but when I made an attempt to pass on to them my newly found carnal information, they shrank back timidly.

I got up and stood in the open door, looking out at the ocean with its steady soft pounding waves. There was, as it should be on that memorable night, a full moon shining in a cloudless star-studded sky. Fina followed me and leaned, naked and slim, in the open door frame. Her eyes were sad since she had now encountered a secret of life that had tempted and confused her but that now had revealed its mystery to her. She was close and yet farther away from me than if she had been on another star. The picture of that glowing white body is still vivid in my mind.

Fina died young of breast cancer. I met Ella when she was a mother of five children, rather voluptuous, but still with that frail look of curiosity and innocence in her large blue eyes. She, too, recalled that full-mooned night and the fragile poesy of our encounter. Then she asked me, "How could anyone be that stupid!" Stupid? I had an answer for that but kept it to myself. I might have lost that memory if our fairy-tale encounter had been fulfilled. Males don't always remember their conquests but surely the lost sexual opportunities all their lives.

In the many novels I wrote, I always inserted an intimate scene that only I and one of my former paramours would remember. I am convinced that every one of my past lovers would pick up a book with my name on it as its author. That is one of my ways to pay homage to the indelible though clandestine love affairs of my life. I used that nostalgic encounter in Ahlbeck in a novel that I wrote ten years after it happened. The book had the title *Sturmflut* (Tidal Wave). It was the story of a judge, a widower, who with his sixteen-year-old son takes a vacation at the Baltic Sea. He had sentenced a man to be hanged, only to discover his innocence after the execution. He almost broke down under the impact of his guilt. His conscience made him act cruelly toward his son, as our father was cruel to us.

When a violent storm broke out, the son of the judge, terrified by the howling wind, sneaked into the bedroom of the daughter of the hotel owner, a girl of fifteen. The two kids were as innocent as I and my two wheat-blonde girls had been. The two children held each other in their arms in the shelter of the bed while the typhoon raged. All they felt was their physical protective nearness.

Hermann Rahn, the editor of *Die Woche*, rejected my novel. "You are a deviate," was his comment. "You have been a student, haven't you? When a boy climbs into bed with a fifteen-year-old broad, he lays her, doesn't he? Don't be arty. When I publish a story I print the truth! Change the scene!"

I didn't change the scene. The *Vossische Zeitung*, the literary newspaper of the Scherl house, accepted that novel. This was in 1930. Years later, when I visited Germany, I tried but could not find a copy of it.

For me, writing is the tangible world and the world that surrounds me a dream, too often filled with nightmares.

The Drei Koenig Schule (Three Kings School) in Dresden, founded eight hundred years ago, perhaps the oldest one in Germany, was the high school where I went. In my time for a few years it became the cradle of contemporary German writers. I don't know the names of the three kings it was named for, but for some unknown reasons the school gave birth to creative talents that became famous not only in Germany but internationally. Erich Kaestner, who wrote the story "Emil and the Detective," was in my class. It was made many times into a motion picture and has not lost its charm. I met him in Berlin in 1962 and tried to induce him, in vain, to come to America and to Hollywood, which could use his talent. When the German Jews after World War I changed their names to Teutonic-sounding ones, Moses Levy became Fritz Stahl, and the writer Johannes Burghardt, a full-blooded Aryan, called himself Ossip Kalenter to ridicule that trend. He found that name in Frank Wedekind's Jack the Ripper play, *Lulu:* Ossip Kalenter, a detective.

There was Ernst Toller, poet and playwright, who was banished by the Nazis and killed himself in Sweden in 1939. My brother Robert also visited that school, though his genius was not visible at that time.

A few years ago I was invited to the Rose Garden of the White House. It was a party to celebrate Helmut Kohl's new Germany in conjunction with German Americans who had left Hitler's Reich, though often not voluntarily. Soon after that festivity, in which Secretary of Defense Carlucci delivered a warm and conciliatory speech praising the new German democracy, in collaboration with German emigrants, I received pamphlets from a neo-Nazi organization that has its quarters in Santa Monica. I found out that most of the anti-Semitic hate propaganda that circulated in Mr. Kohl's Germany is being created in the United States, since the German constitution forbids the printing of this kind of hate literature.

The author of those pamphlets obviously had got hold of the list of the invited, with their names and addresses. The neo-Nazi complained that the list read like an invitation to the 'fortieth anniversary of the inauguration of the Jewish state. He was right, since there were hardly any non-Jewish Germans in existence who "deserted" Nazi Germany when Hitler took over the government.

I know no more than a handful of non-Jewish people who emigrated voluntarily from Germany. One was Conrad Veidt, the internationally famous German actor of that time. Guenther von Stapenhorst, a German aristocrat and successful film producer at the UFA studios, refused to work for the Nazis and went to Switzerland. When Erich Pommer, the Jewish film producer (who had escaped the purge), returned to occupied Germany as the representative of the American government, he rewarded Stapenhorst by making him the head of the newly formed German film industry. Marlene Dietrich, whom Hitler personally offered to promote to the top star of the German theater, secretly deserted Germany against his orders. She entertained American troops during the war.

It is true that Thomas Mann, the Nobel Prize winner, went to live in California, because he had a Jewish wife and was afraid for her life. Would he have left his Vaterland if he had been married to a Christian woman? His brother, Heinrich Mann, emigrated, but he was a socialist, a political concept Hitler did not appreciate.

Erich Maria Remarque left of his free will and lived in Ronco, Italy, near the Swiss border. He took his van Gogh paintings, Manets, and Degas with him. Erich refused to call himself an emigrant, but since his *All Quiet on the Western Front* was an antiwar novel, he surely would have ended up in a concentration camp.

Since I was bored with school and passed the examinations among the top few, my understanding science teacher, Professor Heinz Mueller—nicknamed "Jesus" on account of his blonde beard and gentle manners, who literally starved to death with his wife in 1947—suggested to my father that he send me to the private school of Mr. Hiss. In those days public school did not have advanced classes for especially bright children. Private schools were called "Presse," since they pressed children into a telescoped education. I am grateful to the Drei Koenig Schule that it demanded in its curriculum the study of four languages: German, French, English and Latin or Greek. I chose Latin. "Mons, pons, fons, dens et aries, pais, lapis, grec et caries" have the genitive! That memory, imprinted in my brain, has never left me. "The poor match girl died, far above mortal ken, where neither cold nor hunger could be found." I didn't know what *ken,* an archaic word for heaven, meant, but the word stuck with me forever, though I never used it after having acquired a new language. We learned by rote, and that knowledge saved my life. When I had to leave Germany in a hurry, I was able to converse in French and English.

At Mr. Hiss's school I crammed as much knowledge into my pliable brain as it would hold. I could not wait to get rid of schools and wanted to stand on my own feet, subconsciously to escape my father's dominance. At Mr. Hiss's Presse, I fell in love with my mathematics teacher. Mr. Dieter was a former ship's engineer who suffered from consumption. He had a sunken chest and was extremely thin. But when he taught calculus, an inspired light appeared in his eyes, which made me study so hard that solving mathematical problems became my obsession.

Since our concept is a three-dimensional world, which consists of height, width, length (like a cube), the laws of physics we invent explain this three-dimensional world to us—not the fourth, the fifth, or the hundreds of others. In outer space, according to Einstein, light bends, time shrinks, and there is antimatter, the opposite of gravity. We don't know how the universe works and never will, despite ingenious theories which cannot be proven empirically. Our brain is extremely limited in its conceptions. We are like the fish in a bowl who asks another fish, "If you don't believe in God, you tell me—who is changing the water?" Since we are the fish in the bowl, we create a mystical answer called religion. Only in mathematics do we come closer to the root of the unexplainable. We invent symbols, like the integral, to penetrate the unimaginable. Then, for a fleeting moment, a glimpse of the secrets of creation is revealed to us. But still, when we return to Earth from the unknown, we don't know where we have been, since all our brain is able to understand is a three-dimensional world with its man-made explanations, which science changes from time to time.

My teacher, Mr. Dieter, instilled that love of mathematics in me. It freed me from earthly bounds and gave me a glimpse into a world that I do not and will not share with anybody. With the knowledge of mathematics the universe opened up to me, replacing this earthly "ken" of fantasy where I am forced to live.

I passed my "Abitur" examination at seventeen. The Abitur is the toughest test at the end of all the school years. The student is expected to remember all the knowledge pumped into his brain from the day he entered the school until graduation. The Gymnasium is in Germany the equivalent of the American high school.

The examining teacher gave me a low grade, "3." It should have been a "1." But he resented that I had passed the tests two years before my former class. He said, "I should give you a 1 or 2, but I decided on a 3. I am sure that your private school got hold of the questions and coached you. Accept a 3 or repeat the examination all over again, this time with different problems. It's your choice." I settled for a 3. I didn't fight back. I have made compromises all my life, not spending my energy on fights, getting challenging situations behind me, which, as time passed, didn't have any effect on my life.

I always squeaked through, facing the next one. I never believed that any of my effort as a writer had a big value, convinced that my next book would be better. That's why I never have reread any of my novels, nor have I seen all the pictures I wrote. I believe that life is a jigsaw puzzle of compromises.

A friend of mine, a psychologist, read most of my novels and concluded that I always wrote about the same problem. How could that be? Has *For Kings Only,* a historical novel of a woman who slept only with royalty, the same theme as *Donovan's Brain,* a scientist who keeps a human brain alive, which finally dominates him? They have, my friend declared. "You are writing about people who want to climb to the top of the mountain but never get there. That is the theme of all of your books." But it also is the outcome of everybody's struggle in life.

I visualize that every newly elected American president tries to leave a bigger trail in history than Abraham Lincoln. Then, circumstances beyond his control cut him down to size. I never wanted to reach the top of the mountain. Where would one go after having reached the summit? My life is guided by a joke: A rich Hungarian count bets he can eat fifty pairs of sausages. He eats forty-nine and says, "I don't like them anymore; bring me an omelet." Robert, my brother, as a film director had eaten the fifty pairs, and there was no further summit, only repetition: Academy nominations, festivals of Robert Siodmak motion pictures, his career written up in *Life* magazine, having been for some years the most sought-after director in Hollywood, the city of instant fame and quick demise. The Hungarian count was right: "Never reach the top of the mountain. Let new challenges tempt you. The target should be in front and not in back of you."

After the Abitur, what now? I talked to my father. He asked me, "What can you study in Dresden?"

"Engineering or becoming a veterinarian."

"Then you will be an engineer" was his decision.

I was financially dependent on him and entered the Dresden Technical High School. I was still an American citizen. Ike had renewed his citizenship by visiting the United States in 1913. By an unfair emigration law, a naturalized citizen had to set foot on American soil every seven years or lose his citizenship. That law, since rescinded, made a second-class citizen of every naturalized American.

Being a foreigner in Germany, I was required to pay the university fees in dollars. Since the inflation was still rampant, nobody but the banks were able to produce hard currency. I applied for German citizenship, to be able to pay my tuition in German marks. Father had to sign an agreement that he was responsible for the cost of my education. He did and created a curious citizenship problem for me. During World War I, I was an enemy alien, an American in Germany. When I went to America, having a German passport, I was an enemy alien at the beginning of World War II. Then I received the American citizenship, which made me again an enemy alien for the Germans. That little green, blue, or red book, called passport, decides the fate of everybody's life.

The first year at the university, studying engineering, I developed the idea of a rotary motor, but being penniless, I could not take out a patent on it. Twenty years later a Herr Wankel designed a similar motor that made history.

In 1931 I wrote a novel, *F.P. 1 Does Not Answer*, the story of a platform in the middle of the ocean where transatlantic airplanes were refueled. It was the prototype of the modern airplane carrier. It even had radar on it, ten years before its invention. *Rache im Ether* (Revenge in Space), a silly title that was the publisher's, contained the idea of the laser beam, twenty years before its discovery.

It is not financially rewarding to be too early with new ideas. They are considered science fiction, though the greatest science fiction writer of all times was Leonardo da Vinci, who anticipated the helicopter and the battle tank, developed spherical gears, and explored a future world that only took shape three hundred years after his death. What would he have invented if he had known about the existence of steam power, electricity, shortwaves, high frequencies, atomic power, and the exploration of outer space, of fiber optics and computers? A couple of years at the Dresden Technical High School as a student would have made him change the future of the world!

One of my novels, *The Third Ear,* is based on extrasensory perception (ESP), biochemically created in human bodies. Which young biochemist will pick up that challenge and solve the technical details that I, as a writer of science fiction, am not required to deliver?

At the university the student organization, the Kursachsen, tried to make me a member. But they didn't accept Jews, which increased my insecurities, not being a full-fledged citizen.

Hitler's world, which the German philosopher Johann Gottlieb Fichte created as early as 1793, was always brewing. Alarmed by the French Revolution and the emancipation of the Jews, Fichte suggested cutting off the head of every Jew and replacing it with a new one "in which not a single Jewish idea remained." Adolf Hitler changed Fichte's science fiction fantasy into a lethal reality.

Ike couldn't afford to keep that big house in the Wintergartenstrasse any longer and moved to an apartment in the Mozartstrasse, which was still a socially accepted address. I don't know what he lived on. I believe that he lent money at extremely high interest to Mr. Hub, his skat partner with Richard Strauss. Mr. Hub owned a delicatessen in the Seestrasse. Father had become a moneylender! Years later when Mr. Hub went bankrupt, Father was paid off with merchandise from that bankruptcy—many cases of sweet liquor, which he drank in great quantities. He was a diabetic, and the sugary alcohol killed him. He died of nephritis, on January 30, 1933, the day the Austrian Hitler became Reichskanzler and took over Germany. Ike was spared death in a concentration camp.

The new apartment in the Mozartstrasse 5 was my last stay at home. When I studied engineering, we lived in the same building, which was close to the zoological garden. The zoo had a large restaurant that featured folk dances on Saturday night. That was a ready-made opportunity to pick up girls. My friend, Adolf Brandes, the nephew of the zoo's director, lived in his uncle's elaborate villa inside the zoo. He had the keys to the zoo's gates. We always had a room to take girls for a quick lay. The "room" was the haystack next to the elephant's cage. It smelled of wild animals since at night the lions and tigers were also housed in that shed. The girls got an added thrill of hearing the elephants snort and the lions roar, during our clandestine love affairs.

Adolf and I went to the same Technical High School and often got drunk together on beer. It was a very severe winter when we walked home from a *Bierstube* (beer restaurant). An icy wind was blowing, and the ground was covered with black snow. I saw a fiacre standing in front of the Kuenstlerhaus, the Artists' Hall, where lectures were held and often ballets performed. The night was very dark, and the driver of the fiacre helped an old man to pick up paper that the wind had blown from his hands. I caught one of those papyri as it fluttered through the air. It was a thousand-mark banknote. I caught some more of that heavenly manna, and then a printed sheet, an invitation to the dancing group of Mary Wigman, the originator of the abstract modern ballet. It performed to the sound of drums only, a takeoff on African music, I presume. Forty years later it entered my mind that Henrietta, my wife for thirty years, had been one of her pupils at the same time. Ernestine de Perrot, Henrietta's divorced Swiss mother, had her educated in Dresden where she had joined Wigman's ballet. Since Ernestine, a poor woman, could pay in Swiss francs during the German inflation, she was able to have her child sent to the excellent German finishing school of Mme. Poswick.

That winter night, in my beer stupor, I read the printed page with interest by the light of a street lamp, while money was fluttering around me. After I finished reading, I looked for the hackney. It was gone. I held one thousand and twenty marks in my cold hands. Adolf ran up to me. "I got one thousand and twenty marks," he said in disbelief, the same sum I had collected.

Since the devastating German inflation was still in its infancy, the thousand-mark note still kept some of its original value and was not yet completely worthless. I hid that treasure in my room. So did Adolf. But we both had no bad conscience, since it was Christmastime and a real windfall since the wind had presented us with that loot. Being penniless except for beer money, that heavenly present made me believe in a higher destiny's power. Dutifully, Adolf and I looked up the local paper for an announcement from the man who had lost the money. There was none.

Robert had left Ike's house after a ferocious spat with Father. But my two other brothers, Werner and the youngest, Rolf (Roland), still were staying at home. Werner was eleven and Rolf was seven at that time. Both grew up without a mother. That year, in 1922, I was able to buy Christmas presents for them with the windfall money and hid them in their beds, since Father did not believe in Christmas celebrations.

When Robert was sixteen, he went, as I did, to the Drei Koenig Schule. In the morning he went to the roll call, then left through a window in the toilet, to run to the Albert theater, where he sometimes was hired as an "extra talent." He was stagestruck all of his life. At night, he sometimes took me along, where we became extra talent at performances. Dressed in hirsute clothes, we danced as warlocks in the Walpurgis Night in Goethe's *Faust,* while Satan on the stage performed discreet intercourse with witches.

Robert got a line to speak in *Die Herrmans Schlacht* (The Battle of Hermann) by the nineteenth-century playwright Heinrich von Kleist. Of course, I had to see my older brother, the actor, on the stage. At that time he was sixteen and I fourteen. He told me to enter the theater through a small backstage door and to sit way in the back, since Mr. Berthold Viertel, who directed the play, did not permit visitors.

I sneaked into the Albert theater through the stage door, as Robert had advised me, to see my brother the actor and hid in a faraway corner, the only audience in the morning's dress rehearsal. The curtain was up and Robert, on the stage, was dressed as a Gothic warrior, wearing a helmet too small for his head but adorned with gigantic eagle feathers. A long beard hid his sixteen-year-old face. His shoes were so big that he lost them during the performance. He also carried weaponry—a halbert, a shield, and a sword. I heard in full his important part spoken with a true actor's skill: "The moon has a halo!" I was filled with awe at my brother's talents and adoration, which lasted to the end of his life.

Mr. Viertel, a small, cocky, authoritative man with a thick mop of hair, stepped on the brightly lit stage and rearranged the scene. He discovered me. Walking to the footlights and shouting, "Lights," the theater became ablaze. Stepping up to me, he asked me what I was doing in the theater. I stuttered that I wanted to see my brother the actor and asked Viertel's permission to stay. "Nein! Raus!" he shouted, proving that a Jew could be as tough as a Prussian.

Twenty years later, when I worked as a screenwriter for the British film company Gaumont, in London, his name came up as the director for my screenplay of *Transatlantic Tunnel*. Still remembering the traumatic insult in the Albert theater, I gave the assignment not to him but to Maurice Elvey, a British director, a move that I now regret, since Viertel too was a refugee from Hitler, fighting for his existence. Since that incident in the Albert theater, I held the door open for every mail boy in studios, when he brought me a manuscript or carried a typewriter. Who knows—he might run the studio in the future and give me a job.

Robert was the first of Ike's children to leave the house. Father locked Robert out when he came in late. But Robert, who had inherited Ike's temper, smashed through the entrance door, sending Father, who leaned against it, flying against the wall behind. That night Robert left home, never to return. I stayed on, but I could not stand the tangible misery of home and thought of a way out.

I consulted the dean of the Technische Hochschule, telling him that I was forced to earn a living to finish my education or had to quit. The dean arranged a job for me with the government-owned railway, who trained students to drive steam engines. As a future engineer, I had to show two years of practical work in the field of my future profession. There was an opening for a job in Stuttgart, which also had an excellent technical high school.

Just after the armistice of World War I, Germany had suffered a railway strike that had paralyzed the country. When the dean suggested my learning how to drive a steam engine, I was not aware that I was going to be trained as a future strikebreaker, should the railway workers again dare to defy the dictatorial power of the government. Adolf Hitler's fascist movement was already in the making.

The change from the university in Dresden to that in Stuttgart became an example of a serendipity that only fate can provide. The gods decided to lead me through hardships and despair, and they bestowed that ordeal to prepare me for a reward that changed my life.

Now I had a government income since the railways were state owned. My pay, that of a stoker on a locomotive, was indexed and automatically adjusted to the inflation, which the Weimar Republic had deliberately created to wipe out Germany's World War I debts.

I rented a small room in Cannstadt, a small community at the outskirts of Stuttgart, which consisted of a tiny living room, kitchenette, and an even smaller room with a bed.

At midnight, five days a week, I took the streetcar that ran nightly and hourly to the railway station. There I walked to the depot, where I fired up the locomotive that stood in its shed.

The Allies had, after Germany's defeat, confiscated all of its good rolling stock and had left only the most ancient machines and carriages. The locomotive had no automatic grill, and the cinders of the burned-out coal had to be hauled out with a shovel, instead of being pushed outside by moving a crank that opened the bottom of the firebox. After having brought the team up to its prescribed level, I drove the rusty monster back a few yards on a turntable. With a hand crank, I lined up the turntable rails with the rails of the depot. At two o'clock the train crew arrived, half a dozen sleepy, unshaven men. Then the engineer took over and shunted the old whizzing lady back and forth, while the crew attached the railroad coaches, which had been new in a previous century. After I and the crew had filled the oil boxes of the wheels with heavy oil to prevent the axles from overheating, and after all the safety measures had been checked, the train slowly rolled through the countryside, stopping at small villages where workmen were waiting at dawn to be taken to the factories. They entered the train at four in the morning, to arrive at their workplace at 7 A.M. Their pay started only after they had passed through the factory gate, which meant having to travel six hours for an eight-hour shift.

It was winter and so cold that even the breath froze in midair. My job also was to keep the tanker behind the locomotive supplied with water that spouted from a movable pipe. The splashing water froze my trousers stiff. On the way back to the depot in Stuttgart another fireman took over and I slept on the wooden floor of the empty freight carriage behind the water tender, supporting my head with my leather briefcase. It contained a vacuum bottle and books, which I intended to study but for which I never found time on those trips.

There was a young girl at one of the stations where the train stopped, selling hot drinks. She filled my vacuum bottle with hot milk.

She could not have been older than seventeen, a sturdy country girl, with a peasant's face and large brown eyes. We never exchanged words, not even a greeting. It was a silent love affair, which started and ended with the train entering and leaving the station. She seemed to wait for me since she always stood at the spot where the locomotive would stop. Our mute meetings could not have been more intimate with an embrace.

When I tried to pay she withdrew, as if being paid for her gift would spoil our relations. One day she put highly spiced hot cider into my vacuum bottle. I couldn't take a sip of it, but it might have been her message about how much she liked me. It was a love affair, fulfilled without any personal contact, a mute intimacy, which still has its echo in my memory.

The Technical High School in Stuttgart had a great percentage of foreign students who took advantage of the rampant German inflation, since they possessed Swiss or French francs, English pounds, Dutch gilders, and other "hard" currency that the German student could not obtain. The foreigners, due to the exchange, were rich, could take out the girls, eat in the best restaurants, rent the nicest rooms, and behaved as if they owned Germany. French *chaumeurs* and British unemployed vacationed, living luxuriously on their "dole," their government's unemployment pay.

I had two Swiss friends, who, knowing how poor and hungry I was, never let me pick up a bill when we went to an eating place, which I, anyhow, could not afford.

Raoul Tenier and Edward Schwab came from affluent Swiss families and studied, like thousands of foreign students in Germany, taking advantage of the enormous discrepancy of the different currencies. Their Swiss francs made them German multimillionaires, since the buying power of their hard currency doubled almost every day. For Germans, the impact of the inflation, which made their money worthless, was a numbing experience that deprived them of their energy, since the savings they had accumulated through their lifetime dissolved into worthless scraps of paper. That vacuous time went on for a year. Then the "new" German mark was stabilized with 4.20 mark for 4.2 billion paper marks, and the bonanza for foreigners was over. I felt I again was standing on solid ground.

The Technische Hochschule presented me with a diploma, which stated that I now was a "Diplom Ingenieur" but also owed a bill of four hundred "new marks," a fortune I did not possess.

I went home to Dresden, traveling, to save money, as the third man on the locomotive, a trip for which I did not have to pay, still being an employee of the Reichsbahn. It was a very hard winter, and the journey took twelve long hours on the rattling steam locomotive through a gray, icy night. There was no young girl to fill my vacuum bottle.

I finally arrived in Dresden at dawn, carrying only a satchel with my clothes and books. I walked from the railroad station to my father's apartment on Mozartstrasse 5. I had not seen him in a year, nor did we correspond.

He was just leaving the house when I arrived, and we talked outside at eight in the morning, wet snow falling from dark clouds. The streetlights were still shining.

I told him that I had passed my examinations as a Diplom Ingenieur and that he should pay four hundred marks for my studies, as he had committed himself to the government when I became a German citizen. He saw the opportunity to again dominate one of his children over whom he had lost his power.

"I won't pay. I don't want any of my children to be better educated than their father."

Wasn't it, according to the Talmud, a father's first duty to have his children educated? His decision, seeing the opportunity to dominate me again, was like a physical blow.

Raoul and Edward were appalled that I would lose years of study for the lack of a few hundred marks and invited me to continue my study at the university in Zurich. Sons of rich families, they offered to look after me. Switzerland was as unknown to me and as far away as Patagonia, but I'd have gone to the North Pole to put as much distance as possible between my father and myself. I also had saved a small amount of money and knew that Robert would help financially should he make any money. As a safeguard I had a stamp collection of some value and the knowledge that Raoul and Edward wouldn't desert me. The chance to study in Zurich was a journey powered by pipe dreams, but all I wanted was to get away from my father. I never again entered his house.

If Ike had paid the school bill, I would have stayed in Germany and would not have met my future wife, Henrietta, the companion of my life. It was fate's classic example of serendipity, our inability to fathom the whims of the gods.

Why do we often suffer from the lassitude of the heart and torture each other in our short trip through this green valley? Why can't we live in constant harmony with our parents or friends, those who cannot be replaced?

I wrote an unkind farewell letter to my father and left for a precarious future. I don't know what I wrote, but it was not very complimentary, I guess, since I come from a family of rebels. Now, since I understand him, which I did not in his lifetime, I am sorry for Ike. He must have been very lost, perhaps desperate, since he had no skill at making a living, except as a tradesman in eggs—a business that did not exist anymore. He just didn't know how to cope with life. Due to his harsh life experiences, he wanted to dominate his family in the traditional Jewish patriarchal fashion, as he had been brought up by his father, the stern Rabbi Abraham Siodmak.

But for Ike, there was no family. His wife, married to him against her will, had tried to run away from him but was forced to return to a life she abhorred. The German folklore formulated the expression "*Sich den Krebs and den Hals aergern*" (To die of cancer of the throat, produced by dismay). She died of cancer of the throat at the age of forty-one. Ike, who had her traced by detectives, to bring him proof of her trysts, forced her to return to him. Where else could she go? He banned her to live in the maid's room. Thinking back, I still can't understand how the late Victorian time, which still existed in Germany when she died in 1921, was paralyzing the family, though I had left the house and was already nineteen. The family was completely dominated by the Jewish father, the patriarch, the breadwinner, who exercised his power with unchecked cruelty.

When my mother died in a hospital after a futile operation, I had glanced at a report on the doctor's desk, describing her condition as "*infauste*," which, having studied Latin in school, told me that she had been given up by the doctors. During the last hour before her death, while Ike and his children waited outside her hospital room, I persuaded the nurse to increase the morphine shots, to ease her suffering. Ike was crying, which he frequently did. Too cowardly to enter her room to see her die, he sent Robert and me in to tell her "that he forgave her." Being nearsighted, I took off my glasses not to get an impression of her dying face, which, as I anticipated, would stay forever with me. I wanted to remember her as I knew her when she was still beautiful and not ravaged by death. Robert told me her last words: "I am so happy."

Why, in this short life, do people try to make each other unhappy? What is their fathomless ability to nurse frustrations for which they have no understanding? Robert, who always considered himself her favorite son, never recovered from a shock when, as he told me many years later, he avoided meeting her when she walked lonely across a street, being banned from her husband to see her children.

Though we try to convince ourselves philosophically that the past is over and forgotten, the pains of cowardly actions never leave us. Even a word, wrongly spoken when we are young, might pursue us to the end of our days.

The Romans considered a man grown up when he had reached the age of forty. Only then he was called a *vir,* a man. The word *virility* is based on that conception. But when parents finally have arrived at that age of maturity, their children often have already cut their own path into the jungle of life. How can "unfinished parents" bring up their children without making mistakes? Ike, I'm sure, never outgrew his missing childhood, nor did Robert. Nor did I. It might be that men never really mature. Women do. That's why, having outlived their husbands, women can effectively cope with life. Men rarely do.

To stay alive, Robert and I had too much to do with ourselves and had no time, or means, to look after our younger brother. I stayed with Robert, who, enterprisingly, had opened during the inflation a "bank," which was a money exchange, changing hard currency for almost worthless German money. His "bank" was preferred by call girls, who were supported by foreigners who paid them in their hard currency. The girls, getting dollars or English pounds for their services, lived in splendor.

It was an upside-down world—the foreign poor were wealthy, the German rich were broke.

During the rampant inflation one had to lunch before 12 P.M., since at that time the mark would be devaluated daily.

Being a seasoned hypochondriac, I was always "ailing." That feeling of being unwell started when my mother, who was very superstitious, frequently consulted a fortune-teller. When I was about ten years old, she took me to Frau Stubenrauch (Madame "Smoke in the Room"—a literary translation), who told mother's future from cards. She prophesied that my mother wouldn't need to walk anymore after her fortieth birthday. Mother believed that she would be so rich that her husband could buy one of those noisy contraptions, the automobile, which only the very affluent could afford. She died when she was forty-one. The fortune-teller also predicted that nothing could be said about that little boy, me, then ten years old, after my thirtieth birthday. Until I was thirty, I believed my life, too, would end according to Mrs. Stubenrauch's prognosis. I was plagued by indefinable illnesses, anxiously observing myself to discover the sickness that would do me in before I had reached one score and ten. When that day passed, I immediately recovered.

From that day on I consider every prophecy a menace, a dangerous intrusion into people's subconscious, from soothsaying and cards to palm reading and Bible predictions.

Where were the clairvoyants to predict Germany's future? The Jews should have known, since their history is one continuous Diaspora. "Join the Jews and see the world." Henrietta's uncanny presentiment forewarned her that to live in Germany, even before Hitler controlled Germany's destiny, had sinister implications. But she could not put them into words. Though I worked very successfully in Germany, she preferred staying in Switzerland, her homeland. I could not settle there since, being a writer, my necessary tool was the German language. As it turned out belatedly, it was the wrong conclusion.

Even though I was born and raised in Germany, I always felt like a secondary citizen among the Teutons.

Anti-Semitism was always latent in Germany, especially in schools.

When in 1926 Erich Glaeser wrote his best-selling novel *Jahrgang 1902* (Born 1902), the story of my generation, he started the book with an anti-Semitic scene. The teacher ridiculed a Jewish student, stoop-shouldered, flat-footed, long-nosed, cowardly, as the Nazis depicted the Jews in their newspaper *Der Stuermer*.

That impression has changed considerably since the state of Israel was created. The present Israeli young generation, the Sabras, is athletic, slim, and muscular, the way Hitler would have loved his Braunschirts to look. The Sabras, which is the name of a prickly cactus plant, cannot understand why the European Jews did not defend themselves but let themselves be slaughtered like cattle. Though the Weimar Republic had made anti-Semitism a federal offense, the schoolteacher in Glaeser's novel enjoyed teasing the defenseless Jewish boy. The student's father, who owned a department store, was fearful of his Aryan customers. He exhibited an exaggerated patriotism, hanging out more German flags than his competitors.

Erich Glaeser, who later on became an ardent Nazi, clairvoyantly mirrored the times to come.

The Brothers Grimm in "The Jew among the Thorns" wrote one of the most vicious anti-Semitic fables. That poison was ingrained in Germany's conception of the Semitic race. The teachers, whose strict discipline antedated the regimentation of the Nazis, instilled in their students a deep respect for the law, any law, however inane. Even today, a German friend of mine, now a professor at the University of Southern California, told me that during his latest visit to Germany, he crossed a completely deserted street against the red light, while his German colleagues frantically jumped up and down screaming in protest. Jaywalking, even when there is no traffic, means defying authority. Years later, because it was the law, my former classmates crossed the street to avoid meeting the Jew, who only days before had been their intimate pal.

When the war ended, I received a detailed letter from a classmate, informing me about the fate of some of the teachers and students. Many of them had died in the "Goetterdaemmerung," the prophecy in the German mythology whose gods, like Hitler's Germany, expired in a holocaust of thunder and flames.

Werner Baumgart, who sat on the school bench beside me, was incinerated in the firestorm that destroyed Dresden in 1945. Paul Lauer, who owned a flower shop at the central railway station, committed suicide in 1942 because he had a Jewish father and the Nazis wrecked his shop. Ferdinand Quarck went down with the battleship *Bismarck,* sunk by the British fleet west of Brest, France. Kurt Westler, Rolf Bruene, Gottfried Keil, and Herbert Boehme were murdered by the Poles when they took over Danzig, which they renamed Gdansk. Heinz Lange froze to death on the Russian front in the bloody fight for Stalingrad. Hermann Dufft, who corresponded with me after the war and is now a retired judge in west Germany, spent eight years in a Russian labor camp in which 90 percent of the German prisoners died of starvation and maltreatment. Franz Ernst, a meek boy, as I remember, who sat beside me on the wooden school bench, ran a concentration camp for the SS and was slaughtered by the inmates when the American army approached the city of Halle in Saxony. Dr. Heinz Mueller, our beloved music teacher, tried to make a living copying music but died of starvation and a cruel beating which he had received from Russian soldiers. I came across a former classmate of mine on a trip to Monrovia in 1962. He ran a photography shop in the Liberian capital. I recognized him, but he refused to admit that he came from Dresden, though his Saxonian accent gave him away. He hid in the back room of his shop until I left. Later I found out that he was on the list of wanted Nazi criminals.

Will history ever be able to explain why one man, the worst enemy the Germans ever had, brought out latent cruelties, a hellish sadism, in people with whom I had shared the joys of youth? That warped German mentality did not start with the national socialism. Martin Luther raged obscenely against the Jews and wanted to have them killed, since they would not accept Christ as their Messiah. That anti-Jewish obsession is still rampant in the Vatican, where one pope called the Jewish belief an "unfinished religion." Finished for what? To kill? The Jews were always victims, for two thousand years. That picture changed when they created their own state, built on militarism like their neighbors'. Elie Wiesel, the author who had survived the concentration camp, wrote that the Holocaust signifies not only the defeat of two thousand years of Christian civilization but also the demise of the intellect that tries to find a meaning. Is anti-Semitism essential to keep the Christian religion alive? Does that dogma need to exist, a counterpart that it can hate? If there were no anti-Semitism in the Judeo-Christian theological world, would the Christian religion run empty? I wish I still had the time in my life to study Bible history to explain to myself the dichotomy of the Christian spirit, which, rampant through the ages, will not change as long as there is a cross on a house of worship.

A young couple visited our house. He was Jewish, she Catholic. He was not an orthodox Jew, nor did she practice Catholicism. But they decided that their two children should grow up in some religious belief and looked for the most neutral approach to teach them the Lord's Prayer. Soon he observed that his wife also had taught the children to cross themselves. Very upset, since he believed that she had circumvented their agreement, they argued. She, brought up in a Catholic home, was not aware that the sign of the cross conveys a deadly menace for Jews, since for them the cross still is the symbol of persecution and death.

Rudolf Huebler, a Drei Koenig school student and one of my close friends, became the head of a concentration camp. He spent his days supervising mass executions, going home every evening to unwind with his wife and children as he had relaxed with me on the playground of our school. When my brother Werner was six years old, in 1913, a friend of his age told him, "When I grow up, we're going to kill all Jews, but not you, because I like you." The dichotomy again—the indoctrination of dogmatic thinking clashing with the fair emotions of a child.

The photographic imprint in my mind of innocent children's faces, indoctrinated to hate, to commit atrocities in the name of the country and the party, persist nightmarishly in my dreams. The German educational system of my time did not allow any expression of individuality in school or at home. The schoolteacher was the continuation of the parental powers.

That's why Hitler was called "*unser Papi*" (our Papa). He was the surrogate father of most Germans, and to oppose him was a sin. A joke about him was punishable by being sent to a concentration camp. Does every religion, even the Jewish one, need a fulcrum, an intolerance for any belief that is not their own in order to exist? Until now, no philosopher, no sage since the beginning of the Christian era, has been able to find a plausible explanation, except perhaps by calling that scourge "xenophobia," the fear of strangers.

I like to speculate what kind of turn history would have taken if a dozen Jews named apostles had not declared a gentle young Jew to be the Messiah, elevating him to be the son of God, a belief the rest of the Jewish tribes did not share, since the appearance of a Messiah would destroy their religion. That schism, followed by 2,000 years of discrimination and slaughter of Jews, would not have happened, nor would the Jews, now named Christians, have been fed to wild animals in arenas to entertain Roman citizens. Nor would the intolerance of the Inquisition have existed, or the centuries of religious European wars, in which Catholics and Lutherans, both believing in the same Messiah, fought each other, destroying Europe. The intolerance the Christians have against other religions and the schism within their own ranks—fifty-two different Christian sects in a city like Los Angeles alone—have created the most intolerant religion on Earth, only rivaled by the Muslims. Would the Crusades and their slaughter in innumerable wars have happened, or the sufferings of the believers, based on fear spread by the dogmatic churches? Or would ghettos have existed through the ages, or would the Holocaust have happened? Also the murderous discrimination against the Jews, that small tribe, composed of not even 0.3 percent of the world population, which had delivered the Messiah of the Judeo-Christian religion?

The intolerance of Christianity has followed me all my life, even into the small village where I now live. Racial remarks sometimes expose prejudices of otherwise sophisticated people. Is it possible that the many-thousand-year-old religious bias has altered the genes of the human race, creating the conviction that everyone who does not believe in the religion of his parents is basically a pariah, deprived of the only truth? Is it the fear of the unknown that makes strangers suspect to a humankind eternally looking for a god?

Whoever does believe in absurdities is also able to commit atrocities, of which our present world is a glaring example.

In a small town, ten thousand eligible young men could be married to ten thousand local young women. It would not make much difference who marries whom, if their upbringing falls into the same pattern: kindergarten, local public school, high school, church, perhaps college, then a "secure" job, buying a house, and having children, creating the nuclear family. When the children grow up and leave, the cycle is completed. The question remains: what then is left of life?

A marriage starts with the dessert and ends up with the soup. When the first child arrives, the woman loses the lure of virginity for her husband, and that void has to be augmented by other values. If the marriage is not perfect, the mother or the father transfer too much love on the baby, diminishing the partner's share. They forget that the child is only a temporary visitor in their home. At first the baby is the substitute for the doll the mother cherished in her childhood. When the "doll" begins to test its own personality, the parents believe they have been a failure in its upbringing. But the child wants to test his or her parents' authority. Most children go through similar phases of character development. They are angellike creatures this year, potential murderers the next, unapproachable, obstinate or pliable, changing their demeanor like a chameleon its color. Sometimes they hate their father because he intrudes into their love for their mother, repeating the age-old Oedipus complex. Girls, being in love with their father, might loathe the competition, their mother.

I remember a girl of twelve complaining that on an outing her father, to her dismay, brought "her" along. The "her" was her mother. Then follow the formative and painful "teenage" years, in which the child's own generation exercises influence, superseding that of the parents. When finally the bird flies the nest, the moment of truth arrives: the parents have lost the buffer that has covered the alienation to each other. But then the marriage might have deteriorated to the point of separation. That's one of the reasons that men in their fifties often break up their marriage that has atrophied, by mutual neglect. Some are afraid that life is passing them by and become frightened by the never changing daily routine and encroaching old age. Some divorce their wives, might become promiscuous, or marry a younger woman, who often resembles the first one. Should a man be financially very successful, he invests in a shapely young girl, a "trophy," which enlarges his status among his jealous friends. All humans react in nature's way: a male of any age could still father a child, while a female after her menopause is of no use to nature's circle of propagation, the objective for all living species to continue on Earth.

The human race for thousands of years has vainly searched for the meaning of life, an answer that every blade of grass, every bird, tree, or flower blatantly offers. That's why men are attracted to youthful girls, the symbol of fertility, whose visible sexuality changes an older man's life—for a while.

I once worked with a film director, Jacques Tourneur, who directed *Aloma of the South Seas,* the first screenplay I wrote after my emigration to Hollywood in 1937. He was an ardent collector of French antique furniture but extremely stingy. I sometimes got stuck with his lunch bill at the studio commissary since he had to make an "urgent" telephone call always at the end of the meal. Being a native of French Normandy, he wrote to village priests in his homeland, "Dear Father: I am, a Frenchman, making my living in California, far away from my beloved home. I am very lonely among the strange people of this country, where hardly anybody speaks French. Don't you have in your attic an old piece of furniture you could send me, to make me feel at home in this mental desert?"

Jacques furnished his house in Beverly Hills with museum-quality Normandy antiques. Then, lured by the youth of a teenaged girl, he divorced his wife, who had stood by him during the lean years. He left all of his treasures behind, just taking a small suitcase with clothes along, to start a new life with a renewed virility.

Can the present institution of marriage survive when the divorce rate is, as in California, 62 percent? In my parents' time, my mother was dependent on the whims of her spouse, who earned the money. Now that women are able to earn their own living, and couples live together without the blessings of the church or a paid legal document, an evaluation of that thousand-year-old institution has to be examined. Happiness in marriage cannot be enforced by a legal contract. A marriage needs mutual cooperation. The child is often a fill-in for the slow decay of a union that is supposed to last for a lifetime.

The perfect marriage occurs when any undeveloped character trait in one finds its completion in the partner's. If both characters have equal strength, the fight for adjustment begins at the start of the love affair: a struggle to accept the new partner's intrusion in one's own territory. Who will be the leading one, and who will dominate whom?

A friend of mine's wife died after a long and happy marriage. She had been an absolute slave to his will and whims. He found another woman, and during the marriage ceremony he thanked her for having "rescued" him from his depressing loneliness. But the new wife was much stronger than his departed one. She had been a widow for many years and had learned to fend for herself. My friend could not subjugate her to fit her into his former life pattern. His new marriage was dissolved after two years by mutual and friendly consent. Both had come to the conclusion that they could not reach a decision who was dominating whom, as though a perfect match between two people were not a fusion of their characters into one.

When the children detach themselves, creating their own existence, some parents try to cling to their departed offspring and feel humiliated that they don't get the attention they deserve. Since they are convinced that they have sacrificed their personal lives for them, they now expect to be included in their offspring's existence as before.

At the beginning, Henrietta and I fought constantly, and without her mother's wisdom and patience, our relation might have ended, since I had to return to Berlin. I had to leave Zurich and my studies at the university. Henrietta stayed behind, but strangely, we were not concerned about not seeing each other again. She promised to come to Berlin, and it never entered our minds that this almost impossible occurrence, two people without profession or means, would not happen soon.

Since my landlady, like every landlady in Calvinistic Switzerland, forbade female visitors even in daytime, Henrietta would climb through my bedroom window the old-fashioned way, dating back to Romeo and Juliet. But sexually she drew the line, which was the rule of the youth of that time, before the invention of the Pill, which made women lose their fear of pregnancy.

After my return to Berlin, I moved into Robert's simple room and wrote daily a letter to Zurich. Ernestine, Henrietta's mother, the most liberal woman I ever met in my life, kept us together, though I was without a visible future, an inadequate choice for her only daughter. There was no chance of getting employment as an engineer in Berlin, since a depression was sweeping the country and the whole of Europe.

I began to write, producing voluminous material. That started a writing and film career that gave direction to my later life.

Berlin between 1925 and 1933 was the cultural center of the Western world. It died when Hitler burned the literary works of that time, stopped painters from producing "decadent art," tried to kill the productive mind of every German intellectual. He made a thorough job of that. Germany became a cultural wasteland—and still is, half a century after Hitler lost his war. The same fate happened to Spain, when in 1492 it threw out the Arabs and the Jews. Still five hundred years later, Spain has not recovered from the destruction of those cultures, nor has anything of significant art come out of the postwar European continent. Its geniuses died on the battlefields or in the gas chambers.

In pre-Hitler times, the Berlin literary elite met at the Romanische Café, near the Kaiser Wilhelm Gedaechtniskirche, the Emperor Wilhelm Memorial Church. That majestic building was bombed out during the Allies' raid on Berlin. An architect named Eiermann built a modern church beside it, which the Berlin folk humor named "Powderbox and Lipstick," since it consists of two buildings, a round one and a tall obelisk. He constructed a similar church in Coventry, England, which the Germans had firebombed during the war, to fuse those two inhumanities into one symbol. The British, who had broken the secret German code, knew beforehand of the raid. They had the choice of warning the citizens of Coventry or letting them suffer the ordeal of the attack. Churchill decided to keep the secret of the broken German code, sacrificing hundreds of lives of his countrymen.

How many of the famous pre-Hitler artists' names who hung out at the Romanische Café are still remembered? Only historians recall them today: Ernst Toller (the well-known writer), Hasenclever, Anton Kuh, Hans Tasiemka (who was so famous that I forgot for what he was famous), Carl Zuckmayer (the playwright—one of the very few who voluntarily emigrated, though he was not Jewish or chased by the Nazis). Egon Friedell and Hans Lustig, a feared film critic, who made his way to America and found a safe haven at the film studio of MGM. There are scores of prominent names that time has clouded: Else Lasker-Schueler, whose sensitive poems are still in print, was so impoverished that she owned only one dress. She appeared in the Café with a scarf over her shoulder and a small suitcase, pretending she had just arrived from a trip and didn't have time to change. Now she is buried at the foot of Mount Carmel in Jerusalem. There was the "Rote Lotte," a redheaded hooker, whose most luxurious beat was the Adlon, the most fashionable hotel in Berlin. She had been the girlfriend of a rich German count. When he dropped her, paying her off meagerly, she took revenge by telling about the count's hang-up: he liked to lie naked at his home, on an enormous silver platter, garnished with vegetables, like a suckling pig. Lotte took a blunt knife and pretended to carve him up, which, as she revealed, was the height of his sexual pleasure. That poor man could not show himself anywhere without somebody calling out, "Waiter, serve me that gentleman." He had to change his venue to Brussels, a move that possibly saved his life. Rolli Gero, who, with the well-known journalist "Pam" (Paul Marcus), created the "impossible cabaret." The world-famous satirical caricaturist George Grosz, whom I was fortunate to meet years later in New York, was also a perennial guest at the Romanische Café, like Otto Katz, the Czechoslovakian journalist, who later was beheaded by the Nazis in Prague. Victor Skutezky opened the first cabaret in Berlin featuring black entertainers. He became a well-known film producer in London. I heard the young and Aryan blonde, Marlene Dietrich, sing anti-Nazi songs in Friedrich Hollaender's cabaret, "The Wild Stage."

It was the age of Max Reinhardt and his theaters; of the plays of Bert Brecht, who, with Kurt Weill, left an indelible trace in the theater world; of the novels of Thomas Mann and his brother, Heinrich Mann. Those were the years of the emergence of a German film industry that produced world classics like *The Last Laugh, Nosferatu, Dr. Caligari, M,* and *Metropolis.* The pre-Hitler Germany created a short-lived culture that will be preserved for centuries to come. Artists of many nations congregated in Berlin, as they did in nineteenth-century Paris, fertilizing the culture of that newly chosen country. Berlin created new art forms, dadaism and cubism, which the Nazis tried to destroy. The pictures of the painters of that time now can be found in museums all over the world, since the Nazis sold many of them secretly in Switzerland, leaving the financial loot in Swiss banks as a safeguard against rainy days, which, subconsciously, they must have expected.

Robert and I also were part of the Romanische Café's artistic club. We were very poor, and the head waiter, Herr Nitz, daily gave us credit for a cup of coffee, counting on, should we become affluent, that we would pay him back with large tips. Our table was near the painters' corner, near Emil Orlick, Max Pechstein, Walter Slevogt, Jaeckel, and Kirchner, whose works are now among the classics in international museums. Kirchner, like many German artists, could not exist without his German roots and was driven to suicide.

Nazism was made for Germany like a glove fitting the hand. It certainly did not start with Adolf Hitler publishing *Mein Kampf.* He used the innate German anti-Semitism to lift his party into power. But I suspect that the general German trait and that of the Jews are similar: their drive to excel, their tribalism and intolerance toward other customs, their love for improvement and workaholism—character traits that made Jews fight competitors in every country that permitted them to stay.

The higher the culture of a nation, the more vicious is its cruelty in wars and revolutions. The French and its bloody revolution at the end of the seventeenth century gave a good illustration of it. So did the Germans, who sentimentally listened to Bach's music while shoving human bodies into ovens, or the Japanese in their abhorrent treatment of prisoners of war, and the American settlers for whom a "good Indian was a dead Indian." In 1933, the young English author Christopher Isherwood lived in Berlin. He wrote in his *Berlin Diary*, which became the basis of the musical play *Cabaret:*

> I was sitting every evening in the large, but half-filled Romanische Café, where Jews and intellectual leftists at the marble tables whispered, frightened of each other. Many knew that they would be arrested, if not today, then tomorrow or during the following week. Every night the SA (Nazi storm troopers) in their brown uniforms entered the coffeehouse. As I walked this morning down Buelow Street, the Nazis were just breaking into the apartment of a pacifist writer. They loaded his manuscripts onto a truck, and one of the uniformed brutes read a title to the crowd: "'Never Again War!'" He lifted the manuscripts with disgust as if he were holding an ugly reptile. The people around him screamed with laughter. I looked at my reflection in a window, and was shocked to see a smile on my face.

"It can't be! Germany is the country of poets and thinkers," was the basis for the fact that very few artists found the strength to emigrate after January 30, 1933, when Hitler became "Reichskanzler." Even Bertolt Brecht called that time the "Hitler spook" and was convinced it would end soon. But actors such as Emil Jannings and Werner Kraus, internationally famous names at that time, became ardent Nazis overnight, and appeared later in the vicious Nazi films *Ohm Krueger* and *Jud Suess*.

Very few of the best German brains of Germany had the conviction and strength to emigrate. Those who did continued their work all over the world, thus preserving the German culture—especially the United States, which inherited an infusion of talent of scientists like Einstein and Teller; philosophers like Herbert Marcuse, whose teachings became a "fad" among the young American generation; writers like Thomas Mann; also a great number of gifted filmmakers who created "the golden years" of the Hollywood motion picture industry.

All the roots of fascism were dominant in Germany and, I am afraid, still are: a century-old xenophobia; a smoldering inferiority complex dating from the humiliating defeat of two world wars, which might awaken again; the conviction that the German nation is the superior race in the world but was held in chains by the Allied nations: "Und es soll am deutschen Wesen, einmal noch die Welt genesen" (The world will only become healthy when all nations convert to the German spirit). The world depression of the thirties, with seven million Germans unemployed, the "decadence" of the times that was mirrored in cultural experiments in music, literature, and paintings, wounded the deeply ingrained Calvinistic spirit of the Germans. The Nazis added terror to their power, trying to force conquered nations into the Nazi mold. The Nazis were determined that everybody on Earth who did not accept their creed had no right to live on this planet.

If the Christian churches had found the courage to resist the Nazis, especially the Catholic Church, which for a millennium has been desperately holding onto its earthly possessions, they would have become the unconquerable moral force in Europe and reached the goal that they vainly have tried to accomplish through the ages.

I left for Switzerland. I had some money saved from my salary as an engineer on the German railroad, and I also took my stamp collection along, which I had nursed for a dozen years and had some value. Then there were my rich Swiss friends, Raoul Tenier and Edward Schwab, who were my safeguards should I become destitute. They wouldn't let me starve. Besides, I was never afraid of not meeting scholastic requirements. Anything that was printed in books a normal brain should be able to learn.

I found myself in a foreign country whose way of living was strange to me. The German Swiss are a xenophobic tribe. They only like themselves, and certainly not foreigners, though they worship their money. My applications for enrollment at the Zurich University required passing particular examinations. But there was a way of climbing this hurdle: to be coached by a Presse, a private school like that of Mr. Hiss in Dresden that had prepared me for my early Abitur examination. For years, the Presse in Zurich had collected examination papers, with the questions that the conservative Zurich University regularly asked. All one had to do was to remember them. Besides, I already had the German title "Diplom Ingenieur."

Now I was shooting for a master's degree in mathematics. The Ph.D. would come later, if I could find the money to spend more years on learning.

The Germans have a penchant for titles. A man with a Ph.D. is addressed as "Herr Doktor," which confuses every foreigner since a doctor in any other country is a physician. A judge is addressed as "Herr Geheimrat" (secret counsellor). What kind of secrets does he know? An inspector is "Herr Inspektor." In my early youth the mailman wore a uniform on Sunday and carried a saber. Germany always was full of uniforms. Americans are not fond of them. I saw my son only once in uniform, that of the American Air Force, and he hated to appear in public in it. But in Germany, a title elevates a man's importance.

In America, as I found out many years later, it is the size of the bank account that assures prestige and social standing, also the power to use it. Those people are today's American nobility. I had just completed the last round of preparations for the university examinations and felt exhausted. My finances were at a very low ebb. The future looked bleak. To cheer me up, Edward and Raoul urged me to accompany them to the yearly artists' ball at the Waldhaus Dolder Hotel.

I didn't want to go. But Edward appeared with a tuxedo, which he had discarded when he put on some weight, and glowingly talked about the gorgeous girls in abbreviated costumes who would attend the ball without the supervision of their Calvinistic parents. It was a fancy dress ball, and I found out, to my surprise, that the conservative Swiss girls, who never wore lipstick or makeup and didn't shave their legs, were very attractive in their wild war paints and abbreviated costumes.

There was a chute at the Waldhaus Dolder Hotel that led from the upper balcony to the large ballroom below. Girls came tumbling down to be gathered up by young costumed men and whirled about to the music of a jazz band, the new musical craze of the twenties. I wasn't in a mood to join those gay sprites when out of a cluster of young men a slim figure in white rushed toward me. She might have wanted to get away from that crowd of persistent admirers and picked the first man in her path. Her thick reddish hair, brushed up into a witch's crown, was flying wildly as if made of fine wire. A black mask hid half of her face. Her blue eyes were large. Her mouth was generous and the lips overly painted with red. Her "costume" was a sheet of silk, hugging her shape as if painted on. She dragged me into a dance.

Of course, until this day, Henrietta denies that she had instigated our first encounter and says that it was I who chased her. We danced until a persistent suitor cut in. I gave her up willingly. Not wanting to get rid of my gloom, I withdrew to the second floor where the hotel management had left a few rooms open for guests to relax. I ordered Neuchatel wine to nurse my mental depression. Unexpectedly that white sprite appeared. She had taken off her mask, and I found her eyes too big, her mouth too generous, her hair too unruly. But I liked her nose, which was turned up and finally chiseled. She came to see whether I was still around and reappeared from time to time, while empty bottles of Neuchatel accumulated around me.

Looking back at this strange evening, which might have been the mysterious clue why fate had made me visit Switzerland, I am surprised how much at that age I was able to drink, without getting stoned. We started to talk and I told her that I was studying mathematics and had rented a room at the Scheuzergasse. That's where she lived with her mother. We both marveled at that coincidence! Then to my surprise she posed a mathematical question to me. Her mother, she told me, was dedicated to mathematical problems but could not solve this special equation. That was my moment to show off, and I wrote the formula and its solution on a paper napkin. Since she carried no purse, she put the napkin in her shoe for her mother to see. Then she dragged me downstairs again, since prizes for the best original costume were announced. She got the first prize for that piece of plain white silk her mother had sewn on her. It got her the attention of the judges and not only of the young men around her. Her costume was voted the most original of the evening and awarded 150 gold francs, a sizable sum at that time.

It still was the glorious time before World War II, when gold coins still circulated in Switzerland. Since her costume had no pockets, she asked me to hold the money for her, while I returned to the upstairs room and my bottles of Neuchatel.

From time to time she visited me, the hermit, until the light dimmed in the ballroom. I offered to drive her home in a taxi since we lived on the same street. When I tried to kiss her in the taxi, she lifted her business card between us: "Henrietta Erna de Perrot, architect." She carried that card and some "wild money" in her shoe.

As she told me later, it was the first time that she had permitted a young man to drive her home.

She came from an old Swiss line of barons, who still have their family mansion in the French part of Switzerland, in Neufchatel. There was some significant relationship between her town of birth and my choice of the wine that I had imbibed the whole evening.

The de Perrots had been bankers and engineers for generations, and one of them had built the Jungfraubahn, the funicular leading to the top of that Swiss mountain.

Henrietta lived with her divorced mother. During our long marriage, she never volunteered to talk about her family and I have never inquired. Only much later she started to talk about her youth when she started to write a book: *The Extra Step,* a guide for young women on how to run a house, keep a husband happy, cook memorable meals, and live life "one step above the ordinary." I wish every woman in America would study her book, which took her twelve years to write. Then, I'm convinced, the divorce rate of 62 percent would drop to zero.

In *The Extra Step* she never talks about trying or bad times, of which we had more than our share, only about the happy moments of her life. All of our lives she accepts only the good sides of our existence, a guideline that she has never breached. This has forced us to balance my writer's mind, which, if it doesn't dwell in misery, believes that it doesn't see the world as it really is. It also is a rule in our marriage that we only offer information to each other if we want to and never pry into each other's secrets, as we never would open letters personally addressed to each other.

Henrietta's mother, a resolute woman of German peasant stock, regretted all her life that she had not been born a man. She was liberal far ahead of her time, determined—others would call that human trait stubbornness—and highly independent.

Ernestine had fought her husband's mother, the staid dowager Baroness de Perrot, all through her marriage. The grandmother had resented her son's marriage from the beginning, since in her opinion he had married beneath her station. She finally won out, and her son, Henry, returned to her and her purse strings. His way of breaking up his marriage had been extremely cruel. He had sent his wife and child on vacation and disappeared, leaving them to shift pennilessly for themselves. Ernestine was forced to sew for people to make a living.

She had the foresight and courage to send her daughter to a finishing school in Dresden, which was financially possible for her since Germany was suffering through its horrid inflation and the advantageous exchange of Swiss francs into marks paid for her daughter's education. Returning to Zurich, Henrietta became an apprentice of the architect Frank Zollinger, an innovator like Frank Lloyd Wright, who must have taken a fatherly interest in the spunky girl's talents and abilities.

I couldn't even kiss her once in the taxi. Girls in the twenties didn't give in as easily as those of today. I dropped her at her home, but we didn't remember her gold in my pocket.

Henrietta's mother was elated about her daughter winning the first prize at the artists' ball. 150 francs! A fortune! Three months' rent! "But where is the money?" Ernestine asked. "I gave it to a young man," Henrietta replied. "I couldn't put it in my shoes and dance." "A young man? What's his name?" "But Mother, I wouldn't ask him!" she answered, annoyed.

For Ernestine, that money had gone up in smoke.

The next day I delivered the gold pieces and a children's book for her, *Pechvogel und Glueckspilz*. A *Pechvogel* is a bird that always has bad luck; *Glueckspilz* is a mushroom that experiences only good fortune. Two German folksy expressions that do not make sense in translation, nor in life.

That children's book is still standing on the headboard of her bed, since the day on which we met, seventy years ago.

In our lives together, Henrietta stayed with me through years of hardship, emigrations, hunger, and successes. To have or not to have money never made the slightest difference in our relation, a fact that is the cause of many American divorces.

I can think of no greater anachronism than our perfect unity, that of a grandson of an Austrian rabbi and the offspring of a girl of Swiss nobility, Baroness Henrietta Erna de Perrot, whose family tree started in the Middle Ages. I wasn't impressed, since mine began with the two Jews, Adam and Eve, the first people on Earth.

What turn her life and mine would have taken if my father had paid the four hundred German marks for my education! I would have stayed in Germany, might have became an engineer, but also would have been forced to leave the country to escape death in a concentration camp. What her future would have been, I do not know. But as the protegée of that famous architect Zollinger, she might have found a brilliant career and gotten married to a rich man with a Swiss and not a German accent.

The plus and minus of four hundred marks had decided the fate that we should meet in different countries, hundreds of miles apart, at a romantic fancy dress ball, which we both had been reluctant to attend, living by chance on the same street, the Scheuzergasse.

Though we met daily, we fought, as she remembers, though I don't, to the breaking point. I was too "macho" for her, which was based on my German upbringing. Having whims of iron, she had her own ideas about the relation between a boy and a girl. I remember a night when we took a long walk and were angrily fighting. I don't remember the reason anymore, but I picked her up and dumped her into a melodically spouting fountain in a small deserted little square where we had stopped. Even today, she remembers with amusement the cold water running down her dress and into her shoes. Her mother, Ernestine, who liked me, kept our relationship alive. I exchanged letters with Ernestine but not with Henrietta, but I can't remember what I had written so profusely to her mother.

Even now, after a long lifetime, our marriage has not fallen into a routine.

2

Loss of Innocence

Was it the whim of the gods, Harmatia, or serendipity, or preordained fate that had brought us together? We talk about miracles, fate, *que sera*, "was sein muss muss sein." Others would use the word *luck*.

Even today, the aftershocks of the Victorian era have not completely subsided. A copy of James Joyce's *Ulysses* that contains a passage of fifty pages, explicitly describing a woman's orgasm, could only be found on the Left Bank of the Seine River, where book salesmen dealt in universally forbidden literature.

At the time when Vladimir Nabokov's novel *Lolita* was banned in England and America, I tried to get a copy through my friend André Chanier, the ingenious book salesman on the Left Bank in Paris, who had supplied me with literature I could not find anywhere else. He had never heard about the novel *Lolita*. "Who wrote it?" he asked me. "Vladimir Nabokov," I said. "And what is it about?" "It is the story of a man who has an affair with a twelve-year-old one." "A twelve-year-old what?" André asked. "A twelve-year-old girl." "And what happened?" André inquired. That was France's mentality, liberated from the onus of guilt about sex since the French Revolution of 1789. Americans still recoil from the idea of a sexually active twelve-year-old girl, though now children give birth to children. The fashion of ethics changes with the time. At the times of Louis XIV women of the court displayed their breasts in deeply cut decolleté that would not be permitted to be shown today on television.

What is pornography? "I don't know," the sage Supreme Court Judge Potter stated. "But I know it when I see it." For me pornography is anything that is in bad taste. I lack the understanding for conventions that society tries to impose on people. Conventions are not petrified concepts; they change with the time. There was a fight at the University of California at Berkeley to use four-letter words in daily conversation, a revolution of expression, which shook the American bourgeoisie to its foundation. Four-letter words now have become commonplace. Words like *shit,* which would have made my Victorian grandmother faint, have become a part of modern conversational vocabulary. People live together before marriage and introduce their partners, "This is Jeannie; we live together," or "This is Bob, my boyfriend," which does not arouse resentment but sometimes envy, if the girl and boy are very good-looking. Divorced people might regret that such freedom did not exist in their youth.

Henrietta and I did live together for seven years without paying the fee for a government document, and it never occurred to us to get married, since both had lived through the failures of our parents' marriages. Sexual taboos were still rampant. Even the mentioning of "illicit" relations was taboo. Today television and books examine sexual problems in great detail and discuss former unmentionable themes openly. Mores change constantly. The Greek citizens of Pompeii adorned their rooms with phallic designs. Indian temples depict explicit love scenes, aware of the beauty of sex. The advertising companies could not exist without using sex as a lure as they sell cars or dog food.

By 1932, I had become a known writer and Robert was UFA's top director. We had left poverty row behind us. Henrietta, having joined me from Switzerland, felt the xenophobia of the Germans against all foreigners and Jews much more than we did. She refused to stay in Germany though Robert and I could not understand her antagonism. After all, we were extremely successful, and the idea of leaving that country for an unknown future did not make sense to us. If we had shared her premonition, we would have arranged our lives with foresight and saved ourselves much misery. Looking back, the idea of a Diaspora was inconceivable to future victims of the Nazi terror. If we had only studied Jewish history, we might have anticipated the rising dangers and foreseen that anti-Semitic history with all its horrors would repeat itself.

In 1931, Henrietta and I decided to have a child. "To have a child is as important to me as your writing is to you," she declared. We got married in Switzerland, where we had rented a house in Barbengo for her mother. We didn't tell anybody, not even her mother, about our plan, afraid she would make a motherly fuss about our intended fusion and insist on a family celebration. We got her out of the way by sending her on a pleasure trip to Rome. Our names were officially recorded in the little village of Cadepiano, five miles away from Barbengo. Outside of the Il Sindicado, the mayor's office, our names were posted, informing the citizens of that village of our intent to join in holy matrimony. Nobody objected. Robert was staying a few days with us. He was exhausted from having directed a major UFA picture with Emil Jannings and Charles Boyer, *Stuerme der Leidenschaft* (Storms of Passion). He just slept and ate, not even taking off his pajamas. He resented our decision to get married and didn't want to have any part of it. He wanted his younger brother to marry rich. A few years later he, too, married a poor woman.

On the day of our marriage we drove the narrow mountain road down to the village of Cadepino, Henrietta sitting behind me on my Triumph motorcycle. Robert stayed home and slept. To find witnesses for the legal ceremony we went across the street from the municipality to the public pub. We could pick up only one witness, our friend Luigi, the owner of the local restaurant. He was a stout Ticinese, who, for the ceremony, bravely put on his patent leather shoes. Since he had not worn them since his day of marriage, twenty years earlier, and having gained fifty pounds, he had painfully outgrown them. Il Sindicado, the mayor, was less than five feet tall and had to stand on tomes of old official records to look impressive behind his desk. He married us in the Tessin slang of Italian, of which we understood very little. To supply the second witness, he ran around his desk to join Luigi. Being questioned if I wanted to marry Signorina Henrietta Erna, Baroness de Perrot, a spinster, I said, "*Si,*" and when Henrietta was asked if she wanted to get married to Kurt Siodmak, a bachelor, she also consented in her best Italian, uttering, "*Si.*" After having signed the obligatory documents, Henrietta climbed behind me on the motorcycle, and the newly married couple drove up the narrow winding road to the hamlet of Barbengo, which consisted of a dozen houses. Robert was still asleep. We settled down to our daily routine, now legally joined.

Our marriage day was May 13, 1931. We never have given attention to that day, even forgot to celebrate our fiftieth and sixtieth wedding anniversaries. Birthdays, Christmas, Thanksgiving, and other holidays are of great importance and demand immense festivities. But the legal marriage contract didn't mean anything to us, except that our child had now a legal name. By living together at their free will, a couple can part at any time. But to dissolve a marriage needs an agonizing mental search, trying to patch up character discrepancies that rarely can be changed. Unmarried couples living together today are socially accepted. But in the twenties it was taboo, and the vice squad in Germany had the power to arrest the woman for prostitution.

In a marriage love and and respect for each other cannot be guaranteed by signing an official document. Henrietta planned a big party ahead, on the day when we slept together for the first time. That was the day when our marriage began.

How far can we trust our memories? Do we deliberately forget unpleasant recollections in order not to overload our brain? Many memories stay with us forever, despite our wish to block them out. Those indelible moments torture us to the end of our days.

Since Robert and I were broke, I took a job in a factory that produced photographic paper. But when I, with a group of others, left that evening after work, which consisted of cutting light-sensitive paper in a hall that was dimly lit by red bulbs, there was a line of striking workers outside that building, who shouted obscenities and spat at us. I didn't enter that place a second time, but the humiliation of having worked for a management that wanted to break a union still haunts me today. I went back to my typewriter, to work, seemingly against impossible odds. What to do with my scribbling? No agents existed who would advise or place stories. That profession was created years later. But since Robert and I had written four-line title cards in German for the Mack Sennett comedies and got paid for it by our uncle, Heinrich Nebenzahl, who imported those American shorts, I thought that if I could go to the story department of UFA, they might read my film treatment of *The Brothers*. I would not have remembered that fact, if Professor Harvé Dumont, the erudite film historian at the University of Lausanne, had not published long resumés about my film work in the French magazine *Ecran Fantastique* in 1983. I don't have the faintest idea about that story's content, and no copy exists.

Berlin had a cold winter in 1925, and the only warmth we could find was not in our cheap room, which I shared with Robert, but in the Romanische Café. We both must have been very hungry, since I went on the desperate, seemingly futile journey to UFA's story department, where I had left that film treatment two months previously. Robert was waiting for my return at the coffeehouse. The film company had accepted *The Brothers* and did not know where to find me. For two months there was money waiting for me at the cashier's office—2,500 marks! Stunned, I signed a contract, without reading it, and pocketed the cash, since in 1926 bank checks were rarely issued. Robert was still waiting for me at the coffeehouse. With a composed face I asked him casually why he hadn't ordered a sumptuous meal, as I laid the banknotes on the marble table. That story was never made into a film. Today I would pay the same amount in gold, if I could get a copy of that story, which obviously must have dealt with the life of two brothers who lived together waiting for a miracle to happen.

That miraculous event still stays with me, like a fantasy that only a dream can produce. We had money and could pay our rent, which had been due for months, and continue buying our daily bottle of Klosterbrand, a cheap brandy of which Robert and I consumed one quart every day. It was a habit that might have started Robert's dependence on alcohol in his later life.

I had enough money to persuade Henrietta to come to Berlin. Later I found out that she had sold her beloved racing bike and her violin to get the fare together to travel into the unknown, to live with a young man, whose only asset was that he was imbued with the conviction that he would make a living as a writer.

Henrietta arrived with a large suitcase made of pigskin, an expensive and heavy piece that we, from time to time, took to a pawn shop. Henrietta was a slim girl, with the figure and the pert face of a Vargas painting, a mass of reddish, curly hair, and the strength to face calmly a difficult life and its hardship. She saw, and still sees, only the good in every situation. Her tenet is that negative thoughts conjure unhappiness, an attitude diametrically opposed to my moody and gloomy conception of life. There is a definition, not fully understood, of why two people can complement each other like pieces of a jigsaw puzzle. The Baroness de Perrot, whose family was given that title in the sixteenth century, and the grandson of the Rabbi of Podgorze, whose ancestors went back to the destruction of the temple in Jerusalem in 76 C.E. (Christian era), could genetically hardly have a greater contraposition in tradition and upbringing. It might be, just on account of that contrariety, that we are not only lovers but companions and friends now for more than seven decades. When the first high flame of sexual desire has found its proper level, other values have to fill the gap: companionship and friendship. Two strong characters could not live together without spats of temper, differences of opinion, jealousies, and fights, which are the safety valve of any relationship.

Many years later, on a trip to West Africa, I talked to a wise old black man about the meaning of life. He told me, "Never throw anything of worth away without knowing how to replace it with something of an equal value." We were never looking for that equal value, and as time in life becomes shorter, our comradeship becomes stronger and opens the dreaded question: what would happen to the remaining partner if one died? The wise prime minister of France, Aristide Briand, told his housekeeper of forty years, "I'll make you a present: you may die before me."

After Henrietta's arrival from Switzerland and still having some money left from the sale of *Two Brothers,* we took a honeymoon trip to Hiddensee, a small island in the Baltic Sea. There we rented a bungalow whose wooden shutters had cutouts in the shape of hearts. The lighthouse threw its rotating beam on the white wall of the tiny room. Two hearts lit up and faded to return in unison, a symbol of two people, who, during the course of their lives, would fall in love with each other many times again and again.

We took long walks through the heather of Hiddensee. One day we ran into a huge man who looked at us angrily, resenting that we intruded on his domain, as though he owned the island. How did we dare to cross his path? Was he afraid we would accost him?

I remembered his face from photographs. He was the famous German author Gerhardt Hauptmann, 1912 Nobel Prize winner, whose patrician features and white flowing hair resembled those of Germany's most famous playwright and poet of the nineteenth century, Wolfgang von Goethe. As Hauptmann grew older, he groomed himself to look more and more like his human idol. I don't know whether his arrogance prevented him from admiring Adolf Hitler, whose favorite author he was. He survived Hitler by two months. He was a liberal-minded man, who had written the *Weavers,* a social drama about the starving, exploited linen weavers in Germany's Silesian province. "Die Leineweber haben jedes Jahr ein Kind, das eine is lahm, das andere ist blind" (The weavers have every year another child—one is lame; the other is blind).

When that famous German author stared at us in disgust, he did not know that my brother Robert, thirty years later, would make a successful motion picture of his stage play *Die Ratten* (The

Rats), which revived the German film industry, thoroughly ruined by the Nazis.

We were not aware that we were constantly spied on by a peeping Tom, until one day a twenty-page letter arrived with explicit pornographic descriptions, whose intricacies were unknown to me, innocent of sexual perversions. Of course I never told Henrietta about that pervert. I didn't want her to know that our chaste honeymoon had been shared by a mysterious third person.

Motion pictures do not need Ph.D.'s for their production. Our Uncle Heinrich Nebenzahl, married to a Siodmak, Uncle Usher's daughter, produced "Harry Piel" films, a 1925 forerunner of the Perry Mason TV series. He turned them out like a shoe factory. There was no "art" connected with his enterprise. His son, Seymour, a producer with intuition and imagination, possibly more unique in this business than my idolized producer Erich Pommer, produced the classic picture *M* in which Peter Lorre portrayed a child murderer. I was on the set at the studio when Fritz Lang directed the famous scene of the kangaroo court. A score of criminals, having caught the murderer, force him to confess. Lang, who possessed a sadistic streak, shot that scene innumerable times, starting at eight in the morning and ending at midnight when Lorre finally fainted from exhaustion. That was the effect Lang was aiming at.

The penchant for motion pictures molded Robert's and my life and was the reason that we survived emigration. In motion pictures it is not the style of the written language but the original ideas that count. Imagination is the cornerstone of the visual image. In a business in which few of the film producers were highly educated, we survived, since one could always hire a good secretary to correct the grammar of the written words.

By the time my brother Robert died in 1974, he had directed fifty-six motion pictures in half a dozen countries, of which he only had a smattering knowledge of the language. Picture making was the sole passion in his life. Vacations were a punishment for him. Until the very day he died, Robert was planning new projects. He did not develop a unique style, or he would have given Hitchcock, the master of the macabre, competition. Robert's films are still shown at "Robert Siodmak festivals" all over the world. He left forever a trace in film history.

After having returned from Hiddensee with Henrietta, it was difficult to make a living. I wrote advertising for Van Heusen shirts, basing the announcements on historical research, a sales technique that was novel to the fledgling advertising business of that time. That method is common today.

From time to time I sold a short story to *Scherl's* magazine or its competitor the *UHU*, published by Ullstein, the gigantic publishing house that produced the largest Berlin newspaper, the *Berliner Tageblatt,* and the prestigious weekly, *Illustrierte,* which published the last novel I ever wrote in German: *To the End of the World,* which was a roman à clef, a love story between a star like Greta Garbo and the dishonest Swedish match King Kreuger. But I was more successful with abstract science fiction themes than with intimate life stories.

There is a marked difference between science fiction and science fantasy. Science fiction is the projection of the future on today's world, as the writer visualizes it. Science fantasy often deals with little green men with antennas sprouting on their egg heads. Good science fantasy explores social systems on other planets. But the human brain is strictly confined in its imagination. The medieval painter Hieronymus Bosch depicted monsters with feet and eyes like humans, wings and claws like insects. So did Pieter Breughel, since the human mind cannot conceive other forms than nature produces. The social systems that science fantasy explores are restricted to fascistic, communistic, or utopian societies. So far no writer can conceive of any other political system.

In my science fiction stories, I tried to envision the future. Already in 1924 I wrote about a giant city whose air had become so foul that helicopters, for a fee, lifted people from the deep canyons of the streets high up to let them breathe clean air. Automobiles were not permitted to enter the cities. People moved about on rolling pavements. Advertisements were projected on clouds in the sky, and trains in 1924 whisked passengers with the speed of hundreds of miles an hour through the country. Already, fifty years ago, I visualized the technique of today and tomorrow.

Scherl's printed my short story "The Eggs from Lake Tanganyika." Sixty-four years later, reading an article in *Smithsonian* magazine about the publisher Hugo Gernsback, I found out that he had shaped the format of his new magazine, *Amazing Stories,* after the construction of my short story, since for the first time exact science was mixed with fantasy. His magazine, which still exists, was originally billed as the "Magazine of Scientifiction."

Gernsbach started the scientific trend in his magazine. "*Amazing Stories* is a new kind of fiction magazine," Gernsbach wrote in his inaugural editorial. "Each story will offer science fact and poetic vision. Posterity will point them out as having blazed a new trail, not only in literature but in progress." When he published in 1926 in volume 1 of his magazine the "Eggs from Lake Tanganjyka," he prefaced that story by writing, "We consider this extraordinary story a classic." My story was republished sixty years later, and I received Gernsbach's "Pioneer Award," since he had shaped his magazine on its mixture of science and fantasy.

I based my stories on scientific research. Since I have only a smattering of knowledge in any technical or biological field, I contact the most knowledgeable American scientists on the subject I am writing about. These erudite people, most of them frustrated writers, check my writings for technical accuracy. Dr. David Hare, who was Dandy's (the famous brain surgeon) assistant, corrected my novel *Donovan's Brain* for medical accuracy. Stanford Kraemer, designer of the government's future space lab, advised me on *City in the Sky;* Michael Fulton, on *The Third Ear,* which has as its theme biochemically induced extrasensory perception. My novel *Rache im Ether* (Revenge in Space), published in 1932, was based on a beam that conducted electricity. Fifteen years later science discovered laser. Radar appeared in one of my books, ten years before the British scientists during World War II, thought of it. Some of my anticipated discoveries have been realized by scientific research, like keeping the monkey's brain alive in *Donovan's Brain.* Some are still unsolved, like telepathy based on biochemical substances, the theme of *The Third Ear.* There was, for a time, interest in "space colonies" built fifty thousand miles behind the moon. But the scientists so far have not thought of the more logical "Hotel in Space," a giant satellite that circles the Earth in ninety-six minutes. Passengers board it by shuttle in New York and disembark in Paris fifteen minutes later. Such an international satellite, as described in my novel *City in the Sky,* will be the mode of traveling of the future, and with its hotel in the outer rim, become the "Riviera" of the space age. Now the Japanese have such a structure on their drawing board.

In 1974 I was invited by Stanford University to talk to students about science fiction and fantasy. Living in one of their high-rise apartments, I sometimes in the afternoon was visited by famous Nobel Prize winners, since my martinis were palatable. A clandestine relaxation after a hard day's work was welcome, even to the world famous. I told those austere gentlemen that what they were doing in their research was science fiction, since every idea that is not scientifically proven should be called "science fiction." Scientists test a new idea, sometimes for many years, in laboratories. Should they prove its scientific validity, they drop the word *fiction* from "science fiction," having proven a scientific fact. If their research cannot establish any scientific proof, the idea remains "science fiction."

As a science fiction writer, I am only concerned about ideas. The tedious laboratory work I leave to those whose profession is to explore the unexplored. According to the Bible, "First came the Word." The follow-up is interpretation and exploration. That law has not changed through the ages.

After the return from Hiddensee, our poverty soon became pathetic. The choice was to write a letter to Henrietta's mother in Zurich or to buy bread. I possessed one acceptable shirt that Henrietta washed and dried overnight in our room. The room we lived in was rented in Henrietta's name. I sneaked in at night, unknown to the landlady, Mrs. Keilpflug.

Old houses in Berlin were infested with lice, and we put the bed's feet into cans filled with water, as a barrier against their attacks. But those insects, gifted with technical ingenuity and a knowledge of ballistics, used to crawl along the ceiling to rain from above on the bed.

I wrote stories on a rented Remington portable typewriter and peddled them to publishing houses, or sold them to a newspaper, the *8 O'clock Evening News*. At that time, almost every idea was "original," since that genre of literature was still in its infancy. Now an idea that has not been used before can rarely be conceived, and only the writer's individual approach makes it acceptable for publishing.

Robert found a job as a film cutter with our cousin Heinrich Nebenzahl. When the Harry Piel films were seven years old, Heinrich had them "recut" into "new" ones, which was possible since Heinrich used the same actors. Of course, it could happen that the actors left the scene of the crime in an automobile and arrived in a horse-drawn carriage.

I got a job as a cub reporter at the *8 O'clock Evening News* paper. They paid anemic money based on the lines printed. But it was a job. The *Evening News* had to fight its mighty competitor, Scherl's *Nachtausgabe* (the daily *Night Edition*). The *8 O'clock Evening News* could only exist by digging up sensational scoops to stay competitive.

The editor Franz Schlieffen had heard about a gigantic picture that the UFA studio secretly prepared and that Fritz Lang directed. It was called *Metropolis,* a production so expensive that it nearly broke UFA financially. But Lang did not allow reporters on the set.

Henrietta and I, to gain access to the forbidden territory, signed up as extras. The pay was fifty marks for the night shooting, a great sum for us, three times more than the *Evening Paper* would pay me for the report.

That night Lang was going to shoot the burning of the robot, one of the pivotal scenes of the giant science fiction picture. The actress Brigitte Helm, a blonde Gretchen of eighteen, who played an innocent girl and also its cloned double, the vamp, the personification of evil, was to be burned at the stake amid thousands of extras.

During the Nazi times, Brigitte was one of the few humane Germans who secretly gave financial help to her Jewish friends, who had fled abroad. She kept her former agent, Elizabeth Blumann, who had emigrated to England, by supplying her with British pounds. Blumann turned her bank account in Germany over to her in exchange. Brigitte could have suffered Nazi retaliation if they had known that she helped a Jew. She left Nazi Germany for Switzerland as soon as she was able.

The atmosphere on the gigantic *Metropolis* stage was tense. A strike was brewing among the hired extras. Lang had kept them for more than fifteen hours but refused to pay them for the overtime. I knew I was witnessing an important story for my portable typewriter and pushed my way to the stake where the girl robot, dressed in a shiny material that clung to her body, was to be burned alive. I watched Lang, who wore a monocle in his left eye—which was almost blind and also since he was more Prussian than a Junker—directing Brigitte hypnotically. I don't know how good an actress she was at the time, but here was Svengali and Trilby, and Lang coaxed her into a state of near hysteria.

That motion picture has survived time more than any film I could name, and it was very much admired by Joseph Goebbels, Hitler's chief of propaganda. It telegraphed the coming Nazi domination of a ruling party over the formless masses they governed. The motion picture is still revered and beloved in Germany, where the city of Berlin exhibits its history in a special museum. My good friend Forrest Ackerman, Mr. Sci-Fi (he coined that expression), collected material about that picture and now will have a constant exhibition in Berlin that carries his name: Forrest Ackerman's *Metropolis.*

I am loath to look at that picture with its fascistic overtones, since it evokes buried fears in me of a time when my and my family's lives were threatened by death. That picture for me is devoid of human feelings and has the connotation of the inhuman oppressions millions were forced to endure. Though the Weimar Republic, the forerunner of the Nazis, was supposedly liberal, the German freedom was a coated surface of a police state, tailor-made for Germany.

When the Nazis came to power, Goebbels, who saw in that film the Nazi spirit, tried to keep Lang in Germany, offering him the position as his adviser to the motion picture industry. He suggested that Lang's mother should denounce his Jewish father and sign an affidavit that his genetic father was an Aryan, with whom she had an affair. I understand that Lang enthusiastically welcomed Goebbels's suggestion but wisely left with the next train for England and America. Famous for his international successes, he found assignments in Hollywood. He also imported his Prussian attitude, a behavior not tolerated by American workmen. Workmen do not stand for being shouted at or pushed around, as was the habit of the German directors. After a couple of lamps crashed from the rafter at Lang's feet at the Paramount studio where he was shooting the picture *Manhunt,* the story of an inveterate hunter who stalks the rarest of all beasts, Hitler, and after Lang supposedly had been beaten up by "unknowns," he got the message and adjusted himself to the democratic way of a country where human values have another meaning than that of autocratic Germany.

In the darkened stage, flames shot up at the stake where the robot was to be burned to cinders. But sparks caught Brigitte's dress, setting it afire. Standing as close as possible to the fiercely burning stake, I took advantage of this unexpected opportunity and jumped across the flames, but Fritz Lang and the fire department were even quicker than I and beat out the fire. Brigitte collapsed in Lang's arms, but the cameras had recorded her agony. She was not hurt overlong.

In the tradition of a good reporter, I tried to talk to her, stupidly revealing that I was a reporter. A minute later I found myself outside the stage. Lang had me thrown out instantly.

Twenty years later, in Hollywood, I frequently met Fritz Lang who was directing motion pictures for Paramount Studios. In the studio's commissary, I reminded him of that scene and asked him why he had thrown me, a poor insignificant reporter, out so rudely. He didn't remember and denied that the robot even caught fire.

The *8 o'clock Evening News* paid me a hundred marks for the report. The editor Franz Schlieffen, a notorious womanizer, was very interested in Henrietta and wanted to take her on a trip "as his secretary," knowing that we were not married. She confided in me that she had refused his invitation. His vanity hurt, he did not employ me anymore.

Though I have known a great number of important people during my lifetime, I can't take credit for this advantage, since when I met them they were of my age group and not yet famous. Some of them had even to wait a few scores of years before they became internationally known.

When I worked in London in 1935, one could buy the best seat at the Sadler's Wells Theatre for three shillings and six pence and watch William Shakespeare's *Romeo and Juliet,* with Peggy Ashcroft playing Juliet, John Gielgud as Romeo, Alec Guinness as Mercutio, and Laurence Olivier as Benvolio. Even Charles Laughton, already world famous for his portrayal as Henry XIII in Alex Korda's film, played in *Volpone' or the Fox* for a token twenty pounds' weekly salary at the Old Vic Theatre. A group of aspiring actors and writers met frequently at the Adelphi Terrace at Roger Ackland's apartment.

The Adelphi Terrace was a cluster of old Victorian buildings on the Thames River, which, torn down after World War II, has given way to soulless high-rises.

I couldn't take Henrietta with me on my frequent visits to Roger's apartment, since only men were allowed, according to the time-honored English tradition "gentlemen only." That arrangement makes sense to the English, since men never really relax in the presence of a female. This tribal rite can be found in many countries. There are monasteries in Greece that don't even allow a female goat to enter the compound!

J. B. Priestley, the gray eminence of the gatherings, belonged to the former generation, but he liked to advise young playwrights while bathing in their adoration. The drawback was that he smoked a smelly pipe that he obviously never cleaned, but this practice we accepted since his name was registered in *Who's Who,* the epitome of success. But not many among the contemporaries of that time knew Emlyn Williams, who, acting in the murder mystery written by him, *Night Must Fall,* shocked the audience by carrying a hatbox on the stage which supposedly contained a severed human head. In those days the audience got easily terrified, which seems to be impossible to achieve today, where there are no limits to gruesome excess in literature, on the stage, television, in painting, the screen, photography, or sculpture.

As time progressed, Laurence Olivier became a world star, after his gripping performance as Hamlet at the Sadler's Wells Theatre. So did John Gielgud, Alec Guinness, and others of a time that was pregnant with gifted stage actors. The queen elevated them to nobility, and they were permitted to put the title "Sir" in front of their names. Olivier became Sir Laurence, and Guinness, Sir Alec. Their family names were rarely used, since it was expected that everybody knew of whom one was speaking when the name Sir Laurence was dropped. Even my friend of later years, Anthony Quayle, maybe the best actor ever to play Shakespeare's King Lear, became Sir Anthony, which lifted our personal acquaintance with him onto a higher level. If they had lived long enough, many of our friends might have been included in *Who's Who,* and I might be privileged to brag that I knew VIPs (Very Important People).

When Kaiser Wilhelm II was dethroned in 1918 and his rule replaced by a democratic regime, the Weimar Republic, by law a new nobility could not be created by that democratic government. The "von" as in "von" Richthofen, "von" Ribbentrop, or "von" Krupp, was replaced by other values, expressed in financial success, a measure of importance in which the United States reached the zenith. Success without great amounts of money was not admired. The extremely wealthy people became the heroes of our time, substituting the values of historic family traditions.

At Scherl Publishers, I met Erich Maria Remarque, the author of the worldwide successful novel *All Quiet on the Western Front.* The title was a newspaper quotation that appeared often in German news reports during World War I. The Nazis later tried to defame Remarque by claiming that this name was spelled backward and actually was "Kraemer," which has a Jewish connotation and therefore in the Nazis' eyes lowered him to a nonhuman being. The only accepted social class was the Aryan, though Hitler and Goebbels didn't look like blonde, tall, handsome ideals of the Third Reich, since they were dark-haired, and Goebbels even was handicapped by a clubfoot. But the real Aryan, according to Dr. Joseph Goebbels, could easily be recognized by having red hair in his armpits. I was told about that unfailing distinction by my blonde Aryan friend, the writer Heinar Schilling, who did not accept Henrietta, either, as a true Aryan, since her cheekbones were too prominent for a full-blooded example of the superrace.

Erich Remarque was assistant editor of *Die Elegante Welt* (The Elegant World), a sophisticated magazine like the American *Vogue,* which Scherl tried to emulate. Remarque wrote a gossip column for that slick magazine, reporting who met whom at what party and where. He also composed amusing vignettes, called "Feuilletons," for the social column. Erich sported a monocle, the accepted logo of the sophisticated German. Secretly he wrote the antiwar novel *All Quiet on the Western Front*. Every morning he entered the chief editor's office of *Die Woche,* the weekly magazine for which I wrote short stories, to tell us, an intrigued audience, a new chapter of the book he was composing. Thus I knew the content of that famous novel before it was published.

Scherl was owned by the gigantic Hugenberg Concern, a heavy industrial conglomerate that specialized in armaments. The nationalistic house of Scherl would never have published Remarque's antiwar novel. On advice of his agent, Otto Klement, Erich discarded his monocle and tie, wore his shirt open at the neck, and posed as the front soldier that he was. Klement presented *All Quiet* . . . to Ullstein, Scherl's democratic rival. Their literary editor could not see any financial success in that novel. He told Klement that book would never sell more than a thousand copies. But Hermann Ullstein, his liberal boss, insisted on publishing it. After it had sold its first million, Klement confronted the editor with the novel's international success. But that man still maintained that it should never have sold more than a thousand copies. It is a writer's fate that he has to deal with too many experts, who, secretly envying writers, have the power to reject their work.

Ullstein was later expropriated by the Nazis and published the *Voelkische Beobachter,* their official newspaper. The Ullsteins saved their lives by fleeing abroad in time.

Remarque became a millionaire and wisely shifted his fortune to Switzerland. He had the foresight and courage to invest in impressionistic painters. His collection of van Gogh, Matisse, Degas, and Renoir is still on permanent loan to the Metropolitan Museum in New York. *All Quiet* . . . became a classic motion picture in Hollywood directed by Lewis Milestone, with Lew Ayres in the lead. Ayres in later years became the leading man in one of my motion pictures, *Donovan's Brain,* in which Nancy Davis Reagan, the wife of the later president, played the love interest.

Remarque was the longtime intimate friend of Marlene Dietrich, and wrote a novel about their love affair: *The Arc de Triomphe*. Though he never returned to his native Germany, he did not consider himself a refugee. The Nazis would have sent him to a concentration camp for having written this antiwar novel.

Remarque's house in Ronco at the Italian-Swiss border was a museum of antiques and paintings. A spiral staircase led to the upper floor and ascending or descending it, one passed dozens of Degas drawings. His living room was covered with layers of carpets woven in medieval times. Collecting them was a special hobby of his.

I remember him looking for bargains at Mr. Rosenbaum's antique shop, which was situated in a seventeenth-century baroque building, a historical landmark, belonging to the city of Ascona. It contained treasures that could rival those of international museums, mostly Etruscan, which Rosenbaum bought from Italian farmers. Tuscany, the Italian province at the opposite side of the Lago Maggiore, is the border between Switzerland and Italy. It is rich in unearthed Etruscan statues and artifacts. The farmers of Tuscany sometimes dug up priceless antiques, whose export was forbidden by the Italian government. But at night the farmers crossed the lake in rowboats to conduct underground traffic in Rosenbaum's antique store.

I remember the head of an Etruscan god. Viewed from the right side, the head seemed to sneer in contempt. Viewed from the front of it, the face had an expression of anticipation, waiting for the sacrifice he expected to receive. Observed from the left, its face seemed to smile, thanking for the gift.

Remarque made a sport of "Jewing Rosenbaum down," as he called it—bargaining unfairly—which embarrassed the learned, knowledgeable old dealer. This lowered my admiration for the typical "Aryan" Remarque, contemptuously haggling with a Jew.

Remarque died in his early seventies, helped, I guess, by his love for excellent Swiss red wines.

I needed a literary agent to deal with the publishers. Not many of influence existed in Germany except for one, Helmut Kornfeld, who kept a sumptuous office on the Kurfuerstendamm, the glamorous main street of Berlin. Kornfeld represented scores of contemporary authors: Vicky Baum, who became internationally known with her novels such as *Grand Hotel,* which became a vehicle for Greta Garbo and John Barrymore in Hollywood and also a successful Broadway play. Bernhardt Kellermann, Lionel Feuchtwanger, Jacob Wassermann, and Gina Kauss, illustrious names of pre-Hitler Germany, belonged to Kornfeld's stable.

Kornfeld supported aspiring young writers. He advanced them starvation wages for their future manuscripts. But he asked 50 percent of all proceeds, which made a good income for him. When he had two writers under contract, one worked exclusively for the agent. If he had ten, the output of five went into his pocket. Since he represented most of the young crop of gifted but starving German authors, he drove a big Daimler-Mercedes.

Kornfeld promised to advance six hundred marks, dribbled out in small payments, for my novel that was in progress. When I think back to that time, it is still inconceivable to me that I finally had fourteen novels and half a dozen screenplays published between 1929 and 1933. Those years between 1929 and 1933 were my most productive ones, growing on the fertile ground of the unique culture that Germany produced at the beginning of the twentieth century. It lasted to the day when the Nazis, almost overnight, destroyed its roots, leaving Germany an artistic wasteland that has not recovered, fifty years after the disappearance of the Third Reich.

3

The Golden Years

Then came the "golden years." But were they really that golden?
 The Talmud, that authoritative body of Jewish tradition, states, "It is better not to be born than to be born." It is "Harmatia," the whim of the gods, that the Jews should suffer for millennia. That small breed was often on the verge of being physically wiped out by powerful tribal prejudices. But it wasn't, though its enemies always had the power to eliminate the Jews completely. After the fall and destruction of their Temple in 76 C.E., Jews were scattered all over the world and could be persecuted in every country as an object of hate. Besides, there were obvious reasons to persecute them.
 The world feels threatened by two characteristics: beauty and intelligence. A Jewish boy, when he is thirteen, must be able to read from the Torah, the five books of Moses, at a public ceremony called Bar Mitzvah. Only then can he truly be called a Jew. There is no orthodox Jew who is illiterate, due to the rules of his belief. But among the many explanations of the root of anti-Semitism, every one of them is subjective, none conclusive. Most powers in history who tried to destroy the Jews have vanished. But the Jews have existed for almost six thousand years. The cause may be that most religions are based on mysticism, which does not survive the progress of time, while the Jewish religion is founded on unalterable laws.
 The Germans call Earth "Das Jammertal," the valley of despair. Of course that conviction depends on the circumstances when and where one is born. It must not be too painful to be the king of Luxembourg, living in castles filled with art treasures, in a country that never fought a war and has no army except a colorful palace guard wearing medieval uniforms, carrying fearsome halberts to ward off

enemy armies equipped with tanks and fighter planes. Or to be a billionaire, owning mansions and yachts and scores of beautiful mistresses. But the struggle for existence in one of the republics of the former USSR, in Poland or in the Baltic republics adds certain sense to the Talmud's wisdom about the value of life. The Jews, being practical, never shared the belief that the destiny of the human race on Earth is to suffer.

Werner, the third of my father's sons, born in 1907, emigrated in 1932 to Israel, the year the Germans became openly fascistic. He died at the age of eighty, having lived through a precarious existence in a country constantly under siege by implacable enemies. But he had the compensation of belonging to a country that welcomed him as a Jew, and not as a traveler like his older brothers.

Robert and I wrote him often, and for sixty years he kept every scrap of paper, every postcard, and letter. I retrieved that collection from his family in Israel. I tried to read those communications but could not, since the ghosts of the past appeared like the witches in *Macbeth*. Most letters, sent from Germany, France, England and other countries where Robert and I sporadically worked, guests in foreign lands, had the recurring theme: how to carve out an existence. Or the letters told of hopes, based often on vague possibilities of getting a job or being tolerated to stay for a time in that foreign country. A thousand letters, written during half a century, depicting a condition that had become the basis of our lives. But Werner was "home." Robert never was. Now that correspondence is kept at the Kinemathek, the Museum of Film History in Berlin, since those documents record half a century of a lifetime of two emigrant filmmakers, comprising the development of motion picture history, which would have been forgotten if Werner had not preserved those records in a cardboard box. I regret that I didn't hold on to his correspondence, which recorded the history of Israel, seen through the eyes of a European Jew. Now with the influx of Jews from Yemen, Ethiopia, Tunis, Morocco, and Russia and of the Israeli-born Jews, the Sabras, the European culture and influx are rapidly disappearing. When I visited Werner in Israel in 1974, I could not communicate with his son, David, since, born in Israel, he only spoke Hebrew and Arabic.

Henrietta and I found a new home in America, where I am accepted like millions of other immigrants. We are integrated in this country's customs and ways of thinking. But Robert to the last day of his life preferred being a guest in the country where he had a chance to work. Expelled from Germany, he went to France, then to

Hollywood, and afterward back to Germany, with frequent side trips to England, Spain, Italy, and even Romania, where he directed his last picture, whose hardship might have been the cause of his early death. He died in Switzerland, staying there by the sufferance of the Swiss bureaucracy. He was in limbo, in a constant Diaspora. He elected to live that way, a perambulating motion picture director, who, by design, never wanted any roots except those the film business had to offer for a fleeting time.

I am aware that I am writing too little about my companion in life, Henrietta. Since she went with me through some hopeless-looking times of our perilous existence, she is the most important part of me. We shared the hardships, the joys, and successes. I admire her patience since I wouldn't like to be married to myself. I would have chosen another partner. During times of the greatest stress, Henrietta never lost her optimism. Her female gift, so elusive to men, can evaluate with a sharp bird-eye's vision the vagaries of life. I know that I would not have found the strength to face a life that often did not make sense to me in its inanities, remembering the Talmudistic wisdom that it might be better not to be born than to be born.

Before the golden days started, we hit the bottom of poverty. Since, as we thought, the depth of adversity had been reached—it had become a question of finances to write a letter to Henrietta's mother in Zurich or to buy bread—it was Henrietta's conviction that life from now on could only improve. I didn't see how, since the police made me return my rented Remington typewriter. I couldn't finish my novel and collect the small sum of money that my agent, Kornfeld, had promised to pay me when I turned the finished manuscript over to him.

I went to Robert, who made a meager living as a film cutter for our uncle Heinrich Nebenzahl, but who didn't believe in paying a high salary to his relatives.

"How much is the rent for a typewriter?" Robert asked.

"Thirty marks."

He didn't have thirty marks to spare. An added deposit was also involved, a sum above our financial status. Evidently gifted with psychic powers, Robert climbed to the attic of the large office building at the Potsdamerstrasse where he was working and returned with a small Adler portable typewriter, dusty and deserted among accumulated rubbish. Its ribbon was missing. He could not explain why he had gone to the garret on the tenth floor where he had never been. Now I had a typewriter, though I couldn't afford the ribbon.

I went to Kornfeld for help. His secretary gave me the devastating news that the next day her boss would start his six-week summer vacation. He had no time to see me. In panic I went back to our single room in the Nachodstrasse.

I had sheets of paper and carbon paper left and finished my novel writing right through the night, forty pages of it, by typing ribbonless on the same blank sheet, imprinting the carbon on a sheet of paper underneath.

Next morning I took the novel to the agent. He still would not see me, since I was not one of his moneymaking clients. But the secretary, sensing my despair, took the manuscript to his private office. She returned after a few minutes. Kornfeld had read the first few pages and had scribbled on the soiled cover, "Unsalable. I won't put the good name of my agency on that piece of shit."

We had hit a lower bottom in life than we thought possible. Henrietta suggested that she find a job as a seamstress, a skill she had learned from her mother. I tried to take a job at a filling station. To apply as an engineer at one of the large electric companies would take weeks. And I had no track record except my examinations.

I confided in Martin Stiebing, a former school pal from my hometown Dresden, who had become assistant to the editor of the *Woche*, the most read weekly magazine in Germany. The *Woche* had accepted some of my short stories before.

"Let me read your masterpiece," Martin said, a subterfuge that I suspected was an easy way out to appease me. I turned my only, dirty, pencil-corrected, soiled-by-fingerprints, and partly carbon copy over to him. There was no time or money to have the manuscript retyped professionally.

Martin was a most contradictory character, and I never really understood his way of thinking and acting during our long relationship. He was friend and foe, and I never knew whether he would secretly turn against me. He was unexplainably drawn toward the culture of the Middle East, studied Arabic, and even went to visit Istanbul and the Asiatic mainland during a vacation. Martin was married to a slim, blonde girl, Eva. Both of them flourished during Hitler's time, when gifted writers had been eliminated, killed, or left the country. During the war, he became chief editor of the *Woche*, and Eva wrote novels, one of which even sold one hundred thousand copies. Though I believe that he was not a Nazi in spirit, he must have held a mysterious government job during the Nazi times, which kept him out of the draft almost until the end of the war.

Henrietta had a deep aversion for him and his wife, sensing the shiftless and dangerous opportunist in Martin, who would hurt even his best friends if it were to his advantage.

"I recommended your novel to Rahn," Martin told me next day. Rahn was the chief editor of the *Woche*.

I was speechless, thinking that the only copy I had, smudged and not edited, was in competition with well-known, established authors whom the *Woche* published. But Martin had the inside track. Scherl had story consultants, "lectors," whose job it was to find unpublished novels for their different magazines and newspapers. In those days, magazines and daily newspapers, even those in small towns, printed and reprinted novels in installments. The *Woche* had just published a novel by Gina Kauss, *Luxury Liner*, which had become a huge book success and a blockbuster motion picture in Hollywood. Unable to find a novel, maybe by default or laziness, the publisher's readers had not come up with a follow-up to *Luxury Liner*. The publishing house decided, as Martin told me, to discover new talents, since the established ones had become financially too demanding. Should the author bomb, they had the humanitarian excuse that they had given a struggling writer a chance. Should he be successful, they would become his mentor and be able to buy his output for a low sum.

My novel *Ofen Lehmann Zwei* (Blast Furnace Lehmann Two) seemed to meet that requirement. The background was a steel mill. A time bomb had been attached to one of the blast furnaces by the steelwork's competition, and the story covered the twelve hours before its explosion. "Rahn wants to talk to you," Martin told me a day later. "He wants to buy your novel."

The news didn't impress me, not used to fairy tales happening to me.

"How much should I ask?" I asked Martin, since I had never collected more than a hundred marks for any of my short stories. "Start with fifteen thousand marks," Martin said. "And don't let any agent handle it. Rahn doesn't like agents."

The year was 1929, and inflation had become a memory. Everybody has his or her own conception of money. A couple of thousand marks was a fortune I still could understand. Mr. Getty, the oil tycoon, once stated, "A billion isn't what it used to be." Fifteen thousand marks was a sum beyond my conception. If Martin had asked me to demand a million, I would have shown the same lack of reaction. But Henrietta was unmoved. "They're trying to get you cheap," she said soberly, not even showing excitement about that turn of events. "I've heard that Vicky Baum and Bernhardt Kellermann get forty thousand."

When I entered Rahn's office, Wilhelm Suttner, a redheaded thin bureaucrat and editor of the *Gartenlaube* (the Garden Gazebo), a dull magazine for women, was there. He was the head lector. He made the deals with the authors. "I understand you have joined the poets," Suttner said. "How much do you want for your novel?"

I didn't have the nerve to mention the astronomical sum in the presence of Rahn and his cronies.

"I'd rather see you alone, " I said flustered. He took me to his office, where I told him about the sum Martin advised me to ask.

Suttner emitted a well-studied laugh. "Isn't that rather impudent to ask for such a sum for your first novel? You should be happy even to be published for free in *Die Woche*. But I will be generous and pay you four thousand."

Though that sum also was beyond my comprehension, I confided in Suttner that I was eight thousand marks in debt. He didn't know that I couldn't even raise twenty from my impoverished friends. Four thousand marks would leave me in debt, I lied. My creditors would take the money and leave me in the same state as I was now. I wasn't starving, I told him, though he didn't know that I hadn't eaten breakfast. Fifteen thousand would give me time to pay off my debt and to write my next novel, without being harassed by money troubles.

I left Suttner, convinced that I had blown the biggest chance in my life.

That evening Martin tipped me off that I would get twelve thousand for *Ofen Lehmann Zwei*. The next day Suttner told me that, to assist young writers in their literary efforts, the House of Scherl had magnanimously agreed to pay ten thousand marks for "Furnace Lehmann Two."

I quickly mentioned the sum of twelve thousand, though I'd have taken the ten and run and changed the conversation's subject, talking about my experiences as a fireman and engineer on the State Railroad, my studies in mathematics in Zurich, and my compulsory urge to express myself on paper. Suttner cut me short and produced a contract, wrote into an open space the sum of twelve thousand, and told me that the cashier had the money ready for me. I signed.

I went with my contract to the accounting department. It was twelve o'clock when everybody went to lunch, and the whole city took its traditional lunch hiatus. The cashier had just closed his window. I knocked at it, and I don't know why, maybe because he saw desperation in my face, but he reopened the window. He shoved twelve thousand mark notes over to me. To pay by check was still uncommon. I didn't ask for smaller denominations, afraid something might happen before I could run out of the building.

I had only fifteen but not the twenty pfennig for the streetcar in my pocket. The banks were closed between twelve and two o'clock. There I was, on the Friedrichstrasse in Berlin, with twelve thousand marks in my pocket, unable to board a streetcar or hire a taxi. I walked to our single room on the Nachodstrasse, which was miles away, and had to wait in front of a bank to open its counter. There I changed the twelve thousand-mark notes into fifty-mark ones.

Henrietta was not home. I pushed the few pieces of furniture against the wall and covered the floor with bills. Henrietta returned and looked startled at the wealth at our feet. We took off our shoes and walked on it, supposedly into a new easy life. That was our conception. But world history writes its own message. The day was August 29, 1929.

It is difficult to change from a life of luxury to a simple one. But it is astonishing how quickly one gets used to luxuries that were only dreams during the time of poverty.

I rented a house in Dahlem, a suburb of Berlin, bought a Royal typewriter, the latest model, and, since we lived in the country, a secondhand Chrysler two-seater, the mark of affluence. We had our own egg factory, supplied by Bantam chickens, and lived the life of country squires. I didn't need anymore to put cardboard in Henrietta's shoes, and my collection of shirts with frayed collars and cuffs disappeared.

When during a train ride I watched a passenger engrossed in reading my novel in the *Woche*, I believed that our monetary success was permanent and that I had been accepted as a serious writer by the public. I wanted to tell him, "Hi, I'm the guy who wrote this," still under the same euphoric spell when I read the galley proofs. I then had locked myself into my bedroom to admire and correct them. Scherl had changed the title of *Blast Furnace Lehmann Two* into *Helene Threatens to Burst,* an inane title. Helene was the first name of the owner of the Krupp steelwork, Helene Krupp von Bohlen-Halbach, since the Krupps had no male heir, and Helene married a Count von Bohlen-Halbach. The publicity department of Scherl hoped people would be aware of that sly similarity. They tried to advertise the novel "American-style" by placing small ads in almost every newspaper in Germany: "Helene threatens to burst," expecting to tease readers' curiosity as to who Helene was and why she was going to blow up. But they lost courage during that advertising stunt and did not follow up with an explanation. The public never found out why Helene was in danger to erupt.

I started another novel right away, subconsciously anticipating the Nazi time to come.

It was the custom of the big farms in the north of Germany that the oldest son inherited the ranch and the next in line became a ship's captain on a freighter that traveled to faraway continents. In my story the farmer dies and his seafaring brother takes over the farm. One day a dark-haired young man arrives from Argentina, a son the captain had fathered on his journey. He insists on staying at the ranch among the blue-eyed, Aryan north Germans, a hated stranger who bewitches the girls, dances the tango, and possesses a joy of life, abhorrent to the Bible-thumping villagers. It was a description of the xenophobic frame of mind, which culminated during the Nazi times and which still, more than fifty years after Hitler's death, permeates German thinking. That novel, *Sturmflut* (The Flood), anticipated the coming ethnic cruelties.

I tried to find a copy of that novel when I visited Europe in 1985, but all collections of old newspapers seem to have gone up in flames during the bombings of Germany.

Having studied mathematics, my interest in writing became specialized. I wanted to write about where the world is going, not where it had been. That thematic approach to writing is called science fiction. Every invention starts with a science fiction idea, often put on paper by an imaginative writer. I had the vision of cooling the air electrically in closed rooms, not knowing that the German navy already had solved the problem of lowering the boiler room temperature in its future battleships, an invention that became air conditioning.

In 1929 I witnessed tests in a government laboratory in Kiel, a city at the Baltic Sea. There a small model of the future battle cruiser *Bismarck* was "dragged" through a stream of fast-flowing water, to find the ship's least water friction. It was an experiment prohibited by the Treaty of Versailles. I did get into that restricted place with the help of a friend of mine, an ardent pacifist, who wanted to report this secret test of the navy, conducted, as he thought, without the knowledge of the Weimar Republic's government. His spy mission was futile, since there was already, without a Hitler, a secret rearming of the German forces in progress. Though Germany was forbidden to build airplanes, there existed hundreds of schools of glider pilots, the future members of the Luftwaffe. I now am certain that the Allies helped and financed Germany to rearm, expecting it would turn against that hated bolshevist system, which threatened their capitalist system.

I was trying to find a story that could be made into a film Robert could direct—his most ardent wish. A writer can get a break by writing a successful story or a book. But how does a director get his chance? He first needs a "vehicle," a story, which I hoped to supply for Robert, since he was brother, father figure, and family to me, a substitute for my lonely childhood.

Robert proposed to our uncle Heinrich Nebenzahl, for whom he was working as cutter, to shoot a picture for five thousand marks. Nebenzahl, who spent two hundred thousand marks on each sequence of his *Harry Piel, Detective* series, gave Robert fifty marks and told him to go ahead. That was the full amount of his financial contribution. Later on he distributed that picture, but we never saw a penny.

A small group of film aficionados gathered regularly at the Romanische Café, discussing motion picture themes. In his biography, *Between Berlin and Hollywood,* Robert gives me credit for the idea of his first film. But to gather more glory for himself, since he was always very insecure and needed constant appreciation, even when he became famous in the motion picture industry, he states, "Nothing for my first picture was written down." But I remember that I wrote a fifty-page treatment of a simple idea: A big city, like Berlin, on a Saturday afternoon. A young man meets a pretty girl in the subway and asks her for a date for the coming Sunday. She brings a girlfriend; he, his best friend. The second girl is prettier than the first one, and friction starts between the four young people since the first boy makes love to the second girl. Intercut to the big city, deserted on a Sunday afternoon. The big lakes around Berlin are steaming with life; the beaches are crowded. The whole city has moved to the country. One couple stays in Berlin, sleeping late, leisurely walking the empty streets, relaxing after the rush of the week's work. The Sunday ends. Monday, again the city is crowded.

The country surrounding it, calm and bucolic.

I financed part of that picture with some of my Scherl money. The final cost was nine thousand marks, or $2,500. That avant-garde picture, *Menschen am Sonntag* (People on Sunday), became a milestone in the history of filmmaking, and it is mentioned in most film anthologies.

Five young people who created *Menschen am Sonntag* became internationally known: Billy Wilder, whose name is even mentioned in the *Random House Dictionary,* next to Thornton Wilder; Edgar Ulmer, whose inexpensive Hollywood motion pictures are glorified by the young generation of aficionados; Fred Zinnemann, who collected three Hollywood Oscars. Robert was assisted by the cameraman Eugene Schuefftan, who had invented the "Schuefftan process," the mirroring of miniatures into the camera during shooting. My contribution was the idea for that film and, of course, cash. If the Nazis had not driven these gifted young people into the Diaspora, they would have created a flourishing international film industry in Germany. All of them claim credit for having conceived this milestone of picture making. Zinnemann was Schuefftan's camera-focus man. He left for Hollywood after a few days' shooting. Edgar Ulmer, directing for two days, departed for Hollywood, and Robert took over. He put Billy Wilder's name, an unknown reporter at that time, on the credit title as the author of the screenplay. But there was no screenplay. We devised scenes from day to day. I remember that I climbed on the roofs of enormous apartment houses in Berlin, called mischievously *Mietskasernen* (soldiers' barracks for rent), and shot empty backyards with a still camera, a Plaubel Makina, pictures Schuefftan used in the film.

It was Robert's and Schuefftan's devotion and superhuman endurance, shot under the most difficult conditions during nine months of work, that created that picture. Robert reluctantly put my name on the credits but in such small lettering that it seemed to underline Billy Wilder's name: "After an idea by Kurt Siodmak." For Robert, one Siodmak's prominence in the film business, his, was quite sufficient. He never lost that obsessive sibling rivalry to the end of his life.

The theme of *People on Sunday* has been "lifted" a few times. The Italians created *Dominico d'Augusto* (A Sunday in August), the identical story. The English director Sir Carol Reed made the film *Bank Holiday,* with the same theme. A German emigré writer, Hans Wilhelm, sold him that idea as his. Hans, though a gifted storyteller, must have been desperate, trying to make a shilling, a new currency for him. Besides, I only found out thirty years later. By then he had died of lung cancer, smoking too many Gaulois, French cigarettes, which were his nemesis.

People who have no experience with money are rarely aware of its instability. They believe that the stream of currency will continue to flow forever and that the times of want have vanished like sunshine follows fog. I learned late in my life that this process is working in the opposite. Money has a nasty habit of evaporating like helium, which is lighter than air. Robert never found out about the necessity to live on a budget and died poor. In his lifelong search for love, he gave money to people who knew how to cater to him and never asked for a repayment. He never told anybody about his generosity. It was one of his ways to search for "love." In the last years of his life, when he was in financial troubles, none of his "friends" came to his help.

After I had sold my first novel for a substantial sum to the weekly Scherl magazine *Die Woche,* Henrietta went to Switzerland to find a house for her Swiss mother, and also for me, to be able to work away from the disturbing vibrations of the big city that dilutes the energy of writers. In my case, writing, she knew, did not tolerate diversions and needed a monastic solitude.

Since her mother preferred to live in the Italian part of Switzerland, the Tessin, Henrietta found in Barbengo, a small village close to Lugano, the fifteenth-century Palazzo Cenci for rent. Many villages in Tessin like Barbengo were hanging on hillsides, like swallow nests, fortresses against raiding tribes of Saracenes.

Tessin, with its own Italian language that only Ticenese citizens understand, had retained its own gentle character, different and easygoing to the workaholic German-Swiss. Henrietta left Germany to stay there. Robert and I, with a mounting string of successes, were not aware of the darkness of the future. Nor were the Germans, except the inner circle of the future Nazi government that prepared a coming terror that was beyond any citizen's comprehension.

The human disregard for the life of his own species has not changed since the cavemen cracked each other's skulls. In the span of my lifetime, the twentieth century, the human animal has slaughtered hundreds of millions of its own kind, erasing as many people as inhabit Spain and France combined. And what has that carnage to show for those slaughtered lives, except that it delayed human progress that could have led the world to utopia?

But an eight-century-long peace had existed in Switzerland. Henrietta was happy in the Palazzo Cenci in Barbengo with its sweeping view of the Swiss Alps from its balconies. A large staircase led to the upper floor, but there was no heating except a few fireplaces. It was so cold in winter that Henrietta froze her nose in bed, since the thick walls acted like a refrigerator. But the palazzo's thick walls were protection against the extreme summer heat. In July and August, not even the natives ventured out of their homes at the high noon hours. I bought a tiny Electrolux freezer, not bigger than a square foot, a new invention that had just entered the commercial market. A machine that made ice cubes! The villagers came to the "casa" to admire that miracle. I had a warm-water heater installed, a novelty since the Barbengoians did not know what a bathtub was.

There was no running water in their houses, and the women gathered daily at the fountain in the village square to fetch their drinking water and wash their laundry. We were transported back into the eighteenth century. The unpaved village road was above the Cenci garden, parted from it by a wall that threatened to collapse. Who was going to pay for its repair? A Solomonic judge had decided that if the wall fell onto the road, the community had to pay for it since obviously the road was sinking deeper. If the wall collapsed into the Cenci property, that garden had sunk and was responsible for this disaster. But since that wise judgment had been formulated twenty-two years previously, we hoped that the wall would not topple over as long as Henrietta's mother was alive, and if then, toward the road.

The second unsolved judicial fight was the controversy about the trees in the Cenci garden. They were very old and huge. In fall the strong wind blew their leaves onto the roofs of the adjacent houses, clogging the gutters. The neighbors brought a class action suit against the Palazzo Cenci, demanding the trees be cut down. The judge decided, since the trees were older than their houses, they should move their houses.

Thirty years later I and Henrietta revisited the magnificent palazzo. Some members of the Tentori family still lived across the road, small farmers making a starving existence tilling the infertile stony ground. I remember whenever I visited their home at eating time, the family got up from the table, offering me their own plates of food, a gesture of hospitality for centuries.

Maria Tentori, our neighbor's daughter, a young woman who had worked for us as a maid in the Palazzo Cenci, had died in the meantime. Her doctor had never recognized that she was suffering from extreme high blood pressure and had prescribed the wrong medicine, which produced her early death. I remember her lovely face, the very features the Renaissance painters had used as models for their Madonnas. She never was able to marry, since she had devoted her life to her old mother who, paralyzed, was tied down to a wheelchair. Her brother, Giuseppe, had died of mushroom poisoning, though, as a native, he should have known better. When nobody in her family was able to take care of Signora Tentori, she got up from her wheelchair and looked after herself. For twenty years she had pretended to be paralyzed, to keep her daughter and sons in bondage.

In my memory, the palazzo was huge, the garden large, and the staircase leading to the upper floor like one of those in Versailles. Visiting it again after many years, it had shrunk to a building of ordinary size, the garden small, the "sweeping" staircase narrow. Only the view of the faraway Alps was as imposing as I remembered.

Images we emigrants recall about Europe shrink in size after we have lived in America, which is not a country, as Europeans imagine, but a continent. The palazzo was my vacation home, while my work went on in Berlin.

After the sensational success of *Menschen am Sonntag,* UFA engaged Robert as a director. He was on a comfortable weekly salary but didn't know about the bureaucratic intrigues of the modern motion pictures.

Robert needed a vehicle to direct and was looking for one as unusual and intriguing as his first picture. The head of the story department, Fritz Podehl, rejected every one of his suggestions. He seemed to be afraid of "abstract" young talents.

One day Robert, unhappy and frustrated, visited our home in Dahlem. I had just returned from visiting a friend who had rented a room in a neighbor's house. It was the custom of the time to take in lodgers, but rules of conduct were very strict. No sex was permitted among unmarried couples. The vice squad, which was part of the police and a few years later the nucleus of the Gestapo, the Secret Police, would interfere with illegal cohabitation, booking the women as prostitutes.

When I asked the landlady if Mrs. Lersner was at home, the fat hag's face changed color, like that of a turkey's comb, to a purple hue. She snarled, "Are you sure she is a *Mrs.* Lersner?" resenting that the two lived together without the consent of church or state.

That incident, since I lived with Henrietta without having paid our dues to the Bureau of Marriage, gave me the idea for Robert's picture. It was a short subject, but it paved the way to make him the top director at UFA and opened the door to work with internationally known stars for the most prestigious productions in Europe, those of Erich Pommer.

The title of the short film was *Der Kampf mit dem Drachen* (The Battle with the Dragon). It was the story of a lodger and his mean landlady. The lodger was played by Felix Bressart, who after his emigration became a well-known comedian in Hollywood. In the story, before entering the landlady's apartment, he is forced to change his shoes for slippers at the door. One has the embroidered inscription "To comfort" and the other "The weary." Dust carpets cover the furniture. In his room, cluttered with cheap bric-a-brac, a mysterious toilet roll constantly turns, displaying rules of the house: it is forbidden to smoke; it is forbidden to open the iron blinds that keep out the sun; it is forbidden to turn on the lights in daytime—a dozen "verboten" rules. Bressart noiselessly opens the window a crack and blows cigarette smoke through a long pipe that was hidden in a grandfather clock, to the outside. He leaves the room. Since above every door Chinese chimes inform the landlady which door is being opened, even the toilet door plays an appropriate melody. When Bressart returns, he finds a bill for rent and for cleaning "the smoke-soiled drapes." He is aware that the landlady opened the desk drawer that he had locked and had read his letters. In a sudden frenzy, Bressart pulls down the dust sheets covering the furniture and fastens a hammock above the window. Suddenly the landlady stands in the room. Her part was played by Hedwig Wangel, who was a famous stage and film actress but also became one of Hitler's ardent admirers, playing Queen Victoria as a drink-sodden hag in the Nazi propaganda film *Jud Suess*. Gustaf Gruendgens, a gifted actor, who survived the Nazi Goetterdaemmerung, portrayed Victoria's prime minister, Benjamin Disraeli. He slyly inserted Hitler quotations such as "A lie often repeated becomes the truth." Goebbels never became aware of that hidden treason.

As the landlady in her fury lowers the metal blinds, the hammock descends behind her. With great glee Bressart ties her up and starts a wild dance, destroying the bric-a-brac. At the end of his maniacal dance, he pours the coffee she had brought into a huge glass boot. The coffee is so thin that the liquid is transparent. When he breaks the boot, the landlady dies of heart failure.

So far no dialogue had been spoken in the film.

Friedrich Hollaender, who composed the famous songs for Marlene Dietrich and who ran an anti-Hitler cabaret in Berlin, a daringly defiant act that almost cost him his life, devised the music, recording it simultaneously during the shooting of Robert's short. Scoring a motion picture had not been invented.

The second scene plays in a courtroom. Bressart is accused of murder. The jury are people who live as lodgers: a mechanic, a student, a newly married couple, simple people who are too poor to afford their own home. The judge enters and asks for the verdict. The jury decides that the lodger is not guilty, since all of them have lived in rented rooms, dominated by cruel landladies.

Three spoken sentences were the only dialogue in the twelve-minute film. Robert's conception and the surrealistic treatment of *Der Kampf mit dem Drachen* was a novel approach to filmmaking. It was called by the press "surrealistic," a word coined in the twenties, based on Salvador Dali's painting conception.

Robert finished shooting that short in one day. The story department did not interfere, nor had it bothered to read the screenplay. When the film was shown to UFA's staid board of directors, horrified by its abstract conception and sly social criticism, they refused to release it. But Robert, an ingenious public relations man for himself, managed to show it at a preview of a star-studded UFA film in one of the towns in Berlin's outskirts. The next day the film reporters who went to cover the newest UFA superproduction wrote long articles about Robert's twelve-minute abstract film. They gave the short a glowing send-off, as a masterpiece of the future motion picture art. Still, UFA's board of conservative businessmen did not want the short film to be shown in their theaters. Not to let it die without a fight, Robert showed the short in one of UFA's large projection rooms to crew members, secretaries, mail clerks, and other hired people. Erich Pommer, the genius UFA producer who single-handedly made UFA films with international appeal, came by to see it. I saw Pommer, who became Robert's mentor, for the first time and will never forget his startled expression when he left the projection room, impressed by its daring conception and execution.

Unfortunately no print of this picture can be found. The negative must have burned in the firestorm that destroyed UFA's Babelsberg studios fifteen years later.

Robert followed up *The Battle with the Dragon* with a bittersweet love story, *Abschied* (Farewell), written by Emerich Pressburger and

Irmgard von Cube, who later, in America, wrote the novel *Laura,* which started Otto Preminger's Hollywood career as an important director. The idea of *Laura,* in my opinion, had been lifted brazenly from a novel by the author Timothy Thye, who wrote the story of a reporter who, routinely reporting about the murder of a prostitute, falls deeply in love with the dead woman while digging into her past. In von Cube's Hollywood version, she, naturally, isn't in fact dead—who would do such a tragic thing to Gene Tierney?—and *Laura* has a happy ending. But Timothy's original version did not make that compromise, and his honesty made me never forget his story.

Having an original idea is the gods' gift of creativity, the extreme rare nucleus from which every thought, invention, discovery, story, and play in human history emerges. The mysterious power which spawns a thousand imitators. The gift to create is inborn in selected people, a rare occurrence in the history of existence. It is the force that created human progress from the caveman's compulsion to paint images in caves, to the machines that explore celestial bodies.

The 1930s were pregnant with European motion picture talent. Robert, for his film *Abschied,* scouted around for unknown faces, a genial method that had been his success with *Menschen am Sonntag.* In a record store he found a young girl with high-cheeked, almost Asiatic features, Brigitte Horney. She was the daughter of the well-known psychoanalyst, Karen Horney. Robert, with an unfailing sense for discovering future stars, persuaded her to become an actress. He gave her the lead in *Abschied*. This picture was also a trailblazer. The love scene between boy and girl, set in a rented room, was spoiled by the wrong camera exposure. It could not be repeated since the set had already been "struck"—the film expression for dismantling a set. UFA refused to spend additional money on Robert's picture, since it didn't have the required soapy, happy ending, which UFA believed the public wanted. Circumventing UFA's fatal decision, Robert had his cameraman, Schuefftan, photograph a burning cigarette in an ashtray. Only the dialogue of the two lovers was heard in the darkened bedroom, the final love affair of two young people before they parted. Music came from a piano player, practicing in an adjoining room, endlessly repeating Corelli's etudes.

The ash of the burning cigarette in the tray grew longer and longer until it broke off. The critics hailed that symbolism of intercourse as an innovation, a love scene expressed through a surrogate, a young director's ingenious imagination.

Brigitte Horney became a star of screen and theater. I met her in Zurich after the war in 1948 where she played the lead in Bertolt Brecht's *Mother Courage*. Her face, lined and devastated by her war experiences in a bombed-out Germany, had acquired an ageless beauty.

After the success of *Abschied,* Erich Pommer asked Robert to join his production, a unit separate from the rest of the UFA films. Pommer always included the director in the creation of a screenplay, contrary to the Hollywood custom, in which the director was given a script to shoot and the producer was the ultimate judge of the product.

That method now has changed, and the contemporary film stories in America are a hodgepodge of ideas of writers, the director, the financial group, and stars. That's why many American films have no unity in thought and characterization.

Pommer, who loved to work with writers, had devised an ingenuous method to coax the best efforts out of his writers by making them compete with each other. He put a hundred *Pfennige,* one German mark, on the table at the beginning of the story conference. The writers were awarded with coins according to ideas that they contributed to the screenplay during the working session. It was a hard battle to receive a few *Pfennige* from the kitty. The one who caged most of the coins by the end of the session was the champion of the day.

It is a curse in my life that many of my ideas are ten years ahead of the contemporary trend. There never was a public run for the first edition of any of my books. It always took years before the "trend" caught up with their content. That's why I never made "the big money" like some writers of today. When Alfred Knopf published the original edition of my novel *Donovan's Brain* in 1943, it was sold as a two-dollar hardcover book. I was paid 10 percent, twenty cents, a copy. To find that same novel now in its original edition has a four hundred dollar value for sci-fi aficionados. United Artists, which owns the copyright of that novel, now asks for one million dollars for its television rights. And I had given all film rights away for the grand sum of $1,950, because I needed cash to feed my family.

If I had known at the time that some books of mine would become sci-fi collectors' items, I would have stored away a few hundred copies, also of my screenplays, which I never kept. *Der Mann der Seinen Moerder Sucht* was a film story of the Pommer production that Robert directed. I tried to sell it in London during my emigration, with devastating results since it may have instigated the German producer Frederick Fellner's suicide. It also was the first vehicle for Heinz Ruehmann, who then for half a century became the foremost actor of comedies in German theater and film productions. He became an ardent admirer of the Nazis and was Hitler's pet. He survived the war and died in 1992.

The Pommer version of *The Man Looking for His Murderer* was praised by the critics but unfortunately not by the public. Twenty years later Philippe de Broca, a French director, repeated the idea in *Les Tribulations d'un Chinois en Chine*. His film was a public success. Our version was too abstract in its surrealistic technique to be understood by the general public.

Robert and I parted creative company, he exploding like a comet in Germany's film business, I returning to my typewriter to turn out novels.

I didn't work with Robert again until 1939, when he arrived, penniless, six years later with his wife in Hollywood, one day before the outbreak of World War II.

We were accepting the fact that we lived in Paradise and that this condition would never change, oblivious of the precarious condition that the world, as we knew it, would soon collapse completely and send us penniless into exile.

In 1932 we were convinced that the future had immense possibilities, since at that time I was perhaps the most published author in Germany. I had no difficulty finding a weekly magazine to publish my novels, and my publisher, William Goldmann, accepted every one of my books. As soon as I had completed a novel, I immediately started another one. A compulsive writer, it really didn't matter to me whether I worked in Germany, Italy, or France; at our rented palazzo in Barbengo in Switzerland, in a Bavarian inn, or at our apartment in Berlin. I carried my office with me, a ream of paper and my small typewriter. We drove a Harley Davidson 1200 cc motorcycle, which I had bought from the Barbengo post office. It had been used as a letter carrier up and down the steep mountain, and we drove through Europe, Henrietta in the sidecar, on which our luggage was fastened.

I wrote a novel, *Downtown Madonna*, in Burgebrach, a peaceful village in Bavaria, where I rented rooms in a charming inn. Every village in Bavaria had its own beer brewery. We watched the geese getting drunk on the dregs of fermented brewery hops, swaying on uneasy feet over the country road. We were surprised that guests at the inn guzzled down seven quarts of local beer for dinner. After a few weeks I imbibed four, Henrietta consumed two, to conform with the local habit. The *Muenchner Illustrietre* serialized *Downtown Madonna,* and the Wilhelm Goldmann Verlag published the hardcover. I wrote the first draft of *F.P. 1 Does Not Answer* on Porquerolle, a small island opposite Marseille. Always in flux, staying in each place only for a while, we would change to another location. Europe was our backyard.

Whenever we crossed a border, we put the leftover currency into a wallet, the "General Bum," which took money to keep for the next visit. That small amount of foreign currency saved our lives when we were driven out of Germany.

On the research for my next novel, *To the End of the World,* we traveled on a German tramp freighter from Bremerhaven in Germany to Italy. I had just bought the newest invention, a portable radio, which worked on a wet battery. The dry battery had not yet been invented. I connected that wooden box to the ship's antenna, and sailing through the Bay of Biscay, we could listen to classical music from Sweden. It was as if we owned the boat, being the only passengers except for a honeymoon couple from Sweden.

The captain hated passengers and during a storm came to our cabin, chewing gum and spitting on the floor, trying to get us seasick, which we didn't. But we became friends. He let me steer the boat, which was driven by a turbine, the newest invention in shipbuilding. I learned to keep the ship on an even keel and not to let it sway, a movement that was difficult to stop. The boat, having passed through the Strait of Gibraltar, finally arrived in Barcelona. From there the *Conte Biancomano,* an Italian luxury liner, took us to Genoa. I needed the experience of first-class travel for my novel *To the End of the World,* which had a glamorous ship as its background. That trip, which lasted only nineteen hours, was more expensive than the three-week journey from Bremerhaven to Barcelona. Henrietta resented that expense and ate through the whole first-class ship's menu, but since she did not know the difference between *uova* and *ova,* eggs and grapes, she got eggs ten times that day.

The crew was not cooperative. Genoa was their home port, and they couldn't wait to get off the ship, as did four hundred Italian workers whom the boat carried back to Italy from Argentina.

From Genoa we boarded the train to the seaport of La Specia, and a horse-drawn carriage—the Italians didn't have many automobiles at that time—took us to the small town of Lerici. A strange, overpowering scent accompanied us on this trip. It was the first time that we smelled the blossoms of orange trees, which we could not see since we traveled during a very dark night. In Lerici we rented a small house, "La Scala Santa" (The Holy Stairs), from Signora Barracini, and had to climb 120 steps to reach it, which kept us in good physical shape. The house overlooked the bay with its harbor and the castle where Lord Byron and his friend the poet Percy Bysshe Shelley had stayed a century ago. There Shelley's eighteen-year-old wife, Mary, wrote the original *Frankenstein* novel in 1805. Ten years later that book shaped my Hollywood career.

The Italians were very conservative people, and one had to obey certain rituals to be accepted by them. They are used to foreigners, which they call "Inglesi" (Englishmen), because in the nineteenth century rich British society used to spend the winter months in that country.

It would have been considered bad manners to coldly turn the monthly rent over to the landlady, Signora Barracini. That routine had to follow a social procedure. At the end of the month Signora would be sitting at the open window at the farmer's house, which was situated at number 60 of the 120 torturous steps leading to our rented place. She was always dressed in black and sported a faint black mustache. She was busy knitting. When I passed by, I had to greet her with "Buon giorno, Signora" (Good day, Signora). "Buon giorno, Signor Corrado," she would reply. *Corrado* was "Kurt" in Italian, as I found out. The second day I had to stop at the window *per fare un po' de conversacione*, making conversation in my primitive Italian. On the third day, more conversation took place, ending with the reminder of "il conto," "Domani, domani!" Tomorrow! The next day Signora came puffing up to our little house. She brought a bottle of Chianti, which we emptied. When she was going to leave, I reminded her of the bill, and she produced an itemized slip of paper: rent, charcoal, firewood, wine, and diverse items, like delicious squid that she had bought for us at the fish market. The paper carried the legal tax stamps with the face of Umberto, the king. I checked the items and found that Signora had made a mistake in her favor. She apologized and corrected that error.

That routine never changed during the months we lived at the Scala Santa.

I was busy writing when my friend Ossip Kalenter visited us. His real name was the very Germanic Johannes Burghardt, but when the

German Jews, after World War I, converted their names, like Isaac Levy into Fritz Stahl, in protest he changed his to Ossip Kalenter. He had found that name, "Ossip Kalenter," a detective character in Frank Wedekind's *Lulu,* a morbid stage play in which Jack the Ripper kills prostitutes. Ossip had Maria, a thin, tall, black-haired girl, with him, whom he had found in a circus. He asked us shyly whether we had any objection that he was living with her out of wedlock. We did not object.

Ossip was one of very few of my German friends who left Germany of their free will, in disgust, when Hitler came to power. He was an excellent writer of short stories and essays, a stylist who helped me edit my novel, urging me to take my time in descriptions, a shortcoming that I had to correct. Having started out as a reporter, I was trained to express myself as skimpily as possible. Maria, having escaped the insecure life of the circus, wanted time to stand still forever. Nothing should change. The wind, which blew dead leaves over the road, frightened her, since that was change.

But the gentle Ossip also had a dark soul. He discovered that the local butcher, Ovidio, hated his wife but could not get a divorce, since he was Catholic like all Italians. One day Ovidio asked me whether the Jews have the same religion as the Protestants, a proof of how detached from the world the Italians lived in their small villages. La Specia's newspaper printed a horrible story: "La donna tagliata in pezzi" (The woman cut to pieces). The police had discovered a wicker basket in the storeroom of the railway station with the corpse of a disemboweled woman, a murder that excited Ovidio. Ossip watched the butcher expertly handling sharp knives. He found for Ovidio books in Italian about Landru, the French mass murderer of females. Maybe, just maybe, they might induce the butcher to cut up his wife, which would give Ossip an eyewitness chance to write about a murder.

When the novel was finished we drove the Harley back to Berlin, which was brewing with a fever that destroyed our pleasant way of living.

I wish I had Henrietta's perspicacity about the history in which we lived. Not being German, she saw the situation of that country without my inborn love for it. She insisted on staying in our rented palazzo in Switzerland. It was a pleasant place to work, but I kept our apartment in Berlin and spent my earnings as though they would be perpetual. I should've thought of the future and saved.

Henrietta, very unhappy, could not put her presentiment into words.

Many years later, she confessed that she knew that nothing could have persuaded me to leave my native country, except personally witnessing the coming upheaval. Robert and I dismissed Henrietta's premonition as an outcome of her condition. She was pregnant. Besides, mounting social and political changes happened not only in Germany but in every country of the Western world, even in America with its 25 percent unemployment rate. We disregarded the brewing upheaval, accepting it as just one of the political changes that took place in every country. I, a blind mouse, did not comprehend the urgency to start a new existence abroad. And why should I? The *Berliner Illustrierte* had just accepted my latest novel, *To the End of the World*. It was the ultimate dream of a writer to see his novel serialized in that prestigious weekly magazine. That was the culmination of any writer's fame.

The chief editor of the *Illustrierte* was a Viennese Jew, Georg Froeschl, who had served in the Austrian cavalry in World War I, when there was still heroic fighting with sabers. We met a few years later in Hollywood, both of us refugees. Georg Froeschl—"small frog" in English translation—had Americanized his first name to George. He had found employment at the MGM Studios in Hollywood, which he held until that company collapsed twenty years later. When Froeschl arrived in Hollywood, his agent, Paul Kohner, who represented most Jewish emigrants and looked after them with compassion, introduced Froeschl to Arthur Freed, the successful producer of MGM musicals. The following day Froeschl had a job. Kohner never told him that Freed had phoned him the same night after their meeting, deeply disturbed by the visible desperation in that refugee's face. George always believed that his personality had overwhelmed the MGM producer.

The American Jews in Hollywood helped Jewish refugees from Hitler by offering them small jobs, a charity that the powerful studios could well afford. Froeschl, the ideal company man, complemented the personality of Freed, a man with little formal education. He used the erudite Viennese as an ambulatory encyclopedia, since Froeschl "knew" the answer to any encyclopedic question that Freed threw at him. Freed didn't know that Froeschl sometimes made up those replies, knowing that his boss would never check them. Troubled by insecurities, Freed needed a constant admirer and yes-man, a job that Froeschl fulfilled to perfection. I believe that every one of the highly remunerated studio executives lived in constant fear of losing his job.

When I worked at Universal Studios, I went to my producer's office every Thursday afternoon to tell him what a gifted man he was, expecting he would find out that I was kidding. He never became aware of it and seemed to need that assurance. But the insecurity of executives also created monsters. Stories of studio cruelties were abundant. Harry Cohn, who ruled Columbia Studios like a South American dictator, was a womanizer who liked to invite starlets to studio parties, obviously to soften them up for an affair. To prove his omnipotence, he asked the young women to point out anybody they wanted him to fire. Darryl Zanuck, Twentieth Century's boss, worked in a huge office whose door could only be opened electronically from his desk. A young dancer I knew was ordered to see him for a job. When the door closed, he approached her with his fly open. But she had the presence of mind to tell him that she was married and that her husband was the head of the California Highway Patrol. That information made Zanuck pull up the zipper of his pants in a hurry.

The "casting couch" was one of the routines young actresses had to go through to get signed up for a part. Some studio executives had their preference in women. Zanuck's female stars had buckteeth, an irresistible attraction to him. MGM had call girls on the payroll, booked off as contract players. They visited the producers on demand. Though I worked in Hollywood studios for more than twenty years, I failed to see any improprieties, nor did I come across an illegitimate affair. Being a writer who did not have the power to assign jobs, I only met hardworking people, maniacally dedicated to the task of creating motion pictures, limited in their conversation, which boringly was about stories, assignments, and their frustration that their excellent screenplay had been butchered by the director and stupid, conceited actors.

I believe I only met two really amoral people in my life. Both lacked the ability to consider other people's feelings. One was a German police inspector, Hubert Muehlfriedl, and the other one was Georg Froeschl. When I, in Hollywood, years later reminded him that, as the editor of the *Illustrierte* in Berlin, he had the courage to buy my novel *To the End of the World* for his magazine, despite the rising anti-Semitism of the "Thousand Year Reich," he told me that when he saw me in my black motorcycle coat, he believed me to be a Nazi. He thought like a Nazi and was looking for a Nazi author.

"If I had known that you were a Jew, I'd have thrown you out right away," he told me in his spacious house in Beverly Hills. An Austrian Jew, he forgot that he would have ended up in a concentration camp! Though twenty years had passed since both of us were forced to leave Germany, he still seemed to resent that the freakish incident of having been born a Jew had prevented him from being accepted by a fascistic movement that he, I am certain, admired. He had been married for forty years to his secretary, Else, a charming gentle woman who, though not Jewish, had stuck with him during the hard times of emigration. In her later years, in their home in Beverly Hills, she suffered a stroke and died. George complained that she should have died earlier. That would have given him a chance to get married again to a younger wife.

George had the mentality of a man who, without emotion, runs a concentration camp. He was brought up in the old-fashioned Austrian spirit, music-loving, erudite, of an intelligence that died in Austria and Germany when the "movement" forcibly eliminated the mental elite. Forever admiring the times when Emperor Joseph of Hapsburg ruled that country, George suffered from the injustice of having been ostracized by his native society.

It still strikes me as ridiculous that people are hurt by not being "accepted." The Los Angeles Country Club did not let Jews pass through its gate. But I wouldn't like to be a member of that outfit in any case. The Jews in Beverly Hills have their own golf club and don't accept gentiles. From time to time they grant a non-Jew an honorable membership.

Groucho Marx, the comedian, said, "I would never be a member of a club that accepts me!" pointing out the absurdity of exclusivity. Froeschl's remark that he, a Jew, would have "thrown me out because I was Jewish" explained to me the self-hatred and inferiority complex, which after a millennium of rejection by Christians, exist among members of that Middle Eastern tribe. Is it based on a yearning to be accepted as an equal in countries in which they were only considered as guests? The Jews also are a closed society, basically as exclusive as those nations that have rejected them through history. This would seem to be the fault of that desert tribe, which never had any missionaries and accepts gentiles only reluctantly into their faith.

How often we could have lost our lives, skirting death by inches, walked over a bridge, as Robert and I did, that collapsed minutes later. Once, in the south of France, away from the disturbing distraction of Berlin, Henrietta and I scaled up a sheer cliff in tennis shoes to get to the top of it. Why we tried that perilous ascent I don't know. The reason must have been temporary insanity. Halfway up the soil became brittle and gave way, breaking up in clumps. I remember looking down at the road hundreds of feet below, which skirted the blue Mediterranean. It was impossible to climb back; we had to go on. I already visualized our broken bodies lying at the foot of that cliff, picked up by an ambulance, and being stared at by impassive pedestrians.

It is curious how unmoved we are when we watch the scene of an accident, convinced of our own immortality. Dragging Henrietta along with one hand, I finally reached the top, embracing a small tree with my right arm, lifting her up with a strength I didn't know I possessed. The tree was our anchor between life and death. I assured her that I wouldn't let go of her and that now we were safe. I still clutched the slim wood stem that stood between us and death two hundred feet below, while she wailed that she could not hold the liquid in her bladder any longer.

Looking back, I know it was the same insanity that made me return to Berlin from the safe haven of Switzerland. We had very little cash abroad, and I wanted to collect money due to me from UFA and the Ullstein publishers, though I still was not completely convinced that we would have to leave Germany forever.

A few days before, I had been in Zurich to have my German passport renewed. The local German consul, Wilhelm Franken, extended my passport for four years. He was a confused and frightened old man, afraid for his job, given that position by the then-defunct Weimar Republic. He asked me how long I thought the National-Socialist Party would last. He expected that it would disappear in a couple of months. The hostile faces of the consular employees, wearing the same cruel bellicose expression that I soon was to encounter in many German faces, are still etched in my mind.

At my arrival, Berlin was like a giant carnival. The pressure cooker had blown off its lid. Thousands of Hitler Youth in brown shirts marched to the sound of a song I had never heard before but that soon burned itself into my memory: "The Horst Wessel Song." Horst Wessel was an SA man killed by the "Reds" and had become the Nazis' martyr. The Kurfuerstendamm, Berlin's main thoroughfare, was lined with a hundred thousand people, waving hysterically and screaming, "Our Brown Shirts are coming!" When, shaken and bewildered, I arrived at our apartment in the Pfalzburgerstrasse, I felt that the ground under my feet had given way. Among my accumulated mail I found an official letter, signed by the National-Socialistic Authors Union, an organization I did not know existed, informing me that I was not permitted to publish any of my writings in Germany.

The Nazis had done their homework thoroughly and had every opponent and Jew in their files. There also was a printed notice with the swastika on its letterhead, an "invitation" by Dr. Joseph Paul Goebbels, "Minister of Propaganda and National Enlightenment," to attend a meeting at the Hotel Kaiserhof. The date was March 28, 1933.

I was climbing the cliff again, but without a saving tree on the top. The Nazis could have arrested the Jewish members of the German film industry who attended that meeting: Erich Pommer, Fritz Lang; film directors Hans Schwartz, William Thiele, and half a dozen more; the famous actor's agent Elizabeth Blumann; and dozens of writers, among them me. About three hundred filmmakers were waiting, worrying about what Goebbels had to say. Our lives could have been finished that very day, but the Nazi movement had not yet reached its ultimate momentum, which gave many of us the respite to escape the Holocaust.

Goebbels appeared on the stage in the big swastika-decorated ballroom. I saw the new uniformed breed of Germans now in close-up and discovered the same glassy inhuman look I had discovered in the eyes of the German employees of Mr. Franken's consulate in Zurich.

Goebbels, uniformed, wearing the Nazi logo on his sleeve, limped onto the stage. He was a dark-haired, small man with a clubfoot, certainly not the type the Nazis visualized as a Nordic. Nor was the dark-haired Adolf Hitler a prototype of the blonde Teutonic idol. He was not even German-born. An Austrian, he had been naturalized only a few months previously before the senile General Hindenburg, the figurehead of the German government, had made him "Reichskanzler." Goebbels looked like the caricature of a Jew in Himmler's Nazi paper *Der Stuermer*.

Goebbels announced that he was taking over the German film industry and had certain ideas of the kind of pictures he was going to produce. He stated that the world was not as pictured in the brains of Jewish film directors or writers. He then mentioned the kind of films he was going to produce. Films with national patriotic content, like Sergei Eisenstein's *Potemkin,* Fritz Lang's *Nibelungen* and *Metropolis,* Kurt Bernhardt's *Last Company, F.P. 1 Does Not Answer,* though I was not aware that I had written a film with nationalsocialist tendencies, and others, twelve altogether, of which eleven were written and produced by Jews. Now since the National-Socialists were in power, he confessed that his party had taken advantage of the insipid democratic laws of the Weimar Republic to reach its goal but that from now on a new order would direct Germany, without being softened by Jewish decadence.

Only then it fully dawned on me the truth of Henrietta's premonition, which she could not express as clearly as Joseph Goebbels in his speech. A black void was staring me in the face. When I left the Kaiserhof with a silent subdued crowd, none of the people who had listened to Goebbels dared to voice an opinion. Louis Ralph, the actor and an acquaintance of mine, walked behind me. "Now it will be our turn," he said, with a threatening undertone in his voice as though the Jews had prevented him from becoming a good actor.

That day was the demise of the great German film industry, which has not recovered since. Even today, sixty years later, it supplies only 8 percent of the films shown in Germany. Seventy-two percent of the motion pictures shown in Germany are imported from Hollywood, the rest being produced by foreign countries.

I had to stay two days in Berlin to get a payment from Ullstein, which was still publishing my novel *To the End of the World* in the *Berliner Illustrierte.* Ullstein, the Jewish-owned publishing house, lived up to its obligation.

I also went to UFA, where I still had monies coming to me for *F.P. 1 Does Not Answer.* To my surprise the head of that company, Hugo Correll, received me in his office. I was aware that he was shocked by the bloodless revolution, which did not care about legalities and ruled by fiat. Correll told me that he had received an order to dismiss certain directors, writers, and employees and that all payments to them were stopped and the contracts canceled. He did not mention the word *Jew.*

I asked him, "What's happened to decency?" "This is no time for decency" was his historic reply. It certainly wasn't. The meaning of ethics had changed overnight. Even the churches kowtowed to the new political wave without resistance. The democratic spirit, which the Weimar Republic for fifteen years had tried to instill in the Germans, proved to be hollow. It needed a world war, and the complete destruction of Germany's infrastructure, to instill in the German nation the true meaning of democracy and the understanding of the value of freedom and personal liberties, which had never existed in Germany. Correll died of heart failure shortly after our meeting. It might have been his way to escape the "new order," which had destroyed his concept of honor. He was replaced by a party member.

Afraid to return to my apartment, I traveled about in my Chrysler car. Fred, my mechanic, came with me. He asked me to drive by his apartment house, afraid the Gestapo might wait for him. He belonged to the Socialist Party, whose members were hunted by the new masters of Germany.

We drove to the outskirts of Berlin for a last look at the Wannsee with its sailboats, the beautiful lake where Erich Pommer's villa overlooked the water. Pommer had left Berlin for Paris. He took the train but had ordered his chauffeur to wait for him in Hanover. There, obviously warned by a friend, he left the train and crossed the French border in his car into exile.

The Wannsee was crowded with bathers as if no revolution were taking place in Germany. The picture of a pretty girl, emerging from the water like Venus, is still etched in my mind. Dressed in an abbreviated white bathing suit and pushing back her long dark hair, she looked at me with the innocent come-on smile of a teenager, aware of her sensual attractiveness. Swans crossed the water behind her. By Nazi decree she was off-limits for anybody who was not a full-blooded Aryan and the carrier of suitable genes to build the coming thousand-year Reich.

I remember Fred, the mechanic, painfully pressing my hand, his voice shaking as he said, "Come back soon." It took thirty years to visit Berlin again.

Should you be forced to leave your home in a great hurry, on account of a fire, an earthquake, or any other emergency like the invasion of a horde of Nazis, which of your belongings do you take? If you own a house, might you grab the cat? Should there be a fire, you'd better get out as fast as possible and forget about the cat and save your life.

When you leave a country forever, what do you take with you? Henrietta's ingenious grandmother, Françoise de Perrot, always anticipating emergencies in her life, kept her valuables on a cloth on a small table. In case of an emergency, she could just pick up the tablecloth by its four corners with the jewels inside. I had no jewels to take along.

I was packing my small suitcase, the same with which I had arrived two days previously, with essentials. I had to leave my books behind. My typewriter, the only indispensable tool in my life, was in Barbengo. I hesitated to take along my unfinished manuscript, *The Street of Hope*. What was the use of finishing it? Who would publish it? Half a year later the *Koelner Illustrierte*, a minor magazine, printed it. My friend Ossip signed as the author with his Teutonic name Johannes Burghardt. The editor, who could have gotten himself in deep trouble by breaking the Nuremberg law, since he knew the novel was written by a Jew, told Ossip that he would buy any of my writings, if he could publish it under a fictitious name. Half a century later I found a copy of *The Street of Hope* among my manuscripts. I was shocked by my description of Germany before the collapse of the Weimar Republic. Had the rising nationalism that culminated in the Nazi movement also brainwashed my thinking like that of a jingoistic Teuton? Were we hopelessly conditioned by the pervasive atmosphere around us? I had written about a group of bored, rich young people without ambition or aim, who for the thrill of it, mugged and robbed a man who was carrying a payroll to the bank. They tried to shift the blame onto a poor boy, offering to pay him handsomely if he would confess that he had single-handedly carried out that crime. A government employee, running a youth camp, took over the whole gang and reshaped them into disciplined citizens.

The novel, as it dawned on me fifty years later, had an implied Nazi spirit: a "Youth Camp," the kind the Nazis created a couple of years later, demanding utter subordination toward the "leader," a man whose orders were not permitted even to be questioned. It was a vision of the Nazi rules to come. I regret that I threw the manuscript away, the only copy in existence. It might have helped me to understand better the twisted morality of that period.

When the majority of Germans finally became aware of the spiderweb in which they were caught, their country was lying in ruins, and five million of their young men had been killed.

I was still packing some belongings in my apartment in the Pfalzburgerstrasse, when suddenly all the lights in Berlin went out. The Nazis had shut off the electricity and marched through the streets in endless columns, carrying torches. They wore brown shirts with the swastika on their sleeves. They passed my window, goose-stepping toward the Kurfuerstendamm. The sound of their boots pounding the pavement has never left my ears. They sang their theme song, the "Horst Wessel Song," and a new song that I had not heard: "The trooper storms into the field in a brave and happy mood. If Jewish blood stains the knife he wields, then it is twice as good."

I made the mistake of picking up the telephone and calling Martin, my old friend, who had helped me to sell my first novel to the *Woche*. Eva, his wife, answered. She sounded terrified. Martin was not at home but told me that he would get in touch with me later. I understood. He was afraid to speak to a Jew.

I hung up. My pregnant wife in another country, no substance abroad, no chance to work, no ability to speak any other language fluently—where to go? What to do? There were two nights in my life when I reached the depth of despair. That night in darkened Berlin was the first. It made me a Jew again, a state of mind I had forgotten.

It was the condemnation of the guiltless, Harmatia, the ancient decision of the gods, which even condemned the innocent. There was nothing to repent, nothing that could have changed my condition. My destiny was that I was born in a country that wanted to see me dead, because the Germans were ordered to do so by a pied piper, who, as they found out too late, was the greatest enemy their country ever had. Adolf Hitler, an Austrian, who had become a German by decree, a man whose terrible childhood had created in him a complex too intricate to be analyzed by anyone except psychiatrists. A sociopath, gifted with the persuasion of the rat catcher of Hamelin, who, playing his pipe, led the children of that town to oblivion.

The doorbell rang. Hubert Muehlfriedl was standing outside. Hubert, an inspector of the German police, had been my paid assistant for much of my research for my novels and motion pictures. He was a small, powerfully built man with a round, childlike face. He carried a briefcase.

"Where is your passport?" he asked. It was like sitting in a movie watching an action that was unreal and two-dimensional. It didn't occur to me that Hubert could have pocketed my passport and have me arrested. He was wearing a swastika on his sleeve.

"This is an identification not to be molested in the street. The boys might take me for a Jew, because I'm not blue-eyed like you." I remember that he laughed at his morbid joke. He took a rubber stamp from the briefcase and stamped my passport, then filled out a form that he signed. "Here is your exit visa for Switzerland. Your car is still in front. We better get you out of here fast. Do you have gas in your car?"

I didn't know why he wanted to save me. I soon found out.

"I'm taking you to Basel," he said. Basel was six hundred miles away. It was the town at the German-Swiss border one had to pass. Basel Bad station was in Germany, and Basel Hauptbahnhof was in Switzerland.

"The Gestapo is going to arrest the Jews in Berlin at midnight," he said. "You will be among them."

I asked him what my crime had been. Writing an internationally acclaimed motion picture like *F.P. 1*?

"That won't help you. Your crime is that you chose the wrong parents."

He had changed since I had seen him last. The swastika on his sleeve had instilled a new power in him. Even his voice sounded different. He had shed the cloak of courtesy.

A couple of years ago he had taken a group of filmmakers to the red light district of Hamburg, the "Reeperbahn," which he knew well as a member of the vice squad. My friend Frederick Kohner was with me. Fred, in later years in America, originated the character of "Gidget" in one of his novels. The word *Gidget* is now accepted in American dictionaries as the prototype of the American teenager.

I needed background research for the film *The Man Looking for His Murderer*. Hubert knew the Hamburg underworld well. He took us to a bordello where two women performed with a dildo. They had to send to another house to borrow that gadget. I remember that we, a group of five, unaccustomed to kinky sex, were huddled in a corner like frightened chickens, watching the two women with embarrassment. On the way back to Berlin we passed an accident on the highway. A motorcycle had crashed into a tree. The driver's face was smashed into a bloody pulp. The girl who had been riding with him was unharmed. We gave the hysterical teenager a lift and followed the ambulance. Since there was no room in the back of the car, she sat on Hubert's lap. She buried her face in her hands, while Hubert raped her. He bragged to me later about that act. Maybe I could use that incident in a novel, he suggested, the thrill of using a girl who had just escaped death, her helplessness and submission, the surge of her orgasms that followed in quick succession and that he described minutely with the relish of macho power. He philosophized about the close relation of sex and death, since the sex act is basically one of murderous brutality.

A couple of years ago, when I needed research for my novel *Downtown Madonna,* we drove with my Harley to Moabit, through the darkest ghettos of Berlin. Hubert sat in the sidecar. He took me to a beer restaurant, the hangout of underworld characters and prostitutes. I had never been aware that a place of such depravity existed. The year was 1931, and Germany had seven million unemployed, a fertile ground for Hitler's coming revolution. Hubert was well known at that tavern. The noisy inebriated guests knew that he was a policeman but treated him as one of their own. As soon as he sat down, two steins with beer were set in front of us, but when I wanted to pay, Hubert stopped me. Drinks for him were on the house. He had ordered a couple of young boys to watch my motorcycle. A teenage prostitute came to the table. She was in obvious despair. She told him that her father, whenever she returned home, attacked her sexually, beating her if she refused. Hubert wrote down her address and went to the telephone. He returned after a few minutes. "You can go home in a couple of hours," he told her. "Your father will be arrested for incest, and you won't see him for a long time. The apartment is yours. I will come and see if you are all right." He ended his good deed with an implication: "But don't let me find any dope."

When I was eighteen, studying at the Dresden Technische Hochschule, the use of drugs was common among students. Opium, cocaine, and chloroform were easily acquired. Chloroform was the substitute for ether. I got opium from a friend of mine, a veterinarian who prescribed ten grains of opium, which one could get in any pharmacy, "to administer to a horse." The opium had to be cooked in a special small pipe. Taking a few puffs made me aware that I could solve all the riddles in the world. That knowledge could be so easily obtained that I wouldn't even bother to formulate it. But I didn't trust those powers when I was sober and forced myself to write down the cosmic truth. "The banana has green leaves" was the answer. I gave up smoking that brown gooey stuff, which made me see the world distorted, though as sharply as though looking through a prism, when one day I found myself in a landscape of Hieronymus Bosch's devils, horrifying creatures with wings and claws, fire spouting from their eyes. That "bummer," that terrifying vision, cured me for life from ever using drugs again.

There never was a time in human history without the use of drugs. Our pious grandparents took patent medicines spiked with opium, the men against the cough, the women against their monthly cramps. I once met a Catholic nun in Switzerland. Her only conversation was that in spring she suffered from hay fever and the only cure for it was a sniff of cocaine. She waited the whole year for spring to return. I was sure that the prophets of the Bible were on dope or suffered mental deprivation like the hermits who let themselves be walled in for days, to experience holy ecstasies.

Hubert, with his aberrant kindness toward thieves and whores and his understanding of the inborn instincts of criminals, was never aware of his own amorality.

He enjoyed the power of the Chrysler, of which only a few could be found in Germany. I had bought that car only a couple of months ago from rich Jews, who had studied Hitler's book *Mein Kampf,* in which he had revealed his coming strategy. They were convinced that he would carry out his threats, had cashed all of their assets and left Germany with their fortune intact. They had anticipated what Neville Chamberlain had not foreseen, convinced that no deal was possible with that German "Messiah."

That night we drove through Halle, Ehrfurt, and other sleeping towns. It was a dreamlike, irrational journey, and I had the feeling that the landscape we traveled through sank behind me into a void to disappear forever. Germany, except for Berlin, had no big cities. It was a rural country, the small towns self-contained, populated by hardworking, primitive but efficient people, xenophobic and convinced that Germany was superior to any other country in the world.

We stopped only to fill up the tank, being in a great hurry to reach the border.

Knowing that we would never see each other again, Hubert gave away secrets, which he ordinarily never would have revealed to me. He had been a party member for eleven years, since the aborted Hitler-armed Bierhalle uprising in 1922 in Munich. He now had become a member of the Gestapo, the secret state police. They had sent him to Switzerland to befriend a German who had fled the Nazi revolution and whom the Nazis wanted. Posing as a commercial traveler for Siemens, the huge industrial concern, he described how he became intimate with the official of the labor unions who was hiding in Switzerland. Hubert had been equipped with all necessary documents to prove his fake identity. His victims, knowing they would be sent to a concentration camp if the Gestapo got hold of them, believed Hubert and used his identifications to cross the border. Again and again, the men asked him if they would be safe, and one even put his arms around Hubert. Hubert, hiding behind his boyish, innocent face, assured them that the papers would get them safely across. Penniless, the socialist officials wanted to return to their wives and children. Hubert also found out whom they would contact in Germany, revealing their underground connections. All, including their helpers, were promptly arrested.

He told me that story, his voice choked with sentimental emotion, genuinely sorry for those poor people whom he had sent to their doom. But he had to carry out a job. He talked about his philosophy, which contradicted his emotion: Stage 1 is that your deceitful action hurts you; you hate to deceive your victims. At stage 2, you pretend to be sorry for them. The third stage is enjoyment, to watch the victim's terror and helplessness and complete submission to their fate. A spider wrapping with insects in his net, Hubert was aware that he had reached the third stage.

It was the first time that I became aware of his hidden anti-Semitism, which for years he had cleverly camouflaged.

"Then why do you take me to Switzerland?" I asked him, aware of the abyss that suddenly opened between us.

"I will tell you when we reach the border," he said ominously.

The sun came up when we drove through Mannheim, where we bought some food, which Hubert munched during the journey. I could not swallow a bite. The trip was almost metaphysical and unreal, like the times that followed my forced emigration. Not to look back was my only self-defense left. I could only go forward. If awareness of the difficulties of the times ahead of me had caught up with me, I would not have found the strength to continue living. Now, half a century later, sheltered in a new country where I have lived many years longer than in the land where I was born, ghosts arise from the depth of a snake pit of suppressed fears to torture me.

The sun was setting again when we finally reached the Swiss border. Hubert drove me to Basel Bahnhof, which was guarded by Nazi soldiers carrying machine guns. We had driven for twenty-two hours, stopping also in Frankfurt at midday. That city was in a turmoil, teeming with uniformed Nazis who didn't bother us when they recognized the swastika on Hubert's sleeve.

"Now you can tell me why you did all this for me," I said. Had I misjudged him, and had he been a friend?

"You could have figured that out yourself in your clever Jewish brain. If the SS had gotten you, they would have kept your car and apartment. I will take care of your apartment and your car 'til you come back, if you ever come back," Hubert said.

I safely crossed the border, carrying my small suitcase. I had bought my life for the price of an automobile and an apartment. It was a small fee to pay.

The Swiss put a stamp in my German passport, without asking questions. One year later they added a second stamp: "Jew." The Nazis accepted that racial information. I did not watch Hubert leave in his newly acquired Chrysler. It was like having passed through a tunnel with fear and impending death on one side and freedom on the other. Substantial Swiss citizens were sitting on the terraces of restaurants, drinking hot chocolate and eating cake. No soldiers with machine guns could be seen anywhere, though only half a mile away the horror of an impending Walpurgisnacht was brewing, a nightmare that lasted for twelve years and that, with its government-sponsored cruelties, had no equal in history.

When I visited Germany in 1962, I inquired about Hubert Muehlfriedl. I learned that the Russians had arrested him at the end of the war and imprisoned him. He must have been a very high-ranking Nazi, according to his devotion and unflinching belief in the Fuehrer. After having been in solitary confinement for nine years, he hanged himself.

One of the most potent aphrodisiacs in life is to be wanted. To be inside the business. For that happy circumstance one has to be young. Youth is a club that expels its members without reason when they get older. Sixty-five seems to be the deadline. Even the most famous old motion picture directors, however successful they might have been in the past, cannot find work after a certain age. The writers are not afflicted by age. They send their work in by mail, and no publisher would reject a book because the author is over sixty-five.

The last picture Robert did, Felix Dahn's voluminous historical novel *The Battle of Rome,* he directed under difficult circumstances with a cast of Orson Welles, Laurence Harvey, and the English beauty Honor Blackman.

Since the human body is a battery that in later life cannot be fully recharged, Robert never really recovered from the ordeal after he directed that picture in a primitive country like Romania. He even imported Anne-Liese, his maid for ten years, to look after him and cook for him. He lost forty pounds, and death was marked in his face after he had finally finished that unsuccessful picture for a German company, CCC in Berlin.

But in the early thirties, Robert and I were young, and the idea of becoming tired never entered our minds. We were in demand. William Thiele, the UFA director, was going to shoot a motion picture in Paris. I was to write the screenplay, tutored by the Hungarian writer of plays and films Ladislas Fodor.

Paris! On an expense account! Joe Pasternak, the Hollywood producer, once told me, "Pay me ten dollars' salary a week and an unlimited expense account, and I will be happy!"

I brushed up my school French to be able to talk to the exciting French girls. To be able to tell a joke in a foreign language is the proof of having the facility to speak it.

Ladislas Fodor, an experienced screenwriter and playwright, took me under his wing. We traveled first class, and in the train to Paris I met Alexander Korda, also a Hungarian like Fodor.

Two years later I also worked for him. Korda became Sir Alexander, knighted by the king of England, after having revived the British film industry with his world-successful *Henry VIII* with Charles Laughton. The world in the thirties was full of people who became famous until the Nazis destroyed the brain elite of Europe.

Fodor was in love with Paris as if the city were a woman. The day we arrived at the Lido hotel on Montmartre, he hardly gave me time after the long journey to wash up and change, anxious to show a neophyte the wonders of Paris. Though we had been on a train for ten hours, he forced me to march with him for three hours through the streets of the city, explaining to me with undying enthusiasm its history. Why were the boulevards so wide? Louis Napoleon's architect, Hausmann, had erased the inner city and rebuilt it, broad streets forming a star, converging at the Arc de Triomphe. The streets were built that wide to set up artillery pieces in case of an uprising of which the king was afraid. Why did the mob during the French Revolution at the end of the eighteenth century shout "A la lantern" when they wanted to lynch one of the despised aristocrats? Because the street lamps protrude from the house walls, convenient gallows for hanging. Fodor took me at his expense to the world-famous restaurant La Reine Pedoque, to order *bécassine,* the French name for snipe. An old, dignified waiter brought on a silver platter two tiny roasted fowl and with two knives, one in each hand, cut the meat off their bones in midair, never letting them fall back on the silver platter until only the carcass was left. Then he mashed the meat, added mysterious spices, poured cognac over the food, and set it afire. When it had burned almost to a crisp, he extinguished the flame and presented the bécassines on a thin piece of toast, as a paste, just enough for two bites. The spectacle of preparation was part of the restaurant's fame.

When we left, Ladislas Fodor asked me, "Did I show you my Paris?" He certainly did. "Did I feed you well?" The bill must have been substantial. "Now, when you return to the hotel, a beautiful young lady will be waiting for you. Don't worry, all expenses have been met by me. You are in Paris and what would a Paris night be without a companion?"

There was a young lady waiting for me, and though I didn't understand much of her rapid speech, it actually was not necessary to talk much. France was not Germany where the vice squad invaded hotel rooms, sniffing out unmarried couples. In the morning she took out a little notebook and asked me, "Qu'est que ton nom?" (What is your name?). She wrote my name down and then drew a little flower behind it. If she had a good time, she explained, she painted a flower behind the name. Then she asked me for a little gift, not for herself but for her husband. That astonished me, having been brought up in a Calvinistic country. "*Laver c'est comme nouveau,*" she added, guessing my thought. Take a shower and everything will be like new!

Paris! I had left Berlin, with its restlessness and hectic drive, and had learned in a few hours Fodor's infatuation with the City of Lights. The Revolution had freed the French minds from sexual hypocrisy, the fertilizer on which many religions thrive.

The screenplay Fodor and I wrote was based on the novel *Le Bal* by Irene Nemirowsky. William Thiele the director's leading lady, was the gamin-like redheaded German actress Dolly Haas, who, now living in America, is married in New York to the genius cartoonist Al Hirschfeld.

The director and his writers of our film met at the office of the Vandal/Delac company at the Avenue des Champs Elysées. Suddenly the fun was over. Thiele, the director, was hard to please—so hard that I became quite miserable. Thiele, not one of UFA's first-line directors, was a rude and hysterical man who made life intolerable for anyone working for him. He might have been unsure and insecure about his work, since he hardly spoke any French and was assigned by UFA to also direct the French version of the picture

Le Bal. I hated to sit in conferences with him and started to suffer from stomach cramps, which a doctor diagnosed as an inflamed appendix. That affliction gave me the chance to take a hiatus from my work. I checked in at a hospital, though I could well have waited for that operation until my return to Berlin. I remember lying on a stretcher, being wheeled into the operating room. I asked a pretty nurse—all French girls at that time appeared to me as being pretty— "Are you the sister?" since the German word for "nurse" is *Schwester* (sister). The French one is *infirmière*. The face of a huge bearded intern bent over me and boomed, "I am the sister." Then I woke up without an appendix.

At that time it was the medical fashion to keep the patient after an operation in bed for ten days, depriving him completely of food but supplying him with different waters—Evian, Perrier, Peregrine and other varieties. After a couple of days when the body had shed its poison, the water tastes like different wines.

Since that time of the imposed fast, I yearn for the sensation of purity that a long deprivation of food had created. I think back with pleasure to that short time, a patient in a French hospital, since I had long talks with an exceptional personality, the surgeon, Professor Jean l'Ardonnier, who was a man double my age, with the analytical, seasoned wisdom of a Frenchman. I discussed with him the painful duties in my life to deal with unreasonable people. Returning to the bloody battlefield to fight with Thiele, the director, I had acquired a bird's-eye view of life that helped me stay for thirty years in that erratic business of motion picture production, without ever getting upset by trying circumstances. I had developed a system to overcome the stress of clashing personalities. I just looked into the person's eyes and silently said to myself, "I have lived a long time without you." Then I walked out of the job, if I could afford it at that time.

The story of *Le Bal* was not in my line, either. It was that of a poor French family—father, mother, and daughter—who had a close and happy relationship. By circumstances the father got rich. The family moved to a mansion. Servants, not mother and daughter anymore, did the housework. The father took a mistress, as affluent Frenchmen seem to do, and the mother had a lover, the way Nemirowsky described that nouveau-rich French family. The young girl became lonely, witnessing how her beloved family had fallen apart. Her father arranged a party for his newly found rich friends. The young girl was given the envelopes with the invitations to take to the post office. Disgusted with her new life, she threw the letters in the Seine

River. On the evening of the party, no guests showed up. The father and mother, surrounded by impersonal servants, sat unhappily at the table heaped with expensive food and wine. But the girl insisted that the party should go on and invited the hired help to participate, which culminated in the father dancing with the hired waitresses, the mother and daughter with the cook and hired help. That shock brought the family together, and the film ended as it had begun: a family, again in love with each other, returning to the closely knit group. It was an innocent story, frail even for a television sit-com idea today.

Thiele was in search of a young, innocent-looking actress to play Dolly Haas's part in the French version. A few girls applied for the job at the offices of Vandal/Delac. There was one ingenue whom Thiele liked. She was about sixteen, used no makeup, her shapely legs demurely covered by long woolen stockings. On her thick natural blonde hair she wore a simple toque, as was the fashion of the time. She also could sing, she said. Werner Richard Heymann, the German composer of many world-famous films, like Lubitsch's *Ninotchka,* went to the piano and played the simple, melodic children's song "Frère Jacques." The teenager had a crystal-clear voice, though not of great range, but the microphone would supply that. The next day Thiele made a camera test with her at the Joinville studios near Paris. She went into a corner and crossed herself, then played the part flawlessly. She got the part.

A few weeks later I saw her in a Bugatti cabriolet with her boyfriend racing down the Avenue des Champs Elysées. She wore a very short skirt and heavy makeup, and her fingernails were painted silver. She did not look sixteen anymore but her real age—eighteen. Her name was Danielle Darrieux.

Her mother, a former actress, had dressed and coached her daughter for that audition.

Robert, after his emigration to Paris in 1933, made a picture with her, *La crise est finie,* a film based on my story. Billy Wilder used her in his first director's assignment: *Mauvaise graine* (Bad Seed). Though he swore he would never go through the ordeal of directing, he became one of the top film directors of Hollywood. Danielle Darrieux became a world-famous picture star.

After the war, which ended in 1945, she was accused by the French underground of being a collaborator, but I don't think that she was politically inclined. She might have been attracted all her life by good-looking men of any nation, even German officers.

Twenty years later I met her again at the Twentieth Century–Fox Studios in Hollywood, where she was playing a part in an American picture. She still had that vulnerability of a young girl, which was part of her charm. I invited her to the writers' table to be adored by forty scribblers. "Danielle," I said. "Remember I wrote your first picture, *Le Bal,* in Paris in 1931?" "It was 1943," she replied, taking twelve years off her age. I didn't correct her. In 1943 the Germans had occupied Paris. I was, fortunately, not in France but writing pictures in Hollywood.

I once attended a hanging at the Moabit Prison in Berlin. Since killing a human being is the ultimate crime, how could the state legally commit premeditated murder? Muehlfriedl took me to the execution to prove that since the law was inadequate to cope with major crimes, to send a person to death by state policy was the only solution. Why feed those criminals and take care of them on taxpayers' money? It is common sense to get rid of them.

The hanging was an antiseptic affair. The man, in his late twenties, a pale, slight figure, was led in, supported by two guards. His hands were free. He frantically chewed gum but was not steady on his feet. His eyes were without focus as he was led up the few steps to the gallows. A rope with the traditional hangman's noose was put around his neck, and his head was covered with a black hood. I don't know who released the trap. The body disappeared with a thud into a hole beneath his feet. A few people stood around silently, journalists, the prison warden, and a priest. Why does God's representative have to be witness to a murder?

I was sure that the victim's brain was no longer functioning. It is no punishment to kill a person who has no mind. Executions are the revenge of a society on people who have become threats to their establishment.

The hanged man was a Polish hired hand who had murdered a woman for whom he had worked. To add to my education, Hubert had swiped that man's handwritten memoirs. Only impending death could formulate such a powerful tale. He was an illiterate who probably had never put anything on paper before. At the end of his life story, he started to lie. As long as he had poured out his emotions honestly, his words had a tremendous power of persuasion. When he veered away from the truth, he failed.

There is a similarity between death and emigration. If the emigrant starts evaluating his position, he is doomed. Behind him the road he has traveled dissolves into something nebulous and unreal. That traumatic experience never leaves him as long as he lives, even should he be highly successful in the new country that shelters him. He has lost his homeland and will never completely be integrated into the second one. But also the homeland is flawed forever. He can never return and wipe out the past. Today, many decades after my forced exodus from Germany, I still suffer from nightmares about concentration camps. I never experienced them, but I have met the nattily dressed men in uniform, wearing high shiny boots, whose duty it was to cleanse the world of inferior races and for whom every life, except their own, was expendable.

Being banned from a country of one's birth under the threat of death, not for a crime committed but for a racial bias, is like the sentence of death by a tribunal with preconceived judgment. But the desire to stay alive sharpens the mind cunningly. Thousands of my generation went along that one-way road. It was a forced tightrope walk stretching between life and death, a high-swinging trapeze act with no net to intercept the fall. Too many faltered and failed.

After Muehlfriedl had left me at the Swiss border at Basel, I took the train to Lugano. Henrietta, her mother, and I discussed the bleak future, since I had received an official notice from the Swiss government that my stay in Switzerland had been terminated. I had a few days to leave. Henrietta and her mother were dissolving our household.

Mother, a Swiss citizen, would live in a one-room apartment in Montagnola, a small village in Ticino. I decided to join my brother Robert in Paris, where he already had rented an apartment. He was certain to find a writing assignment for me on one of the pictures that he was supposed to do. But as I found out, all this was fog and smoke.

Switzerland has three distinct citizens: the Swiss Germans in the north, with their thriving capital Zurich; the French Swiss in Geneva and Lausanne; and the Italians in the Ticino—all of whom had vastly different reactions to the growing National Socialist empire at their border. Though the Swiss had a well-trained army led by the able General Guisan and the high Alps, which were almost impossible for any army to conquer, they were no match for the German army. But the Swiss were well prepared for war and had stored food and weapons at the bottom of the deep Alpine lakes. But there was one shortcoming: the German Swiss were very sympathetic to their fascistic neighbor in the north, whose language they spoke.

In 1942, winning the war on all fronts, Hitler poised his army to occupy Switzerland. That army would have been joyfully accepted by the German Swiss but certainly not by the French and Italian cantons, who were determined to fight. The German Swiss would have made excellent Nazis. They tried to follow the Nuremberg anti-Semitic laws. When the Allied bombers in 1944 flew by the thousands over Swiss territory, like clouds of migrating birds, to bomb southern Germany, the Swiss citizens hid in air raid shelters afraid of stray bombs. But Swiss Jews were not permitted to hide in the protective concrete cavern.

Switzerland gave some Jews the permission to stay during the war, since the Red Cross organization, whose logo is a red cross on a white field, was originated in 1852 by Jean Henry Dunant, a humanitarian French-Swiss citizen. He used the reverse colors of the Swiss flag, which shows a white cross in a red background. But the German-Swiss tolerance did not extend to it its racial bias. A refugee Jew I knew, who during the war had fallen in love with a Swiss girl, was by government decree forbidden to marry her or visit her at night. He sneaked into her room after dark. They had a child who became legitimate only after he was able to marry her after the war.

My brother Robert and I fought our separate ways through France and England and then to America. We had the advantage of having had a successful career before the emigration, and we were gifted with a youthful energy that refused to be broken by the difficulties confronting us. Old people who could not tear out their roots and the young helpless ones died in concentration camps. The Jewish exodus also happened during the years of the deep economic depression that ravaged the Western world. No country wanted to accept hordes of refugees, except France, which still had the tradition of tolerance created by the French Revolution.

But even in France it was almost hopeless to obtain a visa for any length of time. Work permits were even more difficult to get, and it was a rhetorical question, since there was no work around, except for the highly specialized. My training as a mathematician was useless. But I had created a skill writing novels and films and Robert by being a director, which opened up the possibility for us to integrate ourselves into foreign countries. Robert successfully did so in France. But there was no chance for me, since my knowledge of French was hardly even colloquial.

Emigrants by the hundreds gathered daily at the police station in Paris for hours to find out whether their permit to stay had been extended. Refusal was tantamount to a death sentence. One had to move on, walking into a void. Some immigrants and their children crossed the Pyrenees mountains that divide France from Spain, in winter, on foot. Many perished. The Catholic monasteries and convents humanely helped the desperate travelers, feeding them and hiding them from the Spanish border patrols. After all, Spain was ruled by a fascist, General Franco, a sympathetic though silent partner of the Germans. The choice to return to Germany to face a certain death was open to all immigrants.

Even America, the traditional haven for the homeless, closed its borders to many displaced people. Joseph Goebbels cunningly permitted a German ocean liner to take two thousand Jews abroad, to prove to the world that Jews were not welcome anywhere. The ship, the *St. Louis,* sailed to America. President Roosevelt, up for election, was afraid to permit the German boat to unload its desperate cargo since the American Congress was highly anti-Semitic. He was careful not to show preference to Jews. Protests by American Jews were of no avail, since the labor unions, plagued by the high unemployment of their members, were afraid that the emigrants might take jobs away from them. WASPs, who ruled America for a century, were anti-Irish, anti-black, and anti-Semitic. Roosevelt's "New Deal" was called the "Jew Deal" by jingoistic Americans. Even during the war against Hitler, the railway lines leading to the concentration camps were never bombed by the hundred thousand Allied planes that otherwise devastated Germany. Roosevelt "could not spare a single bomb before Hitler was defeated" was the explanation. Black soldiers were separated in their own units. Only after a black company was attacked by white American soldiers, suffering high casualties, did Harry Truman integrate the American fighting men, wiping out racial discrimination in the military by decree in July 1948, against the advice of Dwight David Eisenhower, the commander of the Allied forces in Europe during World War II.

Unable to find a haven for his Jewish cargo, the humanitarian German captain, after having tried to disembark his passengers in Cuba, Argentina, and other South American countries, finally ran the *St. Louis* aground at the beaches of Antwerp in German-occupied Belgium. The Jews were returned to the starting point of their tragic predicament.

Robert lived in an apartment at the Place Pereire in Paris. He was almost penniless and had saved nothing. He had his wife Bertha with him. "Babs," socially minded, had married the renowned young film director, lured by the chance of meeting important people and traveling internationally. They did, but not of their choosing. I helped Robert, since I had some money left over from my almost suicidal return trip to Berlin. Half of our money I had left with Henrietta in Switzerland. Babs held a German passport, as I did. Robert was stateless, since he had never opted, as I did, for the German citizenship. Born to American naturalized parents, his passport had expired years ago. That negligence saved Robert's and Babs's lives since the American consul in Paris quickly issued Robert a valid passport, based on some obscure French document, a scrap of paper that mentioned Robert's expired American citizenship.

Robert stayed successfully in Paris until the war broke out in September 1939. Against his wife's objections, he booked passage on the French liner *Champlain*. But Babs wanted to wait for first-class travel on the *Normandie*, which, as she had heard, had a better kitchen. The *Champlain* sailed without lights to avoid German submarines. Instead of eight hundred passengers, the ship carried three thousand; some slept in bathtubs, on billiard tables, or on the open deck. The food was unpalatable, and the French crew was rude and constantly drunk, knowing that the ship had to return to France. It was the last French boat that sailed from Europe before the war broke out. The *Normandie*, with its renowned kitchen chef, never left its harbor. Eventually the *Normandie* did make it to the United States. It was totally destroyed by fire while being refitted as a troopship at a New York pier in 1942.

A few times in my life, I suffered from courage fatigue. Once when I directed a motion picture in San Bernado in Brazil, I had to deal with the lack of raw film; I had to remember every shot since I couldn't find a script girl who could speak English; I had actors who lost their Calvinistic ethics, which many do when they leave the borders of America; and, finally, a workman fell off the scaffold in the studio. The boards of the scaffolding had not been secured. The man was an epileptic who should not have climbed up the ladders. Though everybody rushed to the lifeless man, I was glued to my chair, drained of all energy. I did not care whether he was alive or dead.

Before the outbreak of World War II, a similar condition of courage fatigue existed in Europe. The French, still suffering from the loss of their youth on the battlefields of World War I, did not want to fight, nor did the British. On a questionnaire circulated at

Oxford and Cambridge Universities, students voted overwhelmingly that they would not fight for their own country, a fact that might have influenced Prime Minister Neville Chamberlain to appease Adolf Hitler by allowing him to occupy Austria and Czechoslovakia. When Hitler moved into the Rhineland in 1936, he was not yet prepared for war, and the well-equipped French could have stopped him immediately, which would have been the end of Hitler. They didn't. If one talked to a Frenchman about defending his country against Hitler, his reply was, "*Je m'en fou*" (I don't give a damn). The leaders of the two Western countries did not want to be aware that at their borders an unstoppable dynamic revolution was developing.

A refugee in Paris, I also suffered from courage fatigue. The events had been like hammer blows: a pregnant wife in Switzerland, the loss of my profession, stranded in a country whose mentality was foreign to me. I was very short of money, and had no hope of getting work. In which direction was I to go? Among the thousands of desperate refugees, many I knew from Berlin as intelligent, successful people, not one had an idea what his future would be.

Babs, Robert's wife, who took pleasure in the role of a matchmaker—she amused herself by destroying marriages—introduced me to a young Polish-born woman, a budding writer. Andrea Zbinski was a tall girl with a high-cheeked Slavic face and curiously intense blue eyes. Her masculine tweeds, wool cap, and long strides betrayed her emancipated mind, very different from the rather feminine German girls I had met during my BH (before Hitler) years. Andrea was a type of woman I had never encountered before. She, I thought, took an instant liking to me and promised to teach me a passable French in a short time, so I could converse with French producers and publishers, of which she said she knew many. She offered, for a slight fee, to share her studio with me.

I found myself "*sous les toits de Paris*" (under the roofs of Paris), with tiny gardens, small towers, narrow walkways connecting the tops of buildings, greenhouses, terraces, a whole city hidden from the cavernous street below.

If I thought I had walked into the well-advertised French situation of having a charming mistress cum apartment, and living as her boyfriend, her "petit amour" in a cozy nest, I was mistaken. Through her small studio passed the literary clique of that time, a wave of writers, composers, and painters. I don't know how she was able to collect that many celebrated artists of Paris. I didn't know, either, what attracted that crowd to her. She didn't have anything published, nor was she especially brilliant. I didn't know how she made a living, until I discovered that her guests left some bills in a high vase at the entrance door. She introduced me to André Malraux, famous for his internationally acclaimed novel *La condition humaine* (Man's Fate), for which he had just received the much coveted Goncourt Prize. Malraux, after the war, became minister of art under Charles de Gaulle and had the facades of the historical buildings renewed by having them sandblasted, destroying their patina. Malraux gave me an introduction to the publishing house of Gallimard. Fifteen years later they printed several books of mine, when I no longer needed the money.

Jean-Paul Sartre and his "bonne amie," Simone de Beauvoir, dropped in. Sartre, an ugly man, was a famous playwright and the originator of existentialism, a philosophy that fitted that time of utter confusion. Sartre was blind in one eye, and de Beauvoir was a masculine woman, the George Sand of those days.

Andrea's method of teaching me the right French accent was to take me to plays. She got the tickets for free. When she took me behind the stage of the Comédie Française, I was transported into the times of Toulouse Lautrec, the painter, since the theater attendants dressed like French citizens of the nineteenth century, wearing their hair long and sporting sideburns, called "pork chops," which was the fashion of Louis Napoleon's empire. I hardly understood a word of the rapidly spoken dialogue of the plays. I only knew that the Sartre play took place in hell, which looked much like Andrea's apartment, with its running icy water in a corner kitchen and the toilet, shared by many families, situated between two floors of the building.

When she had her daily guests, the visits became a movable feast. Everybody brought some provisions. The leftovers fed Andrea and me. The *vin ordinaire,* the tasty country wine of France, came in big bottles without a label. The Halles, the wholesale market, which does not exist anymore, provided fresh vegetables. The bread, baguettes, was a yard long. It was not a bad life if one didn't have any ambitions. The world situation was never mentioned by Andrea's artist friends. The interest of the Parisian French stopped at the city's outskirts.

I was sitting on the couch, its springs sticking out like herring bones, when Andrea introduced me to a young woman of ethereal beauty who moved with the grace of a lynx. She was a top model for the dressmaker Poiret. The two talked rapidly in a Paris slang, which I had not mastered and never did. Sitting between them, completely ignored, I was expected to light their Gaulois cigarettes and fill their wine glasses. Suddenly the heavenly apparition bent across my lap and kissed Andrea. It was a long, experienced kiss, like that of lovers who share sexual secrets. I felt as if I were on a deserted island in an ocean with no other land in sight. My macho image faded away, and I became a sexless object. In all my life I have never felt more lonely as at that moment when I was sitting between those two lesbians in love.

Why Andrea accepted me at her studio apartment I could never guess. She knew I was married. It might have been chic at that time to assist a writer of foreign origin. Besides, I was no menace to her and her girlfriends.

A writer's fortune is his stories. The more material he has, the better the chances of selling one. I wrote incessantly, as I had done before in my life and still do, though Andrea was of the opinion that it was more important to read than to write. Robert's last film in Germany was a film that was promptly forbidden by Goebbels. It was based on Stefan Zweig's novel, *Burning Secret*. Zweig, an eminent Austrian author, committed suicide in Brazil where the waves of emigration had stranded him. The theme of the novel was the extracurricular love affair of a woman, the mother of a ten-year-old boy. He witnesses that interlude, between his adored mother and a stranger, which shatters the image of the world of his childhood. After returning home he did not tell his father. That was his "burning secret."

That theme shocked the prudish Nazis, whose sensitivity sent a man to prison for having killed cats with a hammer but thought nothing of throwing live people into ovens. Sexual problems or cruelty to animals was taboo for the Nazis' tender sensibilities. To treat them badly was often punished by years of hard labor.

I still was Andrea's lodger, staying in her studio apartment, which consisted of one big room with a painter's northern exposure and a tiny storeroom for her clothes. That was the "room" I rented. I had given almost all of my money to Robert, since his wife Babs wanted an abortion, which was easy to get in Paris. Babs hated to be pregnant, a condition that would spoil her figure. Sometimes I wonder whether having a child would have made the significant difference in their lives as it did in mine.

As he grew older, Robert regretted not having children. Babs never missed them. She was wrapped up in a social web that included friends devoted to her and a sophisticated lifestyle, which she carried with her wherever she went.

My feelings of an impending doom increased every day. The French sophistication and way of life suited Babs and Robert, but not me. I was searching for a way out but could not find the door. Henrietta, who knew what she wanted, opened it for me.

A telegram from England, sent to Robert's address, reached me. Henrietta had left Switzerland and gone to London. But she didn't know anybody in London. Nor did I. She was in her ninth month of pregnancy. I had hoped she would have the child in Switzerland, where her mother could take care of it. Shocked, I left Paris on the next train for England.

London was shrouded in the dreaded "black fog." It was midday and night at the same time. Particles of coal dust from a million fireplaces had fused with the Channel's dense water vapors to form a black cupola over the city. As the taxi drove me toward the hospital, policemen directed traffic by torchlight, huge gas flames that illuminated a few feet of the street where cars moved at a snail's pace.

The hospital in Hendon was an old-fashioned brick building, built when Queen Victoria was young. They must also have retained the nurses of that period, stern-looking harpies who never smiled. They had put Henrietta in a single room, since delivery rooms were unknown at that time. She was in labor, but nobody was around to help her. Arriving at the border, she had almost had a miscarriage, losing the water that protected the child. Unable to speak English, she told the immigration officer in French that she did not want a German or French child; she wanted a British one.

That must have touched the patriotic veins of the tough British custom officers. They arranged a room for her at the Grosvenor Hotel, the ritziest place in London, so ritzy that its toilets were supplied with two kinds of toilet paper, soft and hard ones. The immigration officer, obviously smitten by Henrietta's innocence and beauty, treated her like a worried father and supplied a German refugee doctor for her, Hermann Herzberg, a refugee who had permission to practice in London. Herzberg transported her quickly to the hospital.

Henrietta told me between waves of labor pains that she did not want me to stay in Paris. She wanted me back, away from Robert's influence. She also considered our stay in England as a stepping-stone to America. It was her dream since childhood to live in the United States. I thought she was feverish. Should I have taken her with me to France? I felt guilty knowing the cause of my guilt. She was in labor for thirty-six hours, and during the waves of pain she tore my Harris tweed trousers to shreds.

From time to time a nurse entered the room, poking at her stomach, which supposedly should accelerate the birth. When I asked the nurse to give Henrietta a medication to alleviate her pain, she told me contemptuously that Queen Victoria had given birth to her children without the help of pills.

I cannot understand why, after the painful ordeal of giving birth, women want to have another child. If men had to go through that ordeal, they certainly would not repeat it. It might be possible that nature, after the child is born, releases an enzyme that makes them forget that torture.

No wonder Queen Elizabeth, in the sixteenth century, offered a prize of one million English pounds for the first man who gave birth to a child—a prize that is still available. Such an event would have smashed the macho world which men had created to dominate women. With the first child born by a man, the female species would become dominant, since women are more clever, more resourceful, and self-contained, and have unfailing premonitions, a mental gift that escapes the male gender. In general, they are stronger than men. They also live longer.

Elizabeth Tudor, queen of England, knew that a million pounds would be money wisely spent to free women from their bondage.

I could not stand Henrietta's sufferings for long and left to find Dr. Herzberg. I had lost my nerve. I walked around the hospital, through streets with their heartless traffic noises. It had started to rain and black soot poured from the sky, soiling my coat and hat. Herzberg was not in his office. Afraid the child, which was a breach, would be born with brain damage due to a lack of oxygen, he had called in an English obstetrician. Our son was born with the assistance of forceps and other medieval hardware.

I bought a bottle of champagne to drink with Henrietta as a beam of happiness in those dark days. The hospital nurses refused to let me see my wife or son. They also did not deliver the champagne to her. She had to wait for hours to see the baby and was convinced that it was deformed. I was not allowed to see her until a day later.

Henrietta had to stay at the hospital for four days. I found a dingy hotel on Kilburn High Street, a thoroughfare where trucks thundered by day and night without pause. But at least, for me, it wasn't the sound of marching boots. The owner of the hotel, a man with a drooping moustache like Colonel Blimp, made the rounds every day to make sure his tenants didn't double up when the room was rented to a single person. He appeared every morning with the stereotypical greeting, "Nice day, isn't it?" even if it rained in sheets or fog had closed in so thickly that from my window I could not see the trucks passing by, only hear their rumble.

The hotel had a small restaurant. I went from the culinary delights of Paris to fish and chips and vegetables pulled through hot water. I could see Henrietta only for a few hours every day, and admired my son, who looked to me like any other baby. In my desperate situation, having to house and feed a family, my sense of a doting father had not yet developed. Henrietta could not feed the baby. The strain of emigration, the precarious circumstances in which we found ourselves, had dried up her milk. The nurses tortured her in vain by applying suction cups to her breasts.

I had to wait. For what? To have Henrietta discharged. What then? There was a young waitress in the hotel, who would sit at my table when the traffic had slackened and the diners were few. To console me she brought me special desserts, like trifle, which she did not put on the bill. Her name was Cynthia. We could hardly communicate, I in my halting English and she in her Cockney slang, which I could often not understand. I didn't know whether she pitied me, a refugee, who just had become a father, or whether she liked me. I believe it was the latter, since she put artificial flowers in my room, where she had to double as maid in the daytime.

With her Cockney accent, she tried to teach me to speak the king's English. Stretched out on my bed, she invited me to admire her small waist. "Don't lead me astray!" she said seductively.

Lead her astray? I could only guess what that expression meant. As a newly created father, I did not take advantage of her invitation. If I hadn't been floating in limbo and worried about the future, which was as obscure as the London black fog, I might have accepted her offer and might have led her astray, if only to prove my mastery of colloquial English.

I remember her fondly, because she was there in those dark hours, and also because I didn't spoil our relationship, creating new difficulties beyond my enormous present ones. Besides, should I have led her astray, I might not have remembered her half a century later.

I had a son, a wife, no job, no permission to work in England, which suffered as much unemployment as the rest of Europe.

Henrietta had to leave the hospital, but the administration refused to deliver the baby before we paid our bill. We had to leave her luggage behind, which contained her clothes. Some old clothes seemed to be of a greater value for the hospital than a child. For the first time I witnessed Henrietta blowing up, shouting at the accountant that she did not give birth to a child to abandon it to an orphanage, as the cold-blooded accountant had threatened.

I changed our last Italian lire into English pounds, and we left with the child to take it to the Wellgard Nursing Home, since we did not know what to do with the baby. Dr. Herzberg had found a home that wanted newborn infants for the training of nurses.

The Wellgard, though based in an old building, was a modern institution, run by a matron, thread-thin, taciturn, her leathery face dried up in a thousand pleats. She showed no emotion when we told her our story.

Every infant had a room to itself. One of the walls could be folded back, opening onto a garden. The child slept from the first day on, in the open air, even when the weather was foggy or rainy. Every day Henrietta was permitted to hold the baby for half an hour, but we had to dress in institutional robes, since the child only knew people in white, or he would cry with fear.

A nurse arrived at six o'clock with a bottle. A stopwatch dangled from her neck. She took the baby in her lap and, on the second of six, put the nipple of the bottle in the baby's mouth. Obviously having a built-in timing device, the child was waiting and never cried. When it was through with the bottle, the nurse took it to a chamber pot and slapped its bottom. He did his business and never wore a diaper.

A Dr. Spock or a modern psychiatrist would be horrified by such a procedure. A baby should be fed when hungry and should have the command of its bowel movement, to avoid inhibitions and incurable complexes. None of them appeared when my son grew up. He became an extremely intelligent and precise human being in his deliberation and business affairs. That discipline might have been created by the Wellgard method of being fed by a stopwatch and having his bottom slapped.

We went to the registry for a birth certificate, since, native-born, he was a British subject. We named him Geoffrey Curt de Perrot Siodmak. It was a long name. The Jewish family tradition prohibited giving several names to a child, since the first name formed the next family name for his future children, as in Slavic languages, where the son of Ivan is called Ivanovich—Ivan, son of Ivan—and similarly, for Jews, Ben Gurion—Ben, son of Gurion. The Swiss add the mother's family name, in this case "de Perrot." That gives a person a chance to trace its ancestry, I suppose.

The clerk at the registration office was an elderly man sporting a long moustache, twisted into a needle-sharp end. He was almost completely deaf and hid his affliction by giggling whenever he could not understand our halting English. He finally wrote Geoffrey's new name down, or our son would still be nameless today.

Geoffrey, thanks to Dr. Herzfeld, was safer at the Wellgard than in a home we could not provide.

We found an inexpensive room at Oxford Terrace. One side of the street was called Oxford, the other Cambridge Terrace. We didn't know that the rooms were rented to couples on an hourly basis. The redheaded landlady, Mrs. O'Day, listened to our plight and offered to let us stay, for a very reasonable rent, as long as we liked. Our first abode in London was a brothel, since Mrs. O'Day had half a dozen girls as steady tenants.

We found ourselves in a cul-de-sac. We had to learn English, and that study took all of our time. To speak English was a matter of life and death. We went to the neighborhood cinema, a cheap run-down place, wrapped up in a blanket, since the theater was not heated, and listened to the English actors from the midday opening to the hour it closed. I wrote English words on sheets of paper that I glued to the wall, adding the German translation in minute letters to it. I hated having to go so close to read the German writing. I had pockets stuffed with notes, English words on one side and the German translation on the other. I had a blotting paper on the table, on which I wrote new words, which disappeared after a day because of the absorbing paper. I read old newspapers with the help of a dictionary Mrs. O'Day lent me. I was certain I would die one day with a unpronounceable "th" between my teeth, a sound no foreigner can ever produce like a native. The difference between *grateful* and *graceful* remained a problem to me.

I ran into a couple of German playwrights, Kurt Goetz and his wife, Valerie von Marten, whose plays had been extremely successful in Germany and, to their luck, also in England, which gave them some much-needed income. Kurt and Valerie, to improve their English, constantly rehearsed sketches he had written.

One of them was "Where is the baby?" "What baby?" "Our baby." On their way to the Dorchester Hotel Kurt and Valerie, driving a Morris Minor car, the smallest automobile available, got lost. Kurt stepped out of the car to ask a policeman, "Where is the Dorchester Hotel?" Instead he fell into his routine and asked, "Where is the baby?" "What baby?" the bobby asked. "Our baby!"

Kurt answered and, aware that he had slipped into one of his scenes, drove off hastily. Kurt was lucky. His plays had been shown in English theaters and he had access to money, and as a produced playwright, the dreaded Home Office let him stay on a visitor's permit.

The German actor Fritz Kortner, who could not speak English at all, rehearsed a whole act of the play *Chu-Chin-Chow* phonetically, not knowing what he was saying. He got the part, which he played for years on the stage, right through World War II, where *Chu-Chin-Chow* was the hit play of the decade.

4

The Cat's Prediction

Our situation seemed to be hopeless. The child was still in an orphanage, which the Wellgard was for us. What to do? Henrietta and I discussed possibilities, all of which were theoretical and which could not be realized immediately. I wanted to give up writing. The possibility of writing for publication in another language looked to me an impossible task. To continue writing in German needs a good translator, for whom we didn't have the money or the connections. I was desperate, with even Henrietta's undying optimism flagging.

The window in our ground-floor room was open. Suddenly a small black cat appeared, went straight to my small portable typewriter, and started to hit the keys. We watched spellbound. Henrietta fed it warm milk. Was the cat a Familiar, a spirit, a female demon telling me what to do? The cat left, never to return again.

Was that fate's message, not to give up writing? Or was it serendipity finding an answer in an unrelated incident? We decided that it was the message that pointed out our future.

To get access to a film studio, I needed an agent. I had a track record, since the English version of *F.P. 1* had been shown in London. I looked in the directory under "theatrical agencies" and picked one with a Jewish name, hoping its representative would be more sympathetic to a refugee Jew than one of the staid Englishmen, who, I suspected, were traditionally anti-Semitic.

The agent, Roger Bernstein of Literary and Film, was a seedy-looking young man. His office was a hole-in-the-wall on Fleet Street, four floors up. He didn't look influential to me. He was impressed by my European credits but didn't recall the film *F.P. 1*, a credit that was my only hope to be recognized. He assured me that he was very much "in" with BIP (British International Pictures) whose production head, Walter Mycroft, was partial to foreign screenwriters, a profession that at that time was rare in England.

Mycroft had a motion picture in mind, using a German director and a gifted Hungarian singer, Gitta Alpar. She had been married to Gustaf Froehlich, the German motion picture star of Fritz Lang's gigantic *Metropolis*. After Goebbels's speech in the Kaiserhof Hotel in Berlin, Froehlich promptly left her, the Jew, jumping on Goebbels's bandwagon. When he came home and greeted Gitta with "Heil Hitler," she replied with "Heil Gustaf" and left him and Germany, which saved her life.

More than half a century later, I met Froehlich in Berlin at the Hotel Kempinski. Though I had known him well, we did not talk to each other. I saw the guilt in his face, for having been an ardent Nazi, and having left Gitta, his then-pregnant wife, shedding her like an old shoe. Almost all German actors who were married to a Jewish wife deserted them, except Hans Albers, the top German film star who during the war stayed in touch with the actress Hansi Burg, his Jewish wife, whom he had smuggled out of Germany in time. She joined the British army and during the invasion parachuted from a British bomber over the Staremberg lake in Bavaria, where Albers had outwaited Hitler's Reich. Hansi, now in British uniform, wanted to be with Hans and to protect him from the invading army. It was a love affair that the Nazis could not break.

Froehlich died shortly after my visit to Berlin in 1985, forgotten and lonely. Gitta died thirty years later in Palm Springs in America. Just before her death, the German film industry of the Federal Republic of Germany invited her to Berlin, to honor the Great Old Lady of the pre-Hitler times.

My agent, Bernstein, made an appointment for me at BIP with Mycroft's secretary by telephone, and I watched him pleading with her to get me a date. I needed an interpreter badly and did not want to see Mycroft alone, but Bernstein claimed that Mycroft did not want agents around when he talked to people he wanted to engage.

It was clammy and cold in London, and the fog seemed to stay forever. I understood why, during the winter, rich Englishmen went to Italy. That wet cold slowly penetrated our bones, and Mrs. O'Day put hot bricks into our bed to warm our feet.

I had trained myself how, during times of great stress, to shut out all negative thoughts. I had no doubt that I would get a job right away. I psyched myself into that belief. Henrietta did not need any psychological crutch. She was absolutely sure that BIP would offer me work right away, though the odds were small, handicapped especially by my lack of speaking English fluently.

A great deal of energy has to be put into every one of our actions, from writing a letter, to filling out a job application, to a love affair. One gets, if lucky, an echo back of the energy spent. Talent or genius is necessary in our volatile world, but without an unflagging perseverance we won't get anywhere. I rehearsed sentences to have ready at my interview with the boss of the studio, whom I visualized being a businesslike, tall Englishman. I entered the BIP complex, enchanted by the particular smell of a motion picture studio, a faint fragrance of celluloid and glue. I was home again.

Mycroft's secretary asked me to wait. Mr. Mycroft would see me presently. He did not show up and the secretary suggested that I should try the next day. For four days I took the bus to Elstree, only to be told that Mr. Mycroft would see me presently. The secretary asked for patience, though I had no choice. But my plight must have moved her sympathy for me, because she advised me, in a hushed voice, not to get up when I saw Mr. Mycroft for the first time. He disliked men taller than he was.

The next day Mycroft showed up. He was less than five feet tall, with a crooked back like Quasimodo. "See you presently," he said, and disappeared into his office for another day. It was a sadistic routine. I guess that due to his affliction, he tried to make people feel inferior. He knew his power over a man looking for a job. I heard that years later he was dismissed by his boss, John Maxwell, the very thrifty Scottish tycoon, and that he starved, impoverished and forgotten, after having served Maxwell for almost twenty years.

A letter arrived from Robert in Paris; there was a chance of selling the story of *La crise est finie* that I had written in Paris with my friend Frederick Kohner. Our cousin, Seymour Nebenzahl, was interested in it. Seymour had an international track record with *M,* the classic Lang picture with Peter Lorre, and the "Dr. Mabuse" horror films. He was able to persuade the French to invest money in his production. Robert asked me to come to Paris. I could not. I had to sit in Mr. Mycroft's waiting room.

It was the week before Christmas. I asked Henrietta to go to Paris. She didn't want me to be alone for Christmas. But Mrs. O'Day, who had become our confidant, assured Henrietta that I would have pleasant company on that day of joy. Most of her girls didn't work on Christmas Eve. She would arrange that the prettiest one would stay with me. I don't know whether that offer was consoling to Henrietta.

I complained to my agent about the inhuman treatment Mycroft was dishing out to me. Bernstein didn't understand what I was talking about. I obviously didn't know the British film business in London. It was not bad will on Mycroft's part. He had something on his mind that hadn't fully crystallized. Of course Mycroft was going to talk to me, and I would see him "presently." That I was flat broke also astonished Bernstein. Why didn't I just overdraw my bank account as every Englishman did in emergencies? The bank wouldn't object, he assured me. I didn't have a bank account.

Henrietta left for Paris with our last money. I went on my eternal trip to BIP in Elstree. This time Mycroft saw me in his office. He had a German film director, Friedrich Zelnick, with him. I knew Zelnick from Berlin as a director of inexpensive pictures and would never have worked for him in my elevated position as a screenwriter for Erich Pommer. Besides, I was a published author and a literary man of substance, and Zelnick was a producer of B pictures. Also present at the conference was a young English writer, Frank Launder. Zelnick was aware of my former attitude to him. Mycroft, sensing Zelnick's antagonism, delighted in putting people together who were at odds with each other. He assigned Frank Launder and me to the screenplay. Zelnick was going to direct.

All Mycroft had bought was the title of a song: "I Give My Heart," which the coloratura Gitta Alpar successfully had rendered in London nightclubs. The song was based on a Viennese operetta, *The Dubarry*. I knew from my school days that Marie Jeanne Becu Dubarry had been the mistress of Louis XV of France. Mycroft wanted to produce a musical, a period piece, in which Alpar would be dressed in elaborate costumes. A spirited lady, she did not need exterior beauty, but she possessed a personality that made men fall in love with her.

I had a job! The studio was going to pay me one hundred pounds.

There was a pay telephone in the corridor of Mrs. O'Day's establishment. With a handful of coins, I called Henrietta in Paris. She was staying with Robert. While I was talking to her, doors opened and closed, couples arrived and left. Amid the traffic of coming and going, I told Henrietta the tremendous news that we had money to rent an apartment and to get the baby out of hock. At first she did not believe me and thought it a ruse to get her back to London.

The next day I received thirty-five English pounds, a fortune, from Roger Bernstein. I didn't know then that he had embezzled the rest. But Bernstein's lawyer, not to have him arrested, made him pay me in installments.

I have rarely met a screenwriter of the thirties or forties who became rich writing for motion pictures. Writers were hired help, like actors or directors. The studios own the negative, which means that they own the motion pictures with all their fringe values, sales in other countries, and later on, television sales. If they were photographed in black and white, they would be colored by laser beams to start their moneymaking cycle again. Thirty-four of the motion pictures I wrote are presently shown on the American television screen. I don't participate in their profits. But, studying the credits, I have realized that almost all the actors and directors have died. Who got the advantage, they and their monies, or I, still being alive?

Zelnick and I with our Katzenjammer accent and Frank Launder with his Liverpool twang made a curiously effective combination. Launder became a well-known screen playwright, and with Sidney Gilliat he wrote *The Lady Vanishes* for Alfred Hitchcock, took over a rundown studio, British Lion, and built it up. With the help of an influential member of the House of Lords, that company was bought later by the British government and made Frank and Sid millionaires.

Gilliat was a soft-spoken, gifted screenwriter. When he intended to get married, he came to me for advice. He confessed that he had never had an affair in his life, which was not uncommon among the young men in England brought up in private boys' schools. I told him not to worry since that was no handicap and that the technique was easy to learn. Afraid of making his young bride pregnant, he asked me, a married man, to supply him with a product that, as he had heard, was sold under the counter in pharmacies. I asked him how many condoms he wanted. He decided that three might get him through the honeymoon. But the day after his marriage, he ordered through me three dozen more. He was a man of quick learning ability, and certainly with Frank Launder one of the most gifted screen playwrights of the thirties.

Friedrich Zelnick changed his name to Frederick Zelnick. Being the boss, he magnanimously invited Frank and me to the literary eating place on Fleet Street, the famous Cheshire Cheese, which was so conservative that it had not even changed its chairs in a hundred years and, I'm sure, never changed their menu of turtle soup and trifle. Each chair was marked with the name of the famous man who had sat there frequently in the nineteenth century. Zelnick occupied the poet Swinburne's chair, mine showed the plaque for Charles Dickens, and Frank's Boswell. I don't know where ideas come from, but sitting in those places, the talent of those famous men might have traveled from the bottom of the seat to my brain.

I told Zelnick an idea for the opening of his picture. The picture should start with the first launching of a hot air balloon, the Montgolfier, which made an ascent of ten minutes at Annonay near Paris, on June 5, 1783. Thousands of Parisians, including King Louis XV, were present to watch the phenomenon of a man leaving the Earth and flying into space. Hired to occupy the gondola, the man who was paid to ascend into the clouds panicked at the last moment and ran away. Not to disappoint the king, the two brothers Montgolfier, Joseph and Jacques, grabbed du Barry's little dog and threw him into the gondola. The balloon took off, the dog barked frantically, and Marie Jeanne ran after her airborne pooch. The king was so amused by the incident and intrigued by the spunky girl that he wanted to meet her. As Madame du Barry, she became his mistress.

Frank and I wrote the screenplay. Frank was a very slow writer. It took him an hour to put down a line. But we had a lifelong friendship. When I visited him in his palatial villa in Nice fifty years later, I finally asked him why it took him that long to put words on paper. He confessed that he did not understand my English. Nor did I his northern English accent.

The black cat's metaphysical prediction had come through. Life suddenly was perfect. Germany and the emigration were a nightmare, disappearing in the mist. BIP got a labor permit for me, that precious bureaucratic document that decides a foreigner's destiny. Convinced that life's problems were solved forever, I conveniently forgot that I was on a day-to-day permit to stay in England. But it was in Henrietta's mind that, after having learned English fluently, we would emigrate to America. She deliberately hid that secret plan from me, as I found out decades later.

Mycroft was pleased with the screenplay for *Gitta Alpar*: "I Give My Heart." Zelnick started shooting. Mycroft, who suddenly was available, asked me to write a story for a German actress, Dolly Haas, who also had emigrated to England.

I got money from France where Robert directed *La crise est finie*, my original screenplay. Danielle Darrieux, whom I had helped to "discover" in *Le Bal* in 1931, was the lead.

Now we had enough cash to rent an apartment for our nuclear family: father, mother, and child.

Unfortunately, our apartment was situated above that of the landlord's, who raised smelly bull terriers and cooked kippers for breakfast. That fish, unknown to us, sent waves of odor of burning fish oil that was mixed with dog odor through our apartment. But it was home, safety, and security. We decided that Geoffrey should be baptized, and I contacted the nearest church, an Episcopal, in the neighborhood. I wanted to divorce the next generation of my family from the Jewish faith, foolishly believing that I could save my son from belonging to a minority whose members for generations had been victims of murder. Besides, I was not religious. Religions are based on inflexible dogmas, and as a writer, I wanted to follow my own mental processes and not what a religion forces on its believers. Who were those people who had laid down those rules? Were they guided by a power that neglected to inspire me? Besides, a child can only be Jewish if the mother is born of that religion. I found dozens of reasons why the new member of the Siodmak clan should not be Mosaic. It would have been smarter not to have him baptized at all and let him choose his own religion when he was grown up. All of my life I was afraid of dogmatic teachings, since I had found out that those who can make you believe absurdities can make you commit atrocities. The world's history proves again and again that theory to me.

Native-born, Geoffrey automatically was a British citizen. I didn't even have him circumcised.

It was the aftershock from my expulsion of my former existence that I wanted to maybe remove myself as far as possible from racial hatred, ethnic troubles, and prejudices. As I found out in life, it cannot be done.

I asked Frederick Zelnick and Frank Launder to be godfather to our son. Henrietta's mother sent a lace veil from Switzerland for the baby to wear. The veil had served Henrietta's family for centuries for those occasions.

We took the child to church. Geoffrey cried. He didn't like becoming an Episcopalian.

The church was clammy and cold. The deacon held the little bundle that protested loudly. Then a beam of sunlight fell through the clerestory, illuminating Geoffrey's face. He smiled. The Jewish godfather Frederick Zelnick kneeled down as is the rule of the ceremony, then took Geoffrey from the deacon's arms. The deacon sprinkled holy water on the boy and mumbled benedictions. The ritual over, we left the church with the first non-Jewish Siodmak in our family history, which had been of the Jewish faith since Adam and Eve.

There was a basic culture in the British nation, different from the robust German types we had dealt with all our lives. Since our knowledge of English was still limited, we only perceived the good in the new country, which did not seem to have the xenophobic viciousness of the Germans. It was a country of innocence, so we thought. My friend Frederick Kohner who, with his wife on his way to America, had rented rooms at the boardinghouse Radnor Hall, on the outskirts of London, shocked the owners when he took a bath together with his wife. He also was "bunking with her," sleeping in the same bed with her. Those things were not officially done in the country that still had an ingrained Victorian tradition.

The story I wrote for BIP, *Girls Will Be Boys,* was geared for the purity of the British mind. The famous actor Sir C. Aubrey Smith played a misanthropic lord who hated women and wanted an heir for his vast fortune. His married daughter had given birth to a child who would inherit the grandfather's wealth, but she was afraid to tell the curmudgeon who lived miles away in his castle (in my conception, ultrarich Englishmen always lived in castles) that he had a granddaughter, and not the grandson he was expecting. Afraid he would disinherit the child, she made him believe that child was a boy. The old man wanted to meet the heir to his name, whom his daughter hid from him as long as she could. Finally she sent her daughter dressed as a boy to the grandfather. Dolly Haas fitted the part, slender, gamin-faced, small-breasted, her red hair cropped short. Her tomboy character deceived the old man right through the first and second acts, until he found out that his "grandson" was a girl. By then he had fallen in love with her, and the happy ending was an expected conclusion.

Today such an idea would be a two-hour TV show for children, but it pleased Mycroft's and the studio owner, Maxwell's, post-Victorian minds. We left the kipper-frying landlord and invited a German refugee, Rudolf Katcher, to move in with us to share the rent. I don't think that there were more than half a dozen emigrant Jews from the film business permitted to stay in England. Rudolf, who made England his home for the rest of his life, Anglicized his German name to Rudolfo Cartier, worked for twenty-six years as a writer and TV director for the staid British Broadcasting Corporation(BBC). Born in Germany, he had the foresight of depositing money in foreign banks and had accumulated a nest egg, a safety net in case of emergencies. Henrietta, the baby, and I shared an apartment, adding the bachelor Rudolf to our family. He bought a refrigerator, the newest scientific invention of that time, and was so awed by its efficiency and beauty that he placed it in the living room, like a precious piece of furniture. There it stood, that modern miracle, created by contemporary science, keeping the milk for the baby always fresh.

My friendship with Rudolf went back to my first efforts in screenplay writing in Berlin in 1926, when Rudolf and I composed a script for a real-life count, Graf Perponchet, who wanted to make a film in the South Seas. Never having been closer to that exotic part of the world than the outskirts of Berlin, we read many books on that mysterious subject.

Perponchet hired two actors and a cameraman to send on the twelve thousand–mile trip, expecting them to return with a full-length picture, featuring dances of exotic and erotic South Sea bare-bellied beauties. One of the actors was Egon Ziesemer, who, being a gentile, later flourished as a director under Goebbels's protection. The other, a funny little Jew, was Max Nosseck, a born comedian. He lisped, and every sentence he uttered sounded like a joke. The two actors went on the ill-prepared trip. They kept only one gag: how to boil eggs in a volcano. The rest of the screenplay they tossed into the South Seas and returned without exotic dancing girls.

Years later I met Max again in Hollywood, where he was under contract to the MGM Studios. He still had his funny delivery, this time in Yiddish-accented English. A refugee, he had gone to New York where he managed to act, produce, and direct inexpensive films in Yiddish. Louis B. Mayer, the MGM tycoon, had screened Nosseck's pictures. A professional Jew, he had shed tears, which he frequently did, moved by Max's story of a poor Jewish family of immigrants in Brooklyn, his birthplace. He put Max under contract to MGM, a gesture of charity that did not cost him anything, since the company paid the salary. In Hollywood Max found nothing to do but collect his weekly check. The year was 1939. Max wouldn't break the ritual of having lunch in the MGM commissary. He always ordered chicken soup, since it was Mayer's contention that chicken soup cured every sickness. When I invited Max to have lunch with me in a better place than the commissary, he refused. Once, Mayer had passed his table, recognized him, and had greeted him with "Hi,

Nosseck!" That miracle could happen again, Max hoped. He sat out his contract, appearing for two years every day at the commissary, eating chicken soup, waiting from eleven to two for the big boss, who never appeared again. But for him, this was making a living.

For us, England was home. We had a native-born son, Geoffrey, and loved that country, which was placid, peaceful, and not hectic as Germany was before the Nazis took over. Mycroft, obviously content with my work for him, assigned me to a third picture: *It's a Bet,* after a stage play by Marcus McGill, *Hide and I'll Find You.*

Suddenly the dream of having found a new homeland became a nightmare. One morning two stout men wearing bowler hats stood at the door of our apartment.

"Which port do you prefer to take," one asked me. "Dover or Folkstone?"

I didn't understand the question.

"You and your wife will be leaving England this week," one said. "You have no labour permit. And without a labour permit, you are not permitted to stay in this country." No labour permit? I had just turned in my screenplay to BIP and was waiting for eventual changes to be made. I went to the accounting office at BIP to talk to the accountant, Percy Stapleton, who had issued my checks. Stapleton was in distress. "Sorry, we cannot get your permit renewed by the Department of Labour," he informed me. Why, he did not know. He suggested that I leave the country and BIP would get me back as soon as possible. "The company owes me seventy-five pounds," I reminded him. Seventy-five pounds was a sizable sum for me. Stapleton was desolate. "We can't pay you, since your contract states that you have to be at the studio in case of script changes, and we might have to pay that money to another writer." "We have roots in England; we have a British child," I reminded him.

"Of course he can stay," Stapleton informed me. "Or take him with you."

Later on I found out that the studio had not asked for an extension of the permit. Mycroft did not have an assignment for me and also wanted to save the company seventy-five pounds.

Henrietta was, as always during times of disaster, calm and collected. She was certain that BIP would call me back, since I had written three screenplays that had been successful films. Rudolf, a bachelor, offered to look after the baby since it was difficult to travel with a child who was only half a year old.

I went to the agency of Vere Barker and Connie's where I knew Elizabeth Blumann. Bluemchen, "little flower," had been the top motion picture agent in Berlin. She was perhaps the wisest woman I have ever met in my life. She had married Mr. Sanders, a British-born gentleman, who, for a certain sum, had made her a British subject. She had no labor problem. Dutifully she met her "husband" Mr. Sanders once a week, but did not live with him. Elizabeth Blumann, now Elizabeth Sanders, had been the confidanté of Marlene Dietrich and German stars like Magda Schneider, whose daughter, Romy Schneider, became an international star, Willy Forst, and Brigitte Helm, who starred in Fritz Lang's *Metropolis*.

I went to the French consulate. They told me it would take weeks before I could get permission to enter France. But I knew that in a couple of days I would be forcibly removed from England. Henrietta, Swiss-born, was permitted to enter France.

The succeeding weeks still seem today a dreamlike experience to me. Was it real or a nightmare that reeled itself up like a horror film? I was on a channel ferry. When the boat arrived in Calais, French emigration officers boarded it. Since I had no entry visa, I was not permitted to leave the ship. Henrietta went ashore, to get me a permit in France. I sailed back to England where I was forbidden to land.

It was the second night in my life when I didn't seem to have enough will to face the shocks of emigration. What kind of world was I living in where a small booklet with government stamps ruled my existence? My ethnic origin decided whether I should live or die. What made me so different from others that I got punished for being born in a country not of my choosing? I was a member of an eternally wandering tribe of which I had little knowledge. I didn't look different than my neighbors. I was educated in the same schools as my peers. Was it the whim of the gods, as Aristotle had described the fate of men, a curse that still lasted after two millennia?

Was Mycroft evil, destroying my livelihood, saving seventy-five pounds for the company? Was Maxwell, the millionaire studio owner, evil years later letting Mycroft, impoverished and lonely, starve to death? I once talked to a Catholic missionary who tried to bring Christian enlightenment to the Muslim heathens in Bangladesh. He told me of the unending cycle of disaster that befell that country every year, of the rains that brought the floods, of the floods that brought cholera, of the thousands of dead people, mostly children and the old, whom the wake of that epidemic left behind. Was nature cruel? Or is death and destruction the seed of the never-ending cycle of nature, with its mysterious laws of renewal? Only when disaster strikes us personally do we learn the inclemency of life. Only people afflicted by it feel the impact of evil and know its nature. My grandchildren might hear or read my life story. They cannot visualize the torture of being a captive on a rickety ferry, crossing a body of water back and forth, just because of a rubber stamp imprint missing on a piece of paper.

The ferry went back to Folkstone, where I was not permitted to go ashore. I had to sail back to Calais, where the French emigration office wouldn't let me off.

The captain of the boat, Roger Greene, became aware of the wandering Jew on his boat who could not pay his fare. A former captain of a destroyer during World War I, he hated the Germans but even more despised the British bureaucracy. He was the counterbalance of evil, a savior, the image of kindness. I told him that my wife was in France to get me the permission to land, and I was searching every time among the crowd on the peer in Calais to see Henrietta's copper head with its unruly hair, before the ferry returned to Folkstone.

Greene permitted me to stay in the empty purser's office. He was bored with his job. He shared his food with me in his comfortable cabin. We played chess. As a boy of fourteen I had been junior champion of the Drei Koenig Gymnasium. I didn't let him win a game, which was a challenge to him, and he waited for one of the channel storms that would paint my face green with nausea. Then he had a chance to checkmate me.

Whenever we arrived in Calais he was afraid Henrietta would show up with entry papers, which would deprive him of his chess partner.

I had thoughts of committing suicide, knowing every wave of the dirty green channel stream. But I thought of Henrietta and my son, my friend Rudolf who had to change his diapers, Henrietta's eternal optimism, which believed that, when having reached the depths, life can only improve. On the ninth day she was standing at the pier, waving papers. I could go ashore. Roger Greene asked me when we were going to finish our chess game, which was in progress. I assured him that we would do it by mail. We never did.

Writers, when they are in trouble, protect themselves by creating a make-believe world on paper, substituting the harsh life that confronts them with one of their imagination. Besides, should they write a salable story, it could have indefinite ramifications and great financial possibility. A story carries its own momentum. It is called a "project," and an author must create many projects, to have material when the opportunity for a sale arrives. A writer without stories on paper is like a shoe salesman without shoes to sell.

For years I had researched an idea that I found amusing, novel, and that contained the ingredients for a book, a motion picture, and even a stage musical.

When I worked in France, in 1931, on *Le Bal* for UFA, I read an anecdote in the *Paris Soir*, the sophisticated boulevard evening paper. The item was, I guess, a filler, to cover an empty space in the paper. It told about the day of the opening of the Paris World Exhibition on the first of April 1867. At that time, there was only one city of glamour in the world: the Paris of Louis Napoleon. Berlin, the capital of Prussia, was a provincial sandbox; New York, after the civil war, a city without direction or shape and that had not found its identity. Victorian London was chained to Puritan traditions by the queen's taboos. Czar Alexander's Moscow was a city forbidden to foreigners. But Paris was the city of lights, of culture, amusing, uninhibited and exciting.

The World Exhibition of 1867 was an enormous complex of halls, built on the Champs de Mars, where now the Eiffel Tower stands. I had found at the National Library in Paris a twelve-volume encyclopedia, describing technical novelties that staggered the imagination of that time. The end of the nineteenth century was the beginning of the mechanical age, the creation of locomotives, steam presses, gigantic machines moved by steam-driven wheels.

The French emperor Louis Napoleon invited the rulers of Europe, Africa, and Asia to build pavilions to exhibit their cultures and wares. On the day of the opening at exactly seven o'clock in the evening, thirty-two thousand gas lamps illuminated the street of Paris for the first time. Thirty-two thousand lamp lighters must have stood at the lampposts to light the gas candelabras at that minute.

The entrance of the Paris World Exhibition faced the Pont d'Iena on the Quai d'Orsay where today embassies are located. At the foot of the bridge, a triumphal arch, formed by sixty-foot columns, had been erected. It flew the banners of the empires and kingdoms participating in the gigantic extravaganza that the emperor had launched to impress the world with France's power and wealth. On the opening day, three emperors, seven kings, a viceroy, nine grand dukes, one archbishop, two bishops, five dukes, twenty-two princes of blood, and a throng of titled personages passed through that gate, which was named Passage des Princes.

By strict protocol, the last one to arrive at the opening was Louis Napoleon and his wife, the Empress Eugenie.

But then a latecomer, the "Duchess of Gerolstein," was announced. A calash pulled by four white horses, the top of the convertible folded back, drove to the grandstand in full view of the royalties. In it sat a blonde young woman exposing enchanting forms in a deep cleavage. But instead of stopping, the carriage went right past the grandstand and disappeared.

The sexy apparition was Hortense Schneider, Jacques Offenbach's leading lady. *The Duchess of Gerolstein* was the title of an operetta by Jacques Offenbach, which was playing at the Bouffe Parisiens, a rickety theater on the Avenue des Champs Elysées.

The crowned heads, of course, wanted to make the acquaintance of that radiant beauty, since it was the fashion of the time for royalty to have a beautiful actress or a famous dancer as a mistress. Leopold, the king of Belgium, had as his mistress the exotic dancer Cleo de Merode, a relationship that lasted so long that he was called by his subjects "Cleopold." From that day of Hortense's daring publicity stunt, the first one in history, Offenbach's theater was filled to capacity as long as the exhibition lasted. Hortense became the mistress of so many kings and emperors that jealous women called her "passage des princes" (a passageway for princes). She died in 1929, still unmarried and rich.

I had told that story, which I had named *For Kings Only*, to the charming young actresses, Frances Day, a singer and dancer who was under contract to the Gaumont British Film Studios in London. There was no more desirable part, I thought, for an actress than playing the pampered mistress of many kings, being feted as a singer and dancer, manipulating world policies, receiving innumerable precious gifts, never getting married, being the toast of Paris, and besides having great fun.

Frances Day had a rival at Gaumont, Jessie Matthews, also a singer and dancer who already had an international reputation. Frances needed an important vehicle to outshine Jessie.

Marooned in France, I hoped that by completing that story my British agent, the Connie Agency, with the help of Frances Day, would sell that story to Gaumont British and I would return to England, protected from expulsion by a labor permit.

Our hopes are our prayers. Hope overshadows all fears and doubts, and I did not permit myself to doubt. Only when a writer gives up creating does he put a stop to his hopes. I had no doubt whatsoever that

For Kings Only would get me out of France and back to England. I worked day and night at my little portable typewriter which the "ghost cat" had blessed.

The small beach hotel in Quiberville near Dieppe where we went to wait out the uncertainties of our life was run by a resolute woman. Her brother was an inventor, devising novelties such as a clever cigarette lighter or a new toy that would make him rich overnight. He worked on his inventions in a hotel room that he had changed into a workroom. The hotel had been recommended to us by Robert as being inexpensive. There I waited for a reply to my numerous letters to Mycroft, who never answered.

Rolf, our youngest brother, had stayed in Quiberville for a time, his upkeep paid by Robert. When the German borders were closed to the Jews, I had taken Rolf to Switzerland to live with Henrietta's mother in Barbengo. There he was happy. He never had a profession, was neglected by our father, he hardly remembered his mother, and we older brothers had no time for him, being too occupied staying alive in countries that were reluctant to accept us. Rolf should have stayed with Ernestine in Barbengo, in Switzerland. Ernestine was a substitute mother whom he loved. Why Robert uprooted Rolf and took him to France, I don't know.

Having met the Haitian ambassador to France, Robert was intrigued by that man's description of that impoverished Caribbean island, run by a crooked dictator. Besides, the ambassador painted a colorful future in his country for young white people. He wrote a letter of recommendation for Rolf, and Robert shipped him off to that most primitive place in the Caribbean with its teeming unemployed blacks, its indescribable poverty. Rolf arrived, turned around, and returned to France and to his death.

He had a love affair with the teenaged daughter of the woman who ran the Quiberville hotel, and he even showed me the receipts, which he carried like a treasure, of the hotel room where he had an affair with the girl.

One day I got a telephone call from the police in Versailles. An impersonal voice said, "Your brother is mortally wounded." It was the police's way to tell me that Rolf was dead. They had discovered one of my letters to him in his pocket and phoned me in Quiberville. He had been found in the Park of Versailles with a bullet in his head. How he got hold of a gun, I didn't know. Many years later I learned that already in Germany he had tried to kill himself by swallowing a handful of Veronal tablets.

He had killed himself because his Quiberville girlfriend had dropped him. Suicide is an attention getter. He might have wanted to punish her with his death. He, a very handsome young man, blew out his brains for her. I remember her mother, the hotel owner, being in a state of terror, afraid her daughter might have been part of a suicide pact.

Rolf was also a victim of Germany's persecution of the Jews, though he might not have been a Jew at all—remembering the fling my mother had with the Crown Prince of Saxony, whom he somewhat resembled. Rolf, being without direction, deserted by everyone, even his brothers, saw no future for himself in the churning cauldron of that time.

There is heroism in taking one's own life, a contempt for the world, a decision shared with no one. It slowly builds to its climax, which culminates in the final exit. As the Talmud states, "It is better not to be born than to be born." The Talmud asks, "Is life worth the struggle, the wars, the despair and pain, if existence on this planet led to the inevitable end of mankind?"

Earth, having started as a fiery rock, will finally cool off, extinguishing all of nature's efforts. The struggle of millions of years and the search for a meaning of life will have ended, taking along the human accomplishments in science, arts, and philosophies. And God, when the planet returns to its original beginning, will be unemployed.

There are people who are born old. Rolf might have lived out his span of life that destiny had allotted to him. According to the coroner, Rolf had shot himself at two o'clock in the morning. Since the Park of Versailles closed its gates at seven, the tortures he must have gone through, lonely and abandoned, during those seven hours, are haunting my life.

I met Robert in Paris. He was cutting his film *La crise est finie*. He insisted on playing the musical tape of that film for me, asking my opinion about the songs that Danielle Darrieux delivered. *La crise* was a pleasant film; the actors were young people, handsome boys and girls. All the girls had a crush on Robert, as he told me.

Robert and I quarreled heatedly about the music, a camouflage that hid the guilt that we had not done enough for Rolf and that we might have prevented his death.

Rolf was buried at the Jewish cemetery in Versailles. A young girl appeared. She had been in love with him and had been his friend to the end. He had never told us about her, but she had visited his body in the morgue several times. We did not. As at the death of my mother, I didn't want to have a last impression of a tortured, possibly crushed face. I wanted to remember him as he was. Nor did I see Robert's body when he died many years later. Was it cowardice or self-preservation to keep the image of people happy in my memory?

A rabbi spoke a few words. He looked desperately poor. He put a wooden stick in the soil to mark the grave as the Jewish desert tribes have done for thousands of years, when they wandered on, leaving their dead behind. A few rocks were put on the grave, to "discourage hyenas from digging up bodies." The people, who had brought the coffin, looked on from a distance, with curiously still, impassive faces.

When Robert's coffin stood, forty years later, in the hall of a crematorium in Locarno, in Switzerland, there were the same impassive and oddly still faces of men in the background watching us, as though they were eternal companions of death, always present at the end of life.

I no longer know where Rolf's grave is located. He left no trace during his short trip on this Earth, for he walked alone, staggering and lost, in a world that, having given him nothing, had taken his only possession from him, his youth. He was nineteen years old when he took his life.

Henrietta and I would not stay in Quiberville, due to our traumatic memories. We moved to the adjoining country, Belgium, traveling by bus, crossing a border that was not guarded since French workers routinely moved daily to Belgium for work, to return to their French villages at night.

We rented a little bungalow at the beach in Knocke, waiting for the miracle to happen, as the black cat had predicted.

We were on the run again, as though by moving constantly we could outrun fate. We didn't look back but went on, afraid we could be deported from France back to Germany.

What next? How to pay for rent and food, stay or take trips? General Bum, the thin leather purse that kept the money, had only a few Italian banknotes left, some French, a few English pounds, and five twenty-franc Swiss gold pieces.

We stayed in Knocke, at the beach outside Bruges. It was the off-season, cold and inexpensive. Small bathing huts on wheels stood along the dry sand. A policeman in a heavy blue uniform and a helmet like an English bobby watched for bathers should they try to bathe in indecent attire. Belgium, a Catholic country with Victorian morals and antiquated decency rules, did not allow bathers to expose any flesh on the beach. One had to have the carriage pulled by a horse into the gentle surf and then step from the bathing house into the ocean. Henrietta, who wore a one-piece bathing suit without skirt, was in danger of being fined for improper exposure. Men had to wear long suits that reached down to their calves. Women wore skirts, stockings, and blouses with long sleeves and frilly bathing caps. One had to get dressed to go swimming.

I revisited Knocke in 1962. Young girls in shoestring halters and G-strings ambled along the beach, which was unchanged. No policeman was around, and the horse-drawn bathing houses had disappeared. Belgian morals, I'm sure, had not been contaminated by the absence of Mother Hubbard bathing suits, and the pretty Belgian girls, parading almost in the nude, were still as bourgeois as when the state watched over their virtue.

Henrietta went back to London. She was permitted entry since she had a British-born son. I was not. Geoffrey was bunked with our bachelor friend, Rudolf Katcher, a composite of substitute father, mother, and nanny. He told Henrietta that Geoffrey liked to watch bridge games until the wee hours in the morning but didn't participate. He was an exceptionally well-behaved child. Once Rudolf had made the grave mistake of feeding the baby plum pudding, with disastrous results.

Henrietta took my precious treatment of *For Kings Only* with her to deliver to my agent, the Connie Agency, on Regent Street, despite that it was written in my faulty English.

I was left in Knocke to wait. Our fate rested on one story that nobody had read. I took a sheet of paper, drew a line down the middle, and wrote all the pluses we had on the left side and the negatives on the right side. On the plus side I wrote that I was convinced Frances Day would like *For Kings Only*. She had clout as a high-priced star at Gaumont. Besides, I had felt a chemistry between her and myself, an affinity that would make her fight for my brainchild. Another plus was that the important agency, Connie's, was looking after us, and our agent, whom we knew from Germany, Bluemchen (a name that she kept to the end of her life), knew that the bridge behind us had collapsed. That small army was going to battle for us.

Sometimes moments of fear broke through my defense. Knowing that I had created a make-believe world, I shut the door to my conscience by starting another story right away, just in case *For Kings*

Only would not be accepted. I had written off British International Pictures, knowing they would never engage me again since they owed me money.

Again I created a private retreat for myself, shutting out the surrounding world. In the hotel lobby I found a tattered book in French, a novel by Henryk Sienkiewicz, a Polish novelist who had received the Nobel Prize for literature in 1905 for his novel *Quo Vadis*. The book I discovered was *Through Desert and Wilderness*. It was the story of a ten-year-old English girl, the daughter of an English archeologist, who with her friend, a fourteen-year-old boy, is kidnapped by the Arabs to be taken to Ahmad Mahdi as hostages.

Times between the present world and a hundred years ago certainly have not changed. The Arabs still kidnap people to blackmail the Western world. The two children are sent to Khartoum and arrive just after its fall. The British General Gordon, who defended that city, had been killed, and the Mahdi had crushed the last resistance of the Egyptian army, which Gordon had commanded. The children escape during the turmoil of the looted and burning city and make their way back to their British parents. They cross the Sudan desert. The boy grows into manhood and the girl into a woman during the perilous voyage. I loved the word *perilous,* which I found in a dictionary, and retitled the story *The Most Perilous Voyage.*

I imagined that Gaumont British would also be looking for a story for the teenaged actress, Nova Pilbeam, who had just had an international success in a Gaumont film where she played the young Lady Jane Grey. Writing every day for fourteen hours, I pulled down a curtain that shut out the "most perilous" world around me, while I was waiting to hear from Henrietta. But I was slowly running out of my frail optimism.

I could not sell that screenplay in England but dug it out thirty years later. In 1966, I went to Cairo to make a deal with the Egyptian government to produce and direct that story. I had it already cast with two adorable teenagers, when the Israeli-Egyptian war in 1967 dashed my hopes. Since the novel was written by a master storyteller, Sienkiewicz, I had little to invent but to telescope it into a screenplay. A book cannot be made into a motion picture without mutilating its content. A film is an extended short story. That is why novels suffer being photographed for the screen. It would require more than the two hours allotted to a film.

Later in America, I tried to find a studio to produce it. *The Most Perilous Voyage* was a perfect vehicle for the Disney studio, which specialized in children's stories. A friend of mine, William Beaudine, who knew Walt Disney and directed motion pictures for that studio, got me an audience with that tycoon.

Walt Disney, surrounded by a permanent halo of tobacco smoke, an affliction that finally killed him, received me in his private office. It contained no writing desk. Disney had risen above the commercial standard of the typical Hollywood producer and liked to talk to his visitors, sitting behind a small round desk, which made the meeting highly informal. We were served tea in English china cups. Walt treated me as if he had known me for years, talking intimately about his studio, revealing privately kept details. There was a cartoonists' strike in progress at the studio, and his employees walked by the window of his office building carrying posters. Walt was notorious for underpaying the people working for him. He was offended by the demonstration and remarked that the Jews always marched in the front of those processions. I don't know how his public relations department handled that racial slur, but they managed to get him a medal from the Jewish organization of Bnai Brith. He must have made that racial slander before, which his PR department, maybe at great costs, defused. Its dissemination would have hurt his company's business since the releasing theaters were mostly in Jewish hands. He also told me, a stranger, that his theme park in Anaheim had been financed to the tune of $65 million by a multimillionaire whose name I had never heard and promptly forgot. As though talking to an old acquaintance, he told me that he regretted not having bought more land adjacent to his project. It now was crowded with cheap enterprises, cashing in on Disneyland's success. It was a curious meeting since I had no chance to talk about my story. When I tried to mention that subject, he told me to get in touch with his story editor, who would report to him.

That visit was the most frustrating "story conference" of my life. But his story editor, obviously alerted by his office, was waiting for me. He had read my screenplay thoroughly. He told me that he would never recommend such a story to his studio. A boy who, though in self-defense, shoots two Arabs? Impossible. Disney Studios, he told me with suppressed anger, prides itself in never showing violence. That remark baffled me, since the Disney cartoons, manufactured for children, contained some of the most gruesome nightmares that ever hit the screen. I left defeated and buried that story in my files.

In 1993, Disney Studios produced this story as its top production of the year. I didn't remind the story department that years ago my screenplay had been rejected by them.

I could not prove that the story department had found my screenplay in its files. Since the Sienkiewicz novel was in public domain, I could only congratulate myself for my superior sense in story judgment, which, unfortunately, was twenty years ahead of its time. The studio people who had rejected my screenplay, among them Walt Disney and his story editor, had died. But good stories are eternal.

At the hotel in Knocke, I had paid my hotel bill, and the General Bum was empty when the Connie Agency called from London. Vere Barker, co-owner of the agency, talked to me. His father was high society, a member of the House of Lords. That's why Vere always wore striped trousers and a cutaway coat and sported a bowler hat, briefcase, and an umbrella, even when the sun was shining. He related to me that he had succeeded in persuading Gaumont British to option *For Kings Only*. I should return to England with the morning ferry. Gaumont had arranged for an entry and labor permit. The boss of the studio, Mr. Maurice Ostrer, wanted to meet me. Though the pay was not what Barker had expected, he got me the labor permission to stay in England. He didn't mention the amount I was to receive. There also was a letter with pound notes in the mail, courtesy of the Connie Agency, just in case I might be short of cash! I wasn't short of it—I was devoid of it, and I guessed that Bluemchen had arranged that financial affair.

That night I walked along the deserted beach. The waves hit the beach in monotonous, eternal sounds. Hidden behind a shroud of ocean fog glowed the white cliffs of Dover. In back of me was the hostile European continent, with Germany and its booted Nazis, blindly trampling over lives to meet their chosen destiny. I promised myself never to return to that nightmare country, nor would I ever write another word of German.

It dawned on me that Gaumont had only offered an option for the story and that my position was still very precarious. But I also anticipated that Frances Day would never let go of that story. She was Hortense Schneider, the rebirth of Offenbach's golden canary, the uninhibited mistress of Louis Napoleon's Paris.

Her home in Kensington was a large studio apartment. A prominent antique piece in that tastefully furnished room was an enormous bed standing prominently on a platform surrounded by a low wrought-iron fence. That fence had a gate. Frances was a modern female spirit, half a century ahead of her time. I knew that wrought-iron door was open for me, since she selected her men like men wish they could choose their women. But, for me, the conduct of business was too intricate to be complicated by an intimate relation.

Next morning the letter with the money arrived. I bought the ticket for the ferry and with the remainder of the money a piece of old Belgian lace for Henrietta.

I knew I would be lucky. Luck is a substance with positive vibrations that almost tangibly manifest themselves. Luck also starts with tiny ripples of good fortune that often are followed by larger, stronger ones, sometimes even becoming enormous waves. So does misfortune. I definitely believe in vibrations: enter a house and feel at once the happiness or unhappiness of its inhabitants. I once owned a French eighteenth-century snuff box, with embossed Fragonard shepherds and shepherdesses. It was made of silver, and its top gilded. It conveyed an unpleasant vibration to me, which I could not explain to myself. One day the top of the box fell off and underneath, scratched in with a sharp utensil, possibly a diamond, was written in German, "Max, Max, where is the father of my dear children? He left me. He does not love me anymore."

I gave that carrier of evil to an actress whom I did not like.

I also remember my father's house when I was a teenager. It was a resplendently furnished place, but none of my friends wanted to stay for any length of time. Was it the ghost of my dead mother's unhappiness who had left distressing vibrations behind? I sometimes wonder what kind of unsound forces we acquire when we buy antique pieces of furniture. It is said that one cannot lead horses past a spot where a murder has been committed, and dogs howl in the distance if somebody is dying.

The Chinese and Japanese consult a wooden horoscope whose magnetic needle tells them whether the house they want to occupy is constructed according to astrological rules.

Now fifty years later in America, I live in a house in the country, which relaxes my friends and makes them feel cheerful. It might be my wife's disposition to live her life in beauty, an attitude that has permeated our home. There, in the large glass-enclosed living room, sits a green Swedish chair with a rounded back. How many of my visitors, arriving edgy from the haste of a big town, have fallen asleep in its soft embrace?

I left the European continent next morning from Dieppe, boarding the channel ferry to Southampton, unfortunately not to Folkstone, where I could have met my friend, Captain Roger Greene, to let him share my good fortune and possibly finish our interrupted chess game, the moves of which he surely had recorded.

Henrietta was waiting for me at the dock. It was foggy and cold, as we took the bus to London, past rows of identical-looking houses. We knew that it was history we were living through.

History is what you experience personally, not what you read in books. History is interpreting time from the present day's perspective. The Americans still write volumes about how they forcibly got rid of the imperial British in 1783, and the British historians tell how happy they were finally shedding those troublesome American colonies. In our case, the elation and the impact of returning to "civilization," and life, cannot be conveyed. It can only be experienced.

Now, living for more than half a century in America, whose inhabitants do not know political instability, how can a displaced emigrant of any nationality convey the insecurities, the proximity of death, menaced by forces that without reason condemn him to be a victim?

But my arrival in England, which promised a continuation of life, turned unrealistic hopes into reality. The impact of that time, which also struck hundreds of thousands of people and still does, has branded its mark in my memory.

I had arrived in a country of political and financial stability. I had been through the German inflation that had completely wiped out the country's internal debt by government manipulations. It had deliberately impoverished its middle class. Here in England, when a person had inherited from his family a trust fund of a few hundred pounds a year, he could manage to exist. In 1934 in England, money still had stability and even, as in Switzerland, could be changed into gold pieces.

My agent, Vere Barker, told me that Gaumont was willing to pay me fifteen pounds a week for twelve weeks for my services, which was three times a mailman's salary, to develop the treatment of *For Kings Only*. If they didn't decide on its production, my streak of luck might run out again, he added cruelly. I talked to Frances Day, who had been present when that deal was made at Gaumont. She told me that Angus McPhail, the studio's story editor, had suggested that I should be paid seven hundred pounds. But Vere Barker, my representative, to stay in good grace with Gaumont, had said, "Give that chap two hundred. But dish it out slowly. He accepts anything." He was a gentleman of impeccable standards, defending an English company against the intrusion of a foreigner.

A few years later he blew his brains out. That's what a gentleman of breeding had to do, according to an unwritten moral code, when he could not meet his gambling debts.

But presently I had an office in Gaumont's studios in Shepherd's Bush. It was an odd building in which to produce motion pictures. Large freight elevators traveled up and down. Pictures were in production at different floors. It seemed impractical to place a large studio in the middle of a city with its congestion and noises. Other film companies were logically situated in quite rural areas, like Elstree, Denham, or along the Thames River. But at the Gaumont studios, every floor had to stop production to permit one set to photograph a scene without sound interference from above or below.

My office was on the fourth floor. It was spacious and had an outer office for the secretary assigned to me, an eighteen-year-old. Mary had the translucent skin of the redhead and dark fawnlike eyes. Voluptuous and flirtatious, she was bait and fish at the same time. What I needed was an old battle-ax of a secretary, who knew the intricate politics and routine of the studio, corrected my faulty English, and advised and guided me through the maze of studio politics.

Mary worked for me for a year. One day I was alone in London, my wife having taken our son to see his grandmother in Switzerland. I drove along Oxford Street in my new Jowett two-cylinder car. There was Mary, walking seductively. I stopped to give her a lift. "I just thought of you," she said. I broke the iron rule and took her to my home. When I found out that she was a virgin, I drove her to her place. Offer a dog a piece of juicy meat, and he will eat it.

The rest of the story I found out years later when I worked at Universal Studios in Hollywood, where my British friend, Charles Bennett, also was engaged. Charles was an English writer whom I had met at Shepherd's Bush Studios. The day after our short tryst, Mary met Charles in the Shepherd's Bush freight elevator and asked him, "Mr. Bennett, do I look different to you?" He was not the only one whose opinion Mary wanted. It was the old story of kiss and tell. Even the head office, without my knowledge, reprimanded her, not me! Men among men are never rebuked for their sexual conduct by their peers. On the contrary, they are admired as being "macho."

After that embarrassing event, all of my secretaries were middle-aged, efficient, and close-mouthed. I learned that well-known truth from my old friend, the director Billy Wilder, whose secretary, though very mod, was in her late forties. "Every young female with whom a writer is confined daily is potential trouble," he advised me. I guess that he, too, must have gathered experience.

I did not know that I had an enemy at the studio, Frederick Fellner, a Jewish refugee, who felt threatened by any refugee from Hitler who also got a job at Gaumont. Fellner had been a successful film producer in Berlin. The shock of the emigration had affected his mind, and he was in mortal fear that his labor permit in England would not be extended. When he read my treatment of *For Kings Only,* he tried to sabotage its sale. A former partner of his, Ferenz Somlo, a Hungarian, who still worked in Paris, knew of a French play entitled *Passage des Princes,* which had the same historical heroine, portrayed by Hortense Schneider. Fellner told his former partner to take an option on the obscure French play. He then informed Gaumont's production department that a play featuring Hortense Schneider was in production in France, which was not true.

The French *Passage des Princes,* as I found out, was a dramatic play. In it, Count Carderousse, a consumptive, was Hortense's lover. A reverse *Camille* plot, it had nothing to do with my musical version of the World Exhibition of 1867.

But suddenly my chances of seeing *For Kings Only* developed became slim. Charles Bennett came to my rescue. Gaumont's top screenwriter, he had just written for Alfred Hitchcock, a young, still unknown director, the worldwide success *The 39 Steps* with Madeleine Carroll, a beauty with violet-colored eyes, and Robert Donat, Gaumont's leading man, the heartthrob of British teenagers.

Charles advised me to inundate Gaumont's story department with ideas. I went to Fellner, who was looking for a vehicle he could produce for Gaumont, and told him the story of *The Man Looking for His Murderer,* which I had written with Billy Wilder for Erich Pommer in Germany and which my brother Robert had directed.

The film started with a young man who wants to commit suicide because of a broken heart. Fellner was appalled. For him the theme of suicide was horrifying and taboo. As a producer he would never suggest such a shocking idea as self-destruction to the production company. I could not convince him that the story was a comedy and even let him read the satirical book *A Handbook on Hanging* by James Dunne, which showed in a "deadly reckoner" from what height a man of a certain weight has to be dropped to be properly hanged. It was a sardonic denunciation of the death penalty that still existed in England and that, contrary to every European law, was lately reintroduced in the United States. Dunne, by publishing his small book, satirized that if murder was society's unforgivable crime, how could the state impose such a cruel, inhumane public revenge?

Hitchcock was an inveterate practical joker. He found delight in sending so-called friends barrels with smelly herrings and found ways to embarrass his actors. He once stated, "I didn't say that actors are cattle. I said that actors should be treated like cattle." It was a sadistic streak in him that was well demonstrated in many of his pictures. But his "friends" found a way to embarrass him. They dropped old house keys with his address all over London. The tags carried the promise of a reward for returning the key personally. "Hitch" got them by the hundreds, people mobbing his house to get their reward. He got angry telephone calls and even threats and had to move for a time to a hotel. But that practical joke did not put a curb in his warped sense of humor.

When Hitchcock heard that Fellner was desperately afraid of being refused by the labor department, which would have meant deportation from England, he spread the rumor that the extension had been rejected by the department of labor. Fellner, a very heavy man, hanged himself from a doorknob, as described as an efficient final exit in Dunne's handbook.

A couple of days later the permission for Fellner to stay came through. It was Sir Alfred's most successful practical joke.

Andrew Sarris, the film critic, wrote after my brother Robert's death in 1974, "He [Hitchcock] manipulated Hollywood's fantasy apparatus with taste and intelligence." He did this directing motion pictures, but certainly not with his life.

I have my first impression of Robert when I was sitting on a chamber pot. The year was 1904, and I was two years old. The living room of the apartment on the third floor on Seidnitzer Platz in Dresden had three windows that looked out on a square. The school where I later went also was on that square, as was my father's egg storehouse. That perhaps is why he chose that location to live, since everything was within walking distance.

On a wall of the living room was a picture that I still remember, executed, as I found out in later years, in Seurat's style of pointillism depicting Mount Ararat, where Noah's Ark supposedly landed after the Flood. Even as a child I could never figure out how Noah could store millions of animal species in that small wooden hull. It was my father's favorite painting.

I remember a little boy with a shock of black hair doing some mischief in that room, while the sun was streaming through the windows. There was a large blue Dresden china tile stove in the corner. Robert had wedged his head between wall and stove and screamed in agony and terror. Father and Mother called the fire department, which came with sirens blasting. The firemen stood there with axes to smash the tiles, which Father prevented. They finally freed the little boy by pouring Mother's salad oil over Robert's head.

That's perhaps why I like to write, since I seem never to forget vivid or even casual impressions. Even snatches of dialogue stay in my mind seemingly forever, as if they were stored in drawers that I have only to open. Robert described in his memoir *Between Berlin and Hollywood,* which he wrote at the end of his life, many incidents that actually happened to me but not to him, as though they had been given to me by default, depriving his life of that experience. When he visited me years later, at my ranch in California, he sometimes secretly pocketed little objects, a miniature painting, a small porcelain dish, something not of great value, which he took with him to Europe where he lived, as if, by some voodoo charm, he could siphon off part of my life. It was sibling rivalry that he, until his death, never overcame but of which he also never was aware.

One day, later in my life when we both were successful in Hollywood, it dawned on me that I, too, was suffering from a "brother" complex. That word, like a psychoanalytic revelation, changed my relation with him to an amused bird's-eye view. From that moment on, his unconscious, sometimes cruel actions could not hurt me anymore. I even watched them with amusement. I remember when, working at Universal Studios, during the time when he was at the height of his artistic success directing the Academy Award–winning film *The Killers,* Mark Hellinger, his producer, was telling me with an amused smile, "Your brother Robert gave me your latest novel to read. He said, 'Mark, you have to read Curt's latest book. If you ever put it down, you can never pick it up again!'"

My success in a field in which he could not claim success for himself produced that Freudian slip. I am sure that he wanted to help me with that remark but here it was again, that sibling competition, which started with my birth, darkening his life.

In his eternal search for love and appreciation, of which he had a great share in his life, he resented his younger brother as an intruder. Two successful Siodmaks menaced his prominence.

But this sibling envy did not pertain at all to my two other brothers, Werner and Rolf, whom he unselfishly helped all his life, as long as he was financially able to do so. Money was his method to curry love. When I was out of a job and he was Universal's top director, he suggested me as the writer of a screenplay. "Let Curt do it; he is an excellent constructionist. For the dialogue take someone else." Of course I didn't get that assignment, though fortunately my relationship with Universal did not depend on his recommendation, having written for that studio twenty-eight motion picture screenplays as a freelance writer. His subconscious emotions, which never penetrated his awareness, made him do things contrary to his love for me.

A short time after his death, examining his life, recalling his attempts to dominate me, I felt hatred for him, as if he had consistently tried to make me feel inferior. But then, despite those contradictory emotions, he was the only person, except for Henrietta, who played a most important role in my life. He certainly was the stronger character, a rebel like my father who ate ham on the Sabbath in the marketplace to hurt my grandfather, the rabbi.

Robert was unbribable and hated to make compromises in his work, not considering any ensuing difficulties that might hurt him. When he directed *The Crimson Pirate* in Italy on the island of Ischia, Burt Lancaster, his star, became extremely difficult to handle. As Robert told in his memoirs, Burt and the producer Harold Hecht conspired to oust him and to shift the director's credit to Lancaster. They did not succeed. When the film was finished, Robert gave a party and invited actors, cast, and crew, except Lancaster, which enraged the actor.

"You invited everybody, but not me," Lancaster said, insulted.

"You behaved so atrociously during the shooting," Robert answered, "that I never want to see you again. You may become the greatest actor in the world and offer me a million dollars to direct you, but I will never work with you again." Robert never again even talked to Lancaster. But in Burt's office in Los Angeles hangs the poster of *The Killers,* the picture that made him a star, with Robert's name as director on it.

It is disconcerting how even very intelligent people cannot handle success without suffering a change of character, possibly to make up for the time when they were, despite their talent, not recognized by their peers or by the public. In every successful person a desire to outshine his peers seems to be the unconquerable desire. Ferenc Molnar, the highly successful Hungarian playwright, said, "It is not enough to succeed, the others must fail." The ephemeral, baseless insecurity of creative people does not seem to abate even when they reach "the top."

Robert never made compromises in his life. I often did, since I never considered my contribution to a film a major one. Filmmaking was not the obsession of my life. It was Robert's, exclusive of all others, including his relations to his wife or to me. There was nothing else for him other than working in a studio. I, a writer of stories, have never found anything more important than putting ideas on paper.

It is my contention that a writer can never really put on paper what he wants to express. A film director's work is final, since it is encased in celluloid. Though it might contain mistakes, the end product cannot be changed. The filmmaker cannot correct anything except by cutting it out or changing its continuity. Even by adding scenes, the picture rarely becomes better. B. P. Schulberg, the head of Paramount at the time when I worked there, stated, "If the picture is a piece of shit and you put a golden crust on it, you still have a piece of gilded shit." Maybe that's why Irving Thalberg, the famous MGM producer, sometimes threw away the first version of a motion picture and had it completely reshot, to create a "perfected" version.

Robert had a strange juxtaposition of ultrahigh sensitivity and kindness toward strangers, with a cutting cruelty for others. Only today am I able to put the jigsaw puzzle of his complex character together. He was a child who never grew up, which was one of his gifts that made him a borderline genius.

He had an unfailing intuition as to how to approach and treat actors to make them rise to the limit of their abilities. He made Burt Lancaster, a young and unknown actor, a world star in *The Killers*. He took a beautiful young girl, Ava Gardner, who could not act, and gave her a lead in the same picture. She emerged from it as one of the top stars of the screen. Tony Curtis (Bernie Schwartz) tells the story of how Robert picked him out from a group of extras during the shooting of *Criss Cross* and let him dance with Yvonne de Carlo, taking close-ups of that handsome couple, which prompted Universal to tie Tony to a long-term contract. Robert found an unknown stage actor, Ernest Borgnine, in New York, and among the great actors in Europe he created Brigitte Horney and numerous others who take their place in film history. Mario Adorf, now a well-known German stage and motion picture actor, whom I met in Munich after

Robert's death, told me, "If Robert had made more films with me, I would have become an international star! Only he knew how to direct an actor to find his ultimate possibilities!"

He always was Svengali in search of a Trilby: as soon as his discoveries reached stardom, Robert lost interest in them. He had to exercise his power over people, a power that he cunningly sugarcoated with humor and unquenchable enthusiasm. He instilled confidence in everyone he worked with. But as soon as they became stars, challenging his authority, he never used them again.

Enforced with a seemingly unlimited energy, a vacation from work was punishment for him. But that childlike "disorder," if I may call it so, interfered with his building a security for his old age. He died, poor and forgotten, as if he had deliberately worked toward that goal. He was looking for love, but when he felt that he was being loved, he fought against that ephemeral feeling as if it were painful to him. Even in his heyday of success in Hollywood, when *Life* magazine printed a ten-page interview of him, he drew in my guest book a caricature of himself and signed it, "Robert is poor!"

Why did he always say that he was born in America, in Tennessee? America! That word seemed to convey exclusiveness to him. My father met my mother in Leipzig in 1898 and they were married there. Robert was born in Dresden, on August 8, 1900. My mother never left Germany in her lifetime. My brother's arithmetic of birth didn't make sense, since even in his memoirs he talked of his Tennessee birth. In that case he would have been borne by my mother before my father met her, in a country where she was not.

When I was born, on August 10, 1902, my father took little Robert to my crib to introduce me by saying, "Here is your new brother." "I don't want your new brother," Robert is supposed to have answered. That antagonistic feeling against me lasted until he died, interspersed with a deep concern and love for me and Henrietta, whom he adored.

When he was Hollywood's top director, he owned a big house and gave memorable parties, inviting the most celebrated people. He suggested that I should change my name to the pen name "Curt Barton." He offered to buy a ranch for Henrietta and me far away from Hollywood. He also wanted to tell me what to write. There was an envious competition in him that he never overcame. He lived for many years a glamorous life that I, shut up with a typewriter in a room like a lighthouse keeper, rarely experienced.

Creativity cannot flourish without a fulcrum, an original idea, a conception. Robert had a visual talent to see a motion picture in his mind to its last detail before the camera recorded it. Fritz Lang and Alfred Hitchcock, who worked with writers on their screenplays, considered the picture as being done when the screenplay was finished. For them the screen realization was a technical job. Not for Robert, who found new ways to change the written word into a moving image. But he lacked the ability to devise the fulcrum. By chance I supplied the original ideas that started his career in Berlin, France, and Hollywood. Whenever I worked in a film studio, wrote a story or a novel, a talent perhaps that permitted me to work in countries that spoke a different language, I was always an "idea man." I was paid for ideas, a gift that saved my life during the Diaspora. There always was a kind secretary or a native writer friend who would correct my lack of knowledge in my newly acquired language.

Robert knew that his first success, *Menschen am Sonntag*, had been conceived by his younger brother, who adored him and whose success vicariously also was his. Since he was anxious to direct, I financed part of that opus with the first big money I had made by selling a novel. That situation repeated itself when he began his career at UFA with *The Battle with the Dragon,* a surrealistic short that I had written for him when the staid bureaucrats at UFA, afraid of young men's talents, tried to break his contract.

Erich Pommer, the gifted German producer, saw the short at the UFA projection room and took Robert into his production to direct a screenplay that I had been assigned to by UFA and that still was in its beginning stage. When he arrived in Hollywood in 1939 at the outbreak of the war, Robert was down and out in this cruel city, which only recognized people with current success. Writing B picture screenplays for Universal and worried about Robert's career, I practically forced my producer, Jack Gross, to give Robert the director's job on my screenplay *Son of Dracula*. As soon as he got the assignment, the power of the sibling competition made him replace me with another writer, Eric Taylor.

It was by chance that I became the "fulcrum" in his life, though he would have reached his success without my ideas or connections. We were "mental" Siamese twins, though he was not consciously aware that this relationship had four times launched his immense success. He made *Son of Dracula,* a classic, ingeniously distributing light and shadows. That inexpensive picture became the cornerstone of his Hollywood success. His meteoric rise in Germany, France, and

America and upon his return later to Germany was based on his extraordinary director's talent. We never worked together, which I understand—who would give orders to whom? Whose idea between us would be accepted by the "director," which he was? Being two years apart in age and looking like twins, who would be in charge?

A director, besides being a craftsman, has to have a touch of sadism, stubbornness, even ruthlessness, to keep the actors and the front office in check. Actors, often coming from nowhere on the social scale, usually lose conception of their own value. They believe, finally, in their paid publicity. It needs a strong character not to be impressed by one's own advertised greatness. Actors come and go, lasting often not as long as firecrackers, shining brilliantly to disappear in darkness. So do directors. Who played in Shakespeare's plays in past centuries? Who directed *A Midsummer Night's Dream* through centuries?

Writers leave a timeless trace, since the written work has permanence in history. They, the sculptors and painters, are everlasting. The books of Plato, the plays of Shakespeare, the statues of Michelangelo and Rodin, the paintings of Rafael and van Gogh will always be part of the human culture. But the image on the picture screen is impermanent and does not survive time for long, except when mentioned by film historians and sometimes, rarely, when shown at motion picture festivals or on late-night television.

Robert was the last "perambulating" motion picture director. He kept an apartment for his wife, where he rarely returned. Whenever he visited me in America, his first words were "I am on my way to Paris" or any other place his restlessness would drive him. Again, he reached Germany, gathering many "Bambis," the equivalent of the American Oscar. He finally settled in Ascona, in Switzerland, where he died of coronary occlusion ten weeks after his wife Babs's death. Though his marriage was a poor one, he must have needed her, because when she was dying of cancer, had lost her hair, and became a mask of death, only he was permitted to visit and take care of her.

I believe that up to his death in 1974, he tried a comeback, though he knew his time had passed. His friends tell me that he never looked as good in later years as at the last time they saw him, when he died. Lonely, but he might have wanted it that way.

Do I still suffer from his domination, the eternal sibling rivalry, even now decades after his death? I don't believe so, but my psychiatrist friend says yes.

5

America

There is a resilience in youth, a perpetual rejuvenation of energies, as though the human body were a battery that constantly recharges itself. Henrietta and I certainly had plenty of amperes in our physical constitution. After a few days in England and now in assumed safety, we were prepared to fight the whim of the bureaucratic labor department. We found a comfortable apartment on Woodchurch Road, a quiet part of Hendon, and engaged a German maid, Martha. Martha took care of Geoffrey, our fast-growing son, sleeping in the same room with him. She also cleaned the house, though Henrietta did not give up her interest in gourmet cooking. We got used to England but not to its food, whose culinary zenith was pulling a dead chicken through boiling water and cooking vegetables until they fell apart, despite the markets having all kinds of exotic items for sale. The preference for simple nourishment seems to be part of the British character. When we left France on one of our previous European trips, we met an Englishman in the three-star Michelin restaurant Chez Monay in Calais, who could not wait to get back to the "roast beef cut off the joint and two veggies," a fare that island thrived on.

    I received my promised two hundred pounds dished out in fifteen pounds a week salary from Gaumont. It was a fortune since one could rent an apartment for eight guineas a month. The British, armed merchants for centuries, knew the value of a shilling. One bought in guineas and was paid in pounds. The guinea was twenty-one shillings, twelve pence more than a pound, though no paper money with the inscription "guinea" existed. It was just the time-honored custom of the merchant to squeeze 5 percent more out of the customer.

We refused to worry about the future and didn't waste a negative thought on it. I plied Gaumont's story department with ideas, trying to sell them *Through Desert and Wilderness* for Nova Pilbeam. Then fate came to my rescue.

The story editor, Angus McPhail, a tall, erudite Scotsman, called me to his office. He had received a cable from the chairman of Gaumont British, Sir Michael Balcon, who was in New York to set up a distribution of British motion pictures. Hollywood, guarding its territory enviously, rarely exhibited foreign pictures in their theater chains to keep every penny of film income for themselves. Sir Michael, to avoid the exorbitant releasing fees, tried to create his own motion picture distribution, since an English picture, *Henry VIII*, with Charles Laughton playing the gluttonous, womanizing king, an Alexander Korda film, had been an enormous success in the United States. Also Hitchcock's and Charles Bennett's *The 39 Steps*, produced by Gaumont, was a smash financial hit. English pictures had become a literary trademark for the Americans.

Angus asked me whether I had heard of the novel *The Tunnel* by the German writer Bernhardt Kellermann. I told Angus that I knew the book by heart, which, by chance, I had read before my emigration. It was the science fiction story of the construction of a tunnel between England and America. Sir Michael had for the first time in English film history engaged American stars for this project. Richard Dix, the popular western film star, was in my opinion the wrong casting to play the engineer who devised that gigantic project. But his American box office returns impressed Balcon, who had contracted the eminent actor Walter Huston to play the president of the United States. George Arliss, whose mere presence in an English or American picture ensured financial success, impersonated the British prime minister. Madge Evans, a pretty blonde and former child star, was cast as the wife of Richard Dix. Helen Vinson and Leslie Banks, well-known British actors, had parts in *Transatlantic Tunnel*, though their British accents clashed with those of the American cast.

"I need the treatment with the proper parts for the actors in three days," Angus told me. "Can you do it?" If he had asked me to write the Bible in three days, I would have convinced him that it was an easy task for me. "Then 'op to it," Angus said, since the hour had come when he could have his first drink.

For the story *The Transatlantic Tunnel*, I envisioned gigantic drills that would gnaw their way to America beneath the ocean floor. When the tunnel between England and France was recently built, the machines that excavated the tunnel were very similar to those that I, a trained engineer, had conceived. I also had the vision of gigantic TV screens, unknown at that time but commonplace fifty years later. My conception of future video phones that replaced the telephone, showing the picture of the speakers, also was premature since television was in its infancy.

I witnessed early television in the home of the cameraman Friese-Greene. At that time a lens that could change focus had not been devised. The projected picture was that of a woman playing the piano. When she bent forward, her face enlarged sideways; when she bent back, it became thin and long. There was a woman and a man talking about their current Indian adventures. When he got stuck, she whispered to him, forgetting that every sound was audible on the screen.

I turned in my fifty-page treatment after twenty-two sleepless hours. Angus cabled its content to his boss in New York. "Mother blind, underwater volcano erupts, forcing closing of tunnel, sacrificing men also engineer's son." Fourteen words, to describe a full-length motion picture. Sir Michael cabled back: "Assign the writer to the screenplay."

We lived happily and securely like an English middle-class family in our rented apartment on Woodchurch Road. The upstairs of our flat was occupied by a retired colonel who had served in India. He sported a most pampered moustache that ended in needle-sharp points. We never talked to each other, except to exchange the usual London greeting, rain or shine: "Nice day, isn't it?" even if the fog was so thick that when I went to the mailbox fifty feet from our apartment, I lost my direction and arrived at our home two hours later. I never saw anybody visiting the colonel, but one day he was found dead, chained naked and handcuffed to the iron radiator in his apartment. It made us search for another abode, one without corpses in upper floors.

Gaumont, after having read my screenplay of *The Transatlantic Tunnel*, offered me a year's contract. Three hundred fifty paid days were security, eternity, and happiness.

We rented a house on the outskirts of London, a sleepy place called Mill Hill where the houses still did not have numbers but names, which tested the memory of the mailman. We lived at "Hathaway," which was Shakespeare's wife Ann's maiden name. It looked out at a common, which is a small park eternally dedicated to the public. No one ever was permitted to build on this time-sacred ground. Half a mile away was a century-old pub, the Red Fox, with flowering vines climbing over its roof. There on Sunday mornings after church one was allowed to buy Colins Spring Ale, a dark brew with an alcohol content of great authority. Each customer was restricted to two small bottles to avoid drunkenness or brawls.

Hathaway was one of many identical tract houses. I frequently tried my key during foggy nights on the wrong houses, which were built as if poured from the same mold. Visiting Mill Hill fifty years later, the suburban village had grown into a noisy traffic-bound city, but the commons were still there, honoring an unshakable British belief that traditions should never be changed.

The National-Socialist revolution in Germany continued, far away from peaceful England. Martha, our German maid, went back to Nazi Germany. She was upset since a Nazi in a brawl had bitten off one of her brother's fingers. Only when she left we found out that she was afflicted with tuberculosis. For years we were afraid that Geoffrey, who slept in the same room with her, had been infected.

We bought an automobile for five guineas, an ancient, tiny, 1926 two-cylinder Jowett convertible. It had to be cranked up. Since it had only one door, and that on the passenger's side, I had to crank the motor by hand, then slide in first behind the wheel since it had the English right-hand steering. Henrietta followed, slammed the door, and we went off at thirty miles per hour top speed. The Jowett's dashboard contained innumerable switches that only I knew how to manipulate. Henrietta could make it start by hitting the dashboard with her shoe. We slowly dismantled the body and painted the hood and the fenders black on our kitchen table. Its reliable motor took us everywhere, though it had the mean habit of dying with a mischievous cough in the middle of traffic in Piccadilly Circus. Then Henrietta had to jump out, and I followed to turn the crank, to start the motor. I jumped back into the right-hand driver's seat. Henrietta slid in, and we drove off, having stopped traffic on London's most busy town square. The London drivers were very courteous and not upset by mechanical mishaps.

Once, when we drove through Greek Street, in the middle of London's bustling Soho district, two men left a sporting goods store, carrying fishing poles. The traffic stopped patiently as the fishermen tried out the poles, casting across the street. Then, obviously satisfied with the efficiency of their choice, they returned to the store and the traffic resumed. Nobody blew his horn, since choosing a fishing rod is for an Englishman an extremely serious business that must not be rushed.

Angus assigned two collaborators to check my still-deficient dialogue. One was a reserved Englishman, Mr. L. du Garde Peach, always dressed in blue, and an enormous woman in a huge flapping hat, the famous Clemence Dane, who in one of her many successful plays, *A Bill of Divorcement,* had mentioned the dreaded word *syphilis.* The young Katharine Hepburn played the lead. Also the word *cancer* was strictly taboo, and in mentioning it, one had to disguise the word by calling that affliction "the big C," as John Wayne, who died of it, did.

I had no interference from the production department writing *The Transatlantic Tunnel.* The brother of Maurice Ostrer, Sean, was the producer. He was a nondescript person, of whom I only remember his contention that a person has to have three bowel movements every day to stay healthy. He died young.

The director was Maurice Elvey. At first Berthold Viertel, the German stage director, was suggested. Viertel didn't get the job because I opposed it, a very mean act, since he too was a refugee who tried to make his living in a foreign country.

Maurice Elvey had a country house in the rural village of Godstone, twenty miles south of London, which he visited during weekends. It was a farmer's house going back to Shakespearean times, filled with Tudor furniture, a thatched roof, and a garden overflowing with roses. When a roof was renewed, the thatcher climbed on it and traditionally stayed there, building it, eating, and drinking, never leaving it until it was finished.

It was the real birth of the British film industry, which hardly existed. Most screenplays were devised by foreign writers. There were only a handful of British motion picture authors, still very young and new in that business. That was perhaps the reason that my screenplay had not been challenged by the front office. When I finally got my year's contract, Frank Alexander, the jingoistic accountant, who discussed the agreement with me, said, "Siodmak, we hate to give you a contract. But you have to teach our young writers how to write a screenplay."

Henrietta and I drove in our five-guinea, hand-painted Jowett car to Godstone to deliver pages of the screenplay. Elvey had a visitor, Sir Seymour Hicks, an important writer and actor, who had arrived in the longest Rolls-Royce I had ever seen. When Sir Seymour wanted to drive home, his chauffeur could not start the ten thousand–guinea behemoth, whose only audible sound, according to its advertising, was the ticking of the dashboard clock. That time it made no noise at all. I drove Sir Seymour to his palatial home in Kensington in our old Jowett. Henrietta sat beside me, the portly Sir Seymour in the rumble seat.

There was a story going around then that, when Sir Seymour bought the latest Rolls-Royce, he objected to the built-in air conditioner. Since he was upset that he could not find one without that convenience, the salesman suggested, "In that case, sir, may I suggest that you just don't turn on the air conditioner?"

My story for Frances Day, *For Kings Only*, was dead. Gaumont was afraid of its production cost, since the company was in financial difficulties, which I didn't know. However, I owned the original story. A writer is often asked how long it takes to write a novel or a story. My science fiction novel *F.P. 1 Does Not Answer*, written in German, published internationally, which became the biggest science fiction film produced in Europe, took two weeks to write. The scenes just fell into place, and the only delay was the time it took to hit the typewriter keys. *For Kings Only* began as a film story, then became the outline of a stage musical, and twenty years later was published as a novel. It still might become a miniseries on television.

Good ideas have a life of their own. Stories only die when the author wants them to die. There is a time in which they become salable, a condition that the writer cannot predict. My novel *Gabriel's Body* took thirty years to find a publisher. It was rejected by a big New York publishing house with the comment that the idea of that book was the silliest science fiction concept and did not make sense, not even to sci-fi aficionados. My prediction was microchips, which were not invented when I wrote that book.

My stage musical, *The Song of Frankenstein,* took thirty years from conception to completion to finding a theater, not in America but in Austria. It now might travel to Germany, then to England and perhaps New York. We are apt to count only the successes and never the failures of our endeavors, but we writers are always as good as our best work.

I had stored two hundred boxes containing story material, novels, plays, screenplays, and film treatments in my garage. An equal amount went up in flames in London during World War II. The remainder of my collection is preserved in a film museum in Berlin, since the Germans are highly interested in the history of motion pictures, contrary to Hollywood, whose prime aim is to turn out a product that produces dollars. It also is possible that my unproduced stories might find their time slot. Stories have a limitless life span. Plays that the Greeks wrote several thousand years ago are still produced. Art is always ahead of the present fashion but has to wait for its acceptance by the public. By then, art will have progressed further. That's why artists are ahead of the trend of acceptance, often live in poverty, even starve to death, and their heirs become wealthy.

In former centuries, writers and musicians were supported by kings and the aristocracy. Their work was always contemporary. Bach and Mozart were subsidized by the Austrian court, as were writers. Today a publisher might prepay an author for his coming work, sometimes with huge sums. The Hollywood film studios engaged writers, who, on salary, would work for those corporations. But they were designated as "hired hands," like carpenters or plumbers. The studios legally kept all rights for themselves, depriving writers of any participation in the success of their life's work.

I sold the picture rights to *Donovan's Brain* for $1,950 to Republic Studios, because I was in a financial bind. The television rights to that book, now owned by another Hollywood motion picture corporation, can be acquired for one million dollars, in which I of course do not participate.

Van Gogh sold only one painting in his lifetime, for eighty francs. The same work was bought at auction by a Japanese businessman for forty million dollars. If the French Impressionists had had the foresight not to die at an early age, they would have become rich. Now the time has arrived when artists may be rewarded during their lifetime. In some cases, the sums flowing into writers' pockets are astronomically high.

An artist must also be a businessman, which very few are. I once had an argument with a producer when I told him that I don't sleep, trying to find the next scene for the screenplay I was writing for him. I was sure he didn't sleep either, figuring out how to cheat me of my money. When we discussed money, I was at a disadvantage. It was true, he acknowledged. He didn't sleep either, trying to find a way to make one dollar ten out of a dollar.

Vere Barker, my London agent, told me that he could get a year's contract for me at Gaumont British, if I took a cut in salary. He did not know that my red-headed secretary was a close friend of Sir Michael's private secretary and that she showed me the memos that went back and forth between the story department and Sir Michael, the studio boss. I told Barker that I would negotiate my own deal. He was furious at my independence. I told the accountant, Sidney

Alexander, that I would only sign a contract if the studio paid my twenty-five pounds' weekly salary, still ten pounds less than my friend Charles Bennett received working for Hitchcock. I could have said twenty-five guineas, in the tradition of the British merchants. But I had seen the memos that Sir Michael sent to Maurice Ostrer, the head of production: "Pay Siodmak—he is worth twenty-five quid." A quid is twenty shillings.

Vere Barker's authority was hurt. He even hinted that Gaumont would cancel my labor permit, that poisoned dagger in the hands of the British companies. But I got that contract. Now Henrietta and I had money. We started to save and bought British sovereigns, gold pieces. We counted them at night in bed, put them in stockings, and slept on that fortune. Now having enough money to emigrate to America, Henrietta wanted to realize her plan to move to the United States. Her unfailing intuition anticipated the upheaval that four years later would devastate the European continent.

The Transatlantic Tunnel was in production. Richard Dix, the burly American western star, did not know how to handle emotional scenes. He asked me how to act when he, according to the screenplay, had to give the order to close the tunnel's steel gates, condemning the men who had not escaped the fiery disaster in the tunnel to their death. His son was among them. I told him that it was the director's job to supply that answer. But Maurice Elvey cruelly told him, "You promised me to be an actor. I was told that you are a top star in America. Find the solution yourself." I asked Dix whether he had children. Three months ago his wife had given birth to a son. I suggested that he should think of his son dying, to understand the impact of that decision. He found the solution logical, and that scene lifted him above his artless macho appearance that had been the success of westerns.

Since I was on the payroll and under contract, McPhail asked me to conceive a story about the famous freebooter, Rob Roy, who had lived in the seventeenth century. To improve my understanding of British characters, he teamed me with another writer, Leslie Arliss. Leslie knew the working of the studio and how to take advantage of its perks. He made the studio supply us with a Humber automobile and ample cash. McPhail told us to drive to Scotland and research the history of that outlaw, Rob Roy. I insisted on taking along Henrietta. We bought kilts to ingratiate ourselves with the Scottish clans.

Driving through the pastoral hills of Scotland, all we learned about Rob Roy was that the Scots brew 2,500 brands of local whisky. Since the individual quantities were just enough to keep the villagers supplied with booze, that precious brew was never wasted on customers outside Scotland. What the distillers sold to the world was trademarked whisky of commercial distilleries but never the really native stuff.

Driving through Scotland, we hit an invasion of thousands of rabbits, which clogged every road and devastated the farmer's crops. It was impossible to drive without running over them. Such a glut of rabbits appears every dozen years. Scientists are unable to explain the cause of their sudden fecundity. After driving through an unavoidable carnage of rabbits, we finally came across a sign set up by the Royal Automobile Club: "Four miles to Rob Roy's Inn." When we arrived at the "inn," we found the remnants of a motion picture set used a dozen years ago that had been elevated to a tourist attraction. The film *Rob Roy* was never made. Still, we delivered McPhail learned material that we had lifted from a novel written by the world-famous author Sir Walter Scott.

The Transatlantic Tunnel was finished. To prepare myself for the evening of the premiere, that pinnacle in the life of a screenwriter's work, I ordered a tailcoat from London's famous tailor, Gieves of Bond Street. I also bought a hat at Locke's.

Acquiring a hat at that prestigious company had its time-honored ritual. One just could not buy the hat and take it home. After the purchase, the store hung the hat for three days on spikes on the roof of the building, to be saturated with the coal dust of London's million fireplaces. Then the felt hat was taken down and cleaned, and the hat band was changed. Only then a Locke hat was ready to be worn, no longer looking shop-new. The upper class even had their new shoes broken in by their butlers.

Gieves, the tailor shop, went back a few hundred years in history. Mr. Quick, the manager, an imposing, heavyset man with effeminate movements, was horrified at my request to close the front of the trousers with a zip fastener. He told me of an incident in which a man had zipped up his fly in a bus and had caught a lady's expensive mink coat. The two people, fused together, had to travel to the end station where mechanics finally succeeded in freeing the mink from the zipper's grip. Mr. Quick also scared me by telling me the case of the fastener having hooked into the delicate skin of the private part of the trousers' wearer, causing immense pain, demanding a clinical operation and creating permanent injury. My pants were fitted with buttons. I paid thirteen guineas, three times my secretary's weekly salary, for that masterpiece in tails, the only one I ever owned in my life.

While I had my third fitting at Gieves, Henry VIII, aka Charles Laughton, entered the store. I had never met him before, but years later he became a frequent guest in my home in Beverly Hills. He had just arrived from Hollywood, where he was to portray the cruel Captain William Bligh in *Mutiny of the Bounty*, a film produced by Irving Thalberg for MGM. Clark Gable had the opposing role of Fletcher Christian, the leader of the rebellion against the sadistic captain, who was set adrift with eighteen loyal crew members in an open boat. Laughton wanted to order the exact replica of Captain Bligh's uniform, which he knew Gieves had tailored.

"One moment, please, sir," Mr. Quick said, limping upstairs on his stiff right leg. He returned with an ancient black order book. "Here it is, the original requisition of March 8, 1787." Laughton ordered two replicas of that uniform. Thalberg never accepted them, since the ship captains of that time wore bowler hats, a drab waistcoat, and many gold watch chains around the stomach. Thalberg ordered what an English sea captain should wear in his film—accurate history be damned. Laughton had to wear a tricornered hat and a multicolored uniform, which the film company's costume designer devised.

For the opening night of *The Transatlantic Tunnel* at the cinema at Leicester Square, Henrietta was dressed in an exquisite long black dress, which she still possesses, and I, of course, in my Gieves' tails. The film was a tremendous success, anticipating future technical inventions like giant television screens, helicopters, and streamlined trains, the kind that the present railroad companies have on their drawing board. The film became a sci-fi classic and is still shown today.

To live in London at that time was like a continuing vacation. Museums, theater, excursions, interspersed with work at the studio. It was a pleasant time, alien to us, being used to the pressure of gloom and work we had experienced for years in Germany.

Our friend Charles Bennett drove his girlfriend, the pretty actress Anne Baxter, Henrietta, and me in his Jaguar convertible to the Thames River at Windsor Castle. There we swam at night in the buff surrounded by swans. All swans in England belonged to the king, and today to the queen. Today Henrietta still complains about the slimy kelp in the river that entwined her body, afraid of monsters hiding in the thickness of that floating weed. We drove our five-guinea Jowett in the evening to Sheppard's Market to have a glass of sherry at the Sherry Bar, spending one shilling. The discussion revolved around the important question: should we have a second one, maybe one for eighteen pence, since money had a high value and even could be exchanged for gold pieces?

We no longer needed to stuff a shilling into Mrs. O'Day's wall heater for twelve pence worth of warm air or take a quick coin-activated shower in the drafty bathroom between two floors under a small stream of lukewarm water spouting from an ancient copper container. In our modern house in Mill Hill, which we rented for two guineas a week, the kitchen stove was heated with coal, automatically producing the luxury of piping-hot water, which rose up to the bathroom above. We rarely heated the house, having, like the British, gotten used to the cold, clammy weather of London. We wore mufflers around our neck, which is standard with true native Britons. When Robert and his wife, Babs, visited us from Paris, we bought oil heaters for the house. My brother and sister-in-law didn't stay long, unable to stand the London cold. They were used to the unhealthy, overheated rooms of their overstuffed apartment at the Place Perrère in Paris.

We had a little garden overflowing with flowers and nice neighbors, an electrical engineer and his family. His wife, having fallen in love with our three-year-old son, stuffed him with Cadbury's chocolate. We asked her not to feed the child sweets. She denied ever having given him any though his mouth was smeared brown. Since I could not contradict her, I saw a sudden gleam in my son's eyes. He understood for the first time that one could lie and get away with it. That's the way we learn in life.

It is not dramatic to recall those times of trouble-free living, but it was the world we yearned to enter, the apogee of a new existence, after that helpless tumbling in a maelstrom of sadistic cruelties and mindless death.

Henrietta took Geoffrey for a visit to Switzerland to introduce him to his grandmother. Frances Day called. She wanted an escort to drive her to the Dorchester Hotel where she was to meet important Hollywood producers. I put on my tailcoat and picked her up, this time in a new Jowett car. Frances was the image of a glorious film star, in a billowing rose skirt, a tight bodice, her blonde hair piled up into a crown. At the Dorchester we met friends of hers, Hollywood tycoons. I had my first encounter with powerful, crude men, the kind that, I found out later, were ruthlessly running Hollywood studios. Maurice Goetz of MGM and his equally unattractive companion looked at me with suspicion: a hunk of a young man, in a tailcoat, obviously Frances's lover, who certainly would inhibit their evening of fun with her. I could not stand the presence of those men, excused myself to Frances, and left, sorry that she had to entertain that kind of people. She told me later that she had tried to interest Goetz in *For Kings Only* and had given him my treatment to take with him to the studio in Culver City.

Years later I located the treatment in MGM's story department, marked "Anonymous," which of course made the story worthless for any studio, since its copyright could not be established.

Since I was under contract to Gaumont, Angus McPhail kept me busy to get the studio's money's worth. George Arliss, the ruling star of Gaumont after his worldwide success as Benjamin Disraeli, wished to play the character of the Italian impostor Count Alessandro di Cagliostro. Though Cagliostro died when he was fifty, he did his confidence tricks when he was much younger; Arliss was already seventy, much too old for that part. McPhail told the Gaumont writers to compete for an original screenplay, with Arliss as Cagliostro in the lead.

Studying the history of that cunning con man (whose real name was Guiseppe Balsamo, born in Palermo, Italy, of poor parentage), I was intrigued by his adventurous chutzpah, which certainly would lend itself to an exciting film character. Arliss had the right hunch by wanting to play him. Balsamo as "Count Cagliostro" visited Greece, Egypt, Persia, and Rhodes. Traveling widely in Europe he posed as a physician, alchemist, and necromancer; sold love philters and elixirs of youth; and pretended to be able to change lead into gold. That was all I needed to know about that colorful con man.

I was certain that my competitors would write about the notorious affair of the "diamond necklace." The old French Cardinal de Rohan had fallen in love with the young Marie Antoinette, the queen of France. Count Cagliostro assured Rohan that he could arrange an assignation. He knew that Marie Antoinette was pining for a precious necklace of rubies and diamonds made for Madame du Barry, the mistress of Louis XV, which the jeweler Boehmer now had for sale for half a million louis d'or. If Rohan would make the queen a gift of that treasure, she would be willing to sleep with him. Cagliostro would make an arrangement between the queen and Rohan at night in the Versailles gardens, where he would present her personally with those precious jewels. The old horny churchman fell for Cagliostro's plot and got the necklace from Boehmer on credit. He presented it in the gardens of Versailles on a moonless night to the grateful "queen." He was duped by Cagliostro's helper, the Countess de la Motte, who, heavily veiled, posed as Marie Antoinette. Of course, the real queen didn't know anything about that conspiracy. That scandal, soon revealed, was one cause that created the atmosphere for the French Revolution, which broke out a few years later.

The "affair of the diamond necklace" was too salient a plot, too natural for a George Arliss film, not to be chosen by all of the competing writers. But I couldn't visualize Arliss as a forty-year-old virile man. A story had to be found that could be played by a man of his age.

I wrote a different one and called it *The Magician*. An aging Cagliostro convinces Maria Theresa, queen of Austria, that he could fuse her many precious diamonds into one gigantic one. But when he tried to melt those irreplaceable stones in a cauldron, they, being pure carbon, went up in smoke. He saved his life by running away, pursued by the queen's horsemen, to his home in Palermo in Italy. Since he only knew two con man's tricks, changing lead into gold and making people young, he left for a country where he was not on the wanted list, to Spain. Madrid, the Spanish capital, was the "Paris" of Europe. Cagliostro's eighteen-year-old daughter, Lorenza, went with him. He used her in that lively city as his shill, pretending she was eighty years old but that his secret treatment had brought back her youth.

Twelve miles outside the gay city of Madrid lived Queen Elizabeth Farnese of Parma, who was so ugly that she was called "Maultasch," having a mouth as big as a handbag. The atmosphere in the Escorial, the twelfth-century castle, was gloomy, run by Cartesian monks who were forever silent, forbidden by their religion to talk. When the ugly queen heard about the mysterious Italian who could change old hags into young beauties, she summoned him to her throne room, whose mirror-covered walls reflected a thousandfold her repulsive features. Vainly Cagliostro tried to convince her that he was a charlatan and that he could not create youth and beauty. Having seen Lorenza, the queen did not believe him. To save himself, Cagliostro invented a clever deception. He admitted that he could create beauty but that mirrors would reveal the former look of his patients. The queen had the mirrored throne hall locked up and decreed that every mirror should be removed from the Escorial, by penalty of death. Cagliostro used beauty treatments, massages, and lotions on his patient, and her sycophants flattered her, pretending to admire the rapid improvement of her beauty. Because she could not see herself, she relaxed, became happier, and therefore looked better, and since she was convinced that she would be beautiful, she became kinder.

Her son, Alfonzo, fell in love with Lorenza, but how could he ever kiss a woman in her eighties? To make sure that she was only eighteen, Lorenza smuggled a small mirror into the castle to prove to her lover her real age. The queen through her spies found out about that breach of law. Lorenza's and the prince's lives were in peril. The queen summoned Cagliostro to the reopened mirrored throne hall where she saw her ugly image reflected. But Cagliostro convinced her that beauty is in the heart, not in the appearance of the flesh. Moved by his eloquence, she forgave him. At once Cagliostro loaded his daughter and the prince in a carriage and left Spain as quickly as the horses could travel. When the queen again looked at herself in the hall of mirrors, she ordered in her fury to bring back Cagliostro. But he and the two young people had already crossed the border into Portugal.

George Arliss liked the treatment and told the studio to deliver a screenplay for his approval. The studio had forgotten to stipulate a price for the story. Since Arliss had liked *The Magician,* I asked for two thousand English pounds, a fortune that would finance my future exodus to America. I wrote the screenplay and the young playwright Emlyn Williams, whose play *Night Must Fall* was the current success on the London stage, was assigned to add to my screenplay. Impressed by his sudden fame, I don't believe that Emlyn was very interested in the job of correcting my dialogue. A good-looking, dark-haired young man, he was rumored to be the boyfriend of two famous men, the actors John Gielgud and Noel Coward. I don't know if that is true, since he married and fathered a son. At the son's baptism in a church in Hendon, Gielgud and Coward were the godfathers of the newborn. I stood next to a cynical old actress, who had been "knighted" by the queen and thus added the word *Dame* to her name. The lady, Dame May Whitty, remarked to me during the ceremony, "Isn't it a lucky child, two fairy godfathers!"

The *Magician* screenplay was completed and accepted by the higher-ups at Gaumont: Angus McPhail, the story editor; Morris Ostrer, chief of production; Sir Michael Balcon, chairman of the company; and a host of others. Then the manuscript was delivered to Arliss, and we were summoned to his home for a conference.

His house, surrounded by a wall, was in the then-expensive part of London called Golders Green. A woman's face scrutinized us through a small window in a narrow wooden door before she let us in. In the entrance hall leading to the living room hung a collection of etchings of naked girls floating on their back in a pool, their pubic hair and vulva minutely drawn, daring pictures for the still Victorian English spirit. Since those well-executed copper etchings of nudes graced Arliss Hall, I wondered what kind of artwork he displayed on the upper floor.

We were led into a living room, served a glass of excellent sherry, while we silently waited for the great mime to make his appearance. When he showed up, a middle-sized, gray-haired man in a white silk bathrobe, his air of authority cowed the big brass of Gaumont. Arliss spoke intelligently about the screenplay, and his suggestions made sense. I watched my superiors relax. One change had to be made, Arliss concluded: he didn't like the mirrors!

That objection, of course, destroyed the screenplay. None of the executives dared to speak up, but I, in my halting English, lacking the jeweler's touch of diplomacy, told Arliss that he was destroying the Cagliostro story and that the screenplay had lost its meaning. Nobody came to my assistance, since to object to George Arliss's criticism was equal to "lese majesty." There was a silence. Then Arliss got up and said, "Gentlemen, you may finish your sherry, then nothing will detain you any longer." He left the room. We were dismissed. But I had the impression that I had gained in stature among my employers, since by defying the great man I had shown bravery and character. The project was dropped and I was loaned out to work for the London Film Company of Alex Korda, which had produced the international success *Henry VIII* with Charles Laughton.

The English motion picture industry fell apart. Korda wanted to produce *I, Claudius,* the story of the cruel Roman emperor, based on the novel by Robert Graves. That film unfortunately never was finished, though I believe it would have been one of the landmarks of the motion picture art. After a few weeks of shooting, the director, Josef von Sternberg, quit because Charles Laughton, playing the insane emperor, was unhappy with his role. Important writers like Lajos Biro, Carl Zuckmayer, Arthur Wimperis, Lester Cole, and Robert Graves had worked on the script. Scenes of the aborted film still exist, with Charles Laughton, Merle Oberon, Flora Robson, and

Emlyn William. I pitied Merle Oberon as Claudius's wife since she had to sleep with that cruel moron. I don't know why Korda deserted that project. An interceding quarrel among Korda, Laughton, and Sternberg might have wrecked the production.

Even my friend, Zoltan Korda, Alex Korda's brother, the gifted director, would not reveal the reason. It was a time of hope and decay: Zoltan, as a producer, wanted me to write and direct my story *For Kings Only*. I remember that he told me, "Don't be afraid of directing."

Then the rumor started that Gaumont was on the verge of bankruptcy. I went to the accountant, Sidney Alexander. Being an Englishman, brought up not to succumb to emotions, his reply was "It is much too early to worry now."

Alfred Hitchcock stuck his head into my office, perhaps prompted by McPhail, and said, "Write me a story of a mute and deaf woman detective!" I solved that problem. I thought of a handsome young woman who had been a crown witness in a murder case. According to McPhail's contention, no story was valid without containing a murder. After the trial was over, my heroine and her girlfriend sign up for a cruise. Not to be accosted by anybody, especially men, her girlfriend informs everybody who approaches her that she is a deaf mute. My heroine needed that isolation for her rest. Returning to her ship's cabin, she enters the wrong room. She sees two men in it and overhears their conversation. When they discover her, one of them pulls a gun, but the other stops him, assuring him that as a deaf mute she could not have heard any of their dialogue. From that moment on, she is forced to be silent and act deaf. Using her voice would have meant her death.

The plot idea would have fitted Hitchcock's request, but I had no chance to talk to him. A studio party, in anticipation of the end of that company, was arranged, a "dance macabre," with music and much booze. Sidney Alexander had too much to drink and, suddenly recalling the terrors of World War I, started to scream in panic, "The tanks are coming, the tanks are coming." We dragged him into an empty room, assuring him that the war had finished eighteen years previously. But he might have had a premonition, since six years later tanks again were rolling through Europe.

The storm clouds gathering over Europe were ignored by the British. World events were seemingly far away, observed but discarded, since we lulled ourselves into the belief that our present life would never change, despite the whim of the bureaucrats in the Labour Department who could expel us at a moment's notice. Henrietta believed that our British-born son would permit us to stay. We felt safe and at home in England, liking its people, their gentleness and traditions, so different from the xenophobia of the French and the murderous nationalism of the Germans. I didn't want to leave for America, to again conquer an unknown future. There was no production going on at Gaumont British though I still received my salary. We writers were very jealous of Noel Langley, also a contract writer, who, through mysterious contacts had been hired by the giant film company Metro-Goldwyn-Mayer in Hollywood. He left in 1936 for America, taking his secret about how and why he got that job with him.

When I arrived in Hollywood a few months later, I visited him in his rented mansion in Beverly Hills. It was one of those homes one finds described only in glamorous architectural magazines. It even had a huge built-in organ like a cathedral in the living room, an Olympic-sized swimming pool, tennis court, and a tropical forest watered every day by artificial rain. The faucets in the bathrooms were gilded. Noel, a handsome young man, had rented that place to impress Diana Churchill, the English prime minister's actress-daughter. He was waiting for her to visit him, since, as he told me, she had promised to marry him. But she didn't show up. Noel contacted a woman in South Africa, a childhood sweetheart, whom he had not seen in decades. He shipped her to America, and they got married.

He was successful for a time, after he got the screenplay credit for *The Wizard of Oz*. I never saw him after my visit in Beverly Hills.

Forty years later, when I was working for Twentieth Century–Fox in Hollywood, a friend of mine visited me at the studio. He was accompanied by his girlfriend, a striking blonde, Jacqueline Langley, born years after my visit to Noel. What are the mathematical odds of such coincidence?

When the English went boar hunting, they added a bulldog to their pack of hounds, because a bulldog has little brains and would charge that big powerful animal, while the pack fearfully hesitated. When the bulldog attacked, the others, encouraged, would follow.

All my life I had that mindless bulldog mentality. Why did I leave for Switzerland to study? With my limited finances it didn't make sense. Why did I travel that poisonous Amazon River for seven months to direct two motion pictures for Universal? Why travel to a country like England to start a new existence or to America on speculation, eight thousand miles from the Europe I knew? Why did I join the OSS (Office of Strategic Services) and later the CIA during World War II, a voluntary "draft" that I had little chance to survive? In daytime the Germans would shoot me, at nighttime the Americans, when they heard my Teutonic accent. Why, for thirty-five years now, do I live hundreds of miles out in the country away from the bread trough of well-paying motion picture assignments? Why did I spend many years writing an "autobiography," five hundred pages, only to discard them to start anew on page one?

A couple of years ago a very gifted photo reporter from Germany, Herlinde Koelbl, visited me at my ranch. She was photographing and interviewing emigrants who had survived the genocide. Among them were Edward Teller, Erich Leinsdorf, Sir George Solti, Theodore Kolleck, and a dozen others of my age, people seasoned by unstable times, who did not often talk publicly about their lives or of their objective observations that supplied the strength to survive. They were aware that part of history would disappear with them if they did not put their thoughts into written words.

I packed five years of work into boxes and started on page one, to formulate my thoughts according to Herlinde Koelbl's conception of her book *Jewish Portraits*. I didn't think of time or the amount of work it entailed.

Though safely cocooned in England, Henrietta insisted that we break up our present existence and move to America, where we had no connections and where my only asset was my knowledge of motion pictures. We had precious little money to start a whole new life, but certainly more than the "General Bum," which had financed our journeys to nowhere until we had new roots in England.

Women possess a core of steel, which the hardest times rarely penetrate. If a woman makes up her mind in an important matter, she becomes deaf and blind, though not mute. Men never really grow up completely. The insecurity of the child never leaves them.

There were logistics to be taken care of: to leave the rented house, to dispose of most of the furniture, some lovely pieces that we had with care bought at the Caledonian Flea Market. That market in London was a mile long. One could buy one single shoe for a farthing, the value of a fourth of a penny, or an antique silver tray for a thousand pounds. We owned treasures that, I regret, were lost during the London bombing raids three years later. But the wisdom of Moses ben Maimonides stated in the twelfth century: "If you have to choose between freedom and wealth, choose freedom and leave your wealth behind. Wealth you can replace. Freedom you cannot."

I applied for a visitor's visa to the United States, which was not difficult since I could prove that we had a bank account. My friend and cowriter, Leslie Arliss, who had never left the British Isles, wanted to come along. Henrietta would stay behind with our now three-year-old son, Geoffrey, and follow after I had canvassed the possibility of living on that new continent.

Henrietta and I looked at the prospectus of ships and chose the *George Washington,* a fairly modern, American, fast luxury liner. The ocean could not yet be crossed by plane. I bought a first-class ticket and was not confined in steerage like my father fifty years ago.

Suddenly an emergency arose: Henrietta, to safeguard our cash, had bought government bonds in our British son's name. She was afraid that since we still had German passports, our money might be confiscated should a war ever break out between England and Germany. I admired her foresight, which I had never questioned, except that there was small print on those bonds that she had overlooked: they could be redeemed immediately, but should they be in the name of a minor child, they could only be cashed in when the bearer was seven years old! Geoffrey was three! We tried to get the money released, but, due to bureaucratic red tape, that would take months. We sold our gold pieces, which paid for my ticket and gave us a thousand dollars' cash to start a new existence.

When we arrived in Southampton, the American line informed us that for technical reasons the *George Washington* passengers would be transferred to the sister ship, the *President Harding*. That boat was thirty years older than the *Washington* and half its size. The Germans had neglected to sink it in World War I.

When I saw New York's skyscrapers, still miles away, from aboard the ocean liner that had carried me across the Atlantic, my impression was not that of a city but that of the spikes on the back of a monster stirring to rise above the haze that covered the ground.

New York was the Metropolis, not the German motion picture—in which dark-clad workmen slave for a social elite, but a medley of faces of all hues, the jetsam of nations that had been poured into a cauldron.

A detachment exuded from the rushing crowd, a palpable indifference to other human beings, void of any human emotions. I felt lost, abandoned by the world as I knew it. In what direction should

I turn, what plan should I conceive to begin a new existence? I also knew that if I did not adjust to this unknown world and conform with its rhythm, I would forever be a misfit in this foreign land. If I belonged to a tightly knit ethnic group, I would get help, directions, and assistance. But a German refugee Jew didn't have such a shelter, not even among the American Jews.

The city looked shabby, though new skyscrapers grew out of rubble, glistening mushrooms, competing with each other in height, each trying to be the tallest, to beat the competition, to dominate. Those blocks of concrete with their rows of sightless windows were reaching for the clouds.

Half a century ago my father had walked the same streets as forlornly as I. Though he was sixteen at that time, an age I could not visualize him ever having been, I understood why he had left the United States after a decade to return to the Europe where he still had roots. He never made it financially big in America, where any immigrant supposedly could become a Rockefeller or a Mellon—a financial potentate.

Immigrants rarely return to their native land. The immense size of this continent, which I, after having lived here for more than half a century, still don't comprehend, expands the conception of everyone's life, fostering the belief that nothing is unattainable if one has the willpower and perseverance to pursue one's dreams.

I called Adele Schulberg, an important motion picture agent. I had met her in Paris, and she had given me her address in New York and Hollywood, promising to represent me.

For a short time in Hollywood, "Ad" was to be my agent. I don't think she ever wasted a thought on getting me a job. Every morning through a flower shop, I had sent to her office desk a bunch of forget-me-nots. She never caught its meaning. Ad also acted as a talent scout for her husband, B. P. Schulberg, the head of Paramount Pictures. On the New York stage Ad had seen a fragile, dark-eyed young actress whom she thought was star material and told her husband about her find.

I had met Sylvia Sidney in London at the Gaumont studios where I worked. She possessed a fey vulnerability, a quality highly appreciated by the American public. When she acted in Hitchcock's picture *Sabotage,* Hitchcock, for reasons unknown to me, disliked her and mischievously addressed her by her original name, Sophia Kosow, as if it were a demeaning name. When her pivotal scene arrived in which she committed a murder, "Hitch," in a travel shot, photographed only her hand in close-up, holding the knife, never her face. I never could fathom Hitchcock's sadistic streaks, which he camouflaged behind a sardonic humor, but I assume he wanted to punish Sylvia for having started an intimate friendship with a newspaper reporter, which he felt interfered with his macho power over her.

Ad's husband, B. P. Schulberg, flew to New York to canvass the young, promising actress Sylvia. He contracted her for Paramount Pictures and promptly broke up his marriage to Ad. His son, Budd, a gifted writer, wrote the best-selling novel *What Makes Sammy Run*. It was a scathing portrait of the devious workings of the motion picture industry. Budd's novel was a "roman à clef" about people he knew in Hollywood where he had grown up. Every one of the powerful studio bosses believed that Budd had portrayed him as a ruthless, scheming heartless monster, void of any human compassion. Budd's description generally fit the frame of mind of most of the tycoons. That book enraged Budd's father and also Louis B. Mayer of MGM, Sam Goldwyn, and Harry Cohn of Columbia Studios so much that they contemplated "banishing" Budd forever from their fiefdom, believing they had the power to keep people out of their personal property, Hollywood.

When B. P. Schulberg lost his position as the head of the powerful Paramount Studios and went broke as an independent producer, he desperately advertised his accomplishments in the trade paper, the *Hollywood Reporter,* begging for a job. None of his friends, with time-honored Hollywood cruelty, reacted. Louis B. Mayer was ignominiously deposed by his stockholders and could never find the money to go back into production. When the much-hated Harry Cohn, the head of Columbia Studios died, hundreds came to his funeral. A wag remarked, "Just give the public what it wants and it will show up in droves."

In 1937 when I arrived in New York, that city was still in the throes of the Depression. "Dance palaces," as in Ruth Etting's socially critical song "Ten Cents a Dance," still existed. The girls, sitting at tables waiting for a dance partner, were young, some of exceptional beauty, even of good breeding. Had the Depression forced them into semiprostitution? At the entrance to the dance hall the customer bought a ribbon of tickets, ten cents each, good for a three-minute dance. The girls collected the number of ten-cent tickets according to their willingness to be held very close. They had a knack to arouse their dance partners, though that propinquity didn't lead to any closer cooperation. To accept a date was against the house rules, since the owner of that enterprise had to protect himself against any suggestion of fostering prostitution.

Food was cheap, entertainment coarse. I went to the variety show at Minsky's, where professional strippers on the stage shed their clothes to the beat of jazz music. Stripping was a strictly American entertainment and did not at that time exist in Europe. The chorus girls, scrawny and undernourished, never undressed, listlessly went through their dance routine. The performing strippers were tantalizingly handsome showgirls.

A nun on the stage demurely took off her habit, except for a thin string across her nipples; another covered the space between her legs. Now a bikini exposes that much. The audience was a beer-guzzling, rowdy male crowd. Wild shouts encouraged the girls to take off their G-strings. A transvestite conducted an indecent act, using the curtain as a partner. Then a picture screen was lowered and a German newsreel was projected: Hitler talking to Mussolini, both in uniform and wearing high boots. Their dialogue was dubbed in Yiddish! The audience screamed with laughter, while I felt my spine freeze in terror. My family had been murdered and the Nazis were marching on. But American Jews like Minsky had no conception of the menace that grew in Germany and that would be the death of millions of their faith.

The day after I saw that show, the mayor of New York City, Fiorello La Guardia, closed Minsky's establishment for good, not on account of the Hitler and Mussolini "joke" but for "decency" reasons. Death as an entertainment, yes, but no stripping nuns! British hypocrisy permitted frontal nudity on the stage if the girl stood still like a statue. Americans did not. France, at the Folies Bergère, with its uninhibited display of sex, never made any secret of the fact that women have two breasts, though Picasso sometimes painted them with three or four. The Hays Office, which guarded Hollywood's sexual purity (on film only), used to draw a hard line. That conception has changed the last decades and nobody seems to care. The time in my youth, when children using a "forbidden" word suffered having their mouths washed out with soap, is gone. Whenever I hear the word *fuck* on the motion picture screen, I know that the film was produced lately. The apothegm *shit* denotes a picture more than five years old. Those without four-letter words are the earlier ones. The use of words has the connotation of its time but loses its poignant meaning when used colloquially.

Those few days in New York disappeared in a staccato of short, disconnected memories. Afraid of not getting a job in Hollywood right away, I had contemplated writing a book called *Ten Men Behind the Screen,* the history of people who were the real originators of the motion picture industry. Though Thomas Alva Edison receives the credit as the inventor of the "fourth art," its roots go back to 1824 and Peter Mark Roget, writer of the well-known *Roget's Thesaurus.* By looking through a Venetian blind, he observed that motion could be broken down into a series of separate phases. I had in mind to write about ten unknown people: John Hershel, Dr. William Fitton, and others who experimented with illusions created by rapid movements of static images.

I found the address of John P. Harris, an old man who lived in a brownstone in Manhattan and was the owner of a museum of early motion picture paraphernalia, cameras, and film posters. He told me that as a young man he had photographed the first kiss ever recorded on film. The shots were taken in the backyard of his house in Pittsburgh in 1896. The backdrop was a bush in his garden. He had been the kisser, the kissee a girl, his own sister. She was sixteen and Harris twenty.

I held in my hand a paper strip about one foot long with the faded images of two young people, his pursuit, his catching and kissing her. It was the first motion picture kiss ever recorded!

I don't know whatever became of this historic, precious piece of film image. I never wrote that book, though I had Harris's permission to use the photographed strip of the kiss, the rarest historical jewel in motion picture history.

I was looking for a used automobile big enough to carry my bulky European luggage. I found a 1932 sixteen-cylinder Cadillac convertible behemoth and bought it for four hundred dollars. Only Marlene Dietrich, when she was at the height of her star power, owned a sixteen-cylinder Cad, a limousine where the chauffeur sat in the open, exposed to sun and rain, while the passengers were sheltered inside, protected from inclement weather. Marlene kept that car polished and pampered for many years in a Los Angeles garage, a nostalgic reminder of her vanished prominence. Fifty years later I saw a picture of a sixteen-cylinder convertible Cad in the *Smithsonian* magazine. Only that one survived, as I had gotten rid of mine. Today that automobile would fetch from collectors a few million dollars, since General Motors had only built two of that model. Of course it would have to be groomed and sheltered in a garage for half a century, at a cost beyond my financial boundary.

From time to time a language creates a new expression, which becomes a buzzword for a short time. The word now is *perks,* which can be found in any dictionary, but not the way of its present meaning, which has become derogative, slightly larcenous. *Perk* also is a polite word for embezzlement of government or company assets or for unauthorized "fringe benefits" charged to stockholders or companies. Every job has loopholes that give people with diminished honesty access to perks.

The many expensive "free" trips company or government employees propelled into sudden prominence take are perks. Those people, convinced of their own importance, having been lifted above the lower-class people who elected or selected them, take whatever advantage they can squeeze out of their job. For them it is a just recognition for their elected positions. Even a secretary of state was "amazed" when he was told how much it costs the taxpayer when he uses his official airplane, the same size as the president's, to fly him to his country club. A commercial one, as he found out to his amazement, also gets him to his golf greens. It is rare that people in high positions, impressed by their high status, don't lose touch with the world of "the common people." Power, quoting the former Secretary of State Henry Kissinger, is the ultimate aphrodisiac, even surpassing sex. The executives of the motion picture industry are experts on perks, which producers and directors take for granted as an added compensation. Everybody in motion pictures, even actors on location, get the hang of it. I didn't catch on.

When I directed a picture, my assistant producer ordered a garden fence for a house of a call girl he liked and charged the cost of it to my underfinanced film. The production manager, Ruby Rosenberg, who died of heart failure on one of the Pacific islands while supervising a remake of the motion picture *Mutiny on the Bounty,* in which Marlon Brando played, was a master of perks. When I, as the director-producer for Universal Studios, was shooting in Brazil, I rented a simple hotel room in Rio de Janeiro, while he booked for himself a suite in a luxury hotel. When he died, he left two apartment buildings in Paris financed by perks he had siphoned off while working for an industry that he knew how to manipulate. I was too simpleminded and innocent in the perk game to understand why the studio accountant who accompanied me to Brazil tried to encourage me to spend picture money for my private use. Universal Pictures had accumulated millions of cruzeiros in Brazil. A rapid inflation reduced their value to almost zero. But since the American company was not allowed by Brazilian law to take money out of the country, it converted its bank account into reams of motion picture film that could be exported. The accountant might have been right: why not use up the money before its buying power had completely melted away?

To travel on an ocean liner also has its perks, as I found out on my journey to America. The unwritten law for a bachelor or a passenger not accompanied by his wife, is to pick during the first hours of the journey an unaccompanied female as a companion partner for the crossing.

I left England without any compunction, suddenly becoming conscious that I had no roots in that country, contrary to my former belief that this stable, peaceful island had become a permanent home for me and my family. There is a Jewish joke with a sad connotation: one Jewish emigrant tells another, "I got a job in Sydney, Australia!" "But that is so far away." "Far away from where?"

I went far away from nowhere, to nowhere, when the *President Harding*, that outdated ocean liner, sailed from Southampton to New York. My family would follow as soon as I had canvassed that unknown continent and was assured of earning a living. My son Geoffrey stayed with Henrietta, who closed our rented house in London, busily getting rid of all that precious junk we had accumulated on our four-year visit in England. She also had to withdraw our savings, which had been frozen earlier, from Barclay's Bank.

To sail away from Europe was as unemotional as taking a bus ride to downtown London.

The *President Harding* seemed almost devoid of passengers. The last spasms of a hurricane blowing from Cuba kept most of the passengers seasick in their cabins. The overaged creaky ship took nine days to make the crossing.

My travel companion Leslie Arliss quickly made friends with an American art student who was returning from a year's study at the Sorbonne, the Paris university. She must have been as eager as he to find a companion for the crossing, since I didn't see them during the trip.

I sat at the first officer's table. The first officer, an old hand at the perk game, had picked for himself a very mod Italian woman. He spoke Spanish to her, and she replied in Italian. Since they had the same objective in mind, there was no language barrier.

The *President Harding* had only lately plied the Atlantic route to America. For years during the Spanish civil war it had transported British tractors to Franco's army. Reinforced with steel plates and machine guns, those agricultural machines were changed into tanks. The first officer didn't have any compunction about having run arms to the fascists on an American boat, though those makeshift tanks might have killed Americans who, like Ernest Hemingway, volunteered for the Loyalist army. The first officer was for Franco and admired Hitler for keeping the human rabble in their place. After that remark, I left his table and sat alone during the crossing.

To venture on deck was hazardous. The Cuban storm was still blowing, heaping twenty-foot waves over the stern. The deck was awash; the water rolled off the wooden planks, taking along everything that wasn't securely tied down. To walk along the ship's corridors one had to support oneself on the walls with outstretched arms. It was a curious sight, seeing passengers shuffle along like Frankenstein monsters from one ship's corridor to the other.

I passed a storeroom whose door was open. There a few of the crew were shoving a dead woman's body into a canvas bag. I didn't see her face, only her white stringy hair.

A crew member told me that she was one of the immigrants who were shipped from Hungary to America. She had fallen out of her bunk and broken her neck. The family had been informed by radio, and the captain was given permission to bury the body at sea. The funeral would take place at midnight. I watched a crew member screwing a bigger bulb into a light fixture on the upper deck. A table was fastened to the railing so it would not be blown overboard. The news of the burial had traveled. Just before midnight, a strange medley of people appeared on deck. At midnight, the ship slowed to a stop. Women in fur coats appeared from the first class, and a group of ragtag people wearing no socks came from the bowels of the ship. They had cards with their names dangling from their chests.

The captain appeared, followed by four crew members carrying a long board covered with the American flag. The canvas bulged with the dead woman's body. As in a horror movie, a sudden hailstorm hit the deck noisily. I remember immigrant men and women, huddling in a tight group, shivering in the cold. The board was put on the table. The captain, taking off his cap in reverence, read something appropriate from the Bible. Then the board with the flag was tilted and the body in its canvas bag slipped over the railing into the gray waves. The sack, weighted with pieces of iron, quickly sank. A few minutes later the table was removed, the lightbulb exchanged for the former smaller one, and the *President Harding* resumed speed. A crew member, whistling a tune, passed me, the folded American flag under his arm.

Some of the first-class passengers met in the ship's bar. A stunning-looking woman took the stool beside me. I had not seen her before. She was dark-haired and green-eyed. Her beauty was aseptic to me, a hothouse orchid, a hybrid. She had discovered a Dutch liquor called Focking. The name amused her, and every few minutes she called the bartender to give her another Focking. She seemed to have picked me as a companion, since I was alone and unattached. She told me that her husband had sent her to Europe hoping the change of venue might help their marriage, which was on the rocks.

I was an innocent abroad, a foreign Mark Twain character, who had never encountered a problem drinker, which the American Prohibition had created by the millions. My innocent European soul was shaken by the forward behavior of that emancipated American female. She acted as self-willed as any male, which made me feel uneasy. Later on, in America, I got used to that kind of strong-willed, independent female type.

We drank that sweet stuff until dusk. I believe that the spectacle of the funeral at sea had morbidly excited both of us. I finally returned to my cabin and went to bed, still confused by having had a glimpse of the world that I was going to enter. Suddenly my drinking companion entered. She was dressed in a silk robe and a nightgown that was slit high along her shapely legs. Her black hair was streaming down her back. She said that she had the "blues" and did not want to be alone. She had with her a bottle of Focking liquor, which she had pried loose from the barman.

That night I shed my European upbringing like a lizard its skin. She had brought the independent spirit of the unknown continent with her into my cabin. She was for me the personification of the New World, since she had a free conception of life that only America provides. Europe and its staid traditions sank in the gray waves of the Atlantic Ocean. It is said that to get rid of pain and memories one has to put a body of water between the present and the past.

Ethics and morals are dogmas, created by powerful people to dominate others, to make them feel guilty if they break the rules, a method that the churches have refined through the ages. I wonder how many pious old women had entered their marriage as virgins. Young whores, old nuns! Morals fade away on cruises. My visitor had decided to end the night in bed with a man. But she lacked the ability of a sexual response, which might have been the cause of her alcoholism. When she left, she was bewildered. Her confession that she had experienced the first orgasm in her life sounded like an accusation. Her frigidity might have been her armor, and her stunning beauty the shield that protected her emotions from entering her consciousness.

Her husband should have sent her to a psychiatrist to unravel her inhibitions instead of to Europe.

When I ran into her again on board, she did not seem to recognize me. I was sorry not for her but for her husband, who was waiting for her at the pier when the ship docked in New York Harbor. He was in his midthirties, handsome and well groomed. Both together could have been Italian tailors' dummies in an ad in *Vanity Fair*.

When we disembarked, she gave me a long, puzzled, and searching look as if she were still confused by our short adventure.

Armed with a visitor's permit for three months, I wasn't even questioned by the immigration officials as I walked through that old building on Ellis Island, over worn stones, which my father also had crossed fifty years ago. He had to go through medical examinations for tuberculosis and other contagious illnesses and also had been checked for lice. This didn't happen to me. As a first-class passenger, the immigration officer even saluted me.

In front of me lay the towers of New York and beyond them America. And Hollywood, a mystical neverland, three thousand miles away. Behind me was the Statue of Liberty. When we passed that giant female, I knew it would shield me from the vagaries of life's struggles and insecurities. I then understood people's speaking of a "religious experience," of being "born again." The multitude of problems that had darkened my existence vanished. A benevolent curtain had fallen protectively behind me. I no longer was a puppet that a capricious government could throw about and destroy at will.

The British-born Leslie, though thirty-six years old, had never in his life been on the European continent, only forty miles away. He was the archetypical Englishman for whom the world fell into two parts: the British Isles and the rest of the globe. He would have never had the idea to leave his protective island without my encouragement. After all, if you have seen England, what else was there to see, since the "sun never sets on the British Empire." That condition changed after World War II.

Curt and Robert, 1905
Kurt (Curt), age three, and Robert, age five in 1905, the year when our sibling rivalry started. It lasted during Robert's lifetime. He had the obsession to dominate, essential for a motion-picture director. I, a writer, was always in doubt about my own work, basic for a writer who is never content with his endeavor. My brother was the stronger character who always needed acclaim, while I lived in the secluded dreamworld of a writer's fantasies.

***People on Sunday,* 1929**
Menschen am Sonntag (German, 1929) (People on Sunday) is one of the most innovating films in the history of motion picture making. It was the creation of 55 young unknown film enthusiasts forced to flee from the Nazis. They influenced the Hollywood film industry for many years. Story by Curt Siodmak.

Schuss im Tonfilmatelier, 1931
Schuss im Tonfilmatelier (German, 1931). Adding sound and dialog to motion pictures opened the chance for new ideas. An open microphone solved a murder case, a device used in many future film stories. Noval and screenplay by Curt Siodmak.

Dolly Haas, 1931
Dolly Haas (1931 and 1934). She played the lead in the first motion picture I wrote in France, *The Ball* (1931) and *Girls Will Be Boys*, (1934) in London after both of us left Germany forever. A forever teenage sprite in spirit and tomboy, sexy but not sensual, a reliable trouper, though she never became an international star. She nevertheless appeared on Broadway with stage stars after her emigration to the United States. She married the gifted American cartoonist Al Hirschfeld.

F.P.1 Does Not Reply (1932)
F.P.1 Does Not Reply (1932) was the most amitious motion picture ever produced in Germany. Then the Nazis took over and the German film industry never again produced a motion picture of international appeal. Novel and screenplay by Curt Siodmak.

***Der Mann der Seinen Moerder Sucht* 1932**
Der Mann der Seinen Moerder Sucht (German, 1932). This film story started my film career. Too cowardly to commit suicide, a man hires a hit man to dispatch him within 24 hours. Changing his mind, he must find and stop his murderer within the contracted time. Screenplay after a story idea by Jules Verne.

La Crise Est Finie, **1934.**
La Crise Est Finie (The Crisis Is Over), French, 1934. Original screenplay by Curt Siodmak.

The Tunnel, 1936.
The Tunnel (British, 1936). Conception of the machine used in the British motion picture anticipated the machine's use half a century later for the construction of the tunnel between France and England. Screenplay by Curt Siodmak.

Letter from German Publisher (1937)
Letter I received four years after my emigration sent me to London from my former publisher Wilhelm Goldman, Leipzig, Germany: "Dear Mr. Siodmak, I herewith inform you that all copies of your books have been confiscated by the Secret Police (Gestapo). Sincerely Wilhelm Goldman.

The Wolf Man, **1941**
This imaginary picture character has added a legend to the American folklore that might still be remembered when the motion picture has been forgotten. Its original title was *Destiny*, and learned explanations have been written about its possible Freudian implications.

***Tarzan's Magic Fountain,* 1941**
Tarzan's Magic Fountain, 1941. There sometimes is fun also for the writer: composing a nonsense story in Palm Springs, meeting handsome people, and getting paid too. Those rare incidences create the illusion of the glamour of working for the motion picture industry. Original screenplay by Curt Siodmak.

The Lady and the Monster, 1941
The Lady and the Monster, (1941), based on the novel *Donovan's Brain*. Miscast with Erich von Stroheim. The star of this novel has been used in three motion pictures, but none of those versions has succeeded in interpreting *Donovan's Brain*, which for over 60 years is still in print. Novel by Curt Siodmak.

***The Invisible Agent*, 1942**
The Invisible Agent (1942). This motion picture was one of the successful Hollywood anti-Nazi propaganda films. Original screenplay by Curt Siodmak.

Son of Dracula, 1943
Son of Dracula (1943). This motion picture started my brother's career as a top director in Hollywood by the employment of light and shadow, creating a new style in motion pictures. Original story by Curt Siodmak.

The Climax, 1944
The Climax (1944). The motion picture art is able to convey visually or audibly human emotions the written word is unable to convey. In *The Climax*, a murderer (Boris Karloff) in a jealous rage kills the woman he loves. The voice of the victim, a gifted singer, reappearing in a young girl, leads to his destruction. Screenplay by Curt Siodmak.

***The House of Frankenstein*, 1944**
The House of Frankenstein (1944). It was the last of the circle of horror pictures, combining all of the film characters, a farewell to a successful period in film history. Original screenplay by Curt Siodmak.

***Four Days Leave*, 1948**
Four Days Leave (Switzerland, 1948). An innocent little picture, but its French star, Suzanne Et Son Marin, was perhaps the most sensual actress I wrote for in all of my motion pictures. Screenplay by Curt Siodmak.

The Invisible Woman, 1949
The Invisible Woman (1949) was a comedy and the last picture in which John Barrymore, perhaps the most famous Shakespearean actor of his century, appeared. Original screenplay by Curt Siodmak.

The Return of the Invisible Man, 1949
The Return of the Invisible Man (1949). How to become a star on screen without being seen? In *The Invisible Man Returns* Vincent Price made himself a successful horror actor for half a century. Original screenplay by Curt Siodmak.

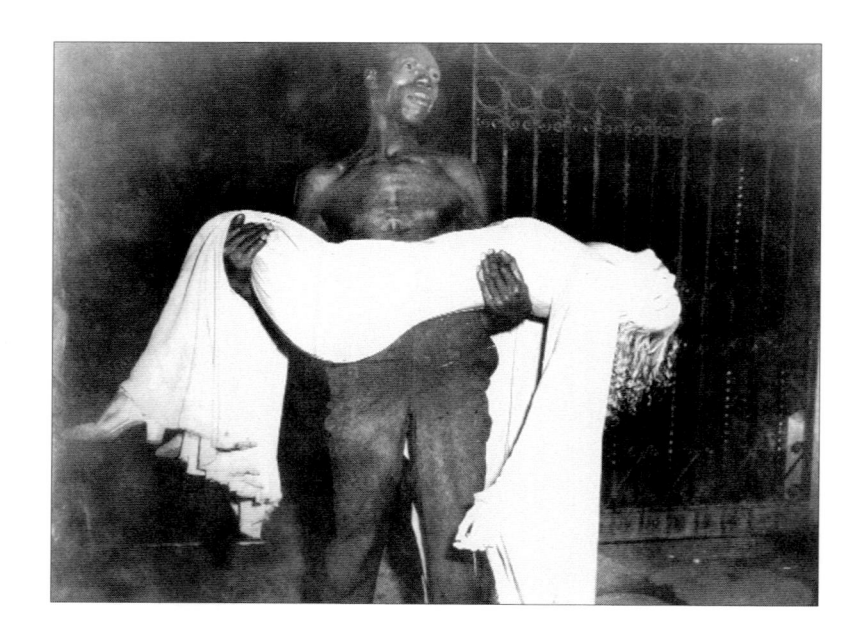

***I Walked with a Zombie*, 1949**
I Walked with a Zombie (1949). Perhaps the most literary film Hollywood had produced in years, a fortunate collaboration of producer, director, and writer. It conveyed a quality rarely achieved in motion pictures. Screenplay by Curt Siodmak.

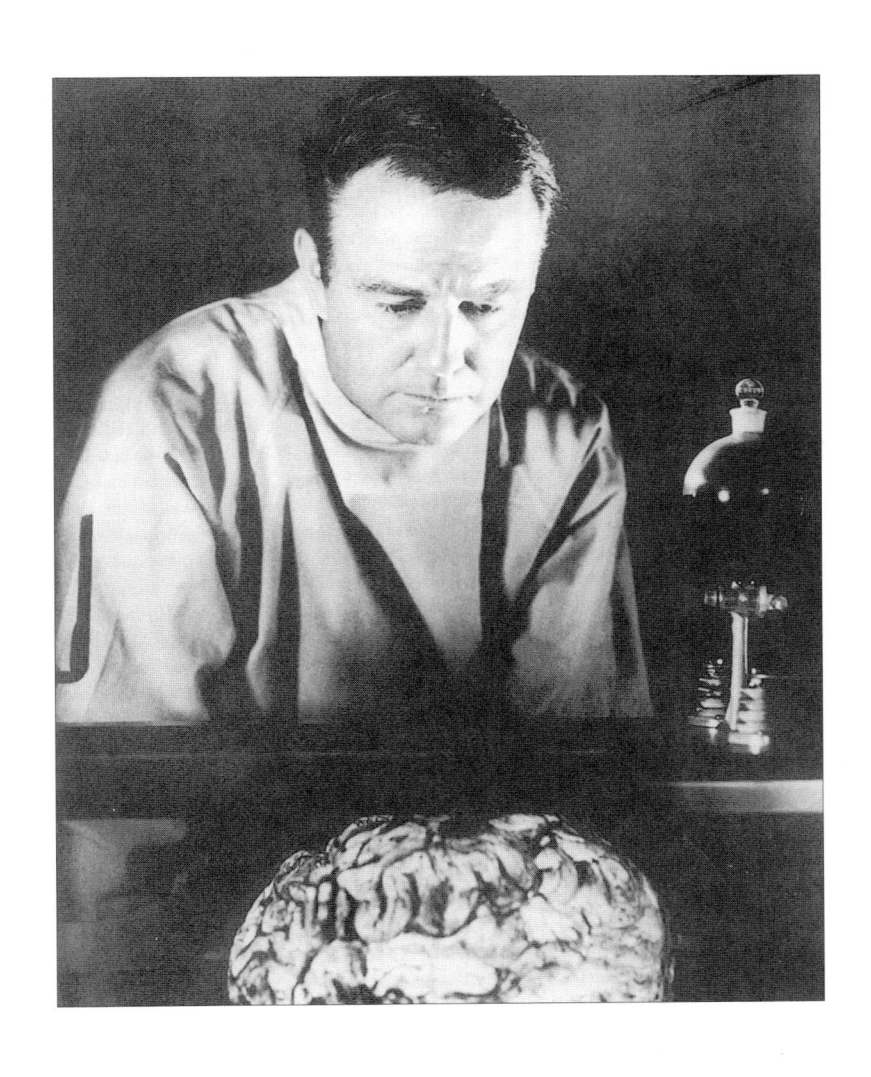

Donovan's Brain, 1953
Donovan's Brain (1953) reproduced under its original title with Lew Ayres and Nancy Davis (the future Mrs. Ronald Reagan).

***Earth Against Flying Saucers,* 1954**
Earth Against Flying Saucers (1954). The special effects, created manually, received the motion picture Academy Award, but 40 years later. Though the picture was reproduced again in 1998 with the latest state-of-the-art techniques, the inexpensive first version remains the favorite among the science fiction aficionados.

***The Beast with Five Fingers*, 1954**
The Beast with Five Fingers (1954). A murderer is haunted by the severed hand of his victim, which finally kills him. The hand is the symbol of his guilt that has taken physical shape but only in this mind. Screenplay by Curt Siodmak.

The Creature with the Atom Brain, 1955
The Creature with the Atom Brain (1955). Today's computer can already outthink the human brain millions times faster than its present capacity. Microscopically small machines, inserted in the human skull, will speed the ability to think millions times faster. The driving force of the human race to explore can never be stopped.

Curucu, Beast of the Amazon, 1956
Curucu, Beast of the Amazon (1956). It was the one and only time that an American motion picture company finished and brought back a full-length picture shot in the Amazon and released for years in America. Original screenplay and direction by Curt Siodmak.

Henrietta
My guiding spirit and for 76 years, my companion and wife, Henrietta, whose spirit never wavered even in situations which seemed hopeless to me.

Robert and Curt, 1962
Robert, 62, and Curt, 60 (1962). Though the closest of friends all our lives, we never worked together in motion pictures. Though I suggested the idea for some of his biggest successes, he only worked with writers he could dominate.

The Lightship, 1963
Das Feuerschiff (*The Lightship,* Germany, 1963). Written in German, it received the German Oscar for the best picture of that year. Screenplay by Curt Siodmak.

VERLEIHUNGSURKUNDE

IN ANERKENNUNG
DER UM DIE BUNDESREPUBLIK DEUTSCHLAND ERWORBENEN
BESONDEREN VERDIENSTE
VERLEIHE ICH

HERRN CURT SIODMAK

DAS GROSSE VERDIENSTKREUZ

DES VERDIENSTORDENS DER BUNDESREPUBLIK DEUTSCHLAND

BERLIN, DEN 7. JANUAR 1999

DER BUNDESPRÄSIDENT

Order of Merit First Class, 1992
Document signed by the president of the Federal Republic of Germany in 1992, of the "Order of Merit First Class," replete with a medal with the German Eagle, possibly given to me for having brought my cultural "baggage" of pre-Nazi Germany with me to America.

Postage Stamp and Postmark, 1997
In 1998 the United States Postal Service for the first time in its history issued a stamp with the imaginary character of a living writer, and also mentioned his name on its cancellation stamp.

Siodmak Brothers Poster, 1998
The International Film Festival in Berlin, Germany, the Berlinale of 1998, had as its theme the motion picture contributions of the Siodmak Brothers, since their work left a trace in motion picture history from silent pictures to the latest state-of-the-art film techniques.

We had worked together on a screenplay for the Gaumont British film *Rob Roy, Prince of Thieves,* a film made half a century later. Since we had no new assignment, we decided to take a look at France. We had sent our wives, Henrietta and Peggy, to wait for us in the south of France, the Côte d'Azur.

I ferried my little Jowett car across the English Channel. I had promised Leslie the best bottle of French Cognac I could find, after a sumptuous lunch in Avallon. That rural village of a few hundred farmers, sixty miles south of Paris, was famous for its Michelin three-star eating place. The food was served by liveried waiters; the liquor was kept in jeroboams five feet high. The bill matched the food. I bought from a native an eighty-year-old bottle of Hennessy Cognac for Leslie. When we finally, after a long and liquid lunch, drove off, the local barber ran after us shouting, "Messieurs, I have a hundred-year-old bottle for sale!" Only in France! Leslie, brought up on the unimaginative cooking of the British middle class, went through a cultural shock, based on our four-hour feast at the Auberge.

In Lyons we saw a huge *affiche,* a painted wooden poster, of Danielle Darrieux, the pretty French star. We knew that our story editor, Angus McPhail, at Gaumont British had a crush on Danielle though he had never met her. We bought that ten-foot-high monstrous poster, had it taken apart, shipped to London, and, after our return to Gaumont, secretly mounted it in McPhail's office. It took one whole wall. It was a rather cruel and childish act and embarrassed Angus. But that foolishness made friends of Leslie and me. He attached himself to me and decided to accompany me to America, though we never became intimate friends. I also suspected that he needed a holiday from his wife Peggy. She sent him a curious radio message to the ship on the high sea that she had had her aquiline nose, which fit her face well, surgically bobbed to make hers look like Henrietta's, whom she envied though she could never match Henrietta's gentle femininity.

I never inquired about Leslie and Peggy's marital relations, though their marriage lasted their lifetime.

Leslie was not creative and needed an assignment, which an unknown freelance writer, without studio connections, could only get on the strength of an original story a studio wanted. He was a company man, not Jewish, not a refugee, taciturn and reserved, all ingredients necessary not to get a studio job.

To be socially accepted in Hollywood, one had to work for a studio. If you said, "I'm writing a novel (or play)," it meant that you didn't collect a weekly check. Then you lost social status and were shunned by your salaried friends. That conception now has changed, and the author who has a novel published or stage play produced is looked upon with envy, since that property might make him or her a fortune. Many very successful Hollywood people—directors, actors, writers—are more interested in impressing their peers than in a high box office return, as the studio took the financial risk and they were paid up front.

MGM foolishly sold the picture rights to the dog story *Lassie* to a producer for two thousand dollars and lost millions of future earnings. Since that disaster, any studio would rather let an unproduced property rot on the shelf than sell the rights to another production, since it might bring in an unlimited financial return. But foolishly it still happens. Universal International refused to add a needed million dollars to a picture, *Home Alone*. Since the Fox distribution needed inexpensive pictures, it invested that missing million, though without enthusiasm. *Home Alone* grossed four hundred million at the box office and became the biggest comedy hit in motion picture history. The child actor was paid seven million for his next job. The producer was elevated to the head of the studio for his brilliant foresight.

Leslie never landed a job and returned to London. There he became successful as a director of some of the Gainsborough costume melodramas for Gaumont British. Leslie was a type of quiet, unassuming Englishman, unaggressive and introverted, a personality in demand in London, where it was considered good breeding never to show ambition.

In New York, Leslie and I loaded our two ship trunks into the sixteen-cylinder Cad convertible and took off, only vaguely aware that we had to travel a distance as far as the boat trip from Southampton to New York. Leslie drove the first hour, then retired to the large backseat to take a nap. He woke up punctually at twelve for lunch, then went back to sleep again, waking up at six in the afternoon, when we stopped in a small town for the night.

American small towns all looked alike to me: the main street, a drugstore at the corner, opposite a rickety hotel, with ancient people sitting on wicker furniture in the lobby, as if they were fixtures of the building.

Motels were not yet popular in America and could hardly be found in 1937. The menu in the "greasy spoon" restaurants was the same everywhere. One could have taken the handwritten menu from one town to the next and ordered the same fare: eggs and bacon, eggs and ham, eggs and sausages, hamburgers, steaks as large as toilet seats, everything served with hash brown potatoes.

Driving through Texas, a barren landscape, along narrow roads, I didn't have the impression that we were moving at all, since we stopped every night at seemingly the same place.

To cross the American continent by automobile was still the exception. Railways carried passenger from city to city. Air travel was only for the rich.

When we turned the motor off at the obligatory small-town hotel, since we avoided staying in big cities for financial reasons, Leslie inquired at the registry about the room numbers where the "girls" lived. The "girls" were the local prostitutes who catered mostly to local farmers and cowboys. The girls had rooms permanently rented with the consent of the hotel proprietor. Leslie didn't see much of the country and even snored during our voyage through the Grand Canyon.

The American continent was seemingly limitless. There was the ever-repeating sign: "Helen's Pecan Stand," which accompanied us in Texas for seven hundred miles until we finally found "Helen's Pecan Stand," a small wooden hut, selling a nut unknown to us Continentals. The two-lane roads, not yet paved into freeway sizes, limited our speed to fifty miles per hour and gave us time to read the "Burma Shave" signs displaying funny two-liners, cropping up every few miles through Texas and Arizona: "The bearded lady tried a jar; she's now a famous movie star." Burma Shave, as I found out, was a shaving cream.

The Cad seemed to have a built-in sensor, since it automatically turned into every one of the rare service stations. The motor swallowed a gallon of gasoline every four miles and my arms got stronger by pumping a yellow liquid that ran through the glass top of the pump. The price of gasoline was nineteen cents a gallon.

When we stopped for the night, Leslie went into the bar for a drink to reinforce himself for his visit to the "girls," possibly to catch up on intercourse that he had missed in staid England. I never saw any of the girls, who might have been too busy to leave their rooms.

At night I fell instantly to sleep, tired from driving and not caring if the worn mattress consisted of hills and valleys. At six in the morning I knocked at Leslie's door. He moaned and groaned and appeared bleary-eyed at the breakfast table, to face the obligatory ham, eggs, hash browns, and coffee. It was a nine-day journey. We were as many days on the road as the *President Harding* churning through the ocean on its way to New York.

In Nashville a girl in a cowboy outfit flagged us down. She wanted a lift but did not know where she wanted to go. She carried no luggage. For the first time I saw blue jeans, encasing a girl's hips like a second skin. She had a trim figure but a hard face with black, piercing eyes. When she heard that we were heading for Hollywood, she decided that this place, too, was her goal. We fed her on the way. Having heard frightening tales about the Mann Act, which made it a federal offense to transport single females across state lines, we made her get out of the Cad and walk across, thus circumventing a law that, we were sure, would have incarcerated us for life. The girl disappeared in the evening and waited for us in the morning. She seemed to know where to sleep in every town. One morning she did not show up and we drove on.

We had to stop over in a small Texas town, to fill up with gas. The attendant, in a cowboy outfit, a young man of huge proportions, was intrigued by our strange accent. He called his father, a person of equally big size. Learning that I was a Jewish refugee, he invited us for dinner at his home. I had never seen such giants as he and his sons were. They were a Jewish family of saddle makers. They asked me what drove me to Hollywood, a town vile, corrupt, and amoral. Shocked by my story that I had to flee Germany in order not to be killed by the Nazis, they offered me a deal. I should stay with them. They would teach me how to shoe horses, build the best saddles in Texas, and see to it that I would make a good living. I should bring my wife and son.

If I had accepted their offer, I might have become a 100 percent American, not a man with two countries. Whoever has two countries has none.

My friend Charles Bennett, author of *The 39 Steps* and many other Hitchcock pictures, had made the same trip a few months previous to our continental crossing, but in six days. He must have traveled day and night in his Packard convertible, a two-seater with a rumble seat. But he was not alone. He had taken his steady companion Nips along, an enormous Manx cat named after a character in *Peter Pan,* and also the original sandbox Nips had used in Charles's London flat. Nips, very particular about his proprieties, would rather die of constipation than be deprived of his favorite sandbox, which Charles had to take out, even in the middle of the Arizona desert, with a thousand miles of soft sand around. Cats like obedient people. Nips died many years later of old age in Charles's Beverly Hills home, still living in his mind in London, the way his master, who died half a century later in Hollywood, did. Charles never applied for American citizenship, a true Englishman, faithful to the Union Jack but loath to live in his native country.

When Leslie and I reached Phoenix, Arizona, Leslie sent a telegram to the only address we knew in Hollywood, the Beverly Wilshire Hotel, to reserve rooms. He signed the message the European way, without his first name, just simply "Arliss."

After two more days of traveling, we arrived at the City of the Angels. There we followed a street sign: Hollywood Boulevard. We thought we had finally reached the end of our journey, having crossed the country Columbus had discovered but named after an unknown Spanish explorer, Amerigo Vespucci. We did not know that we had to drive another twenty miles through streets as drab as London slums. Where were the studios and glamorous stages? Paramount and RKO were hidden among clapboard houses. MGM looked like a prison, as did Warner Brothers.

Years later, after World War II, when Jack Warner, the studio's boss, went to Europe with a group of Hollywood executives, he flew over Auschwitz, the concentration camp. On his return he invited his employees to listen to his report about that trip. Not many writers showed up to listen, since they considered themselves culturally superior to that entrepreneur who had started in vaudeville.

"From the air Auschwitz looks like Warner Brothers Studios," Jack Warner announced. With its main building, its walls, and police guards, it did. But Warner also had a sense of whimsy as I found out when I, in later years, worked in that studio. He was a friend of Salvador Dali, the surrealist painter. They exchanged telegrams daily, consisting of two words, "Petite Marmite," which is the name of a French cooking pot. When Jack cabled "Marmite," Dali replied with "Petite." Or with "Marmite Petite." Jack replied with "Petit Marmite." The two words were their "surrealistic" conversation. That inanity supposedly went on for years.

We finally arrived at the only hotel we had heard about, the Beverly Wilshire Hotel. A uniformed doorman parked the Cad. The hotel management, expecting George Arliss, the famous English actor, and his entourage, had held a score of suites at our disposal. But we cut that extravagance down to two of the least expensive rooms.

Where was the film world that our imagination had painted in our mind, based on what we had seen and read in motion picture magazines: beautiful women and famous actors, the superrich of easy morals who swapped each other's wives with their willing consent, stories of divorces, scandals, of life in glamorous Beverly Hills? Wilshire Boulevard at our arrival looked like London's Oxford Street, with its shops and department stores.

I didn't know anybody in Los Angeles, but Leslie had his British connections, since the British abroad hold together like an exclusive club. Leslie knew the address of a beautiful English actress, Belinda. When Leslie phoned Belinda, she asked whether he would accompany her to a cocktail party that afternoon. We had hardly been in our rooms for an hour but left to pick up Belinda in our mile-long Cad. She was a blonde beauty with a pleasant voice, and an "intercontinental" accent, British and American fused. Foreign actors study elocution at UCLA to tone down their native pronunciation. They know that they never will, and never really want to speak like a native American.

Trained since childhood to use certain muscles in our throats differently than those of other languages, the microphone reveals our origin, German, French or British, Swedish or Slavic. Electronic amplification increases foreign sounds.

Belinda directed us to a house north of Sunset Boulevard in Beverly Hills, the most expensive real estate in California. Driving past mansions with huge gardens, manicured like those of English country homes, we finally stopped at a miniature Versailles. A Filipino servant parked the car. We walked past an Olympic-sized swimming pool with a cabana, five times larger than my little house in Mill Hill. A noisy garden party was in progress. Loose-limbed girls played vicious games of tennis with tanned, athletic young men. The girls looked like cutouts of fashion magazines, their swimsuits as tight as though painted on, which answered all questions about their anatomy. It was the Hollywood fetish not to allow one ounce of superfluous fat to distort the lines of their perfect bodies.

I talked to a handsome German actress. She told me that she was suing a magazine for having published photos of her without her consent. She did not object to being exposed in the nude. Her complaint was that now, after three years of living in Hollywood, she had acquired a much better figure than that in the pictures taken years ago in Berlin.

When I watched Marlene Dietrich being filmed in *The Blue Angel* at the UFA studios in Berlin, she was a rather chubby, round-faced girl. America streamlined her into the shape that made her famous. She even had her wisdom teeth removed to accentuate the heart-shaped face, which became her trademark.

Masculine-looking men are at a premium in Hollywood. That's why Clark Gable, Burt Lancaster, and even Rock Hudson moved into the upper echelon of stardom, which did not mean that the Hollywood male stars were extremely macho in their private lives. Cary Grant, who had a long affair with a female motion picture producer, left her bed one morning. Two hours later the MGM Studio's publicity department informed her that Grant had married Lady Ashley two hours ago. Was it a hatred for women that caused him to break with deliberate cruelty his intimate relationship?

The fate of Rock Hudson, who died of AIDS, is well known. The fact that some Hollywood male stars "switched" at the age of forty or were bisexual, like Cary Grant (who also was addicted to LSD), was never mentioned.

Belinda did not seem to have found a male companion to accompany her to the Sorensen garden party. That's why she asked Leslie, whom she knew from England, to chauffeur her. She introduced us to the host, Cliff Sorensen. Like Howard Hughes in later years, he was a pilot, industrialist and multimillionaire, obviously collecting handsome men and women like postage stamps. A tanned, middle-aged man with a well-trained body but dyed blonde hair, Sorensen politely cracked his face shortly into an impersonal smile when Belinda introduced us to him. He kissed her in a manner the Hays Office, which controlled the morals of the film industry, would have censored.

The large garden door to the mansion was open. Belinda invited us into the house with its collection of South Sea Pacific artifacts. She moved about as casually as if she were the hostess. Sorensen's "office" had hollow glass walls, filled with water in which tropical fish swam. He worked inside an aquarium! The only furniture was a large desk with many telephones. Belinda disappeared, and we did not see her again that afternoon. Left to our fate, Leslie and I drifted back into the garden where food and drinks were served.

A redheaded woman accosted Leslie. She introduced herself as Princess Ostrowska. She was a white Russian who as a child had fled the USSR. So she said. Her girlfriend, a tall model with black hair and violet eyes, a clone of the woman I had met on the boat, attached herself to me. Both ladies were without escorts. One day a wag told me that for every virile man in Hollywood six girls and a hunchback are available. The violet-eyed beauty's name was

Cordelia, and she modeled for the French dressmaker Poiret. She also spoke French but with a midwestern accent.

The cocktail party ended abruptly at six. It was as if a curtain had fallen. The Naiads and their companions vanished. The Princess and the black-haired Cat asked us for a drink at their abode on Tower Road. I'm sure they were intrigued and amused by our wide-eyed innocence.

I don't know who had chauffeured them to the party, but we drove them to their home, which did not have the splendor of the Sorensen residence but had, like every house in Beverly Hills, a lush tropical garden and a pool, whose water looked like blue liquid glass. A Filipino servant dressed in surgical white offered us the typical Hollywood fare, shrimp canapés. We had more drinks at the pool. The night was hot. It was only the end of April, and I wondered what August would be like. It got dark quickly, and the sun suddenly fell behind an unseen horizon. A full moon, brighter than I had ever seen before, lit the sky, and it seemed that all the stars in heaven had congregated over Beverly Hills.

Cordelia told me casually that she had been raped when she was fourteen and had experienced an earth-shaking orgasm. Since then she had never again felt any emotion during her love affairs but instead a deep disgust during that exercise. That's why she avoided physical contact with men whenever possible.

The Princess and the Cat threw off their clothes and swam nude in the glassy water of the pool. They looked like animated lotus petals, frail orchids, but detached with the casual manner that women display who are aware of the beauty of their bodies.

Hollywood! A fairy tale town of radiant beauty, of strikingly handsome people. For decades the most handsome people of the world had emigrated to Hollywood to conquer the movie game. Shapely girls had married handsome boys and produced beautiful children. This was already the fourth or fifth generation of immaculate bodies, future creators of generations of gorgeous human shapes. Why hadn't I gone to Hollywood immediately instead of wasting four years in England with its inhibited xenophobic inhabitants? Here everybody seemed to be an American, even when they were only one generation removed from their European ancestry.

I quickly learned that Hollywood's beautiful people were imbued with a relentless drive. Only the toughest had a chance to succeed. Youth, beauty, sex, sometimes even talent were coins to be exchanged for chances to crash through the icy walls of the motion picture studios.

It also was a city of fear, ruled by cruel insecure men who wielded their power ruthlessly in that competitive, cutthroat industry.

No such night ever happened to me again, not once in twenty years in Hollywood.

Hollywood does not exist. It is just a name for a certain product that is often vilified and despised as the symbol of wickedness but also is secretly admired and envied the world over. The New York film critics love to pan its films. But should they be called to Hollywood for a job, they'd rush to the next plane, lured by the often enormous pay. Money is a powerful substitute for conviction. Many New York critics became screenwriters and, their conscience fortified by a mounting bank account, defended Tinseltown as fervently as they had criticized it.

A few enclaves in Los Angeles produce the Hollywood product: Paramount Studios, situated on Melrose Avenue in a shabby part of Los Angeles; Columbia Studios, not very far away, looking like a giant shoe factory. Metro-Goldwyn-Mayer was part of Culver City, a drab part of Los Angeles. Twentieth Century–Fox is a fortress near glamorous Beverly Hills, which is so elite that it is a separate city with its own police force, city hall, and fire department. It is so detached from Los Angeles that its fire department let a house burn down because it was situated in Los Angeles territory, one hundred feet outside the boundaries of the Beverly Hills enclave.

Universal Studios had built its production stages outside Los Angeles, on land that had been a desert, inhabited by rattlesnakes and coyotes. Warner Brothers and Walt Disney Studios were situated in "Beautiful Downtown Burbank," a rather unattractive part of L.A.

Some black directors, financially successful, left the barrows when the first million dollars poured into their pockets, moved to Beverly Hills, and joined the white Hollywood elite. Such is the lure of Hollywood success. Its glamour and wealth are corruptible and contagious like a drug. It destroys human decency. But it has its ingrained elite of top executives who, protecting each other, move from studio to studio in a game of musical chairs. When one was thrown out for incompetence, he quickly found another, often more lucrative, job at another studio, arranged by his friends, who, of course expected the same courtesy from him should they be fired.

Success in motion pictures, though fleeting, is power, because the screen image reaches an audience of millions in every part of the world.

It creates its own clan that quickly severs its ties with the ordinary human rabble. The studio heads use that dominance like South American dictators, having created the absolute capitalistic system in which all the leadership is concentrated in the top echelon and the hired hands, may they be actors, directors or writers, are ordered what to do. Otherwise their work and salary were suspended, and no member of the "Hollywood cartel" would engage them. Unruly servants were secretly blacklisted. Hollywood studios were run like a benevolent concentration camp.

When Darryl Zanuck, the head of Twentieth Century–Fox, was invited to a sprawling horse ranch in Hidden Hills by one of his top writers, he remarked, "I like people like you with their horses and big overhead. You cannot walk out on me. But there are those s.o.b. writers who stay in hotels, possessing only two suitcases despite the money we pay them. They can pack up and walk out on me. You cannot!"

I got a pass to visit MGM through Joe Pasternak. Joe had produced motion pictures in Berlin and had escaped the Nazis. He quickly became successful in Hollywood, producing cheerful light musicals and comedies, like the *Great Caruso* with Mario Lanza, whose tenor was supposed to equal that of the legendary singer.

Now I was for the first time inside a Hollywood studio, a world of two dimensions. We passed the famous actor Clark Gable, who to my amazement washed off his upper dental plate at a water faucet, brilliant teeth courtesy of MGM, I guess, which he flashed at Vivien Leigh in *Gone with the Wind*. Gable gave Joe a toothless grin. When he, in 1924, got his first job in Hollywood, then an unknown New York actor, he was paid the unreal sum of ten thousand dollars for the lead in *Forbidden Paradise,* a film nobody remembers. He demanded to be paid in cash, convinced that the studio had made a booking mistake. Gable planned to leave Hollywood on the next train for New York before the accounting department found out. He stayed at MGM for nearly thirty years as the "King of Hollywood."

The studio streets were built in many styles, to be used for different demands of shooting backgrounds. They were only empty facades, house fronts supported by posts. Joe pointed out a swarthy, dark-haired Italian to me. "There goes, by the grace of God, the great Mario Lanza." As we passed him, Joe bowed to him exaggeratedly with a smile and whispered under his breath, "Asshole." "I'm, by the wrath of Jehovah, the producer of his picture *The Great Caruso*," Joe said ruefully. "You can't imagine how that bastard can make everybody's life miserable. He does not take direction and thinks he knows everything better. But he has the Voice."

In front of a fake house with a rose garden of artificial flowers, Mickey Rooney (Joe Yule Jr.) and Judy Garland (Frances Gumm), still teenagers, acted in *Andy Hardy*, a perennial series of family pictures that Hollywood turned out like television sit-coms of today, using the same cast and a serialized sequence popular with teenagers and housewives. Mickey Rooney had acted since he was two years old. "I was a fourteen-year-old boy for forty years," Rooney supposedly said, carrying his acting ability way past his middle age, when he appeared highly successfully on Broadway at the age of sixty in *Sugar Babies*. The *Andy Hardy* stories were conceived by young New York writers whom MGM contracted for six months at fifty dollars a week, a starving wage. Their contract was not renewed. It was the studio's intention to clutter up the market with unemployed writers, to rehire some cheaply, a powerful ploy of the studio system.

Judy Garland and Deanna Durbin (Edna May Durbin), teenagers with remarkable voices, became stars at MGM, which decided to keep Judy Garland under contract and dismissed Deanna. Universal gleefully snatched her up. To MGM's dismay, Durbin became an international star. She was intelligent enough to quit at the high point of her career, married a few times, among them my friend the German writer-producer Felix Jackson (Felix Joachimsohn), and then retired to Paris, where she still lives. She despised her acting, which she described as "Little Miss Fix-it, who burst into song." Deanna personified the ideal daughter millions of fathers and mothers wished they had.

Judy Garland's life has been written up in many books. She drifted into drugs and died prematurely. The rumor was, and still persists, that the high echelon of MGM secretly fed drugs to their top actors, even to Greta Garbo. The drug might have been amphetamine, which creates the illusion of superstrength, but since "speed kills," some actors, like Garland, became addicts. Having observed the ruthlessness of the motion picture executives, I can't dismiss that possibility from my mind.

When I entered the men's room at the writers' building, I found myself in an office. A young woman, Dorothy Parker, new in the studio, had put the "Men" sign on her office door to make sure she would meet the male writers. She became so famous that her picture is now on an American postage stamp.

Joe took me to the Lion's Den, where Leo the MGM lion (the roaring logo of their company) resided. Leo the Lion was comfortably housed in a large cage. His handler, wearing heavy rubber gloves, started to masturbate that monster. The lion reached orgasm, rolled over, and slept. The lion tamer must have been used to the astonishment of visitors. "When he is working," he told me, "twice a week, when not, once a week. I feed him and I fuck him. He is like a wife to me." My first day in a Hollywood studio was an education on how that town, where I was going to work for the next thirty years, conducted its scurrilous and heartless business.

We immigrants were lonely people, since we didn't know any Americans intimately. It would also be nice to have a female around in the morning when one brushes one's teeth. But there was no female in our "Berliner Club." The "club," consisting of male members with whom I never had contact while in Berlin, stuck together like people in a lifeboat whose ship has sunk. We played chess or bridge and gossiped. Many of the immigrants looked down on that "land without culture" that was giving them shelter and had saved them from death. That seeming arrogance was an outcome of a deep despair, having lost all roots of a former life and also a lack of strength to begin a new one. What had started as a tightly knit group soon split into fragments. Those who got a studio job left behind those who didn't. The fortunate ones joined the Hollywood pecking order, which is strictly based on income.

Have a sandwich at the Warner Brothers' commissary. At the counter the price for a sandwich was forty cents, forty-five cents when sitting at a table, sixty cents in the "Green room" where the writers had their lunch, one dollar at the directors' and producers' eatery. Invited to Jack Warner's private dining room, the lunch was free.

High-priced actors and writers didn't mix with low-paid ones. During production, the upper echelon had their own bungalows. They kept to themselves, not joining the lower-paid employees. America, which has no nobility like European countries, is fractured into moneyed classes. I lost most of my friends when they entered the rarefied atmosphere of the high salaries. Immigrants with jobs quickly became Americanized. Those who could not or would not adjust themselves to the new country remained Europeans and never changed, like stage directors famous in Europe but unknown in America, successful Continental directors who couldn't find their way into studios. Those who clung to their native language were unable or unwilling to assimilate, couldn't make their living in Hollywood in their former profession, or in despair created their own opportunities like the actor, once famed in Europe, who dubbed heavy breathing into porno pictures to make sex scenes more exciting.

A studio also required a certain "American" personality. Those with the inbred Germanic intolerance and their cultural arrogance, propounding that everything in their homeland was better, had hardly a chance to become assimilated.

To start a new life demands abandoning the former. One has to be reborn, learning the behavior, tastes, and attitudes of the natives. Only by integrating oneself into that flow of customs and habits, a new life could be created. Only after one had been shaped and honed into an "American" could one add the centuries-old European culture, which often gave the immigrant a cutting edge.

There was one oasis of the lost Europe in Hollywood, though exclusive and only accessible to successful foreigners: Salka Viertel's home at 165 Mabery Road in Santa Monica. Salka was the wife of Berthold Viertel, the stage director who twenty years previously had thrown me out of the Dresden State Theater when I wanted to watch my brother act.

Salka fostered an exclusive club for film luminaries. Greta Garbo was one of Salka's close friends. She did not appear with a male companion. Her attractive blonde secretary Helga was a German lesbian. The triangle of Garbo, Salka, who had written some of Garbo's screenplays, and Helga seemed to be very tightly knit, though Garbo once had a tumultuous love affair with the actor John Gilbert, a virile Spanish type, though never a first-rate star.

Though I certainly was no luminary, Salka might have heard my name mentioned in Berlin since she invited me to one of her musical soirees. She might have thought I was an admirer of Arnold Schoenberg, the famous refugee Austrian composer, originator of twelve-tone music. I was finding myself in the same room with Greta Garbo, Thomas Mann and Heinrich Mann, Carl Zuckmayer who had written the screenplay to *The Blue Angel,* and other ultra-famous Europeans. Marlene Dietrich appeared in slacks, a fashion she single-highhandedly created for women all over the world. Baranowski and Piscator, the famous German stage directors, who had been booted out by Hitler, attended, as did Fritz Kortner, who after the war returned to Germany, afraid he would die in Hollywood with the Continental, unpronounceable "th" between his teeth. I certainly did not appreciate Schoenberg's cacophonous music, which was alien to me and felt out of place in the tightly knit German group of Hollywood's literary elite.

I had seen Greta Garbo before, but only in a motion picture in Berlin in 1933. That had been before the invention of dubbing voices and carried German subtitles. I remember vividly one scene: Garbo was talking to John Gilbert during a candlelight dinner scene in her film *Queen Christina*. The subtitle was "blase, blase" (blow, blow), which meant, I guess, to blow out the candles to continue the love affair in the dark. But the German word *blase* has, like in English, the sexual connotation of oral sex. When I was introduced to Garbo, her face did not change its frozen expression, as if I didn't exist, which increased my temerity. Not finding full-blown women exciting, I thought that she certainly was not my type. Nor could I visualize Joan of Arc in any sexual position, though I might be wrong since Kenneth Tynan, the film critic, remarked, "What when being drunk one sees in other women, one sees in Garbo sober." And she herself believed that she was a woman who is unfaithful to a million men. That might have been her mystique: available but impossible for earthlings to reach. James Wong Howe, the famous cameraman, remarked, "Garbo was like a horse on a track. Nothing, and then the bell goes and something happens." It certainly didn't happen to me.

She had come to Hollywood with Mauritz Stiller, whom MGM had engaged. The studio, as a favor to the famous Swedish director, permitted him to bring along his eighteen-year-old protégée. Stiller died a short time after his arrival, but his import, Garbo, became the goddess of the screen. Intimidated, I withdrew close to the door, not daring to mix with the illustrious guests. Schoenberg started his cacophonous music. During the session a dog kept barking in the servants' quarters. Since I was standing close to the door, I left the room quietly, following the dog's sound. I found that noisemaker in the kitchen with the butler, whose ears were stuffed with cotton. I made my presence known, and he reluctantly removed the cotton from his left ear. He kicked the yelping Chihuahua into an adjoining room and confessed that he stuffed his ears because, like the dog, he didn't like Schoenberg's music.

The European culture of the 1930s, injected with the influx of refugees, whose erudition often was very high, seemed to flatter ordinary Americans who rarely had heard of Schoenberg, Brecht, or Thomas Mann. I felt stuffy in the throwback to my former life. This was a new country, demanding a new society. That group was not the society to which I yearned to belong.

At Salka's house I met Margo, a pretty Mexican dancer. I had met her in New York, where Charles MacArthur, the playwright, had given one of his alcoholic parties. Captivated by Margo's pertness and humor, I invited her to a picture show at Grauman's Chinese Theater on Hollywood Boulevard. She accepted without any fuss, which made me believe in the independent nature of motion picture girls, though she was Mexican and only eighteen years old. But I was wrong when I thought I would be alone with her, enjoying a lovely tête-à-tête, late drinks at the Beachcomber tavern, and further possibilities of a pleasant evening. I drove my long Cadillac to the Hollywood Hills, an old, rather run-down part of Los Angeles, and arrived at her house one hour before the picture started. Margo was with her grandmother, her mother, her sisters, Carmelita and Consuela, a brother who played the guitar, and two of her grandfathers. Also a handful of uncles and aunts were present.

The New York actor and matinee idol, Franz Lederer, a Viennese emigré, the heartthrob of many American girls, had proposed to marry her, as I soon found out. A very cultured Austrian, Francis had made her the present of a huge antique Spanish religious painting of the Velasquez school, which hung over the couch in Margo's living room. It seemed to fit the atmosphere of that very Catholic family. I wanted to talk her out of that impending marriage, but of course it was hopeless. When I met Franz half a century later, at the film festival in Vienna, I reminded him of his marriage to that pretty girl. He finally and belatedly agreed that it had been a mistake. His marriage to Maria Margarita Guadalupe Boldao y Castilla had been very short. Later she was married happily to the actor Eddie Albert and become a memorable cook, but she didn't keep her dancer's shape. So I heard by grapevine, since I was never invited.

Margo and I went to the gaudy theater with her mother, sisters, brother and some other relatives, all piling into my mile-long Cad. I bought tickets for the whole family. But I was allowed to sit alone with Margo, holding hands. At the end of the show, we again crowded into the car and drove back to her home. Grandmother had prepared a midnight snack of tacos and burritos, and her brother played the guitar and sang in Spanish. I learned that to date a girl in Hollywood one has to be a bachelor or, if a married man, hide that diminishing fact.

Margo invited me to her wedding to Francis Lederer. It was a double wedding performance, Francis and Margo, and Maria Koretz, a Hungarian singer, and her bridegroom. It took place in the garden of the Koretz villa. Maria was under contract to MGM, but despite her brilliant voice, she never became well known.

I had been warned that much drinking would accompany the Mexican marriage and had taken a few aspirin along, hoping they would keep me sober. There was no escape. A Mariachi band stopped guests and played until they had gulped down a big glass of tequila in honor of the newlyweds. When I felt that the alcohol was befogging my mind, I went to the bathroom and filled a glass from a carafe to swallow the pills. The carafe's "water" was tequila. Many guests landed in the swimming pool, which sobered them up. That's what Hollywood's pools are for.

After a cocktail party at a friend's house, while Henrietta was still waiting for her quota number in London, I gave a handsome red-headed actress a lift home. Her name was Greer Garson. Louis B. Mayer, a knowledgeable collector of female pulchritude, had seen her on the stage in London and signed her to a contract with MGM. Greer was deeply unhappy. She aspired to play in the picture *Toy Wife* but was ordered back to England to appear in the picture *Goodbye Mr. Chips* with Robert Donat. Louise Rainer, who had received an Oscar for her portrayal of a Chinese girl in the international best-seller *The Good Earth* by Pearl Buck, got that part. Greer was heartbroken.

I believe I was high on drinks that night as I drove that enchanting lady home in my small open Buick. I had a vision and explained to her that there was no guarantee that any acting part would lead to success in the motion picture business. Sometimes a job that does not seem important might change an actress's life. In England Greer scored a worldwide hit in *Goodbye Mr. Chips*, which made her an international star. *Toy Wife* with Louise Rainer was MGM's movie disaster of the year, and Louise never worked in Hollywood again.

When Greer returned from England, she phoned me to tell me that since she was a star now, she would have only friends around who believed in her before she became famous. That was the last I heard from her until two years after Henrietta's arrival in Hollywood. Greer unexpectedly invited both of us to her home for Christmas Eve. We accepted since I was curious to find out her reason. I met many Europeans at her expensively catered party. The Austrian film director Reginald Le Borg, whose name was *Grobel* spelled backward, played Viennese songs, and I saw old European acquaintances whom time had discarded.

Later I found out that Greer had planned the party for Hollywood people important to her. After a spat with her Filipino servant, he had thrown the invitations in the trash can. In her disappointment that she had lost her guests who had different plans for Christmas, she might have looked through her address book and invited everybody she could think of.

In 1931 I had written a similar story in *Le Bal,* in Paris with Danielle Darrieux. Of course I cannot verify that story, but as life and imagination sometimes overlap, this is a plausible explanation why we were asked by Greer twenty-four hours before Christmas.

I never met her again though she had a long and successful film career. Pauline Kael, the acerbic film critic, unkindly described her as "one of the most richly syllabled, queenly horrors of Hollywood."

Still floating in limbo between Europe and America, during my first job at Paramount collaborating with Jerry Geraghty, I sometimes forgot which language I was using at the moment. When he replied with "Ja, ja," I had slipped into German. When he answered with "Oui, oui," my mind, still confused, had spoken to him in French. It took a few weeks before I lost that schizophrenic mixing of languages.

Motion picture production in the 1940s was mostly based on nepotism. It depended on whom you knew and what kind of access you had to the "movers and shakers." All of Carl Laemmle's, the boss of Universal Studios, numerous relatives had "studio jobs" but nothing to do. When they received their weekly paycheck they retired to the "laughing room" where they showed their hilarity, having been paid for nothing, and emerged from that room stone-faced.

Carl Laemmle Sr., just five feet tall, was the undisputed dictator of the company he had founded. He had bought twenty-five square miles of desert land outside Los Angeles and, starting with one shed, produced motion pictures. Universal Studios now turns out a billion dollars' worth of negatives, supplying the bulk of the sprawling television industry.

Laemmle was very hard of hearing, and one had to shout to make him understand. If someone said, "Mr. Laemmle, your last picture was a smash hit," he did not understand and made the caller repeat that sentence a few times. But when, even a hundred yards away someone whispered, "Old man Laemmle's last picture stinks to heaven!" he turned furiously on the disseminator of bad publicity. It was his trick pretending that he could not hear well.

Laemmle had a son whom he groomed to take over the studio. Carl Laemmle Jr. became the producer of *Frankenstein*, a perennial moneymaker for the company that spawned dozens of *Frankenstein* pictures.

Carl Jr. was as small as his father. Suffering from being only five feet tall, he exercised strenuously, and he finally gained 1.5 inches in height, just tall enough to be drafted into the army in 1941!

Anybody can become a film producer or motion picture director, but certainly not a creative writer. Studio people are reproductive, except the writer who is faced with an empty page that he or she has to cover with letters, which finally appear on the screen as motion pictures.

Irving Thalberg, the MGM "boy wonder" producer who in the early thirties was responsible for introducing literary flavor into films, was wary of writers. He said, "The writer is the most important film contributor. But never, never give him any power." That condition still exists today. From none of the fifty-nine films I wrote, of which many are still running and highly profitable, have I received any financial return. I was treated as a "hired hand," like a bricklayer or a carpenter. Lacking business sense, I was never successful in amassing a fortune. I also don't know of any writer of my time who died rich unless he had the foresight to buy himself a home in Beverly Hills, which he could sell for a big sum when he couldn't get a job in his later years. His wealth didn't come from his writing business but from selling his real estate.

When the Screen Writers Guild was formalized in 1937, about six hundred professional authors joined. They were able to make a living without Hollywood, receiving income from books and plays. Writing for the screen was a byline, a possibility of making quick money. Now the Writers Guild of America has more than twelve thousand members of which perhaps 2 percent could make a living without writing on assignment. They mostly write for serializations, or sit-coms, "bricklaying" a story based on a preconceived set of characters. Their scripts are then altered, mutilated, dissipated by "executives" and actors, who believe themselves to be better writers than the original author. An artificial laugh track is added, to convince the viewers that the story is funny and that the dialogue line is supposed to be a joke.

I wonder who would ever find the sit-coms humorous if the inane laugh track was not added to the dull dialogue.

For me, to work for TV would be a humiliating business, since the author rarely finds his screenplay on the screen as he had devised it. In its "best years" before TV, Hollywood created about four hundred motion pictures, or six hundred hours of entertainment. Now, adding the TV hours on all stations, there are seventy-two thousand hours to be filled yearly. Subtracting the time for sports, news, reruns, documentaries, and motion pictures, there are still a few thousand hours that have to be covered by "new" material. I believe that all the treasures of the world literature would not fill one week of television shows. That's why TV is called "a literary wasteland." A professional is still an independent creator by publishing a novel that a production company might use as the basis of a motion picture. A Broadway hit can make its author a millionaire, but television writers (well paid for their work including residuals, thanks to the fights, strikes, and constant battles of the Writers Guild with the producing companies) sometimes sit around for months before their brainchild is put into production. Should a writer become successful, he often joins the "hyphenates"—the writer-directors, writer-producers—and becomes an executive, the upper echelon of that industry. Some actors have a chance to become millionaires. But the majority of the two crafts, writers and actors, can hardly eke out a living, since there are not enough jobs to go around.

A producer prefers to engage the same TV writers, to be assured that he is getting a workable script for his money, or assigns the job to a producer-writer friend, keeping the money in the "family." An executive rarely takes chances on newcomers. The perennial comedians, like Bob Hope, Bob Newhart, or Johnny Carson, kept the same crew of writers for decades. Out of that well-paid crowd of gifted writers, some become independent. They rarely work on assignment, since they have the talent to create for the legitimate stage where their plays might earn millions, instead of for a salary, and where they are their own boss.

The entertainment business is cruel, ungrateful, and tremendously unstable. A writer, director, or producer is valued by his last success. There was the joke at MGM, when one employee hopefully tells another employee, "I will be pensioned when I am sixty-five. But how to become sixty-five in this business?" "Overnight."

My Hollywood contact, Howard Bromley, who had been working as a story editor at Gaumont British in London, had become an agent in Hollywood. An agent is the go-between between production and employees. Hollywood is run by powerful agents who control the supply of stories, writers, and acting talent.

Howard was a young man with the clean look of the young Prince of Wales, Edward VIII. Good looks are highly appreciated in American business. A handsome man or woman has a much better chance of getting a job than a plain-looking one.

Howard had a few connections. He introduced me to the story editor of Paramount Studios, Manny Wolfe. The prestigious Little, Brown, Publishers in Boston also had published a translation of my novel *F.P. 1 Does Not Answer* in 1933, and the picture people always were awed by published books or successful plays. They like to control the people they engage but cannot dominate successful authors. The border of their world ended at the studio gate.

Since every office building at Paramount was constructed in another style, to be used as a background in different period pictures, Manny's office was situated in the Tudor building. His office was large, carpeted, and executive serene. When he interviewed me, I was provoked by his pomposity and cockily told him that he reminded me of a Jewish Charles Boyer, with his big eyes and mellifluous voice. That "chutzpah" of a writer who wanted a job surprised him so much that he engaged me.

A job! I didn't care what the assignment was to be. I was again in a studio with its smell of celluloid and glue, the way a new car has its peculiar scent.

I was assigned to two female screenwriters, Lillian Hayworth and Seena Owen. The ladies were more than ten years my senior. My assignment was a musical screen version of *Aloma of the South Seas,* a play by Leroy Clement and John B. Hymer. It certainly was not a story for a musical picture, and I had to invent a complete new plot featuring a pretty eighteen-year-old girl, Dorothy Lamour (Dorothy Kaumeyer), and Jon Hall (Charles Locher), the most gorgeous hunk of the thirties, who had scored a tremendous hit in *Hurricane.* The two ladies were former silent film actresses, who, maybe, had been favorites of powerful producers. Seena had acted in D. W. Griffith's *Intolerance* in 1916. Both were nearly penniless, and Seena confessed that she paid her bills six weeks after she received them. She had conditioned the merchants to wait, just in case she had run out of money. Both women looked physically faded and were given to alcohol and possibly drugs.

Lillian had a similar background to Seena's. Women who trade on their youth and beauty can rarely adjust to the loss of those assets. It is very hard for a female film star to age with grace. Most great beauties like Marlene Dietrich, Rita Hayworth, and Greta Garbo retreated into absolute seclusion. Bette Davis, also Gloria Swanson, actresses who did not rely only on their looks, worked to the day of their deaths, despite their faded exteriors and terminal illnesses. But the two screenwriters I was assigned to on *Aloma of the South Seas* were, as I guessed, charitably kept on the studio payroll, a charity for which the stockholders paid.

A pleasant transformation took place after they had overcome their suspicion of being teamed up with a young writer. The ladies started to spend more time on their makeup. Their way of dressing improved seductively. They seemed to shed a dozen years in age and even became flirtatious. I was wooed by two former stars and had to fight for my honor, not vice versa.

Aloma of the South Seas is still sold on cassettes, an unassuming, pleasant little musical, primitive by today's standards, but with lyrical music by my old friend Frederick Hollander. For the price of twenty dollars for the cassette I can project myself back to a time of innocence that has disappeared forever.

Manny Wolfe told me to take a few days off. He would find another assignment for me. I drove with two friends, Bill and Peggy Wright, to the desert, which Bill knew very well. Wright's father, William Sr., had once written a novel that had become a national bestseller: *The Shepherd in the Hills,* now a long-forgotten book. Bill tried to emulate his father's profession but never succeeded. It is difficult for sons of well-known fathers to compete with their fame.

We drove to a lonely place called Desert Center at Palm Desert, which now has become fashionable and expensive. Desert Center then consisted of half a dozen primitive huts for rent.

Suddenly a sheriff drove up. I still remember the oversized, uniformed man who, walking up to my car, put a flashlight in my face: "You Siodmak?" At once I felt guilty, not knowing what unknown law I had broken. "You go back to Paramount right now. They want you in the morning."

The director, having read the screenplay of *Aloma,* had demanded changes. Paramount had dug up the license number of my automobile. They didn't know where I went when I left town and had asked the sheriff departments all over California to find my car. That was the police routine to trace criminals. I drove in my open Buick back to Hollywood. I don't think I passed any automobile that night on the long empty roads.

I did not know that heaven could be so brightly lit by trillions of stars, each one a luminous moon. On a rock, as I drove by, crouched a very big desert cat with large tufted ears, a lynx, hissing at me. I accelerated, afraid it might jump into my open car. I had never seen a wild animal so close.

As I drove back to the studio that was keeping me on an invisible chain, I wished the night of that silent journey would never end. It didn't, in my memory.

In 1937 the United States was exclusively ruled by WASPs, white Anglo-Saxon Protestants. The rest of the people were considered second-class citizens. One could only enter the States on a time-restricted visitor's permit. Should a visitor apply for naturalization papers, he or she had to leave the country and wait outside its borders for a quota number issued by the Washington bureaucracy. After five years, showing an unblemished police record, one could be sworn in as an American citizen.

The number of accepted new citizens was tilted toward west Europeans, English, Scandinavians, Germans, and French. Hungarians, Rumanians, Turks, and Jews were less welcome and sometimes had to wait decades until a quota number was issued to them. Asiatic countries were not even on the list. Filipinos could not become American citizens, and their visitor permits were restricted to males only. Female Filipinos were not allowed to enter, since a child born on American soil would automatically become an American citizen, and the WASPs didn't want Asians. Now hordes of Latinos illegally cross the Mexican borders and flood California, then branch out all over the United States. Asians, like the tentacles of an octopus, engulf white America. Their children excel in schools, a menace to the WASPs.

At Paramount I had started with a weekly salary of three hundred fifty dollars, a fortune in 1937, where a drink at the Beachcomber Bar, the fashionable watering place of the affluent, was forty cents and a newspaper was five cents, a call girl charged five dollars a "trick," and a studio secretary was paid thirty-five dollars a week. There was Carpenter's Drive-in at Sunset Boulevard and Vine Street, where the "car hops," girls who had come to Hollywood to become stars, picked up a few dollars in secret prostitution. Hollywood was a heaven for bachelors and married men on the prowl.

My salary of three hundred fifty dollars a week was equivalent to seventy English pounds, a salary that I never had received in London. I was so rich that I could order a secondhand convertible Buick by telephone from Howard Buick, to be delivered to the studio. I didn't even choose it myself and left that to the salesman. I paid six hundred dollars' cash for it. That cash deal displeased the salesman, who complained that I would never make a good citizen since I didn't let a fellow American make money by buying "on time," a method unknown to me.

To show a healthy bank account in London was helpful for getting a quota number for Henrietta and Geoffrey. I sent her money since America is extremely partial to the affluent.

But my visitor permit had run out, and I had to leave the United States to reenter legally with a quota number. More humane than in England, where the visitors were kept in bondage by the Department of Labor, the Jewish executives at Paramount helped the uprooted members of their faith. Joseph Karp, Paramount's top lawyer and later head of the studio, called me to his office. He assured me that becoming an American citizen was routine. He advised me to wait in Ensenada, Mexico, for the legal papers. Then the studio would know where to contact me, in case of difficulties. "Just consider it a pleasant holiday and don't worry," he said.

I didn't worry. I was scared to death. The time when I floated between Folkstone and Calais on a ferryboat was still too vivid in my mind. The shock of being adrift again in this world of uncertainty where the color of a passport decided people's fate was still a nightmare. Do we ever overcome those shocks to our existence? Still today I dream that I am stranded in a foreign country without money. In one of my dreams I met Robert, who also was completely lost, and we didn't know where to turn. Henrietta, from whom I received much strength, didn't appear to rescue me in those nightmares. Immigrants are branded people. Fear forever dwells in our subconscious, dragons that appear suddenly and unannounced, seemingly embedded in our dreams.

Jim, an American Hispanic, who now cleans the windows of our ranch in the country, confessed that he wakes up in a sweat, haunted by the thought that he has to bring up his three children and to find money for their education, only to become aware that they have already left home and are standing on their own feet. In his sleep his injured mind turns back to that time of agony.

I had rented a room at the Canterbury apartments on Yucca Street in Hollywood. Hollywood then was still a safe part of Los Angeles. It was not necessary to lock the apartment's door. Nobody would intrude uninvited. The Canterbury also was the favorite abode for young people who aspired to break into the film business, though at thirty-five I felt like an old man, living among a handsome and energetic crowd of twenty-somethings.

For my forced exodus, I left my scant possessions in my rented room and took only the necessary clothes, to assure myself that I would return very soon legally. Then I drove to San Ysidro, to the Mexican border. I left the car in a garage, since it was almost impossible to defeat the Mexican bureaucracy when crossing the border in a car without knowing what bribe to put in whose hand. The highway to the border was well kept and concrete. The road into Tijuana, the town on the other side of the border, was a dirt road. Civilization changed from the twentieth century into the nineteenth within a few feet. I had a little grip with me and waited for the Mexican autobus that would take me to Ensenada, where I hoped to find a clean hotel.

In Tijuana I stepped into a bar, dirty and noisy and as colorful as in an American western. I sat on a bar stool close to the entrance beside a Mexican of immense proportions who wore a sweaty cowboy hat. Beside him sat a middle-aged, shapeless woman, her face disfigured by smallpox scars.

The giant turned to me and asked gruffly, "Do you want to fuck my wife!" I replied that as a married man, I would never be unfaithful. "She isn't good enough for you? You don't like her!" the colossus bent over and I smelled his sour breath. "You are insulting my wife!"

I only knew one reply. I got off my bar stool, threw money on the bar, and left. Who would find me if I got murdered in that strange lawless town filled with characters I had only encountered on the motion picture screen and didn't expect to exist in real life?

Years later I lived through a similar situation in Chicago. It was 1945. When I was returning from my war duties in the Office of Strategic Services (which became the CIA), I had to change trains since the Northern Washington line was not connected with the Santa Fe Railways. The train to California left from another station a mile away. I had to wait two hours for the transfer. Since it was night, I decided to enter a bathhouse adjoining the Santa Fe station, to shave and to change my shirt, which I had worn for days. When I wanted to pay for my short stay, three black men behind the counter at the exit charged me an exorbitant price. I pointed to the prominently displayed price list.

One of the three replied that the price had changed. I suddenly found myself in possible danger, much more immediate than being shot by the Germans, and saw myself disappear without a trace in Chicago. Nobody ever would find my body, since nobody would know where to look for me. I paid and even with a forced smile left a big tip.

The giant in Tijuana followed me when I left the bar. He shouted angrily in a language I did not understand. To fight a man twice my size, surrounded by brown hostile faces? I was aware that it was his routine to shake down a gringo.

Fortunately, the bus stopped in front of me. I quickly mingled with the passengers who boarded it and only felt safe when I sat inside next to a woman who had brought a billy goat with her. I even enjoyed the penetrating stink of that beast.

I didn't see much of the country, too occupied with negative thoughts, which increased by the strangeness of the little villages we passed. There were gangs of starving dogs, people riding on small donkeys, women washing clothes in a fountain, children in rags. The world clock was turned back a hundred years.

I concluded that since the Department of Immigration had made me fill out reams of questions, they must have considered issuing me a quota number. Some questions on those forms didn't make sense to me, or they were spiked with curious pitfalls: Do you intend to overthrow the American government? I assured them faithfully that that thought had never crossed my mind. Was I a communist? I wasn't asked if I were a fascist, which at that time seemed not to offend the American authorities. Even the young John Kennedy had, when he was traveling in Europe, thought that fascism was the right government for Germany and Italy. Thirty years later when he ran for president he was never called on the carpet for that opinion, which would destroy anybody running for high office today.

Some immigrants, contemptuous of seemingly inane official questions, stupidly forget that governments have no sense of humor. If the immigrant sarcastically replies that he intends to kill the American president, he will never be allowed to enter this country. Arrogant, believing in his sophisticated superiority, looking down at the "primitive" Americans, a highly intelligent person sometimes oversteps the line of rationality and behaves like an idiot. The government questions on the quota forms have their reasons. They open up a chance for prosecution, should his future political behavior not please the American authorities.

I got off in Ensenada, then still a small primitive village, and looked for a room. There was the Quinta Chilla courts, a row of primitive bungalows, run by a woman, Carmen Gallo de Maldonaldo. Well educated, she spoke English fluently. Her office also was her bedroom. A huge Parabellum forty-five-millimeter revolver hung at the headboard of her bed, within easy reach. She assured me that the drinking water at the court was purified. I told her the purpose of my visit, and she promised that she would personally collect my mail from the post office, which sometimes forgot to deliver letters or left the bags with mail outside the building during a tropical rain. She also had a telephone that worked, and I could call America at any time, though the call had to go through the Mexico City switchboard, which sometimes took its time to respond.

I found the life rhythm of that Latin country relaxing and peaceful, a peace I was searching for since I had left Europe. I also heard that tourists returned from Mexico with colon diseases, so I lived on bacon and eggs and tortillas. At breakfast in the courtyard, a strange monkey-like animal, a lemur, climbed from a tree onto my table. It was small with big bulging eyes. The lemur liked to sit on my shoulder, his long tail draped around my bald head. With its dexterous little fingers it picked up the milk pitcher, emptying it, then carefully put it back in its place. At night, troubled by thoughts, I went to the adjoining beach and swam out into the darkness. The water was as smooth as that of a lake, though sometimes changing into a wild turbulent ocean. The Spaniard explorer Balboa had named that ocean "Pacific," to appease its viciousness. When I swam through luminous, waveless water, a three-cornered sail emerged from the depth, grew toward the sky until it covered the bright moon. It was obviously a man-eating monster, emerging from the deep. I raced back toward the beach, beating any Olympic record.

After a few days in limbo, Carmen told me that my emigration papers were waiting for me at the immigration office in the United States. I will never forget that kind woman's name: Carmen Gallo de Maldonaldo. She had battled the Mexican telephone company and won and had contacted the American immigration office in San Ysidro. When I left Ensenada, she gave me a small ceramic candleholder, made by local artists for sale to tourists. The Aztec skill in producing pottery effigies had survived the centuries. "It will bring you luck as long as you own it," she said. That three-inch-high animal looks like a llama, its body painted with stripes. I still have it on my desk now for more than half a century, with its spell of luck unblemished.

I crossed the border into the United States on foot. The Mexican dirt road continued into the American paved surface. The small building of the immigration department was antiseptically clean. The emigration officer wore a spotless white uniform. He got off his seat behind a desk and stretched out his hand to greet me.

"Thank you for wanting to become an American citizen," he said, as though he had waited for me. "We want people like you in our country. We'll be proud to have you as an American citizen. But please promise us one thing: always vote! Take part in governing our United States. Welcome to our country."

America! What country in the world would have greeted me that way? Having been an unwanted in Germany, the country of my birth, would a Frenchman, an English official, or a xenophobic Swiss bureaucrat ever have presented me with such a greeting of welcome?

I fell in love with my new fatherland, a love that never left me. I raced back to Hollywood in my open Buick, unlawfully breaking the speed limit, laughing and singing. I was aware that I had not laughed once since I was banished from the land of my birth. I gained a self-respect that, because I was born a Jew, had been suppressed in the country of my birth since the day I was born. The sun was shining hot and bright as I flitted along the Pacific Coast Highway. Europe faded completely from my mind, a continent hostile and menacing. I was reborn, shedding the apprehensions that always had darkened my life. I never had been fully accepted anywhere. For the first time in my life, I felt an inner security. A few kind words from a government official had created a new frame of mind for me.

My room at the Canterbury apartments was as I had left it. Even the bed was still unmade. I always had kept Scotch whiskey in my refrigerator, my favorite brand, Old Rarity, to be sure to find a few friends when I came home from work. Nothing of my few possessions was missing except the Scotch. I didn't mind. It proved that friends were still around.

I reported back to Paramount Studios. Manny Wolfe informed me that the studio would continue paying my salary. He would find an assignment for me. In the meantime, he asked me to ready a few screenplays that needed work. I didn't mind and would have read *Hansel and Gretel* or the Torah. Anything. I found a home that protected me. A father was looking after me. I was being looked after since I was a fellow Jew, who, having been deprived of his former existence, now had returned to his clan, which in Germany had been a curse to me.

The pressure of nightmarish uncertainty, of a nebulous menace that had haunted me since I had left Germany, disappeared from my dreams. I soon would be able to send for my family to share with me this haven of security.

But I soon found out that it was a limited way of living. My new world was restricted to my office at the studio, the commissary at lunchtime, and a plain apartment containing a bed, a closet, a bathroom, and a fire escape outside the window. It was like living in a cocoon. The adrenaline pressure of life had evaporated. Every Friday I got a handsome check from my agent's office. I feathered my nest, the office at the writers' building, with handsome prints. I had a steady secretary, Nell, who having been with Paramount for twenty-five years, was no redheaded, luscious colleen who could get me into trouble. Nell, who had grown-up kids, knew the intricate mechanics of the studio and, motherly, protected and advised me how to keep my job. She told me, "What you don't say, you don't have to retract," a wisdom I have savored all my life.

It was a sheltered living, so perfect that I forgot that conditions might change and life might become again hazardous, insecure, and fleeting.

Manny Wolfe, Paramount's story editor, was a compulsive matchmaker. He liked to pair writers. He had "married" the Austrian immigrant Billy Wilder to Charles Brackett, a wise, highly successful Brahmin, who, fifteen years Billy's senior, gently led the cocky young genius through the intricate maze of studio politics. Brackett and Wilder became associated with the most successful films of the forties and fifties, so much so that their team was referred to as Brackettandwilder, fusing their names. They wrote films such as *Hold Back the Dawn* with Charles Boyer and *Ninotchka* with Greta Garbo for Ernst Lubitsch, the European top comedy director of the 1930s. Billy branched out in another direction with *Lost Weekend, Some Like It Hot* with Marilyn Monroe, and *Sunset Boulevard,* which now, more than forty years later, has become the basis for an Andrew Lloyd Webber Broadway musical.

After years of stormy collaboration, Wilder parted with Brackett and teamed up with I. A. L. Diamond (Itek Dominici), a quiet, shy, highly talented author who was the perfect literary addendum to the gifted young director. When "Izzi" died of cancer after thirty years of collaboration, Wilder, deprived of his "alter ego," never again directed a film.

There are many examples in the history of successful collaborators in which, when one departed, his partner became a basket case, just thriving on his former prominence. Billy, with whom I wrote motion pictures in 1929 in Germany, became the most successful "immigrant" motion picture writer and director Hollywood ever produced, the flagship of the German film group that had found refuge in Hollywood. Billy outshone even his beloved teacher and mentor Ernst Lubitsch, the originator of the "Lubitsch touch," a form of visual sexual innuendo, spicy, but never vulgar. That gift cannot be said of Billy, whose often deliberate coarseness in his direction was cutting and in questionable taste. After Billy eclipsed his master, Lubitsch died in 1947, lonely and disillusioned, in his home at 266 Bel Air Road. Charles Brackett, after his and Billy's collaboration ended, suffered a massive stroke and died in 1969. So strong was his love for his profession as a writer that, his larynx paralyzed, he could utter only one single word, *writer,* which supposedly was his very last.

I was less fortunate in Manny Wolfe's choice of a writing partner. He teamed me with Jerry Geraghty, an amiable but not very inventive writer, my age, who, though with numerous screen credits, lacked Brackett's stature and wisdom. Financially independent, a state that the studios dreaded since they lost the only advantage they had over their contracted writers, Brackett said, "I'm much too rich and too old to take any crap from any studio executives."

By temperament, and also due to my talent of inventing plots—a gift that excluded collaboration—I always worked alone. When I was given a "collaborator" by the studio, I would "block out" the screenplay, which meant that I wrote the first version, the nucleus of any film. The "collaborator," to share the credit, did some dialogue changes but never interfered with my story construction, the most volatile part of a motion picture screenplay. Though dozens of different screenplays can be constructed around a central idea, the project collapses when that idea is tampered with.

Since *Aloma of the South Seas* had successfully starred Dorothy Lamour, Manny assigned Jerry and me to *Her Jungle Love,* in which she also wore a sarong. After *Her Jungle Love,* she became an important star at Paramount as the female partner in the highly successful "road films," goofy comedies played by Bing Crosby (Harry Lillis Crosby) and Bob Hope (Leslie Towns Hope). They were the high point of Dorothy Lamour's career.

Frederick Hollander wrote the songs and music for *Her Jungle Love.* His song "Moonlight and Shadow and You in My Heart," became an "evergreen," a timeless song that brought him a fortune, since he was a member of ASCAP, the musicians' union, the most aggressive one of the entertainment industry. ASCAP payments go to the composer and not, like the film copyrights, to the studios. That's why composers became rich while almost all writers died poor.

Frederick married when he was in his early fifties. Holly was an eighteen-year-old, very pretty, but simplistic blonde. At his wedding party in his garden in the Hollywood Hills at 7357 Woodrow Wilson Drive, Frederick, a compulsive wit, went from male guest to male guest to whisper in a conspirator's voice, "Don't tell Holly that one can have intercourse more than once the same night. She doesn't know."

It was not easy for a studio writer to receive a screen credit, since due to the producer's insecurities, many writers were engaged to work unbeknownst to each other on the same subject. Since the producer often did not trust his own judgment, that method supposedly was his safeguard to compare different approaches to the same theme. It gave the production the chance to "compose" a "workable" shooting script.

I didn't run into that trouble. All of my screenplays, except two, have reached the screen, perhaps based on a craftsmanship that appeased the producer's insecurities, or, since they were B pictures, the limitation of the budget prevented them from hiring an additional writer. For me, writing motion pictures was just a way to make a living. I never took that craft as seriously as writing my novels. I was never content with my motion picture work, whose credits, by their very nature, I shared with many others: the director, actors, film cutters, wardrobe designers, special effects specialists, and a host of others. Watching the credits roll by at the end of a motion picture it is awesome and inconceivable to laypeople how many craftspeople are working on producing a photographed image. Since writing a screenplay is only a part of the end result, a motion picture, like a promiscuous woman, belongs to many. But a novel has only one author. Even should its conversion into a motion picture be a failure, the novel still stands pristine on its shelf.

In 1932 when I lived in Lerici, Italy, taking my beloved portable Remington typewriter along, one of my Italian friends was the town's butcher, Ovidio. He observed that I had "matches" in my brain. They fire up and disappear. Our mind is subjected to a constant rain of thought—meteors, unfinished ruminations, minute ideas, pictures, which flare up not to be remembered when they are of no importance for our present activities. The human brain never goes to sleep, even when we are "sleeping." Some thoughts, important to our daily life, cannot be shaken off; others we never recall, since they disappear without leaving a trace. Some thoughts carry a germ of an idea, insisting to be answered.

Everyone who is not religious is bothered by the question of the meaning of life.

Since time immemorial, philosophers have written and speculated about this many-faceted riddle. Religions have figured out that mystery in their own fashion. Especially the Christian religion, of which fifty-two variations alone exist in Los Angeles. But the answer to that supposedly intricate question is primitive. It is ever-present, not secret or mystic.

The planet called Earth, after having been separated from its source and having established its own existence, is devoid of faculties like emotion, pity, or love.

Now living in the country, I watched a big wasp, a tarantula hawk, fight a tarantula, paralyze it, and drag it into a hiding place to lay its eggs in its body. The larvae would eat the hairy spider alive. There is no sentiment in nature, which is unfeeling like a stone.

When Earth cooled off, a substance called DNA, deoxyribonucleic acid, created living species. If it had not mysteriously appeared, Earth would be like the moon or any other rock in space. Nothing living on this globe is necessary for its timeless existence. Should the elephants disappear, like the dinosaurs, the Earth would not miss them. Nor would it miss the existence of human beings.

The Bible states that Earth was created by God to be enjoyed by man. That was a dangerous assumption, since those human creatures misuse that conception to deplete this planet of its possibilities to sustain the balance of its life. Earth has survived the impact of giant meteors, volcanic eruptions, disasters that paralyzed life for centuries. It will, therefore, outlast the misuse by the featherless bipeds, who might destroy its thin onion skin on which life exists, but not the planet itself. The progression of nature adheres to its own timetable—that is, if "time" exists at all, since time might only be a conception of the human mind. We breathe in and out twelve times every minute. According to the British astronomer Stephen Hawking's theory, the galaxies are "exhaled" into space, to be "inhaled," contracting in a "black hole" the size of a pin, then exhaled again, a process that takes billions of years. Does it take twelve space exhalations and inhalations to equal one human breathing minute? In that case, the meaning of "time" cannot be conceived even in light-years.

Our daily observations are based on a three-dimensional world, and the principles of physics, which we constructed, explain that concept to us. Our brain is not built to comprehend the laws of space or creation—that is, if we don't describe it as the work of a superprotoplasm, a god that has innumerable faces. The different denotations of creation remain theory, which, like "truth," changes from time to time and differs in every religion.

Nature has only one stable objective: propagation and expansion of its species. Every living species is trying to multiply, fighting every obstacle in its way. That force is the only constant. All others are fleeting, replaceable, illusionary. They change with time, conditions, habits, and fashions, to be replaced by other fads and ideas. Nothing the human mind conceives is permanent. Philosophies come and go. So do religions.

Flowers develop colors to attract insects needed for their reproduction. Male animals, displaying features attractive to the female, as the peacock exhibits his wheel of feathers to lure females into intercourse. Only human females try to entrap males sexually by dressing provocatively. The cause might be that the female gender, due to a more sensible bodily construction, outlives the male. How many new fashions are created for the male gender? Those for males hardly change. Females dress provocatively to invite sex. Even little girls wear "training bras" as an education for a future sexual conquest. To curb the sex drive, orthodox Jews cut off the hair of women after they get married. They have to wear a wig and must dress in black, to take them out of sex circulation. So do the Moslems, whose women are forbidden to show flesh or hair in public. Sex through the ages has been the objective of the male species. Anyhow, the male tried. His success is questionable, especially today.

Nature has limited feminine fertility by the creation of the "menopause." If an older woman were able to conceive, her life span would not be sufficient to bring up the child. But a male may be able to cause conception to the end of his life. Men also are mainly attracted to young women, since they promise fertility. Nature is fostering youth for its purpose. That's why a boy of eighteen is at the height of his fertility, before his brain has reached maturity, and a teenaged girl is able to conceive after the first menstruation, even if her mind is still underdeveloped.

The advertising agencies sell the lure of propagation in showing women in their prime of sexual attraction. The film industry uses female allure with great skill. It also appeals to persons of any age with that enhancement of sex—violence. A gun by its tumescent shape is the symbol of active sexuality since its explosive discharge suggests subliminally the equivalent of a violent ejaculation.

When I was looking for a therapist to talk about my increasing state of depression, a sexually attractive young woman therapist, trained for that profession and perhaps well qualified for it, made me decide to choose an older one, a motherly type, in whom I could confide without being aroused by the display of sensuality that the young woman carried, like a matador his red cape. She might have been therapeutically right in her choice of alluring appearance when she had younger male patients. The success of the treatment might be linked to the method of making the patient fall in love with his therapist.

Madison Avenue publicity agents and the film industry are the masters in the game of manipulating sex as a lure to sell their merchandise. When I started at Paramount Studios in Hollywood, I was thirty-five years old, and the starlets, based on my hormone level at that time, appear in my memory much more attractive than the actresses of today.

At Paramount Studios was the starlet Constance Ockleman, whose name a producer changed to Veronica Lake. She created a national fad among young girls by hiding half of her face, that of an angelic witch, behind a cascade of wheat-blonde hair. To escape the producers' sexual harassment, at the height of her career she married overnight a young director. His macho image of himself made the revengeful producer cancel her contract.

At Twentieth Century–Fox Studios, I witnessed the visual creation of a future star. The photogenic look of a young Swedish girl, who couldn't have been older than sixteen, was being fashioned by three makeup men in overalls, expertly and businesslike. They made her take off her shoes to measure her height. She was scantily dressed in a short skirt and a clinging blouse. One man fussed with her blonde hair, another decided that her upper lip was too thin and had to be enhanced. One asked her about her breasts: "Are those your own foundations?" They were. They put her on a scale and decided on her most photogenic weight. I didn't watch the whole procedure, but no expert who knew how to buy a racehorse could be more knowledgeable. She became known as Ann-Margret (Ann-Margret Olsen), a top star of the Fox Studios at that time.

It was the habit of producers to change the names of their actors, a voodoo device to dominate those young people, by shaping their looks, personalities, and names to their own conception. Often the new names that they invented for their protegées where whimsical. Josephine Cottle made her career as Gale Storm, and Roselle Jacobs became Piper Laurie. Marcia Hunt refused to change her name but had to reduce her first name to be Marsha Hunt. I secretly watched her with an unfulfilled desire at the Paramount commissary. She looked like a girl a friend would bring to a prom but who you yourself would never be able to date. I still visualize Marsha as she rose from a table, perhaps looking for somebody she expected. The shape of her young body, her poise, and the ephemeral expression of purity she conveyed stays, static as a photograph, in my mind. Norma Jean Baker became Marilyn Monroe, though she would have become a star under her maiden name. Dorothy Lamour had been Dorothy Kaumeyer, not a name that conveys romance. Also, when you carry a name like Issur Danielowich Demnsky, you'd better change it to Kirk Douglas.

Studio heads tolerated fascism and fostered it. The MGM producer James McGuinness, when he was drunk, denounced during World War II his German-born, very handsome wife, Lucie, who was half-Jewish, to the FBI as a German spy. He did it so often that the Federal Bureau of Investigation soon did not pay any attention to his calls. James McGuinness died of a heart attack. Lucie survived him by half a century. She was a close friend of my brother Robert's wife Babs. Lucie told her that her husband left her, in addition to his large life insurance policy, seven original Coca-Cola shares. I would like to know their current value.

The Canterbury apartments where I had rented a room was a beehive of budding starlets. There was a small commissary in the basement where I loved to have my dinner among dozens of young aspiring actors and actresses.

Ann Sheridan (Clara Lou Sheridan), a cheerful blonde beauty who developed a tough style on the screen, became known as the "oomph" girl and remained a star for thirty years. Still unknown, playing small parts, she had rented a room on the same floor as mine. We had a casual acquaintance, and she liked to join me at the commissary after work. She confessed that she liked writers, whom she found more amusing than the executives and directors, whose presence bored her and whose sexual harassment she had to fight off.

One night I asked her out on an excursion, since I had been invited by Jimmy, the black studio masseur who ran the recreation room at Paramount where many actors and very few executives used to work out. Jimmy wanted to show me a part of Los Angeles that I might never have the chance to see. Ann agreed to come along, and late in the evening we took off in my Buick with Jimmy in the rumble seat. We drove into the part of the city that was all black, where Jimmy lived with his parents and where he had to return by streetcar every night.

In 1937, African Americans would never find a room in a white neighborhood, since the American racial bias was at its height. I met Jimmy's family, the Prentices, in their very bourgeois apartment on a street off Broadway. Mr. Prentice was a person of great dignity, dressed in a dark business suit and wearing a tie, despite the hot California night. He told me that he was a pilot. I didn't find out what plane he was flying, since the airlines engaged black people only as porters. Jimmy's mother, expecting us, had prepared food southern-style, a kind I had never tasted. The family seemed relaxed, as did Jimmy's two teenaged giggling sisters, whose hair was braided in a fashion I had only seen in pictures of tribal women in Africa. Mr. Prentice discussed the century-old suppression and exploitation of the black race by the white man, a theme reminding me of the troubles of my own race. I talked to Mr. Prentice as if he were a fellow Jew. He was surprised that I, a white man, also had suffered discrimination. The story of my reason for emigration seemed to make his own fate look easier to him, since mine was connected with death, and he was physically safe in his country.

The Prentices felt proud that their son had such prominent white friends. It was my first encounter with a family of blacks. Still today, after more than fifty years have passed, the races are even more parted by the color of their skin. Racism seems to be the eternal fate of the world population, xenophobically fostered by the different races themselves. I met a black university professor at Stanford who sent his children to a black university to prevent them from losing their "identity."

At the nocturnal visit to a part of the city where I had never been, I found myself in a fascinating world. I couldn't read Ann Sheridan's mind. She listened silently, an American girl, perhaps brought up with white American prejudices and therefore uncomfortable listening to our discussion. Jimmy felt her discomfort and urged us to leave. He wanted to meet a special friend at the Palladium.

The Palladium was a dance hall of a dimension that baffled my European mind. A jazz orchestra played, though the hall was nearly empty. Jimmy brought a young black girl to our table. She wore a huge black hat, a copy of the one Ann was wearing in white and that was the fashion of that time. The two young women on my left side, the shining white and the dark black face, framed by the large flat hats, two faces of impeccable shape, seemed to have come from different continents. I still wish that I had a camera with me to keep that picture not only indelibly in my mind but to hang in my study, as an example of the unbridgeable dichotomy of the American world.

I ordered drinks, which were confined to beer, and Jimmy brought the orchestra leader to the table. Since I didn't catch his name right away, he repeated it, with an expression of disbelief. "I am Count Basie." I didn't know that Count Basie was one of the most prominent jazz musicians of that time.

Jimmy, who secretly confessed to me that he had slept with white girls, a relation that had been a dangerous liaison for any black in 1937, promised to show us more of a part of Los Angeles that was foreign territory for whites. We drove back to Broadway and stopped on a side street at a house that seemed to be dark, since all curtains were drawn tightly. He knew a secret knocking code. The door opened, and we entered a speakeasy, which served drinks. It was against the California law to serve drinks after 12 P.M., a law that reminded me of my time in London, where alcoholic beverages were sold between 10 A.M. and 2 P.M. and from 5 P.M. to 9 P.M. The curious fact in London was that every part of London had its own closing hours, and there was a bar on Fleet Street whose clientele moved from the north side of the bar to the south side at 10, since the two different precincts met at the middle of the bar. Half of the pub served booze one hour longer than the other half.

Ann uneasily kept close to my side when we passed a room lit by a red bulb, with a large brass bed for hire. I saw only black guests quietly sitting at small tables. They didn't pay any attention to us, even averted their eyes. I had ordered drinks. The air was stuffy and suffocating. I opened a small window to let in the night air. It was a grave mistake. Suddenly two men popped through the window. They were plainclothes policemen, who might have waited to break into the house, since they had no warrant. Nobody moved as they flashed their identifications. There was no excitement. One of the plainclothesmen got hold of the landlord, a heavyset black who seemed to be used to the police intrusion. It was a shakedown. He didn't even argue with that official. The second one advised us, the only white guests, to leave. I told him that I would, after I had received the change of the bill. "I already got it," the city official said, knocking at his breast pocket, "I must keep it by law. It's evidence."

That cancer of dishonesty and shakeups of the police is still a problem in the City of the Angels, where angels are difficult to find.

We left Jimmy behind and drove back to the deserted Sunset Boulevard. It was now about three in the morning. A hamburger stand was still open. Ann wanted a cup of coffee. It was still a time when one could walk the streets of Los Angeles at night without being in peril, held up, robbed, or mugged. Los Angeles had not yet experienced any explosive race riots. As we got our coffee, we watched a tall young woman sitting alone on one of the high bar chairs. She was slim, with the figure of a professional model, wearing an expensive evening dress as if she had just come from a fashionable party. Her movements were slow and her hand unsteady. The man behind the stand filled her coffee cup from a bottle he hid under the table. I asked him what a well-groomed woman was doing at three in the morning at his stand. He told me that she came every night, always alone, wearing the same dress, after her lover had been killed in a car accident on Sunset Boulevard. She never talked, though he had tried to communicate with her.

Sobered up, we drove home. The Canterbury apartments were only minutes away. I took Ann to her door. She asked me in, and the night ended in a fast impersonal clandestine affair, since, as I found, it was "de rigueur" that an independent, bachelor woman thank her escort that way for an interesting evening, a gesture not more significant than a handshake.

Manny Wolfe called me to his office and started the conversation with a compliment, which made me listen warily. "I believe that you are the best writer in Hollywood for creating plots. I have here a special assignment. Henry Hathaway is going to direct *Spawn of the North*. I have half a dozen screenplays here, but Henry doesn't like any of them. Read the novel by Barrett Willoughby. You write the screenplay, but you won't get any credit. You won't get credit since Talbot Jennings, Grover Jones, and Dale Evans worked on it. They couldn't lick it." The names Manny mentioned were the highest-paid Paramount writers.

I heard for the first time that a screenplay had not been written but "licked." "When you're through with it, and if Henry accepts your version, I'll team you up with John McAvoy. He isn't a screenwriter, but he was published in *Readers Digest*." I told Manny that I thought it unfair that the writers who wrote a workable script should not get credit. "The studio decides about credits, not the writers,"

Manny said with implied threat to fire me. "Besides, I have no other assignment for you."

I believe that conversation was the nucleus which made me join a number of writers who wanted to revive the dormant Screen Writers Guild. In front of my eyes appeared the weekly check, and I thought of my anemic bank account, the coming arrival of my family from England, and the drinks at the Beachcomber. Manny dismissed me: "Take all the scripts with you, then you will know what not to do."

That night my old collaborator, Jerry Geraghty, invited me for dinner, telling me that he had a blind date for me. I didn't know that expression and thought he had fixed me up with a blind girl. Charitable-minded, I accepted. He brought a pretty girl along, Jean, an MGM studio dancer. She didn't inquire if I were married, and I didn't mention that small handicap, not knowing the difference that parted the married from the unmarried. I also didn't know that Jean was the captain of a group of about fifty dancers and aspiring actresses, a tightly knit club whose purpose was to protect each other from the cruelties of the Hollywood jungle. When a "club member" was offered a job, she was briefed by her pals about the vagaries and pitfalls of such an assignment; warned about prospective wolves, voracious assistant directors, and oversexed actors; and told how to keep them at bay. Should she have a small speaking part, she was even coached.

Jean soon was known as my "steady." I was in a worse situation than being married to a jealous wife. Wherever I went there was a club member around who reported back to Jean. If I talked to another girl, she asked me whether I had broken up with Jean. When I took Jean out, soon a flock of club girls, often with their husbands, joined us. Nobody ever took advantage of my financially elevated condition and ordered an expensive drink. I bought a few bottles of jug wine, and the crowd retired to my simple apartment at the Canterbury, where we polished off the booze and gossiped. After that they left me alone with Jean.

I liked that bachelor life, which I had experienced for only a very short time, since Henrietta and I had been together for fifteen years. It was a pleasant and carefree life, but drifting and obviously without a future. A couple of Jean's friends got married, and since both had a job in a picture, *Waikiki Wedding*, Frank Tuttle, the Paramount director of routine films, rented for them the bridal suite of a hotel in Hawaii. This was an act of generosity that I, a

European, having been raised to count pennies, greatly admired. Tragedy followed. The young husband, a champion swimmer, dove while drunk into the hotel's swimming pool. There was no water in the concrete basin.

When Jean wanted to introduce me to her mother, I knew I had to cut the ties and told her about my family in London, who soon would join me. She cried and I felt, rightly, like a heel. If a married man has an affair with an unmarried girl, she considers herself abused, since all she has to sell is her youth and sexuality. She obviously is looking for the creation of the American nuclear family: father, mother, two kids, and a house with a white picket fence. If a married man has an extracurricular affair, he is greatly envied by his married male friends.

I remember a certain small restaurant in Beverly Hills on South Beverly Drive, which was frequented by married men and their present paramour. Whoever entered never recognized anybody, even his own brother. That was the unwritten law, never to be broken and never to be mentioned even among deadly enemies.

One week after my confession, Jean got married to a man twice her age, the story editor of Fox Studios. She had never told me that she had known him for years and that he had proposed to her a dozen times. On the eve of her marriage, she appeared in my room at the apartment house. I pleaded with her to give her new husband a chance. It was a scene that Noel Coward could have used in one of his domestic bedroom comedies, a situation, unreal and comical, but heartbreaking for her and painful for me, since I liked her spunk, spirit, and the youthful world she had brought for a short time into my life. That night was the watershed that made me feel middle-aged and strangely confined for having lost forever that uninhibited world of youth. In his heart, every man would like to have the advantage of the security of marriage and keep the abandonment of bachelorhood.

Jean's marriage lasted five years. Though I had not seen her again, she sent me a message through one of her girlfriends, inviting me to start the tribal dance again. I didn't accept her generous invitation. She married again, this time the son of the chairman of a huge aircraft factory. There is a steady reminder of her in my life when I travel in one of the jumbo jets that carries her husband's name.

Since there is a grass widow, is there also a grass widower? And why grass? The pictorial intricacies of languages and their origin have always interested me and are different in every language.

I was tired of my bachelorhood and wanted my family back as soon as possible. An unmarried woman is much more content with her life than a bachelor could ever be. A woman has an inner balance and can spend an evening at home liking her own company. If a bachelor can't get a date for the evening, he usually does not know what to do with himself. Unmarried men are unfulfilled; even their life span is shorter than married men's, especially in the United States. When we lived in England, a man could "retire to bed" when he was fifty, which meant that he gave up his participation in world affairs and tended to his rose garden. Women seem to be an entity, though there also might be a buried fear of loneliness in them.

There are exceptions. An acquaintance of ours, Ann Lazlo, who had been divorced from her husband, a well-known architect, was having breakfast in her apartment, at peace with herself, as she told me, when she heard a scream of agony. As she listened, the scream repeated itself. To her shock, she realized it was she who was screaming without being aware of it.

Do we know about the intricate workings of our subconscious? Since we don't, how can we ever pass judgment on others?

Manny introduced me to his choice for my collaborator, John McAvoy. He had no film credits, no books published, was not a playwright, and I could never find out why Manny thought he would be a good collaborator for me. Possibly since his English was better than mine? Or did Manny expect I should teach him the craft of screenwriting? I didn't like him, and he, an older man, obviously aware of his shortcomings, resented me. We were assigned to the producer, Arthur Hornblow, to find a story for the title *Artists and Models*, which in Hornblow's mind had the connotation of free sex. Whenever I came up with an idea, McAvoy disappeared, supposedly to the toilet to relieve his weak bladder. I soon found out that he went straight to Hornblow's office to tell him "his" brainstorm. I confronted McAvoy, insisting that I be present at those story conferences. When we met Hornblow, the producer of the smash hits *Cat and Canary* and *Ruggles of Red Gap*, I met a very indecisive man. After he turned down every one of our ideas, I finally asked him what he wanted. He replied, "We will know it when we have it," like Superior Judge Potter's definition of pornography: "I don't know what it is, but I know it when I see it." We never found out what Hornblow wanted, and the picture was never made.

My collaboration with McAvoy broke up, and Manny assigned a young female screenwriter, Constance Hill, to me, whose literary assets, or whose assets literary, were that she had a sexy figure, everything of the right size in the right places. We were supposed to work for Albert Lewin, a Paramount executive who wanted to try his hand in production.

Lewin behaved like a schoolteacher, who, to impress his students, flaunts his erudition. Our conferences always took place late in the afternoon, just half an hour before the hired people, mail boys, writers, and secretaries went home and the cleaning crews took over. I soon had the suspicion that Conny, who was somehow primitive and believed that the French made the Champagne and the Americans put the bubbles in it, had known Lewin for some time. He also knew that I was the foil to keep her available to him and on the payroll. After every futile conference in which Lewin expounded his Omar Khayyam fixation, he dismissed me but kept Conny for further instructions in the refinements of the art of moviemaking.

It suddenly dawned on me that my days at Paramount were numbered. I was a writer with nothing to write, a foil for a producer's sexual fling. The seamy side of Hollywood revealed itself. I felt very uncomfortable. There was no chance of talking to Manny Wolfe about my frustration. He would only tell me that supervising sex wasn't part of his job.

Henrietta and Geoffrey were on their way to America. They came by boat from Southampton to Long Beach via the Panama Canal. The time of air travel had not yet arrived.

I rented a house on Marmont Lane, close to the infamous "Garden of Allah," that den of iniquity against which religious zealots raged and where the Barrymore acting clan and many film celebrities had rented bungalows for their supposed orgies. I was never invited to any of them, nor had I ever seen any sexual improprieties at the studio. I only knew people devoted to that "Fourth Art," workaholics, whose atrophied minds had no room but for their singular infatuation with the motion picture art.

I hired a man to run my rented house at Marmont Lane. Frank Kulick, a beefy former wrestler, had worked as a studio janitor. Out of a job, he was recommended to me by Jimmy, the black masseur at Paramount's gymnasium, where a daily workout had put me into excellent physical shape. Frank liked to recline shoeless in the living room, his feet on the table, guzzling beer. He was of the opinion that wealth should be distributed equally among the indigents. I told Frank, since the rooms needed cleaning and since Mrs. Siodmak was soon to arrive from Europe, the house should be put into shape. Frank agreed. He told me that he knew just the right person who excelled in that kind of work. He visualized that the pampered wife of a high-priced writer was helpless without a butler, who also cleaned and could cook. Frank recommended a Filipino who had served for nine years in the U.S. Navy and who could mix an excellent martini. His English was somewhat faulty, so should I be afraid that he might not understand English? I was mistaken. His name was Cypriano Maglaya. He also was known as Max.

I engaged Max. He cleaned the house to perfection. He cooked delicious Asian and American food. He even polished my shoes. Trained by navy admirals in the finer art of mixing drinks, he really knew how to concoct an excellent martini by adding a pinch of salt, which softens the ice in the mixer. He also answered the telephone with "Cook speakin'." Max was the most efficient servant Henrietta could wish for, inasmuch as she always visualized a silent male helper in her future home, a dream she believed would never come true. Max was that.

He also had a girlfriend, Monica Lamarr, whom I never met, only heard, when she visited him twice a month on payday. Since his room was below our upstairs bedroom, I asked Max politely that, if he read the Bible at night, to do it more quietly. The woman's name was on all of Max's paychecks when they returned from the bank. She was one of those professional blondes who were paramours for a score of Filipinos. Those efficient small men were not permitted to import females of their own race. Congress allowed only male Asians to enter the country, a cruel decision that sexually frustrated those virile males. Monica Lamarr collected the wages from her surrogate husbands, a most substantial income, since she had a dozen Filipinos as steady customers. She sold her merchandise to them, and in the morning she had most of the Filipinos' wages but still kept her merchandise, an ideal way of conducting business. Those women sometimes accompanied the Filipinos when they returned home. Somewhere, in the middle of the jungle, one might find a hut with a tennis court, where faded blondes played tennis. That should have been a picture theme for Albert Lewin, who was looking for a story with a quaint background.

Max was the "dream" servant. I tried to inform Max how to adjust to a household headed by a female, since in the navy, he had looked only after males. After Henrietta's arrival a few weeks later, I found out that he was psychologically tuned to a woman's wishes, much more than to a male's. Whenever Henrietta called him, he already brought what she would have asked for. He also secretly ironed her bras and slips and was often standing noiselessly behind her, watching her. That silent presence irritated Henrietta, and she sensed that he was in trouble. When he confessed his love to her in his stammering broken English, of which she understood only the gist, she told him, "Max, why don't you talk to my husband? He is very good at solving personal problems."

Henrietta didn't feel secure with Max around when I wasn't home. We had to let him go. I asked my friend, the composer Frederick Hollander, to take Max over to his household. I later found out that Max had made a pass at Frederick's wife, and Fred (Friedl) passed him on to a bachelor friend.

When World War II broke out, Max again became Cypriano Maglaya. He left for his homeland to join the Filipino army, which was fighting the Japanese. If he survived, he might be playing tennis in the Filipino jungle with blondes, imported from Hollywood.

Albert Lewin had me fired, obviously jealous that I, a much younger man, shared an office with his film student. He might have been afraid that I might make a pass at her, which would decrease her intrinsic value to him. Manny Wolfe had no assignment for me. To again receive a Paramount check, I had to wait two years, until the outbreak of World War II, selling a story called *Pacific Blackout*. But I never again worked for that studio as a writer.

For the first time and many times since, I stood outside a studio, an unemployed writer, feeling like a baby deprived of its bottle. Where was the next check coming from? My knowledge of English was not good enough to write a novel, and I had promised myself never again to write in German. I was optimistic, however. I had an agent, Stanley Bergerman, who had some clout since he was married to Rose Laemmle, the Universal Studios tycoon's daughter. Despite her relation to one of the powerful Hollywood moguls, Rose in later years committed suicide. There is a curtain of tragedy hiding even the most affluent and prominent families.

A writer's job in Hollywood often was based on his track record. I had a novel, *F.P. 1 Does Not Answer,* published by Little, Brown, and two American motion picture credits: *Aloma of the South Seas* and *Her Jungle Love*. Though *F.P. 1,* UFA's top picture, trilingual, with Charles Boyer, a Hollywood top star, and Peter Lorre, was playing all over Europe, the American studios deliberately released no other motion pictures except their own in their monopolistic theater circuit. Foreign-made films had only access to "art houses," catering to a very small and sophisticated minority, though the European films were often of much higher content and spirit than the run-of-the-mill American output.

My future was insecure, but not dark. Besides, I had sent Henrietta cash to accelerate her entry to America. But Henrietta had stopped over in Paris and, guided by my mod sister-in-law, Babs (Robert's wife), had blown that account on elegant French outfits. She had heard much about the beauty of Hollywood girls and was determined to compete with them. When she arrived, she looked glamorous and highly competitive with any of the studio beauties. Though she had only forty dollars in her purse, she brought lots of luggage.

When she and Geoffrey arrived, I waited at the pier at Long Beach where the Norwegian boat *Olafson* had anchored. The passengers were kept on board until the immigration personnel had checked their passports. Their friends and relatives were kept hundreds of feet away from the boat. Only a tiny boy of four was permitted to walk down the long gangway. He carried a tiny suitcase and wore a British cap. He walked straight up to me, and when I asked him who I was, he answered with a clipped British accent, "You are my daddy!"

When Henrietta descended in her Poiret outfit, even the *Los Angeles Times* mentioned in its society column the arrival of "handsome" Mrs. Siodmak, a word she resented since in British English "handsome" only pertains to the description of men.

There was a present for her at the pier, the Buick two-seater with her initials on the doors.

We drove to Marmont Lane, where the house was prepared for her arrival. She always liked a fireplace topped by a wooden beam, which by chance the living room displayed. I had found a very old bottle of Cognac "Le Tour d'Eiffel," which I had placed on the beam next to a big candle without a candleholder, the way she had liked it in London. There was a radio and phonograph with a turntable that changed records, the latest invention. Unfortunately, the mechanism of the changer was perilous to records, since a metal claw grabbed the record and threw it off into a basket, often breaking it. There was, of course, Max, the silent butler, who had prepared a Dutch meal with dozens of Far Eastern dishes.

The news of Henrietta's arrival had spread among my friends. To introduce her, I had invited some guests for an afternoon cocktail, but not as many as showed up, acquaintances who were sad that that convenient halfway house, where the bar was always open, would now be closed to the casual drop-in visitor. Many females came, curious to find out what my wife looked like. There was Ann Sheridan, now a star; Louise Rainer, the twice-Oscar recipient; and Lucie von Wassermann, who later became James McGuinness's, the fascistic MGM producer's, wife. Lucie was constantly surrounded by male admirers, since she exuded a femininity and breeding that the Americans visualized only European nobility possessing. There was Werner Richard Heymann, the well-known European composer of film music and later some of Hollywood's motion pictures, including *Ninotchka,* which starred Greta Garbo. He, an inveterate alcoholic, got hold of the rare bottle of Le Tour d'Eiffel that stood unprotected on the mantelpiece, and quietly emptied it. Then he asked Henrietta "if she had more of that stuff." Henrietta was furious and exiled him forever from our home.

Tyrone Power dropped by with a very handsome young actress, Linda Christian, whom he later married. My friend Dudley Nichols appeared. He, a bachelor, had for weeks been my daily guest in the early morning. On the breakfast table he was composing a screenplay, penciled on foolscap. It became *Stagecoach* with John Wayne, the western that reached such classic fame that it appeared fifty years later on an American postal stamp.

Some girls of Jean's club dropped by, tactfully only married ones, possibly reporting back to her.

I had left London with a very limited amount of cash, and now a few months later, I was able to entertain my wife and son in a large house, introducing them to famous Hollywood people. It was a festivity like New Year's Eve. Like the time following New Year's Eve, life again settled into its insecure routine.

It was a hollow feeling needing a pass to get inside the studio where I used to drive in unchecked. I was a film writer between two jobs, or was employment the time between two layoffs? Could life ever continue without the sheltering, benevolent hands of the studio, by no longer being part of that well-oiled machine that produced moonshine? Where would the next check come from? That problem still haunts Hollywood writers and has not changed since the creation of the dream factories.

I, like my cowriter friends, depended on getting assignments. The studio bought our still-unborn brainchildren, paying in advance, but not knowing whether they would get a maimed one. We were "writers" the easy way, collecting the "seed money" that the studio would lose if we didn't deliver what the production needed. We didn't know the value of our own merchandise and did not fight to retain a part of our brainchildren. The capitalistic studios owned the copyright to the stories and ideas in "perpetuity" and were well aware of the perennial value of produced motion pictures. We did not. If studio writers developed a screenplay on contract, they were like surrogate mothers who give birth to a child who had been adopted before its birth.

Only authors, who in the loneliness of their workroom have enough talent to concoct stories, screenplays, books, plays, or any literary product on their own, have a right to the output of their brain. Studio writers, hired hands, complain that they were cheated by the producers of the fruit of their work. Producers own yachts in the Mediterranean; writers never do, except if they take the chance of developing their work on speculation.

The American copyright, pushed through Congress when the writers had no representation, stipulated that any author had to renew the copyright to his or her work every twenty-eight years; otherwise it would become "public domain." Writing was the only creative profession in the world in which the originator of that craft would lose the right to his or her property during his lifetime. What if a marriage contract would also run out after twenty-eight years and then had to be renewed?

In the American capitalistic system, propped up by its battery of lawyers, writers were legally deprived of all rights to their work. There was even in small print a provision that the writers were not permitted to go on strike, due to their "unique and irreplaceable" profession. That straitjacket was later removed by a court decision. If a writer fought to retain some rights to his work, he ran into a legal stone wall. The studios, knowing the value they possessed, would never give any of their "rights" away. The writer, taking money in advance, lived well. He only thought of supporting himself and his family, as though the ephemeral chance to earn money would go on forever. It never did. His contract with the studio could also be broken for "moral reasons," an expression whose definition was at the studio's discretion. Were the studios also controlling his sex life?

Times have changed, thanks to the guilds, which the writers and directors created through negotiations and strikes, despite the vicious resistance of motion picture producers in a constant running battle. That warfare continues, unabated, and might go on since the time when the Pinkerton men, paid by the sweat factories, shot down workers who wanted to be paid more than a dollar a day. That was in my father's time in the late 1800s.

I remembered my friend Charles Bennett's advice in London: "When in trouble, feed them ideas. Don't depend on an assignment. That kind of work is degrading. Even a dog can be trained to write a screenplay. But how many writers have original ideas? You are an idea man. And that's a rare gift. That's why you are valuable to them despite your lousy English."

I talked to my friend, Collier Young, a producer of my age who also had come to Henrietta's reception. Collier was a company man, knowing the secret of how to stay under contract with a studio. When he finally branched out for himself, he became a millionaire by devising and producing the television detective series *Ironside* with the actor Raymond Burr that ran for years. Handsome and spiffy, Collier, who had the knack of becoming the friend of studio heads and moneyed people, the "movers and shakers" of that business, was a steady guest at their home, since he, a bachelor, was badly needed company for single lady guests.

I told Collier a story I had written: *The Man in the Hound's Tooth Coat.* He saw it as a vehicle for the leading star of that time, Carole Lombard. She was Clark Gable's girlfriend and had much more spunk and exuberance than the handsome but rather dull "King of Hollywood" ever possessed. Collier phoned Lombard; he had her private, well-guarded number. He knew the secret word that opened the doors to the castle of the movie queens and kings.

"Carole will see you at her home on Sunday morning at ten. I told her that you have the exact story she is looking for. Pitch it to her. Don't give her anything in writing. In this town people can't read."

I rehearsed my story in my mind a dozen times. The background was the Studio Club on Larabee Avenue, which I knew from my short bachelor days. That residence was closed to any male visitor. Only unattached girls were allowed. A new lodger, Margene, moves into the club. Margene does not talk, stays always in her room, and never mixes with the studio girls. She never has a date and lives like a hermit, which increases the curiosity of the girls, until they find out that she stutters. She does not talk, afraid of ridicule. To make her get rid of her inhibitions, the girls invent a young and handsome man, which they fashion after a mannequin dummy in the window of a department store. The dummy is dressed in a hound's-tooth coat. The girls plot that "he" was supposedly secretly following Margene, telephoned her, but unfortunately when she was not at the club. He was too shy to visit her there. Margene is mystified and curious to meet him. She loses her stutter, as the studio girls rave about the looks of the man in the hound's-tooth coat, spinning out an ever-increasing net of lies.

The department store sells the coat to a young man who is a shady character. Margene, having fallen in love with the mysterious caller, one day discovers him as he walks past the club. To cure him of his shyness, she boldly approaches him. The crooked character, amused, starts taking advantage of Margene. The studio girls, learning the background of the "mannequin," try to stop the acquaintance, which would bring unhappiness and possible disaster to their new-found friend.

I took a couple of stiff drinks on Sunday morning and drove to Carole Lombard's Beverly Hills home. Collier didn't come along. He didn't think I needed a chaperon.

Carole, whom I had only seen on the screen, in *My Man Godfrey* with William Powell, MGM's debonair leading man, was a striking blonde with a sense of humor, which her lively face constantly mirrored. Though not a stunning beauty, she had that rare faculty that stars like Marilyn Monroe and Zsa Zsa Gabor displayed: whenever they talk to a man, they make him feel that he is the only male in existence. Most women, however beautiful, lack that knack of intense concentration, the ultimate attraction for any male.

I told Carole, haltingly like the stuttering girl, that I didn't expect her to look so lovely. I must have sounded convincing, since it created a chemistry that sometimes happens instantly between opposite sexes. I described the character of Margene to her, as I outlined the story. She loved it. Immediately she went to the telephone and called David Selznick, the famous Hollywood producer of *Gone with the Wind* to whom she was under contract.

Selznick was in the hospital. He couldn't be very ill since he answered the telephone. Carole told him that she had found her next picture story. She mentioned my name and, being an accomplished actress, pronounced it correctly.

"I like the way you tell a story," Carole said. "I'm going to talk also to Clark. I want you to write for him, too."

I left in a daze. Lombard, Gable, Selznick—the top echelon of Hollywood's motion picture industry! I had entered the inner circle of glamour with just a pen and a sheet of paper as my investment.

I told Henrietta we had entered the rare atmosphere of Upper Hollywood. Thinking of the big money the story would bring, I bought a large black Buick sedan for Henrietta. She always wanted a big car, as a protection for our son Geoffrey.

I never heard from Carole Lombard, nor did I see her again. I didn't know then about the noncommittal promises of Hollywood. She might have been honest in her intention, but David Selznick had other plans for her. I wasn't even asked to send in my story.

Four years later, during World War II, as a passenger in a military plane on her way to sell war bonds, the airplane crashed. Carole burned to death. Her remains could not be identified.

Clark Gable never recovered from his loss. He became a notorious womanizer, vainly searching for the perfect love that only Carole had been able to supply.

The author tries to enlighten, while the commercial writer entertains. The word *author* has an elite connotation, but I don't know of any other word in the English language to substitute for it. All my professional writings are based on a central idea, trying to convey information. Though Samuel Goldwyn's opinion was "If you want to send a message, call Western Union," he was wrong. Notwithstanding the budget of a motion picture, for me it had to contain a theme, a point of view, opening an avenue of thought, which might induce the public to think. So do the novels I write. But since the attention span of adults and children has been diminished from hours to minutes in our fast-paced society, the shows Hollywood now produces are mostly devoid of continuity, replacing story development with violence, sex, and, if possible, continuous stimulations, which smother the thinking process. After a picture show, I challenge any viewer to tell the content of the story he or she has just seen, since, deliberately, the audience was kept in a constant state of often meaningless action. I don't think I ever adapted a novel or play, and if I did, I discarded the original, kept the title, and spun an original story around it, whose main objective was to develop a story in continuity.

The experienced screenwriter should be able to write down his central idea on a postcard, as one of my writer friends did. This was the way he sold his stories: "During the war, a shortage of housing facilities existed in Washington, D.C. Unable to find a hotel room, a young man and his wife rented themselves out as butler and maid to a rich family, to have a place to sleep and from where he could conduct his business." That was enough information for a producer to engage the writer, to write the story. Around that pivot of an idea, a thousand different screenplays could be devised. But the hub of the wheel was the idea the writer expressed on the postcard.

Erich Pommer, the eminent German producer, a literary, educated man, always read the writer's original. That honest approach toward a film project then atrophied in Hollywood to a "treatment," to a "two-page outline," then to a "few paragraphs." Now producers don't read anymore. The writer has to "pitch" his story verbally, since producers seemingly have lost the ability to digest the written word.

Today writers on their own time compose screenplays on speculation that the agent peddles, thus relieving the producer from spending money on perhaps futile script development. A screenplay sold that way can fetch a tremendous sum, which might go into hundred of thousands of dollars.

The chance for screenwriters to be hired has been narrowed. They have to switch to the big market of writing for television, a very specialized craft that now feeds three thousand of the twelve thousand Hollywood scribblers. They must write to an established formula, containing the same leading actors, and a cast, whose screen characterization is outlined on mimeographed paper.

Motion pictures, especially those fashioned for TV, are made on an assembly line. If the formula for a television show finds acceptance with the public, which also means that if it attracts advertisers, it might run for years, depicting the same story line in different disguises.

Certain pregnant ideas stick to my mind for decades until I put them on paper.

I was always intrigued by the story of the Taj Mahal, the mausoleum built in 1632 by the Emperor Shah Jahan for his favorite wife, Mumtaz Mahal, near the Indian city of Agra. What fascinated me was that it was not designed by an Indian architect but by a Frenchman, Austin de Bordeaux. He was an adventurer who had drifted into India and found service as the shah's architect. I could not find any reference of Bordeaux's life and had to invent his adventures. I wrote an outline: "No Greater Love," imagining that the Frenchman, having secretly fallen in love with the shah's wife, Mumtaz, had, after her death, built the most splendid poetic mausoleum in the world, not only for the shah but also as a memory for his own unfulfilled love.

I tried to collaborate with the British screenwriter W. P. Lipscomb. It was my constant insecurity as a writer, fearing that I would not be able to put my ideas on paper without the help of a seasoned writer, that made me team up with him. After the story had been written, I found that Lipscomb had peddled that treatment to different studios as the sole creator.

After I had "blocked out" the story, which means that I had written the original draft of *No Greater Love* before I asked Lipscomb to collaborate, I had given the outline, with both our names on it, to Joe May (Joseph Mandel), the German director. Joe had been an important director in Berlin in the twenties and had also escaped from Nazi Germany.

I had met Joe in Berlin on the set of one of his films. When I entered the studio stage, he was way up in the rafters overlooking a set of his recent picture. I called, "Mr. May!" He answered with "Hu, hu." I thought it was a greeting until he finished the sentence: "Hu-hu-hundred thousand marks has cost me that shit of a set!" I had not been aware that Joe May stuttered when he was excited.

When I saw him in Paris a few years later, immigrants, without a job, I asked him if he spoke French. "Im-im Momente nicht," he answered in German. "Not at the moment."

Having been engaged as a director at Universal Studios, he advised me to get rid of Lipscomb, even if I lost the rights to my story.

Lipscomb returned to England without having found a buyer for *No Greater Love*. But the serendipity of that incident turned out to be that Joe May got me the assignment to write a sequel to H. G. Wells's *The Invisible Man,* which he was going to direct. That assignment opened an avenue of writing jobs for me, which lasted for many years. Universal became my home base, and though I sometimes worked for other studios, I wrote twenty-eight original screenplays for Universal Studios. Many of those old films still haunt the television screens today or can be found on videotapes.

Who remembers the directors of Shakespeare's plays? Who knows the names of the famous of yesteryear? They are forgotten, but the bard still exists. Since everyone in his life yearns to leave a tiny trail of immortality, it might be that one of my novels will be found fifty years from now in a secondhand bookstore, while actors and directors have disappeared in the mist of the past. That's why I will stay alive even though my name may be forgotten.

Joe May arranged the job for me to write an original screenplay, *The Return of the Invisible Man.* The original motion picture with Claude Rains had been a great financial success for Universal Studios, and the motion picture industry followed up the success with sequels. Their theory was and still is that since the public knows what to expect, they buy tickets. I never had the ambition to get the Academy Award for concocting a story for motion pictures, because I always considered a studio job the means to make money and certainly not an artistic endeavor. Art is created by the conception of its originator and not by the workmen necessary to carry out that conception, and motion pictures are created by many workmen: the writer, the producer, actors, cameraman, film cutter, and last but not least the publicity department.

Once when I complained to my producer in Germany, Erich Pommer, that I was sharing screen credit with a writer who did not deserve it, he said, "When the picture is a success, it is your picture. When it is a failure, you can blame the others."

Again I was wrapped up pleasantly in the motion picture cocoon, pampered, safe, drawing a weekly check. To work in a studio was like belonging to a benevolent family. Father, the front office, sheltered you, providing sustenance. By today's standards, film writers in 1938 were paupers in comparison to the sums screenwriters now collect for the same kind of work, but they don't know the difference, since there is no way for comparison. Besides, the writers in the forties and fifties were professional literati with books, short stories, contributions to magazines, and stage plays to their credit. They could earn a living without studio assignments. There were different salaries for writers, but even those who received two thousand dollars or more a week, a sizable sum at the time, died impoverished, unless they invested, preparing for their old age. Writers rarely did. If they had bought a home in Beverly Hills during the heyday, they had the chance of selling it with a great profit after being discarded by the industry like old luggage. Their security was gained from real estate, not from studio work.

As a hired writer at Universal Studios, I worked in a wooden bungalow. Air conditioning did not exist for buildings, only for battleships, for which it had been invented. I was sitting shirtless and in shorts behind my typewriter. A fan behind a block of ice simulated cool air. My secretary, Phips, had stripped down to her bra, which was all right since she was only twenty. She also wore shorts. The heat in the wooden shed hit the hundred-plus mark. That was the way writers worked in the forties at the Universal Studios in the Valley.

To drive a car during the California summer heat offered two choices: to leave the windows open and desiccate or close them and suffocate. Air-conditioned cars were unknown. People in the forties lived in conditions that a convict in a prison of today would consider inhumane.

Since the heat cooled off in the evening, I usually stayed on, working late at night. Taking a fresh breath of air, I watched hard hats erect a new stage opposite my bungalow. The foreman asked me about my profession. I told him. "Getting time and a half?" he inquired. I wish I had, but writers, unfortunately, were not paid like construction workers.

I enjoyed writing original screenplays. *The Return of the Invisible Man* did not need much imagination. The subject of "invisibility" was not new to me since my last novel written for the German market, *The Power in the Dark,* dealt with it.

The theme of the story of my book was prophetic: The world was drifting toward a conflagration. The German army moves into Poland (a prognosis written six years before it became fact). A scientist discovers the technique of invisibility. To prevent the coming war he commits acts of terror like sinking a German battleship. He creates mysterious phenomena in every country, which scares the leaders of the nations, forcing them to stop their aggression toward each other and to find the common enemy. Mankind needs a foe stronger than he in order to unite.

The same theme on a small scale I used for my assignment *The Return of the Invisible Man.* It was, I believe, the first picture appearance of a young actor, Vincent Price, who played Geoffrey Ratcliff, who is unjustly accused of having murdered his brother. Sympathetic Dr. Griffin, played by John Sutton, administers a drug that makes Ratcliff invisible, gaining time for him to find the real murderer. But Griffin does not know that the drug carries a debilitating side effect in Ratcliff, a gradual delusion of grandeur that might drive him insane.

The theme of *The Return of the Invisible Man* was the seemingly inevitable corruption of power. The wish to be invisible is deeply ingrained in the human mind. To observe but not to be seen contains a temptation to misuse that potential.

Since *Return* was nominated for an Academy Award because of its special effects and was also a financial success, I had to write every one of Universal's "Invisible" pictures. After a hiatus of years, I was assigned to write *The Invisible Agent.* To send an invisible spy to Nazi Germany during World War II was an obvious theme. Jon Hall played the transparent intruder, helped by the shapely Ilona Massey, a beautiful blonde Hungarian singer. The girl in the film, in love with Jon Hall, was never sure whether the invisible agent was hiding in her bedroom at night and did not dare to undress, jumping fully clothed into her bed.

The German background gave me an opportunity to turn that comedy into a strong propaganda film against the Nazis. It had some very grim scenes depicting the cruelty of the Nazis, even against each other.

To see while not being visible always was part of sexual excitement. When I was about ten and on vacation in Heringsdorf, a small German village on the Baltic Sea, I took a walk on a dark street. There, behind a brightly lit window, a young woman was brushing her hair in front of a large mirror. She was naked, her body almost incandescent in its beauty. She looked stunningly seductive to a boy who had never seen a completely naked young female. I averted my eyes, since I was brainwashed never to look at a female's naked body. The following nights I walked back to that street, but the room was always dark. That fleeting and excitingly shocking incidence in my life was the awakening of spring in my body. Even today the picture of that luminous body still stays with me like a photograph and has not lost its mysterious desire.

For me devising those pictures with the "Invisible" theme was great fun and a challenge since I had a friendly, moving battle with the ingenious director of Universal's special effects department, John Fulton.

He usually appeared in my bungalow asking me the same question: "What trick have you concocted in your twisted mind, which you believe I cannot do?"

My theory, which I did not reveal to him, was that the more difficult an idea was to execute, the more stunning the effect appeared on the screen, and I knew that John Fulton would never give up solving the problem.

"This one is an easy one." I always tried to startle him with an idea. "The mean Japanese agent, Peter Lorre (now with slanted eyes), suspects the invisible man exists. He catches him in a net, which is covered with fish hooks. You see the net move with the captured shape inside, but never the actor himself."

He uttered a curse that insulted my mother. But he never failed to deliver the cinematographic stunts. He had a dozen girls working for him who painstakingly painted out parts of every individual frame, a process that took months.

The last of the "invisible" theme was a comedy, *The Invisible Woman*, filmed in 1941, in which the great actor John Barrymore appeared for the last time in his life. He played a mad scientist, who made a beautiful woman, Virginia Bruce, invisible. I told Fulton that she went into a bathtub, and all one could see was the imprint of her invisible body in the water. She was soaping her long slim legs, which made them appear, then her face. I tried to make her upper body visible, which would have made the picture X-rated. I even talked that scene over with her. Virginia, a fetching blonde, proud of her good looks, would have been game, but not the Hays Office, which controlled the morals of motion pictures. Now, half a century later, that suggestion would not cause a problem. Virginia might even have demanded it. Stunning women do not mind to be shown in the nude, since their beauty is part of their weapon of seduction.

John Barrymore was nearly impossible to work with. The director, Edward Sutherland, had to devise methods to make Barrymore remember his lines, since his love for alcohol had greatly impaired his memory. Sutherland had John walk up and down a staircase, where he read his dialog displayed on the banister. He had to be hung up on wires, to prevent him from swaying out of close-ups. To my surprise, John had just married a handsome nineteen-year-old, Elaine, who was always accompanied by her mother. To solve that riddle of age, since John was close to sixty and looked seventy, I asked him why he had married such a young woman. John stood up, looked down at me and said with the pathos of the Shakespearean actor, "Sir, it fits!"

He died in 1942, sixty years old, of an illness aggravated by his love for booze: "Die? I should say not. No Barrymore would allow such a conventional thing to happen to him." He was right since he remains a legend.

To function, life demands a focus. Without that goal it is disorganized, haphazard, and aimless. The American focus is sharply defined. It is the "nuclear family": father, mother, kids, a house with a white picket fence in the suburbs of a city. But after the kids have grown and leave the home, what then? How to find a new focus? Ken, the postmaster of our little village of Three Rivers, retired after forty-four years of service. He went fishing. He had a truck specially built for his fishing focus. He traveled all over America, caught river fish, and threw them back into the water. His focus seemed to be waiting untroubled for old age and death. My friend Ken, a retired insurance executive, flew every year to faraway Canadian lakes where no human habitation could be found. There he fished in solitude, away from the disturbing vibrations of the world. He didn't kill his prey and threw them back into the lake to swim away. Like Cartesian monks, who deliberately suffered by being walled in to receive illuminations from heaven, those two fishermen had withdrawn into themselves, convinced that they had done their allotted share for society. They were at peace with themselves.

I wish I could, even for a moment, experience the balance those two men had found in their lives as recluses and that one finds in the facial expression of Indian Buddhas.

What drives writers to write every day? Is it an inborn compulsion? What is their focus? To pass the remaining time of life like those fishermen, enjoying their own company, detaching themselves from the daily troubles of a suffering humanity, living perhaps the ultimate state of relaxation by being wishless? That focus does motivate people with a deeply ingrained religious conviction. It doesn't seem to matter what one believes. The act of believing is the goal. A psychiatrist friend told me that truly religious people die at peace. Jews, since they pose questions to the end of their last breath, die the hardest. They are searching for answers, scrutinizing those who pose further questions.

Henrietta and I had reached the American "dream": father, mother, son, and picket fence. We had moved to a small house in a quaint location in Hollywood on Wonderland Avenue, off Laurel Canyon Boulevard. The rent was very low, thirty dollars a month. The living room had a stone-built fireplace, covered with strands of ivy that had grown through the wall. It had a garden and a gazebo where Geoffrey slept. Only three hundred yards away was the Wonderland School, maybe the most progressive junior grammar school in Los Angeles, since the parents kept a psychologist on the payroll, who talked not only to the children but also to parents who had a need for it.

I took over that small house from my friend Curtis Bernhardt, a German refugee who, after having successfully directed a motion picture for Warner Brothers Studios, could afford a more elaborate home. I knew Curtis (then still Kurt) from Berlin, where he had been banned by Joseph Goebbels for being a Jew, despite his patriotic films like *The Last Company,* a glorious epos of German heroism and faithfulness to the flag, a feast of jingoism that no Nazi filmmaker had been able to equal.

We met again in London, where he took me to a ballet at the Sadler's Wells theater. He pointed at a graceful, dark-haired young dancer, Pearl Argyle, who, in 1936, was London's celebrated ballerina. Sacrificing her career, she became his wife and followed him to America. But I believe that she was missing the intoxication of adulation, since she could not find any background for her talents in Hollywood. She also was too sensitive to be able to adjust herself to the picture people her husband had to work with, who didn't possess the refined European culture of her former life. She died young, her death perhaps aggravated by frustration.

I soon became aware that my new country was profoundly altering my personality. My focus had changed completely. It had narrowed its conceptions and, like a laser beam, was concentrating only on writing motion pictures, scripts, and short stories, with the objective of being transformed into films. The world around me had slowly dried up my interest in any ethereal art. The cultural "baggage" that I had brought with me from Europe and enriched me all my life had desiccated. Like the retired people to whom going fishing was their only creative outlet, I had become one-track-minded. I had entered an artificial world, which, though exciting, was two-dimensional, like the screen on which pictures are shown. The explosive world situation and everything outside Hollywood detached itself from my life's interest. The lure of the motion picture world with its potential for gaining recognition, fame, and public adulation has not and might never change.

Life for me had become a pleasant routine: checking in at nine in the morning at Universal. The studio kept me busy. Writing motion pictures also had become a drug, an escape from my still undigested past and the suppressed fears that haunted me since the country of my birth had murdered its native culture.

While the bloody slaughter of World War II was going on in Europe, Hollywood was spinning gossamer dreams, a world detached from the rest of it.

Since the war had broken out between Germany and England, some of my British friends were eager to join their embattled island. My writer friend, George Salmony, suddenly became very mysterious and taciturn. As I found out later, he had joined the British Secret Service, which must have made him feel like an important spy. His British friends gave him a huge, wet farewell party and, to see him off, marched him to the train station. George came back four weeks later, rejected by the military medics because he had flat feet.

I had a friendly, though detached relationship with a producer/director at Universal, George Waggner. He was a commercial director, not like one of the gifted directors such as Huston, Wilder, King, LeRoy, who directed million-dollar blockbusters. George was an expert in Bs, efficient and within the given budget. He had started as a writer, though there wasn't any spark in his imagination. For him I was the perfect complement to his craft, since he depended on a writer with original ideas.

His family, having come to America a hundred years ago, was of German origin, and his pleasure and relaxation were to sing German songs and drink beer with his German pals. He was as undiluted a German as his immigrant great-grandfather must have been. We rarely talked to each other. I was never able to discuss with him the screenplay he was going to direct. He would shut me up with: "I want your ideas, not mine."

Every Thursday afternoon I went to his office to flatter him by telling him what a brilliant director and producer he was. I hoped he would catch on that I was kidding, but, being unsure of himself, he never did. I never knew him well enough to become his friend, since he never talked about himself. Only once he blew his cover: when the news came through that President Roosevelt had died, he blurted out, "High time for that son of a bitch to croak," which made me aware that he had the intolerance of a German.

"I was given a title by the front office," George told me. "*The Wolf Man*. It is Boris Karloff's title. He has no time to play it, since he is on another assignment. Here is the list of our contract players: Claude Rains, Warren Williams, Madame Ouspenskaya, Ralph Bellamy, Bela Lugosi, and Evelyn Ankers, a girl from Australia who can emit a terrifying scream. Take your pick. Lon is going to play the Wolf Man. The budget is three hundred and fifty thousand dollars. We start shooting in ten weeks. Good-bye."

Universal Studios in 1941 was on the brink of financial collapse. The studio had no "focus" and could not compete with the star-studded MGM Studios, which owned Clark Gable, Jeanette MacDonald, the popular Andy Hardy series with Judy Garland and Mickey Rooney, and many actors of international appeal.

Warner Brothers Studios turned out very successful thrillers. It had created a stable of stars: Humphrey Bogart and Susan Hayward (Edythe Marrener), Bette Davis and Jimmy Cagney, who could do nothing that was not worth watching. The world star of Columbia Studios, Rita Hayworth (Margarita Carmen Cansino), had a sensuality and dancing skills that made every film she played in a box office hit. Harry Cohn, the head of Columbia, was lavish with his money when it came to hiring actors. He contracted Gary Cooper for *High Noon* and had the courage to choose subjects like *All the King's Men,* a daring "Americana" of a would-be dictator, a subject that the saccharine Louis B. Mayer would never have touched.

Universal had only one property that perennially brought in money: the Frankenstein series. The character was borrowed from Mary Shelley's 1805 novel, combined with ideas lifted from the German Paul Wegener film *The Golem,* that Jewish legend of an artificially created man.

Sometimes a writer's work, even by writing for a small-budget picture, competes with the giant A pictures, and stays for decades alive when the memory of multimillion-dollar films already have disappeared in the mist of the past.

Though I had nothing to work with but the title *The Wolf Man,* the story fell into shape like a jigsaw puzzle. I saw in it the fight of good and evil in man's soul, and the inescapable working of fate, which also had shaped my life.

Only many years after *The Wolf Man* had been produced did I become aware of the secret of its success.

Many "Werewolf" pictures had previously been written in Hollywood. The werewolf legend can be traced as far back as ancient Greece, with the first extant piece of werewolf fixation appearing in the *Satyricon* by Petronius. My screenplay for Universal gave *The Wolf Man* for the first time a sharply defined character that stuck to him and became the intrinsic part of that legend. I had added a third hairy ghost to American lore, after *Dracula* by Bram Stoker and *Frankenstein* by Mary Shelley. America, which is ghostless, has to import its own monsters from abroad.

Jack Pierce, the genius makeup man, devised a face, half-human, half-animal, an imaginative job similar to the one he had done for the image of the Frankenstein monster.

In 1942 I received a letter from a Professor Walter Evans of the Augusta College in Georgia, who had seen the picture of the Wolf Man. He mailed to me his lecture on popular tragedy, which explains the basic impact of horror stories and movies on the public. He talked about Aristotle's "Poetics," his critique of Greek tragedy, and the Wolf Man.

Aristotle and my screenplay? That conception struck me as a mockery, but studying his lecture, his comparison made sense. In

Greek tragedies, the gods decide a man's fate, from which he cannot escape. When the moon is full, the Wolf Man knows that he is destined to murder. In Greek plays, the gods have ultimate power over the human's life. In *The Wolf Man,* the beast's father exercises an ultimate power over his son. I had, by chance, constructed the film like a Greek tragedy, which seemed to have made that character a classic.

I had given the Wolf Man the name Lawrence Talbot. It stuck. While writing the screenplay, I became aware that all of us are subject to the whim of Harmatia, a predestined fate. Was the Wolf Man a mirror of human life?

Many learned dissertations, even by Sigmund Freud, have been written about the Wolf Man. Professor Cornelius Schnauber, the erudite professor of folklore at the University of Southern California, wrote a treatise giving the film an even deeper meaning by stating that, since Sir Talbot kills the Wolf Man not knowing the monster is his son, he saw in that scene the eternal rivalry between father and son.

> Even a man who is pure in heart
> And says his prayers by night
> May become a wolf when the wolfbane blooms
> And the autumn moon is bright.

That four-liner has now been attributed to "Gypsy folklore." I had made it up. That's how folk history is made.

The Wolf Man died in this motion picture, an impossible task. Since that character is still a moneymaking property, he has been revived many times, which proves that in this capitalistic system, the pursuit of income even defeats death.

That character became so integrated in American folklore that the Postal Service issued a postal stamp with the Wolf Man's image on Halloween in 1996.

Our wonderland abode was a primitively furnished old bungalow with lots of character. It came replete with Bow-Wow, a fierce old tomcat, occasional visits of mountain lions who liked to dine on dogs, and many coyotes, which, having adapted themselves to city life, cleaned out our garbage cans, but only on Thursdays before the garbage pickup arrived.

One evening when the fireplace was going, a half-naked young man with unruly hair and a golden beard reaching to his navel knocked on our front door and introduced himself. "I'm the hermit type and live in a tent above you. I only want to tell you that your roof is on fire." The sparks of the fireplace had ignited the ivy that decorated the chimney. I got the conflagration under control with the garden hose until the fire truck arrived. The hermit later on wrote the song "Nature Boy," which is still being heard over the radio. He might have become a millionaire and left his tent for a mansion in Beverly Hills. That is Hollywood: from the tent to the castle and return.

Further down the street a young actor had rented a house. When I visited him, he was sitting sleepy-eyed on the floor in the corner of the unfurnished living room. I don't think he ever changed that expression of only being half-awake, which became his trademark. As Robert Mitchum, after having been cast in the lead of *The Story of G.I. Joe* (the film about the legendary war correspondent Ernie Pyle, who died in World War II), he became one of Hollywood's leading men for half a century. For the first time I smelled the sweet smoke of marijuana, that hemp plant cannabis, which by its users is considered a "recreational" drug. Mitchum later was busted for smoking the weed and sent to prison by a judge who might have had triple martinis before lunch.

There was a time when many people kept a canary in their homes. The canaries sang beautifully since their food was hemp, or pot. When pot was forbidden by law, the canaries did not sing anymore. During World War II, Nebraska grew hemp for the military, which was essential for making rope. Now nylon is used. But that prolifically growing weed could never be completely eradicated. People who like to smoke pot should take their vacation in Nebraska, where it can be found in abundance.

Across the road lived a young science fiction writer, Robert Heinlein, who in later years became the doyen of that craft, an icon for science fiction aficionados. On the hills way above us, an English lady had rented two tiny bungalows, one for herself, the other for her spry eighteen-year-old daughter, Angela Lansbury, who half a century later was still acting on the stage, on the screen, and in a perennial television series, *Murder She Wrote*.

Affluent people lived on top of the hill, aptly named "Appian Way." There resided the legendary composer Rudolf Friml, a wizened gnome of Austrian decent. His estate was hidden behind a high wall. His companions were three handsome Chinese women. Friml was married to number 1. Number 2 looked after his exquisitely manicured Oriental garden. Number 3 was a gourmet Chinese cook. Living in a sprawling mansion with those lovely females, being famous and getting an enormous income from ASCAP, Friml had his life organized like a musical symphony. He had composed many operas, such as *The Fire Fly, Katinka,* and *Rose Marie,* and songs such as "The Indian Love Song." His friend, Igor Stravinsky, one of the great composers of the twentieth century, a man of his size, lived not far away, on Sunset Boulevard. Henrietta and I were twice invited for dinner at Friml's home with Stravinsky present. I would not have traded for their looks but certainly for their talent and savoir vivre, their style of living.

My friend Bandy (Andrew) Marton, the best second unit film director in Hollywood, had bought a house on Appian Way, which descended four floors down a steep hill. His sprawling building was filled with exotic treasures he had collected during his filming all over the world. Bandy was the codirector of *King Solomon's Mines*. He also filmed the exciting chariot race in *Ben Hur,* an otherwise rather tedious film. That chariot race was the high point of that movie, and I suspect that William Wyler, the film director, got the Academy Award because of Bandy's brilliant chariot race. I heard that a hundred horses died during the shooting, but don't believe it, though cruelty to animals did often occur especially in westerns, to enhance a camera take. But now the Humane Society sternly prevents that outrage.

In the time-honored Hollywood tradition of harvesting every credit, William Wyler didn't mention Andrew Marton in his acceptance speech at the Academy Awards.

Bandy was a man completely without fear. During the filming of *King Solomon's Mines* he flew in a rickety Piper Cub over the jungles of Africa. If there had been an accident, no one would ever have found him. But he balked, when Mike Nichols, directing *Catch-22,* demanded a certain shot be taken from a helicopter. At that time helicopters were not yet equipped for camera work, and the cameraman had to hang out perilously from the door. Bandy refused to take that suicidal shot. Another cameraman tried but did not finish it. As Bandy told me, he died in that attempt.

Bandy was married to Jarmila, a strikingly beautiful, intelligent Hungarian actress. Henrietta confessed that she would understand if I ran away with Jarmila. That handsome woman drove an open Morris Minor, a small topless English automobile. Whenever Jarmila alighted in front of Schwab's drugstore, men quickly clustered around to take a glimpse of her long legs. She regretted not having a child but became pregnant after nineteen years of marriage, as proof that if you don't succeed, try and try again.

Bandy had made a motion picture in Tibet in which Jarmila played the lead with the strapping German actor Gustaf Diessl. Gustaf, as Bandy told me, had stolen a small temple stone from the Tibetans and was convinced that a curse of the monks was threatening his life. On the way back he became so ill that he had to be carried out on a stretcher, wasted to a skeleton, unable to stand up, while Jarmila and Bandy kept their health. As soon as the picture company had crossed the border into India, Diessl miraculously recovered. Bandy had recorded Diessl's decay faithfully on film, also convinced that mysterious powers rule that Asian mountain country.

Schwab's drugstore on Sunset Boulevard was the official meeting place of film actors, producers and directors, budding actors and would-be actresses. The Schwab brothers, three of them, protected young girls who had come to Hollywood to find fame and fortune. The brothers often secretly helped them financially or bought them a bus ticket home, before the girls drifted into prostitution.

One night at Schwab's, Henrietta and I watched a young couple who looked lost and bewildered. The young woman was tall and displayed that elusive quality of "vulnerability," a character trend highly appreciated by film studios. She undoubtedly had star quality. Their names were Jennifer Jones (Phyllis Isley) and Robert Walker, her husband. Jennifer became a major star after her part as a nun in *Song of Bernadette,* a film based on a novel by the German author Franz Werfel.

Twelve years later when we lived in a large house on Lime Orchard Road in Beverly Hills, our neighbor, the real estate tycoon Bill Hollingsworth, invited us to a party. Again we met Jennifer Jones, now the wife of David Selznick, the producer of *Gone with the Wind,* the same mogul who had turned down my story *The Hound's Tooth Coat* for Carole Lombard. Selznick was an uncouth man, and Jennifer seemed defenseless against his coarse treatment of her. But she came up to Henrietta and me and said, "It was in your little home in the Hollywood hills that I heard Brahms's First Symphony for the first time in my life." It was a gracious remark, which showed a sensitivity she had never lost.

Selznick, wanting to be married to her, had cleverly used one of his publicity women to destroy her marriage to Robert Walker. Walker became an alcoholic. He consulted the Viennese psychoanalyst Frederic Hacker, who tried to cure him of his depressions and alcoholism with injections. Though Walker physically fought against them, he was injected forcibly and died in Hacker's office. Years later I talked to Hacker, but he had a learned explanation for anything that I accused him of. Doctors bury their mistakes.

After Selznick died, Jennifer married the billionaire Norton Simon, and when he died she became the trustee of his vast collection of artwork, contemporaries and classics.

Was Jennifer happier than at the time when we met her and her young husband at Schwab's drugstore in Hollywood, "The Sodom-by-the-Sea"?

War is the acme of stupidity, activated by the part of the brain that we inherited from the caveman. We treat each other during wartime with the same cruelties that the Neanderthal exercised against the Cro-Magnon man, or vice versa. That basic killing instinct has not changed in a million years. We are also equipped with a "social" brain that makes it possible to deal with each other civilly, which means that we usually don't stab each other during an argument. The third brain we possess, the mystical one, is still rudimentary. We try to practice humanity, kindness, or other abstract conceptions. The outcome of those attempts is the mystical belief called religion, but it is still overshadowed by intolerance, righteousness, and monetary rewards.

What the joy of pregnancy is for women, the time of war is for men. War for men is a time of relaxation—that is, if they can stay away from the battlefield. Relieved of their family duties, they don't need to hustle to make a living. The trumpet blows three times a day, announcing the feedings. Also, there is always a higher authority that relieves the subordinate from the chore of having to think for himself. War only makes sense for generals, since it proves their necessity. Von Clausewitz, the German military theorist, wrote that war is the continuation of diplomacy by other means. The "other means" are the slaughter of its own kind, who often don't know what they are dying for.

After the wars and their senseless destruction of irreplaceable minds and cultural treasures, the vanquished nations often prosper. They now have a chance to modernize antiquated institutions, replace old machineries with state-of-the-art models, and become competitive on the world market. They are often financially helped by the "victor." The loser becomes the winner like Germany, Japan, and other countries, which gained immensely from being destroyed.

In 1913 my father made a trip to New York, renewing his American citizenship, since as a naturalized American he had to prove every seven years his loyalty to his new country by appearing personally in front of a magistrate on United States soil. It was a stupid law, since a naturalized American remained a secondary citizen. That law now has been abolished. By living in Germany in 1914, our family members possessing a blue American passport were considered enemy aliens, though my mother and we children had never crossed the German border into any other country. In 1921 I had to opt for German citizenship, to be able to pay my university fees in inflated German paper marks. Foreigners had to pay in "hard currency," which I did not possess.

I discarded my blue passport and received a brown one. That brown booklet made me an enemy alien in the United States when America declared war on Germany in 1941. Having applied for American citizenship, I was again issued a blue little booklet in 1942, with the American eagle on it. Fighting on the American side during that war, I was an enemy alien for the Germans. People with red or yellow or green passports were out of luck. They had no protection, many ending in concentration camps, or were slaughtered by people who possessed booklets of another color. The color of an official passport decided people's fate.

When Germany declared war on the United States, Henrietta, Swiss-born, took English lessons at UCLA. I also joined that class, but after one day dropped out since with my acquired grammatically proper English I did not make the colloquial mistakes a born American usually is brought up with—I knew the difference between "I" and "me."

At UCLA, Henrietta, with her charm and extremely good looks, attracted many American males, professors, scientists, often of Nobel Prize quality. When we were invited to their private homes, we had to leave by law before 8 P.M., because, still being "enemy aliens," we were legally under "curfew." I liked that change of venue and invited the most interesting guests to our home. Since Hitler's speeches were broadcast over the radio in German, I translated his provocative ranting to my American friends. I tried to make them understand that war was inevitable, and their country was totally unprepared. My guests could not imagine what a foreign war was like, since that state of human absurdity had never happened on their soil. Half a dozen members of the faculty of UCLA, even if they were exempt from the draft, patriotically joined the Navy

Secret Service in San Diego. I was right. Japan forced the United States into war. Now, half a century belated, that country considers that move a mistake and has apologized, finally considering itself having been the aggressor.

Since America was soon fighting the Nazis, I, still owning a brown passport, again was an enemy alien. But that political handicap didn't prevent me from acting as air raid warden in our hilly district and admonishing the people to turn off their lights or to draw the blackout curtain. Since a lonely Jap sub had lobbed a few shells into a small power station near Santa Barbara, most houses along that coast were for sale at bargain prices, and California prepared itself for an invasion, which, of course, never came.

I suspect I did not do too well as an air raid warden, since my German accent frightened people into believing the Teutons had already landed.

The war didn't disrupt Hollywood's production. The world war couldn't match the importance of photographing fairy tales on celluloid. Besides, the troops needed entertainment.

Every day I went to Universal Studios to earn my weekly check, still supervising my screenplay of *The Wolf Man*. Playing that gruesome-looking monster, my friend Lon Chaney Jr. was sitting during lunch break in the studio commissary, but alone. In his Wolf Man makeup he looked so disgusting that nobody would sit with him. He could only feed himself by sucking liquid food through a straw.

Lon had arrived at 2 A.M. at the makeup department. The makeup people put him into "position," driving a little nail through the skin at the end of his fingernails to prevent him from moving. Then they would build a plaster cast to rest the back of his head. The camera was weighted down with a ton of metal to stop it from quivering during the shooting. The cameraman would expose ten frames, while Lon was told to keep his pupils on a certain spot. Then his position was slightly changed, and another ten frames were exposed. Lon was mostly concerned about his bladder, since the shooting of his transformation into a Wolf Man took six hours. He confessed that was the time when he contemplated killing me. I convinced him that I was only a badly paid writer, had no influence on the production and all of its ramifications, and all I was trying to do was collect a few bucks to feed my family. Lon's *Wolf Man* became the classic werewolf film of all times. In retrospect it makes me believe that I never did anything else of any consistency in my life.

In 1942, with the war raging, I was having lunch in Universal Studio's commissary when George Waggner, my producer, passed me on his way to the executive table. I was sitting with Yvonne de Carlo (Peggy Middleton), perhaps the most beautiful woman I had ever laid my eyes on, and Mary MacDonald (Mary Freye), whose legs were as shapely as those of Betty Grable. I wanted to show off my wit and said, "George, why don't we make a picture, *Frankenstein Wolfs the Meatman*—I mean, *Frankenstein Meets the Wolf Man*." To "wolf" somebody had the connotation of sexual harassment.

I laughed, Yvonne laughed, Mary laughed, but not George. He only looked at me quizzically and walked on.

That was the time during the war when America's factories rolled out tanks, airplanes, and guns, but no automobiles for private use. I needed a different car, since my Buick had passed the retiring age.

A young writer, who had been drafted, wanted to sell his Buick. I wanted to take advantage of that opportunity and asked George if I would get another job when I was through with *The Climax*, a screenplay that I wrote for him with Boris Karloff (William Pratt) and Susanna Foster (Susan Larsen) in the lead.

I didn't have enough cash for that sports car, and for Henrietta, a Swiss, to pay interest on borrowed money was an abhorrent idea. George stuck his head into my office every day, asking me whether I had bought the automobile. When I questioned him with "What's the assignment?" he only answered, "Buy the car."

I found out, to my surprise, that it was easy to get a loan from the bank. They just kept the pink slip of ownership.

"Here is your assignment," George said. "*Frankenstein Meets the Wolf Man*."

"But it was a joke," I said.

"Not anymore," George said. "I give you two hours to find a brilliant idea." He didn't say "to accept the assignment" or ask me "to make up my mind." He knew he had me over a barrel.

Every one of my films has a central idea. In *The Climax*, Boris Karloff in a fit of jealousy murders his paramour, an opera singer with an exceptional vocal range. One day visiting the music conservatory he again hears the dead woman's voice. A young girl, Susanna Foster, a student of the conservatory, had been gifted with similar vocal cords. For Karloff, this is the dead woman's return. He tries to get rid of Susanna, who personifies his bad conscience.

The Wolf Man knows that he is going to kill when the moon is full. A thousand writers can write a thousand screenplays around those ideas, but the original idea cannot be replaced. The wheel would fall apart without its pivot. I had the assignment but needed a central idea for *Frankenstein Meets the Wolf Man*. "Larry Talbot," the name I had given the Wolf Man, knew that there was no way for him to escape his fate of becoming a murderer. He wanted to die, but even if he died, some magical (studio) power would bring him back to life. If Larry Talbot could find Baron Frankenstein, who knew the secret of life and death—didn't he construct a body of human parts?—he might escape his horrible fate and find peace. On his search for the baron he meets the Monster, who also is looking for the baron. The Monster wants to live forever.

That was the idea around which I wrote the screenplay: a search for life and a longing for death.

Lon played the part of Larry Talbot with a sincerity that gave that film a value of fear and pity, which Gotthold Ephraim Lessing, the eminent eighteenth-century literary critic, declared essential to any story.

Being cruelly mistreated as a child by his famous father, Lon Chaney Sr., Lon suffered from clinical depression, which he tried to overcome by his addiction to alcohol. I knew Lon until his premature death in 1973, a tragic character who couldn't adjust himself to life. He *was* the Larry Talbot in *Frankenstein Meets the Wolf Man,* who wanted to die. In that picture, Lon played himself, which made his part frighteningly believable.

In the 1940s and 1950s, there were three permanent family names in the film-producing business: Briskin, Riskin, and Gross. I assume that no studio could operate without having a Briskin, a Riskin, or a Gross as executives. There was an Irving Briskin at Columbia, a Robert Riskin at Fox, and a Jack Gross at Universal. Jack had started in motion pictures by managing theaters in Los Angeles. He got the attention of the highest echelon of Universal, Cliff Wood, since never a piece of chewing gum could be found glued to the wooden seats in any of his theaters. Jack became the master of the B pictures and kept me busy for years with *The Return of the Invisible Man, Invisible Agent, Invisible Woman, The Wolf Man, Frankenstein Meets the Wolf Man, The House of Frankenstein, Son of Dracula, The Climax,* and a few musicals: *Frisco Sal* for Susanna Foster, *Shady Lady* for Ginny Sims, the nightingale of that period, and a few more. I wrote twenty-eight Bs for Universal. I mainly had to invent the story for the screenplay. The studios often had only a title that they believed was salable or some inane property that needed a visual theme I was expected to supply.

It was Jack's policy never to raise any salary. He would pay me the same amount if I got more money from any other studio, but his iron conviction was not to spend more than he had to. That's why he was a good producer for Bs, since he produced films on sensible budgets. Despite that thriftiness, some of those Universal B pictures have become collector's items for the aficionados of horror pictures. Those films have outlived Jack Gross, who tragically died of a heart attack in a men's room in London.

Bs also survived the old Universal Studios, which MCA, then the Japanese, and now a liquor company, Seagram's, gobbled up. The lovers of horror movies, of which millions exist in the world, don't care who owns the motion picture rights to those films, as long as they are available on cassettes or shown at horror festivals, which are held perennially, while the "greatest movies of their time" have sunk into oblivion.

The horror cycle appealed to me because I had been brought up in Germany, where fairy tales were folklore. Those German stories have a deep psychological origin. My German-born friend, Professor Cornelius Schnauber, sees in *The Wolf Man* connections with the theories of Sigmund Freud, Friedrich Nietzsche, and the philosopher Immanuel Kant. He finds in that tale the eternal father-son conflict. In *The Bride of the Gorilla* (1951), which was the first motion picture I directed, he sees the metamorphosis of a human into an animal as an escape from the chains of civilization. In *The Magnetic Monster* (1953) a man-made element becomes a menace to the world, as in Goethe's ballad *The Sorcerer's Apprentice*. He discovered the same theme in my novel *Donovan's Brain*. That film spawned many pictures about scientific experiments that, getting out of human control, menace the world.

Irving Briskin of Columbia Studios knew about the Universal success of the horror cycle, and since he was the "keeper of the Bs" at Columbia Studios, he called for me. He wanted me to create a TV series, *Tales of Frankenstein,* since he had an OK from ABC to develop a pilot. I told him that he would soon run out of ideas to invent another adventure every week for the Baron Frankenstein and Monster. I suggested an anthology, using the Frankenstein saga as a frame, but he did not want to listen. I wrote a half-hour *Frankenstein* show, intrigued by the possibility that I was to direct it. Irving was a great help to me in writing a graveyard scene, since he owned a cemetery.

Directing a motion picture is great fun. A director is able to function even with a Monday morning hangover. The well-oiled film machine runs by itself. All he has to do is to select the camera position, which the cameraman suggests to him. He has to learn to call, "Roll it," "Cut," and "Wrap it." On a big picture he even has his film cutter on the set as an adviser. And he gets paid extremely well, since he controls the budget.

A writer cannot function when his brain doesn't work. Nor can he give work to people, a real power, nor has the writer any say on how the film should be photographed, acted, cut, scored, recorded, advertised, and released. There isn't, and there never was in Hollywood, a writer with authority except when he became a "hyphenate"—a director-writer or writer-producer.

I didn't like directing, which I considered a waste of my time, preventing me from putting words on paper. I also don't have a great respect for actors, whose ego often becomes so inflated that soon they believe that they are the most important part of the show and that the public buys tickets to see them and not the picture.

My brother Robert, who had become one of the top directors of the forties and was paid an enormous salary, lit for a few years the Hollywood firmament like a meteor, sparkling, brilliant, only to disappear like a falling star. He went back to Germany after the war, to become a top director again. Hollywood, with its atrophied memory, never called him back, though years after his departure it bestowed the Oscar on him for the best foreign-made motion picture: *Nachts wenn der Teufel kam* (The Night the Devil Came), a powerful anti-Nazi document, shot in Munich in 1957. Though the film was of international quality, it was not a success in Germany, where even today no anti-Nazi film produced by a German company has a chance of success. That failure might be based on a flaw in the German character, which prevents them from admitting that they ever could be at fault.

Only great directors have a respect for a writer's work. They consider the picture "finished" when the screenplay is finalized to their liking. Fritz Lang and Alfred Hitchcock, King Vidor, Billy Wilder, or William Wyler never deviated from the written word of a script. Most directors are "set decorators" who are more interested in the costumes of their actors than in their dialogue, like Mitchell Leisen, who had worked as a window dresser for the Saks Fifth Avenue department stores before he became a motion picture director.

Robert, who liked to interfere with writers to make himself shine, was at his best if he got a finished screenplay and had no time to "improve" on its construction. That insecurity became his downfall.

Sometimes the miracle happens in the life of a writer that the words fall into place as if they had been assembled in the proper sequence in the writer's brain and now, like an open sluice gate, appear on paper in perfect continuity. That miracle happened to me in Germany when in two weeks I wrote the novel *F.P. 1 Does Not Answer,* which, selling worldwide, became UFA's most prestigious trilingual motion picture, with Hans Albers, Conrad Veidt, and Charles Boyer. Shown sixty years later, it still has the same story impact since it was based on a new conception, an airplane fueling station in the ocean—a conception of the future airplane carrier. *The Wolf Man* also poured painlessly into my typewriter, scene by scene, without the need of much of a change. When I started the novel *Donovan's Brain,* I wrote it as if that book already existed, copying it from my subconscious. The story was abstract for its time: can a human brain exist and function without its body?

The forties and fifties were perhaps my most fertile writing periods, spurred by intelligent friends who visited our little mountain home, writers, painters, decorators, actors, everyone highly creative in his or her field. By chance their sexual preference mostly was gay or bisexual. Since I am interested only in the opposite sex, their leanings were of no interest to me.

I learned a great deal about style from my writer friend, Ellis St. Joseph. Ellis brought Alfonse along, and Alfonse was accompanied by Larry and Larry came with Johnny, Johnny introduced André. The tightly knit club of homosexuals mushroomed. The 1940s were a time of vicious persecution of homosexuals in Los Angeles. The police, to entrap them, visited hotel and restaurant toilets, waved their penis as a come-on to draw out their suspect's "perversion." When the victim responded, the policeman arrested him. Then his friends, often at night, had to scoot around, collecting five hundred dollars' bond, which at that time was a very sizable sum. That entrapment was a police scam of the most insidious kind. I suspect that the police pocketed the blackmail monies, since the court never called on the victim.

One day, when I came home from the studio, thirty-six males strolled in the garden. It was a party of utter congeniality. Henrietta had gone through our address book and had invited that select group to show me how many of those people of special persuasion had become my friends. Jokingly she told me that she had started to worry, since I too put my arm around their shoulders and bent my wrists limply. She was afraid that I might drift into that other world.

After that surprise party, except for a couple of survivors, only heterosexual acquaintances visited our home. Today I wouldn't have lost some of my best friends, since time has eliminated that prejudice. Mostly!

A new life and existence had started in Hollywood but hopefully would not end there. I met only very hardworking people at the studio, highly dedicated to their jobs. The seamy side, kinky parties and wife swapping, the scandals that the tabloids write about and live on, never came my way. Once at Universal, a tabloid wanted to bring out a story about Rock Hudson's homosexual adventures. The studio paid the tabloid off with the unknown story of another leading character, who had, as a young man, been arrested for a bank robbery, a juicy bit of print that saved one of their moneymaking stars but ruined another.

Nobody has ever deliberately tried to make a bad movie. But I have rarely heard a good word spoken about that dream factory which produced their living.

The time span of an actor's success, especially female, was extremely limited. Everybody was considered only as good as his last picture, not as good as his best one, as it should be. The word *loyalty* was missing in the Hollywood dictionary. In Hollywood you can be forgotten while you go out of the room to the toilet. F. Scott Fitzgerald stated, "I accepted the assignment with the resignation of a ghost assigned to a haunted house." But he cashed the studio checks, though his success as a screenwriter was mediocre. Everyone, even stars, should they have the misfortune to appear in a bad picture, were quickly forgotten. Curiously enough, those who received the Oscar rarely appeared again on the screen, as if that much coveted prize also carried a demonic curse.

The tycoons who ran the studios like medieval fiefdoms seemed to find assurance of their power by treating their employees with abominable cruelty. Jack Warner did not permit his own son, Jack Warner Jr., to enter his studio. L. B. Mayer, trying to break the contract MGM signed with Sir Alexander Korda, the eminent English producer and director of *Henry VIII,* had him stopped by the studio police at the gate. But Korda reported every morning for work, knowing that should he not show up even once, he would have given Mayer the legal reason to fire him.

The cameraman at Columbia Studios, Ted Sparkuml, an employee for twenty-two years, read in the *Hollywood Reporter* that he was fired but not told personally, the ultimate insult and humiliation. Jean Osso, a French filmmaker under contract to MGM, went through an ordeal: his son, who during World War II had joined the U.S. Army, was murdered in Chicago. The studio, in a spell of humanity, procured an airplane ticket, which during the war was almost impossible to get, for him to fly to that city. When he returned, he found the lock to his office had been changed. That's how he was told he had been fired. Henry Blanke, the German-American producer, with credits like *The Story of Pasteur* and *The Maltese Falcon*, did not submit to having his studio contract canceled. The studio moved his office and him to a broom closet.

Being a freelance writer, I didn't care about studio politics, since, except for one year at Warners, I was never under studio contract. That year for me was wasted, since I considered myself to be a novelist and not a professional scriptwriter. My reason for accepting a studio assignment was to save enough money to write a book. To be able to cope with a job I didn't like, I took an invisible small altar with me. Whenever I came to the point of frustration and nausea, I, in my mind, went to the imagined altar to repeat the mystical prayer: "My weekly check, my weekly check." That method worked. I always accepted every assignment offered to me. My objective was the printed word, not those sentences often badly mouthed and distorted by actors.

It was on a Sunday, December 7, 1941, when the new world I was trying to create crashed. The Japanese attacked Pearl Harbor. The European war had been raging for two years but was not felt in the cocooned film world. Suddenly the war affected the Americans too. Germany and Japan declared war on the United States. Since Americans are best in teamwork, its huge industrial power started to move, slowly at first, but then in ever-increasing speed. Germany and Japan had awakened a sleeping giant.

One late evening two men from the Federal Bureau of Investigation visited me. One was talking; the other never opened his mouth, just watched me intently. He put a fat file with information about me on the table. I had the uncomfortable feeling that I was back in Germany, constantly watched by the Gestapo. Since I was not politically minded, I couldn't imagine what kind of information the FBI could have collected on me.

They inquired about an older, rather mysterious German who lived on our street. What did I know about him? How often did I see him? What was his profession? What kind of policy did we discuss together? Did we speak German to each other? I told them that I had talked to that man only once and didn't even know his name. The next day that old German had disappeared from sight. Before the two FBI agents left, they told me that I was under curfew, and had to be home every evening not later than 8 P.M. Just because I still had a brown German passport, and not a blue American one, I was a suspected enemy of my new country.

This is a chapter in my life that I haven't fully digested, even after Robert's death, more than twenty years ago. I have not fully come to terms with my relationship with my brother.

A German eulogy called Robert "the world-famous motion picture director." There is a thin line between genius and paranoia, and he was able to balance it until the end of his life, when he fell off that imaginary tightrope. For a time, until my middle age, he was my nemesis. Though our relationship as brothers was very closely knit, he felt his ego menaced by any success I had as a writer. Though for a time he was one of the most sought-after and highly paid directors in Hollywood, and though I never reached even part of his earning power, he could not squelch my faculty to write. I was able to put words in continuity on paper, a prowess that he did not have. Examining the past, I realize how intricate, destructive, and painful the often camouflaged fight for dominance between siblings can be.

One day a single word, which a psychoanalyst would have appreciated, entered my mind: I became aware that I had a "brother complex." That single term changed my relationship and even increased my love for him, since he could not interfere with me anymore. For many years Henrietta was keenly aware of our destructive relationship. But the last twenty years of his life, I could watch our brotherly competition with sly humor, like an audience having figured out a magician's trick.

When he arrived in Hollywood on the day of the outbreak of World War II, he was unknown to the studio heads, despite his great film successes in Germany and France. Robert's knowledge of English was still in its infancy when his agent, Paul Kohner, sent him to the famous writer-director Preston Sturges, who was of French descent, a language Robert spoke well since he had worked in France for nine years. Sturges was impressed by Robert's personality, though his credits in Germany and France were unknown to him. A studio executive's knowledge of the world stops at the studio gate. Sturges called the studio boss, Sol Siegel. "I have the most important European director in my office. You must sign him up right away." Then he turned to Robert and asked, "What's your name?"

Robert got a contract to direct B pictures at Paramount, a dull job for his enormous talent, since the Bs were directed by a rigid technical studio procedure: long shot, medium-close shot, over shoulder shot right, over shoulder left, close-ups. There was no room to show a director's individuality. Robert directed *West Point Widow, Fly by Night, The Night before the Divorce,* and *My Heart Belongs to Daddy,* four easily forgotten program fillers.

Robert was bored. Sol Siegel wanted to get rid of him, and in the time-honored method of making the lives of employees disagreeable for them, Siegel told the cameraman Charles Van Enger to provoke Robert, to have a legitimate reason to fire him. Van Enger refused to carry out Robert's camera directions. "OK, have it your way," Robert told him. "Then why don't you fight, being such a great European director?" the cameraman sneered. "Because this isn't a Siodmak picture; this is Paramount shit," Robert replied. All his life he never lacked personal courage. But that reply also ended his relationship with Paramount.

Robert, trying to find a directing job, soon ran out of money. He even tried to become a wine salesman. I helped him and his wife financially. Every day I asked Jack Gross to give Robert a picture to direct. Gross finally signed him up to direct *Son of Dracula,* a film with Lon Chaney Jr., in which Lon was wrongly cast. Bela Lugosi should have played the part. Lon was on his worst behavior. His pet peeve was the then-reigning studio queen, Maria Montez. One night, Lon, in a drunken bout, threw feces at the bungalow shingle with Maria's name on it. In an alcoholic spell during shooting, he broke a vase over Robert's head. But Robert, always attracted to eccentric people, found Lon's behavior amusing. He was used to high-strung actors.

Son of Dracula had been my original screenplay. It had a pregnant idea: a woman, the beauteous Louise Allbritton, is afraid her lover, the handsome Robert Paige, will die. She invites Count Dracula and demands that she and her lover become vampires. As vampires their love would last for eternity, since they would at night come to life.

When Robert was offered the direction, he was in financial despair. He was offered a weekly salary of only $150. He complained to me that he couldn't accept that kind of money, since not what a writer wrote but what a director contributed to the film was of importance. Keeping two families, I also was running out of cash. He reluctantly accepted Universal's offer and produced a film that still is considered a classic among horror aficionados. It was shot in black and white, which conveyed its eeriness. Robert, having studied Rembrandt's technique, had learned light effects from the master's unique distribution of light and shadows.

That picture was the start of Robert's meteoric rise at Universal. I was relieved that he had gotten a job. The drawback was that the day he moved into the studio, he asked the producer to replace me with another writer. I got fired, and he chose the screenwriter Eric Taylor to work with him. I was shocked at having lost my job, but I also understood that he was aware that we could not work together. Who was going to prevail?

I again was standing outside a studio gate but didn't wait for my agent Stanley Bergerman to peddle me around to find employment for me. I was going back to my original profession: writing novels. I already had the idea for *Donovan's Brain*. I called the then-famous brain specialist, Dr. Jan Jademar, and told him that I was a writer and needed information in his field. Being, like most scientists, a frustrated writer, he coached me about the internal workings of the brain, of which the medical profession still knows very little. I accompanied him on his visits to hospitals in Los Angeles. He introduced me to a carpenter who had suffered a brain injury and had lost the ability to use his plane. I saw terminally ill children with enormous heads and tiny bodies, who smiled when the nurse touched them. I became aware that the medical profession knew less about the working of the brain than astronomers about the constellation and the Milky Way.

Still living in our little house, whose rent had been raised to thirty-five dollars a month, the characters of that novel became more familiar to me than any human being I had ever met. We know little about ourselves. How much do we know even about our closest family members and friends? But the characters a writer creates cannot hide any secrets from him. The author is knowledgeable of all the actions and thoughts of the lives he creates in his mind. If the existence of God could be verified, only a writer would be able to explain it.

Robert heard about my intention to write a novel, of which I had written dozens in the past. This one was the first I wrote in English. My virtue in this newly acquired language was based on the fact that I couldn't camouflage any emptiness of thought by being verbose. The limitation of my English vocabulary forced me to be precise in my telling a story. That shortcoming turned out to be an asset.

Robert, whose salary Universal had raised because of his directing *Son of Dracula,* a box office success, tried to take part in my effort and suggested scenes and situations. To get me away from his influence, Henrietta insisted that I would be much better off writing far away from Hollywood, without interruptions from telephone calls and agents. She had discovered an obscure spa in the Mojave Desert called Coso Hot Springs. There, without my knowledge, she had rented a small bungalow for me. Her plans were strategically laid out: she would visit me with our nine-year-old son Geoffrey every week, bring food, but not the mail. There was no telephone in that part of the desert.

I am married to a very pliable and feminine woman, with a will vastly surpassing mine. She had our big Buick limousine packed for the trip and had not informed Robert, who was busy shooting *Cobra Woman* with Maria Montez in the lead, for my old producer George Waggner as producer at Universal.

Henrietta insisted on getting me away from Robert's "unholy influence," which, as she guessed rightly, would affect the originality of my novel at work.

Coso Hot Springs, hundreds of miles away from Hollywood, consisted of a dozen ramshackle bungalows. Some were built for "therapeutic" purposes. Henrietta abandoned me and my typewriter and drove back with the promise to return in a week. To enjoy the "healthful" steam, one had to lie on a wooden bench in one of the bare "therapeutic" cabins, the head stuck outside through a hole in the wall since the steam in the "bathhouse" was so hot that it seared the throat.

Steam arose from mile-deep holes in the ground, leading to the core of the planet. By lowering a pot with uncooked food into that steaming hell, one received a deliciously cooked meal within an hour. I ate the best boiled beef in my life, carrots cooked to perfection, and potatoes deliciously penetrated by meat sauces.

I settled in a bungalow furnished with a bed, a table, one chair, and a shelf. The weekly rent of seven dollars was collected by some mysterious half-Indian woman who never talked. She might have been mute.

I worked on the novel ten hours a day, since there was not much else to do. That place, which now sports a government air base, was frequented by old people suffering from crippling arthritis. Their relatives dumped them there like used luggage. I cooked for them in my steam holes, since nobody seemed to take care of those ancient citizens who could hardly walk. Small burros, tiny desert donkeys, visited my window at night, baying, begging for a handout of bread.

One day, a large black dog, looking like a Newfoundland breed, was lying on my bed, growling at me. I fed him, and we became friends. He stayed for a couple of weeks. Then an old gold miner appeared. He was searching for his dog. He told me that Navaho, the dog, was waiting in the morning at his breakfast table in his cabin ten miles away. When the miner cooked his eggs and bacon, he sometimes passed out on account of a "nervous" heart. That was the moment the dog was waiting for. Then "that damn dog eats my breakfast." He took my companion home.

Adjoining Coso Hot Springs were the "Devil's Pot Holes," aptly named since nobody could ever live there, nothing grew there, and it was always clouded by steam which exuded from the cracks of surrounding rocks. It was my sauna.

Henrietta appeared every week. Once she had a flat tire and waited into the night until a good Samaritan finally passed by in a truck and changed the wheel for her. It still was a time of peace and trust, the now-vanished courteous America where a single woman could still feel safe wherever she went. It was the time where neighborliness and security were the norm and, except for desert cowboys, nobody carried a gun. Today I would not dare to stay in a godforsaken place like Coso Hot Springs, nor would I ever let my wife drive alone through an uninhabited desert. America has lost its pioneer spirit and with it its innocence.

I finished my novel unimpaired by my brother's suggestions and gladly returned home with a completed book. That novel influenced my future profession, and now, fifty years after its first printing, is still reissued perennially not only here but in many other countries.

I received a call from RKO to meet the producer Val Lewton (Vladimir Leventon). He was a White Russian who had escaped to America with his parents in 1918 during the Bolshevik revolution.

Revolutions are started by the lowest class of society. Their first objective is to murder their elite or force them to flee the country, like the German and Spanish Jews, the Moors, or the Huguenots.

As history proves, the countries that accept the homeless intelligentsia gain immensely from that influx of foreign erudition. The emigrants, bringing the cultural baggage of their homeland with them, enrich the nations that accept them. America is lucky to be in a state of constant evolution, due to the injection of foreign cultures.

Val had seen *Berlin Express,* which I had written for RKO, also *The Wolf Man,* and, as he told me, was intrigued by its Freudian connotations, the fight between father and son, a meaning that I didn't know the film contained. The terror he induced in his motion pictures is implied, carrying a greater impact than graphic violence.

Val had started in the mail room at MGM and had progressed to producer at RKO. His choices of subjects, despite their low budget, were of high literary quality. He produced *Bedlam,* named after the notorious London asylum where the insane were displayed behind bars like animals to the amusement of visitors. In *Cat People,* Simone Simon, a pert French actress, turned into a leopard. I met that glistening black cat in the studio, sleeping in its small cage, one paw extended through its bar. I had the urge to touch a leopard once in my life and put my finger on its paw. The claws closed at once, holding me, and the green eyes opened. I could not withdraw my hand without ripping off its flesh. Then the green eyes closed, the claws withdrew after that display of power and, in this case, cat kindness.

I saw at MGM a small alligator asleep on a chain. When I approached that reptile, it suddenly jumped five feet into the air, its jaws closing with a hiss. Since that time I haven't approached any wild animals or visited a zoo.

Val's motion pictures, despite their abstraction, became good box office for RKO. Universal's commercially minded people did not possess that literary mind and produced pictures whose objective was to "entertain."

H. L. Mencken, the acerbic New York journalist, remarked, "The bad taste of the American public can never be underestimated." He sneered from his elite mountaintop at the rabble of lesser minds, forgetting that those were the people who bought his books for the cash that kept him in caviar.

There is a segment of film audiences that frequent "art pictures." Val's horror pictures could be called "art films," since they had a sophisticated style, closer to my liking than those I had written for Universal Studios. He also was modest about his position, in which, as he told me, the producer's only job was to check the costumes of his actors. That wasn't true since his story evaluations were to the point. He also had the good sense to leave his writers alone after he had assured himself of their ability to work for him. Besides being erudite, he was a man of culture. Val had been the assistant of producer David Selznick. Val was a perambulating encyclopedia for Selznick, a coarse and not highly educated man. When his boss did not know the answer to a historical or literary question, Val unfailingly provided the answer, even if he had to invent it. Selznick, believing him blindly, never checked Val's answers.

Val, a heavyset man of forty-five, was secretly jealous of writers who could, besides writing screenplays, also write novels and plays. He told me that he had read *Donovan's Brain* but that it wasn't a good book, though he remarked that in the sense of Kant's philosophy, it answered the question of whether a brain without a body can experience and digest new information. There he lost me, since the German philosopher Kant had never entered my mind when I wrote that novel.

Val also had a streak of sadism, which made him a perfect producer of horror pictures. He told me that as a schoolboy in Russia, he played "chicken" with his classmates. The game was to put one's hand on the desk and withdraw it quickly before the game's partner could nail it down with a pocket knife. He showed me a faded scar on his right hand where the knife had penetrated his hand. Still, with a glow of pleasure, he recalled the moment when his bleeding hand was nailed to the wooden desk.

The success of a motion picture is not diminished, however silly and tasteless the title may be. Val had bought the film rights to a short story by Inez Wallace with the schlock title "I Walked with a Zombie." He asked me to write the screenplay. I don't know what the story was about, except that a man was married to a beautiful woman who had become a zombie, a living, walking dead, who couldn't react in bed. Franz Kafka slept with a life-sized doll that possessed all necessary parts for intercourse. But that substitute for a warm-blooded woman was a failure, since it didn't have "vaginal warmth," nor did the beautiful zombie in my screenplay. That conversation amused him so much that he accepted me as an equal and not as a hired scribbler.

I cannot deny that there are mysterious powers in superstitions, since they exist, often with deadly results, in every civilization. I had studied the rite of voodoo for Val's zombie picture. Voodoo, though under different names, has been practiced through the ages. It is still practiced today, by propitiatory religious rites and communication with the dead. I am not sure whether there isn't a still-unexplored basis in "superstitions." Several hotels have no thirteenth floor since that number has an evil connotation for many people. The number seven personified "luck." A young man I know never enters a one-way street in his car from the left side and rather motors around the city block. "Left" is called *sinistra,* "sinister," in many languages. One does the "right" thing. "Right" is positive. The writer, Walter Reisch, wrote "WG" in the corner of his screenplays, "with God," believing that God, as his cowriter, would influence the judgment of his producer in his favor. I don't know any country which does not have its secret rites and prejudices. The devil is everywhere in different disguises. In Europe "verified" ghosts haunt houses.

Val had created his own gang of directors, assistant directors, cameramen and cutters, a loyal assortment of people on which he could depend. He elevated cutters to directors, like Robert Wise, who, starting as a film cutter for him, became a top American director with *The Sound of Music.* Jacques Tourneur, a former assistant director, directed the *Zombie* picture, after Val's sensational hit *Cat People.*

Val believed that the audience's imagination is more powerful than watching tomato juice, the films' substitute for blood, oozing out of bodies. Though Val liked my screenplay, I did not fit into his inner circle. He must have sensed that my main interest was not in motion pictures but that I preferred writing my own material, where I had no boss to please.

I Walked with a Zombie, despite its tasteless title, became Val's most literary success, has remained a "cult" film and is rereleased perennially at horror festivals.

Val and I were passionate pipe smokers. Nobody resented the smell of tobacco before smoking became a health issue. A pipe, being lit slowly, gave me pause to think unhurriedly of the right answer during conferences. Pipe smoking slowed the action down. It is important in life to be able to think slowly and deeply. I, a collector of pipes, finally owned 160 of them.

To show my appreciation, I presented Val with a rare straight-grain Dunhill pipe. A few years later he returned it to me, since a severe heart attack forbade him to smoke. He died at forty-seven years of age, a great loss for the film industry, since he had added a missing intelligence and great taste with his pictures. If he could only have outwaited death a few more years, a heart bypass operation, which at his time did not exist, would have prolonged his life.

If you were not you, who would you like to be? Just choose a person of history or of your generation. A young friend of mine, well educated and diplomatic, would have liked to be General MacArthur. MacArthur, that corncob-smoking military genius of unlimited conceit? From that day on I looked at my friend from a different angle. What was buried in his well-camouflaged desires? I know that he liked to lay out a commercial war plan, as MacArthur did for his attacks on the North Koreans, obviously never taking into consideration the casualties, human or in business. For him a business deal was like a planned battle, never mind the victims.

If I could have chosen, I'd have loved to live the life of John Huston, the director, writer, and actor, who, despite lacking handsome features, was blessed with a captivating charm. He possessed the *beauté du diable,* "the beauty of the devil," which passed the line of attractiveness and made him a highly interesting personality.

John was of my generation and grew up in the actor Walter Huston's home. His father told him as a child, "Son, give 'em a good show, but always travel first-class." John certainly did. To match a father's fame demands a great talent, personality, and boundless energy. John had all of those. But one also needs ruthlessness. A certain amount of sadism is a requisite of a motion picture director. To keep the actors under control, a director must have an authority to dominate those actors who are not known for their humility.

Beware of charm, which usually hides imperfection of character, the disregard for other people's vulnerability.

The shedding of a partner or even a close friend, without any consideration of the damage done to their emotions, happens in many people of power. John used to change women like shirts. I met a few of the former Mrs. Hustons. The first one, Leslie, I met at a vacation somewhere at Palm Desert, a pleasant resort, frequented by Hollywood actors. Leslie was waiting there for her divorce from John. If I had not been a married man, I'd have proposed to her right away. She had that indefinable butterfly-dust of a young girl. I don't know and didn't inquire about their parting.

John told me that a man, to live a gentleman's life, has to make and spend twenty million dollars. He earned and spent twenty million, but I don't know if that made him content with himself. For a time he lived in a castle in Ireland and raised thoroughbred horses. But his obsession was creating motion pictures, with women and horses as a byline.

His office at Warner Brothers Studios was next to mine. I was writing *The Beast with Five Fingers,* a film with Peter Lorre. John was given the assignment to write and direct Dashiell Hammett's *The*

Maltese Falcon. This was a difficult and baffling assignment, and he asked the writer and friend, Allen Rivkin, how to tackle that masterpiece of mystery. Allen just marked scenes in the book, telescoping the story into film length, and advised John not to "improve" on that book, a crime that many directors, actors, and producers, unsure of themselves, routinely commit.

John and I had similar preferences: drinking whisky and playing chess. He brought the actor Humphrey Bogart to our home. Humphrey was floating in a stream of Scotch whisky. John, when he drank, could recite all of Shakespeare's plays and alcohol sharpened his mind, while "Bogie" became unpleasant and aggressive when he lost at chess.

Chess is a cerebral game. It is devoid of chivalry and demands logical thinking, which was a difficult task for Bogie when he was in his cups. When I worked for Sol Lesser in Palm Springs, writing *Tarzan and the Fountain of Youth* for him, he expected me to lose, since he was the boss. I didn't cater to him by letting him win, even though that might have shortened my contract. Even former president George Bush found out after his retirement that he didn't win every golf match, nor did Dwight Eisenhower win in poker as often after his retirement as president.

John and I had the same tax accountant, Morgan Marie, the owner of a spiffy outfit of high-priced Hollywood characters he represented. Morgan, who raised Weimaraner dogs, in which he was more interested than in his clients, loved to give parties. Since he collected 5 percent from every salary and investment of his clients, he could charge the high expenses as tax deductions. His hospitable house was the gathering place for many picture coryphées.

Humphrey, always close to the bar, was, to my surprise, gray-haired. He was paid two hundred thousand dollars per film by Warner Brothers, which at that time was the highest salary in Hollywood. He married a pretty model, Lauren Bacall (Betty Jean Perske). When I talked to her, enchanted by her young, clean features, the then-twenty-year-old unexpectedly said, "We like it that way," wrongly believing that I had looked at her cleavage, which didn't indicate much breast. Since it was the time before breast implants, she must have suffered under Howard Hughes's then-fashionable conception that big breasts are essential for female motion picture stars. "Betty" could not cure Humphrey of his drinking habits during their short, happy marriage.

There exists a species of women who, for a few years in their post-teenage youth, exude a high vulnerability that is very attractive, even disturbing for males. That fragility creates a protective shell around them. Marilyn Monroe was gifted with that power, as was Susanna Foster, the young singer at Universal, and Lee Remick, when she started in motion pictures, and some other starlets who flashed through the Hollywood sky, like Susan Kohner, who played in John Huston's *Freud*. That ephemeral condition of youth lasts for only a short time. "Betty" Bogart had that indefinable frail quality, as did a few women who did not become stars but whom I remember all my life, even after brief meetings. That flash of a meeting belongs to my indelible memories.

When John and Humphrey made the picture *The African Queen,* shooting in the poisonous, insect-infested jungles of the Congo, everybody, according to Katharine Hepburn's biography, got sick, except John and his drinking pal. They were so impregnated with alcohol that the insects who attacked them dropped dead, and John and Humphrey never got sick. Peter Viertel, the writer and husband of Deborah Kerr (Deborah Kerr-Trimmer), wrote a novel called *White Hunter, Black Heart,* a roman à clef of that trying film production. He claimed that John wanted a human being to die for him, the ultimate proof of his power. He succeeded: one of the carriers on the crew died of exhaustion during the shooting of *The African Queen.*

After I read Peter's novel I decided I didn't want to become a John Huston after all. He died of emphysema, a deterioration of the lungs, often produced by smoking. But his terrifying illness, a slow death by suffocation, didn't stop him from being active to his last days. Nominated for best director, Huston attended an Oscar ceremony in 1985. Appearing on the stage in a wheelchair, John was handed the envelope for an honorary award he was helping to present. He passed the envelope with the name of the winner on to Akira Kurosawa, the famed director of *Rashomon*. That notice then was passed on to Billy Wilder, who read the name. Kurosawa had difficulty extracting the note fast, and Wilder whispered to him, "Pearl Harbor you could find, but not a small piece of paper."

Nobody heard that remark, not even John, whose wheelchair after two minutes had to be wheeled off the stage to an oxygen inhaler.

I was invited with Henrietta to John Huston's fifth, I guess, wedding, which took place in Ruth Ford's, his bride's, home.

When I entered the living room, John was sitting in an overstuffed chair, intertwined with a young actress, Evelyn Keith, who also could look back on several marriages. Before I could withdraw, Ruth entered. "Don't worry," she said. "I can handle that."

When she saw us leave a few minutes later, she asked, "Do me a favor. I've got a writer here who is very lonely. Could you take him out for dinner?"

The writer was William Faulkner, who I knew belonged to John's and Bogart's wet gang.

We invited Faulkner, who was not yet internationally known, to Romanov's, the then-fashionable eatery. Faulkner didn't care much about food but ordered a whole bottle of Old Forester bourbon. He said that he never touched wine. Faulkner talked about his native Mississippi and complained that the Jews were buying Mississippi. I told him that I was a Jew but that I wasn't buying Mississippi. That seemed to astonish him. Then with a grin, he told us that Louis B. Mayer, the head of MGM, had permitted him to work at home. L.B. thought that Faulkner liked to write in his apartment in North Hollywood. But Faulkner meant home in Mississippi, for which he left the next morning. Then he lectured us about the value of Bourbon whiskies. His favorite one had been the brand Old Crow, but he had started to throw up whenever he took a drink. That condition terrified him. Becoming unable to touch alcohol meant to him inevitable death. When he heard that Winston Churchill had switched from Scotch to French brandy and thus got rid of his crippling allergy, he had tried Old Forester and, by the grace of God, had recovered. Now he imbibed only Old Forester bourbon, which saved his sanity.

Faulkner died of alcoholism. When Oslo bestowed the Nobel Prize on him, he was incapable of rendering his acceptance speech. A substitute read it for him at the dedication ceremony.

When I tell people that I had met William Faulkner, they look at me in awe, then inquire about the nature of our conversation, which historians would record. Did he talk about his work? The theme had been that the Jews were buying Mississippi and that he now drank Old Forester bourbon instead of Old Crow.

I lost touch with John, since making motion pictures is like an amusing cruise, where one makes friends for life whom one never meets again. The last picture he directed was a film based on a short story by James Joyce, appropriately called *The Dead*.

Now, having acquired a bird's-eye view of my life, many of my shortcomings torture me and are the cause of severe mental depressions, whose origin psychoanalysts have not been able to find. To cope with these haunting thoughts of my past, I am spending many hours every day behind electronic writing gadgets. For sixty years I had used typewriters, from manual to electric, word processors, automatic printers, and duplication machines. I now use ten thousand dollars' worth of equipment to put words on paper. But the quality of my writings has not improved since the days of the small portable Adler typewriter, which my brother had found in a deserted attic.

I suffer from "Harmatia." In the Greek tragedies, Harmatia means an error of judgment, resulting from a defect in character, which is based on some personal inequity or traceable fault. I certainly made many errors in judgment because I didn't know better. Henrietta made fewer errors by following her female intuition, which is almost infallible, while my logic has holes like a sieve.

I am aware that I never fought hard enough for myself, convinced that everything I wrote was of doubtful value. To go on living demands the total immersion in a profession that leaves no room for the pursuit of happiness, which Robert and I experienced only for fleeting moments. We were haunted by a fear that afflicts almost every human being. It is called, in German, *"torschluss Panik,"* the panic that the "door" might suddenly close and that there are not enough hours in life for all those tasks one wants to accomplish.

When I look back at the golden years between 1929 and 1933, the time before the wheels of our success became derailed, I still can't understand how I, in a few short years, could have piled up the mountain of work based perhaps on a premonition that my existence was going to change suddenly and completely.

To work for the motion picture industry was like driving an automobile, which might stop at any moment for the lack of gasoline. In Berlin I wrote *Cercasi Modella* for Italia Film, starring "Miss Rome," the eighteen-year-old actress Gina Lollobrigida, whose producer, Arturo Giacalone, vainly tried to make her change her complicated name into one Americans could pronounce. He paid me with a check for four thousand marks, money I badly needed. It bounced. When I went to his office, he was just leaving, spiffily wearing a derby hat and putting on kid gloves to go to the horse races. I told him about the check that the bank had not honored. He looked at me without a change of expression and remarked, "Really?" and walked off, as if I had told him a boring story.

Still, the picture was made in German and Italian. The idea was that a painter has an affair with a rich young woman. He paints her in the nude. An advertising agency used it by putting that naked girl on billboards all over the city. It was a catty story of "kiss and paint."

I went to Paris to write *Le Bal,* this time for UFA, whose checks were solid.

My typewriter never had a moment of respite. When I met the film producer Erich Pommer in Nice, where I was writing the film version of *F.P. 1 Does Not Answer* for him, he reprimanded me with "You're lazy," since he was even more relentlessly driven than I, to squeeze "productive" work out of every minute of his life.

Robert and I had entered the unstoppable squirrel cage of constantly being busy, feeling empty and depressed when we were not involved in some kind of production. That drive never left Robert all of his life, nor was I able to shed that addiction. We were fleeing from life by creating a make-believe world.

We were born with a psychological vacuum, which all our lives we could not completely fill. In 1929, on the opening night of our first motion picture, *Menschen am Sonntag,* at the UFA on the Kurfuerstendamm, the main street of Berlin, the projectionist, who prided himself on an unfailing judgment, predicted a disaster. Robert and I were standing outside the cinema, counting the people who entered. Two went inside and three left. Then one couple entered and three came out. "If one more person enters, the theater will be empty," Robert remarked, depressed.

That night, many of our friends came to our rescue, bought tickets, and even hustled for customers. The theater filled up. That motion picture started the turning point of our lives. It was so novel in its concept that film anthologies of today mention it as a milestone of motion picture history. They didn't know that we were forced to take shortcuts to save money, like using people who never had been in front of a camera and whom we couldn't pay. It was the first film of cinema verité. Even Jean-Paul Sartre wrote about our film in *Nausea,* his existentialist Paris paper: "A formidable, but torturous social event, that film *Menschen am Sonntag.*"

When in 1985 I was invited by the city of Berlin to a science fiction film festival, where some of my pictures were shown, I was standing at the exact spot in front of the identical cinema on Kurfuerstendamm that, half a century previously, had shown *Menschen am Sonntag.* Again one of my pictures, *The Invisible Agent,* which I had written in Hollywood during the war, was running. The past had caught up with my present.

I was surprised that the Germans ran that film since it showed the Nazis in a comical but also cruel light. There was no public reaction when the film ended and the audience left silently. Though German writers, like Guenter Grass and Hermann Boell, were dealing successfully with Germany's Nazi past, the German motion picture industry has yet to produce an anti-Nazi picture. The French repress the memory of their collaboration with the Nazis, as if, by denying its existence, history would vanish. But since the word *Holocaust* has been beautified into the expression *ethnic cleansing,* the cruelties that the human cavemen of today commit have jaded the world's conscience.

There are people one never forgets, due to their genuinely deep humanity. My literary agent Hal Matson in New York was of that kind. A representative of writers, he was fascinated by their work and not concerned about how much money a book could bring. He read their stories and, deeply moved, told me of a short book an uneducated railway employee, whose job was to switch railroad tracks, had written. He had been involved in a railway accident where he had lost both legs and had poured out in writing his emotional gratitude for the care people took of him; of the thrill of seeing a huge ambulance arrive just for him; of his emotions of being pampered by doctors and nurses. For the first time in his life, he, a simple workman, had received attention from neighbors he hardly knew. He had never known that so many people cared. For once in his drab life he felt he was a part of the human species in which he had been only a nonentity. Since he felt his experience so deeply, his writing, which he had never done in his life, had been that of a poet. Hal had tears in his eyes as he read that tale to me.

Literary agents now have become as impersonal as lawyers. An agent I had in Hollywood, Sidney Satenstein, a wealthy man who drove a Rolls-Royce, financed publishing houses, and could commandeer what books had to be printed, represented me as his protégé, as though he were the inspiration of my ideas.

Now books appear and disappear like firecrackers. "Best-sellers" are created by publishers and their spin doctors, and the value of publishing houses is due to the sheer volume of published books, but not by their literary content. The German giant communication corporation Bertelsmann bought the American publishing houses of Doubleday, Bantam, and Dell for billions of dollars. There must be money in writing for some, but only for a few authors.

Donovan's Brain, which Hal Matson represented, had a slow start. It first was printed in a pulp magazine, *Black Mask,* whose copies have become high-priced collectors' items. Nineteen publishers turned the book down until Barney Smith, the literary story editor of Alfred Knopf in New York, acquired it for his company. Knopf always invited his new writers to his estate in Purchase near New York City. He looked to me like an Arabian rug salesman, with his dark Mediterranean eyes and drooping black moustache.

Very congenial, he took photos of us, though I suspect not because of the literary quality of my novel but because of Henrietta's beauty. Katharine Hepburn at her best looked like her clone. The great Alfred Knopf showed Henrietta his extensive greenhouses, since my wife was very knowledgeable about plants. I was left behind to read a small book that he inscribed for me, "Alfred A. Knopf, 1940, a Quarter Century," with paeans written about him by some of his authors, Carl van Doren, Willa Cather, H. L. Mencken, Thomas Mann, Henry Seidel Canby, and other luminaries. I found myself in good company.

After his and Henrietta's tour through his glass houses, he treated us like intimate friends, though he never mentioned my novel. He told us how he had started as a publisher. Since he could not find a manuscript he liked, he decided in frustration on the work of a Syrian poet, Kahlil Gibran, a book not likely to have a big sale. Gibran's writings, especially the book of poems *The Prophet,* are, after seventy years, still in print. Some of his poetry was read at Knopf's funeral. He died at the age of ninety. In a curious premonition I called him two days before his death, and though he did not answer himself, he remembered me.

The Knopf publishing house never promoted the sale of *Donovan's Brain,* though, now after more than fifty years, the dozens of different editions have become collectors' items. If I had been aware of its future secondhand value, I would have stocked up on a few hundred copies of the first edition. An original edition, if a copy can be found, fetches eight hundred dollars among book collectors. Since I was paid twenty cents' author's fee per book sold, I find my share of the earnings a rather unfair distribution of money.

The poisonous virus, television, sneaked into the motion picture business, slowly and inevitably. The motion picture industry, which had ruled for fifty years without competition, didn't take that dwarf seriously—like Sinbad the Sailor, carrying a weak old man who, growing into a giant, threatens to squash him.

Frank Wisbar, a German director, saw TV's possibility very early. I wrote anthology shows for him for a hundred dollars a screenplay. No residuals, no rerun participation. Then an advertising agency (Thompson and Thompson) engaged by Pillsbury Flour contacted me. They needed a writer for a half-hour show: *Front Page Detective*. They had acquired the title from a penny-dreadful crime magazine that had been popular at that time. The producer of the show had engaged Eddy Lowe (Edmund Lowe) for the leading part. Eddy was an insecure, unpleasant man, who, despite his great success in a picture based on the Maxwell Anderson play, *What Price Glory*, never managed to age into a character actor. That show, for which I had to deliver a screenplay every week for five hundred dollars, also paid no residuals. I worked with my friend Bill Danch, whose experience in short story writing was based on having devised Disney cartoons. That show swallowed up all the ideas of my short stories that I had written over decades.

Front Page Detective was the forerunner of all detective serials, which are now the mainstay of commercial television.

More crime and murder seem to appear on the small screen than actually happens in America.

Our show didn't last, since Eddy refused to act and speak dialogue at the same time. I wrote television shows for Studio One, some of which Orson Welles directed. It was as exciting as working for the Broadway stage since the action on the screen was performed live.

Television, by draping the crass commercialism of advertising products with a cloak of entertainment, saved the film industry from extinction, since the small screen became a well-paying income for motion pictures, after they had completed their run in cinema theaters. TV now swallows up seventy-two thousand airtime hours every year, the cinemas less than one thousand.

I met a Hungarian emigrant, Ivan Tors, whose motto was "If I don't get rich, nobody gets rich." For that credo one needs a pinch of ruthlessness, which was the core of Ivan Tors's character. He was a gifted promoter and creator of television series, among them *Flipper*, whose protagonist was a dolphin, an accomplished actor who never spoiled a show.

Trying to get myself a TV series on the television screen, because that's where the money is, I wrote a pilot, *Captain Fathom*, with a former submarine commander, Tom Dykers, as technical adviser.

The pilot was shot in Tampa, Florida. Ivan Tors had watched me develop the novel idea of adventure stories underwater, a background that had not been explored on the big or small screen.

In record time, and without my knowledge, Ivan offered the networks his version of underwater adventures with Lloyd Bridges in the lead, an actor I could not afford. Tors's *Sea Hunt* show ran for many years, while my pilot, coming too late, disappeared into oblivion.

Tors had acquired a ten-minute clip of a German film, *Gold,* a multimillion-dollar extravaganza made in Germany during the Nazi time. The culling he bought was that of a gigantic atom smasher, a set that only a giant film company could afford to build. I had developed a TV series, *A-Men* (Atom Men), based on scientific ideas, in which a group of scientists are the "detectives." Ivan suggested that we form a company with the actor Richard Carlson as the leading protagonist. I wrote a screenplay around that two million–dollar German motion picture set. In my script a scientist creates an element whose growth he cannot stop. It was "the sorcerer's apprentice" in sci-fi. In my screenplay only the giant atom smasher could kill it, but destroying itself in the process. The German footage fit that idea. It was the first time that genetic engineering was mentioned in a motion picture, a science that was still publicly unknown in 1954.

Tors produced, which means that he found the production money, a miserly $150,000 supplied by the Heller Company of New York, an investment bank that liked to speculate in new ventures. We owned that giant set to make the production look expensive. Richard Carlson played the lead. I directed the film in eleven days. Since the film was devoid of sex, it did not catch on, despite that the title *A-Men* was changed to the schlock title *Magnetic Monster,* to lure the horror aficionados. *Time* magazine's science editor, writing a long column about that picture, saw in it a frightening scientific future, with the potential for destroying humankind: a limitless power that might create Utopia or, if not controlled, could make God appear on Earth, with a bunch of keys, announcing, "Gentlemen, closing time!"

Being very short of money, we created special effects, sounds of a squeaking door, mixed with the whine of a compressor, human and animal screams, and other unrelated sounds. We fused them into one sound that conveyed an unearthly effect. I matched the clothes of our actors with those of the Germans in the stock shot. The match was perfect. I photographed the computer, which filled a huge air-conditioned hall at UCLA. Thousands of vacuum tubes in separate chassis were mysteriously connected by scores of students to create electronic circuits. Transistors had not yet been invented. The professor who was supposed to teach them whispered to me, "I wish I knew what they are doing."

Today the multitude of vacuum tubes has been miniaturized into electronic chips. Science, instead of expanding in size, tries to find solutions in the opposite direction, making its gadgets so small that they now can only be created with the help of microscopes.

I also wrote for Ivan *Riders to the Stars*, a sci-fi film, which Dick Carlson directed. Then our company dissolved.

Looking back at that time, I'm glad that none of my efforts to create my own TV series materialized. A success, however financially rewarding, would have forced me into a line of work that would have taken over my life. Only writers with a sense of the value of money can become wealthy. That objective was not in my genes, and even if I had tried, I certainly would have failed.

Tors became rich. He married Constance Dowling, the blonde younger of the two Dowling sisters, starlets, who were an integral part of Hollywood film society. Blonde Connie's dark-haired sister Doris had magnetic appeal for men, who sensed that they would never be bored by and with her.

Connie, a quiet, submissive girl, was anxious to get married, possibly to escape the diet that she had to follow to keep her as ultra-thin as the fashion demanded. She was always hungry but did not dare to break her dietary rules, until she got married.

Her sister Doris was wooed by the writer-director Billy Wilder, who, like most men I knew, was very much attracted by her. He even gave her a small part in one of his motion pictures, but she never was outstanding as an actress. Doris married Artie Shaw, a bald-headed, highly intelligent and intense clarinet player, who had his own orchestra. Artie Shaw's band was for years one of America's top musical ensembles. I understand that he changed professions and worked in real estate. Hearing loss ended his career as a musician.

I met Artie thirty years later. He had been married more than half a dozen times. He told in an interview on TV that he took a new wife whenever he became bored with his present one. He sported an Emile Zola goatee and lots of hair. I liked him better when he was bald.

Connie married Ivan Tors, whom she obviously did not love, and gave birth to a son. Not strong enough to stand up against Ivan's macho domination, she died, still slim, on an overdose of drugs and alcohol.

When I examine the private lives of people, every one of them unfolds like the contrived plot of a soap opera, surpassing the imagination of any professional scribe. Could I have invented Ivan's life story, from his birth in a small Hungarian hamlet to his success in America, where, to honor him, even a street in Miami has been named after him, since he created many jobs and a motion picture studio in that city? Where his longhaired son, with whom Ivan did not get along, with the help of his "hippy" friends saved the animals of the compound Africa USA (of which Tors was a co-owner) from a devastating brush fire in the north of Los Angeles? It united father and son and made them tolerant toward each other.

Ivan emigrated to Kenya in East Africa. After successful years as a TV film producer, he died of a heart attack, far away from any medical help, in the Grand Chaco of the Amazon jungle.

There is no sense or limit to life's quirks of fate.

Sexual aberrations take many forms, according to Baron Richard von Krafft-Ebings, the German neurologist who shocked the Western world with his clinical description of "psychopathic sexualis."

Does the urge to write also have a connotation of sex? Compulsive writing is an addiction impossible to get rid of. It certainly affected my libido as though all energy had been converted into words. When I finished the novel *For Kings Only,* about Offenbach's leading lady, Hortense Schneider, who slept only with kings and emperors, I started the following day on the *Witches of Paris,* which the German publisher Bertelsmann printed. Not sitting at my word machine every day made me feel like rambling through life, useless and guilty. That's why I have hundreds of cardboard boxes with stories, screenplays, plays, ideas, and a full-length unpublished novel, *Despair in Paradise,* about my shocked impression of welfare in Sweden. When I wrote and directed thirteen TV shows with Lon Chaney Jr. in 1960 in Stockholm, the impact of that welfare state on my American mind was overwhelming and disturbing. Now, thirty years later, the United States isn't much different in its social structure from the Sweden of 1960.

It was always my contention that Sweden leads the way in the social development of the Western world. America, for whom the word *socialism* is anathema, was horrified by the socialistic Swedish state. But kicking and screaming, years later, it follows the same pattern.

Several publishing houses in the States were interested in *Despair in Paradise*. But all had it checked by Americanized Swedes, who hated my interpretation of their country. Who in 1960 America would ever have anticipated government stores on Main Street, where white-clothed "nurses" inform everybody, even teenagers, of controlled parenthood and sell birth control paraphernalia? The unwanted pregnancy rate in Nordic countries is less than 4 percent, and prostitution hardly exists. Taxes are immensely high, but every citizen's health and a basic income are guaranteed by law.

Despair in Paradise might remain in its cardboard box for many more years, joining the works of many authors who left unpublished books behind.

Directing adds life to the hermit existence of the writer. I wrote screenplays on speculation. Should I sell one, I could ask the company to let me direct it. Or was that wish a product of sibling rivalry, to show my brother Robert that I also knew where the camera should be placed on the set? My agent Lester Salkow sold my screenplay *The Face in the Water* to Realart Film Production, a company so stingy that before they spent a nickel, they raised the bull on that coin from a calf. I broke even on this deal, since I received two thousand dollars for the screenplay and direction and paid two thousand dollars to the Directors Guild. Without having joined that club, I was not permitted to direct. Robert and Babs, his wife, were shocked when they learned that I wanted to become a director. They rushed to my house very upset, Robert green in the face, as he tried to talk me out of such a dangerous adventure. What if I had a big success? That would cut into his glory as one of the top directors of Hollywood.

I soon found out that directing motion pictures wasn't the ultimate profession I was looking for. Good direction has its roots in the screenplay, and only in the screenplay. Without a good screenplay the director and the actors are lost. The director often calls himself "auteur" to harvest all the glamour of success. But during a long writers' strike the auteur had no job. A writer has to conceive a story and screenplay before the director and actor can "improve" on it and thus claim it as their own creation.

That first attempt to direct happened two years before my second director's debut, *The Magnetic Monster,* became a "classic" for sci-fi aficionados.

Realart, to prove its artistic sense, put a new title on *The Face in the Water*. Jack Broder, the boss, released it as *The Bride of the*

Gorilla. I shot this full-length picture in seven days, a shorter time than in which a TV sit-com is produced today.

The story even had a philosophical idea: a farm on an island in the Pacific. An older man (Paul Cavanaugh) is married to a young woman (Barbara Peyton). She has an affair with the foreman (Raymond Burr). Cavanaugh is bitten by a poisonous snake in Burr's presence. Burr does not call for help and lets the older man die to get the farm and his paramour. But his conscience distorts his mind. Whenever he looks into a mirror, he sees himself in the shape of an animal, since an animal can kill without a feeling of guilt. The policeman of the island (Lon Chaney Jr.) suspects Burr of murder.

When Burr hides in the jungle, envisioning himself a guiltless beast, he is shot by Lon. As he dies, Burr sees his face in a pool of water reverting back to a human being.

There is a difference between writing a scene or standing behind a camera and visualizing that scene and giving it life. In the first minutes of shooting I was in a catatonic state, but the crew and the actors, sensing my mental coma, came to my rescue. I saw Barbara walking through the jungle; the camera moved on its track; the actors spoke their lines. I regained my ability to move and even recovered my voice. The experienced crew guided me through the first hours of production. I was not told that Jack Broder, who had watched me, wanted to replace me, but the actors and crew threatened to walk out. The next day I already felt like an old-timer.

I quickly found out that the art of directing is based 80 percent on public relations, to make the actors believe in the importance of their job, and 20 percent on technique. The actor Tom Conway was contracted for one shooting day. I felt he was only interested in collecting his thousand-dollar salary and then going fishing.

I humbly told him, "Tom, thank you for accepting that very small part. But your scene is the pivot of that film. I depend on your skill as an actor, or I'll have no picture." That plea touched his actor's ego. "My lines should sound like cynical jokes," he said, relishing my accolade. "That will make the public dislike me and feel sorry for poor Barbara." I was safe with Lon and Ray, who disliked each other. Whenever they had a scene together, I watched their antagonism for each other penetrate their acting. Sparks of hatred flew from their eyes. No director could have coaxed more convincing scenes from any actor.

Barbara, a childlike soft blonde, played herself, a sex-crazed kitten, bored with her aging husband and drawn to the younger man.

Hollywood destroyed her, since she did not have the sophistication and knowledge to resist the sexual cruelties of the executives, who knew how to take advantage of a pretty female. She could have become a Hollywood star but had nobody to guide her, like Marilyn Monroe, who was coached by a motherly Mrs. Lee Strasberg.

Gisella Werbisek-Piffl, a famous comedienne, the "Marie Dressler" of Vienna, was an old woman, with a face so lined and homely that it crossed the borderline of ugliness and made her fascinating to watch. She also had a morbid wit. A Jewish refugee in Hollywood, she said she never would be able to understand America, "where the Jews are gangsters and the Goyim are bankers." She also complained that in Austria she was called Gisella, in Berlin Gisela, but her name in America was pronounced "Scheissele," "Little Shit" in German. She was married to Franz Piffl, whose brother was the archbishop of Salzburg. Piffl, on account of his enormous girth and giant body, was in constant demand as an extra in pictures, while Gisella got only one single job, the native witch in my film. In Vienna where she had been rich and famous, she had kept Piffl in Sacher tart and cream. When she was in Hollywood, he had to make her breakfast and serve it to her in bed before he left for the studio.

To American wags, her name sounded hilarious, and she received telephone calls from strangers. The callers pretended having reached the wrong "Gisella Werbisek-Piffl."

There also was a tall, handsome black, who played a native policeman and had half a dozen lines to speak. He was the former top football player Woody Strode. Frightened to have to act and stiff like a wooden Indian, he gained confidence by rehearsing his lines with me so often that I dreamt of them. A natural talent, he quickly caught on to his new profession as an actor. For many years he became a motion picture star, playing in *Spartacus, The Professionals,* and other important pictures.

My little seven-day shooting picture was shown for many years on TV. Every time *The Bride of the Gorilla* was played, Gisella sat in front of the TV set, admiring herself.

6

The War and Hollywood

My five-year quota number waiting period was over. I was again a certified citizen. This time an American, with the right to bear arms that shall not be infringed upon—Amendment II of the Constitution, which led to innumerable deaths of civilians, since there were no British Redcoats or Indians to be shot at, only Americans, family members, strangers to kill, to rob, to blow someone away in a fit of jealousy or a furor of rage. America loses more people by firearms in a year than in the ten years of war in Vietnam. If that killing were a declared war against a foreign country, the sanity of the American public would have stopped it long ago. But in the ongoing slaughter on highways we all are guilty participants.

I had become a citizen of the most stable country on the globe. I owned no gun, I had no debt, and I obeyed the laws of the Constitution, which had lasted unchanged for more than two hundred years. This country is going through a constant evolution, importing thousand-year-old foreign cultures, keeping the United States in a vibrant rejuvenation. Countries like Spain, which in 1492 had thrown out and eliminated its Moorish and Jewish elite, is still, five hundred years later, a culturally barren wasteland. So is Germany and its European satellites, which have not recovered from the losses with its hysterical penchant for National Socialism.

When I received my certificate that made me a member of this country, America was at war with Germany, Italy, and Japan, countries far removed from my new life. I had a permanent new fatherland.

In a champagne-soaked ceremony, I burned my brown German passport, which also carried an eagle, but holding a swastika, and was rubber-stamped "Jew." The burning paper exuded to me a delicious smell of destruction, a past that I would like to eliminate from my memory. I was reborn to shape and form my life without anybody's prejudice or discrimination. "If you are lucky," Albert Einstein had stated, "you are forced to emigrate. Then you can start your life again." He did. So did I and my wife.

Boris Karloff, a frequent guest in our house in the hills, visiting us after shooting my screenplay *The Climax,* liked to relax in the evening by telling my son Geoffrey English fairy tales, explaining their political content of the time. A kind and soft-spoken man, with dark skin like an Indian, he looked in life the antithesis of the Frankenstein monster. He was present when the telephone call came.

It came from a lawyer's office at Seventh and Spring Street in Los Angeles. I was asked to come to the office "at my convenience." A lieutenant opened the door. That "lawyer's office" was the OSS, the Office of Strategic Services, which, run by "Wild Bill" Donovan, later became the CIA, the Central Intelligence Agency.

High-ranking officers with "fruit salad" (many medals on their chest) asked me to consider joining the OSS. They needed German-speaking citizens as writers, publicists, and translators. They didn't tell me that they also were looking for people who spoke fluent German to be dropped behind the German lines.

I guessed that my friends, Joe Kaplan, Mac Jones, Willy Wyler, and others whom I had induced to join Naval Intelligence, had recommended me to the OSS. Since I had received American citizenship, my friends' contention was that I also had to join the war against Hitler.

Since I was a family man and over forty, I was not "drafted" but "invited" by the army. There always exists a play of words that makes a situation legal. To match my Hollywood salary, which was high by army standards, I was offered a lieutenant colonel's pay.

My producer, George Waggner, did not appreciate my joining the army. He believed that I was much more important turning out pictures for entertaining the soldiers.

I certainly had a reason and even a cause to join the fight against the Nazis. I knew the German mentality better than the American brass who ran the OSS did. I had a uniform smartly tailored and packed a suitcase with things that, as it turned out, were not essential since the army had its own idea of what a soldier should possess.

Henrietta, much more clear-minded than I, was in despair but did not show it, since she was fully aware of the danger to my life. But it is a curious fact that going to war, one never believes in one's own death. Being killed only happens to others. Henrietta at once registered at UCLA to continue her study as an architect, anticipating that she would have to earn her own living for herself and our son. Though she never mentioned it, she expected not to see me anymore. But I only thought of that macho adventure of becoming a spy. It is essential to divorce oneself mentally from every connection with the family and start soldiering, mentally detached from the duties of a family man. In my case it was my opportunity to fight a nation that had uprooted me, murdered my relatives, and wanted to exterminate me, since I was an "Untermensch," with the poisonous Jewish blood in my veins.

To be in the army is a vacation from oneself. Brain functions take a holiday; time loses its meaning. Personal initiative vanishes, since the hours of days and nights are rigidly controlled by a machine of which the human being is only an expendable cog. If somebody needs to live in Nirvana, let him serve in the armed forces, since he delivers not only his body but also every ounce of personal initiative. He might be sent to die, but who would think of that, except when being confronted by an equally dehumanized force, the enemy, who also has stopped thinking and only carries out its programming.

That's perhaps why the Jews, not having to kill in battles for two thousand years, had time to develop their special individuality.

I left my family without any deep emotion. A bus took me and a bunch of unknown men, much younger than I, to the El Toro Marine Base near San Diego. We were of different nationalities: Chinese, Russian, Hispanics, and Europeans. I rarely heard English spoken. We lived in barracks and were issued identical fatigues. It was a new experience to shed my privacy and live together with a group of men. My private personality was taken away from me, and I was ordered not to reveal my identity and only reply to the name "Mac." A group of army officers, trained in psychology, tested us for special talents. Many of us obviously were professionals, university professors, scientists, experts in a field of which we might know more than the instructors.

The training was a game, guessing who was who and what his profession might be. We certainly were "elite," picked for special faculties. Young and older people were in our outfit. A vague indication was the color of their shoes. Brown ones might belong to the army, black ones to the navy. The training was conducted in a beach club in San Clemente, where Richard Nixon later lived. He also might have been a member of that beach club but under different circumstances.

The beach club sported a high tower. I was given a flashlight and sent up to a dark upstairs room, furnished like a hotel room. Returning exactly after four and one-half minutes, the newly created spy had to fill out a lengthy form, answering detailed questions about the person who had occupied that room. A he or a she? A he. The questionnaire asked for the man's occupation, his age, his social affiliations, personality, and family background. A bottle of Finch's hair dye told me that he might be past middle age, a man trying to appear younger. There was a snapshot of a baby marked "1922." If that was a picture of his son, the son would now be twenty. There was a photo of a man beside a woman, of about his age. The photo of the same woman, but older. Was he a widower? The occupant might be close to fifty. His clothes lying on the bed came from a company called Phelps Terkel, a medium-priced store where, by chance, I had shopped. He might be a commercial traveler since a suitcase had samples of expensive ties and an order book. I could only take a glance at the notebook in which he had written his expenses. Four and one-half minutes is a short time to examine a life. I was never told whether my findings were right.

There was a swimming pool. We were told to dive quickly and to swim underwater its full length—that is, if people could swim. The surface was doused with gasoline and set on fire. The trick was to come up for air, splash the water, and dive under quickly before the hairs were singed. I am bald, which helped. I guessed that it was a training to stay alive in case a ship was torpedoed and the ocean was covered with burning oil.

A group of officers sitting behind a table questioned me in rapid succession. They tried to rattle me. I was not permitted to give my real name. I had to invent the name of my father, and the questions were shot at me, not giving me time to think. I chose the data of a friend of mine whom I knew well and whose birthday and address were in my mind. I don't think I did too well in that third-degree inquiry because it was suddenly cut short.

As a group, young and old nameless men were led down a path into a wooded area, where we were introduced to plastic explosives. I had never heard of plastic explosives. I thought explosives looked like sticks of dynamite and were not of a pliable, shapeless material. As we walked down a narrow path, small trip mines detonated on either side of us. After the first harmless blasts, the attitude of the group changed into that of wary animals. They watched every step, trying to detect the thin wire that released the explosion.

Now that we had learned to look out for land mines, we were sent to the ocean to arm an innocent little bridge to be blown up. We went through written tests of physics in which I did well, remembering my school days. For two minutes we studied a sheet with different squares, crosses, and irregular shapes and were asked to draw those forms from memory. What for? To recognize the shape of a foreign gun or enemy plane?

Then we were trained to be murderers. The former head of the British police of Hong Kong, Major Fairburn, an Englishman, introduced us to Asian martial art, demonstrating how to scrape the chin of an attacker who held you from behind and to smash his toes with your boots, how to kill a man with any object, even a wooden pencil or a pen, by jabbing it in the soft underside of the chin. Holding a matchbox in the fist would increase the power of a blow. It wasn't a training I relished. I had never even in my horror pictures shown a killing. I abhor violent death, the link of man to a predatory animal.

Highly civilized citizens, who, like me, had never hit anybody in anger, changed into executioners or learned how to rapidly read a document upside down, how to open a safe, how to be inhuman.

When we were dismissed, I was aware that it took two thousand years to spread the kindness of the Gospel and two minutes to revert any man back into a caveman.

I must have passed the OSS examinations satisfactorily since I was accepted as an active spy. My friend Franz Spencer (Franz Schultz) didn't, though I had vouched for him to get him tested by the OSS. Franz changed his name to Spencer to show his dislike for his German name, "Schultz." That change didn't please the judge who swore him in as an American citizen since the name of the judge was "Kaufmann." Franz had motion picture successes in Berlin before his emigration, but he couldn't adjust himself to the American teamwork, which is the nation's strength. He was one of those "diasporatos" who believed themselves to be of a higher level of intelligence than the country that gave them shelter. Besides, he couldn't get a job in Hollywood, though he and I sold at the outbreak of the war a story, "*Pacific Blackout,*" to Paramount. It became a profitable motion picture since it was released shortly after the Japanese attack on Pearl Harbor. I never saw it.

Franz also was sexually and mentally very volatile, had troubles with women, always was afraid he would not be able to perform sexually. He told me that should he have an erection while he took a woman home, he let the woman touch his genitals right away in case of a failure later on. His sexual fears made him unpredictable. He must have hated women since he sometimes attacked them physically. He appeared with a German woman friend, Leda, three times at a Justice of the Peace to get married, but both changed their mind three times at the judge's office.

In Berlin he had an affair with one of Erich Maria Remarque's wives. Remarque was married a few times; the last one, outliving him, was Paulette Goddard (Marion Levy), who also had a few marriages behind her. She had been as a very young girl the leading lady in Charlie Chaplin's *Modern Times*. She married Chaplin, a pedophile, who divorced her when she grew up and he married Oona, Eugene O'Neill's underaged daughter. Paulette married the actor Burgess Meredith and finally Erich Maria Remarque. Since she was Jewish, that might be why Remarque never returned to Nazi Germany.

When Remarque found out about Franz's affair with his then-wife, he hired two thugs and broke into Franz's apartment. The two ruffians were holding Franz while Remarque beat the helpless man. Remarque's cowardice to hire two ruffians lowered my admiration for the "front soldier" who didn't have the courage to carry out his own "macho" vindictiveness. Franz owned a vicious-looking English bull terror that, with a grin, watched the ordeal of his master without coming to his help.

Franz had started with me at the El Toro Marine training camp but disappeared shortly afterward. He didn't seem to have the necessary psychological balance the OSS demanded. The OSS found out that he would crack under pressure.

After the war, Franz retreated to the Canary Islands, where he could live on the "reparations" of the German government and American Social Security. He died of angina pectoris, hating all of his former friends whom he accused of being responsible for his botched-up life. He might have been happy being unhappy.

Our power to help people is very limited. I found out that the only way to help is to loan people money without ever asking for it back. Moses Maimonides wrote about the five stages of charity in the thirteenth century. It is dangerous to find a job for people out of work, since we take the chance of being blamed should they fail. Though I had not seen Franz for seven years before he died, he still thought of me as his enemy, since I had been successful and he had not. There is a saying in German: "We are impossible and you are responsible for it." Some people are failures because they want to fail, due to a masochism deeply ingrained in their character.

Franz, having died unmarried, left no trace. Not even his burial place is known.

During my time in the army, Hollywood had completely vanished from my life. I had entered a world with different laws, the military establishment, which lacked the conception of emotion. A number becomes the substitute for a person's personality. I had become expendable, a soulless part of a killing machine, a dog-tag number, trained to carry preconceived orders. We at the OSS were "kamakazis."

Called to the head office at the El Toro camp, I faced two colonels and one general sitting behind a long table. The way I had been trained, I automatically registered every exit in case I had to leave in a hurry. I was conditioned to be suspicious of everybody, even my uniformed superiors. They might be the enemy in disguise. Was that call a test or a trap?

Two "chicken colonels" and a two-star general faced me from behind a large table. I was "invited" to proceed immediately to Washington, D.C. Soldiers don't travel; they proceed. I was to report to room 2002 of the "Q" (Quonset) building in Washington. I also had to pay for my uniform, since I officially remained a private citizen. I was not permitted to wear my uniform in the United States, only abroad. I had entered a world where murder was a virtue, killing expected, and breaking laws condoned, even rewarded.

Morality supposedly rules human society, but not the military.

I received vouchers good for flights to Washington and was told that as a member of the OSS, I was not recognized by the army as belonging to the fighting force. In case of my decease, as death was called, my widow would not be entitled to any compensation. Since I had volunteered, I had become a shadowy nonentity. The OSS would not protect or recognize me, should I fall into the hands of the enemy.

After that routine information, the three men in uniform shook my hand, possibly to show their sympathy with my fate, which they must have known. Statistically, the odds of staying alive as a member of the OSS were severely limited.

The airplane flying me to Washington was a DC 3, the most reliable passenger plane ever built. It was a two-propeller-driven, small, noisy workhorse and carried less than fifty passengers. It had to land half a dozen times for refueling before it reached its destination.

A friend of mine, Frank Arnold, the only Jewish squadron leader in the army's air corps, wrote a book thirty years after the war, about his war experiences, which started with the following foreword: "Nose" (his anti-Semitic nickname given to him by his group), "should you ever mention any of us in your book, you'll face the biggest libel suit ever. For a Jewish boy we treated you like an American."

Ethnic cleansing on this planet will continue until only the rabble is left and the human elite has been completely eliminated. Then the world will become a cultural wasteland.

The vouchers I had been given at El Toro stated that I had to vacate my seat on the plane to anyone with a higher priority.

During the war, the air corps had assigned my friend Captain Frank Arnold to find out why female pilots had many more accidents than male pilots. It certainly was not the lack of their skill to ferry planes east from the West Coast factories. Frank's conclusion was that the male-ferried planes had urinals strapped to the pilot's thighs, while the female-ferried planes had to land more often to relieve the women of their necessity. More landings, more possibility of crack-ups. Frank constructed a gadget that eliminated the bodily difference. The accidents dropped to normal, thus helping to shorten the war.

Sometimes intricate questions have simple answers.

Our DC 3 came down in Albuquerque, New Mexico, at midnight. I saw a star-studded sky with such clarity that it conveyed to me the conception of eternity. I and a female passenger had to leave the plane to vacate our seats to military personnel with a higher priority. I had to wait for a seat on the next plane to fly east. A young woman, who could not be older than eighteen, was sitting next to me on a cast-iron bench. She wore no stockings on her thin straight legs. Her frail hands held a baby. "My husband is a pilot, he is taking the plane to Nashville, and he wants to see the baby every night. He wants to kiss the baby," she volunteered.

In a wooden hut furnished with a few tables, an old man behind a counter sold coffee and Danish pastry. I didn't know how long I had to wait for the next plane. The young woman who also had been bounced from the DC 3 also waited. She was tall and slim, a replica of the woman I had met on the *President Harding*. It was as if that type of female was destined to cross my path. She carried a slightly worn but elegant flight bag. I, the newly trained spy, concluded that she was used to frequent air travel. I smiled at her, but she did not seem to be aware that I was present.

There was a pay telephone on the wall. I dialed Washington, the number I was instructed to contact three times a day.

"I am held up in Albuquerque," I said. "Field operator seventy-six."

"Roger, seventy-six," the impersonal voice repeated my code number, terminating the call. I sat away from the dark-haired woman. When I heard the sound of a plane approaching, I went outside. The dark-haired one gripped her flight bag. I let her pass.

The silvery DC 3 descended quickly from seemingly nowhere and taxied closer. A stubby gasoline tanker cut a narrow curve toward it. Then the pilot left the cockpit to kiss his baby.

A stewardess came up to me to tell me that there was a seat for me on the plane. "Your priority has been changed to 1-A," she said. "We got a radio message from Washington." She looked at me inquisitively and then at the raven-haired girl, trying to figure our connection.

"What about me?" asked the disacquaintance.

"Sorry, you will have to wait for the next plane. This gentleman has a high government priority."

I picked up my bag to follow the stewardess. Suddenly that night sprite came to life.

"I have to be in New York in the morning," she said. "Tell that stewardess that you will give me your seat. That war will surely go on without you arriving a few hours earlier." I didn't know how she had guessed my military connection.

"I'm sure you're right," I said, "but I cannot change my orders."

"Well, if you show up a few hours later, would they execute you for that?" She tugged my sleeve and smiled at me. Her eyes had a witchlike sharpness.

"They might do that. I wouldn't take a chance with a firing squad," I said, trying to humor her. I had a desperate feeling that time was gliding by. I felt like a man standing in rushing water. It was not the first time that I had to fight that impatience, which sometimes even drove me out of theaters in the middle of a performance. It is a kind of phobia of which I don't know the name but that became stronger as I got older.

"My name is Susan," she said and smiled at me. She had herself well trained to use her looks as a weapon. She repeated her first name again like an intimate invitation: "Susan."

The plane's motor started up. I saw the stewardess in the open door of the plane, looking in my direction.

"I won't forget," I said, "Susan."

When I boarded the plane, she stood slender and streamlined, as if she were cut out of a travel poster. Then the plane took off noisily.

Washington was rainy and humid like a jungle. It seemed to be occupied by a hostile army. There were uniforms everywhere. Now they owned America.

I took a taxi to the Q building, which seemingly was made of cardboard and leftover tin to emphasize its temporary existence. It had been put up during World War I and was still "temporarily" used by the indestructible bureaucracy, which never returns anything lent to them. I looked for room 2002 but couldn't find it. The numbers were jumbled—2013 followed 2340, and other numbers of illogical continuity were written on opposite doors, to make it difficult, I guess, for anybody with evil intent to search for an occupant. Every fifty feet a door parted the corridor. The handles on every one were of a different kind, push button, grips that went up, or had to be pressed down, knobs that had to be turned. I guess if somebody tried to leave the building in a hurry he was delayed by the different mechanisms. Prisons used the same contraptions to delay fugitives.

A few times I asked for direction, and finally I found the right room. A black female secretary announced me to a colonel. I had never seen a black secretary, nor did the Hollywood studios in the forties hire any blacks except as janitors. We once had at Universal a black screenwriter, but he refused to join our writers' table and never hid his resentment toward "honkies." He, an intelligent writer, deliberately perpetuated the racial bias. That picture hasn't changed, and the black students at universities stick together. Their attitude has nothing to do with their mental capacities. Black university presidents exist, men of outstanding abilities. But a black mixing with whites would be called an "Uncle Tom." Even during wartime, although the government in Washington employed many black clerical workers in high positions, racial bias prevailed.

A colonel with a florid face that telegraphed a coming stroke was intrigued by my Hollywood background. He had my files in front of him and also two copies of *Donovan's Brain*. The OSS obviously was dissecting my life and keeping track of my activities.

"I was informed that this book of yours just came out," the colonel said. He didn't say who informed him. "The title intrigued me, and I ordered half a dozen for our files, because I thought you had written about our boss, General 'Wild Bill' Donovan."

The War and Hollywood

I picked up a copy of my book. I hadn't seen it before, though it might be waiting for me at home. I liked the cover, which was done in good taste. "Sign this copy. I'll send it to the general. Write in, 'For William Donovan from Field Operator 76.' He'll get a kick out of that joke. The OSS is independent. No bureaucracy, no interference from Congress, no senators to screw up things."

I signed one book. The colonel put it in a drawer of his desk. "Since you are known as Mac, don't ever respond if someone calls you by your real name, and keep nothing, not even your initials, on yourself." He watched me, a messenger from the enchanting world of Hollywood, with envy. "I've never been to a film studio. Is it true that there are dozens of pretty starlets who like to be banged?"

"Absolutely," I said. "Everything you hear about Hollywood is true."

"That's a life worth living," he said with envy.

"Next time you are in California I'll gladly take you around. But what happens in Hollywood also happens in department stores and wherever boy meets girl."

"And here in the Q building," he laughed. "Have you ever banged a black girl? They really fly. Quite an experience. I don't get that kind from my wife. She doesn't go to bed with me without first getting that absolution from her priest. You are married. Don't let that bother you. It's no more than a scratch."

I didn't answer, and he seemed to be aware of my discomfort.

"Let me call Dr. Scrivener. He runs your department. Now due to your salary of a thousand a month . . ."

"A week," I said, which shocked him. He was a prisoner in a tin foxhole. His future was predictable, and he was bored. "A thousand a week! That's more than a general's salary. Well, in that case we will have to upgrade your status. You will stay at the Old Congressional Club in Maryland. Old-fashioned, but private room, bathroom, swimming pool, an orderly to make your bed and clean up. The works. Dr. Scrivener will take over from here. Report to him."

A jeep took me to the Old Congressional Club, a nineteenth-century building amid a well-manicured garden. I saw uniformed soldiers tending it. They might have been former gardeners, drafted for the sole purpose of keeping the plants of the club alive. Was that the war I had volunteered for?

The room assigned to me was looking out on the swimming pool. It wasn't on fire like that one in San Clemente. "If you need something, sir," the soldier who had taken me to the room said, "ring the bell. Please change into fatigues. We don't use civilian clothes here."

My gear that I had taken to the plane was already lying in the room. My still-unworn uniform, civilian clothes, and the same fatigues I had worn at El Toro were hanging in the built-in closet. I had just changed into my old fatigues, which smelled of disinfectant, when the telephone rang. The OSS didn't seem to waste time. After the long flight I didn't even have time to take a shower. The operator told me to report to room 23.

Room 23 was a large, formerly private room, now changed into an office.

A tall, thin Yankee introduced himself as William Scrivener. He didn't use a cover name, as I had to. Scrivener was a courteous, erudite man of my age. He politely got out of his chair from behind the desk to shake my hand.

"I was an anthropologist at Yale," he said, emphasizing that he treated me as an equal. "I also was 'invited' and accepted the invitation. The OSS might be interesting to you. I read your file. You have experience in journalism, and your German is perfect. We are issuing a newspaper in German, and you will contribute to edit it."

I felt at home. I didn't have to carry a gun, shoot Germans, burn down houses, blow up bridges. Writing was a job I knew.

He handed me a small newspaper. *Die Freiheit,* "Freedom," was its masthead.

"We bring it out twice a month. It is dropped over Germany, especially over German front lines, by plane. We are spreading rumors. It is a part of psychological warfare. I expect interesting contributions from you. The Germans do the same. They use foreign newspapers," Scrivener said, taking the Argentine newspaper *La Prenza* from his desk drawer. "Do you read Spanish?"

"Italian, French, German, but I can make out Spanish," I said.

"The Germans placed this joke in *La Prenza*. That joke makes the rounds even among the British army. A crude joke, but cutting. A plane is crossing the ocean," he said as he folded the newspaper and put it back on the desk, "with an Englishman, a Frenchman, a Russian, a Canadian, and an American as passengers. Overloaded, it throws everything movable out in order to keep the plane in the air. Finally, occupants have to be sacrificed. The Russian jumps out silently. Then the Frenchman, shouting, 'Vive la France!' followed by the Canadian, who yells, 'Long live the king!' The Englishman and the American are left. The Englishman kicks the American out and laughs, 'There will always be an England!'"

"Stupid!" I remarked.

"Maybe so," Scrivener said. "You will come across more of them. The Germans try to put a wedge between us and the British. I found that same joke all over the world, in Swedish, English, and Italian, wherever the Germans have access to newspapers. A joke can never be primitive enough, or people will forget to tell it around. It will be your job to construct some. Also to write small, amusing, nonpolitical stories. That paper should be German-folksy. The *Freiheit* shouldn't read like propaganda. We don't tell about German atrocities or stories of brutalities; we don't tell that Coventry and London were bombed and that we retaliate by burning Germany down."

I found an opening to show off my intelligence and to impress the man from Yale. "Then print in the *Freiheit* that Hitler is going to speak on the fourth of October to the German nation from the 'Eagle Nest' in Berchtesgaden," I said.

"Why?" Scrivener asked, and his face changed sharply, wiping out his polite jovial expression.

"The whole world will wait for that speech. What is he going to say? Surrender? A farewell to his German subjects? Let the world guess. Hitler doesn't know that he is supposed to speak. Since he doesn't, the rumor is created that he might be dead. Maybe the Reichswehr took over. Hitler will be put on the defensive. He will have to deny that rumor, or the people will believe that the Reichswehr hides that fact to continue the war. That will do more damage than a silly joke."

Scrivener sat quietly. He avoided looking at me.

"I see that you know something about psychological warfare. Bring up your idea in our next meeting. Did you think of this before you came to Washington?"

"Just routine," I said. "In the film business you have to throw out interesting ideas, especially when you meet a new producer who doesn't know you. You have to think on your feet. That's how you get a job."

"Think of more," Scrivener said and laughed.

Even today, more than half a century later, there is a discussion in some books of war history why Hitler didn't speak on October 4, 1944, a fact that might have accelerated the assassination attempt. Later on, in the *Freiheit* I anticipated his way of death, but he double-crossed me and shot himself in his bunker in Berlin.

Scrivener told me that the more intelligent an agent is, the less he is able to keep a secret. He belonged to the latter part. He told me that General Donovan, the head of the OSS, and General Wilhelm

Canaris, the chief of the German Secret Police, had been in contact during the war. Donovan informed Canaris that Hitler's life was in danger by a group of German generals and industrialists, who, knowing that the war was lost, wanted to get rid of the Fuehrer. That group had been in touch with the British Secret Service, notifying them of their plan, trying to work out an interim government, should Germany surrender. Donovan delivered the names of that group of assassins to Canaris before they could strike. The Germans arrested the generals, among them Erich Rommel, who was permitted by Hitler's fiat to commit suicide and received a state funeral. The rest they hanged using piano wires, pulling them up and down to increase their agony. Churchill and Roosevelt didn't want Hitler killed and to become a martyr. The two Allied leaders feared post-war German nationalism, like that after World War I. The Germans would believe they would have won the war if their "Papa" had not treacherously been murdered. The Nazis, on Hitler's orders, arrested Canaris, too. He was tortured to death in Auschwitz. Since the German generals who wanted to end the war were expendable to the OSS, what chance did I have, the lowly Field Operator 76?

It was like the old times when I worked in Berlin for the magazine the *UHU,* though now the room was filled with pipe-smoking men in fatigues, whom I only knew by their cover names, Frank, Joe, and Terry, though I recognized some of them from the El Toro times. The Hollywood director William Wyler dropped by in a major's uniform. He was a recognized soldier. We were not.

Wyler, who was born in Alsace-Lorraine and spoke German fluently, was not a refugee. He was the nephew of Carl Laemmle Sr., the head of Universal Pictures. Laemmle had made him a director, the only time I agreed with nepotism. Since then Willy had directed memorable motion pictures like *The Heiress* and *Wuthering Heights.* But he volunteered for the OSS and directed *Memphis Belle,* which describes the mission of an American bomber over Germany that now, more than fifty years later, is still one of the outstanding documentaries of the war. He risked his life for a photographic image.

Wyler was surprised to see me and wanted me to give up writing drivel for a publicity paper and join his outfit. He was looking for a writer of documentaries. But the army had other plans for me, which, when I was told about it, I didn't like.

I met the same faces every day. Some seemed to have followed me from Hollywood to Washington, to defeat the German army. There was Ernoe Kapralik, an overweight Hungarian, who skillfully had drawn actors' faces and assembled them in dioramas. Every one of his creations was a charming work of art. MGM Studios had him under contract. Why he volunteered and what he did for the war effort I didn't know. A young mathematician, Jimmy Stoner, whose greatest wish was to be sent overseas, was also in my group. He was assigned to me. He didn't speak German, but that was the way the army worked, assigning people to tasks for which others had the experience. I wrote "fillers" that had to be amusing and unaggressive among the camouflaged poisoned news of the *Freiheit*.

I wrote about my friend Frederick Hollander, the songwriter of *The Blue Angel*, for Marlene Dietrich, and other songs for her in American motion pictures, including *Desire* and *Destry Rides Again*. He also composed the music for *Guess Who's Coming to Dinner*, the first time that Hollywood showed a love affair between a black man and a white woman, a daring film that shook America, especially Hollywood, to its foundations.

I thought the German readers of our paper would remember Friedl's name and wonder why he worked for the Americans, since they supposedly knew nothing about the government's systematic killings of Jews.

Frederick had lived not far from us in the Hollywood hills. He had bought a small ranch so as not to bother his neighbors with his constant piano playing. One of his neighbors had bought a rooster for his hens. It was fashionable then to grow vegetables and raise chickens to help the war effort. The rooster had come from the east and didn't know about Pacific Standard Time. He lived mentally in the eastern zone and started to crow every morning at 2 A.M., which would be 5 A.M., Eastern Standard Time.

Frederick, a nervous sleeper, woke up every time that bird, which had a powerful voice, crowed two hours after midnight. Frederick's nightly rest was deeply disrupted. He went to the neighbors, asking them to kindly exchange the rooster for one who knew Standard Time. He would gladly supply them with a bird sexually even more vigorous than the eastern crooner. He suggested that they should serve the eastern one with mashed potatoes and gravy. The neighbors refused. Frederick, his nightly sleep in disarray, turned to the city for help. He was informed that the existing ordinance allowed people to keep chickens on their premises if the coop was at least one hundred yards away from their neighbor's dwelling, which was the case here.

In his despair, Frederick resorted to the sleeping pill Amytal. But the delayed aftereffect of that drug interfered with his productivity. He became very irritable, nervously waiting every night for the crowing to start. The quality of his work suffered and he contemplated moving away, until he had the idea of throwing the sleeping pills over the fence into his neighbor's garden, where the rooster gobbled them up. Friedl had his nightly sleep restored, since the bird appeared at 2 A.M., crowed very feebly and went back to his hens to continue his snooze. The hens laid fewer eggs.

That scheme worked well until Friedl received a visit from the Humane Society, accusing him of cruelty to animals. They threatened to take their case to court.

That crime would have made headlines in *Variety*, the influential Hollywood paper, and would have damaged severely Friedl's reputation with the studio people. Rape might quickly be forgotten but not any cruelty to a fowl.

Friedl sold his comfortable home at 7357 Woodrow Wilson Drive and moved to the ocean near Malibu, where studio people lived who bought their chickens cooked and did not bother to raise eggs.

Three hours a day I had to see training films to teach me how to become a spy. One of the films showed a man sitting on a park bench reading a book. It could not have been me since he wore a coat and tie. There were medieval German houses in the background, indicating enemy territory. A stranger sat down next to the man with the book, unfolding a newspaper. After a while he strolled away, casually leaving the newspaper behind. Did the paper contain messages in code? Suppose that man had already been watched by the Gestapo. They would have arrested both right away. Why not supply the second man with an unruly kid? Who would suspect a harassed father to be a spy?

I found those films rather primitive. Would the OSS let me write and direct a new one that conveyed the ideas better?

I had to look at film instructions on how to fold a parachute, to be assured that it would unfold when jumping from an airplane. Since I suffer from acrophobia, the fear of heights, this task didn't appeal to me.

I was shown in agonizingly slow motion how to disarm, fight, maim, kill, or torture people, injuring the weak spots in their bodies to paralyze them. To harden me to face death I had to look at battle documentaries, jungle fights, soldiers blown up fighting an invisible enemy.

I didn't know what the OSS had in mind or what I was being trained for, since I was even shown how to slip on a condom.

At night a group of us took walks to the border of Virginia and Maryland where one could buy cold beer in a wooden hut. Maryland was a dry state; Virginia was not. A score of soldiers walked about with factory girls who picked up a few dollars moonlighting as prostitutes. I never found out what the going rate was. A fierce-looking wiry paratrooper in uniform approached me with, "Your name is Siodmak." My cover blown, I didn't reply. "You arrived in America on the 28th of April 1937 on the *President Harding*." I looked at that muscular, physically well-trained man trying to remember his face and recalled a curious fact: a German refugee, Arnold Auerbach, a former German film producer, had traveled with us. A young man (he might have been this same paratrooper) had walked up to me on deck threatening to beat me up as soon as we arrived in New York. I didn't know what had made him angry until, a couple of days before we arrived, I found out that Auerbach had taunted this young man with the story that I was stalking his girlfriend. Confronting Auerbach, he found pleasure in seeing a fight between two young roosters like us.

A similar incident happened in Hollywood some years later. My brother Robert gave a party in his house for prominent Hollywood actors. I talked to a slim, young actress with an enchanting face, Joan Fontaine. She told me about deprecating remarks Robert had made about me. I was shocked, since it was not Robert's habit to talk meanly about me. He also was cross with me for having supposedly told her that he was to be fired on his last picture, but his agent, Johnny Hyde, had saved his job. Not one word was true. It was a game of hers to test people's reactions. She did the same trick to Billy Wilder and Charles Brackett. She separately told the two men, the most prominent writing team in Hollywood, that they had talked badly about each other. When I confronted the source, the young woman with the enchanting face confessed, amused, that she had invented those stories to test how quickly friends could become enemies. To make friends takes years; to part them, minutes.

I was confronted by a jealous paratrooper who wore a long knife in his high boot. It was a specially constructed murder weapon, given to OSS men being sent into combat. Scientifically, it takes only two pounds of pressure to penetrate a human body. I told the angry man about Auerbach's game on board the *President Harding*. He, obviously a well-educated man, accepted my story. He told me that he never forgot a face. While swimming in the Mediterranean at Casablanca, he had recognized a man whom he had met years previously on a flight from Paris to London.

Then the war struck home: I got a top-secret communication from Scrivener. The Germans had come out with a devastating new jet fighter. It had no propeller but could fly three times the speed of our fighter planes. If their remaining factories had produced that airplane in quantity, the war might have taken a different turn. But Hitler, a man of the infantry, did not trust or believe his air force general, Hermann Goering. He wanted his armies to win the war.

We knew the German air force read the British publication *The Pilot*. Copies were smuggled into Germany via Sweden, and eagerly read by the German Luftwaffe. The air was the last vestige of knighthood. There was no glamour fighting a war when one could kill the enemy from a hundred miles away and never see him. But there were still dogfights and duels in the air, fought with chivalry. My friend Frank Arnold, piloting a Mustang fighter, was shot down. Floating down helplessly in a parachute, he was passed by the German fighter plane and saw the pilot salute him, though he could have killed him. For the air force, this still was a "beautiful war," a reminder of a time when men prided themselves as swordsmen. Captured pilots were treated courteously in special prison camps. The same courtesy existed between high-ranking officers of the warring armies. A captured general was sure to have pleasant quarters assigned to him. One British general, caught by the Italians, lived in a medieval castle and was paid his British salary in lire. Captured German pilots had a special camp in England, as did Allied pilots in Germany. That's why we thought we could influence the German Luftwaffe.

Three more mathematicians appeared in our office, Bert, Bruce, and Will. They were middle-aged men and obviously experts in their fields. We constructed a complicated mathematical formula, proving that the torque of the German jets would at a certain point whirl the plane like a propeller. The pilot would never be able to extract himself from a plane that turned around its axis like a propeller. We hoped that the German pilots felt apprehensive when they were assigned to jet fighter planes, which could outfly and outgun any plane we could put in the air.

After the war, I found out that the Germans didn't have the capacity to build jets in quantity. Their constructions came too late, and our brilliant ideas as printed in *The Pilot* didn't seem to have fooled them.

War has no soul and, like nature, is devoid of any human emotion. The Allies wanted Hitler to commit suicide and not create a myth, as after World War I, which Germans believed was lost due to the "*Dolchstoss von hinten,*" the cowardly stab in the back, a tale that Hitler used in his speeches, stating that it was impossible that the German army could have lost any war without treachery.

My friend, the film director Andrew (Bandy) Marton, shot a picture for MGM in Berchtesgaden, *The Devil Makes Three,* that had the original Eagle's Nest, Hitler's hideout, as its background.

Scrivener called me in his office. I had been assigned to gather information behind the German lines. Though I knew that captured generals were treated with courtesy on both sides, I also knew that spies were treated unpleasantly, then shot. Scrivener assured me that to be caught by the enemy was only a remote possibility. The French underground was well organized. Besides, the Free French Forces, led by General de Gaulle, were now roaring to fight, since they knew that Hitler had lost his war. Scrivener told of the OSS's request for a German-born, not Jewish-looking, volunteer who spoke German preferably with a local accent. I would be shipped out across the ocean soon, but in the meantime I was given a furlough while I was waiting for further orders. He gave me a telephone number to call three times a day. The shipping date was kept secret to avoid leaking it to the German submarines. He also advised me, "Stay away from your family as much as possible. Go to New York and have a good time. The OSS has a room for you at the Plaza Hotel. And don't forget to call three times a day."

He knew that I called Henrietta daily but that I had avoided giving her any information about my life in Washington. Whatever Scrivener told me increased my apprehension, since I knew that I was expendable like everybody else in the OSS. I was convinced that I already had been "expended."

A room at the Plaza, the ritziest hotel in New York! I appreciated the generosity of the OSS. When I checked in, the reception clerk told me to enter the hotel through the servant's entrance. Somebody would show me to my room. That room was a hole in the wall, where the ultrarich parked maids and chauffeurs, their socially inferior entourage. It was so small that even the sun had no room to shine in. But it had a bed and a telephone, just in case the gentry wanted to communicate their wishes to their servants. It also had a small shower, like a coffin standing upright, and a clothes rack.

Maids didn't own many clothes. But the address was tops: I'm staying at the Plaza!

I didn't know anybody in New York, and after a few days I had seen every exhibit at the Metropolitan Museum, at the American Craft Museum, the Frick Collection, the Bronx Museum, even the Mellon Library. I ran out of museums. My favorite refuge was the New York Public Library, which was too vast to cover completely.

I bought a ticket for a Broadway play called *Jacubowski and the Colonel*. I didn't like its theme: a poor Jewish-Polish refugee with a brain had to cater to an elitist officer without a brain. I left in the middle of it.

I still have to see a play on Broadway I like. That might be the outcome of my writing profession. In plays and films I usually am able to outguess the author, anticipating the coming scene. Neither can I sit through to the very end of an opera. The pleasure of listening to singing voices had been exhausted in my early youth when I had to spend, by courtesy of the composer Richard Strauss, too many evenings at the Dresden Opera watching fat women impersonating slim, fair maidens, being in ecstasy about corpulent singers with booming voices. As a teenager I tried to visualize them in sexual situations, of which they sang, but was at a loss to imagine how the lower part of their bodies could ever connect with all those wads of fat around them.

Fortunately I had cash, part of which I spent between the three obligatory telephone calls in bars, where I was watching people, trying to guess their occupations, their home lives, and the reason that they went from their offices to those watering places, instead of going home to their wives and children. I sharpened my education as a spy. I couldn't wait for my departure. But the OSS voice on the phone only answered with "Roger."

I liked the Algonquin Hotel and its owner, Frank Case, who signed his cookbook *Feeding the Lions* for me. He told me that the Algonquins had been an Indian tribe about which Thomas Morton, a British trader and adventurer wrote, in 1622, "The air does beget good stomachs, and they feed continuously, and are no niggard of their vittels." Those were the words that inspired Frank to open a restaurant to carry on that Indian tradition.

Frank Case was an erudite man and fun to talk to, who spent much of his income not repainting his hotel, which it badly needed, but traveling. He told me the secret of how to make the famous Algonquin "Bloody Mary": Churn the gin, fresh tomato juice, and ingredients of your choice in a blender with ice until a foam forms. It makes the drink look festive and alive. I am still using his recipe, now for half a century, and it never fails to impress my guests.

The daily telephone calls with their implied termination immediately prevented me from enjoying myself. But the war in Europe went on without me.

I went to the Mocambo, the "in" watering place at that time. Dean Martin and Jerry Lewis performed. The club was crammed with double the capacity the fire marshal allowed. Suddenly a young woman stood before me.

"Remember me?" she said. She wore her hair long, touching her hips, and I recalled the cat cut of her black eyes, which dominated her face.

"Susan, of course," I said. "Not anymore in Albuquerque? You finally got a seat on a plane."

I looked around for her male companion, since she would not go to this nightclub without an escort.

She guessed my thoughts, a disturbing faculty she possessed as I found out later. "No, I'm not here alone. I'm over there." She pointed to a table with half a dozen smartly dressed young women and an older one, whose wrinkled face I remembered but could not place. "And don't offer me a drink. I don't like the taste," she said. "You are waiting to be shipped overseas, aren't you?" How did she know? Having gone through the OSS training, her question triggered my alarm.

"You don't need to answer," she said. "And since you don't, that's the answer. I wanted to meet you again. I wanted to." She smiled and touched my sleeve with the intimate gesture as she had done in Albuquerque, when she had tried to con the seat from me. Abruptly she left to return to her company, without asking where to find me in that metropolis.

I pointed out that older woman at Susan's table to the bartender. "That's Diana Vreeland," he said, surprised that I asked that question. "Everybody knows her." He turned away, too busy with his job to talk.

I went back to my room at the Plaza. The reappearance of that young woman in a city of millions had disturbed me, an emotion I could not explain to myself. I picked up the slight book about Tao. There was a quotation on the front page from a poem by T. S. Eliot: "Except for the point, the still point, there would be no dance, and there is only the dance.... music heard so deeply, that it is not heard at all, but you are the music, while the music lasts."

Though I didn't like Eliot, a flaming anti-Semite, and therefore my enemy, his poetry made sense to me.

I have read much about religions. A third of my library at home consists of works about different beliefs. None gives me the answers I am searching for, especially not the teachings of Eastern religions, which to me are a negation of life, emphasizing the human limitation to unravel mysteries, thus blocking the road to a sphere that human beings are trying to explore. But Taoism, if it only didn't have a name, might have given me the answer I was looking for.

> The Tao that can be told is not the eternal Tao. The name that can be named is not the eternal name. The nameless is the beginning of heaven and earth. The name is the mother of ten thousand things. Ever desireless, one can see the mystery. Even desiring, one can see the manifestations. These two spring from the same source but differ in name: this appears as darkness. Darkness within darkness. The fate to all mystery.

I had taken a small book about Tao with me and also *Marcus Aurelius,* which Henrietta had given to me when I left. I had glanced at pages and now hoped that the war, which I knew would often be tedious, would give me the time to study, a time I never could afford since I had to concoct stories to make a living. But there certainly was a forever, darkness leading into darkness, ad infinitum, teasing our pea-sized brain with questions to which we arrogantly believe we can find answers. Any answer will open a new darkness. That answer, which I still try to formulate, explains the meaning of "belief" to me, a mystical limitation of life that advises not to search. But should we deliberately curtail our curiosity to penetrate more of the darkness? That would mean, to me, giving up that mental spark that convinces me that there are vast regions that, to stay human and not become a petrified Indian guru, we must continue to explore. That very thinking process is my proof that I am alive. Cogito ergo sum.

I had just telephoned "Roger" and was ready to go out for breakfast, when there was a knock at the door.

Susan stood outside.

"I haven't had breakfast. Have you?" she asked.

How did she know where to find me?

"I found you, since I wanted to find you," she said. "I always find people if I want to find them." That explanation answered my silent question.

"Would you like to have breakfast at the hotel?" I asked.

"At the Plaza? There is a better place nearby, the Café de Paris."

She had her black hair piled up on top of her head like a businesswoman. What was she looking for? I didn't want to complicate my life with a clandestine relation. Men always think of sex when they are accosted by a handsome woman. If they don't follow that macho urge, most men cannot understand why "he didn't go through with it." Do women, too, think that way?

"I guessed you'd need me before you are shipped overseas. And you don't wear a uniform. Why?" It bothered her to find out who I was.

"Do you always treat your assumptions as facts?" I asked her.

We crossed the street to the Café de Paris. The patio was crowded; people were standing around for lack of sitting space. Susan had found a tiny table. How to get a waiter? None stopped when I called. One was boxed in near us. He carried a tray with sandwiches. I took one off the tray. Suddenly I was confronted by the manager. He screamed at me, and as I got up, he tried to hit me. I saw an insane rage in his beady, small eyes. Curiously, today his face is still registered in my memory like a photograph. As he tried to strike me, I redirected the blow, as I was trained, and twisted his wrist. I could have broken it. A group of waiters pulled both of us back. A restaurant manager attacking a guest, just because he had snatched a sandwich? He certainly was the wrong man for his job, cracking up under strain of work or maybe on account of private reasons. I didn't know. I carried my pipe in my hand. The wooden stem was a dagger. Stab his windpipe! I heard the chief of the Hong Kong police, Major Fairburn's, brainwashing scream: "Kill! Kill!" For a sandwich? The situation was too ridiculous to comprehend. If there was a fight, police would question me. My cover would have been blown. The OSS would reconsider their evaluation of me since I would have committed the unforgivable sin: to have broken under strain. I don't know how many thoughts flashed through my mind. I wasn't brought up to be a street fighter. Fight or flight! Part of the training of martial art is to run. I threw money at the table, and taking Susan by the arm, I pushed my way through the crowd.

Susan replaced the museums, the Broadway theaters, the lonely hours in bars. I didn't have to entertain her while waiting for the doom call from Washington. We chatted constantly, about my European upbringing, my work in motion pictures, and, as I soon found out, almost exclusively me. She seemed to avoid talking about herself. I wondered how she had been brought up and by whom, certainly not to become a wife and mother. I wondered whether she knew how to boil water. She asked me how to make a cup of tea. Does one put tea leaves into hot or cold water? What was her upbringing? Did she wish to make herself more attractive by remaining a mystery to me?

She finally let me know that she worked odd hours for *Vogue* magazine in the layout department, which gave her free time at the spur of the moment. That explained to me her infrequent calls at odd times. She talked about *Vogue*'s editor, Diana Vreeland, like a mother.

Diana Vreeland, a powerful society figure, seemed to know everybody in New York. She dictated women's fashions and might have taught Susan how to dress and acquire a grace of movement and bearing, which I had often found in France among members of the higher society or high-priced models.

But did she, a stunning young woman, not have a steady boyfriend? She never again came up to my butler's room and phoned me where to meet her. Waiting for her calls, which came at any odd time, and talking to "Roger" were the punctuation of my lonely waiting days. Whenever she left to go home, she took a taxi and told the driver the address when I could not hear it. When I asked her whether she was married, she replied, "You are married."

I guess that she was twenty-four or twenty-five years old. She never asked any intimate questions about my private life, nor did she inquire about my mystery calls to Washington, but sometimes reminded me that the hour to phone had come. She seemed to know that every one of those calls could terminate our clandestine relation. Every one of our meetings was an implied farewell, controlled by my calls to "Roger."

Since she knew New York very well, it made me believe that the Big Apple had always been her hometown, though once she answered in French when I switched deliberately and unexpectedly to that language. She must have stayed in Europe for some time. Alone? With a lover or a husband? Or did she go to school in France? Was her family French? German she did not understand.

I tried to put her life together like a jigsaw puzzle but didn't get very far. Why did she refuse to tell me her name? Was that part of a game? I asked her what made her call me, since ours was not a love affair, not even an intimacy, since she didn't like that I even touched her hand. She replied that she didn't want me to be lonely before I was shipped overseas. Like Henrietta, she thought that I might not return from the war, though I was only doing what millions of Americans were doing routinely and without a thought of dying.

She had whims: she wanted to ride in one of those horse-drawn carriages for hire near the Plaza Hotel for a leisurely trot around the park and make sure that the pampered horse wore rubber horseshoes. We went to small, inexpensive restaurants. She liked one at 36th Street East, which was hiding in a cellar. It consisted of six tables that were not always occupied. A middle-aged Italian with a strong Bronx accent did the cooking, and his wife and teenaged daughter served as waitresses. I believe they offered the choice of only four different dishes. Susan was convinced that all four were outstanding, which they might have been. She liked Italian food. Was she, dark-haired and dark-eyed, of Italian stock?

Forty-five years later, my cousin Werner Buchold, who lived in New York for decades, invited Henrietta and me and his sprawl of daughters, husbands, and grandchildren to dinner at the same address. That restaurant, though still situated in the cellar, had grown into a noisy, overcrowded place, with uniformed waiters rushing about. It still served Italian food, though of many more varieties, but also had acquired the antlike impersonal hustle of the Big Apple.

When we strolled down Fifth Avenue, Susan wanted to enter St. Patrick's Cathedral. The huge dark nave was empty, except for a few shadowy worshipers. I waited at the door, while she walked down the aisle, obviously familiar with that place, and kneeled down to pray. She had covered her dark hair with a small silk handkerchief. I could not see her face, but I was aware that she was deeply immersed in an emotion that did not fit her lively, cheerful manners. I have often entered these places of worship, since they are a fermata off the noisy, crowded city streets.

When she returned, she casually said, "You will be all right." I told her that I didn't think I was in any kind of jeopardy, but she replied, "I had to pray for you."

Prayers are formulated by dogmatic religions, and their dogmas are man-made rules. But rules impede the freedom of my way of thinking. Of course it is the arrogance of the human mind that believes it can solve any "mystery." A mystery is an unsolved question. Albert Einstein died an unhappy man since he believed that he could resolve the unexplainable.

When Henrietta and I lived in Berlin in pre-Nazi times, I had difficulty breathing, for which no medical cause could be found. That infliction has never left me, and I believe that it is a neurotic escape from unsolved thoughts and undigested emotions. It is, as I have convinced myself, part of the mental ingredient and possibly caused by my profession.

In her despair to help me, as she told me years later, Henrietta went to a Christian Science practitioner for help. That prayer from a person whom she contacted and paid did not know me, had never met me, or heard of me. But whatever thought or prayer by her showed results. My condition disappeared temporarily. The explanation might not be very mysterious. I would have been all right in any case. But still, I can't deny that there is mystery in mysteries, which, when we penetrate them, reveal another mystery.

The human brain is limited in its rationalizations, the way my cat will never be able to run a computer.

A writer I knew, Werner Luedecke, who lived in Rome and was married to an Italian woman, was plagued by misfortunes, also called "bad luck." His Catholic wife forced him to see a priest who "exorcised the devil." Reading from an ancient book of exorcism, *Seraficum Romanum,* the priest called on "St. Michael and all the angels." Then Werner's unfavorable situation turned to the better. "Satan" disappeared. Satan must be present in all religions, since Werner was Lutheran. According to him, the situation would have straightened out anyhow in his favor. Possibly he was right, but otherwise . . .

Susan called and asked me to put on a white shirt and a tie. She wanted to take me to the Waldorf-Astoria Hotel where Harry James, the trumpeter, and his orchestra played on the roof garden. I had been there before and found that hotel to be ostentatious, perhaps based on my dislike for the closed society of the ultrarich, gangsters of the industries.

Susan looked glamorous in a simple, obviously very expensive black dress that left her shoulders bare. How a woman is put together by nature often supersedes the skill of her tailor. For that evening I should have rented a tuxedo. Before we went to the Waldorf, Susan insisted on a dinner at Schratts, a fast-food cafeteria where hurried people, the rich and the poor, mixed democratically.

I would have loved to have taken her to the Waldorf's dining room, just to show off with her.

The terrace on the top of the hotel was a noisy place, its roof covered with a sliding glass dome that had been partly opened. Suddenly the sky exploded, thunder and lightning mixed dramatically with the music of Harry James. A cloudburst drumming on the glass roof almost drowned out the sound of the large orchestra, dramatically complementing the, for me, cacophonous music.

The dancing went on despite the thunderstorm. The floor was so heavily crowded that we could hardly move. For the first time I was close to her. Her body was pliable, but with a lack of intimacy as though she were dancing without a partner. She was a much better dancer than I, and certainly no novice in this kind of place. No screenwriter could have invented the admixture of thunder, lightning, and music except for a Busby Berkeley MGM musical extravaganza. The rain had changed into hail, thundering on the glass roof. The celestial performance stopped as suddenly as it had started.

The impression of unreality that had transported me into an exotic world is still vividly in my memory, as if it had happened only yesterday night. Susan didn't wait for the music to stop. We passed a table with a tall mustachioed man surrounded by half a dozen extremely handsome young women, who, kittenlike, catered to him. Fascinated, he stared at Susan and, getting up, blocked our path. He disregarded my presence as if I didn't exist. I couldn't hear what he said, but Susan's face froze in a witchlike expression. I heard her say, "Occupied. Please later!" Her voice was cutting and contemptuous. "That conceited bore tried to date me," she said, holding on to me as we walked away. "He thinks because he's Howard Hughes, every girl is just waiting for him. He's revolting!"

Years later I met Hughes again. Henrietta and I lived at Lime Orchard in Beverly Hills. I was writing the screenplay *Berlin Express* for RKO Studios, which Hughes had just bought. My producer, Bert Granet, told me that Hughes wanted to talk to me. I had to be at Mulholland Drive and Coldwater Canyon Road at midnight. A two-seater Ford, driven by Hughes, would stop. I felt like I was being transported back into my spy time. Exactly at 12 A.M. an old two-seater Ford coupe drove up and a gangly man stepped out. He wore faded blue jeans and tennis shoes. He didn't introduce himself, and I soon found out that he was hard of hearing. Hughes wanted me to write a few daring love scenes into the picture for Barbara Hale, a pleasant, innocent-looking young actress who was under contract to RKO. In later years she appeared in a successful TV series as the secretary of the criminal attorney, Perry Mason, a role played for years by the actor Raymond Burr. Ray later on acted in the first picture I directed. He was still playing Perry Mason roles until his death in 1993.

I don't know why Hughes wanted to talk to me personally, after midnight, on the deserted Mulholland Drive. Bert Granet could have given me the same instructions. Barbara Hale didn't appear in *Berlin Express*. Merle Oberon was cast in that part.

Hughes was a Texan, a multimillionaire, a bachelor. He kept a dozen young "starlets" he had "discovered" in expensive, rented houses in Hollywood and Beverly Hills. Each had a bodyguard assigned to her, to report, I guess, on visitors. He kept that harem, for which RKO's stockholders were charged. He tried to date every young female star. Many of them, like Elizabeth Taylor, refused to go out with him a second time.

I'm glad that Hughes was not Jewish, or he would have fostered age-old anti-Semitism: a Jew keeping a gaggle of pretty girls? He was all that people envy in a WASP millionaire and would hate in a Jew.

Suddenly the weather vane in my life turned in a direction I had not expected. I had psyched myself to enter a life that might have been the delight of a storm trooper but not of a writer of fantasy and science fiction stories.

I had just talked to "Roger," who had no news for me. By now I had been in New York for three weeks, waiting for the ship to take me to Marseilles. After having crossed the Atlantic in a convoy that could be attacked by German submarines, I was assigned to General Patch's divisions. Trained and brainwashed by the OSS, I had cut my mental cords to my former life and adjusted my mind to another way of thinking.

It was eight in the morning when Susan stood in the door, carrying a large paper bag.

"I was afraid that you hadn't heard," she explained on that early visit. "There's a hurricane warning on the radio. New York is going to be hit in a few hours. You can't get out of the hotel until it's over. That's why I brought some food. I can't let you starve."

I had never heard that hurricanes traveled as far north as New York. I noticed that 56th Street, of which I could see part, was deserted. No cars, no buses, not a pedestrian was around. There was an eerie silence, as if the city were holding its breath.

She could have assumed that I had listened to the radio or that the hotel had alerted me. But she seemed to want to play house as she arranged things bought in a Jewish delicatessen on the tiny table of the butler's room. "They cut off the electricity," she said and turned a light switch. There was no light. She also had been to Brentano's, the bookstore, where she had bought my novel *Donovan's Brain*. I had told her about it.

"It took me the whole night to read it," she said. "Is Donovan your father and Janice your wife? The book is a love affair. People might not know that, but it is about love."

I had never thought of that, but she was right. There was an expression in her face that I could not decode, a probing, a searching and uncertainty, which she covered with small talk. She remarked on the sudden silence of the metropolis and that, should she become mayor of that city, she would declare a silent day once a year, without traffic or any kind of communication, to give people time to contemplate their lives.

Then she got up and slowly started to undress, without any hesitation, as if that action had been the result of a careful decision. I was confused, since that step in our relationship had been given up weeks ago. I had never made a pass at her, convinced that any uninvited intimacy would have been rejected. I also knew that it is the woman who gives the signal.

She took off her clothes, slowly, teasingly, and her eyes never left my face. Her skin was very light, almost luminous. She certainly was aware of her sexual allure, which convinced me that she had teased other men the same way or that possibly a woman had taught her that enchanting graceful striptease of seduction.

Should I have played Joseph rejecting Potiphar's wife? The guilt about sex, which the Western religions have instilled in us, will fade away as we get older but never the regret of having rejected an offered sexual opportunity. Though we might forget our affairs, missed sexual opportunities stay in men's minds forever. To be monogamous is contrary to the male sexual urge. If it were not the case, the world would have a chance to check its destructive overpopulation.

There was an innocence of shape in her unblemished body and a sensuality that nature has created for only one purpose.

She opened the bed, still watching me. But I could not discover any desire or eroticism in her quiet face.

She certainly was experienced and responsive, and without restraint. But I suddenly felt her body stiffen. She pushed me back violently and jumped out of bed.

"I've changed my mind," she said, grabbing her slip and starting to dress.

I got out of bed and also dressed. Of all the experiences I had had in my life with the female gender, this was a new one. My macho pride was in shambles. I felt castrated and very foolish.

Still half-naked, she sat at the table supporting her head in her hands and said, "I was married to a man of your age. One day, when I came home, I found him dead. He died of an overdose of drugs. He had the needle still in his arm. His eyes were open, staring at me."

Suddenly the light in the room went on. Street noise came through the window. There had been no hurricane, just a meteorological warning.

I went to the phone to call a taxi.

"Don't," she said. "If I say I'm sorry that would sound childish." Her eyes were dry, and her face composed, watching not me but thoughts visible only to her.

"They canceled the hurricane," I remember I said. "I wonder how many children were made this morning in New York, since people had time." She did not respond to my joke. She wanted to talk.

Her father, a successful lawyer in New York, died when she was sixteen. She had been extremely close to him. She adored his wit, his looks and was, as she remembered, jealous of her own mother. She smiled. "When I was eleven, we went out camping, Father, Mother, and I. I was cross that he brought her along. I now know that I was in love with him." It was obvious that she must have talked to a psychoanalyst. Two years after her father's sudden death, when she was seventeen, she met a man who strangely fascinated her. He was erudite, had a humor that kept her amused, and fit her conception of what she called "European culture." Twenty-five years older than she, he was of her father's age. A Frenchman, he designed racing cars for the French company Renault. Without her mother's knowledge, she had eloped with him. She was a virgin when she married. When her husband found out, he was gentle and considerate and never forced any physical contact, until she got over her sexual fears. He spoke French to her, which she quickly learned and which made her feel exclusive, worldly, and sophisticated. She didn't know that her husband was using drugs. She did not even know that drugs existed, a fact still unknown in 1945. Only the end of the war in the Far East has brought that curse into the open. Though her father had left a trust fund for her, she took a job offered to her by Diana Vreeland, the editor of *Vogue*, after her husband's death. Diana had been a classmate of her mother's and became a second mother to her. Susan finally told me her dead husband's name, which she still carried: Lefour.

She had been seeing a woman psychoanalyst every week since her husband's death, to control her wish to "self-destruct," as she called it. That woman told her that she had been sexually in love with her father and advised her to mix with people since she had lived like a recluse for a year. But she had dated only men twice her age. When they tried to become physical, she would tighten up and drop the acquaintance. As her psychoanalyst had told her, she was feeling guilty, believing that she was cheating on her father. When she met me and guessed that I would leave very soon, she had made up her mind to make love to me.

I remembered a friend older than I, a seasoned bachelor, who had advised me, "Never sleep with a woman who has bigger troubles than you."

"If you were free, I'd have married you," she said soberly. Did she want to make me understand why she had jumped out of bed? *If, should, would*—three words of the dictionary that rule our lives. Timing rules our life.

That morning of the aborted hurricane was like a movie script, in which the writer was trying to find new and exciting turns and surprises for his story. She had given me a plausible explanation for her brittle rejection of any intimacy, her brave attempt to overcome that past that blocked her emotions. I was almost twice her age and would be getting out of her life, a fact that surely was a safety valve for her. I wonder whether she had talked about me with her psychoanalyst and had gotten her advice to go to bed with me.

The telephone rang. It was Washington. Scrivener was on the line. He told me that my assignment to Europe was off. The FFI, the Free French Army, had been employed to push to the Swiss border. Now that the war was in its last stage in Europe, the French insisted on joining it. Patch's divisions would stay behind. Scrivener asked me to return to Washington and whether I would consider going to Japan. Japan? I knew a great deal about the Germans. I didn't know anything about the Japanese. I had reason to fight the Nazis, though I was no soldier. I told Scrivener that I wouldn't be of any value in the Far East, where I had never been. "I thought so," he said. "Jimmy Stone wants your job. Take the next train home."

Susan was gone.

I went down the long corridor and left the hotel. If I had written such a scene on assignment, the producer wouldn't have accepted it.

Too far-fetched, unreal, artificially constructed. He would have insisted on script changes.

I was floating in limbo between two existences. I was not the happy homecoming soldier, having cheated death, a death I had anticipated, befriended perhaps, but never faced. After I returned to California and a happy family to welcome me home, I felt a deep emptiness I could not fill for many weeks.

> [M]usic heard so deeply, that it is not heard at all, but you are the music, while the music lasts. Except for the point, the still point, there would be no dance, and there is only the dance.

I suffered from severe battle fatigue without having been exposed to enemy bullets. The world I returned to was far removed from the killing fields to which I had mentally adjusted. The OSS had discharged me overnight. It was painful to adjust to the "ordinary" life, to find pleasure in small amenities, to be interested in my family, a condition that Henrietta patiently understood and outwaited. Wasn't I back, unharmed except for that battle of the discrepancy of values? The war in Germany was finished. The FFI, to uphold "*la gloire de la France*," had bravely marched to the Swiss border with American tanks and cannons, flags flying, vainly looking for the Nazi enemy that the Vichy government had too readily embraced.

My OSS detachment, what was left of it, was issued train tickets to return home. No trumpets blew for our "de mortuis." Members of the OSS, when they died, died anonymously. Some of my detachment had been assigned to General Hodges's army in the north. They were caught in the last vicious German attack of the war, the Battle of the Bulge. I never heard from them again.

Henrietta helped me to overcome my depression, not even once asking me about my experiences with the OSS, and I did not offer any information. I believe that anyone who had been brainwashed by the army, especially if he has seen combat, rarely recovers completely from that high and only adventure in his life. For some, war is the high point of their existence, and they love to talk about it and meet their former comrades in yearly gatherings, preferably on foreign shores where death had passed them by but taken their comrades. Harry Kulick, who for decades owned the General Store in Three Rivers where we live, travels every year to the Normandy coast, where on D day, sixty-three of the seventy American tanks of his detachment, without having fired a shot, drowned in the channel with their crews. What makes him visit that watery grave that still holds the now-rusted tanks with their dead crews for more than half a century, I can only guess. As former inmates in German concentration camps suffer from a feeling of guilt that death had passed them by, they often cannot cope with a remorse that they have been spared the gas chambers, where their family members and friends have perished.

Ib Melchior, my close friend and highly disciplined and prolific writer of many books, though having been born in Denmark, had been with the OSS during World War II. His novels deal with the background he has experienced: the enemy, the Nazis. Even now, half a century later, his mind and writing skill still revolve around the deeply cutting adventures when he fought the Germans as a young man.

A few weeks after my return home, a letter arrived from Lieutenant Stoner, who had been assigned to the job I was offered by the OSS. I had met Jimmy during my training in Washington. Jimmy wrote that when he was flying from Cairo to Calcutta, a Chinese member of the OSS who was sitting next to him in the plane lit his cigarette with my lighter. It was a Dunhill with a funnel that could be pushed up for lighting a pipe. When I was with that spy outfit, being anonymous, I shouldn't have kept that gadget since my name was engraved on it.

Jimmy was enthusiastic, wanted to see combat and stay with the army as a career after the war. I wrote a thank-you letter to him, which, after a few weeks, was returned unopened, stamped "deceased." He had been shot by a Japanese sniper when he arrived in Saipan. I didn't even know at that time that Saipan existed. The bullet that killed him had my name on it. For fifty years the lighter has been standing protected by a glass case in my study, a reminder of the fickle vagaries of life and death.

Robert was preparing a picture at RKO that became one of his memorable successes, a film noir of which he was master: *The Spiral Staircase*. He was in the commissary of RKO having lunch with his boss, Dore Schary, who had been engaged by Howard Hughes to run his newly acquired studio. Nobody in the studio, except Schary and a janitor, had ever met Hughes. The janitor told him that Hughes had visited the studio at midnight. His only comment had been, "Paint it."

Dore (Isidore) Schary, a former writer and producer with unlimited self-esteem, had become a power in Hollywood. Schary still had the intelligence of a good writer and had not yet acquired the distant demeanor of men of his position, convinced that their brainpower is superior to everybody who works for them. Schary, in comparison to the Paramount or Columbia executives, was still sympathetic to writers. Having by chance read one of my novels, he pumped me for ideas. I told him of my experience with the OSS. Now that Germany was occupied by Americans, British, French, and Russians, a motion picture filmed with the background of bombed-out Berlin and Frankfurt would make an interesting story. RKO would be the first studio exploring that opportunity. When Schary asked me about the story, I reminded him that just by having smashed up the Wehrmacht doesn't mean that the Nazis, fifty million of them, had melted away. They were still around, seething with humiliation and looking for revenge. Papa Hitler was still adored by many, despite his mistake of having lost the war.

Many Germans, believing they were a superrace, would resist their country's change to a democracy. They would certainly try to keep the Nazi spirit alive.

Schary called in Bert Granet, an affable young producer, and told him to assign me to develop a story with the background of bombed-out German cities. It was a natural task for me since my army training to counteract the German national spirit found an outlet in it. That motion picture screenplay, titled *Berlin Express,* was nominated for the Writers Guild Award as the year's best original story.

Years later, when I wrote for RKO's gifted producer, Val Lewton, I visited my old friend and first film collaborator, the writer-director Billy Wilder, at Goldwyn Studios. Billy was directing possibly his greatest success, *Some Like It Hot,* in which Marilyn Monroe, Jack Lemmon, and Tony Curtis starred. On that day, Billy shot the train sequence. I watched Curtis and Lemmon, dressed in their disguises as women in order to hide from gangsters, as they waited to be called for their scene. It struck me how much pleasure those two stars enjoyed being dressed and moving like females, feminizing their voices and gestures. It was not only "playacting"; it was, as it appeared to me, a deeply buried desire in many actors to impersonate a woman.

When I walked through the RKO back lot to the Goldwyn Studios to see Billy, he was talking to Marilyn Monroe. I had met her years previously on Sunset Boulevard in Hollywood with the photographer Ladislaos Willinger, the gifted portraitist of women. He had used her as his model, even had spent money to have her teeth straightened.

Marilyn was a well-proportioned and more than just pretty woman with the quality of vulnerability that is demanded for stardom. Lazi indicated in her presence that, since she was broke, if I paid her rent, she would invite me to her apartment. That cruel dependency on money might have formed her character. After she became a world star, it made it very difficult for any director to work with her, a retaliation against the power of males who had mistreated her as Lazi did, when she was defenseless.

On the set of *Some Like It Hot*, Billy talked to her about her next scene. She listened for a while, staring at him with a child's big blue innocent eyes. She interrupted him with, "Mr. Wilder, I wish you would not explain that scene to me. You interfere with my conception." Then she walked away.

Shocked, I asked Billy, "How can you take that from her?" He grinned. "She has a brain made of cheese, tits of steel, and I am getting a quarter of a million."

I learned later that Monroe's acting coach was Mrs. Strasberg, the wife of the drama teacher Lee Strasberg, who dominated her. Lee Strasberg originated "method" acting, which young actors like Marlon Brando and his contemporaries adopted. It also gave me an insight to the limited power of a director against the whim and moods of his stars. Should the star player walk out of the picture, the director would be blamed. Nobody can force a star to continue to act. Actors can wreck a motion picture and are very well aware of it. Sometimes they misuse their power. Gottfried Reinhardt, the son of the famous stage director Max Reinhardt, once supposedly had to wait for three days for Kirk Douglas, his star, to appear on the set, and was forced to shoot around him during filming in Germany after the war.

While shooting Arthur Miller's *The Misfits*, Marilyn was unable to appear on schedule and even carried a huge railroadman's watch on a chain around her neck to remind her to be on time. I believe, having been insecure all her life, she also suffered "camera fright," a cousin of stage fright.

The Misfits was Gable's last film. He died of a heart attack soon after the completion of the picture at the age of fifty-nine. Monroe was blamed for his premature death because of the aggravations she had produced during the production. Only a few directors, among them Alfred Hitchcock and Cecil B. DeMille, seemed to have the authority to deal with volatile stars. Hitchcock denied that he considered actors on the same level as cattle but admitted to having said, "Actors should be treated like cattle."

Nobody ever found a movie star in my home as a guest, except for a small group of performers, all of them legitimate stage actors. Every one of them was British-born, erudite, and unimpressed by their personal fame. Since acting is a perishable commodity, some overact when they are cast in important jobs. Many are extremely hard to work with.

But actors can be discarded. So can directors and producers, since they are hired help. When Erich von Stroheim, the then-leading actor-director at MGM, ordered his boss Louis B. Mayer to leave the set while he was directing, Mayer, in a rage, attacked him with a knife. Irving Thalberg, the twenty-four-year-old legendary MGM producer, closed down Erich von Stroheim's half-finished picture. After that confrontation, Stroheim never received another chance to act in a big picture. Stroheim needed an assignment to function. MGM blacklisted him.

The only professional who does not depend on a paid job is the creative writer. If one of my novels has been turned unsuccessfully into a motion picture, that fact doesn't faze me. My books, the way I wrote them, stand on their shelves.

I got a whiff of what it means to live like the rich. The rich are a special breed of the human race. They don't need to stand on their toes to pick the apple. To buy a car, they write a check and drive away with it. Of course I wasn't poor in comparison to 98 percent of American families, but real wealth has a different scent to it.

My agent got an assignment for me to write a *Tarzan* screenplay for Sol Lesser, a tycoon of B pictures, who humbly admitted that his prominence came from being an early pioneer of the motion picture industry. He owned the rights to the film series *Tarzan,* the brawny jungle hero, an English milord who, illogically lost in an African jungle as a baby, was brought up by apes.

The first *Tarzan* story had been written in 1913. Now Tarzan, never aging, has existed through almost a century. Accompanied by his pretty mate Jane and a chimpanzee with more brains than the two together, the lead actor had to be changed from time to time, when he got too old to swing from tree to tree.

Elmo Lincoln, Gene Polar, Demsey Taylor, and many others, great athletes and macho hunks, among them Johnny Weissmuller, the Olympic swimming champion, and a long line of musclemen played Tarzan. I wrote my *Tarzan* when Weissmuller was replaced by Lex Barker in *Tarzan and the Magic Fountain*. Sol (Solomon) Lesser, the owner and producer of that series, was looking for a replacement for Johnny Weissmuller, who had put on a middle-aged spread. I suggested Barker, whom I had met at the Polo Lounge at the Beverly Hills Hotel, that center of the "Who's Who" of the motion picture business at that time.

My assignment had the lure of being able to work in Palm Springs where Sol Lesser owned a winter home.

If you spit at your job, the job spits back at you. That's why I took all assignments very seriously and always wrote the best screenplay I could devise.

Edgar Rice Burroughs was an amusing old man, who, having invented that character, became so famous that a Los Angeles suburb was named after his creation: Tarzana. I don't know of any other writer who has been honored that way. Since all of Burroughs's books had already been motion picture vehicles, Sol had to hire writers to create new Tarzan stories.

Sol rented a comfortable bungalow for me. I was sitting in the well-advertised Palm Springs sun, outside the bungalow with my typewriter, getting tanned while concocting a masterpiece. It was a pleasant and well-paid job, though my conscience bothered me: led by Moses, my forefathers, after forty years of desperately wandering through the desert to find a home, I had returned to that heap of sand for greedy financial reasons!

Sol was a small, slightly pompous but pleasant man in his late fifties, but behind his humor and friendliness I felt the steel of the tycoon that had made him a millionaire. We played chess, but only a couple of times, since he complained that I should have let him win, which I didn't. Never to lose, not even a chess game, is the driving power of very successful entrepreneurs.

The work for Sol went well. I followed Sol's direction, since the Tarzan stories had to be written according to a formula he had devised. Sol, having produced a score of *Tarzans* whose content was predictable, stuck to that moneymaking procedure.

It was Sunday morning. I was pounding the typewriter in front of my bungalow when Sol passed by with Sam Goldwyn (Samuel Goldfish), an even richer motion picture tycoon than Sol. Sol introduced me, and Goldwyn looked at me incredulously. "Your writers work on Sundays!?"

"I never interfere with the creativity of my authors," Sol said, which wasn't quite true. Goldwyn, impressed, asked me to get in touch with him at his office at the Goldwyn Studios in Hollywood.

I never did. I had heard about the difficulties of working for him and left those jobs to writers who had the stamina to endure Goldwyn's vacillating demands.

Sol lived with his wife in a sprawling Palm Springs house. But stealthily he had two young call girls flown in from Los Angeles. He had rented a bungalow for them and used me as a cover-up when he visited them, which he could only do in the daytime. At night he slept at home. In the daytime, he told his wife that he had a story conference and lunch with me. He, being afraid of his spouse, I guess, gave her my telephone number, should she want to call him. I knew where to reach him. We had long daily "conferences," which to me proved his vigor and stamina.

I liked sexually virile people. For me the end of sexual desire also denotes the lessening of creativity. The leaders of America, a country populated by Calvinists, are afraid of mentioning sex and deny having indulged in it. The general public is never shocked by blood and murder but mortified by a display of pubic hair. If magazines or television networks like ABC, CBS, and NBC had existed during the time of Michelangelo, he would never have been permitted to paint a holy picture, showing the genitals of the man that touches God's finger. In 1994, an advertising agency was forced to withdraw a showing of Michelangelo's masterpiece from a TV advertisement, since the male figure had no fig leaf. The ad was scheduled to be shown just before the motion picture *Terminator Two,* which graphically displayed, among tortures, dismemberment, and mutilations, fifty-six murders.

Sol invited me to dinner. He had as his guest Bruno Walter, the German conductor, world-famous for his interpretation of Mozart's music. It might be that I was invited because I spoke German. I was paired with a pert young woman, Paulette Goddard.

I understand the pleasure of "name-droppers." For me, having met Bruno Walter was an indelible event to brag about. I also never forgot seeing Nehru in New York. Years later, in 1962, while flying home from Monrovia in Liberia, where I had visited the Peace Corps in the African jungles to collect material for a novel, I met, in the airport, heads of African governments: Haile Selassie, the Lion of Judah and the king of Ethiopia; Nkrumah of Nigeria, with his ivory walking stick; and other leaders of nations whose features I knew from photographs. They exuded an indefinable aura of power. I savored being surrounded by history.

But when I tried to pull my tiny Minox camera from my pocket, I found myself surrounded by three giant bodyguards. I showed them that I didn't have a gun but wanted to take a photo. They took away my camera and only returned it just before the flight. So the picture of those potentates is etched only in my memory.

Paulette Goddard, after Sol's dinner, asked me to drive her home in my "wolf's car," a red streamlined Buick convertible.

On the way to the Racket Club, where she stayed, a sudden sandstorm blacked out the night. This was a frightening experience since I, blinded, had to stop out in nowhere. Paulette disappeared. When the storm subsided, as fast as it had risen, I found her crouched under the dashboard. A slim woman, she had folded herself into the size of a bag of golf clubs.

Through her I had access to the exclusive Racket Club, with its crowd of young and handsome actors and actresses; a bevy of physical beauties, mostly only covered by a suntan, was a revelation to me that only to be young is worth living. The crooner Dick Haymes, the then-heartthrob of many girls, sat at the pool in an intimate embrace with a dark-haired beauty. I would have loved to change places with him, if I had been a bachelor and if I could sing.

Palm Springs still was a small community. Now, having swallowed Cathedral City and other adjoining towns, it has grown into a large impersonal town. It now has the stale smell of a society whose only measure of value is the amount of money its members have accumulated.

Married Americans yearn for a tract house, detached from their neighbors. Should their income rise, they like to move to a home in a "better" neighborhood. After a measured number of years, their children leave and the house becomes too big and cumbersome. Nothing is as desolate as the child's empty room. The parents change to smaller real estate on equal footing with their friends. Then to escape the nervousness of the city, they yearn for a "home in the country," detached from neighbors with lots of green space, to keep a couple of horses, also to live possibly near a golf course, since to roll a small ball into a hole seems to be the acme of retirement's pleasure.

In our life we had reached stage 2: we were fairly well off. I had well-paying motion picture assignments and cash, enough to pay for a home in Beverly Hills. The house we found was a replica of a small French castle amid two and one-half acres of trees and greenery. It also had the much coveted postal ZIP code 90210, a number so important and impressive that years later a television show by this number was created, depicting the life of the rich and famous.

We were not rich, nor was I famous. I was one of the more successful film writers, who also had a dozen books published, which permitted me to call myself an author. Of course, living in such an abode in Beverly Hills was a financial strain for a writer like me. Henrietta enjoyed the castle on Coldwater Canyon Road, though she never was interested in the social status shared by the rich. Having grown up a member of Swiss nobility, she detested the snobbish atmosphere of titled families. Since childhood she had found them stuffy and dull, and she also hated her grandmother, whose Sunday visit at her father's house was accompanied by the swishing sound of her taffeta skirts, a crackling noise of material which Henrietta still detests. She never owned any clothes made of taffeta. Though she had to accompany her parents to her grandmother's home, she visited not her but the antique furniture, which was like old friends to her, to overcome her dislike for that domineering harpy. Her feelings were, as usual, right. Her grandmother wanted her son back. He had married a woman of common birth. Her grandmother succeeded. Her father, Henry, sent her and her mother Ernestine penniless on a "vacation." Henrietta never saw him again. He returned to his mother's home and bank account. When he died, Henrietta's mother would have been his heir. For reasons still mysterious to me, she never claimed her husband's inheritance for her or her daughter, despite her being so poor she had to make her living as a seamstress. I don't know why she never talked about her past. Henrietta's father never worked and lived on sporadic windfalls from family inheritances. Why wasn't I, after our marriage, included in that very pleasant way of living? We received one thousand Swiss francs from the family trust fund, which I guess still contains a sizable sum. I've never found out why, even during our most financially trying time during our emigration, she or her mother never even contacted her family, claiming their legal rights to their inheritance.

It took Henrietta twenty years before she saw any of the de Perrot family again. She didn't want to introduce me, afraid I might find them stuffy and hopelessly antiquated. But when we lived in Tessin in 1962, I insisted on meeting her relatives whom she had deliberately hidden from me. We finally drove to her town of origin, Neufchâtel, in the French part of Switzerland.

Her uncle, Frederick de Perrot, and his wife, Colette, were aristocratic, gentle people. I found that this ancient, titled family, who had been bankers and engineers for centuries, were extremely gracious and hospitable. Three days before our arrival, Frederick and Colette had ordered an outstanding dinner at the best restaurant in town. After the unhurried meal, we returned to their home, the family mansion, where they introduced us to members of the de Perrot clan, gathered for that occasion. That mansion, built in the fifteenth century, declared a historical landmark by the Swiss government, stands, now incongruously, between modern high-rises.

Henrietta is a part of that five-hundred-year-old tribe, whose knights' armor is exhibited in the Neufchâtel museum. She could never again live in Europe. Her roots are in America, with its freedom and lack of stagnant class difference. She adored our house in Beverly Hills with its eucalyptus grove and generously large rooms. She liked chamber music.

A professional musician is the only performer who gets paid for his work and then plays privately and with pleasure the same pieces for free. The viola player Eric Silverman, a member of the Los Angeles Philharmonic, was the Judas goat who brought musicians from the Los Angeles Philharmonic orchestra to our house. They arrived at night after the performance, were always hungry and expected that there would be enough liquids in our bar to lubricate their talents. Eric also had the knack of inducing famous visiting guests to perform. He created a variety of chamber music quartets, once with Szigetti and Yehudi Menudin, an ensemble even millionaires could not afford to hire.

I am not too fond of music, which after an hour starts to bore me. That honest confession shocked Henrietta, who kept those fiddlers until the weehours in the morning. Of course, they could sleep late, while I had to be at my desk at the studio at nine. One night, when Beverly Hills was shrouded in fog, the group stayed for breakfast, which actually was an elaborate brunch, and only left in the afternoon, to return to their jobs at the Philharmonic. Once the viola artist Eric even brought the conductor Arturo Toscanini, an old man who could not sit down because of bad blood circulation in his legs. I don't know if he drank anything or talked to anybody, certainly not to me. I don't know why he came, though he listened unemotionally and without comment to the excellent quartet. Anyhow, Henrietta's attempt to kindle my liking for Corelli, Telemann, and other Baroque composers was an aborted attempt to share her enthusiasm.

Henrietta's circle of interesting people grew steadily. I was consigned to the job of butler, having to fill glasses and remove plates, and see that everyone was comfortable. One day a Viennese psychiatrist was among the guests. He asked me to talk to him in private. I took him to my studio. He told me that he had studied under Jung and Adler in Vienna. He also had watched my compulsive behavior: the way I couldn't relax, moved my fingers constantly, and other signs a shrink likes to observe. He didn't think I needed professional psychoanalysis, which was a fad at that time, but a few hours of talk would do me good. He told me of a patient who compulsively wrote a novel every week, fifty-two a year, each one containing exactly twenty-nine thousand words. He had found a publisher for them, though they were literarily worthless. After three years of analysis, in which the writer was unable to put anything on paper, he again wrote a novel. "How was that book?" I asked.

"Dreadful," he replied.

7

Did I Really Write That Much?

"Life can only be understood backwards, but it must be lived forward," my granddaughter Carol wrote to me, quoting Søren Kierkegaard, the founder of Danish philosophy. She had gone through a traumatic tragedy in her young life, but had found the strength and wisdom to cope with it by looking forward and keeping the past as an indelible memory.

Did I endure the "*quatre cent fous,*" the "400 blows," with which the French define the limit that breaks the human spirit? Did I absorb the blows without permanent injury? Only now, more than twenty years after my brother's death, have I become aware of our twinlike fate.

A sudden "*torschluss Panik,*" the perception that time has limitations, attacks our consciousness. That moment happens to most males between the ages of forty and fifty, a watershed, which consciously or unconsciously craves for radical changes in life. It is the realization that the goals we set for ourselves are beyond our reach. Then, by changing venue, mentally or physically, we believe that life can still be given a value that has eluded us. But if we don't break the routines of our past existence and radically adhere to different objectives, no significant change can ever occur. This is the moment when we become stagnant and step over the borderline into the territory known as "old." Age is a limit we set for ourselves, independent of dependence on our physical condition.

Not unlike getting a divorce after many years of marriage, Robert and I detached ourselves from Hollywood's regimented studio system. Robert cut his ties abruptly, I slowly. Despite my scores of motion picture credits, a few remaining, but most of them forgettable,

I never felt that writing for the screen was my life's vocation. Working for film studios on a fixed salary was the way to pick up instant cash, a cop-out not to face the hardship of a money-producing profession by turning the financial duties over to the hiring company.

Preserving my writings physically in the shape of a book, my work was solely mine, and not the impersonal jigsaw puzzle of a motion picture production with a hundred names on it.

I have based some of my novels, films, and short stories on science fiction themes, intrigued by ideas that anticipated the future as I visualized it, and though I had studied mathematics with its unlimited conceptions, I was not a scientist who has to prove his ideas empirically. That phase I left to specially trained minds. But, in retrospect, I have witnessed during my lifetime many of my conceptions about the future take shape and become utilized.

I had to divorce myself from the easy way of supporting my family by collecting a weekly check from the studios. Since I was writing novels, a time-consuming and highly speculative business, I was obliged from time to time to work for the cash of the motion picture industry.

Robert's volatile mind was fascinated by the astrologer Carroll Righter. It is surprising how many otherwise intelligent people believe that their lives are ruled by stars, which, though we see them in the firmament, might have died eons before. Even the former president Ronald Reagan and his wife, Nancy, based decisions affecting the fate of 250 million Americans on the stellar configurations of a woman fortune-teller in San Francisco.

Robert believed in Carroll Righter's predictions, though the astrologer had been unable to tell the actress Maria Montez, who never made a decision without Righter's horoscope, that she would die of heart failure in her bathtub the same night she had been at his home for consultation.

Righter told Robert what the stars predicted: he would receive a telegram with an offer on October 23, 1951, that would change his life. A telegram arrived on that date, also one the day before and one the day after, from other companies. Robert chose that date the heavenly powers had reserved for his success to direct the film *The Whistle at Eaton Falls,* produced in New York by Louis de Rochemont. It was a failure that panicked Robert so much that he never returned to Hollywood, had his house sold, and started anew in Europe. But in that picture he gave an unknown actor, Ernest Borgnine, a leading part. It made Borgnine a star for many years. Robert must have been in Borgnine's horoscope.

I also wanted to leave Hollywood, never having belonged to the tightly knit, clubby team of picture makers, who helped each other to get jobs. I felt empty having to write pictures for two half-naked young actors, swinging in a jungle from tree to tree, their only confidant being a chimpanzee.

My childhood friend, Frederick Kohner, who, with his novel of a female Andy Hardy, added the word *Gidget* to the American language, told me that Lazar Wechsler of Praesens Films in Switzerland was looking for a writer who was fluent in German and English. It was a fairly certain job, Fred assured me, but one had to see the producer personally in Zurich.

I don't know which one was more adventurous, Robert's flight from Hollywood on advice of an astrologer, or my flight to Europe on speculation. It was the panicky compulsion to change the direction of my life. I was, like Robert, suffering from "*torschluss Panik*," and also from "Canyon fever." The "Canyon" was Hollywood.

Despite having worked for studios for years, I never had felt comfortable among the Hollywood professionals, whose only talent was to work for the screen. That town was swallowing up my productive years and drying up my energies. A writer's job is the most insecure of that business, a clandestine employment between two layoffs.

A loquacious mynah bird helped me to make up my mind. The bird's cage was standing on Vine Street in Hollywood in front of a jewelry store, where he was sunning himself. The mynah was surrounded by amused passersby, who loved to hear him talk.

I heard him say: "Has somebody been to Reykjavik? Nobody has been to Reykjavik? Oh, hell!" It was obviously repeating a dialog it had heard and not forgotten.

"I've been to Reykjavik," I said. That town, the capital of Iceland, was a fueling station for planes flying to or coming from Europe, since at that time airplanes couldn't carry enough fuel for the transatlantic flight. The mynah bird screamed at me, "Scram!"

I walked away, amused by my anger that I had been insulted by a feathery biped.

A week later I found myself in Reykjavik, the capital of Iceland, waiting for the refueling of the plane that would take me to Ireland, then to Amsterdam. There I had to change planes for Zurich, where hopefully I would work for Lazar Wechsler's company, Praesens Films, six thousand miles away from Hollywood.

The airplane was the first jet that I had flown. It had vibrations that strangely interfered with the speaking voice. They were, I guess, on the same frequencies as the human larynx. It was amusing to listen to a pretty stewardess with a cracked vocal cord.

Praesens Films had gained an international reputation, since twice it had received the Hollywood Academy Award for the best foreign film, *The Search* with Montgomery Clift, and *Tenth of March*, which supposedly was the date when the Swiss expected the German army to attack Switzerland.

I was not traveling alone to Europe, having a knowledgeable expert with me, the film salesman Edgar Heumann. A German refugee Jew, he had outwaited Hitler's "Thousand Year Reich" in Switzerland, and was returning to it for the first time.

The Swiss, who created the Red Cross (the white Swiss cross in their flag having changed to red), are compulsive lifesavers. Some of their citizens sheltered Jews during the Nazi persecution. After the war, young Germans who had run away from their homeland, terrified of a possible clash between the Allies, which now included Germany and Stalin's Russia, found refuge in Zurich. They feared that they might have to fight again on the Eastern or Western side. The menace was unreal to me but not to the war-shocked former Hitler Youth.

Switzerland played a schizophrenic role during the war, a fact that I am not permitted to mention to Henrietta, who, Swiss-born, resents my criticizing the land of her birth. She loves that country of her youth, though she would never leave America to live there.

During the war, Allied bombers took the shortcut across the north of Switzerland to attack Bavaria.

With foresight the Swiss had built air-raid shelters for their citizens, since bomb-laden planes might crash on their soil. The planes crossed that neutral country at night by the thousands with impunity, knowing the Swiss would not shoot at them. The Swiss citizens were advised by their government to seek shelter during that Allied flyover, but Jews were not allowed to use that protection. The Swiss were also the first to stamp the word "Jew" on their passport, a racial logo the Nazis gleefully copied.

The owner of my Viennese literary agency, Thomas Sessler, being Jewish, had escaped Austria and had found refuge in Switzerland. The refugee Jews had to stay at night in one of their "Lager," the camps for refugees.

He had fallen in love with a Swiss girl, but was not allowed, by Swiss government decree, to visit her. The Nazis' Nuremberg law, that a Jew was not permitted to cohabitate with an Aryan female, was willingly accepted by the German part of Switzerland.

Disregarding police orders, Thomas Sessler managed to secretly meet his paramour. They conceived a child, Gabrielle, who became "legitimate" only after the war, when her parents finally were married.

There I was again, traveling into an unknown future, though this time protected by a powerful, highly valued, small blue booklet, the American passport. The plane refueled in Ireland, then landed at night in Amsterdam. Edgar Heumann and I were staying over at a hotel to take the early Swiss airplane to Zurich. That night, sleeping in adjoining rooms, I heard Edgar cry. Shocked, I went to see him. He was lying in his bed in a fetal position, sobbing into his pillow, to muffle the sound. I shook him, believing he suffered a nightmare, but he was awake. I asked if he was in pain, but he shook his head, though he did not stop crying. Not knowing what to do, I could only think of shouting at him, asking him to control himself.

We never mentioned that incident to each other, but it might be that the aftershock of his five years of isolation in Switzerland, the constant fear of Germany getting hold of him to murder him, the implied anti-Semitism of the Swiss government, which, as he feared during the war, would adopt Nazi methods, had broken through his thin defense and was overwhelming him at night.

To return to Zurich after twenty-five years was like moving from the nervous hustle of a big city to a village. It was nostalgic and seemingly centuries ago that I had studied at the university and had met Henrietta, my companion for life. I took a lengthy walk through the medieval streets of that ancient city, and found the little square with the still spouting small fountain where we had a memorable lovers' fight. With my then-macho German upbringing I had picked her up and thrown her into the cold water. She still remembers with amusement the water running into her shoes.

Nothing much seemed to have changed. The narrow streets of the inner city looked ageless, as though time had stood still, untouched by the mayhem of the world.

The relentless pressure of the big studios had been replaced by the leisurely tempo of the Praesens film company, which consisted of three people. Lazar Wechsler, producer and boss, was a heavyset man with an authoritative, overpowering personality. Richard Schweitzer was an author of books and screenplays. Leopold Lindtberg was the director. He was also a musician, who, in his later years, moved to Vienna to conduct the orchestra of the State Opera. Leopold and Richard were my age, and completely under the domination of Lazar Wechsler, who seemed to have an almost medieval, possessive power over them. Richard was an autodidact, a self-taught, knowledgeable, but rather unsophisticated writer. Leopold was erudite, distant, reclusive. Our relationship, though friendly, was never intimate.

Wechsler had become wealthy by importing trainloads of coal from Poland, then a communist country. Creating films was his obsession. He also had the intuition and daring of a motion picture tycoon among the Hollywood moguls. Being Jewish, he had great difficulties during the war, constantly harassed by the pro-Nazi-inclined German-Swiss government.

Richard and Leopold also feared the uncanny, mind-reading power of their boss. It was a love-hate affair, more hate than love since their livelihood was dependent on that forceful man. I found Wechsler similar in character to my father: a Jewish patriarch, sentimental but humanly unapproachable, who demanded absolute obedience from his family. Richard and Leopold had to submit to that demand. Lazar's wife, a gentle Catholic woman, adored him, but, like their only son, was suppressed and insignificant in his life.

When his wife died suddenly of a stroke, Lazar didn't for three days inform anyone of her death and kept her body in the bed. He sat Shivah on a small chair close to the corpse, as his orthodoxy demanded, perhaps angry with God for having taken his wife away without his permission.

Lazar observed the ancient Jewish tradition by giving small presents to even casual visitors. It was the echo of a thousand-year-old tradition, when Jewish tribes were nomads and, crossing deserts, had to seek the hospitality of others, spending the night in their hosts' tents. The traveler depended on tribal hospitality, for which he reciprocated with a small gift.

Now that biblical tradition has been accepted by Western cultures. Today, invited guests normally bring a small present, flowers or a bottle of wine, a reminder of the ancient custom of tribal desert hospitality.

Richard had a novelette, *Four Days Leave,* published. It was the story of an American GI, stationed after the war with the occupation army in Germany. He uses his four-day furlough to cross the border into Switzerland to buy himself a wristwatch. He falls, predictably, in love with the girl who sells him the timepiece. It was an innocent story and so slight that today not even an American television situation comedy would have given attention to it. Wechsler refused to accept that story as the basis of a film, guessing rightly that it would not be a financial success. But in love with his creation, Richard wanted to convince Wechsler to produce it. After all, he and Lindtberg had delivered two Academy Award–winning films. Two Oscars! It was a miraculous feat for such a small company.

When Richard became deadly ill with pneumonia, Wechsler went to the hospital and, breaking out into tears, pledged to produce *Four Days,* if Richard would promise him not to die. That commitment was perhaps a better medicine for Richard's recovery than all the physician's skills.

Wechsler's office was unpretentious, consisting of three rooms at the Limmat Quai. When I phoned him, I got an appointment right away, as if he had been waiting for me.

In his anteroom I met an old acquaintance, the UFA director Gustav Ucicky, who had survived the war directing pictures for Joseph Paul Goebbels. During the early Hitler times he had been a close friend of Walter Reisch, the Jewish UFA author and songwriter, who later emigrated to America, writing with Billy Wilder the classic *Ninotchka* for Greta Garbo. Ernst Lubitsch directed that now classic film.

Reisch kept his friendship with Ucicky even when Ucicky, already in 1932, sported a swastika on his lapel. When I asked Reisch how he could associate with a Nazi, his reply was that everybody had the right to his political opinion and that friendship and politics were different things. I don't think that I ever again talked privately with Reisch, though a year later I had to work with him on the screenplay of my novel *F.P. 1 Does Not Answer,* nor did I ever see Reisch privately in Hollywood after our emigration. By then he might have picked up information about the Nazis, since his family was incinerated in Buchenwald.

At Wechsler's office, Ucicky, with a broad grin, greeted me in the slang of Berlin: "Siodmak! Wo biste denn jewesen?" (Where have you been?). "Not in your ovens," I answered, and I went into Wechsler's office. I never saw Ucicky again but heard that the occupation army did not permit him to work in the revived German film industry.

Wechsler at once offered me his ritual present, a fountain pen. He expected that I would write with it the right screenplay for Praesens Films. He also was well-versed about my past, and knew what I had written, in both German and in English. The weekly salary he offered was slim, but it would be paid to Henrietta in America. He also added a skimpy allowance in Swiss francs.

I had a job and Henrietta an income to run the house and perhaps get us out of debt. I had been a few months without a studio income, which had dried up our bank account. Besides, keeping the Beverly Hills house had been way above my income. The Swiss expense account, though meager, carried me through the days. Besides, there was no time to spend any money since my days were clogged with work.

I was accepted by Richard and Leopold: gentle, gifted people, quite different from Hollywood's commercially minded, efficient personalities.

My American travel companion, Edgar Heumann, found a place for me to live, an almost impossible task since, after the end of the war, there was a shortage of accommodations in Zurich. Edgar got me a room at the same *pension* that had sheltered him during the war. The owner, Frau Grundler, was a spinster, who, I suspect, had been in her youth the mistress of a rich Swiss businessman. He had bought her that apartment, which she had cluttered up with too many furniture pieces, heavy drapes, Oriental carpets, and so many knickknacks that you had to navigate the room carefully without breaking anything. But I had a roof over my head and a bed.

Unfortunately, Frau Grundler owned an old mean tomcat that, hating strangers, sneaked into my room to pee on the drapes, and also, should he find the chance, spray into the breadbasket. After the cat's visit, the room smelled like a lion's cage.

Frau Grundler did not have much money since, whenever I paid the rent, she went immediately to the bank to store the "frankli" in her savings account, not to lose one single day of the 3 percent yearly interest. She also talked about suicide, together with her cat, before she would starve to death, a remote possibility since she was of ample weight.

We worked at Schweitzer's home with a clockwork routine. In the morning Richard religiously wound up his barometer on the mantelpiece, a religious procedure that Leopold hated. At twelve o'clock sharp lunch was served. The menu never varied during the week: Thursday, I remember, was dumplings day, Saturday boiled chicken.

Lindtberg despised Schweitzer's bureaucratic routines and never appeared at the meals. On Sundays Richard liked to drive into the country for lunch, to an old inn, where a young girl served Johannesberger, a fragrant Swiss country wine. A teenager, she wore no makeup, and it was not the Swiss custom for a girl to shave her legs. If reincarnation existed, she might have been an antelope in a former life. Accustomed to American hygiene, I expect a girl to take a shower every day, shave her legs and armpits. The girl had a dark Italian peasant's face in which Richard saw the model for the Renaissance Madonnas.

In contrast to the no-nonsense Hollywood work habits, it was a frictionless way of working among Richard's numerous collection of Swiss music boxes, masterworks of craftsmanship, instruments that cannot be bought but are handed down from family to family. Leopold invited me to his small apartment when Furtwangler conducted the Berlin Philharmonic Orchestra. He and his wife, Sonja, listening to the radio, followed the full score on music sheets, expertly criticizing or praising Furtwangler's renditions. I found myself in the graceful world before World War II, a world of vanished nineteenth-century cultural Europe.

There, fifty miles to the north, was Germany, still digging itself out of mental and physical debris. To write a motion picture about postwar Germany would have been topical and more interesting than describing the leisurely life in Switzerland with its ostentatious prosperity and centuries of ingrained conservatism.

We drove to Zermatt, the ancient village at the foot of Mont Blanc, looking for shooting locations, since a Swiss picture without snow is an anachronism. That year not one snowflake had fallen on Zermatt, and the sun was shining hot, but the newsreel at the small cinema showed the houses and trees in Beverly Hills in California heavily covered with snow, an event that had never happened in people's memory. We contemplated shooting that Swiss picture in Beverly Hills.

Finally, the screenplay was finished. The picture was going into production. Wechsler and Richard had wheedled production money out of the Swiss watch industry, having convinced that powerful cartel about the advertising value of *Swiss Tour,* to which the title had been changed.

Wechsler engaged international stars for his pictures. The French actress Simone Signoret (Simone Kaminker) was to play the Swiss girl. Cornel Wilde, on loan from Fox Studios in Hollywood, portrayed the American GI. To study our female star, Richard, Leopold, and I had lunch with Simone at Baur-au-Lac, the internationally renowned hotel in Zurich. I met the French star, a slim young woman in her late twenties. She had an overwhelming sensuality, with a translucent skin, slanted gray eyes, and a dangerously flirtatious demeanor, which intimidated us three admirers. To fall in love with her, her attitude a visible invitation, would have sapped all my attention and strength.

Simone flirted with the waiters as she flirted with us, a way that improved their service as if she were the only guest. I could have easily fallen in love with her, but was aware that I would have to leave my typewriter to be at her call and whim, by day and at night.

In self-defense I avoided meeting her again, afraid of the lure of that professional mantrap. Even many years later, after she got old and fat, that short hour we talked together never dimmed in my memories.

I encountered that sensual female quality only in one other actress, the Hollywood star Lee Remick: an unexplainable emanation, to which I, though perhaps not every male, was fatally attracted.

Simone married Yves Montand, the actor. Montand had a widely publicized affair with Marilyn Monroe, which would have destroyed any American marriage but not that of a wise Frenchwoman. She outwaited his infatuation and got her husband back with no part missing.

Suddenly the foam of the tide of World War II swept into Switzerland, invading Frau Grundler's apartment. Having sheltered Jews during the war, she now "saved" young Germans by giving them refuge and food. The Germans were between eighteen and thirty, some of the Hitler Youth or the defunct army. Those young men were terrified by the possibility of a new conflagration, since the friction between the USSR and America had created the Cold War. Standing in front of a large map of Europe, which they had fastened to a door, they discussed the safest way to leave Europe via Marseille or Italy.

Those boys owned nothing, not even warm clothes for a harsh winter. I, a Jew who had been driven out of Germany, supplied them with money and clothes I could spare, and gave them even my beloved overcoat with a furry lining.

Those homeless youths were a bewildered group, branded by the terror they had lived through. They were at a loss for how to continue their lives. One seventeen-year-old told me that his father had beaten him senseless when he refused to join the "Werewolves," that secret organization that, after the collapse of Germany, was ordered to conduct, according to Hitler's last orders, a guerrilla war, to continue the fighting, though their "leader" had deserted them by shooting himself. The boy's father threatened to kill his son should he be unfaithful to his beloved "Fuehrer," that ghost that still haunts Germany.

That lost German youth reminded me of the hours when I had had to flee with the only possession I could take with me, my culture. Twelve years later I again wrote a screenplay in German for Lazar Wechsler, *Feuerschiff* (The Fireship), a floating lighthouse in the Atlantic. The film was based on a story by the German novelist Siegfried Lentz. That film received the German Oscar, the Bundespreis, as the best German picture of 1963.

When I left Zurich, Wechsler handed me a golden Pateck Philip wristwatch, not for me to keep, but to give to Darryl Zanuck, the boss of Twentieth Century–Fox, a gift for which Zanuck reciprocated by releasing the Praesens film *Swiss Tour* in his theaters.

It was an expensive gift for Mr. Zanuck, since that movie lost money for Twentieth Century–Fox distribution.

The ambience in the studios changed slowly and became more and more impersonal. For me the fun went out of picture making. Television started as a small competition but soon threw the studio production into disarray. To counteract TV's appeal, giant screens like Cinemascope appeared; multi-sound, even three-dimensional films, were tried, but none worked out. They were too cumbersome to be projected since the audience had to wear Polaroid glasses. In creating a motion picture for cinema theaters, the studios produced in one working day only forty seconds to one minute of finished footage, while the creators of television films had to deliver at least ten minutes to stay within their budget.

Television, to be profitable, had to stay within a tight budget. Directors who did not bring the show in on time were fired. The finished product was presold to advertising companies and television stations. The purpose of television is not to tell stories, but to advertise commercial goods to as great a number of viewers as possible.

Besides, TV was for free, and the studio overhead, the bloated salaries of actors and producers, didn't make sense anymore. To run the big studio machinery the old-fashioned way nearly bankrupted MGM, Fox, RKO, and Paramount.

The actors and actresses often were plain-looking people before their features, enhanced by makeup artists and skillful lighting of their bone structure, became memorable to millions. Their presence was part of the silver screen's allure.

In the fifties, the actress-stars were mostly young and just past their teen years. Sex scenes with post-teenage young girls would have smacked of pedophilia, which, according to Calvinistic ethics, is a crime worse than murder. Today actress-stars are mostly in their thirties, which, since they are consenting adults, seems to make any graphic copulation on the screen acceptable. I find any overt sex actions of adult couples on the screen boring, since photographed fake intercourse is tiresomely restricted by the very lack of variation.

In the fifties, sex scenes were unthinkable, and the censorship to which the film industry of that period was subject harked back to the Victorian age. The Hays Code decreed that any kiss between a male and a female was not permitted to last longer than four seconds on the screen. Even legally married people slept in different beds, kept apart by a nightstand. If a woman was sitting on a bed and a man kissed her, she had to keep one foot on the floor, whatever the situation.

The mentioning of alcohol was likewise taboo. Ronald Colman, the handsome leading man, toasted his paramour with, "I lift this glass of water to drink to our undying love."

Bankers and Jews could not be depicted as villains. Though the film moguls', directors', and casting directors' private lives could fill the pages of any tabloid, the decorum of film purity was strictly enforced, as though sex itself were as dangerous as a loaded gun.

The term *casting couch* was not an empty expression.

For me to work in studios was pure entertainment, especially during the lunch hour in the Fox commissary where everybody mixed, regardless of their financial remuneration. Darryl Zanuck kept a collection of stunningly beautiful, very young women known as the Fox girls under contract. There was Linda Darnell, who applied for a studio job when she was fourteen. She was sent home, despite her Madonna-like beauty, but asked to return when she was sixteen. A talent scout had discovered Brenda Joyce at UCLA. She became a star with her first picture, *The Rains Came,* a best-selling novel so overwhelmingly successful for its author that its success made him blow his brains out. A tall New York model, Kay Aldrich, who, though never becoming a major star, stunned the commissary daily at lunchtime with her statuesque attractiveness.

Some human bodies possess a visual proportion, an acme of abstract beauty, that does not convey the lure of sex.

An Irish girl with flaming red hair in her midtwenties, Maureen O'Hara (Maureen Fitzsimmons), had been brought over by Charles Laughton after he made a picture with the Irish Abbey Players. She played Lady Godiva, a typecasting for her. I regretted that her luxurious waves of hair even covered her thighs when she sat on the white horse. Betty Grable, the pinup girl of World War II, had her legs underinsured for a million dollars. Corbina Wright Jr., a classic beauty, who didn't become a star because she was too well bred to fit into the sex-teasing gaggle of girls, made up for that short-coming by brimming with joie de vivre.

One day I was sitting behind two starlets, Gene Tierney and Jeanne Crain. I was very choosy in picking the right table. Since they both had a small gap between their front teeth, I knew that they were Fox stars. Zanuck had an indefinable affection for very young women whose two front teeth did not touch.

During Marlene Dietrich's heyday, it was the shape of the women's legs that was the sexual attraction. Howard Hughes changed that conception during his short time as a film producer. The rumor went around that Hughes and Zanuck procured girls for each other of the size preferred by those reigning tycoons.

I sat at the table behind Gene Tierney and Jeanne Crain, trying to pick up female speech patterns, which were unknown to me, a foreigner. I eavesdropped, unethically, on their conversation. Since they obviously were very close friends, Jeanne Crain complained about her husband. According to her, he could not wait to make love to her, and would immediately attack her when she entered their home. He didn't bother with preliminaries and often forced her into an interlude with him on the carpet, before she had time to take off her hat. To wear a hat was the fashion in those days. Glancing "casually" at Jeanne, with her translucent skin, purity, sweetness, and gentle demeanor, looking as innocent in real life as in the parts for which she was usually cast, I felt that the sexual impatience of her husband was understandable.

Then Gene, an enchanting beauty whose gentle features expressed her breeding, said something that changed my life and made me aware of a dark uncertainty within me, a painfully vague affliction that no professional psychiatrist could or can explain. Gene complained to her friend that she suffered from deep depressions, a bottomless vague despair, even now at the pinnacle of her success, fame, and fortune, facts that did not prevent her from sinking into a suicidal gloom. She did not know anymore how to be happy.

Reading her autobiography years later, she even tried, vainly, to be cured by the celebrated Menninger Clinic for the Mentally Disturbed in Topeka, Kansas, but without any results. Only constant work that occupied her mind helped her to stay alive. The Menninger Clinic subjected her to drugs and to thirty-eight electric shock treatments, an inhuman torture that blocks out the memory of the patient for a time. It was the modern version of the medieval time when insane people were lowered into a snake pit, believing that the fear of snakes would cure them. But that treatment to which she was forced to submit only created an unspeakable horror in her. She confessed that she had experienced no greater pain or despair in life than her mental depression.

I got up and walked aimlessly through the studio. I used to thrive on the organized commotion of that dream factory, which was a tight, well-oiled organization, where cameramen, grips, makeup artists, electricians, and actors were of impeccable soulless perfection and proficiency. Nobody in that antlike hustle needed to be told what to do or when. The technical machinery operated as precisely as the crew of a racing yacht whose every movement is executed with minute precision and perfection.

I was aware that I suffered, like Gene Tierney, from chronic depressions, which perhaps are based on a psychological condition. That mental anguish, that "darkness visible," as the writer William Styron describes in his memoirs of madness, might have a chemical origin: perhaps a lack or overproduction of serotonin, or other brain substances still unknown to scientists, or the cause might be genetic.

I have no other possibility, to my way of thinking, than to rely on the three pounds and two ounces of brain, no more and no less, that nature allots to every human being. I try not to fall into the trap of the mortal arrogance of believing that the mystery of human existence, with its high peaks and deep valleys, can ever be completely understood by our limited minds.

A change in life's direction often occurs when a man reaches the age between forty and fifty. Then the mental weather vane of his existence starts to move, first imperceptibly, unaware to him, except that he is plagued by a vague feeling of the futility of his existence. In his subconscious an alien growth takes shape, which sometimes seeks release in divorce, a complete change of profession, a flight from the city into a rural background, or any other outlet that he expects will give his mind a purposeful slant on life.

When I came home from the studio, where I had worked under artificial light, the sun was going down. Again one day was crossed out of the span of my life.

At home, I heard the voices of guests. I went to my room to change. A clean shirt lifts the spirit. I looked into the Biedermeier mirror on the wall, the same mirror that now after fifty years hangs in my bedroom as a reminder of the constancy of living that repeats itself like a train schedule. Our daily routine tries to replace what we have used up, nothing more. There is not much variation in making a "living." The clock of time leaves a visible trace—aging.

I looked at my face, which was lined and tired. I had the vague feeling that I must change the pattern of my life. What was I doing to myself? To where did my accumulating years lead?

Working for the motion picture industry is like weaving smoke, its ashes interesting only to film historians. Who of my young friends has heard of Walter Pidgeon; Eduardo Ciannelli, with whom I worked in Brazil; Henry King, the director; John Boles, who played in more than a hundred pictures? Or my friend George Sherman, who directed more than a hundred films and died broke and forgotten?

I had to go back to writing books. Then my ideas would be on paper, and would go on living for a time after me. They might be found a hundred years from now in a secondhand bookstore. Then I still would be alive. Since I was not a trained scientist, the only way open to me was writing fiction.

Every morning I went to the studio office, where I had to switch on the electric lights and sit behind a typewriter in a cramped position, which over the years affected my solar plexus and created chronic nausea. Then I went home, fighting the rush hour. I paid off our maid, Halloween. Halloween lived in my lovely home in Beverly Hills, while I was sitting in that studio outhouse. She enjoyed my home in Beverly Hills while I, in a small room, pressed typewriter keys to make the money to pay for her pleasure? Something was wrong in the way I was conducting my life. Returning home I mostly found "friends" in my bar, which, as a hobby, I had stocked with every conceivable brand of liquor.

Some years ago I had been to the Satire Bookstore on Vine Street, and had climbed up to the attic, where I sometimes had found treasures by rummaging in out-of-print books. A huge old leatherbound Bible, the English Father Brown version of 1820, was lying in a corner, covered with dust. I bought it for $7.50. It was a treasure, which I displayed on my large Renaissance chest, a three-hundred-year-old monster that I had found in an antique store in Westwood Village. I guess that a hundred years ago rich Italian emigrants had brought their furniture, huge cumbersome pieces, with them. That heavy furniture might have come from the captain's cabin of a clipper ship. But those enormous pieces took too much room in a modern apartment, and ended up in antique shops. The one I bought had a patina that only centuries can produce.

I had the Bible rebound by an old craftsman in Pasadena, maybe the last master of that disappearing art. He fell in love with it, used the original leather binding, blending it with some of the same color.

Charles Laughton had become a steady guest in our house since Henrietta, on his first visit, had baked a marzipan soufflé for him that, despite his sexual preference, made him fall madly in love with her. Her cooking magic pleased his palate.

Laughton brought members of the British colony to our home. The British in Hollywood kept mostly to themselves. An exclusive club, they kept away from plebeian American actors.

Once an Englishman, always an Englishman. My friend Charles Bennett, Alfred Hitchcock's writer of memorable pictures, came to America in 1936, and six decades later still held on to his British passport, though he never resettled in his native country.

Charles Laughton brought Michael Redgrave, a tall, distinguished British actor, and his wife, Rachel, along. They had two small children, Vanessa and Lynn, who became well-known actresses. Leo Glenn and his wife, Margaret, joined us. Leo, a former barrister, was an equal match for the Fox Studios lawyers. When he was slated to play the psychiatrist in the film *The Snake Pit,* the studio refused to meet his salary demand. A master in brinksmanship, Leo packed up to return to England. He had already boarded the *Queen Mary* when a telegram reached him, asking him to return to Fox Studios. The studio agreed to all of his demands. It helps being a lawyer when dealing with the capitalistic motion picture companies.

That cultured British crowd used my house with its comforts and Henrietta's gourmet food as a stopover between work and their own homes. From the ceiling in the bar dangled a row of Dutch Churchwarden pipes, each inscribed with the name of a different guest, a time-honored habit I had found in London pubs.

A guest picked up his clay pipe, filled it with my chosen Sobranje tobacco, poured himself a drink, and started a conversation, which was never dull. Laughton read from his next play, Bertolt Brecht's *Galileo.* I was not too enthusiastic about it and said, "But what Brecht wrote is commonplace."

"True," the famous actor said, giving the answer that changed my approach to writing forever, "but he formulated it—you didn't."

He liked to read to us from the Father Brown Bible. "Daniel in the lion's den," he stated, "is basically a comedy." Then he read that chapter with the intonation of a Shakespearean actor, and it became a hilarious tale. Redgrave, to show off his versatility as an actor, contested him by reading the same chapter as a dark tragedy. It was their intonation, the timbre of their voice, their timing and conception, that gave the story a different meaning.

Laughton became so enchanted with his performance that he started to read the Bible in public, then branched out to get a group of British actors together to deliver George Bernard Shaw's *Don Juan in Hell*. He traveled a year with great success throughout America.

Our British club broke up dramatically. Michael Redgrave fell in love with his male secretary and did not join us anymore. His wife Rachel endured that event with a fortitude that I believe only a British lady can muster. But that change of sexual preference I had witnessed before in men around fifty, as in the writers Louis Bromfield and Thomas Mann, that in those days mortified society. Oscar Wilde went to prison for it. In America, some states declared homosexuality a criminal offense. In southern states intercourse was permitted only in the "missionary position," though I never found out how the states asserted that law, also whether all missionaries abided by it.

Redgrave, deserting our pleasant gatherings, destroyed the relaxed atmosphere of our British club, and I soon found the house without guests from the British Isles.

The public interest in horror pictures, which had ensured steady jobs for me, suddenly ceased for psychological reasons. During the war, horror pictures were in great demand. They released the suppressed fear of people during the global killings and murders, especially when their husbands or sons served in the armed forces. Now, since that pressure had disappeared with the end of the war, their anxieties also vanished. Love stories and musicals became the public's preference and took over the market.

Looking back at the history of motion pictures, the image on the screen is a mirror of our present time or of a coming social trend. The Eisenhower years were a fermata of tranquility before a coming storm. Now the world again is in turmoil. Murder, horror, and bloodshed again are depicted on motion picture and television screens, rivaled only by actual bloody news. Films camouflage death as entertainment, even in children's games like Nintendo and in the horror of animated cartoons. Disney films, in juxtaposition to their "children's programs," imprint brutality in the mind of infants, numbing them toward the cruelties of daily life. Those nightmare cartoons are shown mostly on Saturdays as "children's hour." But now we can see public satiation of graphic mayhem that is called "entertainment." Brutality has been augmented with sex scenes. I always change the television station when I see a gun on the screen, or the tiring movements under bedsheets.

Since the amusing circle of our intelligent European friends had disappeared, Henrietta and I wanted to change our Beverly Hills lifestyle, and, as usual, I waited for her to make that decision.

There are "autobiographies," the life stories written by people who are convinced or want to impress others with their prominence, soul exposures of actors, musicians or industrialists, statesmen, madams, even murderers. Those books, written in the first person, are "self-portraits." On the title page, one usually finds an acknowledgement: "Written with Joe Doe," or whatever ghostwriter the author had paid to put his life story on paper. Autobiographies are often doctored to paint the "author" in the most favorable light he wants to be seen by others. Nobody likes to talk about his shortcomings and failures, which inevitably are part of our existence. How often do we succeed in our efforts? If the biographer does not have enough interesting material to tell, he "hypes" his memoirs with "kiss and tell" incidents to document his carnal prowess. He describes encounters with people of name or substance, or, in women's cases, their unfailing female allure. Biographies are written during the last quarter of one's life, a reminiscence of *temps perdus,* to relive past glory. Life stories are looking backward, not forward, and for me are only of interest when they are ventilating the history of the writer's time.

My brother Robert left his memoirs, *Between Berlin and Hollywood,* copious notes that Hans Blumenberg, the gifted author, journalist, and biographer, organized into a book after Robert's death. Robert spiked his life story with anecdotes that were not always true, but often amusing. The book, first called *I Knew Them All,* told about his work with famous actors of his time, names that have lost their meaning for the present generation. Actors such as Thomas Mitchell, Melvin Douglas, Agnes Moorehead, Burt Lancaster, Frank Morgan, Emil Jannings, and others who were well known to the public when he was a successful motion picture director, but they have become ghosts in ancient films on the television screen. Who remembers Louis Bromfield, John P. Marquant, Irving Stone, or John Dos Passos, my favorite authors of thirty years ago? They might be mentioned, but still, who reads their books? If I scan the libraries in private homes, they reveal to me the age group of their owners.

These biographies are read by people whose lives are seemingly devoid of reachable dreams. Then their readers might vicariously identify themselves with their heroes. They are clones of "Walter Mitty" in James Thurber's revealing short story.

The other kind of memoir is the unauthorized biography, written without the famous person's consent, the life history of his victims without their royal clothes, exposing their vulnerabilities, foibles, and warts, often uncovering juicy scandals that "authors" keep out of their biographies.

I am writing my "unauthorized" autobiography, motivated to understand my own failures, and why they happened, trying to cope with them in retrospect. It is curious that the motivations of some of our faulty actions become clear to us sometimes only after decades, actions that we trace to a flaw in our character, or a misjudgment of circumstances, for which our ego refuses to accept responsibility. Sometimes glaring mistakes in our lives might turn out well, changing disaster into luck, a serendipity over which we have no influence. Different causes and times in our lives intersect by chance. The result is called "fate."

Once I heard a German jokingly confess, "We are intolerable and you are responsible for it." There was a grain of truth in his witticism. We try to take credit for successes, and easily blame others for our failures.

In writers' lives, only a minute part of their work finds its realization. That does not mean that their writing lacks quality, or that their ideas are dull, but they are dependent on the "concept of acceptance," uncontrollable elements, like timing, fashion of the masses, fickle elements that may change without forewarning, or which are rejected by their peers, who, content in their position in life, do not want to deal with any change.

The making of a motion picture or the writing of a book or play sometimes takes years of incubation from the idea to the finished product. The vision of the creative artist might be too early, like that of many inventors, painters, and musicians. Being lucky, he might just drop right into the epicenter of the demands of his time. Then he becomes well known, rich, and celebrated, like the two young men who built a computer in their garage, an invention that has already changed the world their parents and peers once knew.

Perceiving the truth, but not being recognized, contains its tragedies. Ignaz Philipp Semmelweis, a Hungarian obstetrician of the last century, warned his colleagues that by failing to disinfect their surgical instruments, they condemned childbearing women to death. The medical profession of the nineteenth century ridiculed his theory. While a large percentage of their patients died of "unknown causes," Semmelweis, whose theory had belatedly changed the concept of medicine, in desperation, committed suicide.

When Mozart's *The Magic Flute* was performed for the first time at the Vienna Opera, the conservative Viennese music lovers pelted the singers with tomatoes. Picasso, through his still-unfinished painting *Les Demoiselles d'Avignon,* was a trailblazer, changing the world of his contemporaries. So were the works of the Impressionists and painters of the abstract: Otto Dix, Miró, Kirchner, and dozens of now accepted and understood works of artists. It is the fate of the innovator that he is decades ahead of his time. Nazi Germany made an issue of this development by banning and even destroying *entartete Kunst* (decayed art). Goebbels "ordered" a new German culture: German writing, German music, German science, rejecting Einstein's "Jewish" theory of relativity. Creating "culture" by fiat doesn't work. Culture is like a tree that slowly grows before it produces fruit.

It is an ego-crushing experience to soberly examine one's own failures. But looking back, while writing my autobiography, unauthorized by my ego, I have spent more than half of my life's work on projects that ended up in boxes heaped in my garage, and have compromised ideas, intimidated by the haphazard and fickle public "concept of acceptance." Now a film museum, the Stiftung Deutscher Kinemathek in Berlin, and the Mugar Library of Boston University see merit in those discarded manuscripts as an example of the customs, thoughts, habits, and foibles of our times.

In my voluntary mental research, many past mistakes, which at the time were shrouded in darkness, have now become painfully visible to me. Why did my brother Robert and I like to associate with shady business characters? Did we resent being dominated by an authoritative film studio? Or did we, since we missed the love of our parents, overestimate our capacity to handle our lives ourselves?

Robert, who found shady people more amusing than honest ones, liked to work in Europe, which has other rules of entrepreneurship than Hollywood, where big film companies are solid factories, whose shares are officially traded on Wall Street. Character shortcomings of Robert's, after a brilliant life, made him fizzle out like a dying meteor, and resulted in his lonely and early death.

A book belongs to its author as long as it is in the process of being in work. He has no influence on its future fate. To overcome his frustrations about his work's uncertainty, a writer has to start another project immediately, and should not wait for the result of the previous one, just as a rider should immediately mount his steed after a fall.

Although everything in Hollywood is for sale, one single element is not within the grasp of the Hollywood producers and studios, nor can it be created by throwing money at it, Hollywood's only weapon. It is the originality of the idea or situation, which cannot be created on demand. Anybody, if willing, can be taught to write a screenplay, to direct a motion picture, to act in it, to edit it, to put it together, though its quality is based on the person's skill. Everybody has original ideas, but one ingredient cannot be taught: transforming those ideas into a legible language, putting words into a continuity until they form logical sentences. Hidden in every block of raw marble is the shape of Michelangelo's *Pietà*. Marble blocks build the mountains of Carrara, but the ability to visualize their hidden inner shapes is the rare gift of creation.

Inspiration resulting from ideas created in other people's brains has happened as long as art has existed. To use another's original creation has happened since time immemorial. Every idea, even the tool of the caveman, started with a nucleus, the original idea. Bertolt Brecht, top writer of my generation, cynically acknowledged, "I don't care on which pile of shit I find my pearls." Didn't he adapt the *Beggars Opera*, the seventeenth-century operetta of the London underworld, without ever mentioning John Gay, its original author? Wasn't Shakespeare's *Hamlet* an adaptation of a medieval Danish play?

Creating without a previous assignment requires vision and a discipline that only compulsive artists have. Michelangelo could clearly see the shape of the *Pietà* in an unhewn block of stone and Rembrandt saw his paintings on the blank canvas. The vision of ideas cannot be expressed in money. Who can measure the power of creative artists who can see where others are blind?

The United States is not a country. It is a continent. Crossing it by air, there are hundred-mile stretches seemingly without signs of life, sometimes dotted by villages and small cities.

When we lived in Europe, we were cosmopolitan. A train would take us in a few hours into countries of another culture, whose language we hardly understood or not at all, like Denmark, Sweden,

France, Italy, or the Slavic-speaking countries, other worlds with their own traditions and habits, their history dating back thousands of years.

It had been exhilarating to walk down the streets of Verona with twelfth-century houses looking down at us, or to stroll through the old part of Prague with its stately palaces and statued bridges spanning the Vistula River. They were built at a time when America wasn't even "discovered."

Hollywood wasn't a continent or a country or city, but a cluster of well-advertised film factories erected in jerry-built structures. I traveled every morning through the same streets, to return the same way, mentally detached from the ongoing history of the world. I became bored, living in a dull world with its monomaniacal love for strips of celluloid, the lifestream of mentally limited people. The studio people's interest in anything else but film production had dried up.

It was a vacuous life, especially for Europeans who were accustomed to mental intercourse in many subjects, and from a place where the film industry was not the major topic. My job in those years was for me without direction, and I knew that middle-aged people didn't have a future. The American society is maniacally youth directed.

I was not a company man who finds his life's fulfillment by going daily to the studio, like William Wright, a minor MGM executive, whose wife told me, "If my Bill couldn't go to the studio every morning, or if he lost his job at MGM, he would die!" I had never been able to integrate myself into the film machinery as my sole profession.

The studios were prisons. With their high walls, the entrance guarded by security men in uniform, they were as difficult to enter as Fort Knox. Fed stories by the studios' publicity departments, the outside world believed those walled-in compounds were inhabited only by glamorous males and females, famous the world over, and deliciously scandal-ridden. The stars whom I daily met looked pretty ordinary to me.

I wanted to change venue, but did not know how.

Then I met Richard Kay and Harry Rybnick, two ambitious young producers who wanted to acquire one of my screenplays that I had written on speculation. It was my conviction that a writer has to turn out words every day of his life, or his brain would dry up. How those two had gotten hold of my screenplay, which I hadn't tried to peddle, I didn't know, but they saw in it a moneymaking picture. I told them I would sell it if they'd let me direct it, and suggested that we shoot it in Brazil. I had heard that in San Bernado, a suburb of São Paulo, a studio with the latest equipment existed.

My screenplay was that of a cocky young American female, a medical biochemist, who, intrigued by the jungle natives' ability to shrink human heads, went to the Brazilian jungles to discover that secret. In her opinion, that chemical concocted of jungle plants might shrink tumors and cancerous tissues in humans. Kay and Rybnick made a deal. My lawyer, Richard Lerner, objected. I should have asked for more money.

But my urge to get out of Hollywood was obsessive. I didn't listen to Dick's objections. I knew that I was grossly underpaid, getting only five thousand dollars for the screenplay, direction, and the months I had to spend on that venture. But as always in my life, money was of minor concern. I wanted to make a picture in South America, which was a challenge since no studio ever had succeeded in bringing back a completed motion picture. Orson Welles, with the RKO money behind him, had come back after months without a completed film. But he had fun spending a fortune during the Rio carnival, which he photographed. The trouble was that he had no screenplay. That couldn't happen to me, a writer.

Dick Kay, a gentle man, had been an assistant director but now sold mattresses and had some knowledge of production. He contracted a young actress, Beverly Garland (Beverly Fessenden), who was anxious to run away from her husband after a turbulent divorce. She told me that she was physically afraid of him and he was still pursuing her. She couldn't get far enough away from him. The Amazon River promised that desire. Pert and pretty, Beverly was a "trouper," the perfect cast for the picture, not afraid of hardship, a courage that I had found in very few actresses.

I intended to include in the film the Iguacu waterfall in Argentina, which rivaled in size those of the Niagara Falls. Since I was shooting in Brazil, I didn't want to endanger my leading actors by sending them to another country without my supervision. I wanted to use a second unit to take the shots. My idea was to have rubber masks made of my actors' faces. The audience wouldn't know the difference. Nobody did, since the second unit, with the waterfalls in the background, never took close-ups of the actors. Matte shots, the technique to integrate actors in a film laboratory with another background, were still unknown.

I took Beverly to a company that specialized in death masks. The company also worked for motion picture studios. Hollow straws were inserted into the nostrils of the actors, a latex concoction was poured over their faces, and they had to lie motionless until that goo had solidified.

I have had a hysterical fear of suffocation since childhood, when my tonsils were removed. Ice cream was promised to me, but my parents fed me chocolate mousse. I felt betrayed. I still remember the chloroform mask that was forced on my face. I was convinced that I was going to be murdered, since I couldn't breathe. The memory of it is still so vivid in my mind that I have never again in my life eaten chocolate mousse.

Beverly, too, was not enthusiastic about my idea until she saw the rubber imprint of the naked body of a young actress of her generation, Carolyn Jones, who appeared in the TV monster show *The Addams Family*. "If she can do it, I can do it," Beverly decided, which assured me that she wouldn't even be scared by giant snakes.

Henrietta, who knows me better than I ever will, knew that I had to leave Hollywood and break the routine of studio jobs. I flew Pan-American Airlines. It took thirty-six hours for that four-motor plane to fly from Los Angeles to Belem, the town where I was going to take the exterior jungle shots. Belem, the Portuguese name for the biblical town Bethlehem, the "town of bread," lies on the mouth of the Amazon where the huge river meets the Atlantic Ocean.

The only food served on the flight was cold, dried-out chicken. Since Pan-Am had no competition on that route, it didn't care about its passengers. I wrote a letter to the chairman of Pan-Am, Juan Trippe, challenging him to take that trip and live on cold chicken. I didn't get a reply. Whenever the plane descended for refueling, in Caracas or Managua, groups of armed soldiers, small in size but big in smell, invaded the plane. They mercifully left the plane at the next descent. Since no surface roads existed between towns that could be traveled by motor vehicles, the plane filled with goats, leaving standing room only. Time jumped from the Stone Age into the twentieth century.

We flew mostly along the coast and finally landed in Belem. Dick Kay was waiting for me. He had made shooting arrangements. Since we were underfinanced, we had to start right away. We stayed at the Grand Hotel Belem, where time had stood still since Portuguese colonial times. In the evening a quartet, three males and a woman, played dinner music from a tiny balcony, adding to the charm of that place. It made up for any kind of unpalatable food, whose consistency was a mystery to me. But fresh fruits, delicious and some unknown to me, were a gourmand's treat. My room had a "bathroom," a completely tiled cubicle, a shower head in the middle of the ceiling, and a hole in the floor. There one took the evening shower, and the opening in the floor served as the toilet, a method that I found more sanitary than an American bathroom.

Beverly arrived with the leading man, John Bromfield, whose good looks replaced his lack of acting ability. The rest of the cast were Brazilians who spoke English, and a crew who obviously had never seen a camera, but tried to advise me after two days' shooting. The excellent cameraman was Rudolf Icsey, a gentle, taciturn Hungarian, who had lived in Brazil for twenty years. He owned a French camera, an Eclair-Tirage, and knew how to shoot in Techniscope and Eastman color. His efficiency saved the film.

There was the enormous Amazon River, miles wide, water shimmering caused by the decay it carried. Sometimes a whole tree-covered small island floated by. Broken loose from the river's shore, it disappeared into the ocean. I never saw any live animals, and we had to borrow them from the Belem zoo. Piranhas, small sharp-toothed fish, existed, but at that time of the year they had, fortunately, migrated a hundred miles upstream. I was told that those fish could strip any living thing to its bones in minutes. To cross the river, the ranchers led a single cow into the water, which kept the piranhas busy, in order to cross with the rest of the herd somewhere else.

Every day, punctually in the afternoon, it rained buckets of water. The curtain of rain was curiously confined, and so restricted that one could step out of it onto dry pavement. The Brazilians have an expression: "See you after the rain," which meant exactly 3 P.M.

Since I was looking for adventure, I didn't have to look any further.

Even in midair, flying away from the Amazon, I couldn't get the picture of the fighting Indians off my retina. The last week I had staged a mock fight between two "tribes" but couldn't stop the untrained natives from cutting each other up. Real blood, not only tomato juice, was flowing, though John Bromfield, who was an expert in film fights, demonstrated to the Indians how to throw a blow, how to fake a stab, how to fall, and how never to hurt anybody in that "fight." But those tribal people got into a real melee, obviously enjoying the brutality of it. That scene was more a bloodbath than a staged scene. Since the shaman was versed in jungle medical arts, which will disappear with the cutting down of the jungle, I depended on him to take care of the cut skins—maybe better than a trained doctor, who didn't exist there.

With every mile flying I got farther away from that constant heat. Beverly badly needed a hairdresser. I couldn't use her emaciated face in close-up. Only John didn't show any sign of wear.

Dick Kay had left for the States, taking the exposed film with him. He assured me that I could finish the job easily without him. I knew that his nerves had become frayed and he was mentally exhausted. I hadn't seen any dailies (exposed film), and had to depend on my memory, a very inept way to shoot a motion picture. In a Hollywood studio, shots can be repeated. I couldn't take the Amazon with me. Beverly and John never uttered a word of complaint, not wanting to make the situation more complicated for me. "Don't shoot the piano player; he does his best" was a sign in a western bar. The worst was over, so I thought. Now we could work in controlled sets, and not step on poisonous snakes.

To direct in Hollywood is not difficult. The "bigger" the director, the easier the job for him. He takes his cutter, who advises him of the camera setups he needs to put the film together, with him on the set. Voice coaches look after his actors, and he has the choice of the most efficient ones. He can shoot twenty takes of a man just walking to a house. He can repeat scenes if the laboratory isn't satisfied; he can expose fifty feet of negative for each one used in the finished picture, whereas I was forced to shoot three to one—that is, three feet of negative for one used in the final cut. Technically nothing bad can happen to a big director with the studio behind him.

But directors of B pictures, like me, especially in a foreign country where the crew speaks another language and where the main objective of the "natives" is to get as much money from the "gringos" as possible, have a tough time. When I found that the crew was underpaid and the chief electrician got only thirty dollars a month, I doubled the salaries. Wrong! Cables broke, lights didn't function, the carpenters worked at snail speed, the grips took twice as long in order to drag out the time. Should, would, if . . . I should have promised them a bonus instead and would have saved money, if . . . Dick had told me that the sets had been built in the studios in San Bernado, that suburb of São Paulo where the interiors of the film were to be shot. So far we had photographed in the Belem jungle. Many things I did not know but soon found out.

Beverly and John wanted to go home to America, where drinking water came out of faucets, and had not been bought in bottles, where plants were not poisonous, people spoke a language they understood, and where the words *yes* and *no* sometimes had opposite meanings.

The size of my waistline had shrunk, and I wore suspenders not to lose my pants. I was a model for anorexia nervosa.

We flew the Brazilian Varig Airline. No more desiccated chicken for lunch and dinner. Since this was a virgin flight of a new model Lockheed plane, we were treated like first-class passengers. The Lockheed representative, Robert Elliot, and his wife Esmeralda, who traveled first-class, mixed with us passengers in tourist class. Elliot, an American, was inspecting the flight. He was Lockheed's salesman to Brazil and received 5 percent commission from Lockheed for every airplane he sold to Varig. Since the cost of the plane was in the millions, his was a lucrative business. Besides, I don't think that he needed money since he was married to a very rich woman of the Brazilian high society.

High-class Brazilians don't call themselves Brazilians. They are proud to be of Portuguese ancestry, descendants of the original European conquerors of Brazil.

Americans are impressed by European nobility. When my friend Rudi von Bismarck arrived at the immigration office in New York, he quickly shed the "von" and then his name, after he was asked whether he still was keeping "subjects"! Some Americans take pride in having one-sixteenth Indian blood in their veins. To be half-Indian might still be socially acceptable but not a full-blooded one from a reservation. I never heard any white American brag about having one-sixteenth black blood in his veins. Asian ancestors might be tolerated, especially when the women are very beautiful, but to be able to trace the family bloodline to the *Mayflower* is the real proof of American aristocracy. Since Americans have no lords, viscounts, even sirs, as the British do; marquises and barons, as the French; or *Grafen* and *Freiherren,* as the Germans, the American nobility is based on the amount of wealth, like the Duponts, Rockefellers, or Dohenys, families who originally started as robber barons or, like the Kennedy family, as rumrunners during Prohibition. Australian families pride themselves that their forefathers were banned from their native land and arrived in chains to the continent "down under."

Since thousands of American families brag that their ancestors arrived on the *Mayflower,* that ship must have been many times larger than the biggest luxury liner ever built.

In Brazil the cleavage between rich and poor is a gap that can never be eliminated except by revolution. If we believe that the upper-class Americans are an extremely rich society, then we don't know about the real wealth of South American society.

The Elliots invited me to their home in São Paulo, which, though staffed with a dozen servants, was not ostentatious. But then Esmeralda displayed her jewels. I held in my hands pounds of gold chains, strands of pearls, exquisitely custom-made bracelets, anklets, brooches, earrings, necklaces, pins, and rings. I touched millions of dollars' worth of jewelry. The evil thought crossed my mind how I could, by a criminal act, take some of that glitter with me and live my life in luxury. There especially was a four-inch-long Cartier golden dragonfly, its wings mounted on quivering platinum springs, each wing a single sheet of diamond. I didn't know that diamonds came in flat sheets. I visualized Henrietta wearing it. Esmeralda casually mentioned that this jewelry was only for her daily use and that her family jewels were safely stored away in banks. Her family's wealth came from beer, and they owned the largest breweries in South America. She offered me land for one dollar an acre in Brasilia, an artificial city built in the middle of Brazil, the new center of the government. She wanted a European as a neighbor, to practice French, English, and German. I declined her offer, since I wouldn't buy an estate that I couldn't reach from my office on a bicycle. I missed that chance to become a multimillionaire.

The passengers on the plane became familiar with each other on the thousand-mile flight to Rio and São Paulo. A stout middle-aged man with a Slavic-English accent, who introduced himself as Itzak Stern and was a jeweler, carried a toucan in a cage with him. The cage door was open and the big-billed bird walked in and out, navigating its large beak skillfully. Stern told me that he always took the bird on his travels, buying the seat next to him for his feathered travel companion. The toucan's name was Carlo. When he laid an infertile egg, he became Carla. She was in love with her master but hated his wife. Carla had the run of his home in São Paulo. Whenever she could, she attacked his wife's silk stockings, tore a hole in them, and, with a giggle, quickly retreated to her cage. When Stern left without her, she screamed constantly. Wherever she flew for exercise, she always returned.

Stern told me that he had left Poland the year Hitler moved into Austria. Since his friends emigrated to North America, he went to South America, not to crowd that continent. A ghetto Jew, he had no conception of the size of the world, and visualized that he had only to "cross the bridge" to visit his friends in North America. He dealt in semiprecious stones—aquamarine, topaz and sometimes emeralds, more rare than diamonds. He dominated the São Paulo gem market. Rio was Louis Simon's, also a Polish Jew, territory. Each one stuck to his own territory.

Since he had no children, Stern was looking for a European partner whom he could trust, and wanted me as a partner. Living in São Paulo for twenty-five years, Stern had become a patriotic Brazilian, but he would always help a fellow Jew, since God had been good to him. He promised me if I would move to São Paulo, which would become one of the most prosperous cities in the world, that I soon would own a house and feed my family. I could keep a young mistress, as he did, and whom he visited at lunchtime for a quick hump, a status symbol all of his rich Brazilian friends observed. I would share the social standing of males in Brazil, where even a man who had killed his wife had been exonerated by an all-male jury, because she had insulted his macho feelings by not having the food ready when he had come home from work. In South America a man was still the indisputable boss.

I found myself in a world that still had one foot in the Middle Ages and where the rich, like medieval nobility, kept slaves. All that was missing was "*le droit du seigneur*," the right of the nobleman to deflower the brides of his workers and servants on her wedding night.

Here a refugee Polish Jew had shed his thousand-year-old traditions and had eagerly embraced the macho powers of a country that was a hundred years behind the social standards of the present world.

The trip to São Paulo was tedious, though interrupted by excellent meals. I talked in the kitchen pantry with a stewardess, an extremely handsome girl, whose skin, like that of Brazilians, had a slightly dark hue. She told me that she had been happily married and that, after a short honeymoon, her husband, a military pilot, had been killed in a test flight. She had made up her mind to commit suicide, but, being Catholic, she could not commit that deadly sin. As a stewardess, her life might end in a plane crash, for which God could not blame her.

Thirty years have passed since our conversation, and Varig has never lost an airplane in an accident. I wonder whether she is still flying.

We landed at night at San Bernado airport. São Paulo was miles away. Since we didn't come from abroad, we were, mercifully, spared the passport and luggage control, and the bribe for custom inspectors.

Having flown halfway around the world, the California winter had changed into South American summer. The stage decorator, Pierino Massenzi, waited for me at the airport. By now I had picked up some Portuguese phrases. I always try to learn as fast as possible some of the language of the country where I work, to be able to listen to what the crew complains about behind my back. Massenzi spoke as much English as I understood Portuguese. He drove Beverly, John, and me through the night to the Hotel Jaragua at the Rua Major Quedinho. I always memorize addresses in strange cities since, during nebulous dreams, I always look for a destination I can never find, a fear that often accompanies me into my waking hours. That fear might be a pathological symbol that I was still looking for a goal of my life, since I was not being fulfilled by what I was doing.

Massenzi turned off the motor whenever the car rolled down a hill to save gas, which in Brazil is very expensive. That method couldn't be very healthy for the motor, an ancient Chevy station wagon. It also did wear out the brake lining. Even the very rich Brazilians, as I found out, drove their cars that way.

We entered the center of São Paulo. New skyscrapers, in the process of being built, were being erected everywhere. Due to rampant inflation, Brazilians, to invest the rapidly declining value of money, put it into real estate. Many signs directed us through detours. Massenzi told me that one of the new buildings had just collapsed and was blocking the main thoroughfare. The builder, to skim off building cost, had mixed the concrete with too much sand. But the city's architecture was stunningly impressive, novel, and experimental. Some buildings had their windows individually turned away from the hot sun, which gave them the shape of giant beehives. The street noise was deafening. The Brazilian loved noise and increased it by fixing whistles to the exhaust of their cars and Lambrettas, small motor scooters of Italian make, of which there seemed to be a million. The traffic, despite the late night, was heavy. Motorized vehicles intermixed with donkey-drawn carriages. The past and the future clashed.

At the Jaragua Hotel, I, like my two leading actors, soaked myself half of the night in the bathtub, to get that musty jungle smell out of my system. Despite the sudden luxury, I was having a numbing premonition of impending trouble. How was it possible that the studios were built next to the noisy airport? Will I have to dub all missing scenes, with no efficient sound system available? Do I have to return to Hollywood with an unfinished film, since it was my pride to bring back a completed picture, which no American company had ever accomplished?

In the morning, Rudolf Icsey, the Hungarian cameraman, who had his home in São Paulo, drove me to the studio in San Bernado. He warned me that I wouldn't find the equipment as perfect as it is in Hollywood. But he assured me that we would be able to manage. It was an ominous confession.

The studio had three stages, like giant warehouses. They were not soundproof. Huge camera cranes, made in France, stood outside. They had not been used since they were bought two years ago and, rusted from the rain, were useless. Mountains of cables, their rubber sheeting cracked, were stacked in heaps. Any kind of lamps, from tiny "spots" to enormous "brutes," were standing in the open. They didn't work. Overhead, planes from the San Bernado airport thundered by every ten minutes. I was too shocked to show any reaction. I asked Rudolf how he visualized that we could record dialogue on a stage that had no sound protection.

"The best time is between 3 and 5," he said.

"In the afternoon?"

"In the early morning."

At the hotel I had received a cable from Dick Kay that Terry Morse, our film cutter in Hollywood, urgently needed more jungle shots with the leading actors. He was running short of film length. I had shot based on my memory, since I hadn't seen one foot of developed film. "We will shoot on stage 1. There the roof is still watertight in case of rain," Rudolf said. "We'll build a jungle, fifty by fifty feet, or less. I just need to hold different branches in front of the lens. Nobody would know the difference between the real and studio jungle."

Then why did I shoot in the Belem jungles, losing thirty pounds and part of my health?

Pierino Massenzi had built interior sets for the film and exteriors of a couple of primitive huts. Rudolf had a secret cache where he had stored usable spotlights and even two working brute lamps. He also had salvaged a few hundred feet of unbroken cable.

Beverly thought getting up at midnight was less trying than being wrapped up in an anaconda. John didn't object to the added times of work, since he got paid by the week.

Curucu was completed in Brazil by an American company. Realart had spent only $155,000 for the entire picture. I sold all the rights to that film to Universal for the same amount. Lacking the skill of a Yankee trader, I didn't ask for more, since in business matters my IQ is that of an idiot. I easily could have gotten more money for *Curucu* from Universal, and that overflow would have belonged to me since Realart was happy to get their production money back.

Curucu after forty years is still haunting the television screen, having returned fifty times the purchase price. But I broke the jinx: I was the only Hollywood director, and still am, who brought back a finished picture shot in the Amazon.

Despite all that hardship, I wouldn't have missed this adventure, nor would Beverly Garland, who gamely had faced many, and sometimes very dangerous, situations. It was my stupidity to have taken such physical chances with her. There was no "stunt woman" as in Hollywood, who stood in for her, when she almost went up in flames running through a burning village.

Two years later, I foolishly shot a second picture for Universal, though under less trying conditions, since I was supported by unlimited funds from the studio. Knowing the pitfalls of working in a foreign country, I should have turned down that job, which Universal offered me, not because they liked my screenplay, *The Amazons*, but to pull their money out of a country whose rampant inflation reduced their cash, which they could not legally export, to almost zero. *Should, would, if!* Three words that cover all of our mistakes. I left part of my health behind, which I never recovered. My leading actress, Beverly Garland, confessed to me years later that filming in Belem, Brazil, with the hostile and poisonous Amazon River, was a challenge and had been the most exciting of the numerous motion pictures in which she had played. She would not have liked to have missed being wrapped up in a live, sixteen-foot-long anaconda.

If you want to know about the character of your friends, take them to a restaurant and watch how they treat the waiters. To have lunch or dinner with my old friend Fritz (Frederick Kohner) was an ordeal that I always tried to avoid. Rude to the waiter or waitress, he sent back every dish with a complaint. But one experience changed his demeanor forever.

A perfectionist in languages, he went to evening school to improve his elocution, to be able to express himself better. Each student had to deliver a speech, which then was analyzed by the teacher. Fritz listened to a head waiter who also had joined that class. The waiter explained how an obstreperous guest was secretly treated. If he sent back, for example, a steak, the waiter took it in the kitchen, spat on it, threw it on the floor, stepped on it, then poured some sauce from a leftover of another guest over it, heated the steak in a microwave oven, then served it again, enhanced with a bunch of parsley.

Fritz never again complained about the food.

If you want to learn about the suppressed desires of your actors, watch how they behave in a foreign country. Most Americans shed their thin Calvinist skin and behave in a manner they would never dare to do at home.

The private activities of my American actors, Beverly Garland and John Bromfield (Farron Bromfield), or those of the crew, didn't interest me. All I demanded was that they did their jobs and knew their lines. Beverly and John were Hollywood pros. The trouble was with the Brazilian actors, Tom Payne, Harvey Chalk, and a few others, who didn't possess the American acting discipline. Tom Payne, a gaunt man with a chiseled face, constantly sipped from a Coca-Cola bottle. I soon found out that he poured *cachaza,* a high-powered rum, in it to overcome his acting inhibitions.

He played a lead in *The Beast of the Amazon.* I had written the screenplay to be shot in the Amazon jungle. In the story the native Indians leave their village to work for the oil companies who denuded the forest and polluted the rivers, digging for oil, destroying two thousand miles of primeval wilderness, and the thousand-year-old Indian culture. A "monster" murders Indians who worked for the foreign intruders, deserting their Stone Age civilization. The "monster" is an educated, patriotic Brazilian, played by Tom, who spoke English fluently. Disguised as a "monster," he frightens the superstitious Indians into leaving their debilitating jobs for the oilmen and to return to their villages and old living traditions. Tom, who in real life resented the intrusion of Mid-Oil and Chevron, played his part convincingly. The producer, Dick Kay, also had engaged a shaman and all the natives of his village. The extras, small, fierce, muscular fellows, had never seen a camera and spoke only their own dialect.

Every night in my bedroom I rewrote the screenplay according to the location I and the cameraman had chosen for the next day. I pushed the revised pages under the hotel doors of the actors, while the actors gathered in the bar or attended to their personal activities, an alcoholic promiscuity that Americans only dare to practice in a country far away from home.

The temperature at the Amazon varied between 93 and 94 Fahrenheit, day and night, and the humidity was always close to 100 percent. An electric light burned constantly in a closet in my hotel room in Belem. When I turned it off, my boots grew green with mildew overnight.

Dick couldn't find a script girl who knew enough English, and I had to remember every shot I had taken, according to the location we chose. There was no technical help as we knew it in Hollywood. Beverly had to take care of her own makeup. She was bored with washing her hair and in her frustration shouted at me, "Damn it, I want you to tell me to wash my hair!"

A trouper, she never once complained, even about the missing toilet facilities in the jungle. Since we shot exterior in the middle of nowhere, a horse-drawn lunch wagon brought food from the Grand Hotel, where we stayed at night. The diet never varied: rice, beans, and beef, carried in open pans. The seasoning was thousands of flies. My native crew didn't mind, but I lived on bananas and chocolate, which brought my weight down considerably. My clothes didn't fit me anymore.

After shooting we returned to the Grand Hotel with its Victorian charm. I was able to sleep only a few hours. At five in the morning, when the sun came up, I wrote my daily letter to Henrietta. The first rays of the sun fell on a slender church tower opposite my window. That quiet of the beginning day recharged the battery of my inner strength, which had teetered on the edge of exhaustion.

Dick Kay acted as assistant director, a job he had learned in Hollywood, securing the physical details of the daily shooting, herding the actors together on time, instructing the grips and camera crew. He broke down under the physical strain of production. He got a bad case of jitters and was unable to get out of bed. For hours I held his hand at night to calm him. I understood why no American company had ever brought a finished picture back from the Amazon.

As we needed them, we rented wild animals from the Belem zoo—tapirs, sloths, and a doped-up leopard who, hoisted into a tree, mercifully slept through the filming. I never saw any native birds or animals or any fish in the river. I guess that everything that could walk, crawl, or fly had been eaten by the indigent population.

But the background of the Amazon River with its small sailing boats, old-fashioned steamers, and Chinese-looking junks was picturesque wherever we pointed the camera. The vast city market was crowded with hundreds of booths and thousands of people dressed in bright native colors. Mixed within that buzzing marketplace, which sold everything imaginable, from tools, vegetables unknown to me, fly-covered meats, to brightly dyed clothes, were booths with mystical voodoo (Macumba) dolls and feather-covered ghostly images. At night I faintly heard the drums of Macumba ceremonies drumming in the surrounding jungle.

Franz, a young handsome German, our chief grip, who knew how to handle snakes, became Beverly's pet. Why he had drifted from Cologne in Germany to Brazil, I don't know. It might be that he was afraid of being drafted into the newly created German army. His West German dialect was so foreign to me that I could hardly understand him. The new generation after Hitler certainly was anti-militaristic. I don't know how he conversed with Beverly since she didn't speak German and Franz not a word of English. Obviously their communication had no language barrier.

Since there was very little to do after work, sex and alcohol were the actors' only entertainment. Larri Thomas, a blonde dancer, arrived from Hollywood carrying a wedding dress on a hanger. She came to marry John and didn't bring any luggage along. She might have thought that Belem was as far as Hollywood is from Beverly Hills. I used her in the picture to charge the cost of her wardrobe to the budget.

I have never mixed personal relations with people I worked with or for. I had never invited my Hollywood bosses or American actors to my home, nor did I go to their parties. Even in Belem, at dinnertime I sat alone, ostensibly working on the script, in order not to show any preference for any one actor. Inevitably, frictions arise during work, and I avoid adding private ones. That I had learned through an early experience, especially among the kiss-and-tell film people. They cannot keep carnal secrets to themselves. Who wouldn't have bragged about having slept with Greta Garbo or Cary Grant?

We rented from the well-equipped Belem zoo an enormous snake, a sixteen-foot-long python. The handlers, led by Franz, lifted that beast into a tree. Those giant snakes defecate only twice a year, and this was the day. The native who stood at the foot of the tree was suddenly covered with the snake's feces, which wrapped him in a gooey blanket from head to foot. He keeled over silently in a faint, stiff like a tin soldier, and had to be hosed off quickly. Nobody went close to him for the next few days.

I wanted my leading actors to pass underneath the tree branch on which the snake was coiled. To stay within camera frame, they had to step on a two-foot-high wooden box. To give them confidence, I covered my fear with bravery and went through a rehearsal myself. The anaconda's enormous fangs snapped at me and I barely jumped out of its reach. Since the snake didn't constrict and devour me, Beverly followed me without hesitation. I was doubtful about John's courage, though he too went through that setup, encouraged by Beverly's true grit.

My opinion of him was verified a couple of days later. I almost lost my two leading actors, and the picture would have ended prematurely. Besides, I would certainly be kept behind Brazilian prison bars for the rest of my life.

I had a native village built of straw, about twenty flimsy huts, which, dried by the sun, were highly flammable. I told Beverly and John that they had to run through the burning village and had to start the very second after I had shouted one of the two sentences a director must know to be a director: "Roll it." (The other is "Cut.") Three cameras were ready, the huts set on fire, and I shouted, "Roll it." John, not a born hero, stood petrified, like a salt figure in Sodom and Gomorrah. Beverly pulled him along. I didn't know how they got through the flames alive, and though Beverly's eyebrows were singed, I had the best shot of the picture in the cameras.

Nobody had warned me that the Amazon produced fourteen-foot-low tides. Sailing back to the hotel, our boat, with the camera equipment and actors, suddenly was mired in mud. John, carrying Beverly, waded ashore, a half mile away. They arrived covered with tiny leeches. I stayed with the fishing boat. The moon, as big as a giant sun, slowly rose on the horizon. All night ragged sailors played guitars, smoked marijuana, and guzzled down cachaza, the homemade native rum brew, so potent I was convinced it would burn holes into the wooden boat. I stayed with that party until the water rose again. It was the night in my life that paid for all the hardship.

The strain and inclemency of our work were etched deeply in everyone's face. I assured Beverly that we had only one more setup, then we would fly to São Paulo, live in a first-class hotel, eat in the best restaurants, and finish the picture in the studio. The last jungle setup for her was that she had to be constricted by the anaconda. There was no danger in that, I assured her. Two men would hold the snake's head and two the end of his tail. A python isn't able to coil as long as it cannot move its head or tail. I don't know how I convinced her, but she accepted the small chance of not being squeezed to death by that monster. To take that shot was pure insanity and would have been done in a Hollywood studio by using an artificial snake. Shooting that scene was like an execution. Beverly's screams were genuine and her close-up showed her terror, which she didn't have to fake.

Twenty years later, when I visited Beverly in her home in the Hollywood Hills, she talked about the snake scene. "You know," I said, "if the snake's tail or head had slipped out of those men's grip, we would have never been able to free you, since a python cannot be uncurled, even if you hack it to pieces."

"Now you tell me," she said.

The shooting at the Amazon was finished. We flew to São Paulo and the studio, which was two thousand miles away. I didn't see my actors for two days. They soaked off the jungle smell in the bathtub in the hotel.

"Who has two countries, has none." Henrietta contests that remark. For her, America has become the roots of her existence as though she had been born here. Even as a child she had the unshakable desire to live in America. For me, all countries, even that of my birth, Germany, have always been alien. "Ubi bene, ubi patria" (Where you feel well is your country). That might be true, but not for the first generation of immigrants. The second springs from its soil. It emerges as native Americans, often gifted with the vibrant energy of this country, where the son of an illiterate Sicilian sharecropper became governor of New York, and the offspring of a similarly uneducated Italian emigrant ran one of the largest automobile factories in the world. There is no nobility in this country. Anybody of any race can become part of this continent's industrial or political or military leaders. A default of success is lack of personal energy. Napoleon Bonaparte, the son of a Corsican peasant, stated that every one of his solders carries the marshall's staff in his knapsack. Everybody certainly can bring it with him to America. All it needs is intelligence, adaptation, and the will to work, taking reverses in stride, and the persistence never, never to give up.

The British prime minister, Lloyd George, was told of a man who is a failure. "Is he dead?" Lloyd George asked.

When I examine the fate of myself and my three brothers, it was an innate lack of adaptability that made us strangers wherever we lived. My youngest brother killed himself in France. Werner emigrated to Palestine, now Israel, in 1932. He lived an extremely hard life but managed to visit the world on a shoestring, canvassing it from Nepal to San Francisco, from the Far East to Australia. That was his hobby, and his life's goal was to see the world. There was not a corner of the world that he did not explore or wished to visit. I don't know how he managed those travels with his limited funds. His Israeli-born son, David, speaks only Hebrew and Arabic. He has the roots of the native-born. He never left or wanted to leave his country.

Robert, though he kept an apartment in Switzerland, went from Germany to France, to England, to America, and restlessly back to Germany after the war to direct motion pictures, wherever he got an assignment. He was rootless to the last day of his life, when he planned to shoot a picture in Italy. From time to time he appeared at our home in Los Angeles or our ranch in the Sequoias. Then his first words were "I am just stopping by on my way to . . . (Munich, Paris, London)." In 1954 he left the safety of a career in Hollywood in search of an inner fulfillment. His job directing pictures was the surrogate. He was in search of himself.

I also never grew roots, despite having written scores of motion pictures in Hollywood, during my twenty years' stay in that city. I, like Robert, detached myself completely from being a company man, whose house is not his home but an office in a studio. I went as a writer-director to Brazil; to Prague, which was still under communist domination; to Switzerland working for a Swiss company. I went to Sweden, Germany, Denmark, always tearing up the roots when I felt them fusing with the ground.

I never was part of a clique of entrepreneurs, servants in the fiefdoms of motion picture tycoons. When they died out or were dethroned, the power of motion picture production slipped into the hands of agents and bankers and moneyed people, who had made their fortunes in oil or in a media other than film entertainment. "Wheelers and dealers," businesspeople controlling "bankable" actors, "bankable" authors, private bankable fortunes. The late agent Irving (Swifty) Lazar was so powerful that he "blacklisted" the giant Universal Studios, refusing to sell them any of his clients, actors, and writers. The five major companies—MGM, Fox, Columbia, Paramount, and Universal—existed only in name. They have become financing companies like banks and rent out studio space to their clients. They are far remote from that creativity that was controlled by private enterprises or actors like Clint Eastwood, Jody Foster, the muscleman Arnold Schwarzenegger, or other "bankable" stars. "Bankable" means that producing companies can raise money on the strength of their participation, since their appearance in motion pictures is a guarantee of getting those pictures released worldwide.

After the original founders, eastern Jews, Japanese money acquired major studios but left the production to Hollywood "experts." Production costs rose astronomically. Some motion picture productions reached the two hundred million–dollar mark. Creativity is measured by the "bottom line," the amount of money a picture is able to create. The time-honored craft of storytelling has become a business as impersonal as selling condoms to China.

The artistic sense of the founders of that industry, their daring, taste, and decisions, has been replaced by "spin doctors," highly efficient publicity people. They are able to wring a quick financial return out of even mediocre films, by clever promotion, smart advertising, and booking the product simultaneously in a thousand theaters, recouping, often over a weekend, the production costs. The craft of telling an interesting story does not depend on a star's name. It is enough that optical machines are able to produce stunning mechanical devices and tricks. They replace the age-old craft of storytelling. Now the audience leaves the theater, possibly stimulated, but unable to formulate what they have seen.

Filmmaking, as it had been practiced for almost a century, can be done by ingenious technical trickery. The gifted film director Robert Altman often related to his actors only the gist of the scene he wanted to photograph and let them invent their own dialogue, believing that their improvisation makes the scene more convincing than any contrived dialogue.

Still, motion pictures of old-fashioned entertainment sometimes successfully sneak by this technical machinery and quietly make their way without the clarion calls of the publicity department, whose budget sometimes exceeds the film's production cost. The success of a motion picture is measured by its financial returns. In the forties and fifties, Hollywood produced motion pictures for a few hundred thousand dollars. Now a budget of less than thirty million dollars is called a B. Big finance, with its almost limitless worldwide distribution—on motion picture screens, on cassettes, through television, satellites, and "merchandising" the blockbusters in toys—reaches a public, not confined to one country, one language, or one culture.

During the forties and fifties, now called the "golden age of motion picture production," it was the story that gave the work its value, enhanced by the personality of actors called "stars," like a "Greta Garbo" picture, or a "Jimmy Cagney," "Humphrey Bogart," "Buster Keaton," "Boris Karloff," "Elizabeth Taylor," "Lon Chaney," or "Cary Grant" film. Or the productions by "Alfred Hitchcock" or "Billy Wilder," names connected with values that fit their time.

I am not a film historian, just a writer, disseminating ideas, looking at his world from his homemade point of view. I believe that we go through changes in vastly different cultures, one fading away, the other emerging.

I try to fit my experiences into a general point of view. The decay of the Victorian age, of which I experienced its last gasps, started with Pablo Picasso's unfinished painting *Les Demoiselles d'Avignon*, passing through the German dadaism period and other groping attempts to shed the frozen style of previous centuries. The breakthrough of the abstract paintings of Miró and Behrman, the emaciated abstracts of Giacometti, to the drip canvases of Jackson Pollock, of Mark Rothko and his contemporaries, are an enigma to me. Wolfgang von Goethe stated, "It is astonishing to me how many mysteries my readers discover in my writings." I force myself to believe that those attempts, called art, have a value and are not transitory illusions like the emperor's new clothes, which only the initiated are able to see. These "mysteries" are bits and pieces, a search not for values but for new expressions, like the rusty bedsprings of Jim Dine, displayed in the Whitney Museum in New York. It is Schoenberg's twelve-tone music, also a mystery to me, and modern jazz, rock and roll, the angry rhythm of rap, and now, in motion pictures, the storyless storytelling, all in incubation, which might unfold their mysteries in the next century.

But, accelerated by an instant global communication and technical developments that outrace the ability of instant comprehension, the human mind might not take enough time to digest and use the rapidly advancing electronic conceptions.

I came across a young man with only a basic high school education, but with a grasp of the intricacies of the digital, microscopically small, electronic chips, who told two scientists with newly acquired Ph.D. degrees, "You idiots, don't you see that the problem is like this," emphasizing that the time they had spent to learn existing techniques had already outrun the newly acquired knowledge. Our impatience expects the world to move during the short span of our life. But all we can do is concentrate our energies like a laser beam, on one of the new intricacies of a floating time that will not reach stability during our life span, perhaps not even during that of our children. Not we, but possibly our grandchildren, might see the new "golden age."

Zealots try to turn back the clock, dreaming of resurrecting past cultures, disregarding the futility of holding on to the past values, the nuclear family, a house in the suburbs, two kids, and a white picket fence. The next picket fence might be green or, like the emperor's clothes, visible only to a generation trained to see.

Jobs for Hollywood-trained screenwriters were available in Germany, since internationally trained German screen playwrights didn't seem to exist. I also had to outwait the German bureaucracy, since my Berlin representative, Heinz Killer, a gentle name for a lawyer, had succeeded in getting for me the obligatory government retribution, payment for German refugees whose assets had been confiscated by the Nazi regime. I was eligible for the pension B 26, that of a postal clerk with twenty-five years' service. I had been on the Nazi extermination list in 1937, since they had traced me through German embassies to London.

The letter from my former publisher, Wilhelm Goldmann in Leipzig, would never have reached me, four years after my involuntary exodus, but for the highly efficient Nazi spy system, which kept track of every emigrant. Had the Nazis invaded England, they would have known where to find me. I guess that the elite of the emigrants, among them prominent German scientists and artists, must have been a pathological threat to Hitler. Goebbels had, during the war, arranged an exhibition, "Depraved Art," but must've been dismayed by the interest of millions of German visitors, a farewell to a vibrant culture. Fortunately, most pictures reappeared after the war, bought by Swiss collectors. The high-ranking Nazis had sold them to keep a nest egg of Swiss francs abroad. It turned out that the death of any moral values was a serendipity to me. I had built a quality of life that I could never have attained in Europe.

Henrietta didn't want to accept any compensation from the Germans. But Babs, Robert's wife, convinced her that it was stupid not to accept restitution from a country that had destroyed my livelihood and confiscated my possessions.

Berlin was still parted by "The Wall," a bulwark that separated East from West Germany. The East German wall was built, the official word is said to have claimed, "to prevent the West Germans from escaping to the Communist paradise." Those concrete ramparts, crowned by barbed wire, were sprayed on the Western side with anticommunist slogans. Henrietta, facing the ghostly symbols of human cruelty, ruins looking like giant broken teeth, started to cry. It was winter, and her tears froze on her cheeks.

We left for Ascona in Switzerland, where Robert had rented a villa at the Lago Maggiore. We had been to Ascona thirty years ago. It then had been a small rural fishing village, where cows grazed on the lake's shore. Now it had become the concentration camp of Jewish refugee millionaires, a movable feast of café society, situated amidst one of the most beautiful mountain views in the world. We moved into a small apartment, the Casa Albertina. Built in the fourteenth century, diminutive rooms overlooked an ancient courtyard where the same families had lived the same primitive life for centuries.

Those peasants were desperately poor, since there was no fish anymore in the shimmering blue waters of the mountain lake. But still the former fishermen had saved, maybe through generations, five thousand Swiss francs to donate to the local Catholic church for a bell to chime as they entered heaven.

There was no more shore for cows to graze. The beach had been taken over by tourists who were streaming in from prosperous countries, France, Germany, Italy, England, and the Nordic ones.

The clique of survivors of the prewar German literary elite met daily at the Cafe Batello for high tea. Those people were remnants of the group that had created Germany's last cultural fling, which the Nazis destroyed. I watched the rapid decay of a small group of the intelligentsia that disintegrated as if eaten by a virus from within. It was the fading away of a culture that Europe, even half a century after the war, could not replace. But those survivors had lost their creative powers, burned out, since their roots were derived from the soil in which they had prospered, unable to revive the culture that had made Berlin before 1933. Berlin's genius—with its directors like Max Reinhardt, Piscator, Baranowski, its music, writers, actors, painters, and exploding creativity—had been murdered overnight.

A few of those fertile brains had settled in Ascona. Erich Maria Remarque lived only a few miles away in Ronco, at the Swiss-Italian border. His collection of French paintings now fills rooms at the Metropolitan Museum in New York. The songwriter Fritz Rotter cohabited with two wives, having become very rich on account of his "evergreens," songs still known the world over. There was Max Kolpe, Marlene Dietrich's private songwriter, poet of immortal songs. Hans Habe was a gifted novelist. Robert Thoeren, who had the lead in my motion picture *The Studio Murder Mystery*, was so handsome that he was called "The Jewish Venus." He wrote the original concept for *Some Like It Hot* and *Victor/Victoria,* a homosexual farce that went through many film versions and plays.

Babs, Robert's wife, hostess of that fading society, collected the rich and famous of the past generation in her house: Orson Welles, Von Karajan, the conductor of the Berlin Philharmonic, and everybody with an internationally known name; Werner Keller, the anthropologist and author whose books, among them *The Bible as History,* were sweeping the literary world. Werner served the best Cabernets I ever tasted.

But then, as if being eaten from the inside by an alien bug, Remarque died of heart failure. The daughter of Robert Thoeren was murdered when she left the UCLA campus at 2 A.M. Driven by a social conscience, she had given a lift to a black "Bible salesman," who was a serial killer the police had been unable to find. Hans Habe's daughter was killed on Mulholland Drive in Los Angeles. Habe, like a Jewish god of revenge, flew to Los Angeles to find and pursue the murderer, but the police advised him not to inquire into his daughter's past. Habe and Thoeren, slavishly in love with their daughters, died soon after of heart failure. The playwright Bertolt Brecht went back to eastern Germany where he died. Babs, addicted to the French cigarette Gaulois, succumbed to lung cancer. Robert followed her ten weeks later. Werner Keller, who had been a member of the Luftwaffe and was cleared by the occupation authorities because he was a rabid anti-Hitlerite, died at only fifty years of age of a stroke. His wife, Vicky, a passionate horsewoman, refused to believe in German atrocities even when her friends had been arrested in Poland for war crimes. They couldn't have been war criminals "since they were horsemen." I witnessed in her the rising denial of facts that was soon to sweep Europe. I asked Werner Keller at what time he became a Nazi foe: in 1942 when Germany won the war or in 1945 when the war was lost for them. They were no Nazis, just opportunists. That generation faded away without a whimper. It had created a past but no future. Strangely no one left any children.

Henrietta and I stayed a few months in Switzerland, a pleasant and peaceful neverland, an oasis among the boiling frictions of the collapse of Europe, trying to find its equilibrium. It was propped up to stay alive by the American Marshall Plan.

Early Italy was Henrietta's and my back garden, with trips to Rome, Siena, Florence, backdrops of a world of dreams that had no knowledge of the time of strife we had been through. Since I had a success with *Light Ship,* written for Bavaria Films, I had writing assignments for a Berlin company, CCC. I soon found out that I was incapable of devising a German motion picture. Any theme that was controversial was threatening to the German film producers. They only chose insipid themes, stories by Conan Doyle and the lesser mystery writer, Edgar Wallace, or saccharin films called "Schnulzen." The German public refused to be faced with problems of their past. Europe tried to wipe out the memory of World War II and, with it, its undigested guilt. There was hardly any mention in the German school books of the time after the turn of the century and the present, as though history could be erased by silence. The teachers in their curriculum taught twenty-eight hours about Napoleon but only six hours about the years between 1930 and 1950. One could travel through France, Germany, Austria and not find a trace of the destruction that only a couple of decades before had devastated those countries. The Germans only remember the cruelty of the Allied firebombings. The French never discussed the times of "occupation." The scars of the war in which one hundred million perished, but which had also extinguished centuries-old cultures, had been buried, physically and mentally.

After every war, the shocked Western civilizations create an organization like the League of Nations to prevent future national mass murder. But, at first imperceptibly, the virus of "patriotism" emerges and grows until it creates a second conflagration. When exhaustion finally stops the slaughter of their own kind, world powers again try to create a barrier against future conflagration, which the German General Clausewitz described as "diplomacy continued by other means." But after the shock of destruction has worn off, again the jingoistic virus blinds the nations. Europe's future is its past. Now, fifty years after the collapse of Europe, again the racial virus grows and strives, as though human insanity has to find an outlet from its confinement. The urge to spill human blood seems to be built into man's genetic system.

But our stay in Switzerland was a flight backward into the past to the cultures of the old world. We often visited the Duomo in Milan, the biggest cathedral in the world. Since its erection a thousand years ago, 120 workmen constantly repair its structure, while 350 stone saints guard the Catholic faith from the roof, as large as a football field. Two of those "saints" had been those of Hitler and Mussolini, though before our visit. But I was told that they wore "halos," golden rings above their saintly features. The statues were removed after Mussolini was murdered by his countrymen and Hitler had killed himself. Suicide is anathema to the church; killing for the fascist is not.

I was writing a potboiler for CCC in Berlin, *Sherlock Holmes and the Necklace of Death*. A motion picture is a long short story, certainly not a novel. The Conan Doyle story didn't have enough content to cover two hours of motion picture. I had to add plot. This wasn't easy, since Mr. Conan Doyle Jr. objected.

A dapper man, he arrived in his two-seater Ferrari convertible with his blonde "secretary." I believe that every one of those expensive cars is factory equipped with a stunning woman, this time a German blonde. She certainly was highly intelligent and impatient with the stupidity of men. I learned that Conan Doyle Sr. was still the most widely read author in the world and that Junior lived off the stream of currency his father's writing created. But Junior resented my added scenes to the story. Though the film, written in English, was finally directed by a British director, Terence Fisher, it became the typical fare for the German market. I never saw it. Though I wrote a couple of more screenplays, based on Edgar Wallace stories, I don't know what happened to them.

The wind again blew from another direction. Henrietta had to leave for home, since her mother, Ernestine, had become very ill. A friend of mine from Three Rivers, Don Nemetz, and his wife, Rowena, visited us in Ascona. He was on his way to Liberia in West Africa, as a business consultant for that country's president, William Tubman. Don invited us to Monrovia. To return home to Three Rivers, I could have flown via London, Iceland, New York, Albuquerque. When Don invited me to Liberia, Henrietta insisted that I accept his offer. I had been to the jungles of Brazil; why not visit the jungles of Africa? I have yet to find a psychologist who can explain to me why it has always intrigued me to visit faraway corners of the globe, teeming with deadly viruses, being exposed to bad water, poisonous food, and physical perils. I now believe that all my life I had been an "adrenaline freak," finding excitement not in dangerous sports, like fighting my way in a canoe through white waters or racing an automobile, but in putting my life and health at stake. I was driven by a relentless curiosity to find novel backgrounds for stories. In retrospect that search doesn't make much sense.

When I returned from Brazil, Henrietta told me an alarming story. Her mother, Ernestine, had called from her quiet home in Canoga Park, complaining that earthquakes were shaking her house apart.

Flames were shooting out of mountains miles away. Her dog, King, was hiding under the bed and the chickens laid fewer eggs. Since she, a sturdy Swiss woman, was not prone to hysterics, and since we hadn't heard about quakes in Los Angeles, we rushed to Canoga Park to witness that phenomenon.

In the ten years since we bought the house in Canoga Park for Ernestine, the state of California had enlarged its net of freeways. The trip to Canoga Park now took only thirty minutes instead of two hours on narrow country roads. Rocketdyne, the missile factory, had moved to Canoga Park. Almost overnight the small town had grown into a city with traffic lights and crowded streets. The old bar where we had seen cowboys on horseback drinking beer had changed into a fast-food restaurant. The local newspaper reported, on the day of our visit, a bank holdup, two robberies, several rapes, and a murder. Capitalistic progress had replaced the bucolic peace of that small pleasant community.

When we responded to Ernestine's distress call, her house was still standing. It didn't show any earthquake damage, but in the evening the Simi Valley mountains in the distance spouted fire. The ground shook. The army was testing long-range missiles, to blow Brezhnev's communist empire to smithereens.

It was obvious that Mother had to be moved somewhere else. But where? Henrietta suffered the compulsive guilt complex of most loving daughters, believing that whatever she did for her mother was not enough. She drove through California with her mother, looking for the ideal house where Ernestine could raise chickens and live with her dog in rural tranquility. I believe that Henrietta canvassed every community in California. But Ernestine didn't like any of the houses available for sale. Some were too far and some too close to Los Angeles. The house also had to have a wooden floor, as she was used to in Switzerland, and not a concrete floor, which she considered unhealthy. She also wanted to be close to her daughter, but not too close. Ernestine was the prototype of Swiss stubbornness, which for eight hundred years and against all odds had fused the multilanguage Swiss cantons together.

Once, when she wrote a check for forty dollars, spelling it "fourty," I tried to explain to her that in that case *forty* was spelled without a *u*. Since she had learned that *four* was spelled *f-o-u-r*, she did not believe me. I showed her the word *forty* in Webster's dictionary. After we had left, she went to her neighbor, Mr. Cook, to ask him how *forty* was spelled.

Anticipating a nascent fascistic Germany, the ancient independent Swiss spirit that Henrietta had inherited caused her to settle her mother, three years before the Nazi putsch, in the Italian part of Switzerland. Neither Robert nor I could understand her premonition, which she carried out with a whim of iron. Being very successful in Germany, the land of our birth, why should we leave for an uncertain life abroad? In 1930, no one, not even the Germans, foresaw the rise of Nazism. It proves to me that male logic makes mistakes, but women's intuition never fails. If we had followed my wife's instincts, much of our life's tragedies could have been avoided.

Writers in those days, not even the successful ones, ever became wealthy. Also, slow inflation gnawed away any savings. Even if a writer were paid one or two thousand dollars a week, a very high sum in the forties, it was not enough to make any significant investment for the future. And what successful young filmmakers, as Robert and I were, thought of securing their future since they were just at the beginning of their success?

Writers were a commodity, shackled and bartered by agents like merchandise. The glamour of the film industry did not exist for writers, and it still doesn't.

Executives, highly paid by the studio, postponed producing pictures as long as possible. They tried to coast along on "projects," avoiding the realization that, should they produce a couple of failures, they might lose their jobs. That's why the producing companies still try to find insurance by imitating the recent successes of their competitors, a theoretical safeguard that often does not work. Studios almost never dare to experiment with new ideas. The big financial successes like *Star Wars* or *Home Alone* were freakish occurrences, their production often previously rejected by many studios.

From time to time a film executive, to prove that he was earning his salary, was forced to produce a picture.

That's where the agent entered. He knew which producer was in the market for a writer and what kinds of stories were in demand. He pitched wares like a commercial traveler, only his merchandise was a human.

He peddled a menu of available scribblers to the producer. The producer looked over the agent's list. There were the $500, the $750, the $1,000 weekly salaried writers. Some demanded an even higher pay. Sometimes the basically insecure producer hired several writers to work simultaneously on the same subject, believing that success could be ensured if he culled the "best" scenes from different screenplays, and fit them together like a jigsaw puzzle. That unfair method was stopped by the Writers Guild, when it grew in power.

I was sent to Fox Studios by my agent, Stanley Bergerman, who believed that he belonged to the inner circle of the Hollywood elite since he was married to Rose, the daughter of Universal Studios' boss, Carl Laemmle. Stan told me to report to Sam Engel, an important producer at Twentieth Century–Fox.

I met a man I had never seen before. I learned that he had been a former rabbi. Jews, having devised the Bible, have a traditional sense for story values. I was allotted twenty minutes of the important man's time, to explain my concept for a moneymaking motion picture. Film stories become interesting for the public when a new, unknown background for them can be found. I told Engel that no studio had tried to produce an underwater film without the timeworn submarine plot or sponge diver story. A monster that lived in the ocean had never been featured. Engel, a heavyset and studious-looking man, asked me what kind of monster I had in mind. I, knowing the game of idea stealing, told him that I had a thought that had to be developed. Engel knew that some of my screenplays for Universal had opened an avenue of horror pictures and had replaced the red in that faltering studio's bookkeeping with black ink. An intelligent man (writers always admire a producer who understands what they are talking about), he believed me. He said that Twentieth Century–Fox ought to produce a science-fiction-underwater-horror film, repeating my words as if he had mouthed them first, that such a background would be novel and could not fail at the box office. Engel had convinced himself of his idea.

My situation with Engel was similar to that of a man who wants to bed a woman. But while wooing her, one wrong sentence would mess up his chance. Since I had convinced Engel of my idea, we shook hands, and I was on the payroll, got an office, a secretary, and a hefty weekly check. The contract was signed weeks later. A studio handshake was as binding as the printed agreement, though small print, worked out by studio lawyers over the years, left loopholes for the administration to slip out of any commitment. One was that the writer has to "conduct his life in a moral fashion," a barn door bigger than the barn itself.

I had a job, but the producer was in trouble, since the studio machinery started to move. The producer had to fight for the script with his boss, who controlled the monies, with the same conviction I had shown to get his approval.

The writer's existence has many mental challenges. One is that first conference with the producer, which is grueling, since it might or might not produce many months of work for him. When he returns home, exhausted, worn out from the ordeal of selling himself and his story, he wants to sit in an overstuffed chair, sip a stiff drink, not talk to anybody, demanding to be left alone, to charge up the depleted inner battery. He doesn't want to meet a bored wife dressed to go out for dinner or be attacked by his kids and their troubles and complaints. The absence of that quiet hour after the writer's homecoming is a stumbling block in many marriages. It needs the wife's complete understanding of her husband's job.

I wrote the first underwater monster story. A writer "friend" to whom I foolishly told the idea passed it on to a smart, young would-be producer and director, who, seeing its possibilities, quickly wrote an underwater horror tale and produced a fly-by-night motion picture for the cost of fifteen thousand dollars, for which he pawned everything, even his house. He established a name for himself and produced a hundred moneymaking quickies. Universal Studios, more flexible than Fox, followed with a string of inexpensive underwater horror films, whose main attraction was to dress an actor in a frightful fish costume.

Since my story was a mixture of science and fantasy, Engel became frightened of the production cost and dropped the subject.

If the studios had been able to overcome their paralyzing insecurities, Hollywood could have been the source and center of original film ideas. Many gifted writers existed. But the lack of courage of the people who were responsible for the costs was the decline of Hollywood. The breakup of the studio monopolies and the initiative of the independent producers brought on a rejuvenation. Due to the end of owning production and cinema chains, the studios had to limit themselves to financing "outside" productions and make their money by releasing the picture. It gave writers of books and plays the chance to participate in the financial returns of this business, which, though built on clay feet, sometimes spouts unlimited fortunes.

My friends miss (and not to my surprise, since I wrote so much about my wife Henrietta) any intimate mentioning of my son Geoffrey, our only child. They might expect a detailed description of our father–son relationship. Did I repeat the pattern of my father's participation in my growing up? My formative years were troubled by tremendous insecurities. Geoffrey's were not. He never went through the psychological trauma of the teenager. He never was in doubt of what he wanted. I always tried to have an ultimate concern about his comforts, his education, and his participation in our family life. Did I miss out on our personal relations? A woman once told me about her sisters, "We exchanged blouses but no secrets." Most fathers and sons are secretive, involved only in the lives of their own generation.

Geoffrey was and is the "don't-touch-me" kind. He feels uncomfortable being hugged by a male. Women consider the scarcity of embracing a lack of love. But most males express their affection differently. Women often don't recognize that men show their love in impulsive deeds, like offering flowers or presents to them, which do not need to be of great value, or men cater to women secretly.

When Geoffrey was born in 1933, no literature existed on how to bring up a child. All Henrietta and I could find was a typewritten looseleaf ring book about child education. Years later Dr. Spock changed all that. Now an abundance of information exists. Psychological research in children's upbringing has become a profession. In my father's time a cruel expression was "*Schade um jeden Schlag der denaben faellt*" (Each hit that misses your child is a shame). I only chastised my son twice during his entire childhood: once when he hid, as a boy of four, a handful of razor blades in his pocket. The other time was when he said, "Why don't you spank me?" I then did, though according to present education my answer should have been, "I don't need to show my affection for you by spanking you." I hadn't read Dr. Spock, since his book didn't exist.

We move within the circle of life in which we are born and which we are unable to leave. Our friends are of our own age group, and we grow up with them. Rarely do we find new ones in later years, then we lose them through death or separation. We talk the language of our contemporaries and live in the same restricted cultural and mental environment, a defined space of thought and time. When children are very young, they are part of their parents' life circle, since they depend on them for shelter and food and need help in their pains of growing up. That dependence changes when children become aware of their own personalities and detach themselves from their parents. "The bird flies the nest," not only physically but mentally. The next generation again creates its own life circle and locks an invisible door to which its parents have no key. Family relations might stay very close, changing from parental guidance to friendship, but never to pal-ship.

I, born in the late Victorian age, had only a scant contact with Ike, my father. It might be that my relationship to my son runs parallel to my experience at my parents' home. I now know that my father tried to bring up his children the best way he knew, but he was handicapped by his upbringing in a stern patriarchal atmosphere, which he vainly tried to emulate.

I possess a painting of my grandfather Abraham, whom I never met, a bearded patriarch, looking stern and unapproachable, and cannot imagine that he ever hugged any of his thirteen children. But my grandmother Sarah's picture portrays a woman with a kind, motherly-looking face.

My father left home for America when he was sixteen. I ran away from Ike, detaching myself from my father's domination.

Do males ever grow up mentally, or do they find their maturity only in retrospect? I'm still convinced that I did the very best I knew to express my love for my son. I was concerned that I should produce all the building blocks for his growing up, though the pressure of having to make a living with my only tools, a pencil and paper, took most of my energy. If I have made mistakes, which I certainly did, I didn't know better.

Children belong to the family circle only for a few fleeting years. Then they build their own world. Close family ties might continue, but only in name, when the offspring are not anymore a part of their parents' life circle. Their interest and even their lingual expressions, their view of the world, are apart from those of their parents. "Never the twain shall integrate." Parents also might appear to their children like petrified relics of a time past. That common image removes the children even further from the intimacy they had experienced in their early youth. We four boys called Ike "the old man." He died at the age of sixty-three.

The kind of friendship children keep with their peers does not seem to be possible with them and their parents. Many parents complain that they "lost" their children, despite that they are sometimes helpful to their children to a fault. That condition is natural for the continuity of the family tree. But when parents, especially Jewish mothers, want to be included in their children's life circle, frictions inevitably arise due to the generation gap.

Parents are by nature proud of their offspring's success in life, since their success reflects on them. They often keep their photographs in their wallets, but I haven't found any son or daughter who carries their parents' with them.

Males compete with the success of their father's life. It is the son's ambition to leave a brighter trail than his father, a natural son rivalry, an essential part in the continuity of the clan. But the identical pattern repeats itself in the life of the children after they have brought up their own offspring.

Human life has the same circle as plants and animals: birth, growing, reaching its peak, then declining, to give way to the next crop of the species.

The job of a writer is like that of a lonely lighthouse keeper. It limits severely the participation of the family. By choice I always worked alone. For that choice I had to pay the price. Did those circumstances form my son's mind, since I see the image of my own loneliness in him? Irving Thalberg, the MGM executive, ordered some motion pictures he produced to be reshot all over again, the second time without the mistakes the first version committed. Would anybody ever wish to have that chance in his life? Then his repeated life might be without fault.

We had to get rid of our White Elephant, that French castle with its two and a half acres of land in Beverly Hills, or go broke. It didn't make sense to work at the studio office, turning the lights on in daytime while the sun was shining brightly, to make the money just to keep our "estate" for the entertainment of guests. For an only sporadically employed writer, it was an overblown expense. The castle demanded a maid, gardeners, and constant repairs. When I had it painted, a contractor arrived with six men in white overalls. They sprayed the outside of the house for the bargain price of four hundred dollars.

Bargain? Even now Henrietta and I have not forgotten the worth of money forty years ago when a dime bought the same amount of goods as a dollar does today. Then there were the "5 and 10 cent" or dime stores. Though they still exist, the 5 and 10 has changed to "5 and 10 dollar bargains."

Of course it was not easy to move from the mansion to a house. Henrietta fondly remembers the exquisite quartets in our music room, where she entertained world-renowned artists, famous names of the music world.

But she would not change our present home in the country with its peace for all the music performances of Heifetz, Szigetti, and Rachmaninoff.

When I arrived in America, money still had stability. Its value dissipated rapidly when President Nixon took the dollar off the gold standard.

In 1886, my father earned one dollar a day for ten hours' work for a Jewish tailor in New York. When Henry Ford raised the daily pay of his workers to five dollars, the industry predicted that those "high salaries" would devastate the American economy. That broke the rule since the entrepreneurs can only become rich by underpaying others. Now, when one loaf of bread in a supermarket sells for two dollars, my grandchildren are unable to comprehend that twenty-five dollars paid the food bill for our family of three for a week.

We found a buyer for the French castle and moved out. Not having found a home, we stayed in a motel and cruised around Los Angeles in search of a roof over our heads.

Hollywood was shrouded in fog while we drove up Sunset Plaza Drive, a street leading from Sunset Boulevard up through the mountains that divide the valley from the ocean. A house was being auctioned off that night at Stebbins Terrace, a side street off Sunset Plaza Drive.

We didn't know that houses were sold that way and curiously joined the few prospective buyers. The house was of an ultramodern construction. It had been devised by the famous architect Neutra.

The living room, with its fourteen-foot-high ceiling, sported a huge view window overlooking the city, with the ocean in the background on clear days. An adjoining bedroom had a sunken bath and an extra exit, the perfect room for our teenage son, Geoffrey. A spiral staircase led from the living room to the master bedroom and to a study with windows facing the panorama of the city. It was a stunning show house, smaller than the French castle but equally impressive. It appealed to Henrietta, as if it were built for her.

The auctioneer was trying to find a buyer. The owners huddled in a corner, seemingly in desperation to get rid of the building before foreclosure. One of the few buyers, who stood around in shirt sleeves, looking as if he had not a hundred dollars in his pocket, bid two thousand dollars above the mortgage of twenty-five thousand dollars. I topped it with four thousand. "Give me five," the auctioneer said. "The furniture is included." Nobody replied. "No sale," the auctioneer decided.

I waited until everybody was gone and offered five thousand dollars' down payment. Had I bid during the auction, the price might have gone higher. "Accepted," the auctioneer said.

We again owned an impressive home, though without the huge garden of the French castle. Opposite the entrance of the new home I planted a monkey puzzle tree, so named because monkeys could climb up but not down, on account of the spikes that pointed upward. That fact would, understandably, puzzle monkeys. Visiting that site after thirty-five years, that tree had been cut down by the new owner who obviously was sorry for confused monkeys.

For a time, our home became the meeting place for a dozen alcohol-drenched actors, directors, and writers. The staircase of the house added to Henrietta's glamour when she descended, as though from Olympus.

One of the steady guests was Richard Lerner, my lawyer, an affable, cultured man who liked to get married. He brought his brother, Alan Jay, to our wet parties. I kept hard liquor in French oak, one-gallon barrels for aging purposes, one containing Scotch whisky, one American bourbon, and one filled with sherry. The sherry was hardly ever touched, while the barrels containing hard liquor never had time to age their contents.

I believe that Richard Lerner was jealous of his famous brother Alan, a sibling theme familiar to me. "Writing musicals is like owning a money press," Richard said, not without envy, though in all of his life he had never been in want of instant cash. He was right. When I met Alan Jay years later, I asked him how much he had earned with the musicals *My Fair Lady,* based on Bernard Shaw's play *Pygmalion,* also *Brigadoon* and *Camelot.* He wasn't sure how much had flown his way. "Maybe eighty-five," he guessed. Eighty-five thousand? Eighty-five million! Money didn't have any meaning for him, since he had never been poor in his life. Both brothers had got from their father, the founder of Lerner department stores, a trust fund of a million dollars on their twenty-first birthdays. More millions followed later.

One-eyed (carrying a black patch over the left one) Jay had been married eight times. I guess that the number of wives was a hobby in the Lerner family. Alan could only perform sexually, as he mentioned, when he was legally married. His taste in women, as in musicals, was outstanding. I only met one of his "fair ladies," the young actress Nancy Olsen, who was so pretty and wholesome that I could well imagine the types of Alan's previous marital adventures.

Mary Martin, the American musical comedy star and perennial Peter Pan in J. M. Barrie's play, was a close friend of Jay's and his collaborator, the Viennese composer Frederick Loewe. When she attended a rehearsal of *My Fair Lady*, before the opening night on Broadway, she was shocked and bewildered. "It's devastating—the two boys have lost their talent," she remarked, proving that only the public is the proper critic of any play, book, or film.

An actor, Ronald Reagan, who never in any motion picture got the girl and who played a small part in one of my brother Robert's films, *The Killers,* joined our group. Reagan was rather taciturn. He might have been troubled, I guess, not having his Warner Brothers Studios contract renewed. Later he did all right in politics.

Alcoholics have spiritual preferences, pertaining to the spirit they consume and not the mystical spirit of belief. Dick Carlson had narrowed his taste to Scotch. When he, by oversight, poured himself a drink not from the Scotch but from the bourbon barrel and took a sip, his face distorted as though he had been poisoned, like Socrates, by hemlock.

A handsome actor, William Holden (William Franklin Beedle Jr.), appeared from time to time with his friend David Niven. David, a well-known British actor, owned a house in Malibu Beach known as "Cirrhosis on the Rocks."

I marveled at the drinking capacity of my guests who never became visibly inebriated, while I felt the impact after a couple of drinks. My visitors became more and more lucid as the evening went on.

The relation between alcoholics is like that of congenial family members, but only as long as that liquid is available in quantity. Erich Maria Remarque lost his cronies when, due to a weakness of his heart that finally killed him, he locked up his excellent wine cellar. An alcoholic deprived of his booze is like an oil lamp running out of oil.

I don't know why Budd (Oscar) Boetticher, a former bullfighter and motion picture director, became the center of a cult of movie fans. He joined our circle. Henrietta never showed up in our group of alcohol aficionados, which was exclusively male.

William Holden, after having been for years one of the most sought-after men in Hollywood, died lonely in his apartment, having bled to death after a fall. He was found by his longtime girlfriend, Stephanie Powers (Stefania Federkiewicz). Richard Carlson, a successful leading man in B pictures, died in 1977 of cirrhosis of the liver.

Richard Lerner moved to Mexico, where, in his opinion, a gentleman could still enjoy life's luxuries in style without being badgered by the IRS. Boetticher disappeared mysteriously, the way he had appeared in our gatherings. He might have gone back to Mexico to enjoy killing bulls. Alan Jay died young.

But it certainly was a lively, animated group of talented and successful men of the entertainment world. Despite their international success, they lived a lonely and frustrated life. They all had numerous girlfriends, and none had been or stayed married for long. They never brought their female partners along. I'm sure that men can only really relax when no females are around. I felt comfortable in London at clubs "for men only."

I never accepted the notion that a writer could be out of a job. He might be out of money, which is a perennial condition of his profession. The rule of my life is to turn out, good or bad, at least three typewritten pages a day. I also never was a television writer, who has to devise story for preconceived characters, like Archie Bunker, Murphy Brown, or Angela Lansbury, in *Murder She Wrote*. Those characterizations never vary the identity. Only the pattern of the story changes. In the first act, the case of the "mystery" is stated, followed by a commercial. The second act probes the case but is wrapped suspensefully in "red herrings." The third, after the commercial interruption, shows the "surprising" denouement, which a trained audience often has guessed. That proven template the television writer must use without variation. To devise those jigsaw puzzle plots needs a polished skill I don't possess.

There are the sit-coms, also devised around established characters of well-defined screen personalities. They are helped by an artificial laugh track, to inform the audience that the dialog or the situation is supposed to be funny.

A new generation of writers is highly proficient in that kind of canned entertainment.

I started in the writing business by recording unrelated ideas, using a pencil and foolscap. I advanced to pounding a small Adler typewriter, replacing it with the bigger Remington, then one with an electrically moved platen, upgraded to the IBM that didn't have keys but a ball that printed letters, then to one with a correcting key, to a word processor, which eliminated the human touch by not needing a secretary. The word processor, an insidious machine that "processes" words, created in my mind the picture of canned goods. I upgraded my computers to a more sophisticated and "faster" one, as though ideas could be replaced by speed. Then came the fax machine and the E-mail, which leaves no trace of words that can be stored in historical archives. The disadvantage was that when one of those intricate components stopped functioning, the writer's working day was lost. But none of all that wizardry improved my writing.

The time of style, of finely honed sentences, of the pleasure of formulating sentences until they reach the shape that the writer has in mind, is fading away. So are the typing mistakes. Now, pressing the key "Ctr," then moving the "window" to "check document spelling," replaces the human and humane presence of the secretary, a companion with the duty of a wife but none of the marital pleasures.

Putting ideas on paper, five hours every day, even on the Holy Sabbath, produced over the years a staggering amount of material, of stories, novels, and plays. I created an "archive" that filled hundreds of cardboard boxes, an inventory of written material. I mostly had a story ready when one was in demand. My archive, which I nourished and guarded, was my fortune and the visual zenith of my life's effort.

Writers basically are manic-depressive: 2 percent manic, 98 percent depressed.

But the 2 percent manic seems to make up for the agony of the depression. Writers, by the very nature of their profession, are not very pleasant to have around. They are self-centered, constantly busy with an "idea" they are trying to formulate. That search for the right expression, which never leaves their minds, supersedes any human contact. A writer belongs to a lonely cult. He seems to be married to himself with no chance of a divorce, though he rarely likes himself. Only the hope that their next idea will bring them an ephemeral happiness that they are searching for but never experience makes them stick to their vaporous profession.

Universal Studios' executive producer, James Pratt, for whom I had written a dozen screenplays, had bought my *Curucu* picture, which I had written and directed in the Brazilian jungles. For forty years it earned money for the studio on TV and abroad and still does. Suffering from a complete lack of business sense, I had sold it to the studio for its original cost.

I decided to become rich enough to pay off my ranch in the Sequoias. Cagily, and on speculation, I wrote a screenplay, hoping that Pratt would like it and assign me to a second picture to direct in the Amazon. I knew that Universal could not turn out any product of quality on such a small budget as I had done with *Curucu*. Universal also had millions of rapidly devaluating cruzeros that could, by law, not be converted into hard currency. But that money could be taken out in the shape of a motion picture.

To write a screenplay was never difficult for me. It was just telling a story as seen through the eye of the camera. It took no more than three weeks to construct the screenplay *The Amazons:* A young archeologist, traveling up the Amazon River to study the cultural habits of the disappearing native tribes, stops at a village that had already been invaded by civilization. That meant that the Indians wore clothes and didn't run around naked, the standard conception of the Western world about Amazon tribes. In a village at the edge of the river, the archeologist meets an old white man, who, after having a few drinks, relates his story. As a young man he went with a small party of prospectors into the unexplored Amazon jungles looking for gold. Hordes of prospectors fifty years later devastated parts of the still virgin forest. He and his group were ambushed by warlike Amazon women, who, blending with the thick overgrowth of trees and plants, became practically invisible.

All of his companions, except him, were cruelly slain. His captors, women whose skin was green, carried him to their village where they lived without men. As the only male, he had fathered many of their children. Sexually exhausted, he escaped.

The archeologist, intrigued by a small golden Chima statue that the old man displayed as proof of his story, hires a safari in search of the "green" Amazons. As in the old man's tale, his group is ambushed and killed cruelly by green-skinned females. They wrap him in a net like a live animal and carry him to their village. There they dive into a mountain stream and emerge as light-skinned young women. The green "skin" was their jungle camouflage.

At the Amazon village, the archeologist meets an emaciated man of his age. He, too, had been captured and for years, the only male, had fathered their children. But only the girl babies were allowed to live.

Playboy magazine would have loved to print such a tale: scores of shapely nubile girls, one single man among them. What sexual stud wouldn't wish such an ultimate macho dream to come true!

But that pipe dream of unlimited sex, no work, and living a hedonistic life has, as the archeologist soon finds out, its pernicious drawback.

His predecessor, his usefulness gone for the women after they had captured a new stud, is used as a target for their arrow practice. The archeologist is forced to swallow a potion, which wipes out the memory of all the sexual pleasures he had experienced. He finally escapes, reaching civilization, but yearns to return to that unfulfilling sexual paradise. Can life, devoid of memory, be called living?

That idea appealed to the mind of James Pratt, the executive producer. But he insisted on a happy ending and a love affair between the leading man and an Amazon woman. That demand gave the story a slant that robbed it of its original conception. Cowardly, I compromised. For a leading lady I asked for Stephanie Powers, a young promising actress Universal was grooming. Pratt promised to look into that matter. Pratt never sent any actress for that part and forced me to find one in Brazil. But I got the concession that the studio would send Henrietta to Brazil with the American actors Pratt had cast for the film. That promise appeased Henrietta, who was very much against my accepting a second film to be shot in South America. She was afraid that the strain would damage my health. She was right as usual.

Sex, for the film industry, which in 1960 still catered to the innocent, was the symbol of evil. Their product was depicting a synthetic approach to life that had never existed. Two decades later the film industry dropped that conception. "Adult" films were produced, displaying explicit love scenes, since the R- and X-rated ones brought in more cash. The film industry had discovered that a glimpse of a woman's breast added thousands of dollars at the box office, though the display of male parts on the screen is still taboo.

Up to the time of the photographed revelation that people are endowed with sex parts, women possessed no breasts, no hair below her head, and a man in motion pictures had no penis. But screenwriters soon ran out of variations of filmable positions in sexual encounters. Sex became spiced with violence, whose coarse cruelties are limitless.

Before the popular display of blood and graphic killings on the screen, the scene where Jimmy Cagney pushed a grapefruit into Mae Clarke's face in the film *Public Enemy* was considered the acme of male sexual sadism. Not her gifted acting but the grapefruit scene made Mae Clarke memorable to the end of her career.

But I sold my integrity for more money than I needed to cover my bank loan for the ranch I wanted to buy. The drawback was that I had to return to a country that had achieved some twentieth-century sophistication but where the social system was still that of a Hammurabi. It was inconceivable to an American mind that the police shoot down, even today, abandoned, parentless children who roam like wild animals through the slums of Rio de Janeiro. Brazil was a mixture of Stone Age cruelties and the most sophisticated modern high-rises in São Paulo and their ultramodern capital, Brasilia.

I still wanted to give the young Amazons that same disregard for the line of the aimless wolf packs of Rio children, the complete lack of any moral compunction, a fact that can now be found in some of today's youth, who, gathering in gangs, have no conception of any human or spiritual value.

The male species has treated women like chattel for thousands of years, the way Aristotle describes them in his treatises. In *The Amazons*, I tried to reverse the power of the sexes.

I was too early with my ideas. Six years later William Golding wrote a book, *The Lord of the Flies*, which describes the absence of any morals and sensitivity in children. I wrote about females, he about boys.

I left Los Angeles for São Paulo. An original screenplay, also producing and directing it, was the acme of a writer's dream. I was blinded by that supposed opportunity. Everything that could go wrong went wrong. I didn't know how to cope with the mysterious workings of a big studio, where everybody tries to grab as much power as possible to improve his status, and with it the weekly check. Never having been under contract, a writer hired for a special assignment, whose screenplays had always reached the screen, I had never encountered any of those internal intrigues, an ingredient necessary to succeed as a company man in the Hollywood jungle.

To ease her waiting for her departure to join me in Belem, I bought gifts for Henrietta's birthday, which was the day I had to leave. In a conspiracy with stores on Hollywood Boulevard, special messengers delivered to her a package every hour on the hour. For twelve hours, the doorbell rang at the apartment on Franklin Avenue, which I had rented, not wanting to leave her alone in our house on Sunset Plaza Drive.

James Pratt had sent, in advance, a production manager, Ruby Rosenberg, known for his skill in handling difficult production in foreign countries. A heavyset, coarse man of fifty, Ruby knew how to manipulate the internal mechanics of a difficult production and how to get the most advantages for himself out of his assignment.

Arriving in São Paulo, Ruby was waiting for me. He had worked on the preproduction, and had assembled a crew. To ingratiate himself with me and also to please himself, he had hired a two-motor Convair plane to fly us to Manaus, the mysterious city on the upper Amazon River. The flight would be a pleasure trip and acquaint me with the country. Besides, it would be educational for both of us. He tried to teach me how to play the studio "perk" game.

Unfortunately, I was a bad student. I had a streak of honesty in me that I could never overcome. It would never have dawned on me to hire an airplane for a pleasure trip and to spend production money as if it came out of a faucet.

The small plane, in which we were the only passengers, flew over the Gran Chaco, the endless rain forest. I watched three rainbows simultaneously in different parts of an endless sky. Once, for refueling, we landed at a tiny airport, a landing strip hewn out of the dense forest. It was a small building built of glass and stainless steel. One of the big windows was shattered. Indians had shot arrows into the pane the day before, as a protest that government people had intruded into their territory. That the airport was guarded by soldiers didn't increase my sense of security.

Deep down below, glittering waterways were snaking their way under the endless roof of greenery to their final destination, a river nine thousand miles long flowing from the north in Peru to the Atlantic, ending at the city of Belem. I didn't see any sign of habitation and was convinced that no human, except perhaps native Indians, had ever entered that primeval part of the globe. Should the plane go down, nobody would ever find the wreck.

After a seven-hour flight, we landed in Manaus. I had read about that inland city thousands of miles away from civilization. At the turn of the century, Manaus had been the richest settlement in the Southern Hemisphere. Surrounded by forests of rubber trees, it was the only supplier of that new commodity the world craved for. While the trees had been cut down savagely without any regard to replanting them, Brazilian entrepreneurs, in conjunction with greedy American and European partners, had robbed the soil of its natural wealth. Unaccustomed to that sudden rain of gold, Brazilian millionaires had squandered their fortunes on creating a fairyland city with sumptuous houses, the sidewalks made of marble. To import European culture, the newly created rich erected an opera house with a golden cupola. To show off their social status, they also invited artistic celebrities from Europe. In 1910 Enrico Caruso sang *Pagliacci* in that theater and the famed Russian ballerina, Anna Pavlova, performed the "Dying Swan" on the opera stage. I went inside that building. The curtain was still hanging but in shreds, and broken windows had been boarded up. The houses on the marbled streets were in disrepair and crowded with Indian families, wearing colorful cotton clothes. To escape the encroaching jungle, the town had moved onto the Amazon River, covering it with small houseboats, moored so close to each other that they created a city of their own.

I should have shot my motion picture with the background of that city, which the impenetrable jungle slowly reclaimed.

Small islands, of the kind I had seen in Belem, floated down the water still carrying trees, plants, and possibly animals, such as monkeys and snakes. Reaching faraway shores in the Atlantic, they carried a new fauna and flora to unknown lands.

When the last rubber tree was gone, so was Manaus's wealth. Though it rained all the time during the motor trip to Manaus, that journey introduced me to the enormity of the river, which I would never have visualized.

That excursion, on which I did not see a Western white face, was the high point of that adventure, poisonous and away from a civilization that might never reach it. It explained to me why American film companies had stayed away from using South American locations.

We returned to São Paulo. Trouble had started that I could not foresee.

Pratt, in his insecurity, must have given Ruby instructions to watch me. Ruby, without my knowledge, telephoned nightly to the studio. I found out that, according to a new law, a motion picture shot in Brazil had to be processed in a Brazilian film laboratory. But no color laboratory existed. A full-length motion picture needs at least one hundred thousand feet of film stock to give the director the possibility of covering the camera angles that produce the necessary fluidity of the finished product. I also needed a troop of young Brazilian female dancers. Ruby could not find an accomplished one, and the woman who trained the dancers never paid them, as I found out later. He engaged the famous composer Radamas Gnattali. His music, which fitted the Brazilian background, Universal replaced with their own music department, to keep Joe Gershenson, their musical director, on the payroll. A grip dropped the sound equipment that had been shipped to me from Hollywood, and I had to rely on the aged RKO sound wagon I had used in *Curucu,* the only one in Brazil. The construction crew in the studio didn't secure the boards on the catwalks. One of the workmen fell from the high scaffold and had to be taken to the hospital. He was an epileptic and should never have been given that job. There was a movement among the crew to strike on account of that accident, though it was not in my power to have prevented it. I remember that when that man fell off the scaffold, and I heard the thud when he hit the floor, everybody rushed to that spot. I was sitting, suddenly numb, drained of all energy, unable to face that new disaster. I had a fight with Ruby who told me to stop the film and go home. It dawned on me that he wanted to sabotage me, though I never found out why. I lost my temper, threatening to send him home, since it was his job to arrange the physical details of this production. Everything on this production ran on the wrong track.

But I was determined to bring back a finished picture.

For the leading lady I engaged a young Italian actress, Giana Segale, a leftover from an unfinished Brazilian picture shot among an Amazon tribe that had never seen a white face. A young Polish director, Jan Segorski, had taken her and an American actor, John Loder, into the interior. He had met Giana Segale in Rome, where she had been a model for "life" photographs, illustrations for story magazines. But Segorski deserted his two actors in the jungle, a thousand miles away from civilization. Giana had bunked with Loder, afraid to stay alone in a small tent. They did not know how to return, when a Jehovah's Witness missionary visited that heathen tribe to convert the wild Indians to Christianity. The holy man was so shocked that a white female and a white male lived together in the same tent that, with his meager funds, he financed their trip back to civilization. That was the film story I should have made.

Before I started the studio production, I returned to Belem with the crew. Universal had sent Don Taylor to play the young archeologist. He was a lightweight actor, with a burning ambition to direct, which he later did in Hollywood for many years. But Pratt had kept his promise and sent Henrietta, who arrived with the American actors Don and Eduardo Ciannelli, also Terry Moore, an experienced film cutter who had put my first film, *Curucu,* together. Without Henrietta and Terry, I don't believe I would have survived that adventure. Looking back at that trying time, when my sleeping hours diminished to three, I did not realize that I was moving toward a nervous breakdown.

Against all odds I completed the shooting and returned to Hollywood with enough footage to put the show together. Still, the picture ran for a time and then for years on television. Don Taylor accomplished what he wanted. He became a motion picture director. Ruby Rosenberg died of a heart attack in the South Pacific during the shooting of *Mutiny on the Bounty* with Marlon Brando. I left in the jungle of Brazil a part of my health that I never fully regained.

Henrietta, her mother, and dog were back from their trip searching for a house. They had visited the greater part of California for a home with the specifications Ernestine demanded, a garden patch for growing vegetables, possibly with an access to a river and also wooden floors. To cut the Gordian knot, I came up with a pregnant idea: contact the real estate broker, Myna de Lespinasse, who ten years before had sold Mother the Canoga Park house. The telephone directory did not register her name. We inquired at the Canoga Park post office. She had left the previous year but had asked that her mail be forwarded to Three Rivers.

Where was Three Rivers? Nobody of our acquaintance had heard of that community. The Automobile Club had the information. Three Rivers was a village at the entrance to Sequoia Park, the home of the giant three-thousand-year-old sequoias, which only grow in the High Sierras and Himalayas. Since Myna wouldn't conceivably have moved to India, we drove to the closer destination, two hundred miles north of Los Angeles, eighty miles south of Fresno.

It was a pleasant drive with no traffic signs to delay us, on Highway 99, built by the army in case of an invasion of Russian hordes, who would strike the American continent from the north, through Alaska, British Columbia, Canada, and the states of Washington and Oregon, to raze Three Rivers to the ground. But we were not alarmed by that possibility and drove north, with Ernestine and her dog, on the search for Myna.

Three Rivers was a quiet rural village, created in 1886 by a commune that followed the rules of the Marxist manifesto of 1848. The colony had cut a road to the top of the seven thousand–foot High Sierra mountain chain to butcher the ancient sequoia trees and live off the sale of the wood. The loggers sometimes cut the wooden behemoths down for fun, just to enjoy the crash of the falling giants. Fortunately, Congress declared the sequoias to be national monuments. The High Sierras were declared a state park where, by law, not even a twig was permitted to be removed. That decision destroyed the lumber business of the Kaweah commune and forced them to leave the county of Tulare, where Three Rivers is situated.

Three Rivers was the only understatement I ever found in America, since it had four rivers, the North Fork, Middle Fork, South Fork, and East Fork, which form the Kaweah River, named after an Indian tribe that used to live there.

Myna, though taking care of wayward teenaged girls, owned a dozen bungalows that she rented out to transient park visitors. She knew of a small house for sale which, though old, was sturdily built, and would fill Mother's request. Did it have a wooden floor? It did. Was it close to the river? It had river frontage.

The property had a small promontory dominated by a huge, vicious gander and his harem, a flock of ducks, which every morning and evening noisily demanded their meal.

Three Rivers was a clone of a western cowboy village as depicted in the then-popular TV shows like *Bonanza* or *Wagon Train*. Its 1,100 inhabitants were nonconformist Republicans who didn't make a distinction between Democrats and Communists. They also rejected any change. In Three Rivers, time had stood still. It had a small market, telephones, and modern technical conveniences, like indoor toilets, running water in the kitchen, a post office, and a three hundred–pound sheriff, who used to sit on unruly people whom he had arrested until the paddy wagon arrived. The Three Rivers spirit had not varied for a century. It was a young community, since only in 1950 Mr. Jeremiah Swanson, the first white child ever born in that village, had died at the age of eighty. Mr. Swanson was the child of the settlers who had arrived from the East Coast in covered wagons a century ago, to settle among a peaceful, guileless tribe of Yokohl Indians. Now the only traces of their thousand-year-old culture are mysterious, ocher rock paintings, and small holes in boulders for grinding acorn, their staple food. Their ancient burial grounds now are underwater, since a reservoir had been built by the Army Corps of Engineers. The enormous dam guaranteed that the newly arrived farmers had enough irrigation to raise their crops of oranges. The Indians lost their land, but the investment in orange groves brought in a very high financial return. Where the well-to-do farmers now live is called Cadillac Row.

Three Rivers was still untouched by the haste of our time, like a Swiss village, the kind Ernestine had known all her life. Next to the house that we bought for Ernestine lived Mr. and Mrs. Cook. They loved to look after Mother, who was a knowledgeable and interesting person. Mr. Cook even installed a bell from Mother's to their house. Manually activated by a thin cable, Mother could call Mr. Cook in an emergency. He and his wife, Louise, were good neighbors until Mr. Cook blew his brains out with a Smith & Wesson two-inch barreled handgun. Despite its outward peace, there were an inappropriate number of suicides, even murders, in that peaceful community, though nobody talked about that flaw.

The difficulty was that the present occupants of the house Myna offered us for sale hadn't paid rent for a year. It took Myna a full year of legal wangling to get them removed. In the meantime, Ernestine stayed in her former abode in Canoga Park.

After a hiatus of fourteen months, Ernestine moved into her new house and lived there contentedly for twenty years, fed the gander and his ducks' harem, grew vegetables, and was very much adored by the natives, though she never joined any of the many civic activities, like the Women's Club, the Chamber of Commerce, or any church, of which Three Rivers had a Catholic, a Protestant, a Baptist, a Community church, a Seventh Day Adventist, and a Hare Krishna settlement, whose members wore distinctive clothes. The Hare Krishnas were expelled because they were selling marijuana, which they grew secretly in the mountains. The police knew about most of those weed patches, watching them grow by helicopter. That weed, having a different hue of green, was difficult to camouflage. Since the police were paid a bonus for every pound they confiscated, they swooped down on the patches just one day before the harvest yielded its highest weight. But these activities were ignored by the churchgoing citizens of Three Rivers, since some of them might have had a hand in growing this "recreational" plant.

After having lived happily in that river house for twenty years, Ernestine, then ninety years old, decided to move into a retirement home. She walked out of the house without glancing back at it even once.

On our first visit, Myna asked Henrietta and me to look at a property on the South Fork Drive, which had just been put on the market. A rich man had bought fifty acres of prime land for his son to make him a farmer. Farmers, essential to feed the population during wartime, were exempt from serving in the armed forces. But the young man and his wife preferred to live at the ocean at Newport Beach, with its yachts and ultrarich society. During the Korean War, they dutifully built that new home on the Three Rivers lot but never occupied it.

When the Korean War and with it the military draft had ended, there was no reason to live in the mountains, away from the five o'clock martini hours at fashionable Newport Beach. The home was for sale.

I certainly was not in the market for a house in the country. The architect Frank Roberts, Frank Lloyd Wright's assistant for a decade, designed and executed that job, the way his master would have built it. Using his client's money, Roberts certainly had not economized where the quality of material was concerned. Huge glass windows opened to a 180-degree view of mountain chains, which in winter were covered with snow. The driveway to it was winding and half a mile long, hiding the building from the country road below. Only the interior needed minor completion. The walls were of choice redwood, the kind hardly to be found today, since coastal redwood trees, having aged a millennium, have been cut down by loggers to be sold to Japan where wood is scarce. The men with the chainsaws were clamoring that they and their families would starve, if the slaughter of those ancient trees were forbidden. But their plight was only postponed. After the trees, which could not be replaced in a thousand years, were gone, the loggers moved somewhere else to create again a wasteland, reminiscent of the disaster of a forest fire.

The Three Rivers ranch, called Blossom Ranch, after the first settler a hundred years ago, and its fifty acres of land, was protected from being subdivided by a surrounding thirteen thousand–acre co-operative than raised cattle. The Williams Act forbade any houses to be built on less than five acres, which prevented the South Fork from being sliced into "city lots" or covered with mobile homes. The water that fed Frank Roberts's creation was an excellent spring. It produced cool, clear water, especially delicious when spiked with Scotch. The floors of the house were heated by circulating warm water. Air conditioning kept it cool in summer.

The Blossom Ranch was safely away from the South Fork River, which was very noisy when the snow was melting in the Sierras and white-foamed waves came cascading down, inundating houses that foolishly had been built along its otherwise docile shore.

Henrietta wanted us to buy the Blossom Ranch.

Hers was the most impracticable idea I had heard in years. I was an author and screenwriter whose livelihood depended on studio jobs. I was connected with the umbilical cord of the telephone, busy with luncheons and dinners with agents, contacts with producers, and was floating in the whirlpool of the motion picture craft. I also had to earn the money to keep up our home in Beverly Hills, to feed my family and many visiting friends. In fact, I was a cog in the machinery of entertainment, which, as I believed, could hardly exist without my input.

I was convinced that, should I move to the country, we would starve and I would climb up the walls of the country home if the daily package of junk mail should cease to arrive, hear the urgent tingling of the telephone, and watch the evening news on TV. How could I live without the input of the studio's exciting atmosphere, which as I secretly confessed to myself, was a waste of my productive years. I had become a slave of an industry, neglecting my craft as a writer of novels, short stories, essays, and any other literary output. I certainly was no country boy, though the bucolic life suited Henrietta, who as a young girl had herded goats on the mountain meadows of Switzerland.

I told Henrietta that ten diesel engines could not drag me out of Hollywood and that, due to my mental makeup and training, I would never be able to live away from a metropolis and would dessicate mentally in the stale atmosphere of a rural community. Besides, I was perennially short of cash, and a quantity of story material was an important asset, as a shoe salesman must offer different styles of shoes.

Fate has its own way of asserting itself. A friend of mine, the gifted surgeon Dr. Arthur Lesser, whose income demanded a yearly tax shelter, asked me if I knew of a property in which he could invest and write off the taxes. For some people losing money seems to be a lucrative income.

To help Arthur in his predicament, I mentioned the Three Rivers property to him. I described the ranch in such glowing terms that Henrietta, listening to my sales talk, wondered why we didn't acquire it ourselves, since it was of such beauty and also within our financial possibilities. Besides, to live in the country was much cheaper than an expensive house in Los Angeles.

To raise cash for the down payment, I put our house on Sunset Plaza up for sale. But it was a time when the real estate market hit its perennial cycle when nobody bought property. Still, I paid a couple of thousand dollars down and wisely asked for a ninety-day escrow. During those three months, we didn't even receive a telephone call from anybody interested in our Sunset Plaza home. I found a party who rented the house, and we moved into a small apartment on Franklin Avenue. Since house sales move in cycles in Los Angeles, the real estate market had dried up. After three months of financial frustration and not to lose my down payment on the Blossom Ranch, I tried to raise a second mortgage on our townhouse but was shocked by the demand of high interest and the insidious "points" added to the loan. Also, the title search and red tape that accompany every real estate transaction would take too long to find the cash.

My doctor friend, Arthur, was versed in dealing with capital. As a surgeon, he was used to opening up people, helping himself and sending a bill. He suggested we try a bank. Why a bank? "Let me tell you a secret," Arthur said. "The banks have walls. The walls are covered with shelves. On those shelves the banks store batches of money. That money they rent out for a percentage. The difference between lending that money and the borrowing public is the reason why banks are in business."

His advice, though abstract, made little sense to me. I had been dealing with the Bank of America since the day I arrived in Hollywood in 1937. I knew the bank manager of the Bank of America on Sunset Strip, Wilson Asdel. Defying Henrietta's Swiss conservative mind, I for years had borrowed small sums and paid them back promptly. I had learned that in America, to be a good citizen, one has to make debts, to keep the economy rolling.

I talked to my bank manager, in my mind a futile attempt, to get a second mortgage loan, which banks on principle don't give. Banks also don't like to lend money on property outside the city limits. But used to writing fictitious stories, I tried. "Mr. Asdel," I asked the bank manager, a gray-haired, middle-aged and cold-blooded Yankee, "how much is my character worth to you?"

"Character, shit," Mr. Asdel said. "How much money do you want?" "Nine thousand dollars to meet the escrow on a ranch in the country," I said. Asdel opened the drawer of his desk, took out a form, scribbled something on it, and said, "Sign it." He didn't ask for collateral for the loan, which in 1958 was a very big sum. He also didn't ask for what length of time I needed the money. But he might have known that I always had paid my loans back on time.

Now I had an apartment in Hollywood, a house on Sunset Plaza Drive for sale, a ranch in the country with lots of acreage on which nothing grew, no cash, no job, but I had acquired something invaluable: the gambling spirit of the pioneer, which keeps this country vibrant and progressive.

Two weeks later I sold my screenplay *The Amazons* to Universal Studios for a sum that covered not only Asdel's loan but also the price of the ranch.

It also meant the return to Brazil, with its hardships, as producer, writer, and director. I didn't repay Wilson Asdel his loan immediately. I paid off the loan in droplets, to make him feel right in his decision, which had defied the bank rules.

Now we have lived at the ranch in Three Rivers for thirty-five years, a fermata of peace in our action-packed existence. Sitting on our hilltop, watching the snow-covered hills around it; the giant sequoias silhouetted on mountaintops, miles away; waiting for the moon to climb into the star-studded sky, a burst of eternal light, slowly exposing its golden disc; listening to the noise of the South Fork River, angry in spring, soft in summer, but unseen from our vantage point; the changing seasons that remind us of the limitation of our time; the herons greeting each other in midair when one flies to the lake to catch the evening meal of fish, the mate returning from it; the variety of birds, the titmouse, the nuthatch, the jays, quail, the clownish woodpeckers, the giant ravens, which circle us, asking to be fed; the wildlife, raccoons, bobcats, foxes, bears, and occasional mountain lions; the herds of grazing cows on the other side of the river, away from our mountain peak—this is an oasis of a peace of which we had so little in our lifetime.

It was the midlife crisis, the male menopause. Mine was not based on a search for a return to a youth passed, personified in a younger wife, who often resembles the former one, or being stymied by the realization that the future could only be a slow descent into an empty old age. My discontent was triggered by a question: What to do with the rest my life? Writing motion pictures, strings of celluloid that disappear, leaving hardly any ashes? I wasn't born with the innate sense of many native Americans who look forward to retirement, to go fishing, play golf, or other shallow rewards for a lifetime of toil.

Though I now owned a many-acre ranch in the country in one of the most beautiful parts of California, in the foothills of the High Sierras, halfway between Los Angeles and San Francisco, my biological time clock told me to "find myself," if there was anything to find in that mental void. Besides, Hollywood, as it did from time to time, was again shedding its skin like a lizard. There were no studio writing assignments anymore. The writer had to be part of a "package" of an independent unit. A still-infant industry, television, was trying to cut a groove for itself in the entertainment world. For a time I took part in it, writing half-hour shows for a fly-by-night producer, Frank Wisbar, and a weekly one for the soap factory Procter and Gamble,

Front Page Detective. The leading man, Edmund Lowe, was so burned out that he refused to act and speak dialogue at the same time.

I had ideas for TV series: *The Couch*, an anthology based on the profession of a psychoanalyst; *Ship's Doctor*, using the background of a luxury liner; *James and Vasco*, a detective and his shepherd dog, which had more brains than his master. I wrote a show for Martin Melcher, the husband of Doris Day (Doris von Kappelhoff), the popular singer who played a perennial virgin in sixty comedies. For Melcher I created a detective whose partner was a computer. But the deal blew up when Melcher supposedly tried to relieve his wife of her sixteen million–dollar fortune. I wrote a stage play and screenplay of an Asian woman who gives birth to a monster, a "demon." The film producers rejected it, shocked. A few years later the writer Ira Levin had a world success with *Rosemary's Baby*, the same theme, only the actress, Mia Farrow, played the junior devil's surrogate mother. Skirting my idea, *The Couch* was later produced as *The 50 Minute Hour*, since a psychiatrist works only for fifty minutes but charges his client for sixty. *Ship's Doctor* became *Love Boat*. I even wrote and produced a pilot called *Captain Fathom*, which inspired my former partner, Ivan Tors, to do the show *Sea Hunt* with the actor Lloyd Bridges. All those shows ran for years, though without me. CBS "adapted" *No. 13 Demon Street*, calling it *Thriller*, with Boris Karloff in the lead; *A-men*, which I wrote and directed as *Magnetic Monster*, was lifted by a production company owned by an entrepreneur, Sam Harris, who just changed the title to *Top Secret*. I could have sued that company since the similarities were glaring. But I have never sued anybody, ever. Suing uses up money, time, and energy—three limiting factors of my life. I lack the conviction to fight the "system." I also might have a subconscious apprehension that a TV series would tie me down, demanding years of my life, forcing me to become a company man, a dried-out businessman, since I never could see any value in tailor-made jobs. I didn't need to play the popular game of "the great idea robbery." I was the "idea man," whose ideas were "realized" by others. Not to fight back also was an easy way to avoid any responsibility to have to produce something in which I didn't see value. This, of course, is a thought incomprehensible to any person whose life's objective is to gather green strips of paper.

Now the "entrepreneurs" of my generation are gone. They often lived lives of affluence, were part of the Hollywood elite of "wheelers and dealers," a crowd I arduously avoided and Henrietta deeply resented. My life's companion, besides Henrietta, was my typewriter and its incorruptible taskmaster, the blank piece of paper. When I had no paying job, I certainly was never out of work.

I put my ideas down in novels: *Donovan's Brain* (Knopf), *Hauser's Memory* (Putnam), *Sky Port* (Crown), *City in the Sky* (Putnam), *Gabriel's Body* (Leisure), *Whomsoever I Shall Kiss* (Crown), *For Kings Only* (Crown), *The Third Ear* (Putnam), *The Witches of Paris* (Bertelsmann), and *Despair in Paradise,* a novel about the Swedish welfare state, which is still looking for a publisher. I don't count the short stories, essays like "Epistles to the Germans," the correspondence after the war, replying to German "friends," who wrote to me when they found out that I hadn't gone up in smoke in Hitler's ovens. That collection of letters became a "classic," first published in Will Burnett's *Story* magazine, which had launched Hemingway, Tennessee Williams, Bunin, Saroyan, and many other contemporary, well-known writers. That was my reward, not the growing bank account.

The publisher Alfred Knopf told me, "My client Thomas Mann religiously turns out one written page every day, between eight in the morning and twelve in the afternoon. He delivers one completed book to me every year." His advice became a guide for my life: I compulsively wrote every day, as the assertion of my existence.

The search for ideas never became stale since science opened a new and intriguing frontier to be explored: space. Not the fantasy world of little green men with antennas on their bald heads, but the challenge of its scientific background. I wrote a novel, *Sky Port,* the construction of the first hotel in space. It was followed by *City in the Sky,* bought by the producer that produced the James Bond films, cannibalizing it for its film *Moonraker,* since I described a novelty: intercourse in antigravity, the perfect ending for their film.

I realized the possibilities that space exploration offered to the world, which, though still a fantasy, is within the range of possibility. I became aware of the limited size of the planet Earth when watching the Echo, a weather satellite. I could observe as it appeared every night in the south, crossing that part of the sky in nine minutes before disappearing in the north. Since it circled the Earth in ninety-six minutes, I was able to see 10 percent of this planet's atmosphere from my restricted vantage point. That observation gave me the idea for the novel *City in the Sky.*

Hollywood money isn't money; it is congealed snow, the writer Dorothy Parker remarked. It is Monopoly money, carrying a curse, since everybody I knew, including me, lived beyond his income, to compensate for the shallowness of his existence. Hollywood also is a town where inferior people make superior people feel inferior.

Hollywood has a bad name among the famous film workers. D. W. Griffith, the great motion picture director, who died poor, remarked, "It is a shame to take this country away from the rattlesnakes." Though Hollywood had been good to me, I never understood the disdain and hatred of the people who made their living in motion pictures. It might be that its shallowness leaves a nostalgic impression on their lives. But the legendary director Ernst Lubitsch gratefully acknowledged, "I've been to Paris, France, and to Paris, Paramount. Paris, Paramount is better." For me Hollywood had the personality of a paper cup. The price to stay a lifetime in that paradise was to surrender one's talent.

Henrietta, who never was happy in Hollywood, felt that I was wasting my productive years by just trying to make money. For her, Hollywood was a cage that prevented me from doing what she believed was my vocation: broadcasting thoughts. Though I am not a scientist, I knew how to drape scientific ideas in a cloak of entertainment.

The only way to get out of the "City of Nets," which is how Bertolt Brecht called that motion picture factory, was to leave Hollywood. I was helped by a letter I received from the Bavaria Film Company in Munich, saying, should I be in Germany "by chance," I should contact their director, Ladislao Vajda. "By chance" meant that Bavaria wanted to save the expense for my fare but offer me work.

Later I found out why Bavaria contacted me. German writers didn't have the experience to construct a screenplay for the international film market. Besides, I had worked for a partner of Bavaria, Praesens Films in Switzerland. Bavaria was looking for a Hollywood-trained writer who also was proficient in German. I grabbed that opportunity, though Henrietta was very reluctant even to visit Germany. We found a caretaker for the ranch and left, as if in flight. I wasn't aware that I had embarked on a journey that would divorce me from Hollywood studios forever.

Returning with Henrietta to Germany was a traumatic experience. After a hiatus of thirty years, I found myself in a country unknown but at the same time familiar to me. I, of course, was prepared to run into remnants of Nazism, that frame of mind that is innate in almost every German. I again had made friends in Germany, by letter and on their visits to America, intelligent and pleasant people, that mental elite that exists in every nation. But even fifty years after that insane destruction of humans and cultures, I haven't come across one single German who could bring himself to utter one single word of apology about his own participation in Germany's psychotic cruelties.

The memory of man's inhumanity toward man can never be erased from the annals of history. Intolerance and racism seem to be part of the human genetic code, DNA.

Soon the horrors of war are forgotten or denied or relished by men as the most exciting time of their life. Excesses are cloaked in the shiny coat of patriotism, and the surviving warrior prepares the new generation again for the next slaughter that the human species seems to need to fulfill its destiny. The national flag is declared an untouchable and noble symbol. But it is just a colored rag, representing "national honor," that nebulous conception whose meaning nobody can explain.

Born in Germany, I had lived for a time under the Kaiser's sacred flag of black-white-red, then during the Weimar Republic's flag, but fortunately not under Hitler's swastika rag. Now there is another one, that of the German Federal Republic, also a powerful symbol. Four different flags representing the honor of one country during my lifetime, all of them of equal value or perhaps of no value at all? The American flag became for a time a symbol of the right wing that flirted with fascism, and it lost its meaning of national unity. An amendment to the Constitution now makes burning the flag a federal offense, as if love for one's country can be ordered by government fiat.

The new generation does not feel any guilt about their predecessors' inanities. Germans born after the war enjoy *"die Gnade der spaeten Geburt,"* the luck of not having been alive during their nation's former inhumanities.

Horace, a Roman consul in 440 B.C., exclaimed, "*Dulce et decorum est pro patria mori*" (It is sweet and honorable to die for one's country). He was an old man who wanted the young to perish for him. He also might have been the originator of patriotism. The Germans put their wish for death into poetry: "*Kein schoeneren Tod gibts auf der Welt als wer vom Feind erschlagen*" (There is no sweeter death than being slaughtered by the enemy). The French die "*pour la gloire de France*" (for the glory of France), though nobody can explain what "glory" means.

After every human slaughter, the shocked survivors create organizations like the League of Nations or the United Nations, proclaiming that they had fought "the war to end all wars." But then in the name of national pride old men again order the young to arm themselves, to protect the nation's security. Friedrich II, called "the Great," king of Prussia, impatiently reprimanded his soldiers: "*Wollt ihr Kerle denn ewig leben?*" (Do you guys want to live forever?). Leading killers of their own species are honored in statues, like Napoleon Bonaparte, in impressive mausoleums. The many thousand-year-old sequoia trees in the High Sierra National Forest suffer the names of soldiers: "General Sherman" or "General Grant," but not "Walt Whitman" or "John Muir."

We traveled, on Bavaria's invitation, to Hamburg, the gateway on the Elbe River to the Atlantic Ocean. Though inland, Hamburg, the liveliest harbor town in Europe, is brimming with the exciting commotion of international trade. Where were the bombed-out houses, razed by firestorms of a war only twenty years ago? The city had been rebuilt in the style before the British bombers incinerated it, only two decades ago.

German cities rose from the rubble. The Germans called that rejuvenation "*das Wirtschaftswunder*" (the miracle of commerce), creating the most powerful commercial state in Europe. That they were helped by four million Turks, imported for that purpose, is not mentioned. Foreign labor, paid by the Marshall Plan, erected a bulwark against the Slavic hordes, the way Charlemagne in 811 C.E. had built on the same ground a fortress against the threat of a Slavic invasion. History lacks variety. If you want to know the future, study the past.

In 1962 when we arrived in Germany, which was still suffering from the traumatic effects of the Nazi regime, I found myself in a country trying to emulate the American style of freedom. Had Nazism gone up in smoke, leaving no ashes, or had it dug itself underground, to wait for its day of rebirth?

German cities and villages have a medieval charm, since they have existed for a millennium. Henrietta and I found an old restaurant in Hamburg, its walls wood-paneled, the dining room decorated with antique paraphernalia. The British bombs might have overlooked that ancient tavern, or it had been refashioned in the patrician atmosphere of that ancient Hansa City. It was the right place to order the famous flounder, a flat fish only found in the Atlantic Ocean. Only one dining room table was occupied, by six substantial-looking men, sitting behind their steins, having a noisily good time.

I am married to a woman who smiles at everybody, a whim appreciated in America but looked on with suspicion in Germany. For Germans a woman's smile might invite intimacy. Henrietta smiled at six substantial males at the round beer-wet table. One came over. He had heard us talk in English. I answered him in German.

"You speak German," the man said.

"I was born in Saxony," I told him in German.

He said, "Why do you speak in English?"

"I live in America."

"Did Hitler throw you out?" he asked, using the German *du*. That intimacy is only used among family members and close friends and carries, without having been invited to use it, an edge of disrespect among strangers.

"Yes, Hitler threw me out," I said.

"Are you Jewish?"

"I'm Jewish."

"Didn't we catch you?" The varnish of postwar democracy disappeared, and I was transported back into Hitler's world.

"No. You didn't catch me. And what are you doing?" I also used the German *du,* the intimate way he had addressed me. He pulled up a chair and sat down, jovially, without any rancor. For him, a middle-aged man and survivor of the Hitler generation, there was no rancor in his talking to a Jew. He might never have met one. "I'm the boss of the biggest insurance company in Hamburg, and the boys at my table had been in my outfit at the SS. I look after them. They work for me," he said with pride.

I watched Henrietta freeze, as I had witnessed twenty years ago, when she insisted on leaving Germany. I did not understand her then. Now I did.

"How much do you pull down?" I asked, still addressing him with the familiar *du*.

"Me?" he said. "Sixty thousand [marks], a free apartment overlooking the Alster River, and a free Mercedes." He was pleased with himself.

"Sixty thousand?" I said. "Man, if you were boss of a big insurance company in America, you'd get at least five hundred thousand dollars. But you have to be Jewish."

He laughed and painfully squeezed the skin of my belly, obviously knowing body torture points. He insisted on buying drinks and bringing his SS friends to our table.

That encounter would have been different in 1937, when these SS men were looking for me, to prevent a Jew from contaminating the Nazi spirit.

The next day I was back in the motion picture business, assigned to write a screenplay in German for Bavaria Films. The job was to adapt a novel by Siegfried Lentz. It was a challenge to write again in German. The director was Ladislao Vajda, a Hungarian refugee of the Nazi times who had settled in Spain. The film had an English lead, James Robertson Justice, a Shakespearean actor who spoke an accent-free German. The theme was, in essence, an American gangster story: bank robbers escape by boat, occupying a lightship that is anchored outside the Hamburg harbor. That picture received the film prize, the Bambi, the award for the best German motion picture of the year 1962. It was remade twenty-five years later in English with the Austrian actor, Klaus Maria Brandauer. That version disappeared without a trace, though I tried to find a copy.

Ladislao Vajda was a "pro," a craftsman impossible to find among German filmmakers. He was a raging Americaphobe and hated everything America did or stood for, though he had never been to that country. His antagonism was perhaps based on the fact that he had not been invited to Hollywood, where his Hungarian compatriot, Michael Curtiz (Mihaly Kertesz), had become one of the top directors for Columbia Studios. Curtiz was best known for his motion picture *Casablanca*.

Spain, Vajda's chosen new country, had, after its Franco fascistic period, gone through its first free election. Vajda bragged that only a dozen voters had been killed. That there were no violent deaths among American voters, he brushed aside.

I witnessed the filming on a large lightship that the company had rented. It was an ambulating location, traveling to Malmö in Sweden. I enjoyed the freedom of movement and inspiration of that floating film location. I had a perambulating job, away from the confined Hollywood studio offices, where I had to dream up stories by artificial light. With that freedom of movement and being a perambulating writer, it was as though the past before Hitler's Germany had returned and the war had made me a prisoner of world events. I, but not Henrietta, liked this mobility. I didn't even dream that a couple of months later I'd find myself without Henrietta, deep in the jungles of West Africa.

On our trip to the Côte d'Azur in 1932, Henrietta and I traveled on our Harley Davidson, she in the sidecar. I was commanded by my producer Erich Pommer to meet him in Nice for a story conference. I was writing for him the screenplay *F.P. 1 Does Not Answer,* which became his and my last picture ever produced by UFA.

One year later, in 1933, we didn't leave Germany—Germany left us. Pommer left Germany at the same time as I. For seventeen years, his chauffeur Max had been his "vox populi," his Gallup poll. Max had viewed every picture of the Pommer production. Sitting alone in a projection room, Max was the oracle for Pommer, which, of course, was pure nonsense, since not even a seasoned filmmaker knew whether the public would like that show. The history of picture making is filled with misjudgments of experts.

When Henrietta and I attended the Writers Guild awards dinner in 1988 at the Beverly Hilton Hotel, we were placed at the same table with the legendary Jules Stein, an ophthalmologist who had created the powerful film agency MCA and acquired the giant Universal Studios. That tycoon, a man in his eighties, intrigued by Henrietta, had to find support by putting his hand on her thigh, while he related the story of *Star Wars,* one of the biggest financial successes of the motion picture industry. George Lucas, a young filmmaker who had written and directed the film *American Graffiti,* which Universal had financed and turned out to be a great success, had offered that studio his screenplay of a space saga, *Star Wars.* The screenplay to *American Graffiti* had been rejected by every studio until Universal had agreed to finance it. According to Jules Stein's version, *Star Wars* had been offered to Universal but was rejected. Twentieth Century–Fox finally agreed to finance Lucas's screenplay, budgeting four million dollars, a small sum to produce a major motion picture.

It went over budget, and Fox found itself in a dilemma, having spent nine million dollars. To minimize its loss, the finished picture was offered for sale for seven and a half million dollars without finding a buyer. Columbia Studios finally bought 50 percent interest in it for three million dollars. It grossed one billion, much more than *Gone with the Wind.* Jules Stein inquired at his studio why the Lucas screenplay had been rejected, since *American Graffiti* had grossed fifty million dollars. He couldn't find any producer in his studio who admitted ever having seen the screenplay, heard of it, and so, of course, had not rejected it. In the motion picture business everybody wants to share a success but nobody ever accepts any responsibility.

I always was susceptible to "vibrations." The depressing misery in hospital waiting rooms stymies my breathing. I dislike hotel beds, aware of the exudation of foreign bodies, an odor that penetrates even the freshly washed sheets. Whenever I enter a house, I can sense whether its inhabitants are happy or whether some tension is lurking. But flying to Liberia, "vibrations" didn't warn me. I didn't anticipate that I was on the way to Poltergeistland.

My neighbor in Three Rivers, Donald Nemetz, was a business adviser to William Tubman, the president of that West African republic. Tubman wanted to rid his government of corruption and to design a new constitution, streamlining that country into American efficiency. Don had invited us to visit them, but Henrietta could not go.

Nemetz, meaning "German" in Czech, possessed the rigid Teutonic traits of stubbornness, obstinacy, but also, in his case, unbribable honesty. In a country ruled by graft called "dash" and pork-barrel politics since its inception more than a century ago, Don was an excellent choice for a job that never could succeed.

Since Henrietta wanted to return home to her ailing mother in California, I went with Don and his wife Rowena, pricked again by an adventurous spirit, since Don had told me stories about that country, which nobody possessing a rational mind would ever believe. Nobody since Graham Greene in his book *Travels with My Aunt* had written about Liberia from an inside view. My excuse was that I wanted to find new material to write about, a flimsy excuse to cater to my "adrenaline freak" condition, that insatiable curiosity. I was like a flea that jumps in the air, not knowing where he will land.

Our SAS airplane landed in Lisbon airport for refilling. I expected the plane to be half-empty, since I could not visualize why any people wanted to fly to Monrovia. In Lisbon the airplane took on a huge cargo of women and children. They were wives and children of company employees from every conceivable European country: Swedish, German, English, Danish women in their late twenties and early thirties. None of their brats were older than ten. At once the peace of the plane changed into mayhem. Those women joined their husbands, most of them accountants, employees of European industries who had their offices in Monrovia, with the intent to rob that African country of its mineral wealth.

A blonde, tall, young woman had sat next to me as we left in Zurich. She was a stunning beauty, wearing a white dress with a two-colored seaman's collar. I had tried to talk to her once, but she didn't answer, possibly jaded by being bothered by men. I wondered how it would be to be so beautiful, knowing that wherever she went every gaze follows her automatically. She left, in Lisbon, with a small, bald-headed, middle-aged man. I had seen those kinds of beauties before, mostly in the company of older men. Since she obviously was a menace to her peers, she might not have been accepted by them and attached herself to wealthy men more than double her age, who treated her not like a Volkswagen but like a Rolls-Royce. Such beauty must be lonely.

I was never bored during the long flight along the coast of Africa. At the end I was holding a baby, bottle-feeding it while the mother collapsed with fatigue. But I didn't have to change its diapers.

Finally, late in the evening, we landed at Robertson Airfield in Liberia.

Liberia, though an "independent" democratic republic, was an American colony. Its currency was American banknotes. The highest denomination was twenty dollars.

The immense Robertson airport, where the SAS plane landed, was forty miles outside the capital city, Monrovia. It had been built by the U.S. Army's Air Corps during World War II, to fly supplies from Belem in Brazil to Liberia, for the Allied armies that fought the German General Rommel's divisions in Algiers. Liberia had inherited that abandoned installation.

When we landed late in the evening, heavily armed police surrounded the plane. They spoke a singsong English that I hardly understood. Don jokingly suggested that I should hire a lawyer the moment I arrived, since too many laws had stymied every freedom in that country. Of course, those laws could be circumvented by "dash." Customs inspectors in a Quonset hut were meticulous and slowly rummaging through the passengers' luggage, looking, I guess, for contraband cigarettes and booze. It was almost midnight, and the children, most of them tired out, were sleeping or crying. But then, exactly at midnight, customs slapped labels on the luggage without opening it and locked up the office. The passengers left with their uninspected suitcases and traveling bags. It was my first impression of Liberian efficiency.

The night was darker than any I had ever experienced in my life. The sky, though it glowed with the pinpoint lights of billions of stars, was like a black glass bell enclosing the Earth below. The police had disappeared. There was a Chrysler station wagon waiting for us. The driver was fine-featured like many West African blacks. He drove us to the capital. That trip seemed endless. From time to time the station wagon stopped at a water hole and the driver doused his head. Don explained that the Liberians suffered from a lack of protein in their diet and tired after even small exertions.

In a ritual that Don had practiced with me on the plane, the polite greeting was touching the flat of the hand with that of the other person, then snapping the middle finger with his, a trick I never really mastered. That "greeting" also transferred a sweetish smell of palm oil, an odor that stayed with me during my visit.

Victor Stoloff, a film director who had shot a motion picture in Africa, told me that he had been intrigued by a young Zulu dancer of exceptional grace and beauty. When the interpreter introduced her to him, she shrank away from him. He, too, stepped back, since she reeked of rancid butter. The interpreter apologized for her. She was shocked, since Victor to her smelled like a corpse. The Zulus only wash their dead but keep butter in their hair as protection against the sun. To meet her, Victor should have rubbed himself with rancid butter.

Liberia had been created by a white American, Jehudi Ashmum, in 1822 to give American slaves a homeland in Africa. Though no more than 1 percent of Liberia's present population, descendants of the black families that had been returned to Africa at the beginning of the nineteenth century ruled that country the way their forefathers had learned from their slave masters in the South, now suppressing two million tribal people. The Firestone Company, which de facto owned the country and ran its plantations like a medieval fiefdom, paid their black workers one dollar a day for an eight-hour work shift. Firestone was not allowed to raise that pay since the large plantations were owned by Liberian millionaires, who kept their workers underpaid. But they supplied them with rice, their staple food, at a minimal cost. When the workers finally revolted, demanding better pay, their salary was doubled but so was the price of rice.

That policy laid the groundwork for a bloody revolution that, twenty years later, would wipe out both the ruling class and the Firestone Tire Company in Liberia.

Our Chrysler station wagon finally arrived in Monrovia. White houses, those of executives of the Firestone Company and high Liberian officials, had bright street lamps hanging from rafters to keep burglars away. Armed guards stood in the darkness of the houses. There was an ominous overtone in that tranquility.

Don's house was modern, whitewashed, and spacious. It was refrigerated, the rooms without carpets and only furnished with bare necessities, to prevent insects from taking over the house. Lassie,

Nemetz's old shepherd dog that Rowena had taken along from Three Rivers, greeted us. He attached himself to me during my stay. He was bored, I guess, since Don and Rowena were rarely home. I was shown to my room. Fist-sized house spiders clung to the ceiling. I brushed them down, and the dog ate them. But the bed was clean. I was nervous in a tired and edgy way, but it was just the atmosphere I was looking for. It was less hot than I had anticipated, though the humidity was like that of the Amazon jungle, very unhealthy for Rowena, who suffered badly from asthma.

If I were looking for a background for stories, I was in the midst of it. But there was too much to digest in the short days I visited that schizophrenic country. I thought of that old saying: "If you want to write truthfully about Rome, stay three days or stay thirty years." The house servant, Peter, a gray-haired, distinguished-looking black, served breakfast: American Quaker oats and canned milk, canned California pears, bread baked by Langendorf. Modern markets in Monrovia, owned by Lebanese, sold all kinds of American food, shipped in refrigerated freighters that flew the Liberian flag, though they belonged to American companies. The price of that imported food was prohibitively high, way out of the reach of the native population, except the ruling Liberians. I also never knew what time it was since the change of time between Switzerland and Liberia was eight and three-quarters hours' difference, not easy to compute.

Rowena drove me to the center of Monrovia. I took my camera, but she warned me never to photograph a pregnant woman. I would be arrested and go to prison for that. I saw a picturesque row of wooden Victorian buildings, though badly in need of repair. When I tried to photograph those colorful buildings, two women shouted angrily at me, telling me to photograph the modern government structures, offended that I wanted to show the impoverished side of their country.

The center of the city was its harbor. There stood enormous half-finished buildings, equipped with very modern comforts, to house the government officials. A few workmen crawled over them slowly. At that pace it might take years to finish, if ever. Next to that coming grandeur stood dilapidated shacks, worse than those I had seen in Belem or Manaus, among them an empty shell, a schoolhouse. The children had to bring their own chairs. There were no school books. A heap of sand behind the house was the latrine for the kids to relieve themselves. The country was 90 percent illiterate, though the country's leaders, as I found out, studied at Oxford, Cambridge,

Harvard, and Stanford. The government did not want people to be educated, which they believed would foster revolutions.

Blacks aimlessly drifted about, tribal people from the interior hoping to find work in Monrovia. Groups of them were standing around, motionless, like driftwood. Waiting. For what? Who fed them? Relatives? They should have stayed in their villages, as they had done for centuries, raising vegetables. Rowena told me that it had been much worse on her former visit. This was her second one. Worse? It was a country without direction. What was Don going to do about that? This country was dying or going to explode. I could not organize my thoughts. I certainly would not write a story based on the political structure of that black "republic," which to me looked like a state run by gangsters. The black immigrants from the United States had destroyed an age-old tribal culture, infusing it with their alien society, which only knew how to emulate all the bad traits of their former American slave masters.

To write about Liberia's racial structure requires a learned ethnologist and not a writer of fiction like me. The material was so overwhelming that I was unable even to digest the first impact of my impressions. I was not informed enough to write about such an intricate problem. A British survey written in 1890 described the financial situation as hopeless. It was and still is.

I wondered what Don's mission was. How could he ever bring order into a chaos that only a revolution could resolve? That revolution came twenty years later, and it was bloodier than I had visualized. It didn't change anything, except exchanging one cruel, corrupt dictator for another. I believe that the American State Department deliberately did not interfere. The CIA would rather have a fascist dictator run that country than to have another "Castro" in its backyard.

The Peace Corps! That might be the background for a story. President John F. Kennedy created the Peace Corps, a group of devoted, enthusiastic young people bringing the knowledge of the white man to the Third World! The Peace Corps in Liberia was headed by a retired professor of economics of an eastern university, Francis Garret. He had rented, with American monies, a big building from the Firestone Company. The large entrance hall, designed for entertaining, was temporally decorated with palm leaves, since a marriage between two Peace Corps members was scheduled. The palm leaf decorations were executed with such dexterity and skill that the

Smithsonian Museum in Washington ought to exhibit them in their collection of folk art.

Rowena told me that "little William" and some other teenaged friends had done the decorating work.

William, ten years old, had left the bush to find refuge in Don's house where his father, Peter, worked for the Nemetzes. Rowena, for the first time in her life, had a company of servants, girls who washed and cleaned and made her and Don's bed; Peter, who also could drive a car; a cook; a gardener; and Willy, who did errands for her.

Willy had run away, since his mother beat him. Peter had five wives in the jungle and might not know himself how many children he had fathered during his short monthly visits. None of his family had ever left the bush or been in Monrovia. Peter had tried to teach William to open a door by pressing down the door handle and pushing it. A chimpanzee would have learned that trick, but not Willy. But Willy could weave palm leaves, an ancient jungle art. How does one measure intelligence?

Rowena paid Willy a dollar a week. Peter took that money away from him, and when his son objected, he beat him like his mother had done. When the boy was still "obstinate"; Peter called the police, who arrested Willy for being "unmanageable." Willy was thrown in prison.

Rowena brought him back. I insisted on seeing the jail. Rowena first objected, but drove me to the "beach" prison. It was a stockade, overstuffed with human beings. A slave ship in the eighteenth century would have been a luxury liner in comparison. The open yard was enclosed by giraffe-high fences. Human hands and feet were sticking out through the iron enclosure like corkwood. I talked to one of the prisoners. He was sent to that hell since he owed eight dollars. How could he ever pay back his debts if he couldn't earn any money? He stuck his hand through the iron grill, and I pressed dollar notes into it, enough to get him free. But could he? Would the guards or prisoners rob him of his money? Rowena paled when I told her. She whisked me back to her car, a small Simca coupe. Cars with open roofs were forbidden, since a sniper might use them for a drive-by shooting. Rowena told me the danger of my crime: I might be arrested for helping and abetting a criminal. That would create an international incident. I had to promise her never to act independently without telling her first. She would give me a book of rules that were strictly enforced by the police.

Rowena suddenly stopped the car at the blaring sound of loudspeakers. "The national anthem," she said. "Everyone must stop and take off his hat." The anthem was played every day a few times. Why, nobody knew. Taxis were cruising about, always driving the same route, picking up passengers for twenty-five cents. White men rode next to the driver, black ones in the rear. The cars were painted with inscriptions: "Look easy, you fool." "Where were you?" "David Wayne says money is his best friend." "Carnivorous." A few days later I saw two of the taxis wrecked at the side of the road. The Liberians, not accustomed to automobiles, didn't know the difference between the gas pedal and the brakes.

I became more and more confused by the wealth of impressions that rained down on me and that I could not correlate. To bring a system into this mayhem would mean writing a thousand-page book about it.

The wedding ceremony was dignified and short. It was conducted by the Catholic bishop of Monrovia. He was a tall, heavyset black, dressed in flowing expensive linen with brocaded collar and sleeves. A huge golden cross dangled over his ample stomach. People were supposed to kiss the bishop's ring, given to him in Rome by Cardinal Pacelli, the future pope. His fingers on both hands were covered with golden rings. I talked to the bishop but didn't kiss his ring. He was upset about the Freemasons, who wanted to rule the world and were anticlerical. I didn't come across any Freemasons during my stay in Liberia.

One of the Peace Corps members, a young man of about twenty-five, had joined the Corps a year ago to bring enlightenment to the blacks. He was a plumber by trade and taught the village people how to construct septic tanks. He was anxious to return to Vonjema, a town of one thousand in the bush, near the Sierra Leone border.

When he told me his story, his voice was choked with tears. His parents in Wisconsin had forbidden him to join the Peace Corps since he would have to mix with "niggers." If he did, he was not welcome anymore in his father's house.

Peter, the head of Rowena's work crew, saw to it that nobody would use any of the Nemetzes' plates and glasses. He drank from a small tin cup he carried on a chain and had his own plate and cutlery. A missionary woman, a Latter-Day Saint who taught school, had a tiny chimpanzee baby as a pet, which she carried around like a child. That monkey ate from her plate and slept in her bed. But should a black use her china, she would smash the plate or the cup.

That missionary woman, not a Peace Corps member, forbade her students to dance, since Negro music was created by the devil. Not knowing how to get rid of their teenaged, hormone-driven energies, many girls became pregnant.

There were Catholic missionaries, Episcopalians, Methodists, Seventh-Day Adventists, Jehovah's Witnesses, Lutherans—all preaching their interpretation of the gospel to the heathens. On account of the missions, the Moslem religion made great strides in Africa. They didn't set themselves aside as the Christians did. Their darker skin color helped them too. Israelis were also around, medical people and architects. Jews never try to convert anybody. It is difficult even to become a Jew. The mother has to be Jewish, since there is no absolute certainty who the father was. The Jews built houses and hotels like the luxurious Pan-Am Hotel and always left when the job was finished. They also ran the hospitals.

Don introduced me to the Honorable Norman Talbot, the minister of the interior. Talbot had graduated from Stanford University, to return to his country, where he was sure to be employed in a high position. He was married to a pretty, lively, though overweight young wife. Liberians speak English fluently, but to my ear it had only a faint resemblance to the English language I knew. Twenty years later, Talbot, who had become president of Liberia, was executed with his cabinet by a revolutionary firing squad, thus ending the rule of the descendants of American slave settlers.

Talbot told me that in the bush he had been bitten by a snake. The witch doctor, who fortunately was with him, picked up some herbs that grew nearby, chewed them, and put that "medicine" on his foot. The rest of the "medicine" he spit into a hole in the ground. A snake wiggled out and died. Talbot walked away. His wife told me about her father who could talk underwater from Monrovia to Harper. Harper is a harbor two hundred miles away at the Nigerian coast. News that happened that day at the Ivory Coast became known in Monrovia the same day, due to underwater communication. I guess there must have been sounds in Morse code. Fishermen sailed in pitch-black nights, only guided by the stars. That I believed. Also, that the rainfall of the seasons could be foretold, and food had been planted accordingly. That wasn't mysterious to me since sudden squalls of rain, dropping without warning from a seemingly transparent sky, drenched me completely and so often that I didn't even bother to open my umbrella. My cotton clothes dried in minutes.

Talbot's wife told me that her father owned a mystic mortar and pestle and three white sticks of unknown material. If he pointed the sticks at a person, he could cut people in half by making the sticks touch each other. The sticks also could down trees a mile away by throwing a fiery thunderbolt. Unfortunately, her father died without telling her where he had hidden that mortar.

There were witch doctors, who, as a Jesuit priest told me, could heal sicknesses that modern medicine could not, like gangrene. An insane girl, whom the Jewish doctors could not cure with their pills, was sent to the witch doctor in the bush. He kept her in the jungle for three months. She returned completely normal, got married, and had children. This I believe, but most of that ancient medical knowledge is getting lost since it is not passed on to the next generation.

Since this was Poltergeistland, I heard innumerous tales of mysterious happenings, though I have never seen any myself. I'm not superstitious, and believe it is silly that some American hotels have no thirteenth floor or room number 13, but when I spill salt, I do throw a pinch over my left shoulder.

Francis Garret, the head of the Peace Corps, suggested that I should go with members of the Corps to the bush country. He would arrange transportation to Vonjema and a hut to stay in. Vonjema was the seat of the district government in Bongo County, with its courthouse and a school. It also had a power plant, recently installed. As I found out, electricity was installed when President Truman was expected to visit that town of five thousand. All government employees were taxed 50 percent of their salaries for two months to pay for the generators and electric lines. This may be a way to improve the living standard in Liberia, but that method of financing wouldn't work in the United States.

Since Rowena stayed mostly in bed, nursing her asthma, and Don left for his office early in the morning, I was glad to get away from Monrovia, a dirty, run-down city, except for the modern villas of government people and ultrarich Liberian landowners. But there was a strip of lovely beach of white sand where I went with Lassie, the dog, to swim. The beach was owned by a government minister who charged a fee that the poor could not afford. I saw a white-haired Englishman, working for a European mining company, accompanied by a young black girl of great symmetry of body. A fat woman in her thirties, white like a huge madder, her hips and breasts oozing out of a tight bathing suit, was accompanied by a handsome young black with a figure as though carved in ebony. When a rich black will ever be able to buy for himself a young white woman, only then Liberia will have caught up with the multinational America. The American government was preserving apartheid in Liberia and didn't seem to be concerned about it.

I had heard about the jungle judicial system of "trial by ordeal," which was still practiced in tribal communities. Great faith had been placed in the trial by ordeal, from the Old Testament, to the clergyman, to Increase Mather's Salem witch-hunts, and it was still practiced in Africa and Brahmanic India. The idea is that something, not somebody, out there "knows" who is guilty and will point to him or her if only given a chance. The chance usually involved fire, water, or poison. Poison, recommended in the Bible, was still used in Liberia. The innocent would survive, the guilty perish. Under Saxon law, if the accused could walk over red-hot plowshares without burning himself, he was not guilty. I was constructing a story in which a member of the Peace Corps has to go through the native ordeal or has the chance of returning home, but he decides to go through with the native ordeal, to prove his innocence and to save the mission of the Peace Corps. I had found my theme; all I had to do was write 120 pages of screenplay.

I had come across a book about justice in Liberia, in Don's library, that seemed the basis for an interesting story.

"The trial by native ordeal shall not be allowed where the bark Sassawood is administered. Ordeals, however of minor nature and which do not endanger the life of the individual, are hereby authorized." The interpretation of the word *minor* was left to the judge, who made up his mind before the trial about the guilt of the accused.

Sassawood bark is a deadly poison when swallowed. Mixed with minerals and vegetables, its fatal effect could be controlled. Or the accused had to retrieve a metal ring from boiling oil without burning himself. But the hand of the accused could be protected by a secret paste the judge knew how to brew.

Since there was no court trial, as in the British code of law, the guilty was coerced to reveal himself.

I packed a suitcase with my portable typewriter and stationery to write my daily letter to Henrietta. Mailing was impossible. I saw sacks of letters, rain-drenched and rotting, standing in the open in front of the post office. Only registered mail had a chance to be delivered. Don gave my correspondence to the American Embassy, who send their communications by diplomatic pouch.

Rowena lent me a sleeping bag and bedsheets. I fortified myself with a bottle of whisky. Booze of any brand one could get in Lebanese supermarkets for an exorbitant price. I packed my medicine chest, Scripps antimosquito sticks, digestive pills, shirts, and a tie. A tie was essential, since when visiting a government official, one had to wear one as a sign of respect. In Vonjema, where I was headed, the district governor, the judge, and visiting dignitaries wore ties and white shirts with golden cufflinks to indicate their elevated social station.

The unpaved road leading into the interior is passable only during dry weather. The rain changes it into mud. Now it was powdery with red dust, slowly grinding out the moving parts of any vehicle. A Peace Corps girl drove the jeep. She had a sore throat, being allergic to the red dust that the jeep churned up. Also a young man, Joseph Bissell, rode with us. He was the son of the owner of the American multimillion-dollar company that produces vacuum cleaners. His was a religious family, whose tenet demanded that its members serve the Lord for a couple of years by teaching the heathens a skill. Joe was a trained mechanic. That made sense to me, in contrast to the golden-ringed bishop and the salvation-teaching missionaries.

Why the American government was interested in educating Liberian children I didn't know. To get the permission to open schools, the State Department had "dashed" the district's governor with eighty thousand dollars.

The jungle on both sides of the road was covered with small growth, not with trees like the Amazon country. We stopped when a jeep with four young Peace Corps members came from the opposite direction and a palaver started. There was, to my surprise, a modern restaurant building in the middle of nowhere, where the group went. We, the only guests, sat at comfortable tables and well-made wooden chairs. Tea was served along with stale English biscuits.

When, after my return to Monrovia, I told Don about that visit to a restaurant in nowhere, he was angry that I went there. The district governor had imprisoned every stonemason and carpenter in Bongo County and forced them to build this restaurant. When the work was finished, he released them without pay. The ruling Liberians had learned from their ancestors how to have houses built by unpaid labor. In southern American states, blacks, haphazardly arrested for imaginary crimes, had been forced to build houses for judges and sheriffs. The tradition of nineteenth-century slave labor had been exported back to Africa.

The farther we drove into the bush, the cleaner the native villages looked. Gone were the shacks with the roofs covered with rusted tin. The round native huts were whitewashed, and they carried large metal tanks with water that the sun heated, an ancient way of a solar system. This was Kru country, the most numerous native tribe of Liberia. I saw blacks with scar marks on their faces, an age-old custom to give them tribal identity. The women wore long batik skirts, and their breasts were bare, which looked good on the young girls. I was careful to hide my tiny Minox spy camera. Some of the superstitious natives believed that to be photographed would steal their soul.

How many centuries was this country still away from the thoughts and technical accomplishments of the twentieth century? The blacks had been the white man's burden. Now the white man had become the burden of the blacks. He had destroyed the rhythm of an ancient culture that had been working well until his arrival, importing industries producing toxic waste, unemployment, family destruction, telephone, television. The worldwide distribution of cheap pocket radios had given Africans access to a world that was upsetting their tribal equilibrium with the *fata morgana* (mirage) of a better way of living, a shell that hid frustrations, strife, and discontent.

I lived in one of the small huts that the embassy had built for the Peace Corps. Behind my primitive hut, containing a cot, a cold shower, and a propane burner, rose the Mountain of the Ghosts, jungle covered, stretching its crest into the clouds. It exuded an atmosphere of mystery that I picked up like a radio its signals.

I bought my food in a general store run by a lively, amusing, middle-aged Lebanese. I liked the weekly market, with its turmoil and wonders, bustling with commotion, its stands with vegetables, baskets woven with great dexterity. There one could buy colorful batik material. I brought some back to Henrietta, but it was not colorfast and imprinted its vivid design on the wearer's skin. Dutch Heineken beer was for sale in gallon cans for forty American cents. I never found out how that kind of beer, expensive in America, had made its way into a jungle city like Vonjema or what the real cost of making Heineken beer was. Women were weaving long ribbons of delicately dyed sheep wool. Already among the beautiful native-made clay pots, cheap colored tinware, imported from India, had crept in, signaling the death of an ancient culture.

I suffered from an *embarrass de richesse,* too much interesting material for my story. All I had to do was to write the screenplay!

Home again! There are conveniences that we accept in civilized countries as a matter of fact, like turning a faucet that spouts clear drinking water. We don't know about the existence of the *Wuchereria bancrofti* worm that infests the marrow of a human leg. To get rid of that murderous madder, one had to catch its head in a slit piece of bamboo and slowly, slowly turn that wooden stick, carefully pulling that monster out of its lair. Should its fragile skin break, thousands of tiny worms would infest the bloodstream and enter the body and feed on it. The *Wuchereria* worm is the curse of western Africa—that and malaria, leprosy, virus diseases, sleeping sickness, and lately polio, which was absent before. We have no snails in our lakes that carry schistosomiasis. When we get sick, there is a pill to cure it. Our lives are protected by "rights." We travel on paved roads at great speed, buy food that is pasteurized. We live by laws created to protect us. A government chosen by-the-people for-the-people of-the-people looks after us. The African states might never be able to bridge that crevasse that separates government power from personal liberty. The African ghosts refuse to be expelled. Africa, losing its cultural past, glides further back into a time that can only be compared with the darkest frames of mind of the European Middle Ages.

When I returned to Monrovia after three weeks in the bush, I showed Don the screenplay I had written about the clash of ancient superstitions with the Peace Corps' often futile attempt to introduce Western knowledge to tribal people. Don became upset. "One more bad publicity about the Peace Corps, and they can pack up and go home," he told me. "The government only waits for a reason to expel us." He even demanded that I destroy my diary notes, which I had mailed home. Since he was working for the Liberian government, there were diplomatic frictions between him and the American State Department. The American ambassador was opposed to the Peace Corps, an independent government unit that he did not control. As usual, in the fight between bureaucrats jockeying for positions of power, the victims were the people.

Nostalgically, I watched my last sunset in Monrovia, a kaleidoscope of colors, illuminating trees with thin stems and tops as flat as though cut into an inverted funnel by a landscape gardener. Bird nests hung from its branches on threads like tiny church bells. Giant hibiscus and bromelia and an explosion of flowers exuded their pungent scent.

I was leaving a fermenting world, whose future I could not visualize. Was it sinking into oblivion, detached from an expanding world, leaderless, ravaged by sickness, drifting farther away from the technical developments of the Western Hemisphere?

Don's driver took me to the airport. Don and Rowena's life circle never touched me again. Whatever good Don may have created in this backward country got wiped out completely in a gruesome revolution. As the Jesuit priest predicted, nothing ever changes in West Africa. Modern techniques are only a thin layer covering the tribally fossilized frames of mind.

The SAS plane on its way to New York stopped in Dakar for refueling. In the airport lobby, I was enclosed in a historical time capsule. Haile Selassie, king of Ethiopia, a frail, bearded man, sat listless in a chair, two bodyguards behind him. Kwame Nkrumah, prime minister of Ghana, handsomely dressed in a tailored white cotton suit, supported by an ivory walking stick, strutted around like an oversized rooster. Sese Seko Mobutu of Zaire was drinking from a Coca-Cola can, and Jomo Kenyetta, the kingly ruler of Kenya, swarthy and very dark-skinned, should have worn a golden crown.

Those was faces of people whose features I recalled from newspaper prints. Some I remembered but could not place. That group, waiting for a plane, was on their way to an African summit conference; where, I didn't know. Nobody talked. When I took out my tiny Minox camera to take pictures of those luminaries, I suddenly was surrounded by bodyguards. I showed them my "weapon," but they took it away from me, though I got it back when I left. I imprinted those waiting minutes in Dakar in my memory, adding them to my mental photo of Nehru of India, whom I had once seen in New York; Joseph Goebbels in Berlin; August, the king of Saxony of my youth; Charles de Gaulle driving by in Paris in an open cabriolet, standing up, his hand never leaving his soldier's cap in a constant salute; and other wheelers and shakers of world history who, by chance, had crossed my life.

Now I was back home, and that African venture, so far detached from our lives in California, became static, like photographs. But having visited an enigmatic world, did the power of Macumba I had encountered in Brazil really exist? What force does voodoo possess? What occult phenomena rule minds and keep them in mental chains? The Western world with its multitude of religions (in the

United States alone there are over fifteen hundred) is only a segment of it. All through history an innate, genetic power has directed human actions, often in the names of ghosts and figments of religions, generating cultures, decays, and wars. Tribes fought for territorial gains, like the mass migrations in history, or made wars for profits, like the Crusades, or for religious causes, like the Thirty Years' War.

Back in our glass house in the High Sierras protective mountains exuded a peace I had not found anywhere else. Being sixty-two years old, I discussed with Henrietta how to create a quiet future. "Why don't you talk in schools and universities? Write your books, your stories. You don't have to consider a deadline anymore. You've made your point. What else do you want?" my son Geoffrey, then thirty-one years old, asked me. He was as old as I was when I had been forced to leave Germany to start a new life from scratch. His advice made sense.

I didn't know that the busiest time in my life was just ahead of me.

First was the "Word." But before the word was spoken or written down came the "Idea." Without a primary idea the Word can convey nothing. The Idea is not dependent on the Word. It can reach its meaning physically. The Cro-Magnon man who shaped clay into a vessel, filling it with oil or any other burnable liquid and discovering a twig that siphons fuel, started the world's most revolutionary progress. His idea changed night into day. It grew and became, like all major discoveries, more and more sophisticated. The artificially created light source went through many stages: oil lamps, candles, gaslight, electric light, glass rods filled with mercury vapors. An oil-soaked twig doubled man's waking hours since he could see in the dark.

The Wright Brothers replaced the hot air balloon by propelling the first flying machine 120 feet through the air. One of the brothers ran in front of the contraption, chasing cows out of the way. In less than a century, their original idea went through its sophisticated development. Jet engines now propel man-made vehicles around the globe in supersonic speed.

When I watched the shuttle at Cape Canaveral being blasted into space, the complicated method of hurling a hundred thousand–pound rocket into thin air seemed to me to belong to a time of development paralleled in history, when, before the discovery of electricity, ornate gas lamps lit the room. Space exploration has reached a technical impasse, despite the communication satellites that, from a distance of thousands of miles, can register the size and color of a mouse.

How are ideas born? They always wait in limbo in some of our brain cells until an observation lifts them into consciousness.

I decided to leave forever the giant toy train called "motion pictures" and with it a profession that was working for the eye of the camera and not for the written word. Since I was fortunate not to have to depend on earning a living anymore, I returned to my original profession as a scribe of novels, which, because of my emigrations, change of language, and financial insecurity, had forced me to work for thirty years in a medium that does not depend on the written word.

For the next eighteen years, I turned out literary material: essays, short stories, and novels. Some of them were bought by motion picture companies. I didn't have to write screenplays for motion picture companies that paid me to write the blueprint for their production. I again could choose subjects I wanted to explore. I wrote a trilogy using the same character, Dr. Patrick Cory, looking at life as a thirty-year-old scientist in *Donovan's Brain,* a fifty-year-old in *Hauser's Memory,* and at age seventy in *Gabriel's Body*. It explored a character's approach to life, who, at different ages, probed his mental functions that change with the added years.

I might have been Dr. Cory myself, but I had to wrap my private thoughts in a cloak of entertainment.

Then came this book, in which I judge my life backward. It sometimes sounds as if it had not happened to me but to one of my fictional characters in my novels. I titled the first version of this autobiography *Masada Two,* since I always was beleaguered by the genetic flaw in humans, racism. I changed the title to *Mosaic,* since the book is put together in small details. *Mosaic* is also the German name for Moses. Its third version I call *Unfinished Ruminations,* since we react differently to identical situations, according to our age. For a time I chose the title *Even a Man Who Is Pure in Heart,* from the four-liner I had made up for *The Wolf Man*.

Epilogue

Writing is a catharsis, a cleaning up of mental debris left on the path of life. What is the question? What is the answer? The Jews reply to a question not with an answer, but with another question, which for thousands of years gave their existence continuation.

Our span of life is the arousal from an eternal limbo, a short awakening of consciousness, and the return to the state of oblivion. Prompted by its limitation of years, we try to take stock of our accomplishments, if any, to discover a trace by which we could be remembered.

The literary and motion picture elite looks with disdain on the kind of work I did, which, as it has turned out, has more substance than their fleeting macrosuccesses.

There is a deep psychological desire in human minds to be the originator of an idea, especially in re-creators like producers, directors, and actors. The reason for often not buying ideas from the creator, which are only a minute part of the film production, is that they imagine that they also possess the elusive, intangible gift of creativity. They want to convince themselves that, though they are mortal, their name will live on through their work. But that is a fallacy. Only a few writers' names in world history are remembered, fewer than painters. Of course, warriors, leaving a bloody trail in history, are remembered. The bloodier the trail, the more their memory is imprinted in the world's history. Since the human race has been created with murderous instincts, even against its own kind, the worship of death is the root of true immortality. The monsters that roam our literature belong to that category.

I got a telephone call from a person unknown to me. He introduced himself as Pius Fischer. Pius? A holy man? Fischer? The Shoes of the Fisherman, the symbol of the papacy? Has the pope sent an emissary? I first believed it to be a joke, until that person introduced himself as the German consul stationed in Los Angeles. He said that the Federal Republic of Germany, headed by President Weizsecker, wanted to bestow on me The Order of Merit First Class. He asked for my acceptance.

Though I am aware that the world is filled with the most bizarre inconsistencies, I was bewildered and asked for time for contemplation.

I had to explore that mystery and asked Mr. Pius Fischer to visit us at the ranch in Three Rivers, an invitation that he accepted without hesitation.

A few days later, an affable German arrived with his wife, Marie-Louise, a slim woman with the grace of a ballet dancer. But I couldn't find out from him why I was selected to get the highest German cultural decoration.

I discussed the mystery with Henrietta. Should I accept a medal from a country that had wiped out my family and forced me into exile? Swiss-born and highly sensitive to the cruelties in the German character, she suggested that I reject that honor. But, since the German Federal Republic had been trying for almost half a century to erase the Nazi spirit of its country, instilling in Germans a democratic way of thinking, a conception in which the Weimar Republic had failed, I believed that it was important to support the German struggle for liberal political independence. I told Mr. Fischer that I would gladly accept the president's award. I had met President Weizsecker in Berlin in 1991 at a reception at the Schloss Charlottenburg and had a twenty-second conversation, which impressed me, since he pronounced my name properly.

The German intellectual elite love their country but don't like to live there. Even the German court of the eighteenth century conversed not in German but in French. That dichotomy can only be understood by Germans. Dr. Cornelius Metternich, the then–German general consul stationed in 1992 in Los Angeles, owns a farm not in Germany but in the south of France, in the Pyrenees. I haven't yet found educated Germans who don't aspire to own a foreign piece of real estate or to travel for their vacations abroad. My German friends, now American citizens, some of whom even served in the American army during World War II, speak in glowing terms about their former fatherland.

It might be a matter of love-hate that German-born American citizens wouldn't dream of returning to live in their native country but gloat when America loses even a soccer game to another country. They love to visit their country of birth, but once having lived in America, they seem to be incapable of returning "home." They would never give up the independence and informalities of a life that is alien to their former country. They can only find mental freedom in their adopted country, this vast and multinational continent, boiling with a constant evolution and where every immigrant is fighting for "equal rights and opportunity under the law," rights that do not exist on the European continent.

I was permitted to invite guests to the decoration ceremony at the general consul's home in Bel Air. I wanted to ask a group of immigrants who had contributed immensely to the cultural success of the country that had accepted and shelters them. There was pride and a hidden sense of implied retaliation in my choice of guests, to demonstrate to Germany the great loss of culture and progress that their former homeland had suffered by banning, for racial reasons, that group from their land of birth.

Our flagship in Hollywood was the director Billy Wilder, a friend of mine since 1929, who had garnered a few dozen honors, one even bestowed on him by then-president George Bush at a nationally televised ceremony at Kennedy Center in Washington. There was Professor Cornelius Schnauber, who as a young man had fled East Germany during its communist period, and, having found an intellectual haven at the University of Southern California, had built up the Max Kade Institute. Max Kade, a German immigrant chemical engineer who had discovered Vaseline and named and wisely patented that goo, had left millions to USC, to keep the cultural ties between German-speaking countries and America alive.

I had other immigrants on my list, especially the group of Jewish-German filmmakers who had been expelled by Dr. Joseph Goebbels. That infusion of creative talent had greatly fertilized Hollywood's film industry.

The consul general gave a well-prepared speech. He mentioned that I had written about laser beams in 1932 and had "originated" in 1928, in a novel, the modern airplane carrier. Just before Hitler took over Germany, UFA Studios in Babelsberg near Berlin had converted the book into its last film with international appeal.

The consul general spoke of my vision of genetic engineering, a decade before biochemistry understood the laws of DNA, of future visions, not yet realized, like radar and a "Hotel in Space," a giant satellite described in a novel that reached the screen in a James Bond film. I wish Theodore van Karman, the Hungarian aerodynamic genius and designer of the Mustang fighter for the air corps in World War II, and other outstanding brains who were adopted by this country were alive. Without their genius, the outcome of World War II and therefore history would have taken another turn.

I accepted that decoration, shaped like a Maltese cross, as an acknowledgment that I had brought with me my German "cultural baggage," as the consul general named it. I understood what he wanted to say: the basis of all immigration is that the culture of the country of their birth that new citizens bring with them has always added to the cultural and scientific development of America, that multiracial country that has accepted them without prejudice.

The local physician in Three Rivers, my friend Arthur Molina, is one of the few people who can "read."

There is a difference in being able to read and to read with the perception to analyze what ideas the writer has meant to convey, also to interpret its meanings of which the author mostly is not aware. Art has the gift of analysis, which is based on his profession of diagnosing his patients, not only their illnesses but also underlying causes, which often produce symptoms that won't respond to medication. Besides, he is a mystic, having experienced incidents in his life that defy rationalization.

For me, mysteries do not exist. They are phenomena whose origin has not yet been discovered. Mysticism evaporates as soon as an explanation of its source has been found. Since the age of the caveman, people have believed in myth, to explain a godly power, whose sometimes pitiless cruelties have to be endured without complaint, since they surely must serve a higher purpose only the gods know.

Art and I have discussions about the origin of myth. He couldn't endure life without a belief that has its roots in Catholicism, imposed on him in childhood. I once talked to a Catholic priest who confessed that if there were no God, he would commit suicide. I met him in the house of a motion picture producer, from whom he wanted a large donation for his church in Palm Springs.

I stopped seeking answers in dogmatic religions when the weekly offering in an Episcopalian church was held up in a chalice to the image of Christ nailed to a cross and when the Jewish worshipers were charged on high holy days in the synagogue a fee for the right to pray.

Since I don't believe in myth, I am convinced that "unexplainable" occurrences are just a lack of our knowledge and a dilatory way of finding their origins. Art considers me a crass materialist, though not in the monetary sense. I don't accept his evaluation of me since we understand only what can pass through the sieve of our brain. To believe in myth is, for me, an abrogation of rationality, the end of a probing curiosity that is the fertilizer of human progress. To blindly accept enigmas as unsolvable manifestations of a superior power leads to the dead end of our ability to think. To accept without investigation is contrary to my awareness that I am alive.

The human species, in comparison to the animal breeds, is endowed with two extraordinary genetic faculties. One is the human mind's affinity for mathematics. A piece of rock that, according to carbon 14 testing, showed human-made incisions made twenty-five thousand years ago, proves that fact. Archeologists deciphered those man-made marks as a device to predict the start of the four seasons. Stonehenge, that group of rocks standing for 3,500 years on Salisbury Plain in Wiltshire in England, points directly at the rising sun on the summer solstice. There was an Egyptian, an Aztec, an Asian, and a medieval astronomer. All were trying to chart the mystery of the heavens. The human brain has built-in disciplines that progressed from the first primitive tool, which might have been a sharp-edged rock, to computerized machines sent into space to explore planets.

The second unique human faculty is the search for a "truth," the intent of which always is the riddance of evil. Once a person has been indoctrinated with a dogmatic religion or has convinced himself of the validity of his "truth," that myth becomes an unshakable power, overshadowing even the sense of self-preservation, the sexual drive, the compassion for loved ones, and even paternal love. It sacrifices all human values to conform with the demands of the chosen god. Religion often believed in human sacrifice to appease a god. The human body was replaced by the slaughter of the "innocent" lamb, as if only the death of something alive could please the gods. Religious rituals and the spilling of blood coalesced thousands of years ago, at first physically, then symbolically. Today, "the body of our Lord," in the shape of an oblate, is fed by ordained priests to their congregations, an atavistic remnant of cannibalism. I read in

Sweden on a stone with (translated) runic characters, "The warriors returned from their invasions of foreign countries, bringing with them the 'sweet' meat." This must have been human flesh.

Abraham, in Jewish mythology, was ordered by a god he had never seen and who never revealed himself except in his visions to sacrifice his firstborn. The happy end of that tale is that one of his god's angels prevented him from murdering his own child. His god's existence is formulated in the Bible, a book of history, philosophy, common sense, myth, and, surely, innumerable contradictions, since it was conceived by mortals at different times of the ever-changing human conception of good and evil. For those human-conceived beliefs, martyrs willingly suffered horrendous tortures and died in ecstasy. The believers of a contemporary myth went on crusades, trying to annihilate tribes who had chosen a different god-image. Still today, to disseminate their "gospel truth," missionaries travel to the remotest parts of the planet to convert other tribes to their belief.

Though the chosen god of all Christian dogmatic religions is Jesus of Nazareth, who preached, for the first time in religious history, kindness toward man, the interpretation of how to worship him created an aggressive intolerance, unbendable righteousness, torture, and wars, some of which ravaged countries for centuries with pitiless cruelties.

On this planet exist hundreds of gods from which to choose, such as Allah, whose message is disseminated in the Koran, and the gentle Jewish boy Jesus, who has been elevated to the son of God, though the descendants of his tribe, the Jews, until today, have been mercilessly persecuted and murdered. They suffered for centuries confined in ghettos to keep them separated from the true believers. Among the thousand different religions in the United States, each one is convinced that it is the only guardian of the "truth."

Gods were physically depicted, until a Jewish rabbi named Moses decided that the god of his tribe was invisible. It was a clever idea that facilitated the lives of the Jews, since they didn't have to carry the heavy idol, a golden calf, on their long trek through the desert to a homeland which took them almost two thousand years to find.

I believe that human genes carry roots of discrimination, of racism and intolerance, that explode through the ages into wars. Blood has been spilled endlessly, and still is, now called "ethnic cleansing," a term that camouflages a holocaust.

Americans do not like to mention death. People "pass away," a circumvention of the word *dying*. I could not find a second word for death in any other language. When I visited the publisher William Randolph Hearst in his castle in San Simeon in 1937, I was instructed never to mention the word *death* in his presence, as if he could ban that final human outcome by ignoring it.

To compute my age, I just take the last digits of the present year and subtract two. The result is almost a century, which creates a slight pang of guilt in me, since only very few of my contemporaries are still alive. What will I, my doctor friend Art asks, leave behind, of my writings, to be remembered?

Certainly not my name but perhaps a fairy-tale legend that I, by chance at a motion picture assignment, created in 1942. In my screenplay I delineated the character of the Wolf Man, a figure that has haunted people's fantasy for two thousand years. Ovid, the Roman poet (17 C.E.), wrote that Jupiter changed Lycan into a wolf. That's where lycanthropy got its name.

Books, contemporary plays, and stories, which entertain, are vulnerable to the passing of time. But fairy tales have a life of their own, enduring, and seemingly eternal.

America is too rational to have created its own ghosts, which England especially has in abundance. But due to the emergence of moving pictures, America now has three lasting specters.

By writing *The Wolf Man,* I added one of the three ghosts to the American lore. Every one of the three specters is a European import. Count Dracula, the protagonist of a novel written by an Englishman, Bram Stoker, in 1897, is a corpse that comes to life at night and lives forever by feeding on human blood, a love bite that carries sexual connotations. The third is the man-made Frankenstein monster, based on Mary Shelley's 1815 novel that she wrote to entertain her husband, Percy Bysshe Shelley, and their friends Lord Byron and others.

The early nineteenth century was a literarily pregnant time when, to amuse themselves, those people competed in trying to compose the most frightening story, based on Wolfgang von Goethe's Faust legend. Mary won, and her character of a man-made monster, sewn together of human parts, has survived the years.

Of course, those mental exercises could only happen before the invention of mass media entertainment, but all have a connection with religious inquiries, deeply hidden in the human brain since the caveman believed that gods created the thunder and lightning.

A good idea never dies. It might be plagiarism that I take credit for *The Wolf Man,* as the third ghost in the American folklore, though that credit should go to Ovid.

The level of my education is spotty, and my knowledge of philosophy and other mental disciplines is almost nonexistent, though my library contains many books written by eminent scholars, authors of biblical history, philosophers whose ideas shaped the course of the world from the ancient Greek times of Aristotle to Martin Buber, Niemeyer, and other notable thinkers of the twentieth century. Since I haven't studied them in depth, which would demand a mental background I don't possess, I always ventured to create my own explanations of life. As a layman, I'm trying to find the psychological roots of my existence that, as I have become aware, escape my grasp.

I have to base my very subjective understanding of the world on the short life span that I experience, a time of history as fleeting as the blinking of an eye. I have never tried to force my own thoughts on others, the way many dogmatic religions exercise their power: believe as I do or remain a heathen. Do you choose to go to heaven, or do you want to fry in hell?

The power of the dogmatic religions is based on creating fear and guilt in their followers, and to convince them that only their church knows the eternal truth.

Religious zealots ring my doorbell uninvited because their religion demands that they contact disbelievers and convince them of the "truth," which God had revealed only to them. I like to talk to them, especially adult ones, not the young boys and girls who are sent in pairs to distribute pamphlets, a task that has been forced on them by their church or their parents.

An older woman, whose husband drove her to our house, waiting outside in their Cadillac, which made me believe that there is profit in their religion, was belligerently imbued with fire-and-brimstone fervor. When I asked her how many people belonged to her faith, she proudly told me that they had two and a half million members, every one certain to be admitted into heaven. I inquired about the fate of the Buddhists, Shintoists, Hindus, Jews, and other beliefs. She was convinced that all those billions of people would be better off forever dead but that all could be saved if it weren't for that bottleneck: the lack of missionaries of her faith! Her attitude was, to me, the essence of dogmatic religions, the selfishness of its members who take only the salvation of their own souls into account, discarding the remainder of mankind as food for Satan. She was the personification of the single-mindedness into which her religious belief had deteriorated, a religion that originally had been based on kindness and love.

Is my mind also walled in by a selfish "truth"? To disseminate my subjective thoughts and ideas, I stealthily hide them in a cloak of entertaining storytelling, since the depth of my thinking, shallow at best, might be challenged by erudite experts. I continue to explore their conceptions about philosophy and religion with the concentration and pleasure of replaying a chess game of masters. But to me, their conclusions remain variable at best. Truth is what the brain accepts as being the truth. One could argue about it, but thoughts are moves of a chess game, whose outcome for me is invariably a draw.

I talked to a friend of mine, whose whole existence is involved in studying Buddhism. He even spent years in India to find certification of his belief. In our arguments, I tried to explain to him that his deep understanding of that faith has been recorded in books, written by scholars, disseminated by brains, who had digested those beliefs and had, in profound wordings, put them in formulation. My friend had accepted knowledge predigested by others. His contribution to his belief was that he believed in that faith without having added to it one single thought of his own. But he is content with life, since he has found his truth, while I am still searching, comparing, examining a hundred approaches to the mysteries of our existence, which we, due to a freak of nature, will never find. To come to a conclusion we must accept a preconceived belief that, by its very nature, can only be based on myth.

My singular conception has narrowed down to the contention that nature had once been perfect, like the Garden of Eden myth, until an alien curiosity distorted its balance.

The country is still inhabited by species of animals whose ancestry goes back hundreds of thousands of years, longer than that of humankind, and who have not changed shape or habits, like the birds, who leave us in winter to return in spring; raccoons, which appear at our door at night; bears emigrating from the mountains, to break our garbage cans in search of food; the million varieties of insects, which, I'm convinced, are going to be the heirs of this planet; the ravens that circle our house, arriving from miles away as soon as I put some scraps of meat on the rock where they like to be fed. How do they know that food has been dished out to them? I remember that when we went with our recreation vehicle to a remote spa in the Mojave Desert, far away from any habitation, only desert sand circled us for miles. But when I threw out a few handfuls of bird feed, in a short time hundreds of blackbirds appeared to gather up the seeds. How did they know? When there is fresh blood in the ocean, how do schools of sharks suddenly appear? Does the water carry smell instantly for miles? What senses direct the existence of those creatures? I am surrounded by a concerted collaboration of a nature whose functions, unknown to us, scientists attribute to "instinct." But the instincts that once adjusted the human species to nature have dissipated.

I believe that the original *Homo,* but not the *Homo sapiens* he later became, also once belonged to the finely tuned concert of nature, a nature without sentiment that ruthlessly discards imperfection, making disappear from this planet everything that disturbs its rhythm but fosters those creations that fit into its life pattern. Once the Earth was in equilibrium, changing in a slow evolution, which might have begun with the first living thing, amoebas in the ocean, life that developed into fish that finally climbed out of the water and became air-breathing animals, a world in which "human" creatures with a diminutive brain smoothly fit.

But then, by a freak of evolution or by deliberate mysterious intent, the brain of that biped grew in complexity, steadily adding functions to its size. Until that time, no gods or beliefs had unbalanced the rhythm of nature. That featherless, hairy biped began to think, branching out into mental regions where he searched for an answer to his queries. He started to reason, a process that, though it had a beginning, has no limitations.

The questions he asks can never be answered and will always be arbitrary, and the "truth" he finds is the "truth" he decides to be the only "truth."

The first *Homo sapiens,* smitten with bigger brain cells, tried to find an answer to the mystery of thunder and lightning, and since he could not discover any that could stand the proof, he attributed that phenomenon to an all-powerful god. That chosen god opened Pandora's box. Man's endless search for knowledge began, but it will never penetrate completely nature's enigmas. Since our thinking had a beginning, we wrongly assume it will also discover an end.

That search for the mystery within mysteries has also guided my inquisitiveness as a writer. I have come to the conclusion that, should I ever give up trying to find for myself the answer to the seemingly unexplainable, it also would mean the end of curiosity, which is the focus of my life.

Filmography

Hauser's Memory (1970) (TV) (novel)
Ski Fever (1967)
    aka *Liebesspiel im Schnee* (1967) (West Germany)
Das Feuerschiff (1962)
Sherlock Holmes und das Halsband des Todes (1962)
    aka *Sherlock Holmes and the Deadly Necklace* (1962) (U.S.)
    aka *Sherlock Holmes et le collier de la mort* (1964) (France)
    aka *Sherlock Holmes la valle del terrore* (1962) (Italy)
    aka *Valley of Fear* (1962) (U.K.)
Ein Toter sucht seinen Mörder (1962) (novel *Donovan's Brain*)
    aka *The Brain* (1964) (U.S.)
    aka *A Dead Man Seeks His Murderer* (1962)
    aka *Over My Dead Body* (1962)
    aka *Vengeance* (1962) (U.K.)
Devil's Messenger (1961)
Love Slaves of the Amazons (1957) (also story)
Curucu, Beast of the Amazon (1956)
Earth versus the Flying Saucers (1956) (story)
    aka *Invasion of the Flying Saucers* (1956)
Creature with the Atom Brain (1955)
Riders to the Stars (1954)
Donovan's Brain (1953) (novel *Donovan's Brain*)
The Magnetic Monster (1953)
Bride of the Gorilla (1951)
Tarzan's Magic Fountain (1949)
    aka *Tarzan and the Arrow of Death* (1949) (U.S.)
Berlin Express (1948) (story)

The Beast with Five Fingers (1946)
Frisco Sal (1945)
Shady Lady (1945)
Climax (1944)
The Lady and the Monster (1944) (novel *Donovan's Brain*)
   aka *The Lady and the Doctor* (1944) (U.K.)
   aka *Monster & Tiger Man* (1949) (USA: reissue title)
   aka *Tiger Man* (1949) (USA: reissue title)
House of Frankenstein (1944) (story)
False Faces (1943)
The Mantrap (1943)
The Purple V (1943)
Son of Dracula (1943) (story)
I Walked with a Zombie (1943)
Frankenstein Meets the Wolf Man (1943)
London Blackout Murders (1942)
   aka *Secret Motive* (1942)
Invisible Agent (1942)
Aloma of the South Seas (1941)
Pacific Blackout (1941) (story)
   aka *Midnight Angel* (1941)
The Wolf Man (1941)
The Invisible Woman (1940) (story)
The Ape (1940)
   aka *Gorilla* (1940)
The Invisible Man Returns (1940) (also story)
Black Friday (1940)
Her Jungle Love (1938) (story)
Non-Stop New York (1937)
   aka *Blood Oath* (1937)
Abdul the Damned (1935) (treatment; uncredited)
It's a Bet (1935)
The Tunnel (1935)
   aka *Transatlantic Tunnel* (1935) (U.S.)
La Crise est finie (1934) (novel)
   aka *Finie la crise* (1934)
   aka *The Slump Is Over* (1934) (U.S.)
Girls Will Be Boys (1934)
F.P. 1 (1933) (also novel)
   aka *F.P. 1 Does Not Answer* (1933) (U.S.)
   aka *Secrets of F.P. 1* (1933)

   aka *The Secrets of F.P. 1* (1938) (U.K.; reissue title)
   aka *Where the Lighthouse Shines across the Bay* (1933) (Australia)
   aka *I.F.1 ne répond plus* (1933) (also novel)
   aka *F.P.1 ne répond plus* (1933)
   aka *F.P.1 antwortet nicht* (1932) (novel)
   aka *F.P.1 Doesn't Answer* (1932) (U.S.)
Le Bal (1931)
   aka *Der Ball* (1931)
Der Mann, der seinen Mörder sucht (1931)
   aka *Looking for His Murderer* (1931)
Der Kampf mit dem Drachen, oder Die Tragödie des Untermieters (1930)
Mord im Tonfilm Atelier (1930)
Menschen am Sonntag (1930)
   aka *People on Sunday* (1930)
Flucht in die Fremdenlegion (1929)
Mascottchen (1929)

Index

Ackerman, Forrest, 81
Adorf, Mario, 171
Albers, Hans, 144, 273
Aldrich, Kay, 352
Allbritton, Louise, 277
Alpar, Gitta, 144, 146, 148
Altman, Robert, 379
Ankers, Evelyn, 260
Ann-Margret, 235
Arliss, George, 176, 186-189, 207
Ashcroft, Peggy, 83
Ayres, Lew, 85

Bacall, Lauren, 285, 286
Banks, Leslie, 176
Barker, Lex, 334, 335
Barker, Vere, 152, 163, 165, 181, 182
Barrymore, John, 86, 257
Baum, Vicky, 86, 94
Baxter, Anne, 184
Bellamy, Ralph, 260
Bennett, Charles, 22, 166, 167, 176, 182, 184, 206, 207, 249, 356
Bergerman, Stanley, 245, 278, 388
Bernhardt, Kurt, 115, 258
Bernstein, Roger, 143, 144, 146, 147
Blackman, Honor, 123
Blanke, Henry, 275
Blum, David, 5

Blum, Rosa Phillipine, 5, 10, 20
Blumann, Elizabeth, 81, 114, 152, 153, 160, 163
Blumenberg, Hans, 358
Boehme, Herbert, 55
Bogart, Humphrey, 260, 285-287, 379
Boles, John, 355
Bolito, Hector, 12
Borgnine, Ernest, 171, 342
Boyer, Charles, 17, 73, 230, 245, 273
Brandes, Adolf, 46
Brando, Marlon, 198, 333, 404
Brecht, Bertolt, 62, 63, 105, 216, 356, 361, 383, 413
Bressart, Felix, 102, 103
Bridges, Lloyd, 293, 411
Briskin, Irving, 270, 271
Broder, Jack, 296, 297
Bromfield, John, 365-367, 370, 371, 373, 375, 376
Bromfield, Louis, 357, 358
Bruce, Virginia, 257
Bruene, Rolf, 55
Buchold, Werner, 323
Buck, Pearl, 218
Burg, Hansi, 144
Burghardt, Johannes, 40, 108-109, 177
Burr, Raymond, 249, 297, 325
Burroughs, Edgar Rice, 335

Cagney, James, 260, 379, 399
Carlson, Richard, 293, 294, 395
Carroll, Madeleine, 167
Carson, Johnny, 221
Case, Frank, 318
Cavanaugh, Paul, 297
Chaney Jr., Lon, 29, 260, 268, 270, 277, 295, 297, 379
Chanier, André, 71
Chaplin, Charlie, 304
Christian, Linda, 247
Ciannelli, Eduardo, 355, 403
Clarke, Mae, 399
Clift, Montgomery, 344
Cohn, Harry, 16, 111, 195, 260
Colman, Ronald, 352
Conan Doyle, Arthur, 384, 385
Conway, Tom, 297
Cooper, Gary, 260
Correll, Hugo, 115, 116
Coward, Noel, 188, 241
Crain, Jeanne, 353
Crosby, Bing, 231
Curtis, Tony, 171, 332

Dane, Clemence, 179
Darnell, Linda, 352
Darrieux, Danielle, 127, 128, 148, 158, 203, 219
Davis, Bette, 223, 260
Davis, Nancy (Reagan, Nancy), 85
Day, Doris, 411
Day, Frances, 156, 160, 163-165, 180, 185, 186
de Beauvoir, Simone, 134
de Carlo, Yvonne, 171, 269
Diamond, I. A. L, 230
Diessl, Gustaf, 265
Dietrich, Marlene, 41, 62, 85, 103, 153, 197, 208, 215, 223, 313, 353, 382
Dine, Jim, 380
Disney, Walt, 162
Dix, Richard, 176, 182

Donat, Robert, 167, 182
Douglas, Kirk, 236, 333
Dowling, Constance, 294
Dufft, Hermann, 55
Dunne, James, 167, 168
Durbin, Deanna, 213
Dykers, Tom, 292

Eastwood, Clint, 378
Elliot, Robert, 367, 368
Elvey, Maurice, 48, 179, 182
Engel, Sam, 388, 389
Evans, Madge, 176
Evans, Dale, 239

Farrow, Mia, 411
Faulkner, William, 287
Fellner, Frederick, 106, 167, 168
Feuchtwanger, Lionel, 86
Fischer, Pius, 436
Fitzgerald, F. Scott, 274
Fodor, Ladislas, 124, 125
Foster, Jody, 378
Foster, Susanna, 269, 270, 286
Fox, William, 15
Franz, Ernst
Freed, Arthur, 110
Friedell, Egon, 61
Froehlich, Gustaf, 144
Fulton, John, 256, 257

Gable, Clark, 184, 209, 212, 249-151, 260, 333
Gabor, Zsa Zsa, 250
Garbo, Greta, 78, 86, 213, 215, 216, 223, 230, 247, 347, 375, 379
Gardner, Ava, 171
Garland, Beverly, 363-367, 370-373, 375-377
Garland, Judy, 213, 260
Garrett, Frances, 423, 427
Garson, Greer, 218, 219
Geraghty, Jerry, 219, 231, 240
Gero, Rolli, 62
Giacalone, Arturo, 288

Gielgud, John, 83, 84, 188
Gilbert, John, 215, 216
Glaeser, Erich, 54
Goddard, Paulette, 304, 336, 337
Goebbels, Joseph, 8, 33, 81, 82, 102, 114, 115, 131, 135, 144, 151, 258, 347, 360, 381, 432, 437
Golding, William, 400
Goldmann, William, 106, 381
Goldwyn, Samuel, 15, 195, 251, 335
Grable, Betty, 269, 352
Granet, Bert, 325, 326, 332
Grant, Cary, 209, 375, 379
Greene, Graham, 419
Griffith, D. W., 222, 413
Gross, Jack, 173, 270, 271, 277
Grosz, George, 62
Guinness, Alec, 83, 84

Haas, Dolly, 125, 127, 148, 150
Hacker, Friedrich, 24, 265, 266
Hale, Barbara, 325, 326
Hall, Jon, 222, 255, 256
Hammett, Dashiell, 284
Harris, Sam, 411
Harvey, Laurence, 123
Hathaway, Henry, 239
Hauptmann, Gerhardt, 76
Hayes, Helen, 12
Haymes, Dick, 337
Hayward, Susan, 260
Hayworth, Lillian, 222
Hayworth, Rita, 223, 260
Hecht, Ben, 12
Hecht, Harold, 170
Heinlein, Robert, 263
Hellinger, Mark, 169
Helm, Brigitte, 81, 82, 153
Hemingway, Ernest, 200, 412
Hepburn, Katharine, 179, 286, 291
Heumann, Edgar, 344, 345, 348
Heymann, Werner Richard, 127, 247
Hill, Constance, 242, 243
Hitchcock, Alfred, 22, 77, 147, 167, 168, 173, 176, 190, 194, 195, 206, 272, 333, 356, 379
Hoffmannsthal, Hugo von, 10
Holden, William, 395
Hollaender, Frederich, 103
Hollander, Frederick, 223, 231, 232, 245, 313, 314
Hollingsworth, Bill, 265
Hope, Bob, 221, 231
Hornblow, Arthur, 242
Horney, Brigitte, 104, 105, 171
Horney, Karen, 104
Howe, James Wong, 216
Hudson, Rock, 209, 274
Huebler, Rudolf, 56
Hughes, Howard, 285, 325, 326, 331
Hunt, Marsha, 236
Huston, John, 260, 284-287
Huston, Walter, 176, 284

Isherwood, Christopher, 63

Jackson, Felix, 213
James, Harry, 324, 325
Jannings, Emil, 17, 63, 73, 358
Jennings, Talbot, 239
Jones, Grover, 239
Joyce, Brenda, 352
Joyce, James, 71, 287

Kael, Pauline, 219
Kaestner, Erich, 32, 40
Kafka, Franz, 282
Karloff, Boris, 260, 269, 300, 379, 411
Karp, Joseph, 225
Katz, Otto, 62
Kauss, Gina, 86, 93
Kay, Richard, 362-364, 366, 371, 373, 374
Keaton, Buster, 379
Keil, Gottfried, 55
Keith, Evelyn, 286
Keller, Werner, 383
Kellermann, Bernhardt, 86, 94, 174
Kellogg, Frank Billings, 35

Kennedy, John F., 227, 423
Kerr, Deborah, 286
King, Henry, 260, 355
Knopf, Alfred, 105, 291, 412
Koelbl, Herlinde, 192
Kohner, Frederick, 119, 145, 150, 343, 372
Kohner, Paul, 110, 276
Kohner, Susan, 150, 286
Kokoschka, Oskar, 10
Korda, Alexander, 83, 124, 176, 189, 190, 274
Kraemer, Stanford, 79
Kraus, Werner, 63
Kulick, Frank, 243
Kulick, Harry, 330
Kurosawa, Akira, 286

Laemmle Jr., Carl, 220
Laemmle Sr., Carl, 16, 219, 220, 312, 388
Laemmle, Rose, 245
Lake, Veronica, 235
Lamarr, Monica, 244
Lamour, Dorothy, 222, 231, 236
Lancaster, Burt, 170, 171, 209, 358
Lang, Fritz, 77, 81, 82, 114, 115, 144, 145, 153, 173, 272
Lange, Heinz, 55
Lansbury, Angela, 263, 396
Lanza, Mario, 212
Laughton, Charles, 83, 124, 176, 184, 189, 190, 352, 356, 357
Laurie, Piper, 236
Leigh, Vivien, 212
Leisen, Mitchell, 272
Lemmon, Jack, 332
Lerner, Richard, 363, 394, 395
Lesser, Sol, 285, 334-337
Levy, Moses, 40
Lewin, Albert, 243-245
Lewis, Jerry, 319
Lewton, Val, 280-283, 332
Lincoln, Elmo, 334
Lindtberg, Leopold, 345-349

Lipscomb, W. P., 252, 253
Loewe, Frederick, 394
Lollobrigida, Gina, 288
Lombard, Carole, 249-251, 265
Lorre, Peter, 77, 145, 245, 256, 284
Lowe, Edmund, 292, 411
Lubitsch, Ernst, 127, 230, 231, 347, 413
Luedecke, Werner, 324
Lugosi, Bela, 260, 277
Lustig, Hans, 61

MacArthur, Charles, 12, 217
MacDonald, Jeanette, 260
MacDonald, Mary, 269
Maglaya, Cypriano, 244-246
Malraux, André , 134
Mann, Heinrich, 41, 62, 215
Mann, Thomas, 41, 62, 63, 215, 216, 291, 357, 412
Marquant, John P., 358
Martin, Dean, 319
Martin, Mary, 394
Marton, Andrew, 264, 265, 317
Marx, Groucho, 112
Massenzi, Pierino, 370, 371
Massey, Ilona, 255
Matson, Hal, 290, 291
May, Joseph, 253
Mayer, Louis B., 15, 151, 195, 218, 261, 274, 275, 287, 334
McAvoy, John, 239, 242
McGuinness, James, 236, 247
Melcher, Martin, 411
Melchior, Ib , 331
Mencken, H. L., 281, 291
Meredith, Burgess, 304
Miller, Arthur, 333
Mitchum, Robert, 263
Molina, Arthur, 438
Monroe, Marilyn, 230, 236, 250, 286, 298, 332, 333, 350
Montez, Maria, 277, 279, 342
Moore, Terry, 403
Morton, Thomas, 318

Mueller, Heinz, 41, 55
Mycroft, Walter, 144-146, 148, 150, 152, 153, 157

Nabokov, Vladimir, 71
Nebenzahl, Heinrich, 74, 77, 80, 91, 97
Nemetz, Don, 385, 419-429, 431, 432
Newhart, Bob, 221
Niven, David, 395

O'Hara, Maureen, 352
O'Neill, Eugene, 304
Olivier, Laurence, 83, 84
Orlick, Emil, 62
Ouspenskaya, Maria, 260
Owen, Seena, 222

Paige, Robert, 277
Parker, Dorothy, 213, 412
Pasternak, Joe, 124, 212, 214
Pechstein, Max, 62
Perrot, Frederick de, 338, 339
Peyton, Barbara, 297
Pidgeon, Walter, 355
Piel, Harry, 80
Piffl, Franz, 298
Polar, Gene, 334
Pommer, Erich, 17, 41, 77, 102, 103, 105, 114, 116, 167, 173, 252, 254, 289, 418
Powell, William, 250
Power, Tyrone, 247
Powers, Stephanie, 395, 399
Pratt, James, 397, 399, 400, 402, 403
Price, Vincent, 255
Pyle, Ernie, 263

Quayle, Anthony, 84

Rahn, Hermann, 40, 93, 94
Rainer, Louise, 218, 247
Rains, Claude, 253, 260
Ralph, Louis, 115
Rathenau, Walter, 33
Reagan, Ronald, 342, 395

Redgrave, Lynn, 356
Redgrave, Michael, 356, 357
Redgrave, Vanessa, 356
Reinhardt, Gottfried, 333
Reinhardt, Max, 62, 333, 382
Reisch, Walter, 283, 347
Remarque, Erich Maria, 41, 84-86, 304, 382, 395
Remick, Lee, 286, 350
Riskin, Robert, 270
Rivkin, Allen, 285
Rooney, Mickey, 213, 260
Rotter, Fritz, 382
Ruehmann, Heinz, 106
Rybnick, Harry, 362, 363
Ryder, Carroll, 342

Salkow, Lester, 296
Salmony, George, 259
Sarris, Andrew, 168
Sartre, Jean-Paul, 134, 289
Satenstein, Sidney, 290
Schary, Dore, 331, 332
Scheidemann, Philip, 33
Schilling, Heinar, 84
Schlieffen, Franz, 81, 83
Schneider, Hortense, 156, 163, 167, 295
Schulberg, Adele, 194, 195
Schulberg, B. P., 171, 194, 195
Schulberg, Budd, 195
Schwab, Edward, 50, 51, 64, 65
Schwartz, Hans, 114
Schwarzenegger, Arnold, 378
Schweisinger, Johannes, 31, 32
Scrivener, William, 309-311, 316, 317, 329
Segale, Giana, 403
Selznick, David, 250, 251, 265, 266, 282
Shaw, Artie, 294
Shaw, George Bernard, 357, 394
Shelley, Mary, 108, 261, 441
Sheridan, Ann, 236, 247
Sherman, George, 355

Siegel, Sol, 277
Signoret, Simone, 349, 350
Silverman, Eric, 339
Simon, Simone, 281
Siodmak, Abraham, 24, 25, 52, 391
Siodmak, Babs, 131-133, 135, 136, 174, 184, 246, 296, 381, 383
Siodmak, Geoffrey, 139, 149, 156, 160, 175, 178, 185, 193, 199, 225, 243, 246, 250, 258, 279, 300, 389, 390, 393, 433
Siodmak, Ike, 5, 9, 24-27, 45, 47, 48, 51-53, 391
Siodmak, Robert, 10, 16-18, 24, 28, 29, 40, 43, 44, 47, 48, 53, 62, 72-77, 90, 91, 97-99, 101, 103-105, 110, 112, 123, 124, 127, 129-133, 135, 136, 145, 146, 148, 157-159, 167-174, 185, 225, 272, 273, 276-279, 288, 289, 296, 315, 331, 341-343, 358, 360, 378, 382, 383, 387, 395
Siodmak, Roland, 11, 21, 47, 157, 158, 170, 377
Siodmak, Werner, 11, 18, 47, 56, 90, 170, 377
Slevogt, Walter, 62
Sorensen, Cliff, 209
Spencer, Franz, 303-305
Stein, Jules, 418
Stiebing, Martin, 92-94, 118
Stiller, Mauritz, 216
Stinnes, Hugo, 37
Stoloff, Victor, 421
Stone, Irving, 358
Stoner, Jimmy, 331
Storm, Gale, 236
Strasberg, Lee, 298, 333
Strauss, Richard, 8-10, 18, 45, 318
Strode, Woody, 298
Sturges, Preston, 276, 277
Sutherland, Edward, 257
Suttner, Wilhelm, 94
Sutton, John, 255
Swanson, Gloria, 223

Talbot, Norman, 426
Taylor, Demsey, 334
Taylor, Don, 403, 404
Taylor, Elizabeth, 326, 379
Taylor, Eric, 173, 278
Tenier, Raoul, 50, 51, 64, 65
Thalberg, Irving, 171, 184, 220, 334, 392
Thiele, William, 114, 124-127
Thoeren, Robert, 382, 383
Thomas, Larri, 375
Thurber, James, 359
Thye, Timothy, 104
Tierney, Gene, 104, 353, 354
Toller, Ernst, 40, 61
Tors, Ivan, 292, 293, 295, 411
Toselli, Enrico, 12
Tourneur, Jacques, 59, 283
Tubman, William, 385, 419
Tynan, Kenneth, 216

Ulmer, Edgar, 98

Vajda, Ladislao, 413, 417
Veidt, Conrad, 17, 41, 273
Viertel, Peter, 286
Vinson, Helen, 176
Vreeland, Diana, 319, 322, 328

Waggner, George, 260, 269, 279, 300
Wallace, Edgar, 384, 385
Wallace, Inez, 282
Walter, Bruno, 336
Warner, Jack, 207, 214, 274
Warner Jr. Jack, 274
Wassermann, Jacob, 86
Wassermann, Lucie Von, 247
Wayne, John, 179, 247
Wechsler, Lazar, 343, 345-349, 351
Weill, Kurt, 62
Weissmuller, Johnny, 334, 335
Welles, Orson, 123, 292, 363, 383
Wells, H. G., 253
Werbisek-Piffl, Gisella, 298

Westler, Kurt, 55
Wigman, Mary, 46
Wildau, Arthur, 11, 30
Wilde, Cornell, 349
Wilder, Billy, 98, 127, 167, 230, 231, 260, 272, 286, 294, 315, 332, 333, 347, 379, 437
Williams, Warren, 260
Willinger, Ladislaos, 332, 333
Willoughby, Barrett, 239
Wisbar, Frank, 292, 410
Wise, Robert, 283
Wolfe, Manny, 222, 223, 229-231, 239, 240, 242, 243, 245
Wood, Cliff, 270
Wright, Frank Lloyd, 68, 407
Wright, William, 223, 362
Wyler, William, 264, 272, 300, 312

Young, Collier, 249, 250

Zanuck, Darryl, 16, 111, 212, 351, 352
Zinnemann, Fred, 22, 98
Zollinger, Frank, 68
Zuckmayer, Carl, 61, 189, 215
Zuckor, Adolf, 17
Zweig, Stefan, 135

About the Author

Curt Siodmak, born in 1902, was a major contributor to both Germany's influential interwar film industry as well as Hollywood's golden era, working on fifty-six films. Among his works are the Wolf Man movies, featured as part of Universal Studios' classic horror genre along with Frankenstein and Dracula pictures. Siodmak has also written more than two dozen novels, including *Donovan's Brain* and *For Kings Only,* selling millions of copies around the world. His personal story itself reads like a riveting drama, with his having experienced two world wars, immigration to England and the United States, and countless adventures in between.